NARRATIVE AND DRAMATIC SOURCES OF SHAKESPEARE

Volume VI
OTHER 'CLASSICAL' PLAYS:
TITUS ANDRONICUS
TROILUS AND CRESSIDA
TIMON OF ATHENS
PERICLES, PRINCE OF TYRE

Volumes published

I. EARLY COMEDIES, POEMS, ROMEO AND JULIET

II. THE COMEDIES (1597–1603)

III. EARLIER ENGLISH HISTORY PLAYS:
HENRY VI, RICHARD III, RICHARD II

IV. LATER ENGLISH HISTORY PLAYS:
KING JOHN, HENRY IV, HENRY V,
HENRY VIII

V. THE ROMAN PLAYS:
JULIUS CÆSAR
ANTONY AND CLEOPATRA
CORIOLANUS

VI. OTHER 'CLASSICAL' PLAYS:
TITUS ANDRONICUS
TROILUS AND CRESSIDA
TIMON OF ATHENS
PERICLES, PRINCE OF TYRE

NARRATIVE
AND DRAMATIC
SOURCES OF
SHAKESPEARE

Edited by
GEOFFREY BULLOUGH
Professor of English Language and Literature,
King's College, London

Volume VI

OTHER 'CLASSICAL' PLAYS:
TITUS ANDRONICUS
TROILUS AND CRESSIDA
TIMON OF ATHENS
PERICLES, PRINCE OF TYRE

LONDON: Routledge and Kegan Paul
NEW YORK: Columbia University Press
1966

First published 1966
by Routledge and Kegan Paul Ltd
Broadway House, 68-74 Carter Lane
London, E.C.4
and Columbia University Press
Columbia University, New York
Made and printed in Great Britain
by William Clowes and Sons, Limited
London and Beccles

Library of Congress Catalog Card Number: 57-9969

To Kenneth Muir

PREFACE

THE plays treated in this volume have little in common, but they are all based on themes which, if not classical in any modern historical sense, were in the sixteenth century regarded as authentically of the ancient world. Thus Timon, the prototype misanthrope, emerged from the pages of Plutarch to become a vehicle of Lucianic satire and a favourite 'Morality' allusion during the Renaissance. Troilus and Cressida were to Chaucer and later writers as real as the more truly Homeric participants in the Troy story. Apollonius-Pericles was a typical hero of Greek romance as Christianized by the Middle Ages and revived for Elizabethan popular reading. And Titus Andronicus was a figure (whether fictitious or not made no odds) from the last days of divided Rome when the darkness of savagery was falling over the Mediterranean world. Being written at very different periods of Shakespeare's career the plays afford scope for interesting comparative studies in his handling of source-material at the beginning, middle and towards the end of his development. In bringing together the chief sources and analogues I have tried to provide texts as full as possible within the limits of my space; but I have not sacrificed what Shakespeare may have used in order to include what he certainly did not. His omissions are often significant, but by no means always. There seemed, also, no good reason for giving the whole of the anonymous *Timon*, which he almost certainly never saw; on the other hand for *Pericles* I print Twine's and Wilkins's narratives entire, the latter because it is still a centre of controversy and because it may derive in part from a previous *Pericles* play.

My thanks go out to the staffs of the libraries where I have worked, at King's College and the Goldsmiths' Library of London University, at Edinburgh University and the British Museum. I am grateful to Dr L. B. Wright and the authorities of the Folger Library, Washington, for permission to print (for the first time in its original form) the Titus Andronicus chap-book; to the Delegates of the Oxford University Press for allowing me to reproduce the late Sir W. W. Greg's invaluable transcript of the Troilus and Cressida 'plot' in B.M. Add. MSS. 10449; and to the Victoria and Albert Museum for allowing me to collate the anonymous *Timon* MS. Many scholars have kindly sent me offprints of relevant articles, and I have as usual made use of the invaluable work on Shakespeare's sources published over many years by Professor Kenneth Muir, to whom this volume is gratefully dedicated. Miss Rosemary Jackson has given constant help, and my wife has toiled over the proofs and generally made it possible for me to complete the work.

CONTENTS OF VOLUME VI

PREFACE   *page* vii

LIST OF ABBREVIATIONS   xiii

1. *Titus Andronicus*. Introduction   3
   Texts
   I. Probable Source [A] and Analogue [B]. *The*
      History of Titus Andronicus. Anon. n.d.   34
      A. The Tragical History of Titus Andronicus   35
      B. The Lamentable and Tragical History of
         T. Andronicus (ballad)   44
   II. Source. From Ovid's *Metamorphoses*, Book VI,
       translated by Arthur Golding (1567)   48
   III. Source. From *Thyestes*, by L. A. Seneca; trans-
        lated by Jasper Heywood (1560)   58
   IV. Analogue. *A Lamentable Ballad*. Anon.   71
   V. Probable Source. From Plutarch's *Parallel Lives*,
      translated by Sir Thomas North (1579).
      (Scipio Africanus)   77

2. *Troilus and Cressida*. Introduction   83
   Texts
   I. Source [A] and Analogue [B]
      A. *The Seaven Bookes of Homers Iliads*, translated
         by George Chapman (1598)   112
      B. *The Iliads of Homer*, translated by George
         Chapman (1611)   138
   II. Probable Source. From Ovid's *Metamorphoses*,
       translated by Arthur Golding (1567). (Books
       XII–XIII)   151

III. Possible Source. From *The Hystorye Sege and Dystruccyon of Troye*, by John Lydgate (1513)   157

IV. Source. From *The Recuyell of the Historyes of Troye*, by Raoul Lefevre; translated by William Caxton (*c.* 1474)   186

V. Analogue. From *The Testament of Cresseid*, by Robert Henryson (1593 ed.)   215

VI. Possible Source. The *Troilus and Cressida* Plot, BM. MS. Add. 10449   220

3. *Timon of Athens*. Introduction   225
Texts

I. Source. Plutarch's *Lives of the Noble Grecians and Romanes*, translated by Sir Thomas North (1579). (From The Life of Marcus Antonius)   251

II. Source. Plutarch's *Lives of the Noble Grecians and Romanes*, translated by Sir Thomas North (1579). (From The Life of Alcibiades)   252

III. Translation of Possible Source. *The Dialogue of Timon*, by Lucian, from the Italian version by N. da Lonigo (1536)   263

IV. Analogue. From *Timone*, by M. M. Boiardo (*c.* 1487)   277

V. Analogue. *The Palace of Pleasure*, by W. Painter (1566). (The Twenty-Eighth Novell)   293

VI. Analogue. From *Theatrum Mundi*, by P. Boaistuau, translated by John Alday (1566?)   295

VII. Analogue. From *Timon*. Anon (after 1601)   297

VIII. Possible Source. From *Campaspe*, by John Lyly (1584)   339

4. *Pericles, Prince of Tyre*. Introduction.   349
Texts

I. Source. From *Confessio Amantis*, book VIII, by John Gower (1554 edn.)   375

II. Source. *The Patterne of Painefull Adventures*, by Laurence Twine (1594? edn.)   423

III. Analogue. From *The Countesse of Pembrokes
Arcadia*, by Sir Philip Sidney (1590) 482

IV. Analogue. *The Painfull Adventures of Pericles
Prince of Tyre*, by George Wilkins (1608) 492

V. Analogue. From *The Orator*, by Alexander
Silvayn, translated by Lazarus Piot (1596) 546

APPENDIX. *Pericles* and the Verse in Wilkins's *Painfull
Adventures* 549

BIBLIOGRAPHY 565

INDEX TO THE INTRODUCTIONS 575

LIST OF ABBREVIATIONS

1. *Shakespeare's Works and Apocrypha*

Ado	*Much Ado about Nothing*
AFev	*Arden of Feversham*
AShrew	*The Taming of A Shrew*
AYL	*As You Like It*
CE	*Comedy of Errors*
Cor	*Coriolanus*
Cym	*Cymbeline*
Ham	*Hamlet*
1H4	*Henry the Fourth, Part I*
2H4	*Henry the Fourth, Part II*
H5	*Henry the Fifth*
1H6	*Henry the Sixth, Part I*
2H6	*Henry the Sixth, Part II*
3H6	*Henry the Sixth, Part III*
H8	*Henry the Eighth*
KJ	*King John*
LComp	*Lover's Complaint*
Lear	*King Lear*
LLL	*Love's Labour's Lost*
Luc	*The Rape of Lucrece*
Mac	*Macbeth*
MM	*Measure for Measure*
MND	*A Midsummer Night's Dream*
More	*Sir Thomas More*
MV	*The Merchant of Venice*
MWW	*The Merry Wives of Windsor*
NobKin	*Two Noble Kinsmen*
Oth	*Othello*
Per	*Pericles*
PhT	*The Phoenix and the Turtle*
PPil	*The Passionate Pilgrim*
R2	*King Richard the Second*
R3	*King Richard the Third*
RJ	*Romeo and Juliet*
Son	*Sonnets*
TA	*Titus Andronicus*
Tem	*The Tempest*
TGV	*Two Gentlemen of Verona*
Tim	*Timon of Athens*
TN	*Twelfth Night*
TrC	*Troilus and Cressida*
TSh	*The Taming of The Shrew*
VA	*Venus and Adonis*
WT	*The Winter's Tale*

2. *Modern Editions and Other Works*

Arden	The Arden Shakespeare
Camb	The New Cambridge edition, edited by J. Dover Wilson, A. Quiller-Couch, &c.
Coll	*Shakespeare's Library*, ed. J. P. Collier.
Conf	John Gower, *Confessio Amantis*.
ELH	*English Literary History* (Johns Hopkins University, Baltimore, Maryland)
ElSt	E. K. Chambers, *The Elizabethan Stage*, 4 vols.
EngHist Soc	English Historical Society
EngStud	*Englische Studien*

xiii

Hol.   Holinshed's *Chronicles*

JEGP   *The Journal of English and Germanic Philology*

Jest Books   *Shakespeare Jest Books*, edited W. C. Hazlitt

Lee   Sir Sidney Lee, *Life of Shakespeare*

MalSoc   Malone Society Reprints

MedSt   E. K. Chambers, *The Medieval Stage*, 2 vols.

MLN   *Modern Language Notes*

MLR   *The Modern Language Review*

MPhil   *Modern Philology*

New Arden   The Arden Edition of Shakespeare (revised and reset)

N&Q   *Notes & Queries*

Oxf.   The Oxford Edition of Shakespeare, text by W. J. Craig; Introductory Studies by E. Dowden

PhilQ   *Philological Quarterly*

PMLA   Publications of the Modern Language Association of America

RES   *The Review of English Studies*

ShJb   Jahrbuch der deutschen Shakespeare—Gesellschaft

ShLib   *Shakespeare's Library*, 6 vols. 2nd Edn. 1875, edited J. P. Collier and W. C. Hazlitt

ShQ   *Shakespeare Quarterly*

Sh.Soc. Trans.   *Transactions of the New Shakespeare Society*

SPhil   *Studies in Philology*

Sh Survey   *Shakespeare Survey*

Texas   *University of Texas Studies in English*

TLS   *The Times Literary Supplement* (London)

TR   *The Troublesome Raigne of King John*

Var.   *The New Variorum edition*, ed. H. H. Furness, &c.

WSh   E. K. Chambers, *William Shakespeare.*

3. *Other Abbreviations*

Arg   Argument

Chor   Chorus

Prol   Prologue

Rev.   Review

F   Folio edition

n.d.   No date

Q   Quarto edition

S.R.   The Stationer's Register

STC   *A Short-Title Catalogue of Books printed . . 1475–1640* (1950)

TITUS ANDRONICUS

INTRODUCTION

ON 6 February 1594 'a Noble Roman Historye of Tytus Andronicus' was entered in the Stationers' Register to John Danter along with a ballad on the same subject. The play was printed in the same year (Q 1). A second Quarto, printed in 1600 by James Roberts for Edward White, corrected the text somewhat. A third Quarto was printed for Edward White in 1611, and the first Folio text was set up from this, with the addition of some stage directions, the whole of Act III, Scene 2 (in which Titus expatiates on his grief and anger) and two other lines.

Another entry in the Stationers' Register, on 19 April 1602, allowed the transfer from Thomas Millington to Thomas Pavier of 'A booke called Titus and Andronicus'. It has been plausibly suggested[1] that both the 1594 entry and this of 1602 referred, not to the play, but to a prose story which together with a ballad survived in, or influenced, an eighteenth-century chap-book, now in the Folger Library [Text I]. On 14 December 1624, an entry of 128 ballads, made to John Pavier, Edward Wright and four other men, included a 'Titus Andronicus', probably the ballad of the 1594 entry. Two years later, after Thomas Pavier's death, his 'rights in Shakesperes plaies or any of them' and 'His parte in any sorts of Ballads' were made over to Edward Brewster and Robert Birde. The ballads included 'Tytus and Andronicus'.

Some items of stage history have a bearing on the play's date. Was it the *Tittus and Vespacia* played for Henslowe by Strange's men between 11 April 1592 and 25 January 1593; a new ('ne') play? This may have been a play on Titus Vespasianus, the virtuous monarch famed for the Siege of Jerusalem and for his conversion from profligacy on achieving the purple; perhaps on his relations with his father Vespasian—which resembled those of Prince Hal with Henry IV. Since Strange's men had

[1] Cf. J. Q. Adams, ed., *TA*, 1936; J. C. Maxwell, *New Arden*, 1953, p. 9.

3

another play *Jerusalem* in 1592 there may well have been two plays on different periods in the life of Titus. Sussex's men acted a 'ne' *Titus Andronicus* for Henslowe between 24 January and 6 February 1594. Later in the same year the Admiral's *or* the Chamberlain's Men played it on 7 and 14 June. [The Chamberlain's company had previously been Lord Strange's, before he became Earl of Derby in September 1593.]

Was our play really 'ne' when played by Sussex's men in 1594? The title page of QI refers to performances by men of the Earl of Derby (Strange) and the Earl of Pembroke, as well as those of Sussex. There may have been joint performances; or Henslowe may have taken over the play from Derby's or Pembroke's Company. Maybe it was rewritten for the 1594 production; this (or later revision) would help to account for some of its peculiarities. Ben Jonson in the Induction to *Bartholomew Fair* in 1614 declared satirically:

> 'Hee that will sweare, *Ieronimo*, or *Andronicus* are the best plays, yet, shall passe unexcepted at, heere, as a man whose Judgement shews it is constant, and hath stood still, these five and twentie, or thirtie yeeres.'

The number of years should perhaps not be taken too literally, since Jonson's purpose was satire, but he classed *Andronicus* with *The Spanish Tragedy*, which was probably written about 1589.

Francis Meres in 1598 included *Titus Andronicus* among Shakespeare's plays and this is good evidence that Shakespeare had a major part in it. Is it a very early piece by Shakespeare, or a work of collaboration dating from about 1590, or does the play as we have it represent a rewriting of someone else's play by Shakespeare as late as 1594, alone or in collaboration? Certainly *Titus* was old-fashioned in themes and style for 1594. But the evidence is diverse and contradictory, and cannot be discussed fully here. The First Folio editors, like Meres, attributed it to Shakespeare. Long afterwards, in 1687, Edward Ravenscroft, who 'improved' the play, declared that he was

> 'told by some anciently conversant with the Stage, that it was not Originally his, but brought by a private Authour to be Acted, and he only gave some Master-touches to one or two of the Principal Parts or Characters; this I am apt to believe,

because 'tis the most incorrect and indigested piece in all his Works; It seems rather a heap of Rubbish then a Structure.' (*WSh*, II, 255)

Ravenscroft was the first of many critics to doubt that Shakespeare was the sole or chief author. Others, while admitting that Shakespeare may have had a hand in it, have doubted whether he would have done so as late as 1594 and have suggested various dates from 1589 onwards.

Evidence of an early date for a *Titus* play comes from the anonymous *A Knack to Know a Knave*, in which someone is as welcome

> As Titus was unto the Roman Senators
> When he had made a conquest on the Gotts[1].

A Knack was registered on 7 January 1594, but entered in Henslowe's *Diary* as new when Strange's men played it on 10 June 1592. Was this reference caught up into *A Knack* from performances of *Titus*? Professor J. C. Maxwell (*New Arden*, xxvi–xxvii) points out two resemblances in *The Troublesome Raigne of King John* (printed 1591):

> *TA*, AARON Even now I curse the day, and yet, I think
> Few come within the compass of my curse,
> Wherein I did not some notorious ill.
> (V.1.125–7)

> *TR*, JOHN How, what, when, and where, had I bestowed a day
> That tended not to some notorious ill?
> (Pt. II.1060–61 Cf. Vol. IV, p. 147)

> and *TA*, No funeral rite ...
> But throw her forth to beasts and birds of prey
> (V.3.196–8)

> *TR*, Cast out of doors, denied his burial rite,
> A prey for birds and beasts to gorge upon
> (Pt. II.1.35–6)

The Troublesome Raigne might have taken this from *Titus*, but the indebtedness might equally be on the other side.

---

[1] Cf. Hazlitt's Dodsley, VI.572.

The external evidence is too elusive to disregard Henslowe's note that *Titus* as played in 1594 was new. But it may have been a revision of an earlier play written by Shakespeare or (more probably) by someone else.

Two foreign versions of the story have been thought by some scholars to spring from earlier English plays. These are the German *Tragædia von Tito Andronico*, printed in 1620,[1] and a Dutch play by Jan Vos, *Aran and Titus*, printed in 1641.[2] In the Dutch play there is no mention of Alarbus, Tamora's son, but a similar incident, when the victorious Titus proposes to sacrifice the Moorish prisoner Aaron to the god of war, but is prevented from doing so when Tamora begs the Emperor to spare him. It has been argued that this was probably the original incident and that Shakespeare changed the sacrificial victim to Alarbus in order to give the Queen a stronger motive for revenge; but in view of her guilty passion for Aaron a change would scarcely be necessary. The sacrifice of Alarbus, like the killing of Mutius, does not occur in the prose narrative which may derive from the original source (*inf.* 38), and both may have been inserted by the dramatist into the play to reveal Titus's Roman qualities.[3] This suggests that the Alarbus-episode was altered by the Dutch playwright rather than by Shakespeare.

In the German play the names of all the characters except Titus's are changed, and Lucius becomes Vespasian. This led to the suggestion that the piece derived from Henslowe's *Tittus and Vespacia* of 1591/2. But Lucius' part is too small for him to have been a titular hero, and Henslowe's play is more likely to have been about the Emperor Titus. H. de W. Fuller argued very neatly that the Dutch play was an adaptation of Henslowe's 1594 *Titus*, that the German play came from *Tittus and Vespacia*, and that our play combined features of both English originals.[4] But the case is not proven, and it seems more likely that both continental plays descended from Shakespeare's play.

---

[1] Trans. by A. Cohn in *Shakespeare in Germany*, 1865.
[2] Cf. Cohn, *ShJb*, xxiii, 1888, 11ff.
[3] W. W. Greg noted that Mutius seems to be an extra son, for Titus had twenty-five and lost twenty-two, yet brought four to Rome.
[4] *PMLA*, xvi, 1901, 1ff.

Of all the other analogues of *Titus Andronicus* the one which comes closest to its plot is the prose story in the Folger Library chap-book. This work, printed in the mid-eighteenth century, probably goes back to a sixteenth-century original, possibly to the *Noble Roman Historye* of 1594, and may well represent a major source of the play [Text IA]. A modernised text was given in the Signet Library edition by Sylvan Barnet (1964).

The first two of the six chapters of the chap-book history describe how Titus Andronicus raised the siege of Rome but was forced to fight for ten more years, during which he slew Tottilius, King of the Goths, and captured his queen, Attava, himself losing many of his twenty-five sons in battle. Tottilius's sons Alaricus and Abonus continued the struggle until the Emperor obtained peace by marrying Attava. By opposing this union, for fear of the Emperor's weakness and Attava's bad influence, Andronicus excited the latter's hatred. She had him exiled but he was recalled owing to the popular outcry.

The Queen has a black child by her paramour, an unnamed Moor who seconds her plots against Titus. She persuades her astonished husband that the child is his and regains his favour. Soon however her power is threatened when the Emperor's son by a former marriage falls in love with Titus's daughter Lavinia and is betrothed to her. To prepare for her own sons' accession she removes the Prince with the help of the Moor and her sons by having him shot 'through the Back with a poyson'd Arrow'. His body is cast into a pit, into which Lavinia's three brothers fall when Lavinia persuades them to go searching for her fiancé. Being discovered with the corpse, they are condemned for murder.

The Queen plays a heartless trick on Titus, sending the Moor to offer him the lives of his sons in exchange for one of his hands. The Moor cuts off the hand and Titus is sent the heads of his three sons. Horror increases when Lavinia, mourning her lover in 'Woods and Groves' is raped by Alaricus and Abonus, who then, following the Moor's advice, cut off her tongue and her hands. Discovered by her uncle Marcus Andronicus, she is taken to her father, and writes in the sand the identity of her ravishers.

Titus now feigns madness, and shoots arrows 'towards Heaven, as in Defiance, calling for Vengeance'. The Empress and her sons feel secure, but the citizens are alarmed, and some of Titus's friends help him to take bloody revenge on the Queen's sons. After cutting their throats he makes their flesh and ground-up bones into 'two mighty Pasties'. The Emperor and Empress accept an invitation to Titus's house, 'thinking to make sport with his frantick Humour'. After they have eaten of the pasties he tells them their contents, and his friends, emerging from hiding, kill the Emperor and his wife. The Moor is captured and confesses his crimes; he is punished horribly by being smeared with honey and left to starve among bees and wasps. Expecting dire punishment, Titus kills his daughter at her own request and then falls on his sword.

The temporal setting of this prose story is supposedly 'in the Time of Theodosius', presumably towards the end of the fourth century A.D., for Theodosius the Great (son of the Roman General who in Britain drove back the Caledonians and created the province of Valentia between Hadrian's Wall and the Forth and Clyde) was made Gratian's colleague and Emperor of the East in A.D. 379. By this time the Roman Empire had long passed its height, and barbarian invaders, and especially the Goths, were roaming about the Eastern Empire—not as yet, however, in Italy. Theodosius shattered the vast army of the Goths in four years, made peace with Athanaric and tried to use the Goths in Thrace against other tribes, but they were unruly and contemptuous of the Romans. When Maximus (elected Emperor of the West in Britain) was warring against his rival, Valentinian II, Theodosius incorporated Huns, Alani and Goths in his army and defeated Maximus at Aquilegia in A.D. 388. Later he defeated the Franks (394) and ruled as sole Emperor for four months only. A pious Christian, he did penance in 390 for massacring 7,000 citizens of Thessalonica, and died in 395 in the arms of his friend, St Ambrose. This Emperor had little in common with the Theodosius of the prose story. His grandson Theodosius II (A.D. 401–50) however was Emperor of the East from 408 to 450, and was greatly under the influence of his wife Eudocia; but she was not a Gothic princess. During his reign, when Theodosius' second son Honorius (384–423) was Emperor of the West, Italy was invaded and only the strenuous efforts of Stilicho his general (a Vandal by birth) whose daughter Honorius married in 398,

kept them at bay. Stilicho repulsed Alaric the Goth in Greece
and defeated him at Pollentia in 402 and again at Verona. He
saved the Empire a second time in 406 when the Gothic Rada-
gousius, with 200,000 or more men, ravaged Italy as far as
Florence. Shortly afterwards, when hordes of Vandals, Alani
and Suevi invaded Gaul, Stilicho made an alliance with Alaric
against them, but he was accused of treacherously seeking to
be Emperor, and was forced to flee to Ravenna, where he was
murdered in August, 408. Alaric now marched on Rome and
besieged the city in A.D. 409. The Romans, blaming Stilicho
for their collapse, had his wife Serena strangled, but the city,
as Gibbon (combining Jerome and Zosimus) relates,

'gradually experienced the distress of scarcity, and at length
the horrid calamities of famine. The daily allowance of
three pounds of bread was reduced to one-half, to one-third,
to nothing; and the price of corn still continued to rise in a
rapid and extravagant proportion... The food the most
repugnant to sense or imagination, the aliments the most
unwholesome and pernicious to the constitution, were eagerly
devoured, and fiercely disputed, by the rage of hunger. A
dark suspicion was entertained, that some desperate wretches
fed on the bodies of their fellow-creatures, whom they had
secretly murdered; and even mothers... even mothers are
said to have tasted the flesh of their slaughtered infants.'
(Decline and Fall, Chap. XXXI)

Alaric agreed to ransom the city and raised the siege, but later
in the year was back again, capturing the port of Ostia and
investing the city until its gates were opened to him and he
made Attalus Emperor for a short time. In A.D. 410 Rome was
besieged a third time and, being taken, was sacked with cruel
slaughter, after which for four years the Goths pillaged Italy
at will until they withdrew voluntarily under Alaric's successor
Adolphus.

There are traces of these historic events in the first pages of
the prose story, which may derive from some semi-fictitious
chronicle. When Theodosius II was Emperor at Constantinople
the feeble Honorius was Emperor at Rome. The author has
confused dates and persons. His Titus Andronicus has something in common with Stilicho, who kept the barbarians at bay

for many years and in the end was barbarously treated by the Emperor (Honorius) and others whom he had protected. There was no Gothic King Tottilius, but there was a Tottila who lived in the sixth century. Attava is unknown to history; Alaricus is a very different person from Alaric the Goth who inspired an epic by Southey. Moors occur occasionally in later Roman chronicles. The Emperor Maximus had Moorish guards, and Ammianus Marcellinus describes at length the exploits of a prince of Mauretania who campaigned against Theodosius in A.D. 376 in North Africa.

The Andronici belong to a much later phase of history, and to the Eastern Empire rather than to the West. Andronicus Commenus was Emperor of Byzantium (1183–5), and very unlike Titus, being a tyrant, but when the populace rebelled against him he was mutilated before being killed, and his right hand was cut off. There were other Andronici whose lives showed even less resemblance to anything in the chap-book.

The prose story had little or nothing to do with either the history of Rome or that of Byzantium. It was a tale of horror in which names were taken from dark periods of violence and strife; the late Roman setting was probably chosen because the history of that period was obscure and the Gothic element already suggested mystery, cruelty and the downfall of Rome; and had not the Goths in the reign of Theodosius sworn never to keep faith with the Romans?[1]

Shakespeare seems to have realized the unhistorical nature of the story, for the names which he adds are no more systematic-ally chosen. There was an emperor, Antoninus Bassianus Caracalla (d. 217), as cruel as Saturninus in the play, and the subject of a Latin University play.[2] According to the *Excerpts* of Valesius (Pt. 1, 14, Loeb), a Bassianus, married to Con-stantine's sister Anastasia, was made Caesar so that he would hold Italy, but took up arms against his brother-in-law and was executed. There was an emperor in the third century named Saturninus. Ammianus Marcellinus in his *History*[3] tells of a Roman general Saturninus who under Valens during the reign of Theodosius the Great was given command of the

---

[1] Gibbon, *Decline and Fall of the Roman Empire*, Ch. XXVI.
[2] Referred to by *New Arden*, xxxvii and *Camb. Bibliog. of English Lit.* I, 661.
[3] *The History of Ammianus Marcellinus*, tr. J. C. Rolfe (Loeb edn.), Vol. 3, 1939.

cavalry but was unable to prevent the barbarians from getting through the passes into Thrace (Bk. xxi.8.6–8). Later (in A.D. 378) this Saturninus escaped from the battle in which Valens was killed (Bk. xxxi.13.6–10). But the name could have been taken (like many others in this play) from Plutarch, whose life of Caius Marius contains a Lucius Saturninus who urged Marius to accept the consulship for a third time when the latter was pretending not to want the office. This Saturninus later slew a man who competed with him for a tribuneship. None of these suggestions however is at all satisfactory.

The ballad given in the chap-book was printed with some variants by Richard Johnson in his *Golden Garland of Princely Pleasures and Delicate Delights*, a collection of mainly historical ballads (1620) which contained 'A Lamentable Song of the death of King Leare and his three Daughters' apparently based somewhat on Shakespeare's tragedy. The Titus ballad was also printed in a broadside by Edward Wright and later included in Percy's *Reliques* (No. XIII) and in the Roxburghe and Shirburn volumes of ballads. The *Golden Garland* variants are given below with the chap-book text (*Text* IB).

The relationship of the ballad to the prose tale is close. R. M. Sargent concluded that it 'contains no information beyond that of the prose history; no incidents, characters, or even names not found in the prose history are added in the ballad; nothing whatever is introduced from the play alone' (*SPhil*, xlvi, 169). The ballad seems to be derived almost entirely from the prose version. The lines written by Lavinia in the sand are the same in both. In the ballad they 'are set off in quotes, and stand out metrically as obviously composed by another hand than the rest of the ballad' (*ibid.*). The inverted commas prove nothing, but the metrical difference suggests that the prose version came first. Moreover in the poem 'only by reference to the prose narrative can the reader understand the causal sequence of events' (*ibid.*); for example, why the Emperor suddenly married the Gothic Queen, and why she wanted Lavinia's betrothed out of the way. The ballad is closer to the prose-story than to the play in making the fiancé the son and natural heir of the Emperor, not the latter's brother.

On the other hand the ballad agrees with the play in placing the rape of Lavinia before the cutting off of Titus's hand and

the execution of his sons. Sargent thinks that an editor or
printer who knew Shakespeare's play may have changed the
order of some three quatrains in the original ballad. Except for
this, he claims, 'it owes nothing to Shakespeare's play'.

There are however other similarities between *Titus Andronicus*
and the ballad. Thus whereas in the prose story Titus kills his
daughter last, after his friends have helped him to kill the
Emperor and his cruel wife and to punish the Moor, in the
poem Titus first kills his daughter and then the Empress and
Emperor before slaying himself; the Moor's punishment
follows. In the play he kills first Lavinia and then the Empress,
but the Emperor kills him, and it is Titus's son Lucius (not in
the ballad) who kills the Emperor. The punishment of the
Moor too is nearer to that in the play: he is half-buried and
left to starve but not smeared with honey.

There are verbal resemblances too:

No Tongue at all she had to tell her harms. (Poem)
Nor tongue to tell me who hath martyr'd thee (*TA*, III.1.108)

I tore the milk-white Hairs from off my Head (Poem)
Rent off thy silver hair . . . (*TA*, III.1.260)
he tore his hoary Hair, which Age . . . had made as white
as Snow . . . (Prose)

She writ these Words upon a plat of Sand (Poem)
This sandy plot is plain. (*TA*, IV.1.69)

Was the ballad derived in part from *Titus Andronicus* or vice
versa? Considering that the structural changes made by the
dramatist were theatrical in effect, it seems likely that the poem
came after the play, and that the few verbal resemblances were
picked up during a quick perusal of the latter. The title of the
poem, 'The Lamentable and Tragical History of Titus
Andronicus', recalls the titles of the Quartos. The ballad, a
dramatic monologue by the dead Titus, belongs to the *Mirror
for Magistrates* tradition. Such pieces were still being written in
the early seventeenth century, and it is impossible to say whether
it was composed before or after 1600.

The prose tale contained incidents of a kind associated with
the Dark Ages and the history of the Turks, but some of its
ingredients came from Ovid and Seneca. Thus the rape and

mutilation of Lavinia derived from the tale of Philomela, sister of Tereus's wife Procne in *Metamorphoses*, Bk. vi [Text II]. Lusting after Philomela, Tereus takes her to a lonely house in the woods and ravishes her, then seizes her by the hair, binds her hands, and cuts off her tongue with his sword. She is kept a close prisoner but weaves into a sampler words which describe the wicked deed, and sends it to her sister, who frees her during the mad rites of Bacchus. The sisters kill Itys, Procne's son (Philomela 'slit his throte') and cook his flesh, which they give his father to eat. When he tries to kill them they are all three changed into birds. The father of the women dies of grief.

From Ovid the prose narrative takes the seizing of Lavinia by the hair, the binding of her hands, the rape and the cutting out of her tongue (the mutilation of her hands is added), the throat-cutting, the cooking of the flesh, and the cannibal banquet. The writing in the sand may come from the story of Io in *Met.* i. 649–50, where the woman transformed into a cow writes with her foot to let her father know who she is. In the chap-book Lavinia does not help avenge herself as she does in Ovid, except to hold the bowl.

The prose tale may also owe something to Seneca's *Thyestes* in which Atreus ritually sacrifices the sons of his brother Thyestes and serves up their flesh at a feast, mingling their blood with the wine [Text III].

The punishment of the Moor by smearing him with honey and leaving him to be stung by insects is found in the *Metamorphoses* of Apuleius (viii.22), who may have got it from a Greek story by Beo (closely parallel to that of Philomela) in which when Politecnos has violated her sister Chelidon, his wife Aedon kills their son Itys. The father-in-law Pandareus prepares to punish Politecnos with the honey-torture but Zeus intervenes.[1] The original of Iachimo in *Cymbeline* suffered thus (Boccaccio, *Decam.* ii. 9).

In the incidents connected with the Moor the prose history combines two features thought in the Middle Ages to be characteristic of Moors, their eroticism and their cruelty. In numerous tales Moors had intrigues with white women. Thus in *Il Novellino* of Masuccio of Salerno (Novella 22), a lady of Trapani

---

[1] Cf. I. Cazzaniga, 'Il Supplizio del Miele e delle Formiche...' *SPhil*, 46, 1949, 1–5.

falls in love with a Moorish slave brought home to Sicily by her husband, and 'considering naught either that this fellow was a slave and she a free woman, or that she was fair and he beyond measure hideous, or that she was a Christian, he a Moor, or that by reason of this last-named consideration she would give offence to God, to the law, and to her honour, remembered only that he was young and lusty, and would on this account satisfy her carnal desires better than could her husband.'[1] She elopes to Barbary with the Moor, who quickly turns against her lechery, and ill-treats her. Her husband follows them and, helped by his wife's maid, kills them both and later marries the girl.

A story with some features parallel to those in the prose history appeared in Matteo Bandello's *Novelle* (1554),[2] and was translated into French by François de Belleforest in his *Histoires Tragiques* (1570).[3] Later it was retold by Simon Goulart (1610)[4] who wrote that the tale had been told 'in Spanish, Italian and French very fully; but I have little desired to make it longer, it being so strange that I tremble every time I think of it' (p. 508).

Bandello got the story of a slave who kills his owner's wife and her three children from the Latin of Pontano. In his version the setting is Majorca, where lives a rich man Rinieri Ervizzano, with his wife and three small sons, the eldest seven years old. There is a tower beside the house, linked to it by only a little bridge. The father has chastized his Moorish slave. One day when the master has gone hunting the Moor binds the wife's hands and rapes her. Rinieri, coming back, hears her cries, and finds that the Moor has broken down the bridge. The Moor throws down the eldest son, who is killed on the

---

[1] *The Novellino of Masuccio*, trans. W. G. Waters, 1895, ii, 25–35. Masuccio asserts that owing to the alternate war and peace between Sicily and North Africa 'there are to be found very few Trapanese who are not as well acquainted with the country of the Moors as with their own' (p. 26).

[2] *La Prima, Seconda, Terza Parte de le Novelle des Bandello*. In Lucca per il Busdrogo, 3 vols. 1554, iii, Nov. 21, pp. 97ff.

[3] *Des Histoires Tragiques. Tome Second. Extraicts de l'Italien de Bandel, contenant encores dix huict Histoires, traduites et enrichies outre l'invention de l'Autheur.* Par François de Belle-Forest. Comingens. A Turin, par César Farine, 1570. Histoire 31ᵐᵉ, pp. 622ff.

[4] *Thresor d'Histoires Admirables et Memorables de nostre temps* ... Mises au lumière par Simon Goulart, Senlisien. Par Paul Marceau, 1610.

rocks. When the father begs him to spare the other two boys, the Moor says that he will do so if Rinieri will cut off his nose. This the father does, and the Moor then batters both children against the wall and throws their bodies down. 'The cruel Moor laughed, thinking he had done the finest thing possible' (cf. *TA*, V.1.111). He then cuts the mother's throat and tosses her corpse out through the window. 'I am only sorry that I could not do the same to you', he cries (cf. *TA*, V.1.143 etc.). Then he throws himself down from the lofty tower. At the end Bandello says that black slaves are in every way untrustworthy, 'but all these [vices] are nothing compared with the great cruelty that reigns in them'. Negroes, he asserts, are of 'the worst possible nature'. Belleforest also, in his Introduction, writes of the wickedness of black men.

In England a story on the theme was entered in the Stationers' Register on 22 July 1569 and 22 July 1570 to Richard Jones, who paid 3d. for the licence to print it.[1] A ballad made on the theme was printed in *Ancient Songs and Ballads* (1774) and Charles Hindley's *Roxburghe Ballads* (1873/4)[2] [Text IV]. The discoverer of this parallel, E. Koeppel,[3] who did not know the chap-book, believed that Shakespeare combined two separate stories, one about the Goths and Titus, the other about the wicked Moor. But the prose history made this combination, and we need not suppose that Shakespeare knew either Jones's 'petiefull novell' or the ballad.

The dramatist alters the prose story considerably, to increase its sensational qualities, its political implications, and its characterization. The play begins in Rome soon after the death of an emperor, when two of his sons, Saturninus and Bassianus, are quarrelling over the succession. The people of Rome, however, through the Tribune Marcus Andronicus, ask Titus Andronicus Pius to stand as candidate for the vacant throne. Titus has

---

[1] '22 July 1569, & 22 July 1570. Rd. of Ryc. Jounes, for his lycense for pryntinge of a history intituled a strange and petiefull novell dyscoursynge of a noble Lorde and his Lady, wth thayre tregicall end of them and thayre II cheldren executed by a blacke morryon . . . III^d.'

[2] *Ancient Songs and Ballads*. Written on Various Subjects and printed between the Year MDLX and MDCC, chiefly collected by Robert Earl of Oxford, 2 vols, London, 1774. *The Roxburghe Ballads*, ed. Charles Hindley, 2 vols, Hertford, 1873/4.

[3] E. Koeppel, 'Beiträge zur Geschichte des Elisabethanischen Dramas', in *EngStud*, XVI, 1892, 365–71, traces these versions of the wicked Moor story.

just returned to Rome in triumph but sad, bearing the coffin of one of his sons and accompanied by the four survivors of his twenty-five boys. In response to Lucius' request Titus sacrifices to the *manes* of the dead sons the eldest son of the captive Gothic Queen Tamora, despite her plea for mercy. With her other sons Chiron and Demetrius she longs for revenge. Titus refuses to stand for election as emperor, and when he is asked to choose between the rival brothers he chooses Saturninus, 'your emperor's eldest son' (I.1.224) although Saturninus has already displayed an arrogant and unruly disposition (I.1.202–7), less promising than the dignity of his brother Bassianus.

To reward Titus Saturninus wishes to marry the General's lovely daughter Lavinia, and Titus agrees, but Bassianus claims her as his betrothed and carries her off. Angered by this Titus kills his son Mutius who tries to prevent his pursuing the pair. But Saturninus, accusing the Andronici of mocking him, now says that he will marry the Gothic Queen. With difficulty Titus is persuaded to let Mutius be buried in the family tomb (I.1.341–86). Titus is not invited to the new Emperor's wedding, but Saturninus is persuaded to forgive the old General and his family. Tamora hypocritically assists in the reconciliation, but she promises her husband to punish them for affronting him and for killing her son.

Most of this material is not in the prose history. By inserting it Shakespeare has greatly enriched the tale and effectively contrasted the ancient Roman ideals of Titus with the imperial decadence represented by Saturninus. The public rivalry of Saturninus and Bassianus reveals their different natures and their rivalry for Lavinia's hand brings her into the story from the beginning and also explains why Saturninus mourns little when his brother (not his son, as in the prose tale) is murdered. Titus Andronicus is presented as a stern old Roman, ruthless in sacrificing to his sons' *manes*, and in punishing filial disobedience. By the end of the first Act a strong dramatic expectancy has been excited and we await the results of the Gothic barbarian Tamora's desire for revenge.

The beginning of Act II shows another alteration of the story. The Moor Aaron is not just the Queen's instrument but the dominant partner in their guilty relationship, ambitious 'to mount aloft' with her (II.1.1–24). A Machiavellian mischief-maker, he is delighted to think that Tamora will ruin Saturninus and Rome, and quick to use the lustful rivalry of Chiron and Demetrius for the chaste Lavinia. He (not the Queen) suggests that she may be taken 'by force, if not by words', and makes a plan by which they may 'revel in Lavinia's treasury' (II.1.103–31).

Shakespeare has shifted incidents in order to make the triple scheme, against Lavinia, her husband, and Titus's sons, unified and prominent. Keeping the birth of the blackamoor child till later he makes the plot against Lavinia's virtue precede the murder of Bassianus. In II.3. Tamora expresses her passion for Aaron, who tells her of the imminent rape of Lavinia and engages her help against Bassianus (by a forged letter not in the prose story). The entry of Lavinia and Bassianus leads to a crude passage of reproof and heavy irony[1] after which Tamora accuses them of plotting against her life, whereat her sons murder him and seize his wife. Lavinia pleads lengthily for mercy before being dragged off. Aaron brings in two of Titus's sons to see a fictitious panther in the pit where the body of Bassianus has been thrown. They both fall in, and the Emperor is brought to find his brother murdered. Tamora produces a letter purporting to be from Titus's sons to a huntsman whom they have bribed to kill Bassianus. Aaron finds the 'bribe' (which he has hidden for the purpose), and Saturninus is convinced of their guilt. As soon as they have been led away, Lavinia enters, mutilated and mocked by her ravishers, to be found by her uncle Marcus (II.4).

Thus Act II rearranges the prose material so as to get a crescendo of intrigue and horror, making the murder of Bassianus, the false accusation of Titus's sons and the rape of Lavinia occur on the same day. As Professor Maxwell declares, 'Here the play shows effective concentration' by bringing the three vile plots into one continuing action, and setting them 'into close connection with the intrigue between the empress and the Moor'.[2]

Act III, Scene 1, is occupied with the pathos of Lavinia, the

---

[1] It recalls somewhat the hunting-scene in Marlowe and Nashe's *Dido Queen of Carthage*, into which Iarbas introduces a jarring note.

[2] *TA, New Arden*, p. xxxvi.

grief of Andronicus (first at his sons' condemnation and then at the sight of his daughter), Aaron's deceitful scheme to get the old man to sacrifice his hand, and the latter's speedy disillusionment. Titus is near to madness and begins to think of revenge, and his one surviving son Lucius, being banished, flees to the Goths 'To be reveng'd on Rome and Saturnine'. In III.2 Titus revels in his grief. The suspense before the identity of Lavinia's assailants is discovered is heightened by moving the cutting off of Titus's hand and the execution of his sons from before Lavinia's rape until after it. The identification is made in IV.1 with the help of Lucius' son, with whom Lavinia has often read the classics, using a copy of Ovid's *Metamorphoses* which in Bk. vi 'treats of Tereus' treason and his rape'. Lavinia writes the names in the sand. Marcus swears revenge, but Titus in his 'ecstasy' is more cautious and makes his brother believe that he is 'yet so just that he will not revenge' (IV.1.128). Titus does not take Marcus into his confidence when he pretends to be mad. In IV.2 he sends weapons to Tamora's sons with an ambiguous inscription from Horace which hoodwinks them but not Aaron, who however is pre-occupied by the birth-pangs of his mistress, the Queen. The bringing in of the blackamoor baby infuriates Tamora's sons, but Aaron will not let them kill 'this my first-born son and heir' (IV.2.93). He kills the nurse to keep the secret and arranges for a fairer (but still Moorish) child to be substituted at Court for his own, which he will take to the Goths. Obviously Shakespeare could not make dramatic use of the absurd credulity shown by the Emperor in the prose history. By delaying the birth of the blackamoor baby he was able to use it as a means of punishing Aaron and making him confess his atrocious crimes.

IV.3 shows how Shakespeare could develop the germ of an idea from the source, which tells how Titus 'feigned himself distracted and went raving about the City, shooting his Arrows towards Heaven, as in Defiance, calling to Hell for Vengeance'.[1] On the phrase 'shooting his Arrows towards Heaven' the drama-tist built a scene in which the 'mad' old man teaches young Lucius to shoot his arrows upwards, tipped with messages to

[1] Marlowe's Tamburlaine threatens to shoot cannon against heaven after Zenocrate's death (Pt. 2, II.4) and later sends Theridamas to fetch down Apollo to cure his sickness (V.3).

the gods; but Marcus directs them into the Court where they are taken to prove Titus's insanity. Titus sends a clown with pigeons and a letter which angers Saturninus; but when news comes (IV.4.61ff.) that Lucius is at hand with an army of Goths, Tamora plans to play on Titus's weakness, 'To pluck proud Lucius from the warlike Goths'. The prose history has no parallel to this, since none of Titus's sons survived.

Act V, Scene 1, shifts to the Gothic army. Aaron, captured with his baby, promises a full confession if Lucius will spare the child. He boasts of his misdeeds and curses the day 'wherein I did not some notorious ill' (V.1.127).

Pursuing her plan, Tamora and her sons, disguised as Revenge, Rape and Murder go to Titus, who at first says that he is not mad but then enters into their game in a long scene of ambiguous speeches through which his hatred appears (V.2.28–109). Urged by Tamora he sends for Lucius to attend a banquet at his house to discuss the political situation with Saturninus and the Queen, but as soon as Tamora leaves he and his friends seize Demetrius and Chiron. The ravishers are ritually murdered, Titus cutting their throats and Lavinia catching their blood in a basin. Titus will make of their flesh and bones a pasty for the banquet.

At the feast (V.3) Titus, attired like a cook, serves the food. He asks whether Virginius was right to kill his daughter 'Because she was enforc't, stain'd, and deflow'red' (though in fact she was only threatened with violation). When the Emperor says yes, Titus kills Lavinia (not at her request as in the prose story), reveals the crime of Tamora's sons, and announces that they have been served up as food. He stabs the Empress and is himself killed by Saturninus, whom Lucius at once slays. Marcus allays the people's fears and Lucius tells his story. The blackamoor baby is produced and Lucius is acclaimed Emperor. Marcus kisses his dead brother farewell and Lucius greets his son Lucius. Aaron is condemned to be buried breast deep and starved to death (not smeared with honey and left to the insects). He is evil to the last:

> If one good deed in all my life I did,
> I do repent it from my very soul.

Tamora's body is to be flung out to be the prey of beasts and birds.

3

The order of the climax is altered from the prose story. The death of Lavinia comes earlier, and is used as a means of leading up to the accusation of Tamora's sons and the revelation of their end. Climax is thus achieved, and Lucius is introduced to avenge his father's death and to become the next Emperor of Rome.

In developing the character of Aaron [1] Shakespeare clearly intended to increase the horrific features, the strangeness which appalled Goulart in the actions of Bandello's villain, black, barbarous, vengeful, heartless and cruel in the extreme. Aaron is also ambitious, rejoicing in his erotic power over Tamora and her ability to cause the Emperor's 'shipwrack and his commonweal's' (II.1.1–24), not because he sympathizes politically with the Goths, but because he is a wrecker. 'Blood and revenge are hammering in [his] head' (II.3.39). But he is also a lover of 'policy and stratagem' (II.1.104–5), of any plot

> Which cunningly effected, will beget
> A very excellent piece of villainy.   (II.3.5–7)

His combination of bloody-mindedness and Machiavellian intrigue recalls Barabas in *The Jew of Malta*; and it is significant that *Titus Andronicus*, like Marlowe's play, has been thought by some critics to be something of a burlesque, a comic melodrama. I see no burlesque, for the dramatist is not mocking at the form or characters or plot; but Barabas is a humorous villain as Richard III is (though to a less extent), for he is gleeful about his own cleverness and has, as he says, a saturnine humour (II.3.31). This must be distinguished from comedy however; and the crude asides in which he expresses his fathomless villainy for the audience's benefit, e.g.

> Let fools do good, and fair men call for grace,
> Aaron will have his soul black like his face
>
> (III.1.204–5)

are serious melodrama. When he sees his black baby a trace of more normal humanity mingles with his paradoxical praise of

---

[1] Wolfgang Keller pointed out that the name of the Turkish slave Ithamore is biblical, and connected with the name Aaron in Numbers iv.28: 'Ithamar the son of Aaron the priest.' 'Perhaps Shakespeare took the name of Aaron from this source.' *ShJb*, lxxiv, 1938, 137–62.

blackness (IV.2) and he is proud of his offspring and cries genially

> Look how the black slave smiles upon the father
> As who should say, 'Old lad, I am thine own.'
>
> (IV.2.120–1)

To save the child he takes him to the Goths, intending to have him brought up a hardy barbarian, 'To be a warrior and command a camp.' The paternal love which makes him confess all to save his bastard is not however allowed to make us waste sympathy on him since he proceeds to 'curse the day... Wherein I did not some notorious ill' (V.1.127) and give examples of other enormities which he has done 'As willingly as one would kill a fly'; and he goes unrepentant to a horrible death, a damned soul. Aaron is not so much a Senecan villain as the antithesis of all Christian goodness.

The portrait of Titus Andronicus suits well the hero of a revenge play, but he is much more than a mouthpiece of violent sentiments. He seems to go through three phases. At first he is the great general of the prose story, dignified and loyal, but his loyalty is displayed in peace as well as in war, and the dramatist shows that he is wise and unambitious when he refuses to stand for election as Emperor. A modern critic has blamed Titus for choosing the arrogant Saturninus instead of the amiable Bassianus; but any Elizabethan would regard it as natural and right for him to support the elder son rather than the younger. This may not have been a Roman custom, but it was a modern one. In other respects Titus is the stern old Roman of the ancient legends. He at once accedes to Lucius' request that an important Goth be sacrificed to his brothers' spirits, and is unmoved by Tamora's entreaties. His is indeed a 'cruel irreligious piety' (I.1.130) but it was Roman as well as Greek in kind, though the idea came from Seneca's version of the *Trojan Women*. This ruthlessness is shown again when he kills his own son Mutius for opposing him when he has promised Lavinia to Saturninus (*ibid.* 244–5, 289–91), and for a time he refuses to let Mutius be buried with his brethren, so great are his sense of paternal dignity and his loyalty to the Emperor he has created. Titus's behaviour towards Mutius is strictly in accordance with the Roman father's unlimited powers of life and death (*patria potestas*) over his children, which were traditional and confirmed by the Laws of the XII Tables. But 'in extreme cases it was the custom to summon a domestic court, composed of the nearest relatives of the family, before whom the guilt or innocence of the child was investigated'.[1] 'Long before the close of the republic, the execution of a son by order of his father . . . was regarded as something strange, and . . . monstrous.' Lucius Brutus had two of his sons executed for plotting to restore the Tarquins.[2] But Mutius has committed no crime save disobedience, since Lavinia was betrothed to Bassianus, whose rights could not lightly be set aside. Titus's action is apparently intended to be regarded not only as 'strange, and . . . monstrous' but also as a proof that he belongs to a different age and moral order from that in which he finds himself, an age of rigorous devotion to duty and honour. There is no pervasive sense in the rest of the play that the evils which fall on Titus are a just punishment for his austerity.

Titus's second phase, of passionate grief, belongs to Act III. The first scene shows him distraught and pleading for his condemned sons, lamenting over his daughter, then sacrificing his hand and praying for his sons, and lastly swearing revenge. III.2, found only in F1, mingles grief with vengeful thoughts. After this revenge occupies Titus, but he warns Marcus that care will be necessary (IV.1.95–9) and his talk of going to the court with presents makes Marcus think that he has forgotten revenge in madness. Like Hamlet later he makes cunning use of ambiguities, relying on his enemies' belief that he is mad. His friends too think that 'his sorrows are past remedy' (IV.3.31). But the Emperor (like Claudius in *Hamlet*) is made suspicious by young Lucius's flights of arrows and the knife folded in the Clown's petition. Tamora brings their doom upon them by imagining that she can win over the senile Titus, who fools her and her sons in V.2 and sweeps to his revenge.

In choosing to write a play of horror and revenge in which the revenger is an old man who goes mad or nearly mad with grief and then pretends to be insane in order to attain his ends, Shakespeare was following the example of Kyd in *The Spanish Tragedy*. His Titus is not so complex a figure as Hieronimo, nor

---

[1] W. Ramsay, *Manual of Roman Antiquities*, 1870 edn. pp. 247–8.
[2] Cf. Plutarch's *Life of Publicola*.

is he subject to such influences—wife, Bellimperia—as was the latter. The outline of *Titus Andronicus* is simpler and grander, and the political threads, which, again following Kyd, Shakespeare has interwoven with those from the prose history, are not so confused. But if the source provided the climax of the cannibal banquet, Kyd's use of the play within the play probably suggested the disguise of Tamora and her sons as allegorical figures in a Senecan playlet which Titus turns to great advantage, seizing them in their assumed identities before killing them as what they really are.

The author of *Titus Andronicus* realized that some of the incidents in the story belonged to the traditions of Seneca and Ovid, and treated his play as a Senecan drama with a strong Ovidian flavour. Considerable expansion was used however, and other elements were added which broaden the scope and significance of the action. In particular some attempt was made to make it a Roman play with political implications. Opportunity for this came from the need to substitute for the preliminary biographical material of the first two chapters of the prose tale other incidents which would show the nobility of Titus and contrast him with the Emperor and the Gothic Queen. The designer of the plot seems to have been interested both in the political ideal of order and unity in the State and in the ancient traditions of Rome from which the later Empire departed. He therefore filled out the cruel theme with political matter not in his main source, introducing the quarrel between the two brothers, the refusal of Titus to stand for election, his choice of Saturninus, and other incidents which increase our sympathy for the central figure by making him a Roman of the finest traditional kind.

The source of much of this new material seems to have been Plutarch's *Parallel Lives of the Greeks and Romans* (1579), which Shakespeare was to use for his later Roman plays. Plutarch did not discuss the later emperors, but the ingratitude of the Emperor towards the General who has saved him reminded the dramatist of two great Romans who had suffered similarly. These were Scipio Africanus and Coriolanus.

Scipio conquered the Carthaginian Hannibal as Titus Andronicus conquered Tottilius the Goth. He was offered a kingship in Spain but refused it [Text V]. Like Titus he captured a beautiful princess. For a time he was held in high esteem but the Roman people showed the utmost ingratitude to him and his brother Lucius, and he left Rome for Laternum, where he died in voluntary exile, 'content rather to leave the citie, then by civill warres to destroy it'. Plutarch contrasts Scipio's behaviour with that of other disaffected leaders who 'would solicite straunge nations and mighty kings to come with force, . . . to destroy the citie, . . . as *Martius Coriolanus, Alcibiades,* and divers others did, by record of auncient stories.'[1]

Turning to the *Life of Coriolanus* the dramatist took from it several ideas which would distinguish the Titus story from that of Scipio. Coriolanus is a candidate for the consulship; Titus is named as *candidatus* for the imperial throne, but whereas Coriolanus behaves arrogantly, Titus refuses the honour because he is old and loyal to the last Emperor's son.[2] The friends of Titus who in the prose story help him in his revenge are not described as Goths. The dramatist however takes another hint from Plutarch's *Coriolanus*, and since Titus cannot leave Rome, gives him a son, Lucius, who would be exiled (III.1.50–1) like Coriolanus (and like Lucius Scipio) and, like Coriolanus, march against Rome with a foreign army (V.1). Tamora's scheme (IV.4) 'To pluck proud Lucius from the warlike Goths' was suggested by the attempts made to win over Coriolanus ere he reached the city, and Aemilius declares that Lucius

> threats, in course of his revenge, to do
> As much as ever Coriolanus did.   (IV.4.67–8)

Lucius describes himself much as Coriolanus might have done:

> Lastly, myself unkindly banished,
> The gates shut on me, and turn'd weeping out,
> To beg relief among Rome's enemies;
> Who drown'd their enmity in my true tears,
> And op'd their arms to embrace me as a friend:
> And I am the turn'd forth, be it known to you,
> That have preserv'd her welfare in my blood,

---

[1] Cf. R. A. Law, 'The Roman Background of *Titus Andronicus*', *SPhil*, 40, 1943, pp. 145–53.
[2] Plutarch's Numa Pompilius refuses to be King but is persuaded with difficulty. The parallel there is closer to *Richard III*.

And from her bosom took the enemy's point,
Sheathing the steel in my adventurous body.

(V.3.104–12)

But Lucius comes to Rome not to destroy but to save, as Marcus
explains when, calling his nephew 'Rome's dear friend' and
'Rome's young captain' he declares that they will restore civil
unity to a sad people 'by uproar sever'd':

> O, let me teach you how to knit again
> This scattered corn into one mutual sheaf,
> These broken limbs again into one body;
> Lest Rome herself be bane unto herself.

There is an echo here perhaps of *The Troublesome Raigne*:

> Let *England* live but true within it selfe,
> And all the world can never wrong her State

(1187–8)[1]

As the late E. M. W. Tillyard demonstrated, *Titus Andronicus*
points the same lesson as Shakespeare's English Histories.[2]
But the situation in *King John* is here reversed; the fact that
Titus urged his son to go to the Goths is not held against him,
and once Lucius is acclaimed as Emperor we hear no more of
his awkward allies, for after all this is not a historical, nor pri-
marily a political, drama.

As Mr R. A. Law has well shown, the debt to Plutarch's
Scipio extends in curious fashion into the names of several
characters, for which the dramatist seems to have done little
more than turn to the *Life* at the end of North (1579):

> 'Titus is the praenomen of Titus Flaminius, the censor . . .
> Marcus, the praenomen of Marcus Claudius Marcellus,
> another Roman censor; Lucius and Martius constitute the
> full name of a Roman knight serving under Scipio; Quintus
> is the praenomen of Quintus Fabius Maximus, Scipio's great
> adversary; Caius, the praenomen of Caius Caelius, consul
> with Scipio's brother; Aemilius recalls the name of Lucius
> Paulus Aemilius, Scipio's father-in-law; Publius is the

[1] Cf. Vol. IV, p. 151.
[2] E. M. W. Tillyard, *Shakespeare's History Plays*, 1944, 135–41.

praenomen of Scipio himself, and also of his father; while Sempronius Longus was the consul with whom Scipio served, the son of Sempronius, earlier overcome by Hannibal. A tenth name, Mutius, is given as that of a friend of Tiberius Gracchus, grandson of Scipio, and recurs several times in Plutarch's *Life of Tiberius*.'[1]

Titus, of course, Shakespeare got from the prose tale. For the rest he probably wanted common Roman names, and there is no special significance in most of them. But Lucius was the name of Scipio's brother who after him suffered from Cato's animosity but was finally rewarded by the Romans. Mutius may come from Plutarch, but the name was that of Mutius Scaevola, who, failing to assassinate Porsenna the Etruscan champion of the tyrant Tarquin, proved his fortitude by laying his right hand on a pan of burning coals.[2] The sacrifice of Titus's hand may have reminded Shakespeare of this celebrated incident, when choosing a name for the gallant son who dies defending the right.

In supplementing the prose source the dramatist went directly to Seneca and Ovid. So the relationship between the Emperor and Lavinia's lover is changed in order to introduce a Senecan as well as a political motif. The rivalry of Saturninus and Bassianus recalls faintly that between the brothers in Seneca's *Thebans* which originated in Euripides' *Phoenissae* and reappeared during the Renaissance in Dolce's *Giocasta* (translated by G. Gascoigne and F. Kinwelmersh in 1566) and in *Gorboduc* (1562). The ruthless piety of Titus in sacrificing Alarbus was invented not only to make him a stern old Roman but also to introduce another Senecan theme, this time from the *Troades*, where Hecuba's daughter Polixena and Andromache's son Astyanax must be sacrificed to the shade of Achilles. Titus's petition to Pluto to send Revenge from Hell (IV.3.13–17; 37–8) may come from the prose story, but Titus's language shows an acquaintance with the Senecan underworld, for instance, in *Thyestes* where Megaera sends out the shade of Tantalus to afflict the house of Pelops [*inf.* 59], and in the *Agamemnon*, where the ghost of Thyestes acts as prologue. *Thyestes* has other

---

[1] R. A. Law, *op. cit.*
[2] Plutarch, *Life of Publicola*, North ed. G. Wyndham, i, 1895, 269.

connections with *Titus Andronicus* since in it Atreus avenges himself on his brother Thyestes by killing his sons and serving them up at a feast of reconciliation [Text III]. 'In Seneca as in *Titus*, there are elaborate preparations for the killing, the killer is also the cook (this is at most implied in Ovid), the feast is public, and the head is not shown . . .'[1] Tamora's description of the 'barren detested vale' in which her sons murder Bassianus and ravish Lavinia may owe something to the darksome wood in *Thyestes* where Atreus murders his brother's children (Act IV, 1897ff.).

The confusion of divine and zodiacal names in IV.3 may be a reminiscence of the derangement of the heavens foretold by the fourth Chorus in *Thyestes* after Atreus's crime (844ff.). There are also some verbal reminiscences: the words of Phaedra declaring that she will madly pursue Hippolytus over Styx and through rivers of fire ('Per Styga, per amnes igneos amens sequar' (l. 1180)) are distortedly echoed in II.1.135 where Demetrius, lusting after Lavinia, says that until he can possess her, 'Per Stygia per manes vehor' ('I am borne through Stygian regions among ghosts'). In IV.1.81–2 after Lavinia has revealed the names of her attackers Titus cries,

> 'Magni dominator poli,
> Tam lentus audis scelera? tam lentus vides?'

('Ruler of the great pole, art thou so slow to hear crimes and to see them?'), which is a conflation of two passages from Seneca, one from *Phaedra*, 671–2 ('Magne regnator deum, / tam lentus audis scelera? tam lentus vides?') with one from *Epistle* 107 ('parens celsique dominator poli').[2]

Even more powerful than the influence of Seneca is that of Ovid. The rape of Philomela is referred to by Marcus at some length when he has found Lavinia:

> 'But, sure, some Tereus hath deflowred thee,
> And, lest thou shouldst detect him, cut thy tongue,'

and having told how Philomela 'in a tedious sampler sew'd her mind' he goes on:

---

[1] J. C. Maxwell, *New Arden*, xxxix.
[2] J. A. K. Thomson, *Shakespeare and the Classics*, 1952, p. 52. Had Shakespeare been reading some editor's notes on Seneca?

But, lovely niece, that mean is cut from thee;
A craftier Tereus hast thou met withal,
And he hath cut those pretty fingers off,
That could have better sew'd than Philomel.
(II.4.26–43)

Later, in IV.1, the account in the prose tale of Lavinia's revelation is elaborated and delayed when Lavinia runs after the little boy Lucius who, thinking that, like Hecuba of Troy in *Metamorphoses*, xiii, 538ff. she has run 'mad for sorrow', flies from her with his books under his arm. We learn that she used to read poetry and Cicero's prose to him. She takes up Ovid's *Metamorphoses* and tosses it in her handless arms until it opens at 'the tragic tale of Philomel', whose rape occurred, like hers 'in the ruthless, vast and gloomy woods'. Titus wonders if the ravisher was the Emperor:

Or slunk not Saturnine, as Tarquin erst,
That left the camp to sin in Lucrece' bed? (62–4)

But with his staff Lavinia writes 'Stuprum,[1] Chiron, Demetrius.'
Marcus makes them all swear vengeance

as, with the woeful fere [husband]
And father of that chaste dishonour'd dame,
Lord Junius Brutus sware for Lucrece' rape. (IV.1.89–91)

These and other references to the rape of Lucrece come probably from Ovid's *Fasti*, which Shakespeare used for his poem on the subject.[2]

As in Ovid Lavinia helps her father in his vengeance. She carries his hand in her mouth (III.1.282), and she holds the bowl to catch the murderers' blood (V.2.182–3), but she appears at the feast only to be killed. Several mythological allusions in the play may also come from Ovid.

One of the most obviously Senecan features of the play, though modified by the Machiavellian love of trickery and the Elizabethan liking for disguisings, is the device of Tamora in V.2 to mock and win over Titus by disguising herself as Revenge and her sons as Rape and Murder. Both her language in this

---

[1] Latin for 'rape'.
[2] Cf. Vol. I, 189–96.

scene (28–40) and Titus Andronicus's (44–59) are in the Elizabethan Senecan tradition of *Jocasta* and *Locrine*. But, as Mr J. C. Maxwell has suggested,[1] the personification of Rape (called Rapine at ll. 59 and 83) may have been suggested by the story of Tereus and Philomene in Gower's *Confessio Amantis*, which is told by the master to his student as an example of Ravine, which is a vice 'in the lignage of Avarice'.

> For whan him faileth paiement,
> Raviné maketh non other skille,
> But taketh by strength al that he wille.
> So ben there in the same wise
> Lovers, as I the shall devise,
> That whan nought elles may availe,
> Anone with strengthe they assaile
> And get of love the sesine
> Whan they se time, by ravine.   (Bk. V.)

Tereus is called a 'raviner', but there is nothing else in Gower's narrative to mark it as a source for *Titus Andronicus*.

On the whole, apart from a few passages of portentousness and gloom which can be paralleled in other Elizabethan plays, the Senecan qualities are found in the incidents rather than in the style, which owes more to Ovid; but both influences were combined to make *Titus Andronicus* a formal artificial tragedy in which balance and rhetoric are very important.

In structure the play makes great use of balance and contrast between groups, persons and incidents.[2] There are contrasts between the Romans and the Goths, between Titus and Aaron, the gentle, virtuous Lavinia and the fierce lustful Tamora, between Titus and his brother Marcus, who acts as a pointer to normality. The sacrifice of Tamora's son Alarbus is followed by Titus's slaying of his son Mutius. Tamora's two sons are balanced by Titus's two boys. The Queen pleads in vain for Alarbus, and soon Titus pleads in vain for his two sons. Their dishonourable deaths contrast with those of their two brothers. When Bassianus snatches Lavinia from Saturninus the latter calls it a rape (I.1.404); soon Lavinia is really raped. Her

---

[1] *New Arden*, p. 112n.

[2] Cf. the admirable analysis of the play by H. T. Price in 'The Authorship of *Titus Andronicus*', *JEGP*, XLII, 1943, 55–81.

mutilation is avenged by the murder, cutting up and cooking of her assailants. The Moor has Titus's sons killed, but his son is spared, thus showing the greater mercifulness of the Romans. The 'banquet' in III.2 foreshadows the loathsome feast in V.3. The main tragedy is set between and has an important bearing on two national events, the choosing of two emperors, Saturninus (in I.1) and Lucius (V.3). Shakespeare's additions to his source were thus often intended to give balance to the design of the drama.

The play is fairly closely knit considering the nature of its sources. Theatrically it is remarkably varied, including all kinds of spectacle, scenes of state, hunting scenes, feasting, bloodshed and cruelty, an army on the march, disguising; the whole bag of tricks beloved by producers.

Obviously a great effort has been made to make a formal tragedy not on the strict classical lines of the Countess of Pembroke's *Antonie* (1592) or the Kyd–Garnier *Cornelia* (1593), but in a way suited to the English popular theatre. As in these dramas rhetoric is very important, for tragedy to the Italians and French and their English imitators meant not only horrifying and grievous events but also violent and pitiful emotions.[1] In Senecan tragedy the display of passions was of primary importance—the incidents in *Medea*, *Troades* and *Phaedra* were arranged to allow the characters to reveal diversity of passion through words and gestures. This is true of many scenes in Shakespeare's early Histories. So also in *Titus*, where the expression of emotion either through long individual speeches or through contrast by dialogue is a major aim—e.g. in the political speeches of Marcus and Titus, Tamora's pleading (I.1), Aaron's ambition (II.1), Tamora's love-speech contrasted with his vengeful one (II.3), the dialogue between Lavinia and her captors, Marcus's grief on finding her (II.4); the turns of Titus's emotions in III.1; III.2 which exists mainly for its emotional effect and was probably cut in performance because it did not advance the action; Aaron's defence of his child (IV.2) and his gloating confession (V.1), Titus's mock-madness in IV.3, the mock Senecan speeches of V.2, etc. Such speeches—like the play as a whole—differ from Seneca in that

[1] See *Les Tragédies de Sénèque et le Théâtre de la Renaissance*, ed. J. Jacquot, Paris, 1964.

action and passion are closely related. The dramatist is too much the theatrical presenter of a tale packed with incident to be satisfied with static analysis of feeling and motive.

On the other hand, as Mr E. M. Waith has well argued,[1] in style and attitude the author was plainly under Ovid's influence. The compendious Senecan portentousness is replaced by expansive figuration. The characters revel in their feelings; they appeal directly to each other and the audience to note the justice or vehemence of their passion. So Titus cries:

> Is not my sorrow deep, having no bottom.
> Then be my passions bottomless.

and

> If there were reasons for these miseries,
> Then into limits could I bind my woes.   (III.1.217–21)

And Marcus a little later expects of Titus a passion even greater than before: 'Now is a time to storm, why art thou still?', but Titus disappoints him by laughing hysterically. Obviously the dramatist, like the characters, was wondering how such extreme emotions might be fitly expressed. Mr Waith concludes:

> 'like Ovid, he was more interested here in portraying the extraordinary pitch of emotion to which a person may be raised by the most violent outrage ... Character in the normal sense of the word disintegrates completely. What we see is personified emotion' (*ibid.* 46).

Often the impression given is of detachment rather than of complete immersion in the story. Again this recalls Ovid's urbane presentation of strange happenings. As Miss M. C. Bradbrook, exaggerating a little, has written, 'the horrors are all classical and quite unfelt, so that the violent tragedy is contrasted by the decorous imagery. The tone is cool and cultured in its effect.'[2] The 'psychic distancing' of the horrors is achieved often by the slow movement of the speeches, the fanciful, 'aesthetic' imagery, by which 'the suffering becomes an object of contemplation' (Waith). Sometimes this results in bad taste, as in Marcus's prettifying of Lavinia's mutilation

---

[1] *Sh Survey* 10, 1957. pp. 39–49.
[2] *Themes and Conventions of Elizabethan Tragedy*, 1935, p. 99.

(II.4.15–32), but it is remarkable how nearly this attempt to write revenge tragedy in terms of Ovidian rhetoric succeeds.

Could any other dramatist but Shakespeare have written this *tour de force*[1]? The combination of interest in political order, Roman customs, Plutarch, Seneca and Ovid, with constructive skill, the 'inset' device, a theme of ingratitude, a varied characterization which even within this crude tale can make Aaron not wholly evil, Titus not wholly admirable; the rhetorical skill and flexibility, the sustained power of dramatic movement shown throughout, all these and other characteristics suggest that Shakespeare planned the play and probably wrote most of it. There are passages reminiscent of Peele, Marlowe and Kyd, but Shakespeare may have been imitating them while experimenting in styles different from those in his early Comedies and English Histories. If Shakespeare had a collaborator it was probably Peele. [2]

A somewhat similar display of passions marks *2* and *3 Henry VI* and *Richard III*,[3] in which however the rhetorical method is subordinate to historical chronicle and to political ideas which are confined to the beginning and end of *Titus Andronicus*. That these ideas are there at all, and that some attempt is made to present the Senecan-Ovidian plot within a new pseudo-historical framework, are evidence for Shakespeare's authorship and for a date not far from 1592.

But *Titus* has also many parallels with *Venus and Adonis* and *The Rape of Lucrece*, which were also experiments in Ovidian themes and modern poetic rhetoric. Shakespeare's interest in Ovid is apparent in *The Taming of the Shrew* (1592/3) when Sly is offered a choice of mythological pictures based on Ovid's stories, but that play has little of the glow or artifice of *Titus*. I incline to date *Titus* at about the same time as *Venus and Adonis* (entered in S.R. 25 June 1593). The subject of *The Rape of Lucrece* (1594) may have been suggested by the rape of Lavinia rather than *vice versa*, though it made an excellent companion-picture to the passion of Venus for Adonis. The detached

---

[1] For a fuller argument see H. T. Price, *op. cit.* and *New Arden*.

[2] Cf. J. D. Wilson, *Camb.* Introdn. and J. C. Maxwell, *JEGP*, xlix, 1952, 557–61. A. M. Sampley, *PMLA*, li, 1936, 688–701, doubts that Peele could have written this 'on the whole, well-constructed' play.

[3] V. Whitaker, *Shakespeare's Use of Learning*, San Marino, 1953, pp. 66, 68, 104, notes resemblances to *R3* in the Senecan references.

contemplation of emotions in the act of expression already mentioned as a feature of *Titus Andronicus* is also found in the two narrative poems, and was developed into a characteristic of the self-conscious Richard II in his fall.

As a collection of theatrical and rhetorical devices *Titus* is in tragedy what *The Two Gentlemen of Verona* is in comedy. Both were not wholly successful yet valuable exercises for a playwright exploring new techniques and new dramatic material, and moving away from tragic English chronicle and 'classical' comedy towards more romantic and lyrical themes.

I. Probable Source [A] and Analogue [B]

THE HISTORY OF
TITUS ANDRONICUS

Anonymous[1]

THE HISTORY OF TITUS ANDRONICUS, The Renowned Roman General. Who, after he had saved *Rome* by his Valour from being destroyed by the barbarous *Goths*, and lost two-and-twenty of his valiant Sons in ten Years War, was, upon the Emperor's marrying the Queen of the *Goths*, put to Disgrace, and banish'd; but being recall'd, the Emperor's Son by a first Wife was murder'd by the Empress's Sons and a bloody Moor, and how charging it upon *Andronicus*'s Sons, tho' he cut off his Hand to redeem their Lives, they were murder'd in Prison. How his fair Daughter *Lavinia* being ravish'd by the Empress's Sons, they cut out her Tongue, and Hands off, &c. How *Andronicus* slew them, made Pyes of their Flesh, and presented them to the Emperor and Empress; and then slew them also. With the miserable Death he put the wicked *Moor* to; then at her Request slew his Daughter and himself to avoid Torments. Newly Translated from the *Italian* Copy printed at *Rome*. *London:* Printed and Sold by *C. Dicey* in *Bow* Church-Yard, and at his Wholesale Warehouse in *Northampton*.

[1] I am indebted to Dr Louis B. Wright, Director of the Folger Library, Washington D.C. for permission to print the text of this chap-book.

34

[A] Probable Source

THE
TRAGICAL HISTORY
OF
TITUS ANDRONICUS, &c.

CHAP. I

How Rome *being besieged by the barbarous* Goths, *and being at the Point to yield, thro' Famine, it was unexpectedly rescued by* Andronicus, *with the utter Defeat of the Enemy, for which he was receiv'd in Triumph.*

WHEN the Roman Empire was grown to its Height, and the greatest Part of the World was subjected to its imperial Throne, in the Time of Theodosius, a barbarous Northern People out of Swedeland, Denmark, and Gothland, came into Italy, in such Numbers, under the leading of Tottilius, their King, that they over-run it with Fire and Sword, plundering Churches, ripping up Women with Child, and deflowring Virgins in so horrid and barbarous a manner, that the People fled before them like Flocks of Sheep.

To oppose this destroying Torrent of the Goths, a barbarous People, Strangers to Christianity, the Emperor raised a mighty Army in Greece, Italy, France, Spain, Germany, and England, and gave Battle under the Passage of the Alpine Mountains, but was overthrown, with the Loss of threescore thousand of his Men, and flying to Rome, was besieg'd in it by a numerous Host of these Barbarians, who pressed so hard to beat down the Walls, and enter with a miserable Slaughter of the Citizens, that such as could get over the River TYBER, fled in a fearful manner to a distant Country. The Siege lasting ten Months, such a Famine arose, that no unclean Thing was left uneaten, Dogs, Cats, Horses, Rats and Mice, were curious Dainties; Thousands died in the Streets of hunger, and most of those that were alive, looked more like Glass than living Creatures; so that being brought to the last Extremity, the vulgar Sort came about the Emperor's Palace, and with piteous Cries implored him either to find some means to get them Food, to stay their fleeting Live, or make the best Terms he could, and open the Gates to the Enemy.

This greatly perplexed him; the former he could not do, and the latter he knew would not only uncrown him, if he escaped with his Life, but be the Ruin of the Roman Empire; yet in the greatest of this Extremity, he unexpectedly found Relief.

4

Titus Andronicus, a Roman Senator, and a true Lover of his Country, hearing in Græcia, where he was Governor of the Province of Achaia, what Straits Rome and his Sovereign were brought into by the barbarous Nations, got together Friends, and sold whatever he had of value to hire Soldiers; so that with his small Army he secretly marched away, and falling upon the mighty Army of the Enemy, (when they were drowned as it were in Security, Wine and Sleep, resolved to make a general Storm the next Day, in which they had undoubtedly carried the City) he and his Sons entering their Camp, and followed by the rest, made such a Slaughter, that the Cry and Confusion were exceeding great; some changed Sleep into Death, others vomited Wine and Blood mixed together, through the Wounds they received; some lost Heads at once, other Arms: Tottilius, in this Confusion being awakened, had his first care to convey away his Queen and two Sons, who were newly come to the Camp, and then labour'd to rally his flying Men; but being desperately charged by Andronicus, he was thrown from his Horse and much wounded, many Lives being lost in remounting him; whereupon, seeing the Slaughter so great by the pale Beams of the Moon, and not knowing the Number of his Adversaries, having caused the Retreat to be sounded, he fled in great Confusion, and left the rich Spoils of his Camp, the Wealth of many plunder'd Nations, to Andronicus and his Soldiers; who being expert in War, would not meddle with them that Night, but stood to their Arms till the Morning.

CHAP. II

How in ten Years War, with the Loss of two and twenty of his valiant Sons, he won many famous Battles, slew Tottilius, *King of the* Goths, *and did many other brave Exploits, &c.*

THE Watch, upon the Walls of *Rome*, having heard a confused Cry and the clashing of Arms, were greatly astonish'd, but could not think what it should mean; for the Camps of the barbarous Goths extended in a large Circuit about the famous City; however the Captains of the Guards advertized the Emperor of it, who sent out Scouts but they, fearful of approaching too near the Enemy in the Night, could get certain Intelligence, only, that they heard the Groans and Cries, as they thought of dying Men: However the Shades of Night being dispelled, and the glorious Sun casting forth a chearful Light, the Porters of the Gate espying three Men coming towards it, and soon after being come up, knocked with great earnestness, they took the Courage to demand what they were, and what they required?

I am, said one of them, Andronicus, your Friend, and desire Admittance to speak with the Emperor, since the News I bring will no doubt be pleasing to him.

Upon this, lifting up his Helmet, they knew him with Joy, knowing him to be a very worthy Patriot, thinking he came to do them good, as he had often done in their great Distress, when the Huns and Vandals invaded the Empire some Years before, and were beaten out by him.

The Emperor no sooner heard he was come, but he ran from his Palace to meet him, and would not suffer him to kneel, but embrac'd him tenderly as a Brother, saying, Welcome Andronicus, in this the Time of our greatest Misery; it was thy Counsel I wanted, to know how to free us from this barbarous Enemy, against whose Force the City cannot long hold out.

May it please your Majesty, replied Andronicus, let those Fears be banished, the Work is done to you unknown; I and my twenty five Sons, and what Friends and Soldiers I could get, have this Night fallen into their Quarters, cut off fifty Thousand of them, and their scattered Remains with their King are fled.

At this the Emperor was astonished, and scarce could believe it, though he very well knew the Integrity of Andronicus, till his own Captains came and told him the Siege was raised, with a miserable Slaughter, but by whom they knew not, unless the Enemy had fallen out among themselves, and the Troops they could yet see in view were but inconsiderable; now these were those that belonged to Andronicus, who as soon as it was Day were in pursuit of the Enemy, under the Command of his five and twenty Sons.

This surprizing News was no sooner spread in the City, but the Joy of the People was exceeding great; and when they knew who was their Deliverer, they went in Procession and sung his Praises; after that, he rode in a triumphant Chariot through the City, crowned with an Oaken Garland, the People shouting, Trumpets sounding, and all other Expressions and Demonstrations of Joy, that a grateful People could afford their Deliverer, in which he behaved himself so humble, that he gained the Love of all.

This was no sooner over, but he desired the Emperor to join what Forces he could with those that he had brought, and speedily pursue the Enemy, before he could gather new Strength that he might beat him out of Italy and his other Countries, where he yet held strong Garrisons: This was embraced as good Counsel, and the Senators, by the Emperor's Mandate, assembled with Joy, who chose with one Consent Andronicus their General; he was not slow in mustering his Forces, nor in the speedy Pursuit; he found they had passed the Alps, and that their Army was increased by new Supplies, yet he gave them Battle, and charging through the thickest of their Squadrons hand to hand, slew Tottilius, and beat down his Standard; whereupon the Goths fled, and the Slaughter continued for many Miles, covering all the Lanes and Roads with the Bodies of the Dead; and in the Pursuit he took the Queen of the Goths Captive, and brought her to Rome[1]; for which signal Victory he had a second Triumph, and was stiled the Deliverer of his Country[2]: But his Joy was a little eclipsed by the Loss of five of his Sons, who died couragiously fighting in Battle.[3]

CHAP. III

How the Emperor, weary of so tedious a War, contrary to the Mind and Perswasions of Andronicus, married the Queen of the Goths, and concluded a Peace; how she tyrannized, and her Sons slew the Prince that was betrothed to Andronicus's Daughter, and hid him in the Forest.

THE Goths having found the Pleasantness of these fruitful Countries, resolved not so to give them over, but, encouraged by Tottilius's two Sons Alaricus and Abonus, sent for fresh Forces, and made a Desolation in the Roman Provinces, continuing a ten Years War,[4] wherein the valiant Andronicus, Captain-General of the Empire, gained many Victories over them, with great Effusion of Blood on either Side; but those barbarous People still encreasing in their Numbers, the Emperor, desiring Peace, it was agreed to, in Consideration he should marry Attava,[5] Queen of the Goths, and in case he should die without Issue, her Sons might succeed in the Empire. Andronicus opposed this very much, as did many other; knowing, through the Emperor's weakness, that she being an imperious Woman, and of a haughty Spirit, would govern him as she pleased, and enslave the noble Empire to Strangers: however, it was carried on with a high Hand, and great Preparations were made for the Royal Nuptials, though with very little Rejoicing among the People, for what they expected soon followed.

The Queen of the Goths being made Empress, soon began to shew her Disposition, according to the Cruelty of her Nation and Temper, perswading the easy Emperor to place the Goths in the Places of his most trusty Friends; and having above all, vowed

---

[1] The play begins here.
[2] In I.1 he is elected Emperor but refuses the honour.
[3] I.1. 33–7. At I.1. 195–7 he has lost twenty-one sons. Cf. the rubric of this chapter.
[4] Hence I.1. 31–3 perhaps.
[5] Tamora in *TA*, which alters the circumstances of the marriage.

Revenge on Andronicus, who most opposed her Proceedings, she procured him to be banished[1]; but the People, whose Deliverer he had been in their greatest Extremity, calling to mind that, and his many other good Services, rose unanimously in Arms, and went clamouring to the Palace, threatning to fire it, and revenge so base an Indignity on the Queen, if the Decree which had been passed against all Reason was not speedily revoked. This put her and the Emperor into such a Fears, that their Request was granted; and now she plotted by more private Ways to bring the Effects of Revenge and implacable Hatred about more secretly.[2]

She had a Moor as revengeful as herself, whom she trusted in many great Affairs and was usually privy to her Secrets, so far that from private Dalliances she grew pregnant, and brought forth a Blackmoor Child: This grived the Emperor extreamly, but she allayed his Anger, by telling him it was conceived by the Force of Imagination, and brought many suborned Women and Physicians to testify the like had often happened. This made the Emperor send the Moor into Banishment, upon pain of Death never to return to Rome; but her Lust, and Confidence she had put in him as the main Engine to bring about her Devilish Designs, made her Plot to have that Decree revoked; when having got the Emperor into a pleasant Humour, she feigned herself sick, telling him withal she had seen a Vision, which commanded her to call back the innocent Moor from Banishment, or she should never recover of that Sickness: The kind good-natur'd Emperor, who could not resist her Tears and Intreaties, with some difficulty consented to it, provided he should be commanded to keep always out of her Sight, lest the like Mischance might happen as had been before: This she seemingly consented to, and he was immediately sent for, and the former Familiarities continued between them, though more privately.

Andronicus, besides his Sons, had a very fair and beautiful Daughter, named Lavinia, brought up in all singular Virtues, humble, courteous and modest, insomuch that the Emperor's only Son,[3] by a former Wife fell extreamly in Love with her, seeking her Favour by all vertuous and honourable Ways, insomuch, that after a long Courtship with her Father and the Emperor's Consent she was betrothed to him.[4]

The Queen of the Goths hearing this, was much enraged, because from such a Marriage might spring Princes that might frustrate her

---

[1] In *TA* I.1. 428–95 Tamora pretends to befriend Titus.
[2] I.1. 442–55.
[3] Bassianus is Saturninus' brother.
[4] Contrast I.1.

ambitious Designs, which was to make her Sons Emperors jointly;
wherefore she laboured all she could to frustrate it, by declaring
what a Disgrace it would be to the Emperor to marry his Son to the
Daughter of a Subject, who might have a Queen with a Kingdom
to her Dowry: But finding the Prince constant, she resolved to take
him out of the Way; so it was plotted between her, the Moor, and
her two Sons, that they should invite him to hunt in the great
Forest,[1] on the Banks of the River Tyber, and there murder him.
This was effected, by shooting him thro' the Back with a poysoned
Arrow, which came out at his Breast, of which Wound he fell from
his Horse and immediately died[2]: Then they digged a very deep
Pit in a Path-way, and threw him in, covering it lightly with
Boughs, and sprinkling Earth on it[3]; and so returning reported they
had lost the Prince in the Forest, and though they had sought and
called every where, they could not find him.

CHAP. IV

*How the wicked Moor, who had laid with the Empress, and got into her
Favour above all others, betrayed* Andronicus's *three Sons, and charged
the Prince's Murder on them, for which they were cast into a Dungeon,
and after their* Father *had cut off his Hand to save them were Beheaded.*

THE fair Lavinia no sooner heard the Prince was missing, but she
fell into great Sorrow and Lamentation, her Heart misgiving her of
some Treachery, and thereupon she entreated her Brothers to go
in search of him, which they did with all speed; but being dogged
by the Moor and the Queen of Goths two Sons, they unluckily
coming in the Way where the Pit was digged, they fell both in upon
the dead Body, and could not by reason of the great Depth, get out[4];
their cruel Enemies no sooner saw this, but they hasted to the
Court, and sent the Guards in search of the murdered Prince, who
found Andronicus's two Sons with the dead Body, which they drew
up, and carried Prisoners to the Court, where the Moor and the
other two falsely swore against them,[5] that they had often heard
them threaten Revenge on the Prince, because he had put them to
the Foil, in a Turnament at Justing. This, and the Circumstances of
their being found, with the vehement Aggravation, was a sufficient
Ground to the Emperor to believe, who loved his Son entirely, and
was much grieved for his Death, and tho' they denied it with all the

[1] Cf. I.1. 492–4 where Titus invites the Emperor.
[2] In *TA* II.3.116–17 Bassianus is stabbed.
[3] II.3.186.
[4] Cf. II.3.192–245.
[5] Compare the letter in II.3.246–92.

Protestations imaginable, and pleaded their Innocence, demanded the Combat against their Accusers,[1] which by the Law of Arms they ought to have been allowed, they were immediately loaden with Irons, and cast into a deep Dungeon among noisome Creatures, as Frogs, Toads, Serpents, and the like, where notwithstanding all the Intercessions that were made, they continued eating the filth that they found in that Place.

At last the Queen designing to work her Revenge on Andronicus, sent the Moor in the Emperor's Name, to tell him, if he designed to save his Sons from the Misery and Death that would ensue, he should cut off his right Hand and send it to Court. This the good-natur'd Father scrupled not to do, no, nor had it been his Life to ransom them, he would have freely parted with it; whereupon laying his Hand on a Block, he gave the wicked Moor his Sword, who immediately struck it off, and inwardly laugh'd at the Villainy; then departing with it, he told him his Sons should be sent to him in a few Hours[2]: But whilst he was rejoicing with the Hopes of their Delivery, a Hearse came to his Door with Guards, which made his aged Heart to tremble. The first Thing they presented him was his Hand, which they said would not be accepted; and the next was his three Sons beheaded.[3] At this woful Sight, overcome with Grief, he fainted away on the dead Bodies; and when he recover'd again, he tore his hoary Hair, which Age and his lying in Winter-Camps for the Defence of his Country, had made as white as Snow, pouring out Floods of Tears; but found no Pity from the hardened Villains,[4] who left him with Scoffs in the midst of his woful Lamentations with his sorrowful Daughter: Yet this was not all, for soon after another to be deplored Affliction followed, as shall in the next Chapter be shewn.

CHAP. V

How the two lustful Sons of the Empress, with the Assistance of the Moor, in a barbarous manner ravish'd Lavinia, Andronicus's beautiful Daughter, and cut out her Tongue, and cut off her Hands, to prevent Discovery; yet she did it by writing in the Dust with a Wand, &c.

THE fair and beautiful Lavinia, for the Loss of her Lover and Brothers, so basely murder'd by Treachery, tore her golden Hair, shed Floods of Tears, and with her Nails offer'd Violence to that

---

[1] Cf. II.3.301: 'Let them not speak a word'.
[2] III.1.151–91.
[3] Cf. III.1.234–7.
[4] Cf. the Messenger's shame at III.1.238–40.

lovely Face Kings had adored and beheld with Admiration; she shunned all Company, retiring to Woods and Groves, to utter her piteous Complaints and Cries to the sensless Trees, when one Day, being watched thither by the Moor, he gave notice of it to the Queen's two Sons, who, like the wicked Elders and chaste Susanna, had a long Time burned in Lust,[1] yet knew her Virtues were proof against all Temptations, and therefore it could not be obtain'd but by Violence[2]; so thinking this an Opportunity to serve their Turns, immediately repaired to the Grove, and setting the Moor to watch on the Outborders, soon found her pensive and sorrowful, yet comely and beautiful in Tears, when unawares, before she saw them, like two ravenous Tygers,[3] they seized the trembling Lady, who struggled all she could, and cried out piteously for help; and seeing what their wicked Intentions bent at, she offered them her Throat, desiring they would bereave her of her Life, but not of her Honour[4]; however in a villainous Manner, staking her down by the Hair of her Head, and binding her Hands behind her, they turned up her Nakedness, and forced their Way into her Closet of Chastity, taking it by Turns, the Elder beginning first, and the Younger seconding him as they had before agreed on; and having tired themselves, in satiating their beastly Appetites, they began to consider how they should come off when such a Villainy was discovered; whereupon, calling the Moor to them, they asked his Advice, who wickedly counselled them to make all sure, seeing they had gone thus far, by cutting out her Tongue to hinder her telling Tales, and her Hands off to prevent her writing a Discovery[5]: This the cruel Wretches did, whilst she in vain intreated 'em to take away her Life, since they had bereaved her of her Honour, which was dearer to her. And in this woful Condition they left the Lady, who had expired for the Loss of Blood,[6] had not her Uncle Marcus happened accidentally, soon after, to come in search of her,[7] who at the woful Sight, overcome with Sorrow, could hardly keep Life in himself; yet recovering his Spirits, he bound up her Wounds, and conveyed her home.

Poor Andronicus's Grief for this sad Disaster was so great, that no Pen can write or Words express; much ado they had to restrain him from doing Violence upon himself[8]; he cursed the Day he was born to see such Miseries fall on himself and Family, intreating her to

---

[1] Cf. II.1.26–119.   [2] II.1.108–9.
[3] Cf. II.3. The tiger-image appears at l. 142.
[4] Lavinia to Tamora, II.3.168–78.
[5] Cf. II.4.1–8.   [6] II.4.29–30.   [7] II.4.11ff.
[8] Plenty of words in III.1.63–150.

tell him, if she could any ways do it by signs, who had so villainously abused her. At last the poor Lady, with a Flood of Tears gushing from her Eyes, taking a Wand between her Stumps, wrote these Lines.

> The Lustful Sons of the proud Emperess
> Are Doers of this hateful Wickedness.[1]

Hereupon he vowed Revenge, at the Hazard of his own and all their Lives, comforting his Daughter with this when nothing else would do.

CHAP. VI

How Andronicus, *feigning himself mad, found Means to intrap the Empress's two Sons in a Forest, where binding them to a Tree, he cut their Throats, made Pyes of their Flesh, and served them up to the Emperor and Empress, then slew them, set the Moor quick in the Ground, and then killed his Daughter and himself.*

ANDRONICUS, upon these Calamities, feigned himself distracted,[2] and went raving about the City, shooting his Arrows towards Heaven, as in Defiance, calling to Hell for Vengeance,[3] which mainly pleased the Empress and her Sons, who thought themselves now secure[4]; and though his Friends required Justice of the Emperor against the Ravishers, yet they could have no Redress, he rather threatening them, if they insisted on it; so that finding they were in a bad Case, and that in all Probability their Lives would be the next, they conspired together to prevent that Mischief, and revenge themselves; lying in Ambush in the Forest when the two Sons went a hunting, they surprized them, and binding them to a Tree pitifully crying out for Mercy, though they would give none to others, Andronicus cut their Throats whilst Lavinia, by his Command, held a Bowl between her Stumps to receive the Blood[5]; then conveying the Bodies home to his own House privately, he cut the Flesh into fit Pieces, and ground the Bones to Powder, and made of them two mighty Pasties, and invited the Emperor and Empress to Dinner, who thinking to make sport with his frantick Humour came; but when they had eat of the Pasties, he told them what it was[6]; and thereupon giving the Watch Word to his Friends, they

---

[1] IV.1.79–80.
[2] IV.2.3; IV.3.25–31.
[3] Hence IV.3.10–44.
[4] Cf. IV.4.1–38. Here Tamora yet seeks his death.
[5] V.2.152–206.
[6] V.3.60–3.

immediately issued out, slew the Emperor's Guards, and, lastly, the Emperor and his cruel Wife, after they had sufficiently upbraided them with the wicked Deeds they had done. Then seizing on the wicked Moor, the fearful Villain fell on his Knees, promising to discover all[1]; but when he had told how he had killed the Prince, betrayed the three Sons of Andronicus by false Accusation, and counselled the Abuse to the fair Lavinia, they scarce knew what Torments sufficient to devise for him; but at last, digging a Hole, they set him in the Ground to the middle alive, smeered him over with Honey, and so, between the stinging of Bees and Wasps and starving, he miserably ended his wretched Days,[2] After this, to prevent the Torments he expected, when these Things came to be known, at his Daughter's Request, he killed her[3]; and so, rejoicing he had revenged himself on his Enemies to the full, fell on his own Sword and died.[4]

[B] Analogue

The Lamentable and Tragical History of Titus Andronicus, *with the Fall of his Sons in the War of the* Goths, *with the manner of the Ravishment of his Daughter* Lavinia, *by the Empress's two Sons, through the means of a bloody* Moor, *taken by the Sword of* Titus, *in the War: With his Revenge upon their cruel and inhuman Act. To the Tune of,* Fortune my Foe, &c.

YOU noble Minds, and famous martial Wights,
That in Defence of Native Countries[5] fights
Give ear to me that Ten Years fought for Rome,
Yet reap'd Disgrace at my returning home.

 In Rome I liv'd in Fame, full threescore Years,
My Name beloved was of all my Peers;
Full five and Twenty valiant Sons I had,
Whose forward Virtues made their Father glad.

 For when Rome's Foes their warlike Forces felt,
Against them still my Sons and I were sent;
Against the Goths full ten Years weary War[6]
We spent, receiving many a bloody scar.

---

[1] Cf. V.3.176–90.   [2] V.3.35–53.
[3] At V.3.64 Saturninus kills Titus.
[4] G (*Golden Garland*) *has* countrey.
[5] V.1.53–151   [6] I.1.31, 'Ten years'.

Just two and twenty of my Sons were slain,
Before I did return to Rome again;
Of five and twenty Sons, I brought but three[1]
Alive the stately Tower of Rome to see.

When Wars were done, I Conquest home did bring,
And did present my Prisoners to the King;
The Queen of Goths,[2] her Sons,[3] and eke a Moor,
Who did such Murders, like were none[4] before.

The Emperor did make the[5] Queen his Wife,
Which bred in Rome debate and deadly strife;
The Moor with her two Sons did grow so proud,
That none like them in Rome might be[6] allow'd.

The Moor so pleased this new[7] Empress's Eye,
That she consented to[8] him secretly,
For to abuse her Husband's Marriage Bed,
And so in Time a Blackmoor[9] she bred.

Then she, whose thoughts to Murder were inclin'd,
Consented with the Moor with bloody Mind,
Against myself, my Kin, and all my Friends,
In cruel Sort to bring them to their Ends.

So when in Age I thought to live in Peace,
Both Care and Grief began then to encrease;
Amongst my Sons I had one Daughter bright,
Which joy'd and pleased best my aged Sight.

My[10] Lavinia was betrothed then
To Cæsar's Son,[11] a young and noble Man,
Who in a Hunting, by the Emperor's Wife,
And her two Sons, bereaved was[12] of Life.

He being slain, was cast, in cruel wise,
Into a darksome[13] Den, from Light of Skies;

---

[1] I.1.69 *s.d.* names four. [2] *G.* Goth.
[3] The sacrifice of Alarbus is omitted; also the quarrel about Lavinia.
[4] *G.* was here. [5] *G.* this. [6] *G.* was then.
[7] *G.* new made. [8] *G.* with. [9] *G.* blacke a moore.
[10] *G.* My dear. [11] Brother, in *TA* [12] *G.* were.
[13] *G.* dismall.

The cruel Moor did come that Way as then
With my three Sons,[1] who fell into the Den.

The Moor then fetch'd[2] the Emperor with speed,
For to accuse them of that murderous Deed:
And when my Sons within the Den were found,
In wrongful Prison were they cast and bound.

But now behold what wounded most my Mind,
The Empress's two Sons of Tygers kind,[3]
My Daughter ravished without Remorse,
And took away her Honour quite by Force.[4]

When they had tasted of so sweet a Flower,
Fearing this[5] sweet should turned be[6] to Sour,
They cut her Tongue, whereby she could not tell,
How that Dishonour unto her befel.

Then both her Hands they basely cut off quite,
Whereby their Wickedness she could not write,
Nor with her Needle on her Sampler sow
The bloody Workers of her dismal Woe.[7]

My Brother Marcus, found her in the[8] Wood,
Staining the grassy Ground with purple Blood,
That trickled from her Stumps and handless Arms.
No Tongue at all she had to tell her harms.[9]

But when I saw her in that woful Case,
With Tears of Blood I wet my aged Face,
For my Lavinia I lamented more
Than for my two and twenty Sons before.

When as I saw she could not write nor speak,
With Grief my aged Heart began to break;
We spread a heap of Sand upon the Ground,
Whereby the bloody Tyrants out we found.

---

[1] Only two in *TA*. Lucius survives. *G*. two.
[2] *G*. seetht.
[3] Cf. the tiger-image in the prose tale and *TA* II.3.142.
[4] *G*. perforce.   [5] *G*. their.   [6] *G*. shortly turne.
[7] Cf. II.4.38–43. *G*. direfull woe.   [8] *G*. a.
[9] III.1.107, 'Nor tongue to tell me who hath martyr'd thee.'

For with a Staff, without the help of Hand,
She writ these Words upon a plat of Sand[1]:
The lustful Sons of the proud Empress,[2]
Are Doers of this hateful Wickedness.

I tore the milk-white Hairs from off my Head,[3]
I curst the Hour wherein I first was bred;
I wish'd the Hand that fought for Country's Fame,
In Cradle rock'd, had first been stricken lame.

The Moor delighting still in Villainy,
Did say, to set my Sons from Prison free,
I should unto the King my Right Hand give,
And then my three Imprisoned Sons should live.[4]

The Moor I caus'd to strike it off with speed,
Whereas I grieved not to see it bleed,
But for my Sons would willingly impart,
And for their Ransom send my bleeding Heart.

But as my Life did linger thus in vain,
They sent to me my bootless Hand again,
And therewithal the Heads of my three Sons,
Which fill'd my dying Heart with fresher Groans.

Then past Relief, I up and down did go,
And with my Tears writ in the Dust my Woe;
I shot my Arrows towards Heaven high,[5]
And for Revenge to Hell did often cry.[6]

The Empress thinking then that I was mad,
Like Furies she and both her Sons were glad,
So nam'd Revenge, and Rape, and Murder, they
To undermine and hear what I would say.[7]

I fed their foolish Veins a little space,[8]
Until my Friends did find a secret Place,

---

[1] IV.1.69. 'This sandy plot is plain.'   [2] IV.1.79–80.
[3] III.1.260. 'Rent off thy silver hair.'
[4] The order of events agrees with III.1.151–245.
[5] IV.3.1–4; 50–6.
[6] IV.3.13–15; 37–8.
[7] Obscure unless we know IV.4.88–93; V.2.1–148.
[8] Explained by V.2.64–9; 142–4.

Where both her Sons unto a Post were bound,
Where just Revenge in cruel Sort I found.

    I cut their Throats, my Daughter held the Pan
Betwixt her Stumps,[1] wherein the Blood it ran.
And then I ground their Bones to Powder small,
And made a Pasty for Pies straight therewithal.[2]

    Then with their Flesh I made two mighty Pies,
And at a Banquet serv'd in stately wise;
Before the Empress set this Loathsome Meat,
So of her Sons own Flesh she well did eat.[3]

    Myself bereav'd my Daughter then of Life,
The Empress then I slew with bloody Knife;[4]
And stabb'd the Emperor immediately,
And then myself, even so did Titus die.[5]

    Then this Revenge against their Moor was found,
Alive they set him half into the Ground,
Whereas he stood until such Time he starv'd[6];
And so God send all Murderers may be serv'd.

FINIS

II. Source

OVID: METAMORPHOSES
translated by Arthur Golding (1567)

The XV. Bookes of P. Ovidius Naso, entytuled Metamorphosis, translated oute of Latin into English Meeter, by Arthur Golding Gentleman. A worke very pleasaunt and delectable. 1567. Imprynted at London, by Willyam Seres.

---

[1] V.2.182–4.   [2] V.2.190.   [3] V.3.54–63.
[4] As in V.3.47, 63.
[5] In *TA* the Emperor kills Titus and Lucius kills the Emperor, V.3.64–6.
[6] Nearer to V.3.179–83 than to the prose tale.

From The Sixth Booke
(The story of Philomela)

The neyghbor Princes thither came, and all the Cities round   526
About besought their Kings to go and comfort *Thebe*: as *Arge*
And *Sparta*, and *Mycene* which was under *Pelops* charge.

. . . .

Alonly *Athens* (who would thinke?) did neither come nor send: 538
Warre barred them from courtesie the which they did entend.
The King of *Pontus* with an host of savage people lay
In siege before their famous walles and curstly did them fray.
Untill that *Tereus* King of *Thrace* approching to their ayde,
Did vanquish him, and with renowne was for his labor payde.
And sith he was so puissant in men and ready coyne,
And came of mightie *Marsis* race, *Pandion* sought to joyne
Aliance with him by and by, and gave him to his Feere
His daughter *Progne*. At this match (as after will appeare)
Was neyther *Juno*, President of mariage wont to bee,
Nor *Hymen*, no nor any one of all the graces three.
The Furies snatching Tapers up that on some Herce did stande   550
Did light them, and before the Bride did beare them in their
      hande.
The Furies made the Bridegroomes bed. And on the house did
      rucke[1]
A cursed Owle the messenger of yll successe and lucke.
And all the night time while that they were lying in their beds,
She sate upon the bedsteds top right over both their heds.
Such handsell[2] *Progne* had the day that *Tereus* did hir wed:
Such handsell had they when that she was brought of childe
      a bed.
All *Thracia* did rejoyce at them, and thankt their Gods, and
      wild
That both the day of *Prognes* match with *Tereus* should be hild
For feastfull, and the day likewise that *Itys* first was borne: 560
So little know we what behoves. The Sunne had now outworne
Five Harvests, and by course five times had runne his yearly
      race,
When *Progne* flattring *Tereus* saide: If any love or grace
Betweene us be, send eyther me my sister for to see,
Or finde the meanes that hither she may come to visit mee.
You may assure your Fathrinlaw she shall againe returne

---

[1] squat.   [2] lucky gift.

Within a while. Ye doe to me the highest great good turne
That can be, if you bring to passe I may my sister see.
Immediately the King commaundes his shippes a flote to bee.
And shortly after, what with sayle and what with force of Ores,   570
In *Athens* haven he arrives and landes at *Pyrey*[1] shores.
Assoone as of his fathrinlaw the presence he obtainde,
And had of him bene courteously and friendly entertainde,
Unhappie handsell entred with their talking first togither.
The errandes of his wife the cause of his then comming thither
He had but new begon to tell, and promised that when
She had hir sister seene, she should with speede be sent agen:
When (see the chaunce) came *Philomele* in raiment very rich,
And yet in beautie farre more rich, even like the Fairies which
Reported are the pleasant woods and water springs to haunt,   580
So that the like apparell and attire to them you graunt.
King *Tereus* at the sight of hir did burne in his desire,
As if a man should chaunce to set a gulfe of corne on fire,
Or burne a stacke of hay. Hir face in deede deserved love. ⎤
But as for him, to fleshy lust even nature him did move.   ⎬
For of those countries commonly the people are above   ⎦
All measure prone to lecherie. And therefore both by kinde
His flame encreast, and by his owne default of vicious minde.
He purposde fully to corrupt hir servants with reward:
Or for to bribe hir Nurce, that she should slenderly regard   590
Hir dutie to hir mistresseward. And rather then to fayle,
The Ladie even hirselfe with giftes he minded to assayle,
And all his kingdome for to spend: or else by force of hand
To take hir, and in maintenance thereof by sword to stand.
There was not under heaven the thing but that he durst it
         prove,
So far unable was he now to stay his lawlesse love.
Delay was deadly: Backe againe with greedie minde he⎤
         came,   ⎮
Of *Prognes* errands for to talke: and underneath the same ⎬
He workes his owne ungraciousnesse. Love gave him power ⎮
         to frame   ⎦
His talke at will. As oft as he demaunded out of square,   600
Upon his wives importunate desire himselfe he bare.
He also wept: as though his wife had willed that likewise.
O God, what blindnesse doth the heartes of mortall men
         disguise?

----

[1] Piræus.

By working mischiefe *Tereus* gets him credit for to seeme
A loving man, and winneth praise by wickednesse extreeme.
Yea and the foolish *Philomele* the selfe same thing desires.
Who hanging on hir fathers necke with flattring armes,
    requires
Against hir life and for hir life his licence for to go
To see hir sister. *Tereus* beholdes hir wistly tho,
And in beholding handles hir with heart. For when he saw   610
Hir kisse hir father, and about his necke hir armes to draw,
They all were spurres to pricke him forth, and wood to feede
    his fire,
And foode of forcing nourishment to further his desire.
As oft as she hir father did betweene hir armes embrace, ⎫
So often wished he himselfe hir father in that case.   ⎬
For nought at all should that in him have wrought the ⎭
    greater grace.
Hir father could not say them nay they lay at him so sore.
Right glad thereof was *Philomele* and thanked him therefore.
And wretched wench she thinkes she had obtained such a
    thing,
As both to *Progne* and hir selfe should joy and comfort bring, 620
When both of them in verie deede should afterward it rew. ⎫
To endward of his daily race and travell *Phebus* drew,   ⎬
And on the shoring side of Heaven his horses downeward ⎭
    flew.
A princely supper was prepaarde, and wine in golde was set:
And after meate to take their rest the Princes did them get.
But though the King of *Thrace* that while were absent from
    hir sight,
Yet swelted he: and in his minde revolving all the night
Hir face, hir gesture, and hir hands, imaginde all the rest
(The which as yet he had not seene) as likte his fancie best. 629
He feeds his flames himselfe. No winke could come within his
    eyes,
For thinking ay on hir. Assoone as day was in the skies,
Pandion holding in his hand the hand of *Tereus* prest
To go his way, and shedding teares betooke him thus his guest.
Deare sonneinlaw I give thee here (sith godly cause constraines)
This Damsell. By the faith that in thy Princely hart remaines,
And for our late aliance sake, and by the Gods above,
I humbly thee besche, that as a Father thou doe love
And maintaine hir, and that as soone as may be (all delay ⎫
Will unto me seeme over long) thou let hir come away   ⎬
The comfort of my carefull age on whome my life doth stay. ⎭ 640

5

And thou my daughter *Philomele* (it is inough ywis
That from hir father set so farre thy sister *Progne* is)
If any sparke of nature doe within thy heart remayne,
With all the haast and speede thou canst returne to me
    againe.
In giving charge he kissed hir: and down his cheekes did
    raine
The tender teares: and as a pledge of faith he tooke the right
Handes of them both, and joyning them did eche to other
    plight,
Desiring them to beare in minde his commendations to
His daughter and hir little sonne. And then with much a doe
For sobbing, at the last he bad adew as one dismaid: 650
The foremisgiving of his minde did make him sore afraid.
   Assoone as *Tereus* and the Maide togither were a boord,
   And that their ship from land with Ores was haled on the
      foord,
The fielde is ours he cride aloude, I have the thing I sought
And up he skipt, so barbrous and so beastly was his thought,
That scarce even there he could forbeare his pleasure to have
    wrought.
His eye went never off of hir: as when the scarefull Erne[1]
With hooked talants[2] trussing up a Hare among the Ferne,
Hath laid hir in his nest, from whence the prisoner can not
    scape:
The ravening fowle with greedie eyes upon his pray doth gape.   660
Now was their journey come to ende: now were they gone a
    land
In *Thracia*, when that *Tereus* tooke the Ladie by the hand,
And led hir to a pelting graunge that peakishly did stand
In woods forgrowen. There waxing pale and trembling sore
    for feare,
And dreading all things, and with teares demaunding sadly
    where
Hir sister was, he shet hir up: and therewithall bewraide
His wicked lust, and so by force bicause she was a Maide
And all alone he vanquisht hir. It booted nought at all
That she on sister, or on Sire, or on the Gods did call.   669
She quaketh like the wounded Lambe which from the Wolves
    hore teeth
New shaken, thinkes hir selfe not safe: or as the Dove that seeth

---

[1] Eagle.
[2] talons.

Hir fethers with hir owne bloud staynde, who shuddring still
 doth feare
The greedie Hauke that did hir late with griping talants teare.
 Anon when that this mazednesse was somewhat overpast,
 She rent hir haire, and beate hir brest, and up to heaven-
 ward cast
Hir hands in mourningwise, and said: O cankerd Carle, O fell
And cruell Tyrant, neyther could the godly teares that fell
A downe my fathers cheekes when he did give thee charge of
 mee,
Ne of my sister that regarde that ought to be in thee,
Nor yet my chast virginitie, nor conscience of the lawe   680
Of wedlocke, from this villanie thy barbrous heart withdraw?
Beholde thou hast confounded all. My sister thorough mee
Is made a Cucqueane[1]: and thy selfe through this offence of
 thee
Art made a husband to us both, and unto me a foe,
A just deserved punishment for lewdly doing so.
But to th'intent O perjurde wretch no mischiefe may remaine
Unwrought by thee, why doest thou from murdring me
 refraine?
Would God thou had it done before this wicked rape. From
 hence
Then should my soule most blessedly have gone without
 offence.
But if the Gods doe see this deede, and if the Gods I say   690
Be ought, and in this wicked worlde beare any kinde of sway,⎤
And if with me all other things decay not, sure the day   ⎟
Wille come that for this wickednesse full dearly thou shalt ⎬
 pay.   ⎦
Yea I my selfe rejecting shame thy doings will bewray.
And if I may have power to come abrode, them blase I will⎤
In open face of all the world: or if thou keepe me still ⎬
As prisoner in these woods, my voyce the verie woods shall⎟
 fill,   ⎦
And make the stones to understand. Let Heaven to this give⎤
 eare   ⎟
And all the Gods and powers therein if any God be there. ⎬
 The cruell tyrant being chaft, and also put in feare   ⎦   700
 With these and other such hir wordes both causes so him
 stung,
That drawing out his naked sworde that at his girdle hung,

[1] female cuckold.

He tooke hir rudely by the haire, and wrung hir hands behind
hir,
Compelling hir to holde them there while he himselfe did
binde hir.
When *Philomela* sawe the sworde she hoapt she should have dide,
And for the same hir naked throte she gladly did provide.
But as she yirnde and called ay upon hir fathers name,
And strived to have spoken still, the cruell tyrant came,
And with a paire of pinsons [1] fast did catch hir by the tung,
And with his sword did cut it off. The stumpe whereon it hung   710
Did patter still. The tip fell downe, and quivering on the
ground
As though that it had murmured it made a certaine sound,
And as an Adders tayle cut off doth skip a while: even so
The tip of *Philomela's* tongue did wriggle to and fro,
And nearer to hir mistresseward in dying still did go.
And after this most cruell act, for certaine men report
That he (I scarcely dare beleve) did oftentimes resort
To maymed *Philomela* and abusde hir at his will.
Yet after all this wickednesse he keeping countnance still,
Durst unto *Progne* home repaire. And she immediatly   720
Demaunded where hir sister was. He sighing feynedly
Did tell hir falsly she was dead: and with his suttle teares ⎫
He maketh all his tale to seeme of credit in hir eares.   ⎬
Hir garments glittring all with golde she from hir shoulders ⎪
teares   ⎭
And puts on blacke, and setteth up an emptie Herce, and
keepes
A solemne obite [2] for hir soule, and piteously she weepes
And waileth for hir sisters fate who was not in such wise
As that was, for to be bewailde. The Sunne had in the Skies
Past through the twelve celestiall signes, and finisht full a
yeare.
But what should *Philomela* doe? She watched was so neare   730
That start she could not for hir life, the walles of that same
graunge
Were made so high of maine hard stone, that out she could not
raunge.
Againe hir tunglesse mouth did want the utterance of the fact.
Great is the wit of pensivenesse, and when the head is rac[k]t
With hard misfortune, sharpe forecast of practise entereth in.

[1] pincers.
[2] obit, funeral rite.

A warpe of white upon a frame of *Thracia* she did pin,
And weaved purple letters in betweene it, which bewraide
The wicked deede of *Tereus*. And having done, she praide
A certaine woman by hir signes to beare them to hir mistresse.
She bare them and delivered them not knowing nerethelesse   740
What was in them. The Tyrants wife unfolded all the clout,
And of hir wretched fortune re[a]d the processe whole
    throughout.
She held hir peace (a wondrous thing it is she should so doe)
But sorrow tide hir tongue, and wordes agreeable unto
Hir great displeasure were not at commaundment at that ⎫
    stound, ⎪
And weepe she could not. Ryght and wrong she reckeneth ⎬
    to confound, ⎪
And on revengement of the deede hir heart doth wholy ⎭
    ground.
   It was the time that wives of *Thrace* were wont to celebrate
   The three yeare rites of *Bacchus* which were done a night-
    times late.
A nighttimes soundeth *Rhodope* of tincling pannes and pots: 750
A nighttimes giving up hir house, abrode Queene *Progne* trots,
Disguisde like *Bacchus* other froes,[1] and armed to the proofe
With all the frenticke furniture that serves for that behoofe.
Hir head was covered with a vine. About hir loose was tuckt
A Red-deeres skin, a lightsome Launce upon hir shoulder
    ruckt.
In post[2] gaddes terrible *Progne* through the woods, and at hir
    heeles
A flocke of froes: and where the sting of sorrow which she feeles
Enforceth hir to furiousnesse, she feynes it to proceede
Of *Bacchus* motion. At the length she finding out in deede   759
The outset Graunge, howlde out, and cride now well, and
    open brake
The gates, and streight hir sister thence by force of hand did
    take,
And veyling hir in like attire of *Bacchus* hid hir head
With Ivie leaves, and home to Court hir sore amazed led.
   Assoone as *Philomela* wist she set hir foote within
   That cursed house, the wretched soule to shudder did begin,
And all hir face waxt pale. Anon hir sister getting place
Did pull off *Bacchus* mad attire, and making bare hir face

---

[1] women.
[2] In haste.

Embraced hir betweene hir armes. But she considering that
Queene *Progne* was a Cucqueane made by meanes of hir, durst
    nat
Once raise hir eyes: but on the ground fast fixed helde the
    same.   770
And where she woulde have taken God to witnesse that the
    shame
And villanie was wrought to hir by violence, she was fayne⌉
To use hir hand instead of speache. Then *Progne* chaft[1] a ⎬
    maine
And was not able in hir selfe hir choler to restraine,   ⌋
But blaming *Philomela* for hir weeping, said these wordes.
Thou must not deale in this behalfe with weeping, but with
    swordes,
Or with some thing of greater force than swords. For my part, I
Am readie, yea and fully bent all mischiefe for to trie.
This pallace will I eyther set on fire, and in the same
Bestow the cursed *Tereus* the worker of our shame: 780
Or pull away his tongue: or put out both his eyes: or cut
Away those members which have thee to such dishonor put:
Or with a thousand woundes expulse that sinfull soule of his.
The thing that I do purpose on, is great what ere it is.
I know not what it may be yet. While *Progne* hereunto
Did set hir minde, came *Itys* in, who taught hir what to doe.
She staring on him cruelly, said, Ah, how like thou art   ⌉
Thy wicked father, and without moe wordes a sorrowfull part ⎬
She purposed, such inward ire was boyling in hir heart.   ⌋
But notwithstanding when hir sonne approached to hir neare, 790
And lovingly had greeted hir by name of mother deare,
And with his pretie armes about the necke had hugde hir fast,
And flattring wordes with childish toyes in kissing forth
    had cast:
The mothers heart of hirs was then constreyned to relent, ⌉
Asswaged wholy was the rage to which she erst was bent, ⎬
And from hir eyes against hir will the teares enforced went.⌋
But when she saw how pitie did compell hir heart to yeelde,
She turned to hir sisters face from *Itys*, and behelde
Now t'one, now t'other earnestly and said, why tattles he,   799
And she sittes dumbe bereft of tongue? as well why calles not
    she
Me sister, as this boy doth call me mother? Seest thou not
Thou daughter of *Pandion* what a husband thou hast got?

---

[1] chafed, fretted.

Thou growest wholy out of kinde. To such a husband as
Is *Tereus*, pitie is a sinne. No more delay there was.
She dragged *Itys* after hir as when it happes in *Inde*
A Tyger gets a little Calfe that suckes upon a Hynde,
And drags him through the shadie woods. And when that they
    had found
A place within the house far off and far above the ground,
Then *Progne* strake him with a sword now plainly seeing
    whother
He should, and holding up his handes, and crying mother,
    mother,   810
And flying to hir necke: even where the brest and side doe
    bounde,
And never turnde away hir face. Inough had bene that wound
Alone to bring him to his ende. The t'other sister slit
His throte. And while some life and soule was in his members
    yit,
In gobbits they them rent: whereof were some in Pipkins ⎫
    boyld,   ⎬
And other some on hissing spits against the fire were broyld: ⎪
And with the gellied bloud of him was all the chamber soyld. ⎭
    To this same banket *Progne* bade hir husband, knowing
    nought,
    Nor nought mistrusting of the harme and lewdnesse she had
    wrought.
And feyning a solemnitie according to the guise   820
Of *Athens*, at the which there might be none in any wise
Besides hir husband and hir selfe, she banisht from the same
Hir householde folke and sojourners, and such as guestwise
    came.
King *Tereus* sitting in the throne of his forefathers, fed
And swallowed downe the selfe same flesh that of his bowels
    bred.
And he (so blinded was his heart) fetch *Itys* hither, sed.
No lenger hir most cruell joy dissemble could the Queene,
But of hir murther coveting the messenger to beene,
She said: the thing thou askest for, thou hast within. About ⎫
He looked round, and asked where? To put him out of dout, ⎬ 830
As he was yet demaunding where, and calling for him: out ⎭
Lept *Philomele* with scattred haire aflaight[1] like one that fled
Had from some fray where slaughter was, and threw the
    bloudy head

[1] afloat, overflowing.

Of *Itys* in his fathers face. And never more was shee
Desirous to have had hir speache, that able she might be
Hir inward joy with worthie wordes to witnesse franke and
free.
The tyrant with a hideous noyse away the table shoves,
And reeres the fiends from Hell. One while with yauning
mouth he proves
To perbrake up his meate againe, and cast his bowels out.
Another while with wringing handes he weeping goes about.   840
And of his sonne he termes himselfe the wretched grave. Anon
With naked sword and furious heart he followeth fierce upon
Pandions daughters. He that had bin present would have
deemde
Their bodies to have hovered up with fethers. As they seemde,
So hovered they with wings in deede. Of whome the one away
To woodward flies,[1] the other still about the house doth stay.[2]
And of their murther from their brestes not yet the token goth,
For even still yet are stainde with bloud the fethers of them
both.
And he through sorrow and desire of vengeance waxing
wight,
Became a Bird upon whose top a tuft of feathers light   850
In likenesse of a Helmets crest doth trimly stand upright.
In stead of his long sword, his bill shootes out a passing space:
A Lapwing named is this Bird, all armed seemes his face.
   The sorrow of this great mischaunce did stop *Pandions*
   breath
   Before his time, and long ere age determinde had his
   death. . . .

III. Source

From THYESTES

by Lucius Annaeus Seneca, translated by Jasper Heywood (1560)

The Seconde Tragedie of Seneca entituled Thyestes
faithfully Englished by Jasper Heywood fellowe of

---

[1] Philomele becomes a Nightingale.   [2] Progne becomes a Swallow.

Alsolne College in Oxforde. Imprinted at London in
Fletestrete in the hous late Thomas Berthelettes.
Anno. 1560. 26. die Martii.

The fyrst Acte.

TANTALUS.   MEGÆRA.

What furye fell enforceth me to flee thunhappie seate,
That gape and gaspe with greedy jawe, the fleeyng foode to
eate?
What god to Tantalus the bowres where breathyng bodies
dwell
Doth showe agayne? is ought found worse then burning
thurst of hell
In lakes alowe? or yet worse plague then hunger is there one,
In vayne that ever gapes for foode? shall Sisyphus his stone,
That slypper restles rollying payse[1] upon my backe be borne?
Or shall my lymms with swyfter swynge of whirlyng wheele
be torne?
Or shall my paynes be Tityus pangs thencreasing lyver styll,
Whose growyng gutts the gnawyng grypes and fylthie foules
doe fyll?   10
That styll by night repayres the panche that was devowrde
by daie,
And wondrows wombe unwasted lythe a new prepared praie.
What yll am I appoynted for? O cruell judge of sprights,
Who so thou be that torments newe among the soules
delights
Styll to dyspose, adde what thou canst to all my deadly woe,
That keper even of dungeon darke wolde sore abhorre to knoe,
Or hell it selfe it quake to see: for dreade whereof lykewyse
I tremble woulde, that plague seeke out: Loe nowe there dothe
aryse
My broode, that shall in mischiefe farre the grandsiers gylt out
goe,
And gyltles make: that fyrst shall dare unventred ylls to doe.   20
What ever place remaineth yet of all this wycked lande,
I will fyll up: and never once while Pelops house dothe stande
Shall Minos idle be.   MEG. goe foorth thou detestable spright,
And vexe the godds of wycked house with rage of furies might.
Let them contende with all offence, by turnes and one by one

---

[1] weight.

Let swoordes be drawen: and meane of ire procure there maie
    be none,
Nor shame: let furie blynde enflame their myndes and wrath-
    full wyll,
Let yet the parents rage endure, and longer lastyng yll,
Through childerns childern spreade: nor yet let any leysure be
The former fawte to hate, but styll more mischiefe newe to see,   30
Nor one in one: but ere the gylt with vengeance be acquyt,
Encrease the cryme: from brethern proude let rule of kyng-
    dome flyt,
To runagates: and swarvyng state of all unstable things,
Let it by doubtfull dome be toste, betwene thuncertayne kyngs.
Let mightie fall to miserie, and myser clyme to myght,
Let chaunce turne thempyre up so downe both geve and take
    the ryght.
The banyshed for gylt, whan god restore theyr countrey shall,
Let them to mischiefe fall a freshe: as hatefull then to all,
As to them selves: let Ire thinke nought unlawfull to be doon.
Let brother dreade the brothers wrathe, and father feare the
    soon,
And eke the soon his parents powre. let babes be murdered yll,   40
But woorse begotte: her spouse betrapt in treasons trayne to
    kyll,
Let hatefull wyfe awayte. and let them beare through seas
    their warre,
Let bloodshed lye the lands about and every feelde afarre:
And over conqueryng captaynes greate, of countreys farre to
    see,
Let luste tryumphe: in wycked house let whoordome counted be
The lightst offense: let trust that in the breasts of brethern
    breedes,
And truthe be gone: let not from sight of your so heynous
    deedes
The heavens be hyd, about the poale when shyne the starres
    on hye,
And flames with woonted beames of light doe decke the
    paynted skye.   50
Let darkest night be made, and let the daye the heavens
    forsake.
Dysturbe the godds of wycked house, hate, slaughter, murder
    make.
Fyll up the house of Tantalus with mischieves and debates.
Adorned be the pyllers hyghe, with baye and let the gates

Be garnysht greene: and woorthie there for thy returne to
    syght,
Be kyndled fyre: let myschiefe doone in Thracia onse, there
    lyght
More manyfolde. wherfore dothe yet the uncles hande delaie?
Dothe yet Thyestes not bewayle his childerns fatall daye?
Shall he not fynde them where with heate of fyres that under
    glowe
The cawdern boyles? their lymms eche one a peeces let them
    goe   60
Dysperste: let fathers fires, with blood of childern fyled bee:
Let deynties suche be dreste: it is no myschiefe newe to thee,
To banquet so: beholde, this daie we have to the releaste,
And hunger starved wombe of thyne we sende to suche a feaste.
With fowlest foode thy famyne fyll, let bloode in wyne be
    drownde,
And droonke in syght of thee: loe nowe suche dyshes have I
    founde,
As thou wouldst shonne. staie whither doste thou hedlong waie
    nowe take?
  TAN. To pooles and floods of hell agayne, and styll
    declynyng lake,
And flight of tree full fraight with fruite that from the lyppes
    dothe flee,
To dungeon darke of hatefull hell let leefull be for mee   70
To goe: or if to light be thought the paynes that there I have,
Remove me from those lakes agayne: in mydst of worser wave
Of Phleghethon to stande, in seas of fyre besette to be.
Who so beneath thy poynted paynes by destenies decree
Dooste styll endure, who so thou be that underliest alowe
The hollowe denne, or ruyne who that feares and overthrowe
Of fallyng hyll, or cruell cryes that sounde in caves of hell
Of greedy roaryng lyons throates, or flocke of furies fell
Who quakes to knowe, or who the brands of fyre, in dyrest
    payne
Halfe burnte throwes of, harke to the voice of Tantalus:
    agayne   80
That hastes to hell. and (whom the truthe hath taught)
    beleve well mee
Love well your paynes, they are but small. when shall my
    happe so bee
To flee the lyght? MEG. disturbe thou fyrst this house with
    dyre discorde:

Debates and battels bryng with thee, and of th'unhappie
    swoorde
Ill love to kynges: the cruell brest stryke through and hatefull
    harte,
With tumulte madde.   TAN.   To suffre paynes it seemeth well
    my parte,
Not woes to woorke: I am sent foorth lyke vapour dyre to ryse,
That breakes the ground, or poyson lyke the plague, in
    wondrowse wyse
That slaughter makes. shall I to suche detested crymes, applye
My nephewes hartes? o parents greate of godds above the skye,   90
And myne, (though shamde I be to graunte,) although with
    greatter payne
My tounge be vexte, yet this to speake I maie no whit refrayne,
Nor holde my peace: I warne you this, leaste sacred hand with
    bloode
Of slaughter dyre, or fransie fell of frantyke furie woode
The aulters stayne, I will resyste: And garde suche gylt awaye.
With strypes why dooste thou me affryght? why threatst thou
    me to fraye
Those crallyng snakes? or famyne fyxt in emptie wombe,
    wherfore
Dooste thou revyve? nowe fryes within with thyrst enkyndled
    sore
My hart: and in the bowels burnte, the boylyng flames doe
    glowe.
    MEG.   I followe thee: through all this house nowe rage and
    furie throwe.   100
Let them be dryven so, and so let eyther thyrst to see
Eche others blood. Full well hathe felte the cummyng in of thee
This house: and all with wycked touche of the[e] begun to
    quake . . .

The seconde Acte.

ATREUS.   SERVANT.

. . . SER.   What thyng seekste thou to bryng to pas?
ATR.   I note what greater thyng my mynde, and more then
    woont it was
Above the reatche that men are woont to woorke, begyns to
    swell: 240
And staythe with slouthfull hands. What thyng it is I can not
    tell:

But great it is. Beete so, my mynde now in this feate proceede,
For Atreus and Thyestes bothe, it were a worthy deede.
Let eche of us the crime commit. The Thracian house did se
Suche wicked tables once: I graunte the mischiefe great to be,
But done ere this: some greater gilt and mischiefe more, let yre
Fynde out. The stomak of thy sonne o father thou enspyre,
And syster eke, lyke is the cause: assist me with your powre,
And dryve my hande: let gredy parent all his babes devowre,
And glad to rent his children be: and on their lyms to feede.   250
Enough, and well it is devysde: this pleaseth me in deede.
In meane time where is he? so long and innocent wherfore
Dooth Atreus walke? before myne eyes alredie more and more
The shade of suche a slaughter walkes: the want of children
    cast,
In fathers jawes. But why my mynde, yet dreadst thou so at last,
And fayntst before thou enterprise? it must be doone, let be.
That whiche in all this mischefe is the greatest gilt to se,
Let him commit. . . .

. . . .

The fourth Acte.

MESSENGER. CHORUS.

What whirlwinde may me hedlong drive and up in ayre me
    flyng,
And wrappe in darkest cloude, wherby it might so heynous
    thyng
Take from mine eyes? o wicked house that even of Pelops ought
And Tantalus abhorred be.   CHO. what new thing hast thou
    brought?
                                               530
  MESS.   What lande is this? lythe Sparta here, and Argos,
    that hath bred
So wycked brethern? and the grounde of Corinth liyng spred
Betwene the seas? or Ister ells where woont to take their flight
Are people wylde? or that whiche woonts with snowe to shyne
    so bright,
Hircana lande? or els do here the wandryng Scythians dwell?
  CHO.   What monstrous mischefe is this place then giltie of?
    that tell,
And this declare to us at large what ever be the ill.
  MESS.   If once my minde may stay it self, and quakyng
    limms, I will.
But yet of suche a cruell deede before mine eyes the feare

And Image walkes: ye ragyng stormes now far from hens me
    beare   540
And to that place me drive, to whiche now driven is the day
Thus drawen from hens. CH. Our mindes ye holde yet still
    in doubtfull stay.
Tell what it is ye so abhorre. The author therof showe.
I aske not who, but which of them: that quickly let us knowe.
    MESS.   In Pelopps Turret highe, a parte there is of palaice
        wyde
That towarde the southe erected leanes, of whiche the utter
    syde
With equall toppe to mountayne stands, and on the citie lies,
And people proude agaynst theyr prince yf once the traytours
    rise
Hath underneathe his battryng stroke: there shines the place
    in sight
Where woont the people to frequent, whose golden beames so
    bright   550
The noble spotted pillers graye of marble dooe supporte.
Within this place well knowen to men, where they so ofte
    resorte,
To many other roomes about the noble courte dothe goe.
The privie Palaice underlieth in secret place aloe,
With ditche full deepe that dothe enclose the woode of privetee,
And hidden partes of kyngdome olde: where never grew no
    tree
That cherefull bowes is woont to beare, with knife or lopped be,
But Taxe, and Cypresse, and with tree of Holme full blacke
    to se
Dothe becke and bende the woode so darke: alofte above all
    these
The higher oke dothe overlooke, surmountyng all the treese. 560
From hens with lucke the raygne to take, accustomde are the
    kyngs,
From hens in danger ayde to aske, and doome in doubtfull
    thyngs.
To this affixed are the gifts, the soundyng Trumpetts bright,
The Chariots broke, and spoyles of sea that now Myrtoon hight,
There hang the wheeles once won by crafte of falser axell tree,
And every other conquests note: here leefull is to see
The Phrygyan tyre of Pelops hed: the spoyle of enmies heere,
And of Barbarian triumphe lefte, the paynted gorgeous geere.
A lothesome spryng stands under shade, and slouthfull course
    dothe take,

With water blacke: even such as is, of Yrksome Stygian lake   570
The ugly wave, wherby are woont, to sweare the goddes on hie.
Here all the night the grisly ghosts and gods of death to crie
The fame reportes: with clinkyng chaynes resoundes the
    woode eche where,
The sprights crie out: and every thyng that dredfull is to heare,
May there be seene: of ugly shapes from olde Sepulchres sent
A fearfull flocke dothe wander there, and in that place frequent
Woorse thyngs then ever yet were knowne: ye all the wood full
    ofte
With flame is woont to flasshe, and all the higher trees alofte
Without a fyre dooe burne: and ofte the wood besyde all this
With triple barkyng roares at once: full ofte the palaice is   580
Affright with shapes, nor light of day may once the terrour
    quell.
Eternall night dothe holde the place, and darknes there of hell
In mid day raignes: from hens to them that pray, out of the
    grounde
The certayne answers geven are, what time with dredfull
    sounde
From secret place the fates be tolde, and dongeon roares within
While of the God breakes out the voice: wherto when entred in
Fierce Atreus was, that did with him his brothers children
    trayle,
Dekt are the aulters: who (alas) may it enoughe bewayle?
Behynde the infants backs anone he knyt their noble hands,
And eke their heavie heds about he bounde with purple bands: 590
There wanted there no Frankensence, nor yet the holy wine,
Nor knife to cut the sacrifice, besprinkt with levens fine.
Kept is in all the order due, least suche a mischiefe grette
Should not be ordred well.   CHOR. who dothe his hande on
    swoorde then sette?
  MESS.   He is him selfe the preest, and he him selfe the dedly
    verse
With praier dyre from fervent mouthe dothe syng and ofte
    reherse.
And he at thaulters stands him selfe, he them assygnde to die
Dothe handle, and in order set, and to the knife applie,
He lights the fyres, no rights were lefte of sacryfice undone.
The woode then quakte, and all at ones from tremblyng
    grounde anone   600
The Palaice beckte, in doubte whiche way the payse therof
    woulde fall,
And shakyng as in waves it stoode: from thayre and therwithall

A blasyng starre that foulest trayne drewe after him dothe goe:
The wynes that in the fyres were cast, with changed licour floe,
And turne to bloud: and twyse or thryse thattyre fell from his
     hed,
The Iverie bright in Temples seemde to weepe and teares to
     shed.
The sights amasde all other men, but stedfast yet alway
Of mynde, unmoved Atreus stands, and even the godds dothe
     fray
That threaten him, and all delay forsaken by and bye
To thaulters turnes, and therwithall a syde he lookes awrye.   610
As hungrie tygre woonts that dothe in gangey woods remayne
With doubtfull pace to range and roame betweene the bullocks
     twayne,
Of eyther praye full covetous, and yet uncertayne where
She fyrst may bite, and roryng throate now turnes the tone to
     teare
And then to thother straight returnes, and doubtfull famine
     holdes:
So Atreus dire, betwene the babes dothe stand and them
     beholdes
On whome he poyntes to slake his yre: fyrst slaughter where
     to make,
He doubtes: or whome he shoulde agayne for seconde offryng
     take.
Yet skylls it nought, but yet he doubtes, and suche a crueltie
It him delights to order well.   CHOR. Whome take he fyrst
     to die?   620
     MESS.   First place, least in him thinke ye might no piete to
     remayne
To grandsier dedicated is, fyrst Tantalus is slayne.
     CHOR.   With what a minde and countnaunce, coulde the
     boye his death sustayne?
     MESS.   All careles of him selfe he stoode, nor once he woulde
     in vayne
His prayers leese. But Atreus fierce the swoorde in him at last
In deepe and deadly wounde dothe hide to hilts, and gripyng
     fast
His throate in hand, he thrust him throughe. The swoorde
     then drawne awaye
When long the body had uphelde it selfe in doubtfull staye,
Whiche way to fall, at lengthe uppon the unkle downe it falles.
And then to thaulters cruellie Philisthenes he tralles,   630

And on his brother throwes: and strayght his necke of cutteth
    hee.
The carcase hedlong falles to grounde: a piteous thyng to see,
The mournyng hed, with murmure yet uncertayne dothe
    complayne.
    CHOR. What after double deathe dothe he and slaughter
    then of twayne?
Spares he the childe? or gilt on gilt agayne yet heapeth he?
    MESS. As long maned Lyon feerce amid the wood of
    Armenie,
The drove pursues and conquest makes of slaughter many one,
Though now defiled be his jawes with bloude, and hunger gone
Yet slaketh not his Irefull rage, with bloud of bulles so greate,
But slouthfull now, with weery toothe the lesser calves dothe
    threate: 640
None other wyse dothe Atreus rage, and swels with anger
    straynde,
And holdyng now the sworde in hande with double slaughter
    staynde,
Regardyng not where fell his rage, with cursed hand unmilde
He strake it through his body quight: at bosome of the childe
The blade gothe in, and at the backe agayne out went the same.
He falles, and quenchyng with his bloud the aulters sacred
    flame,
Of either wounde at lengthe he dieth. CHOR. O heynous
    hatefull acte.
    MESS. Abhorre ye this? ye heare not yet the ende of all
    the facte,
There followes more.   CHO. A fiercer thyng, or worse then this
    to see
Could nature beare? ME. why thinke ye this of gilt the ende
    to bee?   650
It is but parte. CHO. what coulde he more? to cruell beasts
    he cast
Perhapps their bodies to be torne, and kept from fyres at last.
    MESS. Would god he had: that never tombe the deade
    might overhyde,
Nor flames dissolve, though them for foode to fowles in pastures
    wyde
He had out throwen, or them for pray to cruell beasts woulde
    flyng.
That whiche the worste was wont to be, were heere a wisshed
    thyng,
6

That them theyr father sawe untombde. but oh more cursed
crime
Uncredible, the whiche denie wyll men of after time:
From bosomes yet alyve out drawne the tremblyng bowells
shake,
The vaynes yet breathe, the fearefull harte dothe yet bothe
pante and quake: 660
But he the stryngs dothe turne in hande, and destenies beholde.
And of the gutts the sygnes eche one dothe vewe not fully colde.
When him the sacrifice had pleasde, his diligence he putts
To dresse his brothers banquet now: and streyght a soonder
cutts
The bodies into quarters all, and by the stoompes anone
The shoulders wide, and brawnes of armes, he strikes of every
chone.
He laies abrode theyr naked lymms, and cutts away the bones:
The only heds he keepes, and hands to him comitted ones.
Some of the gutts are broachte, and in the fyres that burne
ful sloe
They droppe: the boylyng liccour some dothe tomble to
and froe   670
In moornyng cawdern: from the flesshe that overstands alofte
The fyre dothe flie, and scatter out, and into chimney ofte
Up heapt agayne, and there constraynde by force to tary yet
Unwillyng burnes: the lyver makes great noyse uppon the spit,
Nor easely wote I, if the flesshe, or flames they be that cry,
But crie they doe: the fyre like pitche it fumeth by and by:
Nor yet the smoke it selfe so sadde, like filthy miste in sight
Ascendeth up as woont it is, nor takes his way upright,
But even the Goddes and house it dothe with filthie fume
defyle.
O pacient Phœbus though from hence thou backward flee the
whyle,   680
And in the midst of heaven above dooste drowne the broken
day,
Thou fleeste to late: the father eates his children well away,
And lymms to whiche he onse gave lyfe, with cursed jawe dothe
teare.
He shynes with oyntment shed full sweete all rounde aboute
his heare,
Replete with wyne: and often times so cursed kynde of food
His mouth hath helde that would not downe. but yet this one
thyng good
In all thy ylls (Thyestes) is, that them thou dooste not knowe.

The fifth Acte.

The thyrde Sceane.

ATREUS. THYESTES.

Let us this daie with one consent (o brother) celebrate. 800
This day my steptors may confyrme and stablyshe my estate,
And faythfull bonde of peace and love betwene us ratyfye.
   THY. Enough with meate and eke with wyne, now satysfyde
     am I.
But yet of all my joyes it were a greate encrease to mee,
If now about my syde I might my little children see.
   ATR. Beleve that here even in thyne armes thy children present
     bee.
For here they are, and shalbe here, no parte of them fro thee
Shall be withhelde: theyr loved lookes now geve to the I wyll,
And with the heape of all his babes, the father fully fyll.
Thou shalt be glutted, feare thou not: they with my boyes as
     yet 810
The joyful sacrifyces make at boorde where children sit.
They shalbe callde: the frendly cuppe nowe take of curtesy
With wyne upfylde. THY. of brothers feast I take full
     wyllyngy
The fynall gyfte, shed some to gods of this our fathers lande,
Then let the reste be droonke. whats this? in no wyse wyll my
     hande
Obeye: the payse increaseth sore, and downe myne arme
     dothe swaye.
And from my lypps the waftyng wyne it selfe dothe flie awaie,
And in deceived mouthe, about my jawes it runneth rounde:
The table to, it selfe dothe shake, and leape from tremblyng
     grounde.
Scant burnes the fyre: the ayre it selfe with heavy chere to sight 820
Forsooke of sunne amased is betwene the daye and night.
What meaneth this? yet more and more of backewarde beaten
     skye
The compasse falles: and thicker myst the worlde doth overlye
Then blackest darkenes, and the night in night it selfe dothe
     hyde.
All starrs be fledde: what so it bee, my brother god provyde
And soons to spare: the gods so graunte that all this tempest
     fall
On this vyle head: but now restore to me my children all.

ATR. I will, and never daye agayne shall them from the withdrawe.

THY. What tumulte tumbleth so my gutts, and dothe my bowells gnawe?

What quakes within? with heavy payse I feele my selfe opprest, 830

And with an other voyce then myne bewayles my dolefull brest.

Come neere my soons, for you now dooth th'unhappie father call:

Come neere, for you once seene, this greefe wolde soone asswage and fall.

Whence murmure they? AT. with fathers armes embrace them quickely nowe,

For here they are loe come to thee: dooste thou thy children knowe?

THY. I know my brother: suche a gylt yet canst thou suffre well

o earth to beare? nor yet from hens to Stygian lake of hell

Dooste thou bothe drowne thy selfe and us? nor yet with broken grounde

Dooste thou these kyngdomes and theyr kyng with Chaos rude confounde?

Nor yet uprentyng from the soyle the bowres of wicked lande 840

Dooste thou Mycenas overturne? with Tantalus to stande,

And auncyters of ours, if there in hell be any one,

Now ought we bothe. now from the frames on eyther syde anone

Of grounde, all here and there rent up, out of thy bosome deepe

Thy dens and dungeons set abrode, and us enclosed keepe,

In botome lowe of Acheront: above our hedds alofte

Let wander all the gyltie ghosts, with burnyng frete full ofte

Let fyry Phlegethon that dryves his sands bothe to and froe,

To our confusion overroon, and vyolently floe.

O slouthfull soyle unshaken payse, unmoved yet arte thou? 850

The gods are fled. ATR. but take to thee with joy thy chyldren now,

And rather them embrace: at length thy chyldren all, of thee

So long wysht for, (for no delaye there standeth now in mee,)

Enjoye and kysse, embracyng armes devyde thou unto three.

THY. Is this thy league? may this thy love and fayth of brother bee?

And dooste thou so repose thy hate? the father dothe not crave

His soons alive (whiche might have bene without the gylt,)
  to have:
And eke without thy hate, but this dothe brother brother pray:
That them he may entoombe, restore, whom see thou shalt
  straight way
Be burnt: the father nought requyres, of the that have he shall,   860
But soone forgoe. ATR. what ever parte yet of thy children all
Remaynes, here shalt thou have: and what remayneth not,
  thou haste.
    THY. Lye they in feeldes, a foode out floong for fleeyng
    foules to waste?
Or are they kept a praye, for wylde and brutyshe beasts to eate?
    ATR. Thou hast devourde thy sons, and fylde hy selfe
    with wicked meate.
    THY. Oh this is it that shamde the godds: and day from
    hens dyd dryve
Turnde backe to easte. alas I wretch what waylynges may I
  gyve?
Or what complayntes? what wofull woordes may be enough
  for mee? . . .

IV. Analogue

A LAMENTABLE BALLAD

[1] Text from *The Roxburghe Ballads*, ed. Charles Hindley, 2 vols. 1873/4, ii, 339–47.

Anon

A Lamentable Ballad of the Tragical end of a Gallant Lord and a Vertuous Lady, with the untimely end of their two Children, wickedly performed by a Heathenish Blackamore their servant; the like never heard of.

The Tune is, The Ladys Fall.

In *Rome* a Noble man did wed,
  a Virgin of great fame.
A fairer creature never did
  dame nature ever frame;
By whom he had two Children fair,
  whose beauty did excel:
They were their parents only joy,
  they loved them both so well.

The Lord he loved to hunt the buck,
   the tiger and the bear: 10
And still for swiftness always took
   with him a Blackamoor:
Which Blackamoor within the wood,
   his Lord he did offend,
For which he did him then correct,
   in hopes he should amend.

The day it grew unto an end,
   then homewards it[1] did haste,
Where with his Lady he did rest,
   until the night was past: 20
Then in the morning he did rise,
   and did his servants call;
A hunting he provides to go,
   straight they were ready all.

To cause the wil the lady did
   intreat him not to go;
Also,[2] good Lady, then quoth he,
   why art thou grieved so?
Content thyself I will return
   with speed to thee again;   30
Good Father (quoth the little Babes)
   with us here still remain.

Farewell, dear children, I wil go,
   a fine thing for to buy:
But there therewith nothing content,
   aloud began to cry:
The Mother takes them by the hand,
   saying, come go with me
Unto the highest Towre, where
   your Father you shall see.   40

The Blackamoor perceiving now
   (who then did stay behind)
His Lord to be a hunting gone,
   began to call to mind:
My Master he did me correct,
   my fault not being great;

[1] he
[2] Alas

Now of his wife I'll be reveng'd,
  she shall not me intreat.

The place was moted round about,
  the bridge he up did draw;   50
The gates he bolted very fast,
  of none he stood in awe:
He up into the Tower went,
  the Lady being there:
Who when she saw his countenance grim
  she straight began to fear.

But now my trembling heart it quakes
  to think what I must write;
My senses all begin to fail,
  my soul it doth affright:
Yet I must make an end of this
  which here I have begun,   60
Which will make sad the hardest heart,
  before that I have done.

This wretch unto the Lady went,
  and her with speed did will,
His lust forthwith to satisfie,
  his mind for to fulfill:
The Lady she amazed was,
  to hear the villain speak,
Alas (quoth she) what shall I do?
  with grief my heart will break.   70

With that he took her in his arms,
  she straight for help did cry;
Content yourself Lady (he said)
  your Husband is not nigh.
The bridge is drawn, the gates are shut,
  therefore come lie with me,
Or else I do protest and vow
  thy Butcher I will be.

The chrystal tears ran down her face,
  her children cryed amain,   80
And sought to help their mother dear,
  but all it was in vain:

For that outrageous filthy Rogue,
   her hands behind her bound,
And then perforce with all his might,
   he threw her on the ground.

With that she shriekt, her children cry'd,
   And such a noise did make,
That towns-folks, hearing her lament,
   did seek their parts to take: 90
But all in vain, no way was found
   to help the Ladies need:
Who cried to him most piteously,
   oh help, oh help, with speed.

Some ran into the Forest wide,
   her Lord home for to call,
And they that lord still did lament,
   this gallant Ladies fall.
With speed her love came panting home
   he could not enter in.   100
His Ladies cries did pierce his heart,
   to call he did begin.

O hold thy hand thou savage Moor,
   to hurt her do forbear,
Or else besure if I do live,
   wild Horses shall thee tare:
With that the Rogue ran to the wall,
   he having had his will,
And brought one child under his arm,
   his dearest blood to spill.   110

The child seeing his Father there,
   to him for help did call:
O Father help my Mother dear,
   we shall be killed all:
Then fell the Lord upon his knee,
   and did the Moor intreat,
To save the life of his poor child,
   whose fear as then was great.

But this vile wretch the little child
   by both the heels did take,   120

And dasht his brains against the wall,
  whilst Parents hearts did ake:
That being done straightway he ran
  the other child to fetch,
And pluckt it from the Mothers breast
  most like a cruel wretch.

Within one hand a Knife he brought,
  the Child within the other;
And holding it over the wall,
  saying, thus lye shall thy Mother: 130
With that he cut the throat of it,
  then to the Father he did call:
To look how he that head had cut,
  and down the head did fall.

This done he threw it down the wall,
  into the mote so deep,
Which made the Father wring his hands
  and greviously to weep.
Then to the lady went this Rogue,
  who was near dead with fear!   140
Yet this vile wretch most cruelly
  did drag her by her hair.

And [? haled her] to the very wall,
  which when the Lord did see,
Then presently he cryed out,
  and fell upon his knee:
Quoth he, if thou wilt save her life,
  whom I do love so dear;
I will forgive thee all is past,
  though they concern me near.   150

To save her life I thee beseech,
  O save [her?] I thee pray,
And I will grant thee what thou wilt
  demand of me this day;
Well, quoth the Moor, I do regard
  the moan that thou dost make;
If thou wilt grant me what I ask,
  I'll save her for thy sake.

O save her life and then demand
   of me what thing thou wilt: 160
Cut off thy nose, and not one drop
   of her blood shall be spilt:
With that the Lord presently took
   a knife within his hand;
And then his nose he quite cut off,
   in place where he did stand.

Now I have bought the Ladys life,
   then to the Moor did call:
Then take her, qd. this wicked Rogue,
   and down he let her fall.   170
Which when her gallant Lord did see,
   his senses all did fail:
Yet many sought to save his life
   yet nothing could prevail.

When as the Moor did see him dead,
   then did he laugh amain
At them who for their gallant Lord
   and Lady did complain:
Quoth he, I know you'll torture me,
   if that you can me get,   180
But all your threats I do not fear,
   nor yet regard one whit.

Wild horses shall my body tear,
   I know it to be true,
But I'll prevent you of that pain,
   and down himself he threw:
Too good a death for such a wretch,
   a Villain void of fear,
And thus doth end as sad a tale,
   as ever man did hear.   190

Printed by and for A. Milbourn, and sold by the Booksellers
of London.

V. Probable Source

PLUTARCH'S PARALLEL LIVES OF THE NOBLE GRECIANS AND ROMANES

translated by Sir Thomas North (1579 edn.)

From THE LIFE OF SCIPIO AFRICANUS

For he had not only a noble corage in him, beeing indued with many singuler vertues, but he was also a goodly gentleman, and very comly of person,[1] and had besides a pleasaunt countenaunce: all which things together, are great meanes to winne him the love and good will of every man. Moreover, even in his gesture and behavior, there was a certaine princely grace. Now, the glory of martiall discipline, being joyned unto those his rare gifts of mind and nature: it was to be doubted, whether his civil vertues made him more acceptable unto straungers, then wonderful for his skil in warres. . . . Scipio greatly praysed his souldiers, and did reward them, for that they had done so valiant service. . . .
Afterwards he sent unto all the cities of Spayne, the hostages that were found in the city, which were a marvelous number: the which wanne him great fame for his curtesie and clemency, whereby he allured many nations to yeld them selves unto the Romanes, and to forsake the Carthaginians. But one thinge above all the rest, chiefly increased his prayse, and wanne him great love and good will, as a myrror and example of all vertue. There was a young Lady taken prisoner, that in beautie excelled all the women in Carthage: whome he carefully caused to be kept, and preserved from violence and dishonor.[2] And afterwards when he knew that she was maried unto Luceius, Prince of the Celtiberians: he sent for her husbande that was a verie young man, and delivered her unto him, untouched, or dishonored. Luceius not forgetting his noble curtesie unto her, did let all his subjects understand the great bounty, modestie, and rare excellencie of all kinde of vertues that were in this Romane Generall: and shortly after he returned againe to the Romanes campe, with a great number of horsemen. . . .

---

[1] *In margin*: Scipioes great mind and goodly personage.
[2] *In margin*: The great chastitie of Scipio.

After this battell, Scipio according to his maner, caused all the Spanish prisoners to be brought before him, and then gave them libertie to depart, without paying of raunsome.[1]

From THE COMPARISON OF ANNIBAL WITH P. SCIPIO AFRICAN

This may truely be sayd of Annibal, that he obtayned many great victories in the warres, but yet they turned to the destruction of his contry. Scipio in contrary manner did preserve his contry in such safetie, and also did so much increase the dominions thereof: that as many as shall looke into his desert, they can not but call Rome unthankefull, which liked rather that the African (preserver of the citie) should goe out of Rome, then that they would represse the fury and insolency of a few. And for myne owne opinion, I can not thinke well of that citie, that so unthankfully hath suffred so worthy and innocent a person to be injured: and so would I also have thought it more blame worthy, if the citie had bene an ayder of the injurye offred him. In fine, the Senate (as all men doe report) gave great thankes unto Tiberius Gracchus, bicause he did defend the Scipions cause, and the common people also, following the African, when he visited all the temples of Rome, and left the Tribunes alone that accused him, did thereby shewe how much they did love and honor the name of the Scipioes. And therefore, if we should judge the Citizens harts and good wills by those things, men would rather condemne them for cowards, to have suffered such outrage, then unthankfull for forgetting of his benefits: for there were very few that consented to so wicked a deede, and all of them in manner were very sory for it. Howbeit Scipio, that was a man of a great minde, not much regarding the malice of his enemies, was content rather to leave the citie, then by civill warres to destroy it. For he would not come against his contry with ensignes displaied, nether would he solicite straunge nations and mighty kings to come with force, and their ayde, to destroy the citie, the which he had beautified with so many spoyles and triumphes: as Martius Coriolanus, Alcibiades, and divers others did, by record of auncient stories. For we may easily perceive howe carefull he was to preserve the libertie of Rome, bicause when he was in Spayne, he refused the title and name of king which was offred him: and for that he was marvelous angry with the people of Rome, bicause they would have made him perpetuall Consul and Dictator: and considering also that he com-

In margin: Scipioes liberalite to his enemies.

maunded they should set up no statue of him, nether in the place of the assembly, nor in the judgement seate nor in the Capitoll. All which honors afterwardes were given by the Citizens unto Cæsar, that had overcomen Pompey. These were the civill vertues of the African, which were great and true prayses of continency.

TROILUS AND CRESSIDA

INTRODUCTION

THIS PLAY was first printed in Quarto form in 1609. There had been two entries in S.R. The first, in 7 February 1603, was to 'Master Robertes. Entred for his copie in full Court holden this day to print when he hath gotten sufficient authority for yt, The booke of Troilus and Cresseda as yt is acted by my lord Chamberlens Men.' Obviously Roberts had some rights to the play, but he did not print it. Pollard has suggested that the entry may have been made to stop anyone else pirating the piece. On 28 January 1609 the book was entered to Richard Bonian and Henry Walley who published it, in a good text, though not all editors agree with Peter Alexander that it was set up from Shakespeare's manuscript. The first Folio text presents problems.[1] It should originally have been printed after *Romeo and Juliet*, which occupies pp. 53–77 (misnumbered 79). *Timon of Athens*, which now comes next, occupies pp. 80 (really 78)–98, followed by *Julius Caesar* ((107)–130). *Troilus* now appears between *Henry VIII* and *Coriolanus*, between the Histories and the Tragedies. Its second leaf is numbered 79–80; there is no other pagination for this play. It is generally agreed that probably after the first pages of *Troilus* had been set up in type, a hitch occurred. Permission to print the play may have been refused by Walley. So *Timon* was printed after *Romeo*, though it was too short to fill the estimated gap. When permission to print *Troilus* was given, the catalogue of plays had already been run off, so *Troilus* does not appear in it. The play however was printed in its present position with a new first page (but five extant copies include the cancelled one) and the print already set up for the second leaf was used. The Folio text may well have been taken (as W. W. Greg and E. K. Chambers

---

[1] Discussed by J. Q. Adams in *JEGP*, vii, 53–63; P. Williams, *Studies in Bibliog.* (Virginia) 1950, 131–43; Alice Walker, *MLR*, xlv, 1950, 459–64; J. G. McManaway *Sh Survey*, 5, 145; and in *Variorum* p. 347.

argued) from a copy of the Quarto collated with a manuscript.

As usual, doubts have been raised about Shakespeare's total authorship of the play. The Prologue appears in F1 but not in the Quarto. Was it Shakespeare's? The Epilogue has been considered out of keeping, and the last few scenes unworthy of the rest of the play. Speculations based on subjective judgements are hazardous. Shakespeare may possibly have had an old play to draw on (or reject) but there is no evidence to support J. M. Robertson's contention: "All that is broadly clear is that the opening matter is not originally Shakespeare's, even if touched by him; that Pandarus and Thersites are not creations of his; that the Thersites scurrility is from other hands; and that the huddle of events in the fifth act, and the poor finish, are also alien."[1] In what follows the play will be taken as it stands and as substantially Shakespeare's, for the whole thing has unity of tone. I see no basis for supposing (with L. Hotson) that a first draft of *Troilus* was Shakespeare's lost play *Love Labours Wonne* mentioned by Meres in 1598, or that the play was composed at different periods of Shakespeare's career.

How long before the 1603 entry in S.R. *Troilus* was written has been much debated. The Admiral's Company gave a play in June 1596 which Henslowe noted as 'troye'. In April 1599 Dekker and Chettle were paid for 'Troyeles & creasse daye'. Next month they were paid for an 'Agamemnon' (first entered by mistake as "troylles & Creseda") (Henslowe, *Diary*, I, 109; II, 202). This play was probably a sequel to their *Troilus* piece. Shakespeare's play may well have been commissioned by the rival company to vie with Henslowe's epic drama, the contents of which may be suggested by the 'plot' extant in the British Museum (MS. Add. 10449)[2] [Text VI]. Chapman's *Seaven Books of the Iliad* were published in 1598. The line 'The fool slides o'er the ice that you should break' (*T & C*, III.3.216) may allude to a story given in the Chamberlain's actor Robert Armin's *Foole upon Foole* (1600). Jonson's *Poetaster* (1601) had a 'prologue arm'd', like that of *Troilus*, l. 23.

---

[1] J. M. Robertson, *The Genuine in Shakespeare*, 1930, 114–16.

[2] W. W. Greg, Henslowe Papers, 1907, 129, 142; J. S. P. Tatlock, 'The Siege of Troy in Shakespeare and Heywood', *PMLA*, 30, 1915, 697–703.

The poem *Saint Marie Magdalens Conversion* by I.C., printed in 1603, has Shakespearian references:

> Of Helens rape and Troyes beseiged Towne,
> Of Troylus faith, and Cressids falsitie,
> Of Rychards stratagems for the English crowne,
> Of Tarquins lust, and Lucrece chastitie,
> Of these, of none of these my muse nowe treates.

Attempts have been made to prove that *Troilus* was one blow in the 'war of the theatres', and that by depicting Dekker as Thersites and Ben Jonson as Ajax Shakespeare routed the opposing party; cf. *The Return from Parnassus* (acted at Cambridge, 1601–2).

> 'O that Ben Jonson is a pestilent fellow, he brought up *Horace* giving the Poets a pill, but our fellow *Shakespeare* hath given him a purge that made him beray his credit'[1]

But Ajax may just be Ajax, a character somewhat inconsistent because he is made out of two men in the sources, Ajax Telamon and Ajax Oïleus. In tone the play certainly resembles *Hamlet* and *Measure for Measure*, and we may confidently ascribe it to 1600–3.

The ambiguous if not directly satiric treatment of epic and romantic themes in *Troilus and Cressida* has been variously explained by critics who have usually regarded the play as harsh and repellent. Dowden thought it full of 'inexpressible pain ... bitterness and loss of faith in man'. 'Did Shakespeare write *Troilus and Cressida* to unburden his heart of some bitterness by an indictment of the illusions of romance, which had misled him?'[2] Middleton Murry thought it the product of 'a wounded and bewildered spirit'.[3] Tucker Brooke imagined that Shakespeare was 'however subconsciously, anatomizing the England of the dying Elizabeth'.[4] G. B. Harrison made a brilliant parallel between the sulking Achilles and Essex's

---

[1] Edited by J. B. Leishman, 1949, 1766ff. Cf. W. Elton on Shakespeare's Ajax in *PMLA*, LXIII, 1948. Jonson's pill was *Poetaster* (1601) against Marston and Dekker.

[2] E. Dowden, Introduction in Oxford edition, 3 vols, 1939 edn.

[3] J. M. Murry, *Countries of the Mind*, 1922, pp. 11–22.

[4] T. Brooke, *Yale Review*, n.s. xvii, 1928, 576–77.

withdrawal from court in 1598, noting that Chapman not only dedicated his first Homer translation to Essex, but wrote of his 'Achilleian virtues' and apostrophized him as 'Most true Achilles'. Harrison therefore concluded that Shakespeare was mocking at Essex either in 1598 or in 1600 after his return from Ireland. (In that event Shakespeare must have blushed to remember his own Prologue to *Henry V*.) J. D. Wilson suggested that on the contrary he was trying 'in the last bitter months of 1600 when Essex moped and sulked . . . to goad the earl into action'.

Taking a less personal view O. J. Campbell[1] regarded the play as a 'comical satire' against individualism (in the camp story) and sensuality (in the love story)—a comedy which adapted for drama the aims and methods of the Roman satirists whose work had become so influential in the 'nineties that in June 1599 the printing of satires and epigrams was forbidden. The play might be treated as a fashionable exercise in social criticism, which would be very suitable if, as has been suggested,[2] it was performed only at the Inns of Court; hence the Quarto preface asserted that it was 'never stal'd with the Stage, never clapper-clawd with the palmes of the vulgar . . . sullied, with the smoaky breath of the multitude.' It would appeal to an audience which enjoyed reading the Satires of Marston and Hall and the Elegies of Donne. Without accepting all the details of Campbell's interpretation of the play I believe that he and Alexander are right, and that *Troilus*, with its Latinisms, its mingling of noble ideals with cynicism about human conduct, its mockery of the heroic and the romantic was probably written for a cultured audience which prided itself on its unshockable 'realism'. Certainly Shakespeare's handling of the available source-material tends to make us agree with this view.

The story of the Trojan War as told by Homer and Virgil was of course well known in the Middle Ages and Renaissance, and before Chapman there were several translations of the

---

[1] O. J. Campbell, *Comicall Satyre and Shakespeare's Troilus and Cressida*, San Marino, 1938, pp. 184–234.

[2] By P. Alexander, 'Troilus and Cressida, 1609', in 4 *Library*, ix, 1928, pp. 267–86 and *Shakespeare's Life and Art*, 1939, 195–6. His assertion that the cynicism was 'a device to startle these simple wordlings out of their complacency' ignores the brutal fashion which would make them enjoy even Pandarus's epilogue.

Iliad which Shakespeare might possibly have seen had he so desired.[1]

It has been suggested that Shakespeare read a French version of Homer,[2] and Tatlock pointed out[3] that a reference on the title-page of the second 1609 quarto to '*Pandarus* Prince of *Licia*', showed knowledge of the Latin or French translators, or of Arthur Hall, not of Chapman's 1598 version. It is unlikely however that the dramatist was responsible for this title-page.

George Chapman's translation of the *Iliad* appeared in three stages. The *Seaven Bookes of the Iliades* (1598) contained Bks. I–II, VII–XI. In the same year the description of Achilles' shield from Bk. XVIII was also published. Twelve books were printed in 1609 (the year of the *Troilus* quartos), and the complete *Iliad* only in 1611. I have no doubt that Shakespeare read the *Seaven Bookes*, and suspect that his satiric treatment of the Greeks and his use of high-sounding language was partly to mock at the hero-worship shown by Chapman in the prefatory material to his versions. But the following summary of Shakespeare's possible debt to Homer implies that he read more of the *Iliad* than Chapman gave in 1598—perhaps in Salel's version. Since Chapman greatly altered his version between 1598 and 1611 the excerpts below are taken where possible from the 1598 text,[4] otherwise from the 1611 edition [Text I].

The action of *Troilus and Cressida* passes over the early events of the war, begins in the middle with the withdrawal of Achilles, and ends, not with the destruction of Troy, but with

---

[1] 'Accessible to Shakespeare there were the following translations of the *Iliad*. *English*: (1) Arthur Hall's, printed in London, 1581, translated from the French of Salel, first ten books only, in fourteeners. *French*: (2) Jehan Samxon, Paris, 1530, in prose, from the Latin. (3) Hugues Salel: Bks. I–X., 1545, 1555; XI, XII, 1554; I–XII, 1570; complete, 1580, 1584, 1599; in verse, from the Greek, completed by Jamyn. *Latin*: (4) Lorenzo Valla, in prose, 1474, 1502, 1522 (Cologne). (5) H. Eobanus Hessus, in verse, 1540, 1543 (first three books), 1545, 1549 (complete). (6) Greek and literal Latin, 1551, 1560–7, 1561, 1570, 1580, etc. (7) V. Obsopoeus and others, in verse, complete, 1573. (8) Spondanus, Basle, 1583. Any one of these, except one or two incomplete versions, would have given Shakespeare the knowledge he shows.' J. S. P. Tatlock, 'The Siege of Troy in Shakespeare and Heywood', *PMLA*, XXX, 1915, p. 742.
[2] By Salel or Samxon. Cf. *ShJb*, ix, p. 37.
[3] *Op. cit.* pp. 743–4n.
[4] Comparison of this with Chapman's final version suggests that he may have read *Troilus* and taken from Shakespeare one or two ideas about degree which he incorporated into his revised Bk. II.

the death of Hector. In these respects the play resembles the *Iliad*. As J. F. Palmer showed,[1] much of the epic action seems closely to follow Chapman's *Seaven Bookes*, for after we have seen the Greek heroes and the first effects of the quarrel between Agamemnon and Achilles (as in Books I and II), the story 'passes on at once in the first Act to the subject-matter of the Seventh Book,[2] the challenge of Hector to the Greeks, and its acceptance by Ajax Telamon'. Palmer points out that this material is used until Act IV. 'There are also allusions to other matters in the Seventh Book, including the embassy to Achilles; while the Third, Fourth, Fifth, and Sixth Books, which relate the acts of Diomede, Hector's prophecy, and the wound of Menelaus, are entirely passed over' (Palmer).[3] The reason given for Achilles' withdrawal in Shakespeare is different from that in Homer, but his insubordination and pride are Homeric, and his friendship with Patroclus is from Homer, although Shakespeare gives it an unpleasant homosexual tone. Shakespeare was probably led to make an important motif of the dissensions in the Greek camp by Homer's insistence on them (though they appear also in medieval authorities), and perhaps Ulysses' great speech on order was inspired by Homer's account of how he spoke in Book II to the Greeks who wished to return home [*inf.* p. 120]. Hector's challenge and the embassy to Achilles follow Homer to some extent, though the part played by Aeneas in I.3.215–309 and Ulysses' device to use Ajax as a bait to lure Achilles out are not in the *Iliad*.

The characterization of Ajax probably owed something to Homer's Ajax Telamon, the noble 'bulwark' who in Bk. XI becomes temporarily a 'dull mill-ass'; also to Lydgate's boastful Ajax Oïleus (*inf.* 157–8). But Shakespeare undoubtedly recalled the quarrel between Ajax and Ulysses over Achilles' armour in Golding's translation of Ovid's *Metamorphoses*, XIII, [Text II], where Ajax shows his boastful folly and Ulysses uses expressions found in II.3 etc. The dramatist had already used this Ovidian passage in *The Rape of Lucrece* (1394–1400) for the

---

[1] J. F. Palmer, Royal Soc. of Lit. *Transactions*, 2nd ser. XV, 1893, 64ff.

[2] 'The Third Book' in Chapman, 1598.

[3] For other material on the Homeric influence I am indebted to J. S. B. Tatlock, *op. cit.* pp. 738–42, and to R. K. Presson, *Shakespeare's Troilus and Cressida*, Madison, 1953.

painting of Priam's Troy which contained contrasting portraits of Ajax and Ulysses:

> In Ajax' eyes blunt rage and rigour roll'd;
> But the mild glance that sly Ulysses lent
> Show'd deep regard and smiling government.

But the Ajax who fights Hector and is praised by the latter in IV.5.113–47 is the Ajax Telamon of *Iliad*, Bks. VII, XVII and elsewhere, who depressed the spirit of Hector. Several incidents in *Troilus* may derive from parts of Homer not yet translated by Chapman. In Shakespeare as in Homer (XVIII), Achilles is moved to return to battle by the death of Patroclus (V.5.30–2); but Shakespeare takes from medieval authorities another cause, the slaughter of his Myrmidons. When Achilles has the body of Hector tied to his horse's tail (V.8.21–2; V.10.4–5) it reflects his unworthy act in *Iliad*, XXII, when he ties Hector by the feet to his chariot and drags him through the dust. But the horse's tail is from Caxton or Lydgate [*inf.* 214 and 185]. Previously, Shakespeare's Achilles, like Homer's, looks for the best place on Hector's body whereon to strike and kill him (IV.5.230–45). The allusion to Ajax: 'They say he yesterday coped Hector in the battle and struck him down' (I.2.33–4) may come from *Iliad*, XIV–XV rather than from Ovid, since Homer makes much of Hector's 'sickly fare' and 'grief of mind', after Ajax had felled him with a stone. The references to the Gods as taking sides come from Homer. Thus III.3.188–90 where Achilles' deeds are said to have

> Made emulous missions 'mongst the gods themselves,
> And drave great Mars to faction,

probably derives from *Iliad*, XXI where Mars attacks Pallas.

The problem of Shakespeare's indebtedness is greatly complicated by the variety of mediæval stories which dealt with the Trojan story and combined the wrath of Achilles with the tale of Troilus and Cressida.

In Homer Troilus, Cressida, Diomedes and Pandarus all appear, but not in their later relationships. Troilus, the youngest son of Priam, is a gallant warrior but scarcely mentioned. Chryseis is one of two Trojan maidens captured by the Greeks, and given to Agamemnon and Achilles respectively.

When the Greeks refuse to let Chryseis' father, the priest Chryses, ransom her, he invokes a plague upon them. Chryseis is then returned to her father, and it is Agamemnon's selfishness in taking Briseis from Achilles in recompense that causes Achilles' withdrawal.

Homer's Pandarus is a brutal warrior. In Book IV when the Gods wish to make one of the Trojans break the truce, 'By offering in some treacherous wound the honoured Greeks abuse', Pallas goes down

> And sought for Lycian Pandarus, a man that, being bred
> Out of a faithless family, she thought was fit to shed
> The blood of any innocent, and break the covenant sworn;
> He was Lycaon's son, whom Jove into a wolf did turn
> For sacrificing of a child, and yet in arms renowned
> As one that was inculpable.

A great archer, he shoots at Menelaus and wounds him. Finally he is slain by Diomedes, whom Homer treats as second only to Achilles in strength and valour.

Long afterwards, in the fourth century A.D., Dictys the Cretan wrote an account of the Trojan War, the *Ephemeris Belli Troiani*, pretended to be based on a journal kept by a Greek during the siege. In the sixth century this was countered by the *De Excidio Troiæ Historiæ* of Dares Phrygius, written from the Trojan point of view. This work was put into Latin hexameters by Joseph of Exeter in the twelfth century, and in this form probably influenced Chaucer. Dares described Troilus, Diomed and Briseis, but did not bring them into an amorous triangle. This was effected by Benoit de Sainte-Maure whose vernacular *Roman de Troie* tells the love-story of Troilus and Briseida as a minor episode in an immense romance in which classical epic is narrated and expanded in chivalric terms. Benoit describes the meetings and love between Troilus and Briseida quite briefly. He is much more interested in their parting, Diomed's wooing of her, and the consequent duel between Diomed and Troilus.

Benoit's French verse was put into Latin prose by the Italian Guido delle Colonne, whose *Historia Troiana* (1287) became the chief medium by which the story of Troilus was disseminated. Boccaccio's *Il Filostrato* however went largely to the French poem, 'since Benoit's treatment of the episode of Troilus and Briseida is far more extensive and attractive than Guido's'.[1] Boccaccio eked out the episodic material thus obtained with matter from his own *Filocolo*. For Troilus's falling in love he drew on the love of Achilles for Polyxena in Benoit's *Roman de Troie*. What was only an episode for previous authors has become for Boccaccio the main theme of a long poem to which the heroic siege is only a background, and in which the emotions of the chief characters are emphasized lyrically—for Boccaccio himself was 'Filostrato', laid low by love. Boccaccio also first made Pandarus an important figure. The go-between had of course occurred frequently in Plautus, whether as a professional matchmaker or as a servant helping his master. Unlike these, Boccaccio's Pandaro is Troilo's friend, thus resembling Laris in the French *Claris and Laris* who encourages Claris in his love for Laris's sister Lydame, the wife of King Ladont. Lancelot has a friend Galehont who arranges a meeting between him and Guinevere. Tristano in the Italian Tristan story has an amorous adviser. Perhaps Boccaccio owed something to the rather indistinct friend of Achilles in Benoit who negotiates with the parents of Polyxena.[2] His Pandaro is Griseida's cousin, a gay young fellow, eager to help his friend.

For Chaucer in the *Hous of Fame*, 1429ff. the Troy story had been written by Homer, Dares, Dictys, Boccaccio, Guido and also Geoffrey of Monmouth, whose *Historia Regium Britanniae* (*c.* 1139) told how Aeneas, fleeing from Troy, settled in Italy. His great grandson Brute was driven out and came to Albion and on the Thames founded New Troy, later called London. The legend that the British kings were of Trojan descent had much to do with the sympathy felt in mediæval and Tudor times for the Trojans.

Troilus and Criseyde was a *rifacimento* of Boccaccio's *Filostrato* in which Chaucer developed the characterization, increased the humour and pathos, debated the erotic issues in the light of the courtly love code, and, while presenting the story of the lovers fully for the first time in English, produced one of the greatest of our poetic works. As W. P. Ker wrote, 'It is a tragic

[1] K. Young, *The Origin and Development of the Story of Troilus and Criseyde*, Chaucer Society, 2nd ser. 40, 1908.
[2] K. Young, *ibid*. pp. 45–7.

novel, and it is also strong enough to pass the scrutiny of that comic Muse who detects the impostures of inflated rhetoric and romantic poetry.'[1]

There were several versions of the Troy story in the Middle Ages. From Dares Phrygius came the six books *De Bello Troiano* by Joseph of Exeter (Josephus Iscanus), and an anonymous octosyllabic poem in Middle English, *Seege of Troye*. From Guido's *Historia* descended at least four metrical and two prose versions. These are the *Gest Hystoriale* in 14,044 alliterative lines[2]; a Scots poem by Barbour, now extant only in two fragments; John Lydgate's *Troy-Book*, a free rendering of Guido delle Colonne's *Historia*; a version of Lydgate's poem ascribed in the Bodleian Library MS (Laud 595) to Lydgate but probably by another poet; Caxton's prose *Recuyell of the Historyes of Troye (c.* 1474). Of these works the only two printed by Shakespeare's time were Lydgate's and Caxton's, and it is likely that Shakespeare knew them both.

That Lydgate's *Troy-Book*[3] was a result of Henry V's patronage of the monk of Bury St Edmunds we know from the poet himself, who states in his Prologue that he received his commission at 4 p.m. on Monday, 31 October 1412. Lydgate based his account on Guido's Latin, but expanded the work to over 30,000 lines, partly to please the King by developing the chivalric possibilities of the tale, partly for rhetorical, and partly for didactic reasons. The work is in five books, of which the first tells of Jason's voyage in search of the Golden Fleece, of the abduction of Hesione to Greece and the destruction of the first city of Troy. In Book II Priam rebuilds the city, sends Antenor to ask for the return of Hesione, and then sends Paris, who seizes Helen, whereupon the Greeks prepare to besiege Troy. Books III and IV trace the events of the long war, culminating in the capture and burning of the city. Book V relates the misadventures of the Greeks on their return home, and of the surviving Trojans, such as Aeneas.

---

[1] W. P. Ker, *Essays on Medieval Literature*, 1905, p. 84.

[2] Edited in *E.E.T.S.* 39 and 56 by G. A. Panton (1869) and D. Donaldson (1874). For this and other poems on the theme see J. E. Wells, *Manual of the Writings in Middle English*, New Haven, 1923, pp. 106ff.

[3] Edited by H. Bergen, 4 vols. *E.E.T.S.*, ExS, 97, 103, 106, 126 (1906–35). Cf. W. F. Schirmer, *John Lydgate* (1961), Ch. 5.

Despite its length and some tedious rhetoric in speeches and digressions, Lydgate's poem holds the interest surprisingly well. A disciple of Chaucer, to whom he frequently pays tribute, Lydgate owes much to his master. He gives colour and life to Guido's dry narrative, especially when describing festivities, tournaments, duels, battles and the qualities of important characters. Being a monk, he moralizes the theme, pointing out the evils of war and dissension and the ephemeral nature of all things human under the rule of Fortune.

On the whole Lydgate sides with the Trojans more than with the Greeks, partly perhaps because the Trojans lost the war, but mainly because they were more knightly, less treacherous, than their foes. Hector and Troilus in particular he praised for their chivalric virtues, in which he found Achilles wanting. In this Lydgate's attitude anticipates Shakespeare's, who may have read the *Troy-Book* either in the edition printed by R. Pynson in 1513 as *The hystorye / Sege and dystruccyon of Troye*, or in that revised by Robert Braham and printed by Thomas Marshe in 1555. Some excerpts from Pynson's edition are given below. From Lydgate's poem Shakespeare may have obtained the account of Troilus's character (IV.5.95–112), the episode of Hector and the resplendent knight (V.6 and 8), and Achilles' orders to his Myrmidons (V.7) [Text III]. In the main, however, the dramatist got his chivalric material from Caxton.

Caxton's *Recuyell of the Historyes of Troye* (1474?), the first English printed book,[1] was a translation of a fifteenth-century French prose work by Raoul Lefevre, a priest and chaplain of Duke Philip the Good of Burgundy, 'in which is comprehended [wrote Caxton] how Troye was thries destroyed and also the labours and histories of Saturnus, Titan, Jubyter, Perseus and Hercules.' Caxton also incorporated a translation of Lefevre's history of Jason. The third Book of Lefevre's *Le Receuil* extended from the rebuilding of Troy by Priam to the death of Ulysses (Ch. XXXII) and followed Guido's account closely, although he mentioned other authorities (e.g. Dares, Ovid and Virgil) whom he did not use. Caxton translated Lefevre as literally as he could—though with many errors. His work was repub-

---

[1] Edited by H. O. Sommer, 2 vols. 1894.

lished several times before Shakespeare's death, first by Caxton's helper Wynkyn de Worde in 1502 and again in 1503; then by William Copland in 1553; then in 1596 and 1607 by T. Creede, 'Newly corrected, and the English much amended. By William Fiston.'

There has been much discussion about the degree of Shakespeare's indebtedness to Lydgate, Caxton and Chaucer. He certainly used Caxton, and in an early edition, not in the 1596 modernized version where, for example, the word 'orgulous' (found also in Shakespeare's Prologue) was changed to 'proud'. The excerpts below are from the first edition [Text IV]. The name 'Sagittary' for the dreadful archer of V.5.14 is not found in the printed editions of Lydgate (although it appears in a manuscript) but it is repeatedly used by Caxton. Lydgate spells 'Pollicene' where Caxton has 'Polixena', 'Polyxena' or 'Polixene'. (But Shakespeare could have got his spelling from many other sources such as T. Cooper's *Thesaurus Linguae latinae* (1565).) In Caxton and Shakespeare (IV.5.120) Hector calls Ajax his 'cousin-german' and embraces him after their combat. This is not in Lydgate. The scene in Shakespeare is otherwise indebted to Caxton, for whereas in Lydgate Criseida is welcomed to the Greek camp only by Calchas, in Caxton as in Shakespeare she is met by a great many Greeks.[1] Other parallels are pointed out in my notes.

In his edition of Caxton's *Recuyell* (I.xlv) H. O. Sommer asserted that Shakespeare drew 'not ... from Chaucer, but from Lydgate's *Troy-Book*, or, still more likely, from Caxton's *Recuyell*'. He gave no evidence. Fuller comparison led R. A. Small to a different conclusion. The character of Pandarus, the affectionate jester, comes from Chaucer. Caxton never mentioned Pandarus in connection with Troilus and Cressida, and Lydgate only briefly, referring to Chaucer. Caxton prefers to call Criseyde Briseyde, although he mentions Chaucer's name for her. He refers his readers to Chaucer for their full story, and completely omits their meeting and Troilus's wooing of her, but, like Homer, goes straight to the exchange and Troilus's

---

[1] These distinctions were pointed out by R. A. Small, *The Stage-Quarrel between Ben Jonson and the So-called Poetasters*, Breslau, 1899, pp. 153ff.; and E. Stein, 'Caxton's *Recuyell* and Shakespeare's *Troilus*', *MLN*, xlv, 1930, 144–6. Cf. *Variorum TC*, pp. 424–5.

sorrow at it. Briseyde forgets Troilus quickly because of the welcome the Greeks give her, their presents and promises to protect her, and because life with them is so pleasant.

Caxton makes more of Diomedes' love than of Troilus's [*inf.* 204]. For Caxton Troilus is more a warrior than a lover. In him they had 'a newe Hector ... who was little lesse strong and worthy than Hector'. He did 'marveiles of armes, for to revenge the death of his brother', and overthrew Diomede. Briseyda, realizing that she would never recover Troilus, went over entirely to Diomede.

Obviously Shakespeare's Troilus in love is from Chaucer. As Small writes: 'The scene in which the Trojan heroes pass and Pandarus points them out to Cressida, with especial commendation of Troilus (I.2.183ff.) is suggested by the passage in Chaucer in which Cressida watches Troilus come home with battered helmet amid the acclamations of the people (Bk. II, 610–51) and that in which Pandarus makes Troilus ride by the window in which he and Cressida are sitting (II, 1009–1022; 1184–92; 1247–88). Pandarus' bringing a letter from Troilus to Cressida (I.2.291) is from Chaucer (II, 1002–1204). The mental confusion of Troilus and Cressida at their first meeting (III.2.17ff.) is suggested by Chaucer's description of the first meeting of the lovers (II.1751–57; III, 50–203); Cressida's declaration of her love, by Chaucer (III, 1239); and the last of the same scene (III, 2) by Chaucer's account of how Pandarus finally brought the lovers together (III, 953–1253). . . . Cressida's protestation of fidelity (IV.2.106) is suggested by Chaucer's IV, 1534–54. . . . Cressida's letter, received by Troilus as an aggravation of her unfaithfulness (V.3.108ff.) is from Chaucer V, 1590ff. Troilus' threats at Diomed are paralleled in Chaucer V, 1702ff.'

Some of these parallels might be imaginative coincidences; but enough remains to make it certain that Shakespeare was indebted to Chaucer for many important features of the Troilus–Cressida relationship.

One concludes therefore that Shakespeare owed something to Homer, Chaucer, Lydgate and Caxton. But in his handling of his material, both in the camp scenes and in the love story he departed greatly from them in tone. That his treatment of Cressida and Pandarus was not entirely novel was shown by

Hyder E. Rollins[1] who traced the popularity of the Troilus story after Chaucer and the variable opinions held of its characters.

In a play given at Eltham on Twelfth Night 1515/16 Cornish and the Children of the Chapel Royal played the 'Story of Troylus and Pander'. According to Bale, Nicholas Grimald wrote a Latin comedy, *Troilus ex Chaucero*. In *The Rare Triumphs of Love and Fortune*, a piece played before the Queen in 1582 and published in 1589, a play of Troilus and Cressida is given before the Gods in which the lovers 'Cries out on Love, that framed their decay'.[2]

There were various attitudes to Cressida. Thus the balladist William Elderton, in 'The panges of Love and lovers fittes' (1559/60) told of her pity for Troilus which led her 'To slepe with him and graunt him rest'.[3] Skelton, on the other hand, in *Philip Sparrow* (1507) declared that in her love 'she did but fayne', that 'Troylus also hath lost / On her much love and cost', and Pandarus 'for a speciall laud / He is named Troylus baud'. The reputation of Cressida took on a moralizing tone with the *Testament of Cresseid* of Robert Henryson. This fine narrative poem by a Scottish Chaucerian was published in Thynne's edition of Chaucer (1532) and in all subsequent editions until 1721, including that by Speght, who regarded it as Chaucer's. The poem was published separately by Henry Charteris in Edinburgh in 1593, and the extract below is given in his text [Text V].

Henryson's poem is a sequel to Chaucer's, and imagines the punishment of her infidelity. Diomed tires of her and dismisses her, and she lives 'As some men sayne, in the courte as commune' (76–7). Returning to her father Calchas she dreams in the temple that Venus demands that she be punished and the gods afflict her with leprosy. On waking she finds that she has the disease. Her father sends her away, and she goes to the spitalhouse and becomes a beggar. One day Troilus rides by, is reminded of his lost love, and gives her alms. Cresseid dies

---

[1] 'The Troilus-Cressida Story from Chaucer to Shakespeare', *PMLA*, 32 (n.s. XXV), 1917, pp. 383–429.

[2] Dodsley, *Old Plays*, ed. Hazlitt, VI, p. 155.

[3] Cf. J. P. Collier, *Old Ballads*, Percy Society, Vol. I, p. 26.

after sending her ruby ring to Troilus, who mourns her and puts up a monument.

The grim beauty and pathos of Henryson's poem made a great impression on Elizabethan love-poets. Thus Turbervile called his faithless mistress 'faire Cressid's heire' and in a poem 'The Lover in utter dispaire of his Ladies returne, in eche respect compares his estate with Troylus' writes:

> I naythlesse will wish hir well
> And better than to Cresid fell:
> I pray she may have better hap
> Than beg hir bread with dish and clap.[1]

George Gascoine in his *Posies* (1575) 'mentions the lovers on nearly every page' (Rollins), and George Whetstone's *Rocke of Regard* (1576) contained a 'Cressid's Complaint' in the preface to which he declared:

> 'The inconstancie of Cressid is so readie in every mans mouth, as it is a needelesse labour to blase at full her abuse towards yong Troilus, her frowning on Syr Diomede, her wanton lures and love.'

Whetstone's aim was to warn all men against 'Cressid's heires', who were 'more cunning then Cressid herselfe in wanton exercises, toyes and incitements'. For him Cressid was always a wanton and a whore, and he rejoiced in her downfall. On the whole there was much less pity than blame for her in the references in poems and ballads at the end of the century.

As for Pandarus, his reputation declined more swiftly than hers, and few would disagree with Skelton's view of the character whom Chaucer had treated kindly as a benevolent, trustworthy and ingenious uncle mindful of his own amorous griefs. The Elizabethans saw him as the 'pander', the 'pimp'.

As we have seen, the Troy story and the Troilus story was staged in the fifteen-nineties. The Admiral's Men played a 'troye' in 1596 when Henslowe noted it as a new play ('ne'), with receipts of £3. 9s. 0 on 22 June, 24s. on 2 July, 29s. on 7 July, and 21s. on 16 July. There is no real evidence that this was (as Sir W. W. Greg once thought)[2] an earlier draft of

---

[1] *Epitaphes, Epigrams, Songs and Sonets* (1567), ed. J. P. Collier, p. 249.
[2] *Henslowe Diary*, ed. Greg. II, 180.

part of T. Heywood's *The Iron Age* (not published till 1632, and
now thought to date from 1611–13). Henslowe's company
owned a 'great horse with his leages'.[1] This was probably
needed for the end of a Troy play. On 7 April 1599 Henslowe
advanced Dekker and Chettle three pounds 'in earneste of ther
booke called Troyeles & creasse daye', and nine days later
twenty shillings 'in parte of payment of ther boocke called
Troyelles & cresseda'.[2] Two entries in May 1599 of payment to
the same dramatists for 'ther boocke called the tragedie of
Agamemnon', and another on 3 June to the Master of Revels's
man for licensing this play, probably refer to a sequel to their
Troilus play.

Of great interest in relation to these facts is the fragment of a
'Plot' of an Admiral's play preserved in the British Museum in
MS. Add. 10449. Written on two columns on a single sheet
of paper, now mounted on pasteboard, this represents less than
half, perhaps the second and fourth quarters (or fifths) of a
'plot' made for a call-boy or stage-director and now covers
thirteen scenes, with entrances, exits, sound-effects and names
of characters. Actors' names occur which date it 1598–1602
and Sir W. W. Greg's suggestion that it refers to the 1599
Troilus and Cressida of Dekker and Chettle is more likely than
that it concerned the *Troy* play of 1596.

The 'plot' was briefly analysed by J. S. P. Tatlock who
thought that the play was based on Caxton and Lydgate
Homer, with material from Chaucer and Henryson. I agree
with much of Tatlock's argument but differ from him in some
respects.[3] So much of the 'plot' is missing that we can only
guess at the action of the play, but it seems to include some
matter in common with Shakespeare. Greg's transcript is given
below [Text VI].[4]

The fragment begins with a council scene (A), between the
Greeks and Trojans. Scene C may correspond to the Hector–
Ajax encounter in IV.5. Scene D probably showed the capture

---

[1] *Henslowe's Diary*, ed. R. A. Foakes and R. T. Rickert, 1961, p. 320.
[2] *Ibid.* pp. 106–7.
[3] Cf. J. S. P. Tatlock, 'The Siege of Troy in Shakespeare and Heywood'.
PMLA, xxx (n.s. xxiii), 1915, 697–770. My analysis will be found in *Essays and
Studies of the English Association*, ed. W. A. Armstrong, 1964.
[4] By kind permission of the Delegates of the Oxford University Press; from
W. W. Greg, *Dramatic Documents from the Elizabethan Playhouses* (1931).

of Antenor by the Greeks which led to the exchange of Cressida. Scene E may have shown the coming of Pandarus and Troilus to Cressida, as in Chaucer and in Shakespeare's III.2. In F. Ulysses talks to Priam, perhaps to propose the truce during which the exchange of Antenor for Cressida and Thoas was arranged. Presumably then the scenes missing at the top of the right-hand column included the exchange, the parting of Troilus and Cressida, and Diomed's wooing of her. In Scene H the war is on again and the presence of the women on the walls may indicate the occasion when the Trojans fled, and Hector though wounded felt shame because the Trojan ladies were watching (cf. the allusion at I.2.1–36). In Scene J Achilles in his tent is visited by Diomed, Menelaus and Ulysses, probably in an attempt to persuade him to join them in battle. No doubt he is refusing to fight when Ajax enters with the dead Patroclus on his back. (For this action there is no warrant in the sources.) Scene K showing Cressida 'with beggars' is probably taken from Henryson's *Testament*, and Troilus and Deiphobus would pass by and give her alms. In Scene M, the last on the fragment, Troilus probably fights Diomed, and as Tatlock argues, Achilles 'probably kills Hector in the sight of the Trojans on the walls', and 'Priam perhaps descends to beg his body back'. We cannot be sure that this was the last scene of the play, since the 'plot' may have continued on the other side of the sheet; but it seems likely that the piece would not continue long. We cannot tell whether Troilus was killed or not.

Like Shakespeare's play the Admiral's piece combined the themes of war and love, the Hector-Ajax, Hector-Achilles motifs and the Troilus–Cressida, Troilus–Diomed themes. It may (L) have introduced Achilles' love for Polyxena. If the foregoing summary is correct it must have been a very episodic play, and not satiric. Achilles kills Hector without using his Myrmidons, despite the presence of Deiphobus (Scene M). Henryson's influence probably gave the end of Cressida a moral and pathetic turn. This agrees well with Dekker's customary attitude.

Any conclusion about the relationship between this play and Shakespeare's must be tentative. But the Admiral's piece was probably written before *Troilus and Cressida*, and the parallels in structure and content are close enough to suggest that

8

Shakespeare conceived his play as a 'realistic' answer to the unsophisticated mixture of epic and didactic sentiment likely to have characterized the piece by Dekker and Chettle.

Shakespeare could have treated both sides of his plot with the high seriousness proper to epic and romance. Chapman gave warrant for a heroic attitude to the war, and Chaucer and Lydgate for a sympathetic handling of Cressida. On the other hand, in the British tradition the Greeks were already unpopular, and Troilus was the victim of an unscrupulous wanton. In his previous plays Shakespeare had taken up both romantic and unromantic attitudes to the story. Thus Petruchio (*TSh*, IV.1.147) had called his spaniel Troilus, whereas Lorenzo (*MV*, V.1.4–6) at Belmont had waxed sentimental about him, and Rosalind (*AYL*, IV.1.95) had laughingly called him 'one of the patterns of love'. But Benedick (*M. Ado*, V.2.31) calls Troilus 'the first employer of panders' and this is the usual attitude to Pandarus (e.g. *H5*, IV.5.14), except that Pistol may refer absurdly to the Homeric Pandarus (*MWW*, I.3.76) when he cries, 'Shall I Sir Pandarus of Troy become, And by my side wear steel?' Cressida is chiefly referred to as Troilus's bedmate, and as a beggar (*TN*, III.1.55–8)[1] while in *Henry V*, II.1.78 Doll Tearsheet is called "the lazar kite of Cressid's kind". Thus Shakespeare was well aware of Cresseid's fate in Henryson's poem (which he doubtless thought was by Chaucer), and may refer to it in *Troilus and Cressida*, V.2.102 when she says, 'I shall be plagu'd'. The fact that he ends his play long before this event, and when Troilus is raging for revenge on Diomed is highly significant. He was not writing a tragedy but a savage comedy in which he mocked at romantic conceptions of war and love and accentuated the weaknesses of human nature which he found in his sources so as to show the evil effects of passion on the judgment in both the political and erotic stories combined in the play. Accordingly he modified both the tone and the incidents he found in his classical and medieval sources and (as a short analysis of the play will show) he set out to shock lovers of Homeric heroism and medieval chivalry by the deliberate distortion of character and motive and by the expansive treatment of personages capable of base interpretation.

---

[1] These references were collected by H. E. Rollins, *op. cit.* 424–5.

The Prologue sets the scene in magniloquent, heroic language ('princes orgulous', 'instruments of cruel war', 'warlike fraughtage' etc.) which recalls Chapman's attitude to Homer, but comes even nearer to the first edition of Caxton's *Recuyell* (1474?) where the words 'orguylous and prowd' (simplified in later editions) often occur. Since the Prologue shows other debts to Caxton (e.g. 'port of Athens', 'sixty and nine', and the names of the six gates) it was probably written by the author of the play, who drew so much from the *Recuyell*. Nothing is said of Troilus and Cressida; the expectation aroused is of epic events ('Beginning in the middle') equal in grandeur of tone to that found in Chapman's *Seaven Bookes* and probably in recent plays on Troy.

Shakespeare is jesting ironically, for Act I, Sc. 1 at once belies the epic manner when Troilus enters with no heart to fight because of his love for Cressida. Pandarus, while pretending not to 'meddle' reveals himself as the quintessential go-between. Aeneas's news that Paris has been wounded by Menelaus makes the young man realize how 'womanish it is to be from thence' (I.1.112). Already love is seen as the enemy of heroism.

I.2. introduces Cressida talking merrily with Paris and Pandarus, mocking at Ajax and at Pandarus's praise of Troilus (yet eager to hear it). We learn something of Ajax's character— a confusion of humours (I.2.19–30) got by combining Ovid's Ajax and Homer's Ajax Telamon—and of the Trojan heroes as they come from battle (182–239). The women on the walls and Hector's shame come from the occasion (in Lydgate and Caxton) when he was wounded in the face and the Trojans forced back in view of Queen Hecuba and his sisters (*inf.* 173, 203). Caxton or Lydgate may have suggested the review of Trojan heroes (*inf.* 157) which also recalls Portia's comments on her suitors (*MV*, I.2). Cressida is coquettishly interested in Troilus, and shows a lively mind with a fondness for bawdy talk.

I.3 moves to the Grecian camp and the more serious political aspects of the war, as the Greek lords discuss their failure to take Troy after seven years' siege. Agamemnon ascribes it Homerically to 'the protractive trials of great Jove' (I.3.20). But Ulysses gets to the heart of their trouble in the great speech on order in which he develops ideas found in *Iliad*, Bk. II, where

Agamemnon speaks of wrangling and strife and Ulysses, reminding a soldier of his duty, asserts the need for leadership (*inf.* 120). He blames the insubordination of Achilles and Patroclus and their bad influence on Ajax and others in opposing the policy of gradualness operated by their elders. In Shakespeare (unlike his classical and mediaeval authorities) there is no mention of the quarrel about Chryseis. Disunity among the Greeks is the result of a moral rot and Achilles is moved solely by vanity and general discontent. Shakespeare's Ulysses praises the speeches of Agamemnon and Nestor and Agamemnon refers to the kind of speech Thersites might have made—an obvious allusion to what Thersites actually says in Homer.

The length and solemnity of this discussion prove that it had special significance for Shakespeare, and so it would for the audience either in 1600–1 when Essex was sulking, out of favour, or after his execution when the oration would remind hearers of the dangers inherent in a social unrest still far from settled. In neither case should the parallel between Achilles and Essex be pressed closely.

The coming of Aeneas with Hector's challenge gives a fine chivalric tone to the epic incident from *Iliad*, VII, with his description of the Trojans ('Courtiers as free, as debonair unarm'd As bending angels' (235ff)), and the vaunting of Hector's 'lady' which stirs Agamemnon and Nestor. In Homer and Ovid's *Metamorphoses*, Bk. XIII Ajax becomes the Greek champion by chance of lottery. In Shakespeare the lottery is 'faked' in order to reduce Achilles' pride, ridicule Ajax, and reveal the 'policy' and trickery behind apparently heroic actions.

In II.1, after a long passage of mutual mockery between Ajax and Thersites revealing the stupidity of the one and the vicious railing of the other, Achilles shows his annoyance at the lottery and that he has not been directly challenged by Hector. 'It is put to lottery: otherwise, He knew his man'; that is, he would have fought Hector if asked to do so.

II.2 parallels I.3 when Priam invites his sons' opinions about Nestor's offer to end the war if only Helen be restored. Hector's view is eminently sensible: 'Let Helen go', but Troilus prates of honour and spurns 'fears and reasons', and when Helenus the priest points out the need for 'reasons' in state affairs, grows impatient:

> Nay, if we talk of reason,
> Let's shut our gates and sleep . . .
> reason and respect
> Make livers pale and lustihood deject. (46–50)

In confessing that Helen is not worth the holding Hector lays bare the weakness of the heroic code (whether in war or love) to which Troilus vows himself:

> 'Tis mad idolatry
> To make the service greater than the god;
> And the will dotes that is inclinable
> To what infectiously itself affects,
> Without some image of the affected merit. (56–60)

Troilus's great speech defending Trojan honour expresses a boyish delight in gallantry and daring as he praises Paris's action (as told by Lydgate and Caxton) in abducting Helen (61–96). Cassandra's woeful prophecies do not recall him to 'discourse of reason'. He regards her as insane and will protract a quarrel 'Which hath our several honours all engag'd'. Paris will not surrender Helen 'On terms of base compulsion' (153), and Hector, while insisting that to do so would be in accord with the 'moral laws of nature, and of nations', weakly votes for keeping Helen for Pride's sake. So the impetuous Troilus with his passionate talk of honour has overborne his eldest brother's sagacity.

In the Greek camp (II.3), after Thersites has played the licensed jester to an indulgent Achilles the latter refuses to see the generals and sends word that he 'will not to the field tomorrow' (161). His 'savage strangeness' shows that he is 'plaguy proud'. Ulysses works cleverly on Ajax's foolish vanity and makes him think himself superior to Achilles. The arguments in Homer Bk. IX and Caxton are not used since Achilles does not face Ulysses and Agamemnon.

III.1 takes us back into Troy where Pandarus jests gaily with Paris and Helen (who will not let her lover fight that day). Troilus too is out of the battle: 'He hangs the lip at something.' So on both sides martial duty is at the mercy of private feelings.

Later that evening, in III.2 we can sympathize fully with Troilus when his sensitive soul experiences the delights of expectation, and of dalliance, before he is taken in to bliss. The oath-swearing of the lovers endows their passion with irony. Chaucer is behind all this, for neither Lydgate nor Caxton shows the coming together of Troilus and Cressida.

The irony deepens in III.3 when Calchas asks, as a reward for his treacherous service to the Greeks, that Antenor be exchanged for Cressida. Diomed is charged with the mission and ordered to discover whether Hector will fight Ajax. In the same scene Achilles is treated contemptuously by the Greek generals. Then Ulysses plays subtly on him, sympathizing, and preaching a noble sermon on 'perseverance' which 'keeps honour bright', and on the fickleness of men and 'calumniating time'. Such a speech would have special significance in England if the play were written before Essex's revolt, while he was in despair after his failure in Ireland. Ulysses introduces a new aspect of Achilles' character, his love for Priam's daughter Polyxena (which in Lydgate and Caxton did not begin until a year after Hector's death, but then prevented him from fighting the Trojans). Patroclus urges him to fight, and Achilles is so far moved as to wish 'To see great Hector in his weeds of peace'.

IV.1 moves to Troy, where Aeneas and Diomed greet each other as friendly foes (6–34). Paris asks Aeneas to go before and warn Troilus that he must give up his mistress. Diomed speaks disparagingly of Helen:

> For every false drop in her bawdy veins
> A Grecian's life hath sunk; for every scruple
> Of her contaminated carrion weight
> A Trojan hath been slain . . . (69–74).

Whereas in Chaucer (IV.141ff) Troilus was present in 'parlement' when Priam agreed to exchange Criseyde for Antenor, in IV.2 Troilus is parting from Cressid after spending the night with her when Aeneas brings news of the exchange concluded 'by Priam and the general state of Troy'. Troilus takes the blow manfully but Cressida bewails:

> O you gods divine!
> Make Cressid's name the very crown of falsehood
> If ever she leave Troilus . . . (102–4)

Troilus never questions the need for her to go, and in IV.3
says that he himself will hand her over to Diomed. They part
in IV.4 with protestations of fidelity, exchanging tokens (a sleeve
to her, a glove to him). He fears (as in the mediaeval sources)
that she may be tempted by Greek graces, but she swears to be
true.[1] Troilus bids Diomed 'use her well', and Diomed indignantly declares, more truly than he yet knows, 'when I am
hence I'll answer to my lust' (131).[2]

When Diomed brings Cressida to the Greek camp (IV.5)
she is free with her kisses and Ulysses is disgusted by her
'wanton spirits' (54–63). The duel between Ajax and Hector
takes place, and 'The issue is embracement' between the
cousins (113–50). Hector, invited to the Greek tents, is lauded
by Agamemnon and Nestor, but Achilles insolently views him
as a future victim and promises to meet him next day in the
field (265–9). Ulysses, who has praised Troilus as the 'second
hope' of Troy, promises to bring him to Calchas's tent where
Diomed is already amorous of Cressida.

In V.1 Thersites brings Achilles a letter from Troy and while
he is reading it insults Patroclus by telling him that he is
rumoured to be Achilles' 'masculine whore'. Achilles reveals
that the letter comes from Hecuba,

> A token from her daughter, my fair love,
> Both taxing me and gaging me to keep
> An oath that I have sworn. I will not break it. (39–46)

His oath is not defined, nor when he made it, but it will prevent
his fighting Hector. This passage must be interpreted with
reference to Lydgate's and Caxton's account of Achilles'
communications with Troy about his sudden passion for
Polyxena and the conditions made that he should work for
peace (*inf.* 207). Like Menelaus, Paris, Troilus and Diomed, he
is in the toils of love. Thersites comments, 'Nothing but
lechery! all incontinent varlets!'.

Troilus discovers (V.2) the speed and depth of Cressida's

---

[1] Cf. Chaucer IV, 1422–1589.   [2] Cf. Chaucer V, 78–91.

duplicity when, guided by Ulysses, he spies on her interview with Diomed during which she gives him Troilus's sleeve and tempts him to return. Troilus's struggle not to generalize upon her behaviour is well portrayed. He turns his disillusionment into rabid hate of Diomed. In this scene Shakespeare compresses and intensifies the emotional implications of Chaucer Bk. V, 1233ff. There, after Criseyde has not kept her promise to come back to him within ten days, Troilus dreams that she is being loved by a boar, and his sister Cassandra's interpretation makes him desperate.

> And ofte time he was in purpos grete
> Himselven lik a pilgrim to disguise,
> To sen her; but he may not contrefete
> To ben unknowe of folk that weren wise,
> Ne finde excuse aright that may suffise,
> If he among the Grekes knowen were:
> For which he wep ful ofte, and many a tere. (1576–82)

He writes to Criseyde and she replies, putting him off; then he finds on a coat-armour taken by Deiphebus from Diomed a brooch which he had given to Criseyde at their parting. Henceforth he seeks out Diomed in battle. Probably Shakespeare took a hint from the lines just quoted and so created the eavesdropping scene in which Troilus watches the seduction of his mistress and her betrayal of his trust, while his just passion is itself cynically mocked by the base Thersites: 'Lechery, lechery; still, wars and lechery: nothing else holds fashion' (V.2.190–2).

In contrast with this scene of infidelity, V.3 presents the faithful Andromache, supported by the prophetess Cassandra, with Priam himself, attempting to stop Hector from going out to battle. Troilus rebukes Hector for his 'vice of mercy' (which Ulysses has already noted at IV.5.105–6), and shows his lack of judgment when he calls Cassandra a 'foolish, dreaming, superstitious girl' (79). (Compare his attitude in Chaucer (V, 1520–6) when she has interpreted his dream as signifying his lady's infidelity:

> Thou seyst not soth, quod he, thou sorceresse,
> With all thy false gost of prophecye!
> Thou wenest ben a gret devineresse . . .)

Troilus tears up a letter from Cressida, dismissing it as 'Words, words, mere words, no matter from the heart' (108). In Chaucer he receives a long letter from her explaining her continued absence, but his reaction is different, 'Him thought it like a kalendes of chaunge' (V.1633) but cannot believe her untrue, for he has not had the proof Shakespeare has afforded in V.2.

The next scenes (4–8) show how thoroughly both sides 'begin to proclaim barbarism, and policy grows into an ill opinion'. The battle swings both ways: Troilus chases Diomed; Thersites grovels to Hector; Diomed, as in Lydgate and Caxton, sends Troilus' horse to Cressida; Patroclus is killed off-stage, and Achilles, roused by this and the massacre of his Myrmidons, rages against Hector (V.5). Troilus takes on both Diomed and Ajax. Hector courteously spares Achilles when he has him at a disadvantage (V.6), and pursues a Greek clad in sumptuous armour. This, as in Lydgate and Caxton, causes his death. Achilles (as in Lydgate and Caxton against Troilus) plans to use his Myrmidons to overcome Hector (V.7), and kills the latter unchivalrously when he is unarmed (V.8), and maltreats his corpse.

The play now comes rapidly to a close. In V.9 the Greeks see Hector's death as spelling the fall of Troy, and in V.10 Troilus raves of destruction, grief and revenge, dismissing Pandarus to well-earned disrepute. Pandarus however is unashamed, and in his epilogue assumes that he has sympathizers in the audience. When he says, 'Some two months hence my will shall here be made', is he promising a sequel to the play?

Even so short an account as this makes it obvious that Shakespeare has given a different interpretation of both the epic and the erotic theme from those he found in his sources, while basing that interpretation on points of character and incident already there. Both sides in the war are disillusioned by their losses and the scant promise of victory. The Greeks are weary and disunited, and though there is no question here (as in Homer and Caxton) of giving up the siege without the return of Helen, she is represented and recognized as not worth the blood shed for her. There is division between the older and wiser leaders and their younger colleagues, whose faults are more apparent than their virtues.

Ajax is brave but (except when he meets Hector in IV.5) has the stupidity and boastful vanity of Ovid's doltish Ajax. Achilles is deliberately debased. For Shakespeare the Achilles who sulks petulantly through most of the *Iliad* could not be the glorious hero Homer yet makes him out to be. So his whole personality is interpreted in terms of his failings in the epic, and supported with material from Lydgate and Caxton, so that he kills Hector in a doubly villainous manner. Even his friendship with Patroclus is given a cloying, faintly homosexual tone, and in avenging his Myrmidons and Patroclus he breaks his oath to Hecuba.

Ulysses, the wisest of the Greeks, will stoop to play a deadly practical joke on Ajax in order to get Achilles back into the war by appealing to the latter's injured self-esteem and desire for glory. The end justifies the means; 'policy' governs all his actions and speeches. Nevertheless Shakespeare does not use the aspersions on his character cast by Ovid's Ajax (Text II). Ulysses is the noblest of politicians.

On the other side the wiser Trojans know that they are in the wrong and that Hesione is not well avenged by the abduction of Helen. But pride, both personal and national, sustains their resolve to keep her, and Hector's reasonable arguments yield to Troilus's ill-considered appeal to prestige and dignity. Both Greeks and Trojans are driven on by pride in various forms. The difference between them is not, as Professor G. W. Knight has argued, between 'reason' and 'intuition', but between pride veiled with policy and pride openly admitted and glorified.

The theme of honour is as important in this play as in *1 Henry IV*, and more deeply considered. Above all other Greeks towers royal Agamemnon, a massive but remote figure preaching courage in adversity, a doctrine of stoical endurance which his counsellor Nestor seconds, declaring that 'valour's show and valour's worth divide In storms of fortune' (1.3.46–7), and that

> then the thing of courage
> As rous'd with rage, with rage doth sympathize,
> And with an accent tun'd in self-same key,
> Retorts to chiding fortune. (I.3.51–54)

For these truly heroic men honour stands 'in the reproof of

chance'. For Achilles it is bound up with a sense of his own importance which makes him insolent and insubordinate to them and, when he falls in love, capable of secret negotiations with the enemy. Troilus has the faults of youth. He is the embodiment of adolescent ardour, sensitive at times, the prey of illusions, like Hotspur in his passion for war; impatient of cold reason in his pursuit of glory by

> valiant and magnanimous deeds,
> Whose present courage may defeat our foes,
> And fame in time to come canonize us (II.2.195–206)

In the erotic pursuit which briefly but disastrously distracts him Troilus's boyish moods, his sensual ecstasy and chivalrous devotion, excite our sympathy, which turns to pity but not to mockery when we realize that he is deceived. He is not a tragic figure but he is not a satiric butt and certainly he is not meant to suggest 'the educated sensuality of an Italianate English roué'.[1] When he is shocked out of his illusions about Cressida (Shakespeare does it much more swiftly than Chaucer) he still loves her, but with a jealous rage that turns against Diomed (V.2.162–73), and henceforth war is the means of savage vengeance. He is a boy still, as Hector says (V.3.33–6), but he has cast honour and chivalry to the winds in his bloodlust.

Cressida is a shallower person than in Chaucer or Lydgate, and though she is not patently wanton from the first, she is so conscious of her power, and uses it so obviously ('Yet hold I off' etc . I.2.297–8) that we are not surprised when Ulysses sees through her, and when she uses on Diomed the devices she used on Troilus. Yet she is a delightful creation, engrossed in the moment and the love it brings, and aware of her inability to withstand male flattery or passion and her own desire to yield. She has far more charm than the cold, glossy, sophisticated Helen, and Shakespeare does not punish her, nor even clearly foretell the fate Henryson gave her. She drops out when she has done her work, which is to reveal to Troilus the need to distinguish what seems from what is, and to raise doubts in our minds about the value of romantic love, as Achilles raises doubts about epic heroism.

Both war and love are further soiled through the running

---

[1] O. J. Campbell, *op. cit.* p. 210–12.

comments of Thersites, who scatters his filth over everything in life. We must not believe all that he says, but some of the mud sticks, and there are bitter home-truths in his railing. That Shakespeare developed him so expansively from the thumb-nail picture in Homer is highly significant, and proves that the play has in it much of the 'comicall satyre' fashionable between 1598 and 1603. Thersites has something in common with Carlo Buffone (in Jonson's *Every Man Out of His Humour* (1599))[1] of whom Macilente says:

> O, 'tis an open-throated, black-mouth'd cur,
> That bites at all, but eats on those that feed him;
> A slave, that to your face will, serpent-like
> Creep on the ground, as he would eat the dust,
> And to your back will turn the tail and sting
> More deadly than a scorpion. (I.1.)

Buffone helps the satire by exposing the follies of fools and pretenders in a tone of constant derision. He thinks and speaks the worst of all men, but his special field is in manners, whereas Thersites denigrates motives and morals, and, being a licensed jester, abuses people to their faces. The tolerance shown to his vilification demeans the society he lives by insulting and makes us suspect its values as well as his. So long as Hector is alive and Troilus keeps his charming if immature idealism the hatred of Thersites, based on envy, malice and all uncharitableness, makes us eager to redress the balance. But the end of the play may seem to justify his strictures.

This ending has caused much critical discussion. It is strangely inconclusive, say some writers; Shakespeare would never have left it so; someone else must have finished it. Cressida should have been punished, Troilus killed; Pandarus's epilogue, with its leering familiarity, is a blot on the piece. I can agree with none of these criticisms. John Palmer came near the truth when he suggested that Shakespeare was here 'trying, against the grain of his nature, to stand apart from his creatures, to play the absolute just judge of Molière, to see them in the light of simple intelligence . . . to write the pure comedy of reason'.[2] Reading both classical and mediaeval

---

[1] Cf. O. J. Campbell, *op. cit.* pp. 64–9.
[2] John Palmer, *Comedy*, 1914, pp. 18–21.

accounts of the Trojan war in the light of reason Shakespeare must have smiled ruefully at the evidence of base human nature there hinted but usually cloaked by heroic or romantic narrative. Lydgate saw this when he occasionally rebuked his characters for their moral failings; at other times he blamed Fortune, as Homer blamed the partial gods. Shakespeare frequently seems to blame Time, but to call this the central theme of *Troilus and Cressida* is to mistake temporal accident for substance. For the changes which occur are the result of human error, not of the clock. The play is full of ambiguities, of the 'confusion of humours', of characters with contrary streaks in their natures, so that our attitudes towards them must shift. The piece comes to its natural end with the downfall of its two most likeable young heroes. Hector has been mistaken more than once, but he exemplifies a noble magnanimity unique among the warriors, and his death foretells the destruction of Troy through intrigue and deceit. As Troilus declares (V.10.22), echoing one of Lydgate's favourite phrases: 'Hector is dead; there is no more to say'. Here is true tragedy, in nobility and heroism wasted. After this, the strong words of defiance spoken by Troilus and his hope of revenge seem futile, for though he is a 'second Hector' we know that the end of Troy is near. But since his martial ardour is at least more manly and public spirited than his erotic weakness and jealousy it is right that Pandarus (as if in reminiscence of Falstaff after Hal's coronation) should be dismissed to the 'ignomy and shame' he has deserved as a misleader of youth. His epilogue may well have been written by Shakespeare as a reminder that such men are shameless, that heroes in all ages fight and die to make the world safe for Thersites and Pandarus, and that the modern age is maybe one of panders rather than of Hectors. Finally, as Theodore Spencer wrote,[1] the play 'marks an extension of awareness in Shakespeare's presentation of man's nature. Whatever name we give it, whether we call it a tragedy, or a history, a comedy or a "comicall satyre", it describes in a new way the difference between man as he ought to be and man as he is . . . Troilus is the kind of experiment which was necessary before *King Lear* could be written.'

[1] Theodore Spencer. *Shakespeare and the Nature of Man*, N.Y. 1942, pp. 111-21.

I. Source [A] and Analogue [B]

From THE ILIADS OF HOMER
translated by George Chapman

A. Source

THE SEAVEN BOOKES OF HOMERS ILIADS
translated by George Chapman. ... J. Windet, 1598

BOOK I

[The cause of Achilles' refusal to fight.]

The Argument

Appollos *Priest to th'Argive Fleete doth bring*
Gifts for his daughter, prisoner to the King:
For which her tendred freedome he intreates:
But being dismist with contumelious threates,
At Phœbus *hands by vengefull prayer he seekes,*
To have a plague inflicted on the Greekes:
Which done, Achilles *doth a Counsell cite,*
And forceth Chalchas *in the Kings despite*
To tell the trueth why they were punishte so:
From whence their fierce and deadlie strife doth grow.
In which Achilles *so extreamelie raves,*
That Goddesse Thetis *from her Throne of waves*
(Ascending Heaven) of Jove *asistance wonn*
T'afflict the Greekes, *by absence of her Sonne,*
And make the Gennerall himselfe repent
To wrong so much his Armies Ornament.
This found by Juno, *shee with* Jove *contends,*
Till Vulcan *with Heavens cuppe the quarrell ends.*

An other Argument

Alpha, *the prayer of* Chryses *sings,*
The Armies plague, th'incensed Kings.

Achilles banefull wrath, resound great Goddesse of my verse
That through th'afflicted bolt of *Greece* did worlds of woes disperse,
And timelesse sent by troopes to hell, the glorie-thirsting soules
Of great Heroes; but their lims, left foode for beasts and foules:
So *Joves* high counsell tooke event, from whence that Jarr begun.
Twixte *Agamemnon* King of men, and *Thetis* Godlike sonn.
What God did give them up to strife. *Joves* and *Latonas* seede,
Who Angrie with the King for wrongs, against his Priest decreede,
Excited sicknes through the host, which much life put to flight:
His Priest came to the Greekes swift Fleete, with ransome infinite.
The golden Scepter and the Crowne far-shooting *Phœbus* wore,
To free his daughter: which in hand he did propose before
The Peeres of Greece, whome he besought, but both th'*Atrides* most,
Who were most mightie in the rule of all th'imperiall Host.

Atrides and the wel-greavde Greekes; Gods that in heavenlie hals
Make blest abodes, renowme your swords, with *Priams* razed wals,
And grant you safe retreat to Greece: meane tyme accept of mee
This holie ransome, and returne my dearest daughter free,
Approving your religious mindes to him: from *Jove* descends
Divine *Apollo* that his darts through all the earth extends.
The generall presence well allowd the Priest and his demands,
And thought the shyning presents fitte to free his daughters bands:
But *Agamemnon* was displeasde, and did his gifts refuse,
Dismist him with unfitte repulse, and this hard charge did use:

Hence doating Priest, nor let me find thy stay protracted now
In circuite of our hollow Fleete, or once hereafter know
Of thy returne: for if I doe, the Crowne thou doest sustaine
And golden scepter of thy God, thou shalt present in vaine:
Thy daughter I will not dissolve, till age deflower her hed:
Till in my Royall Argive court, her bewties strow my bed
And shee her twisting spindle turnes farre from her native shore;
To which if thou wilt safe returne, tempte our contempte no more.

This answere strooke the Priest with feare, who servd his sterne
　command
In silence shunning his abode, and walkt along the strand;
Of *Neptunes* high resounding rule, when from the Fleete farre gone....

[Chryses prayed to Apollo, who sent a plague upon the Greeks.
Achilles asked Chryses why, and promised to protect him.]

Then tooke the blamelesse prophet hart, and saide they were not
　vowes,
Yet unperformd, nor Hecatombes, but love that *Phœbus* showes
In honor of his priestes disgrast by *Agamemnons* will,

That skornd his ransome, and reserves his dearest daughter still.
For this *Apollo* sends this plague, and yet will send us more,
Nor will containe from our distresse his heavie hand before
The blacke eyde virgin be releast, unbought and ransomlesse,
And convoyed hence with Hecatombes, till her chaste foot do presse
The flowrie *Chrysas* holie shoore, and so if we shall please
Th' offended God perhaps he may recure this keene disease.
    He sat: the great *Heroe* rose; the far commanding king
Atrides, full of frowarde griefe, excessive angers sting:
Sperst blacke fumes round about his brest, his eyes like burning fire
Sparcled beneath his bended browes as lightnings of his ire,
And looking sternelie on the priest, Prophet of ill (said he)
That never dist presage my good, but tookest delight to be
Offensive in thy *Auguries*, not one good worde proceedes
From thy rude lips, nor is performd in anie future deedes,
And now thou frowardlie dost preach, in midst of al the Greekes,
That heavens farre-shooter in this plague the restitution seekes
Of my faire prisoner, who retaind is cause of our annoy:
And all because thou knowest, in her I take such speciall joy,
And wish to bring her to my Court, since I esteeme her more
Then *Clitemnestra*, that to me the nuptiall contract swore
When shee was yet a maide and young: nor doth she merite lesse
Both for her bodies comelie forme, her native towardenesse,
Her wisedome and her huswiferie, yet will I render her
Yf it be best, for to my good my Souldiers I preferre.
But in her place some other pryse see quickelie you prepare,
That I alone of all the Greekes loose not my honors share,
Which needes must bee confest unfit, but thus my friendes you see
That what by all your mindes is myne another takes from mee.
    To him the excellentest of foot, divine *Achilles* said,
Ambitious and most covetous man, what prise can be repaid
By these our nobleminded friendes for thy desirde supply?
All know how scantlie we have storde our common treasury.
For what the spoiled Citties gave, ech souldier for his paine
Hath duelie shard by our consentes, which to exact againe
Were base and ignominious, but to the God resigne
Thy pleasure for our common good: and if the most divine
So grace us that this wellwalled towne we leavill with the plaine,
We fourefold will repay the losse thy fortunes now sustaine.
    The king replide, be not deceyved nor thinke though thou art
        strong
And godlike framde, thou canst perswade my patience to my wrong,
Or that thy feet into thy breath can transmigrated bee

To passe me with thy sleightes as well as in outrunning mee,
Wouldst thou thy selfe injoy thy prise, and I sit dispossest?
Then let the Greekes apply themselves as much to my request
And with some other fit amendes my satisfaction make,
If not, Ile make mine owne amendes, and come my selfe and take
Thyne *Ajax*, or *Ulisses* prise (men of most excellence
And most admitted to thy love) and let him take offence
On whome I shall performe my vow, but touching this designe
We will hereafter or elsewhere decide what shall be mine.

  Now let us lanch the Sable barke into the holy seas,
Shippe chosen rowers in her bankes, and *Hecatombes* to ease
Our instant plague, and wee wil cause bright *Chrisys* to ascend
Whose charge to some Greeke prince in chiefe t'is fit we should
     commend,
Or to the royal *Idomen* or *Ajax Telamon*,
Or to the prudent counsaylor, *Divine Laertes* sonne,
Or to the terriblest of men, thy selfe *Æacides*:
That offrings made by thy strong hands *Apollo* may appease.

  Æacides observing well the urgte authoritie
Of his proud foe, with browes contract returnd this sharp reply:
O thou possest with Impudence that in command of men
Affectst the brute mind of a Fox, for so thou fill thy denne
With forced or betrayed spoiles thou feelest no sence of shame,
What souldier can take any spirite, to put on (for thy fame)
Contempt of violence and death, or in the open field,
Or secret ambush, when the heyre his hie desert should yeeld
Is before hand condemnd to glut thy gulfe of avarice?
For me I have no cause t'account these *Ilians* enemies,
Nor of my Oxen nor my horse have they made hostile spoile,
Nor hurt the comfortable fruites of *Pthyas* populous soyle,
For manie shadie distances hils and resounding Seas
Are interposde: but our kinde armes, are lifted to release
(Thou sencelesse of all Royaltie) thyne and thy brothers fame,
Imprisond in disgracefull *Troy*, which nothing doth inflame
Thy dogged nature to requite, with favour or renowne,
Our ceaslesse and important toiles; for which what is myne own
Given by the generall hands of Greece, yet by the valure got
Of my free labours thy rude lust will wrest in to thy lot:
In distribution of all townes, wun from our Trojan foes
Still more then mine to thy heapt store th'uneven proportion rose,
But in proportion of the fight the heaviest part did rise,
To my discharge, for which I find much praise and little prise.
But Ile endure this ods no more, t'is better to retire,

And to my countrie take my fleet, not feeding thy desire
Both with the wracke of my renowne and of my wealth beside,
Exhausted by the barbarous thirst of thy degenerat pride.
  Affects thou flight? replyed the king, be gon and let not me
Nor anie good of mine be cause to stay the fleete or thee.
There are enow besides will stay and do my state renowne,
But chiefely prudent *Jupiter* (Of all his hand doth crowne).
Thou still art bittrest to my rule; contention and sterne flight
To thee are unitie and peace; if thou exceed in might,
God gave it thee, and t'is absurde to glorie as our owne
In that we have not of our selves, but is from others growne.
Home with thy fleet and *Myrmydons*, there let thy rule be seene:
I loath so much to feare thy rage, or glorifie thy spleene
That to thy face I threaten thee, and since th'offended Sunne
Takes *Chryses* from me, whome by right of all consents I wun,
Yet I with mine owne shippe and men must send her to her Syre,
My selfe will to thy tent repayre, and take thy harts desire,
Even bright-cheekt *Brysis* from thine arms, that then thy pride may
    sweare
Atrides is thy better far, and all the rest may feare
To vaunt equallitie with mee, or take ambitious hart,
To stand with insolence comparde in any adverse part.
This set *Peleides* soule on fire, and in his brisled brest
His rationall and angrie parts a doutfull strife possest,
If he should draw his wreakefull sworde, and forcing way through all
Make *Agamemnons* braverie fit for bloudie funerall,
Or else restraine his forward mind, and calme his angers heat . . .

[But Pallas appeared to him and forbade him to attack Agememnon.]

She gone, *Pelides* did renew breach of his tempers peace
And gave the king dispightful words, not yet his wrath wold cease.
Thou great in wine with dogged lookes, and hart but of a Hart
That never with the formost troups, in fight darst shake thy dart
Nor in darke ambush arme thy selfe, these seeme too ful of death
For thy cold spirite; t'is more safe, with contumelious breath,
To show thy manhood gainst a man, that contradicts thy lust,
And with thy covetous valour, take his spoiles, with force unjust
Because thou knowest a man of fame, will take wrong ere he be
A generall mischiefe; nor shamst thou though all the armie see.
Thou souldier-eating king, it is on beasts thou rule hast won,
Or else this wrong had beene the last thou ever shouldst have done,
But I protest and sweare to thee a great and sacred oath. . . .
So since thy most inhumaine wrongs, have such a slaughter made

Of my affections borne to thee, they never shall renew
Those sweet and comfortable flowers, with which of late they grew,
But when the universall hoast shall faint with strong desire
Of wrongd *Achilles*, though thou pyne, thou never shalt aspyre
Helpe to their miseries from me, when underneath the hand
Of bloody *Hector* cold as death their bodies spred the sand,
And thou with inwarde hands of griefe, shalt teare thy desperate
minde
That to the most kinde, worthie Greeke thou wert so most unkind.

    This said, he threw against the ground, the scepter he susteind,
Through which in bright transfixed droppes a shower of gould was
    raynd.

    So sate the king and he inragde, when up old *Nestor* stood,
The thundering *Pylean* Orator, whose tong powrde forth a floud
Of hony-sweeting eloquence; two ages he had liv'de
Of sundrie languagde men, all which were dead, yet he survivde,
And now amongst the third he raignd: he thus bespake the peeres.

    O Gods what mightie woes wil pierce through all true *Achive* eares,
And how will *Priam* and his sonnes with all the *Ilion* seed
Even at their harts rejoyce to heare these haynous discordes breed
Twixt you who in the skill of fight and counsels so excell
All other Greekes! let my advise this bitternes expell;
You are not both so old as I, who livde with men that were
Your betters far, yet ever held, my exhortations deare
I never saw; nor ever shall behold the like of them: . . .
Let not the king officiously by force the damsell take,
But yeeld her whome the Greekes at first *Pelides* prise did make.
Nor let a kings heire against a king, with such contempt repine,
Since never scepter-state attaind an honour so divine,
And rightfully by *Joves* high gift: though better borne thou bee
Because a goddesse brought thee foorth, yet better man is he
Since his command exceedes so much. Then let the king subdue
His spirites greatnesse, and my selfe to *Thetis* sonne will sue
That he depose his furies heat who is the mightiest barre
Betwixt the Grecians safe estate and power of impious warre.

    With good *decorum* reverend Syre, *Atrides* did replie,
Thou givest us counsell, but this man, above us all will flie;
All in his power he will conclude and over all men raigne,
Commanding al, all which I thinke his thoughtes attempt in vaine.
What if the ever being state to him such strength affordes
Is it to rende up mens renownes with contumelious wordes?
Achilles interrupted him; Thou mightst esteeme me base,
And cowardlie to let thee use thy will in my disgrace:

To beare such burthens never were my strength and spirites combinde,
But to reforme their insolence, and that thy soule should finde:
Were it not hurt of common good more then mine owne delight,
But I not soothing *Nestors* sute, for rights sake reverence right,
Which thou dost servilely commend but violate it quite.
And this even in thy intrayles print, Ile not prophane my hand,
With battell in my lusts defence. A gyrle cannot command
My honour and my force like thine who yet commandes our hoast.
Slave live he to the world that lives slave to his lusts engrost:
But feed it, come, and take the dame, safe go thy violent fleet:
But whatsoever else thou findst, aborde my sable fleete
Dare not to touch without my leave: for feele my life mischance,
If then thy blacke and lustburnt bloud flow not upon my Lance,

   Contending thus in wordes opposde they rose, the counsaile brake.
Pelides to his tents and ships his friend and men did take.
Atrides lancht the swiftsayld shippe into the brackish seas,
And put therein the Hecatombe that should the God appease.
Twise ten selected rowers then, then *Chrysys* foorth he brings,
Made her ascend the sacred shippe; with her the grace of kings,
Wise *Ithacus* ascended too: All shipt together then,
Neptunes moist wildernes they plow, the king chargde all his men
Should hallowed Lustrations use, which done, into the floud
They threw the Offall, and the barke purgde from polluted blood.
Thus sweet and due solemnities they to *Apollo* keepe,
Of Buls and Goates, neere to the shore of the unfruitefull deep.
The savor, wrapt in cloudes of smoake, ascended to the skies,
And thus they sanctified the Campe with generall sacrifice.
Yet *Agamemnons* froward thoughts did not from discord cease,
But cald to him *Talthibius* and grave *Euribates*,
Herralds and carefull ministers, of all his high commandes,
And this injurious Ambasie committed to their hands.
Goe to *Achilles* tent and take the bright-cheekt *Brysys* thence.
If he denie, tell him my selfe with more extreame offence
Will come and force her from his armes, with unresisted bandes.
The Herralds all unwilling went along the barren sands:
The tentes and fleet of *Mirmodons* they reatcht and found the king
In his blacke shippe and tent, his lookes markt with his angers sting,
Greeting their entrie, which amazde and made them reverend stand
Not daring to salute his moode, nor what they sought demande.
He seeing them loath th'injurious cause of his offence to be,
Welcome ye Herraldes, messengers of gods and men (said he)
Come neare: I blame not you, but him that gainst your wils doth
        send

To have the lovelie *Brysis* brought. *Patroclus*, princelie frend,
Bring foorth the dame and render her; pleasd be their soveraign
then!
But here before the blessed gods, before the eyes of men,
Before your ignominious king, be faithfull witnesses
Of what I beare: if ever worke in future bitternes
Of anie plague to be remoovde from your unhappy host,
Be needefull of my friendlie hand, wrong hath your refuge lost.
Your king not present harmes conceives, much lesse succeeding woes,
But led by envious counsell, raves and knowes not what he does:
Nor how to winne his name renowne, being carefull to foretell
How with lest death his men might fight, and have them bulwarkt
well.
    This said *Patroclus*, well allow'd the patience of his frend,
Brought *Brysys* forth, and to her guides her comforts did commend
With utmost kindenesse, which his frend could not for anguish use;
Shee wept and lookt upon her love; he sight and did refuse
O, how his wisdome with his power did mightilie contend,
His love incouraging his power, and spirite that durst descend
As far as *Hercules* for her; yet wisdome all subdude.
Wherein a high exploite he showd, and sacred fortitude.
Brysys without her soule did move and went to th'*Achive* tents;
Achilles, severd from his frendes, melts anger in lamentes
Upon the shore of th'aged deepe vewing the purple seas,
And lifting his broade hands to heaven he did with utterance ease
His manlie bosome, and his wrongs, to *Thetis* thus relate: . . .

[He begged his mother Thetis to ask Jove to let the Trojans defeat
the Greeks. She agreed, but the gods were divided in their sym-
pathies. Ulysses delivered Chryseis to her father.]

BOOK II

[Agamemnon tested his troops by urging them to leave Troy. Many
of them made for the ships, and the chiefs had to persuade them to
return.]

    Ulisses met the king, from whome he was so bold
To take the scepter never staind held in his line of old,
With which he went amongst the troupes to stay them from the fleete:
And with what prince or gentleman, his royal steps did meete,
In these faire termes he willed him, pretended flight forbeare:
Sir, t'is not fit for such as you to flye as checkt with feare,
But rather stay, and with bold wordes, make others so enclinde:
For you as yet not rightlie know king *Agamemnons* minde:

He makes but try all of such spirites as he may most renowne,
And hee will quicklie punish such as flying humors drowne:
All we in counsel heard not all comprisde in his command,
Nor durst wee prease too neare for feare of his offended hand.
The anger of a king is death; his honor springs from *Jove*.
His person is in spight of hate protected in his love.
But if he saw the vulgar sorte, or if in crie hee tooke
A souldier with exclaimes for flight: him with his mace hee stroke,
And usde these speeches of reproofe: wretch keepe thy place and
    heare
Others besides thy Generall that place above thee beare:
Thou art unfit to rule and base without a name in war
Or state of counsaile: nor must Greekes be so irregular
To live as every man may take the scepter from the king:
The rule of many is absurd, one Lord must leade the ring
Of far resounding government: one king whome *Saturnes* sonne,
Hath given a scepter and sound lawes, to beare dominion. [1]
Thus ruling, governd hee the host: againe to counsayle then:
From ships and tents in tumults swarmde these base disordred men,
With such a blustring as against, the Ponticke shore reboundes,
A storme driven-billow, with whose rage, the sea it selfe resoundes.
    All sate, and sylent usde their seates, *Thersites* sole except,
A man of tongue, whose ravenlike voice a tuneles jarring kept,
Who in his ranke minde coppy had of unregarded wordes[2],
That rashly and beyond al rule usde to oppugne the Lords,
But what soever came from him was laught at mightilie:
The filthiest Greeke that came to *Troy*: he had a goggle eye:
Starcke-lame he was of eyther foote: his shoulders were contract
Into his brest and crookt withall: his head was sharpe compact,
And here and there it had a hayre. To mighty *Thetides*[3]
And wise *Ulisses* he retaind much anger and disease:
For still he chid them eagerlie: and then against the state
Of *Agamemnon* he would rayle: the Greekes in vehement hate
And high disdaine conceipted him: yet he with violent throate
Would needes upbraide the General, and thus himselfe forgot.
    Atrides, why complainst thou now? what dost thou covet more?
Thy thriftie tents are full of coine, and thou hast women store,
Faire and well favorde, which we Greekes at every towne we take
Resigne to thee: thinkst thou, thou wantst some treasure thou mightst
    make,

---

[1] Cf. his 'degree' speech and its context. I. 3.
[2] I.3.73, 'rank Thersites'.
[3] Achilles. Cf. II. 1. 33–6.

To bee deduc't thee out of *Troy* by one that comes to seeke
His sonne for ransome, who my selfe, or any other Greeke,
Should bring thee captive? or a wench, fild with her sweets of youth,
Which thou maist love and private keepe for thy insaciate tooth?
But it becomes not kings to tempt by wicked president
Their subjects to dishonestie: O mindes most impotent,
Not Achives but Achian gyrles, come fall aborde and home:
Let him concoct his pray alone, alone Troy overcome,
To make him know if our free eares his proud commandes would
    heare
In any thing: or not disdaine his longer yoke to beare,
Who hath with contumely wrongd, a better man then hee,
Achilles, from whose armes, in spight that all the world might see,
He tooke a prise won with his sword, but now it plaine appeares,
Achilles hath no splene in him, but most remislie beares
A femall stomacke: else be sure, the robberie of his meede,
O *Agamemnon*, would have prov'd thy last injurious deede.
Thus did *Thersites* chide the king to whome al Greece did bow,
When wife *Ulisses* straite stoode up, and with contracted brow,
Beholding him usde this rebuke: Prating *Thersites*, cease,
Though thou canst raile so cunninglie: nor dare to tempt the peace,
Of sacred kings, for well thou knowest I know well what thou art:
A baser wretch came not to *Troy* to take the Grecians part.
Prophane not kings then with thy lips; examine our retreate:
Whereof our selves are ignorant, nor our states so greate,
That we dare urge upon the king what he will onelie know:
Sit then and cease thy barbarous-tauntes to him whome all wee owe
So much observance though from thee these insolent poisons flow:
But I protest and will performe if I shall deprehend,
Such phrensie in thy pride againe, as now doth all offend:
Then let *Ulisses* loose his head: and cease inglorious
To be the native father cald of yong *Telemachus*,
If from thee to thy nakednes thy garments be not stript,
And from the counsayle to the fleete thou be not soundlie whipt.
    This said, his backe and shoulder blades he with his scepter smit:
Who then shrunke round and downe his cheekes the servile teares
    did flit:
The golden scepter in his flesh a bloody print did raise,
With which he trembling tooke his seat, and, looking twentie waies,
Ill favoredlie he wipte the teares from his selfe-pittying eyes,
And then though all the host were sad they laught to heare his cries.
When thus flew speeches intermixt, O Gods what endles good
Ulisses still bestowes on us? that to the field of bloud

Instructs us: and in counsaile doth, for chiefe director serve,
Yet never action past his hands that did more praise deserve,
Then to disgrace this rayling foole in all the armies sight;
Whose rudenes henceforth will take heed how he doth princes bite.
   This all the multitude affirmd, when now againe did rise,
The razer of repugnant townes, *Ulisses* bolde and wise,
With scepter of the Generall, and prudent *Pallace* by
That did a Heraldes forme assume and for still silence crie,
That through the host the souldierye might understand th'intent,
The counsaile urgde; and thus their flight his wisedome did prevent:
Atrides, if in these faint driftes the Greekes have licence given,
Thou will be most opprobrious of all men under heaven,
Since they infringde their vowes to thee at our designes for *Troy*,
From horse-race *Argos* to persist, till *Ilion* they destroy:
But like young babes amongst themselves, or widdowes, they lament,
And would goe home: and I confesse, a tedious discontent
May stirre some humor to returne: for if a man remaine
But twyise two sevenights from his wife, much moode he doth
   sustaine
Within his many-seated ship, which winters stormes enfoulde,
And fierce commotion of the sea: where thrise three heavens have
   roulde
About the circle of the yeare since this our ankerd stay.
I cannot then reproove such Greekes, as greeve at this delay:
Yet were it shame to stay so long, and emptie handed flie:
Sustaine a little then my friendes, that we the trueth may trie
Of reverend *Chalchas* prophesy . . .

[Ulysses reminded the Greeks that Calchas, the renegade Trojan
priest, had prophesied success after ten years.]

Ulisses having spoken thus, his words so liked were,
That of his praise, the Ships, the tents, the shore did witnes beare:
Resounding with the peoples noice, who gave his speech the prise.
Th'applawse once ceast, from seate to speake old *Nestor* doth arise.
Fy Greekes, what infamie is this? ye play at childrens game,
Your warlike actions thus farre brought, now to neglect their fame:
O whether from our lips prophane shal othes & compacts fly?
The counsailes and the cares of men now in the fire shall die:
With those our sacred offringes made by pure unmixed wine:
And our right hands, with which our faiths we freely did combine;
The cause is, since amongst our selves we use discursive words,
And goe not manlike to the field to manage it with swords,
Nor with the finenes of our wits, by stratagems devise

In all this while against a world to worke our enterprise.
But (great *Atrides*) as at first, thy counsell being sound,
Command to field, and be not led corruptly from the ground
Of our endevors by the moodes of one or two that use
Counsails apart; they shall not goe to Greece till *Jove* refuse
To ratifie his promise made, or we may surely know
If those ostents were true or false that he from heaven did show . . .
But if some be so mutinous, whom nothing may restraine,
Let him but touch his black-armde Bark, that he may first be slaine,
Then great *Atrides* be advisde, and others reasons see:
It shall not prove an abject speech that I will utter thee.
In tribes and nations let thy men be presentlie arraide,
That still the tribes may second tribes, and nations nations aide:
Of everie chiefe and soldier thus the proofe shall rest in sight,
For both will thirst their countries fame and prease for single fight.
What soldier when he is allowde his countryman for guide,
Will not more closely sticke to him then to a strangers side?
Thus shalt thou know, if Gods detaine thy hand from *Ilions* harmes,
Or else the faintnes of thy men and ignorance in armes.
    This to autentique *Nestors* speech *Atrides* answer was:
All Grecian birth (thryse reverend King) thy counsails farre surpasse:
O would King *Jove*, *Tritonia*, and he that guides the Sunne
Would grant me ten such counsellers, then should our toyles be done.
Then *Priams* high-topt towers should stoope, outfacing us no more,
But fall beneath our conquering hands, dispoylde of all her store:
But *Jove* hath storde my life with woes, that no good houre can
                    spend,
And throwne me in the midst of strifes that never thinke of end,
Since with *Achilles* for a Gyrle in humorous termes I strove,
And I the Author of the strife; but if intreated love
Make us with reunited mindes consult in one againe,
Troy shall not in the left delay her lothed pride sustaine:
But now to foode, that to the fight, ye may your valours yield:

[The Greeks ate and made sacrifices to the gods, then went to arms.
Homer gives a catalogue of ships and heroes, with brief portraits
of some leaders.]

BOOKE VII.[1]
[Hector challenged the Greeks to single combat.]

Hector exceedingly rejoycde to give such counsaile eare,
And fronting both the hosts advanst, just in the midst his speare:

[1] In *1598* Chapman calls it 'The Third Booke' of his 'Seaven'.

The *Trojans* instantlie surcease, the *Greekes Atrides* staide.
The God that beares the silver Bowe, and warrs triumphant maide,
On *Joves* beech, like two *Vultures* sate, pleasde with the Peres high
 harts,
And to behold the thickned hostes, joine shields, helmes, horrid darts:
And such fresh horror as you see, driven through the wrinckled
 waves
By rising *Zephyre*, under whome the sea growes blacke and raves:
Such did the hasty gathering troupes of both the Armies raise,
Betwixt both which the Challenger his challenge thus displaise:[1]
Heare Trojans and ye well armed Greekes, what my strong mind
 diffusde
Through all my spirits, commaundes me speake: *Saturnius* hath not
 usde
His promist favor for our truce, but studying both our ills
Will never cease till *Mars* by you his ravenous stomacke fills
With ruinde *Troy*, or we commaund your mightie Seaborne fleete.
Since then the Generall Peeres of *Greece* in reach of one voice meete,
Amongst you all whose brest includes the most impulsive minde,
Let him stand forth as combattant, by all the rest designde.
This I propose and call high *Jove* to witnesse of our strife:
If he with home-thrust Iron, can reach th'exposure of my life
(Spoyling my armes) let him at will convey them to his tent;
But let my bodie be returnd, that *Troys* two-sixt descent
May waste it in the funerall Pyle; if I can slaughter him,
(*Apollo* honoring me so much) Ile spoyle his conquerd lim,
And beare his armes to *Ilion*, where in *Apollos* shryne
Ile hang them as my trophies due: his bodie Ile resigne
To be disposed by his friends in flamie funerals,
And honored with erected tombe where *Hellespontus* fals
Into *Egæum*, and doth reach, even to your navall rode:
That when our ages in the earth shall hyde their periode,
Survivors sayling the blacke sea may thus his name renew;
This is the monument, whose bloud long since did fates embrew:
Whome passing farre in fortitude illustrate *Hector* flew:
Thus shall posteritie report, and my fame never dy.
This said, dumbe silence shut all lips; they shamed to denie,
And fearde to undertake: at last did *Menelaus* speake,
Checkt their remissives and so sighd as if his hart would breake:
Ay me, but onelie threatning Greekes not worthy Grecian names:
This more and more, not to be borne makes grow our huge defames.
If *Hectors* honorable proofe be entertaind by none,

---

[1] In *TC*, I.3. the challenge is delivered by Æneas.

But you are earth and water all, which symbolisde in one,
Have framde your faint unfirie brests: ye sit without your harts,
Simplie Inglorious: but my selfe will use acceptive darts,
And arme against him, though you thinke I arme gainst too much
    ods:
Faire conquestes boundes are held aloft amongst th'immortall gods.
He armd and gladlie would have fought, but *Menelaus* then
By *Hectors* farre more strength thy soule had fled th'abodes of men,
Had not the kings of Greece stood up and thy attempt restraind:
And even the king of men himselfe that in such compasse raignde
Who tooke him by the boulde right hand and sternelie pluckt him
    backe:
Mad brother t'is no worke for thee; thou seekest thy wilfull wracke:
Conteyne though it despight thee much, nor for this strife engage
Thy person with a man more strong, and whome all feare t'enrage:
Yea whome *Æacides* himselfe in men renowning warre
Makes doubt t'encounter: whose huge strength surpasseth thine by
    farre:
Sit thou then with thy regiment; some other Greeke will rise,
(Though he be dreadlesse and no war wil his desires suffice,
That makes this chalenge to our strength) our valors to avow:
To whome if he can scape with life he will be glad to bow.
This drew his brother from his will, who yeelded, knowing it true:
And his glad souldiers tooke his armes: when *Nestor* did pursue
The same reproofe he set on foote, and thus supplied his turne:
What huge indignitie is this! how will our countrie mourne?
Old *Peleus* that good king will weepe: that worthy counsaylor.
That trumpet of the Mirmidons who much did aske me for.
All men of name that went to *Troy* with joy he did enquire
Their valor and their towardnes: and I made him admire.
But that ye all feare *Hector* now if his grave eares shall heare,
How wil he lift his handes to heaven, and pray that death may beare
His greeved soul into the deepe: O would to heavens great king,
Minerva and the god of light, that now my youthful spring
Did floorish in my willing vaines as when at *Phæas* towers,
About the streames of *Jardanus* my gathered Pylean powers,
And dart-imployed Arcadians fought neare raging *Celadon*[1]: . . .
O that my youth were now as fresh and all my powers as sound.
Soone should bould *Hector* be impugnde: yet you that most are
    crounde
With fortitude of all our host, even you me thinkes are slow,
Not free and set on fire with lust t'encounter such a foe.

[1] Cf. I.3.291–301.

With this nine royall princes rose, *Atrides* far the first,
Then *Diomed*: th'Ajaces then, that did th'encounter thirst:
King *Idomen* and his consortes, *Mars*-like *Meriones*,
Evemons sonne *Euripilus*, and *Andremonides*
Who all the Grecians *Thoas* cald, sprong of *Andremons* bloud,
And wise *Ulisses*; everie one proposde for combat stoode.
Againe *Gerenius Nestor* spake, let lots be drawne by all,[1]
His hand shall helpe the well-armd Greekes on whome the lot doth
    fall,
And to his wish shal he be helpt, if he escape with life
The harmefull danger breathing fit, of this adventrous strife.
Ech markt his lot, injecting it to *Agamemnons* caske.
The souldiers prayed, held up their handes: and this of *Jove* did aske
With eyes advanst to heaven: O *Jove* so leade the Heraldes hand,
That *Ajax* or great *Tideus* sonne may our wisht champion stand:
Or else the king himselfe that rules the rich Micenian land.
This said, old *Nestor* mixt the lots; the formost marke survaide
Strong *Ajax Tellamon* inscribde: as all the souldiers praide
One of the Heraldis drew it forth, who brought and showde it rounde,
Beginning at the right hand first, to all the most renownde:
None knowing it everie man denide, but when he forth did passe
To him which markt and cast it in, which famous *Ajax* was,
He stretcht his hand and into it the Heralde put the lot,
Who viewing it th'inscription knew. The Duke denied it not,
But joyfully acknowledgde it, and threw it at his feet:
And said O frendes the lot is mine, which to my hart is sweet,
For now I hope my fame shall rise in noble *Hectors* fall,
But whilst I arme my selfe do you on great *Saturnius* cal,
But silentlie or to your selves, that not a Trojane heare;
Or openlie (if you thinke good) since none alive we feare,
None with a will if I will not can my bould powers affright,
At least for plaine fierce swindge of strength, nor want of skil in fight.
For I have good conceipt my birth and breede in *Salamine*,
Was not all consecrate to meate, or mere effects of wine.
This said the wel given souldiers prayed: up went to heaven their
    eyes,
O *Jove* that *Ida* dost protect, most happie most divine,
Send victorie to Ajax side, fame-grace his goodlie lim:
Or if thy love blesse *Hectors* life, and thou hast care of him,
Bestow on both like power: like fame: this said, in bright armes
    shone,
The good strong *Ajax*: who when all his warre attire was on,

---

[1] In *TC*. Ulysses rigs the draw, I.3.374–6.

Marcht like the hugelie figurde *Mars* when angrie *Jupiter*
With strength on people proud of strength sends him forth to
    inferre
Wreakeful contention: and comes on with presence ful of feare:
So th'Achive rampire *Tellamon* did twixt the hostes appeare:
Smiling with terrible aspect, on earth with ample pace
He bouldlie stalked, and did shake his dart with deadlie grace:
It did the Grecians good to see, but hartquakes shooke the joynts
Of all the Trojanes; *Hectors* selfe felt thoughts with horrid points
Tempt his bould bosome but he now must make no counterflight,
Nor with his honor backe retire, that had provokte the fight.
Ajax came neare, and like a tower his shielde his bosome barde:
The right side brasse, and seaven Oxe hydes within it quilted hard:
Old *Tycheus* the best cooryer that did in *Hyla* dwell
Did frame it for exceeding proofe, and wrought it wondrous wel.
With this stoode hee to *Hector* close, and with this brave began:
Now *Hector* thou shalt clearelie know, thus meeting man to man,
What other leaders arme our host, besides great *Thetis* sonne[1]:
Who with his hardie Lions hart, hath armies overrunne.
But he lies at our crookt-sternde fleete a rivall with our king.
In height of spirite yet to *Troy* he manie kings did bring
Coequall with *Æacides*, al able to sustaine
All thy bould chalenge can import: begin then, wordes are vaine.
Helme-graced *Hector* answerd him: Well honorde *Tellamon*,
Prince of the Souldiers came from Greece, assay not me like one
Yong and immartiall, with puft ayre, or like an amazon dame.
I have the habit of all fights and know the bloodie frame
Of manlie slaughter: I well know the readie right hand charge:
I know the left, and everie sway of my securefull targe;
I triumph in the crueltie of fixed combat fight,
Manage my horse to all designes. I thinke then with good right
I may be confident as farre as this my challenge goes,
Without detection of a vaunt borne out with empty shoes;
But (being a soldier so renownd) I will not worke on thee,
With lest advantage of that skill I know doth strengthen mee,
And so with privitie of sight, winne that for which I strive,
But at thy best (even open strength) if my endevors thrive.
Thus sent he his long javeline forth; it strooke his foes huge shielde
Neere to the upper skirt of brasse, which was the eight it helde:
Six fouldes th'untamed dart strooke through, & in the sevinth
    tough hide
The point was checkt; then *Ajax* threw: his angrie lance did glyde

---

[1] Shakespeare builds on this implied rivalry.

Quight through his bright orbiculare targe, his Curace, shirt of
    mayle,
And did his manlie stomacks mouth with dangerous taint assayle.
But in the bowing of himself blacke death too short did strike;
Then both to plucke their javelins forth encountred Lion like,
Whose bloody violence is increast by that raw foode they eate,
Or Bores whose strength wild nourishment doth make so wondrous
    great:
Againe *Priamides* did wound in midst his shield of brasse,
Yet pierst not through the upper plate, the head reflected was!
But *Ajax* following his lance smote through his target quite,
And stayd bold *Hector* rushing in, the lance held way outright,
And hurt his neck; out gusht the blood, yet *Hector* ceast not soe,
But in his strong hand tooke a Flint (as he did backwards goe)
Blacke, sharp and bigge, laied in the field. The seavenfolde targe
    it smit,
Full on the bosse, and round about the brasse did ring with it:
But *Ajax* a farre greater stone lift up, and wreathing round,
With all his bodie layd to it, he sent it forth to wound,
And gave unmeasured force to it. The round stone broke within
His rundled target: his strong knees to languish did begin:
He streaking leand upon his shield, but *Phoebus* raisd him straight,
Then close to swords they would have gone, and laid on wounds
    of waight,
Unlesse the Heralds, messingers of gods and godlike men,
(The one of *Troy* the other *Greece*) had held betwixt them then
Imperiall scepters: when the one, *Idæus*, grave and wyse,
Said to them, now no more my sonnes, the soveraigne of the skyes
Doth love you both; both soldiers are, all witnesse with good right:
But now Night laies her mace on earth; t'is good t'obay the night:

    Idæus (*Telamon* replied) to *Hector* speake, not me,
He that cald all our Achive Peeres to station fight was he.
If he first cease, I gladly yield: great *Hector* then began:

    Ajax, since *Jove* to thy bigge forme made thee so strong a man,
And gave thee skill to use thy strength; so much that for thy speare
Thou art most excellent of Greece, now let us fight forbeare:
Hereafter we shall warre againe, till *Jove* our Herald be,
And grace with conquest which he will; heaven yields to night, and
    wee:
Goe thou and comfort all thy Fleete, all friends and men of thyne,
As I in *Troy* my favorers, who in the Phane divyne
Have offerd orisons for me; and come, let us impart
Some ensignes of our strife to shew each others suppled hart,

That men of *Troy* and *Greece* may say, thus their high quarrel ends;
Those that encountring were such foes, are now (being separate)
    friends.[1]
He gave a sword whose handle was with silver studs through driven,
Scabard and all, with hangers rich: by *Telamon* was given
A faire wel-glossed purple waste: thus *Hector* went to *Troy*,
And after him a multitude fild with his safties joy,
Despairing he could ever scape the puisant fortitude
And unimpeached *Ajax* hands: the Greekes like joy renued
For their reputed victorie, and brought them to the King,
Who to the great *Saturnides* preferd an offering. . . .

[Nestor advised the Greeks to build walls and a dyke to protect
their fleet.]

    The Kings doe his advise approve: so *Troy* doth Court convent
At *Priams* gate in th'*Ilion* tower, fearefull and turbulent.
Amongst all, wise *Antenor* spake: Trojans and Dardan friends,
And Peeres assistents, give good eare to what my care commends
To your consents for all our good: resolve, let us restore
The Argive *Helen*, with her wealth to him she had before[2]:
We now defend but broken faiths: if therefore ye refuse,
No good event can I expect of all the warres we use.
    He ceast and *Alexander* spake; husband to th'Argive Queene:
Antenor to myne eares thy words harsh and ungratious bene:
Thou cast use better if thou wilt, but if these trulie fit
Thy serious thoughts, the Gods with age have reft thy healthfull wit:
To warrelike Trojans I will speake. I clearely doe deny
To yield my wife: but all her wealth I render willingly,
What ever I from *Argos* brought, adjoyning to it more
Which I have readie in my house, if peace I may restore.[3]
Priam surnamde *Dardanides*, godlike in counsels grave,
In his sonnes favour well advisde, this resolution gave:
My royall friends of everie state, there is sufficient done
For this late counsell we have cald in th'offer of my sonne:
Now then let all take needefull foode; then let the watch be set,
And everie court of guarde held strong, so when the morne doth wet
The high raisd battlements of *Troy*, *Ideus* shall be sent
To th'Argive Fleete and *Atreus* sonnes t'unfold my sonnes intent
From whose fact our contention springs: and (if they will) obtayne
Respit from heate of fight, till fire consume our soldiers slayne:

---

[1] No reference here to their blood-relationship. Cf. IV.5.92–3, 119–50.
[2] Cf. II.2.1–25.
[3] Contrast Paris in II.2.130–62.

And after our most fatall warre let us importune still
Till *Jove* the conquest have disposde to his unconquered will.
    All heard and did obay the King, and in their quarters all
That were to set the watch that night did to their suppers fall.
Ideus in the morning went, and th'Achive Peeres did finde
In counsell at *Atrides* ship: his audience was assignde:
And in the midst of all the kings, the vocall Herald said:
Atrides, my renowned King, and other Kings his aide,
Propose by me in their commands the offer *Paris* makes,
(From whose joy all our woe proceeds) he princely undertakes
That all the wealth he brought from *Greece* (would he had died
before)
He will (with other jemmes adjoynde) for your amends restore.
But famous *Menelaus* wife he still meanes to enjoy,
Though he be urgde the contrarie by all the Peeres of *Troy*.
And this besides I have in charge; that if it please you all,
They with both sides may cease from warre, that rites of funerall
May on their bodies be performde that in the fields lie slayne:
And after to th'instinct of Fate renew the fight againe.
    All silence held at first, at last *Tytydes* made replie:
Let no man take the wealth, or dame; for now a childs weake eye
May see the imminent blacke end of *Priams* emperie.
This sentence quicke and briefly given the Greekes did all admire;
Then said the King, Herald thou hearest in him the voice entire
Of all our Peeres to answere thee, for that of *Priams* sonne;
But for our burning of the dead by al means I am won.

[In Book IX Agamemnon's proposal to give up the struggle was
indignantly opposed and efforts were made to placate Achilles]

                        So *Agamemnon* mournde:
And sighing deepelie, thus he breathde his griefes that inward burnde.
    O frendes and princes, adverse *Jove* hath wrapt this life of mine
In helpelesse ruine: since he vowde, and bound it with the signe
Of his bent forehead, that this *Troy* our vengeful hands should rase,
And safe returne: yet now engagde, he plagues us with disgrace,
After our trust to him hath drawne so much bloud from our frendes:
My glorie nor my Brothers wreake were the proposed endes
For which he drew you to these toyles, but your whole countries
    shame
Which had beene huge to beare the rape of so divine a dame
Made in despight of our revenge: and yet not that had movde
Our powers to these designes if *Jove* had not our driftes approvde:
Which since wee see he did for blonde t'is desperate fight in us
To strive with him then let us flie; t'is flight he urgeth thus.

Long time stil silence held them al; at last did *Diomede* rise:
Atrides, I am first must crosse thy indiscret advise,
As may become me, being a king in this our martiall courte:
Be not displeasde then, for thy selfe didst broadelie misreporte
In open field my fortitude, and calde me faint and weake,
Yet I was silent, knowing the time, loth any rites to breake
That appertainde thy publike rule, and all the Greekes knew well
(Of everie age) thou didst me wrong: as thou then didst refell
My valour first of all the host, abhorring men dismaide,
So now, with fit occasion geven I first blame thee afraide:
Inconstant *Saturns* son hath given inconstant spirites to thee,
And with a scepter over all, an eminent degree:
But with a scepters soveraigne rule, the chiefe power, fortitude,
To bridle thee he thought not best thy brest should be endude[1]:
Unhappie king, thinkst thou the Greekes are such a sillie sort,
And so excessive impotent as thy weake words import?
If thy mind moove thee to be gone, the way is open, go,
Mycenian ships enow ryde neare, that brought thee to this woe.
The rest of Greece will stay till *Troy* al terrors overcome
With her eversion, or if they be doters of their home,
And put on wings to flie with thee, my self and *Sthenelus*
Will fight till firme perseverance, bring home *Troys* end with us:
And least this madnesse seeme, observe what reasons I pursue:
We fight with love of *Jove*, with which one man may worlds subdue.
  This speech was likte, which *Nestor* markt, who like a right old
      man
Would fayne preferre his graver yeares; and therefore thus began:
Tydides, thou in warre art best, in counsails best, and none
Can blame or contradict thy speech: yet hast not undergone
The depth of that the cause requyres: for Certes thou art young,
And mightst be but my youngest sonne, yet wiselie-bold thy tongue
Gives counsaill to our Grecian Kings: since with such good respect
Thou hast opposde thee to our chiefe: but now thine eares erect
To me profest thy Seignor King; Ile speake, Ile handle all
Should be proposde, which none shall check, no not our Generall.
A hater of societie, unjust, unhousde is he
Loves civill warre, and for his right does all men injurie.[2]
I call that our intestine warre where still growes the offence
Sprung twixt our King and *Thetis* sonne: let him then fetch from
      hence
The remedy we have to reape, whom thys assumpt concernes:

---

[1] Contrast Agamemnon's strength in I.3.1–30.
[2] This may have suggested I.3.75–137.

A wise man by words briefe, well urgde, a large intention learnes.
Now let us yield to night, take foode, and set without the fort
Upon our wel-rais'd trench the watch, which to the youngest sort
I give in charge: *Atrides* then, thou that art generall King,
Bid all thy Princes to a Feast, t'is fit in everie thing,
Leade thou in bountie as in Power . . .
Hunger and thirst being quickly quencht, to counsaile still they sit.
And first spake *Nestor*, whom they thought of late advysde so well;
A father grave and rightly-wise, who thus his tale did tell:

   Most high *Atrides*, since in thee I have intent to end,
From thee will I begin my speech, to whom *Jove* doth commend
The impyre of so many men, and puts into thy hand
A scepter, and the use of lawes, that thou mayst well command;
It therefore doth behove thy self, of all to speake the best,
And so to heare that sound advyse may be with use imprest
In thy conceipt by others given: be rulde still as obayde;
First marke, and then thy judgement forme of whatsoever saide:
For me, what in my judgement stands the most convenient
I will advyse, and am assurde advice more competent
Shall not be given: the generall proofe, that hath before bene made
Of what I speake, confirmes me still, and now may well perswade:
Because I could not then, yet ought, when thou (most royall King)
Even from his tent, *Achilles* love didst violentlie bring,
Against my counsaill urdging thee by all meanes to relent:
But you, obaying your high minde, would venter the event,
Dishonoring our ablest Greeke, a man th'immortall[s] grace
And so oppose yourself to *Jove*, and his high forme deface,
For which he staynes and blots us out, with our owne bloud in dust:
Even now yet let us seeke redresse, we see that needs we must
Confesse to *Jove*, and to our friend fitt compensation yield,
Whom fayre sweete speech and royall gifts, must supple for the field.

   O father (answered the king) my wrongs thou numbrest right;
Myne owne offence, myne owne tongue graunts, one man must
      stand in fight
For our whole armie; him I wrongde, him *Jove* loves from his hart:
He shewes it in thus honoring him, who living thus apart
Proves us but number: for his want makes all our weaknes seene:
Yet after my confest offence, soothing my humorous spleene,
Ile sweeten his affects againe, with presents infinite,
Which (to approve my firme intent) Ile openly recite . . .

[He would return Bryseis 'untoucht', and make great gifts in compensation for injuring Achilles.]

All this I gladlie will performe, to pacifie his hate:
Let him be mylde and tractable; t'is for the God of ghosts
To be unrulde, implacable, and seeke the blood of hosts,
Who therfore men doe most abhore. Then let him yield to mee.
I am his greater being a King, and more in yeares then hee.
Brave King (sayde *Nestor*) these rich giftes must make needes him
    relent:
Chuse then fitte legates instantly to greete him at his tent.
But see ile chuse them at first sight, and let them soone be gone:
Jove-loved *Phœnix* shal be chiefe, then *Ajax Telamon*,
And Prynce *Ulysses*: and on them let these two heraldes wayte,
Grave *Odius* and *Euribates*: come Lordes, take water strayte,
Make pure your hands, and with your tongues urge t'*Achilles* minde
Whilst we pray *Jove* his rigorous moods may kindlie stand inclinde.
    All likt his speech, and on their hands the Heralds water shed:
The youths crownde cups of sacred wine to all distributed.
But having sacrifisde and drunke to every mans content,
(With many notes by *Nestor* given,) the Legates forward went.
With courtship in fit gestures usde he did prepare them well,
But most *Ulysses*, for his grace did not so much excell:
Such rytes beseeme Ambassadors, and *Nestor* urged these
That their most honors might inflict exempt *Æacides*.
They went along the shore and prayed the God that earth doth
    bind
In brackish chaines, they might not faile but bow his mightie minde.
The quarter of the Myrmidons they reacht and found him set,
Delighted with his sweet-voic't harpe, which curiously was fret
With worke conceipted through the verdge: the bawdrick that
    embraste
His loftie necke was silver twist; this, when his hand laide waste
Aetions citty he did chuse as his especiall prise;
And loving sacred musicke wel made it his exercise:
To it he sung the glorious deedes of great Heroes dead,
And his trew mind that practise fayld, sweete contemplation fead.
With him alone and opposite, al silent sate his frend,
Attentive and beholding him, who now his song did end.
Th'ambassadors did forwards prease; honorde *Ulisses* led;
And stood in view: their suddayne sight his admiration bred,
Who with his Harpe and all arose: so did *Menetius* sonne,
When he beheld them: their receipt *Achilles* thus begun:
    Helth to my Lord: right welcome men, assure your selves ye be[1]:
Though some necessitie I know doth make you visite me

---

[1] Contrast their reception in II.3.106-11.

That take some stomacke gainst the Greekes. This said, a severall
  seate
With purple cushions he set forth, and did their ease entreate,
And said: now frend our greatest bowle, with wine unmixt and neate
Oppose these Lordes: and of the depth let everie man make proofe;
These are my best-esteemed frendes, and underneath my roofe.
Patroclus did his deare frendes will, . . .

. . . hunger and thirst alaide,
Ajax to *Phenix* made a signe as if too long they staid
Before they told their legacie; *Ulisses* saw him winke,
And filling the great bowle with wine, did to *Achilles* drink.

   Health to *Achilles*, but our plights stood not in need of meat,
Who late supt at *Atrides* tent, though for thy love we eate
Of many things, whereof a part would have suffisde a feast,
Nor can we joy in these kind rites, that have our harts opprest
(O Prince) with feare of utter spoile: t'is made a question now
If we can save our fleete or not, unlesse thy selfe indow
Thy powers with wonted fortitude, now *Troy* and her consortes,
Bould of thy want, have pitcht their tents close to our fleete and
  fortes,
Lighting a firmament of fires; and now no more they say
Will they be prisond in their wals, but force their violent way
Even to our ships and *Jove* himselfe hath with his lightnings showde
Their bould adventures happie signes, and *Hector* growes so proude
Of his huge strength borne out by *Jove* that fearfully he raves,
Presuming neither men nor Gods can interrupt his braves;
Wilde rage invades him, and he prayes that soone the sacred morne
Would light his furie: boasting then our streamers shalbe torne,
And all our navall ornaments fall by his conquering stroke;
Our ships shall burne, and we our selves ly stifled in the smoke;
And I am seriously afraide, heaven will performe his threates
And that t'is fatall to us all, far from our native seates
To perish in victorious *Troy*. But rise though it be late,
Deliver the afflicted Greekes from Troys tumultuous hate;
It will hereafter be thy griefe, when no strength can suffice
To remedy th'effected threates of our calamities.
Consider these affaires in time, while thou maist use thy power
And have the grace to turne from Greece fates unrecovered howre.
O frend thou knowest thy royall Syre, forwarnd what should be done,
That day he sent thee from his courte to honor Atreus sonne.
My sonne (said he) the victorie let *Jove* and *Pallas* use
At their high pleasures, but do thou no honorde means refuse
That may advance her: in fit boundes contayne thy mightie minde,

Nor let the knowledge of thy strength be factiously enclinde,
Contriving mischiefes; be to fame and generall good profest
The more will all sortes honor thee; benignity is best.
Thus chargde thy Syre, which thou forgetst, yet now those thoughts appease
That tortures thy great spirit with wrath: which if thou wilt surcease,
The king will merite it with giftes; (and if thou wilt give eare)
Ile tell how much he offers thee, yet thou sitst angrie here.

[He repeated Agamemnon's offer of compensation.]

Al this hee freelie wil performe, thy anger to allay:
But if thy hart to him be more then his giftes may represse,
Yet pittie all the other Greekes in such extreame distresse,
Who with religion honor thee, and to their desperate ill
Thou shalt triumphant glorie bring, and *Hector* thou maist kill
When pride makes him encounter thee, fild with a banefull sprite
Who vauntes our whole fleete brought not one equal to him in fight.
   Swift foote *Æacides* replide, divine *Laertes* sonne,
T'is requisite I should be short, in refutation
Of thy grave speech, affirming nought but what you shall approove
Establisht in my setled hart, that in the rest I moove
No murmur nor exception, for like hell mouth I loath
Who holdes not in his wordes and thoughtes one indistinguisht troth:
What fits the freenes of my mind my speech shall make displaide:
Nor *Atreus* sonne, nor al the Greekes shall winne me to their aide:
Their sute is wretchedlie enforst to free their owne despaires:
And my life never shalbe hyrde with thankeles desperate prayers:
For never had I benefite ever t'impugne the foe.
Even share hath he that keepes his tent, and he to field doth goe.
With equall honor Cowardes dye, and men most valiant.
The much performer and the man that can of nothing vant.
No overplus I ever found, when with my mindes most strife
To do them good, to dangerous fight I have exposde my life,
But even as to unfeatherd birds the carefull dam brings meate,
Which when she hath bestowde her self hath nothing left to eate,
So when my broken sleepes have drawne the nights t'extreamest length,
And ended manie bloudie dayes with stil-employed strength
To guard their weaknes, and preserve their wives contents infract,
I have bene robde before their eyes; twelve citties I have sackt,
Assailde by sea; eleaven by land, during this siege neere *Troy*:
And of all these, what was most deare and most might crowne the joy

Of Agamemnon, he enjoyde, who here behinde remainde;
Which when he tooke, a few he gave, and many things retainde:
Other to Optimates and Kings he gave, who hold them fast,
Yet myne he forceth; only I sit with my losse disgra'st.
But so he gaine a lovelie dame, to be his beds delight,
It is enough, for what cause els doe Greeks and Trojans fight?
Why brought he hether such an host? was it not for a dame?
For fayre-hayrde *Helen*; and doth love alone the harts inflame,
Of the Atrides to their wyves, of al the men that move?
Every discreete and honest minde cares for his private love
As much as they; as I my self lov'de *Brysis* with my life,
Although my captive, and had will to take her for my wife:
Whom since he fors't preventing me, in vaine he shall prolong
Hopes to appease me that know well the deepenes of my wrong.
But good *Ulysses*, with thy self, and all you other Kings,
Let him take stomacke to repell *Troys* firie threatnings.
Much hath he done without my helpe; built him a goodlie fort,
Cut a dyke by it, pitcht with pales broad, and of deepe import,
And cannot all these helpes represse this kil-man *Hectors* fright?
When I was armde amongst the Greeks, he would not offer fight
Without the shadow of his wals, but to the Scæan ports,
Or to the holy beech of *Jove* come backt with his consorts,
Where once he stoode my charge alone, and hardlie made retreate;
And to make new proofe of our powers, the doubt is not so great. . . .

[Achilles threatened to sail for home next day, and rejected the
appeal of his old friend Phœnix, although he invited him to stay
the night. Ajax was indignant.]

              . . . soldierlike brave *Ajax* Telamon
Spake to *Ulysses*, as with thought *Achilles* was not worth
The high direction of his speech, that stoode so sternlie forth
Unmov'de with th'other Orators: and spake not to appease
Pelides wrath but to depart: his arguments were these:
  High-issued Laertiades, let us insist no more
On his perswasions; I perceave, the world will end before
Our speeches end in this affaire: we must with utmost hast
Returne his answere, though but bad: the Peeres are els where plast,
And will not rise till we returne: great *Thetis* sonne hath storde
Prowde wrath within him as his wealth, and will not be implorde:
Rude that he is, nor his friends love, respects doe what they can:
Wherein past all we honorde him; O unremorsfull man,
Another for his brother slayne, another for his sonne
Accepts of satisfaction: and he the deed hath done
Lives in belov'de society, long after his amends:

To which his foes high hart for gifts with pacience condiscends,
But thee a wilde and cruell spirit, the gods for plague have given,[1]
And for one gyrle, of whose fayre sex we come to offer seaven
(The most exempt for excellence) and many a better prise;
Then put a sweete minde in thy breast, respect thine owne allyes.
Though others make thee not remisse, a multitude we are,
Sprung of thy royall family, and our supreamest care
Is to be most familiar, and hold most love with thee
Of all the Greeks, how great an host so ever here there be. . . .

[Achilles rejected Ajax's counsel, but with moderation, then dismissed the ambassadors.]

This said each one but kyst the cuppe and to the ships retyrde,
Ulysses first. *Patroclus* then the men and mayds requyrde
To make grave *Phœnix* bed with speede, and see he nothing lacks:
They strayte obayde; and laide thereon the subtle fruit of flacks,
And warme sheep-fels for covering, and there the old man slept,
Attending till the golden Morne her usuall station kept.
Achilles lay in th'inner roome of his tent richly wrought,
And the fayre by his side that he from *Lesbos* Lady brought,
Bright *Diomeda, Phorbas* seede. Patroclus did imbrace
The bewteous *Iphis* given to him when his bold friend did race
The loftie *Syrus,* that was kept in *Enyeius* hold.
Now at the tent of *Atreus* sonne, each man with cups of gold
Receav'de th'Ambassadors returnde, all clusterd neare to know
What newes they brought: which first the King would have
    Ulysses show:
Say most praise-worthy *Ithacus,* the Grecians great renowne,
Will he defend us? or not yet will his prowde stomacke downe?
Ulysses made reply: Not yet will he appeased be,
But growes more wrathfull, prising light thy offerd gifts and thee;
And wils thee to consult with us, and take some other course
To save our Armie and our Fleete, and sayes with all his force,
The morne shall light him on his way to *Pthyas* wished soyle . . .
All wondred he should be so sterne, at last bold *Diomede* spake:
    Would God *Atrides* thy request were yet to undertake;
And all thy gifts unoffered; hee's prowde enough beside:
But this ambassage thou hast sent will make him burst with pride.
But let us suffer him to stay or goe at his desire,
Fight when his stomacke serves him best, or when *Jove* shall inspire:
Meane while our watch being stronglie held let us a little rest
After our foode: strength lives by both, and vertue is their guest;

[1] Cf. Agamemnon, II.3.115-37.

Then when the rosy-fingerd Morne holds up her silver light,
Bring forth thy host, encourage all, and be thou first in fight.
   The kings admirde the fortitude that so divinely mov'de
The skilfull horseman *Diomede*, and his advice approv'de:
Then with their nightlie sacrifice each tooke his severall tent,
Where all receavde the sovereigne gifts soft *Somnus* did present.

B. Analogue

THE ILIADS OF HOMER

translated by George Chapman. R. Field for N. Butter. [1611][1]

Booke XIV.

[Neptune heartened the Greeks by leading them against the enemy.
Ajax encountered Hector.]

        But when they joynd, the dreadfull *Clamor* rose
To such a height as not the sea when up the North-spirit blows
Her raging billows bellows so against the beaten shore:
Nor such a rustling keeps a fire, driven with violent blore
Through woods that grow against a hill: nor so the fervent strokes
Of almost-bursting winds resounds against a grove of Okes
As did the clamor of these hosts, when both the battels closd.
Of all which, noble *Hector* first at *Ajax* breast disposd
His javelin, since so right on him the great-soul'd souldier bore;
Nor mist it, but the bawdricks both that his brode bosome wore
To hang his shield and sword, it strooke; both which his flesh
    preserv'd:
Hector (disdaining that his lance had thus as good as swerv'd)
Trode to his strength, but going off, great *Ajax* with a stone
(One of the many props for ships that there lay trampl'd on)
Strooke his broad breast above his shield, just underneath his throat,
And shooke him peecemeale. When the stone sprung backe againe
    and smote
Earth, like a whirlwinde gathering dust, with whirring fiercely round
For fervour of his unspent strength in setling on the ground:
And as when *Joves* bolt by the roots rends from the earth an Oke,
His sulphure casting with the blow a strong unsavoury smoke;
And on the falne plant none dare looke but with amazed eyes
(*Joves* thunder being no laughing game) so bowd strong *Hectors* thyes;
And so with tost up heels he fell: away his lance he flung;

---

[1] In these excerpts the punctuation has been considerably lightened.

His round shield followd; then his helme, and out his armour rung.
  The *Greekes* then showted and ranne in, and hop't to hale him off;
And therefore powr'd on darts in stormes to keepe his aide aloofe;
But none could hurt the peoples guide, nor stirre him from his
    ground:
Sarpedon Prince of *Lycia*, and *Glaucus* so renownd,
Divine *Agenor*, *Venus* sonne, and wise *Polydamas*,
Rusht to his rescue and the rest: no one neglective was
Of *Hectors* safetie; all their shields they coucht about him close,
Raisd him from earth, and (giving him in their kinde armes repose)
From off the labour carried him to his rich chariot,
And bore him mourning towards *Troy*[1] . . .

Book XVI

[The slaying of Patroclus.]

Then *Hector* bad *Cebriones* put on; himselfe let goe
All other Greekes within his reach, and onely gave command
To front *Patroclus*. He at him jumpt downe, his strong left hand
A Javelin held; his right a stone, a marble sharpe; and such
As his large hand had powre to gripe, and gave it strength so much
As he could lye to: nor stood long in feare of that huge man
That made against him; but full on with his huge stone he ran
Discharg'd, and drave it twixt the browes of bold *Cebriones*:
Nor could the thicke bone there prepar'd extenuate so th'accesse,
But out it drave his broken eyes, which in the dust fell downe,
And he div'd after; which conceit of diving tooke the sonne
Of old *Menœtius*, who thus plaid upon the others bane:
  O heavens! for truth this Trojan was a passing active man;
With what exceeding ease he dives! as if at worke he were
Within the fishie seas. This man alone would furnish cheare
For twenty men, though twere a storme; to leape out of a saile
And gather Oysters for them all; he does it here all well,
And there are many such in Troy. Thus jested he so neare
His owne grave death; and then made in to spoyle the Charioteere
With such a Lyons force and fate as (often ruining
Stals of fat Oxen) gets at length a mortall wound to sting
His soule out of that ravenous breast that was so insolent;
And so his lifes blisse proves his bane: so deadly confident
Wert thou *Patroclus* in pursuit of good *Cebriones*;
To whose defence now *Hector* leapt. The opposite addresse
These masters of the cry in warre now made, was of the kinde

---

[1] Cf. I.2.33–6.

Of two fierce kings of beasts, opposd, in strife about a Hinde
Slaine on the forehead of a hill, both sharpe and hungry set,
And to the Currie never came, but like two Deaths they met:
Nor these two entertain'd lesse minde of mutuall prejudice,
About the body, close to which when each had prest for prize,
Hector the head laid hand upon, which once gript never could
Be forc't from him; *Patroclus* then, upon the feet got hold,
And he pincht with as sure a naile: so both stood tugging there,
While all the rest made eager fight, and grappl'd every where. . . .
    As long as *Phœbus* turn'd his wheeles about the midst of heaven,
So long the touch of eithers darts the fals of both made even:
But when his waine drew neere the West, the Greekes past measure
        were
The abler souldiers, and so swept the Trojan tumult cleare
From off the body, out of which they drew the hurl'd in darts,
And from his shoulders stript his armes, and then to more such parts
Patroclus turn'd his striving thoughts, to doe the Trojans ill:
Thrice, like the god of warre he charg'd; his voyce as horrible:
And thrice nine those three charges slue, but in the fourth assay,
O then *Patroclus*, shew'd thy last, the dreadfull Sunne made way
Against that on-set, yet the Prince discern'd no deitie,
He kept the prease so, and besides obscur'd his glorious eye
With such felt darknesse, At his backe he made a sodaine stand,
And twixt his necke and shoulders laid downe-right with either hand,
A blow so weightie that his eyes a giddy darkenesse tooke,
And from his head, his three-plum'd helme, the bounding violence
        shooke,
That rung beneath his horses hoofes, and like a water-spout,
Was crusht together with the fall. The plumes that set it out,
All spatterd with blacke bloud and dust, when ever heretofore
It was a capitall offence to have or dust or gore
Defile a triple-feather'd helme, but on the head divine,
And youthfull temples of their Prince, it usde, untoucht, to shine.
Yet now *Jove* gave it *Hectors* hands, the others death was neare,
Besides whose lost and filed helme his huge long weightie speare,
Well bound with iron in his hand, was shiverd, and his shield
Fell from his shoulders to his feet, the bawdricke strewing the field:
His Curets left him, like the rest, and all this onely done
By great *Apollo*. Then his minde, tooke in confusion,
The vigorous knittings of his joynts dissolv'd, and (thus dismaid)
A Dardan (one of *Panthus* sons) and one that overlaid
All Trojans of his place, with darts, swift footing, skill, and force,
In noble horsemanship, and one that tumbl'd from their horse

One after other twenty men; and when he did but learne
The art of warre; nay when he first did in the field discerne
A horse and chariot of his guide: this man with all these parts
(His name *Euphorbus*) comes behind, and twixt the shoulders darts
Forlorne *Patroclus*, who yet liv'd, and th'other (getting forth
His javelin) tooke him to his strength, nor durst he stand the worth
Of thee *Patroclus* though disarmd; who yet (discomfited
By *Phœbus* and *Euphorbus* wound) the red heape of the dead
He now too late shund, and retir'd. When *Hector* saw him yeeld,
And knew he yeelded with a wound, he scour'd the armed field,
Came close up to him, and both sides strooke quite through with
    his lance.
He fell, and his most weightie fall gave fit tune to his chance.
For which, all Greece extremely mourn'd. And as a mightie strife
About a little fount begins and riseth to the life
Of some fell Bore, resolv'd to drinke, when likewise to the spring
A Lyon comes alike disposde; the Bore thirsts, and his King,
Both proud, and both will first be serv'd; and then the Lyon takes
Advantage of his soveraigne strength, and th'other (fainting) makes
Resigne his thirst up with his bloud: *Patroclus* (so enforc't
When he had forc't so much brave life) was from his owne divorc't.
And thus his great divorcer brav'd: *Patroclus*, thy conceit
Gave thee th'eversion of our Troy; and to thy fleete a freight
Of Trojan Ladies their free lives, put all in bands by thee:
But (too much prizer of thy selfe) all these are propt by me.
For these have my horse stretcht their hoofes to this so long a warre,
And I (farre best of Troy in armes) keepe off from Troy as farre,
Even to the last beame of my life, their necessary day.
And here (in place of us and ours) on thee shall Vultures prey,
Poore wretch; nor shall thy mighty friend affoord thee any aid,
That gave thy parting much deepe charge; and this perhaps he said;
Martiall *Patroclus*, turne not face, nor see my fleete before
The cures from great *Hectors* breast, all guilded with his gore,
Thou hew'st in pieces: if thus vaine were his far-stretcht commands;
As vaine was thy heart to beleeve, his words lay in thy hands.
    He languishing replide: This proves thy glory worse then vaine,
That when two gods have given thy hands what their powres did
    obtaine,
(They conquering, and they spoyling me, both of my armes and
    minde,
It being a worke of ease for them) thy soule should be so blinde
To oversee their evident deeds, and take their powres to thee;
When, if the powres of twenty such had dar'd t'encounter me,

My lance had strew'd earth with them all, Thou onely dost obtaine
A third place in my death; whom first a harmefull fate hath slaine
Effected by *Latonas* sonne; second, and first of men,
Euphorbus. And this one thing more concernes thee; note it then:
Thou shalt not long survive thy selfe; nay, now Death cals for thee,
And violent fate; *Achilles* lance shall make this good for me.
    Thus death joyn'd to his words, his end; his soule tooke instant
      wing,
And to the house that hath no lights descended sorrowing
For his sad fate, to leave him young and in his ablest age.
He dead; yet *Hector* askt him why in that prophetique rage
He so forspake him? when none knew, but great *Achilles* might
Prevent his death, and on his lance receive his latest light.
Thus setting on his side his foote he drew out of his wound
His brazen lance, and upwards cast the body on the ground;
When quickly, while the dart was hot, he charg'd *Automedon*,
(Divine guide of *Achilles* steeds) in great contention,
To seize him to: but his so swift and deathlesse horse, that fetcht
Their gift to *Peleus* from the gods, soone rap't him from his reach.

Book XXII

[The slaying of Hector.]

The Argument

All Trojans housd but *Hector*, onely he
Keepes field, and undergoes th'extremitie.
Æacides assaulting, *Hector* flies,
Minerva stayes him: he resists, and dies,
Achilles to his chariot doth enforce,
And to the navall station, drags his corse.

Another Argument

Hector (in *Chi*) to death is done,
By powre of *Peleus* angry sonne.

    Thus (chac't like Hindes) the Ilians tooke time to drinke and eate,
And to refresh them; getting off the mingl'd dust and sweate,
And good strong rampires on in stead. The Greeks then cast their
    shields
Aloft their shoulders; and now Fate their neare invasion yeelds
Of those tough wals, her deadly hand compelling *Hectors* stay
Before Troy at the Scæan ports. *Achilles* still made way
At *Phœbus*, who his bright head turn'd and askt: Why (*Peleus* sonne)

Pursu'st thou (being a man) a god? thy rage hath never done.
Acknowledge not thine eyes my state? esteemes thy minde no more
Thy honour in the chace of Troy, but puts my chace before
Their utter conquest? they are all now housde in Ilion,
While thou hunt'st me. What wishest thou? my bloud will never
　　　runne
On thy proud javelin. It is thou (repli'd *Æacides*)
That putst dishonour thus on me (thou worst of deities).
Thou turndst me from the wals, whose ports had never entertaind
Numbers now enter'd, over whom thy saving hand hath raign'd
And robd my honour. And all is, since all thy actions stand,
Past feare of reckoning: but held I the measure in my hand,
It should affoord thee deare-bought scapes. Thus with elated spirits
(Steed-like, that at Olympus games, weares garlands for his merits,
And rattles home his chariot, extending all his pride)
Achilles so parts with the god. When aged *Priam* spide
The great Greek come, sphear'd round with beames, and show'ng
　　　as if the star
Surnam'd *Orions* hound, that springs in Autumne, and sends farre
His radiance through a world of starres of all whose beames his owne
Cast greatest splendor: the midnight that renders them most
　　　showne
Then being their foile and on their points cure-passing Fevers then
Come shaking downe into the joynts of miserable men:
As this were falne to earth; and shot along the field his raies,
Now towards *Priam* (when he saw in great *Æacides*)
Out flew his tender voyce in shriekes, and with raisde hands he smit
His reverend head, then up to heaven he cast them, shewing it,
What plagues it sent him; downe againe then threw them to his
　　　sonne,
To make him shun them. He now stood without steepe Ilion,
Thirsting the combat; and to him thus miserably cride
The kinde olde King: O *Hector*! flye this man, this homicide,
That strait will stroy thee. Hee's too strong, and would to heaven
　　　he were
As strong in heavens love as in mine. Vultures and dogs should teare
His prostrate carkasse, all my woes quencht with his bloudy spirits.
He has robd me of many sonnes and worthy, and their merits
Sold to farre Ilands: two of them (aye me) I misse but now;
They are not entred; nor stay here. . . .

　　　　　　. . . take the towne, retire (deare sonne) and save
Troyes husbands and her wives, nor give thine owne life to the grave,
For this mans glory: pitty me, me, wretch, so long live,

Whom in the doore of Age, *Jove* keepes, that he may deprive
My being in Fortunes utmost curse, to see the blackest thred
Of this lifes miseries, my sonnes slaine, my daughters ravished,
Their resting chambers sackt, their babes torne from them on their
    knees
Pleading for mercy; themselves dragd to Grecian slaveries,
(And all this drawne through my red eyes). Then last of all kneele I
Alone, all helpelesse at my gates, before my enemy,
That (ruthlesse) gives me to my dogs: all the deformitie
Of age discover'd, and all this, thy death (sought wilfully)
Will poure on me. A faire yong man, at all parts it beseemes,
(Being bravely slaine) to lye all gasht and weare the worst extremes
Of warres most cruelty, no wound of whatsoever ruth
But is his ornament: but I, a man so farre from youth,
White head, white bearded, wrinkl'd, pin'd, all shames must shew
    the eye:
Live, prevent this then, this most shame of all mens misery.

    Thus wept the old King, and tore off his white haire, yet all these
Retir'd not *Hector*. *Hecuba* then fell upon her knees,
Stript nak't her bosome, shew'd her breasts, and bad him reverence
    them,
And pittie her: if ever she had quieted his exclaime,
He would cease hers, and take the towne, not tempting the rude field,
When all had left it: thinke (said she) I gave thee life to yeeld
My life recomfort; thy rich wife shall have no rites of thee,
Nor doe thee rites: our teares shall pay thy corse no obsequie,
Beign ravisht from us; Grecian dogs, nourisht with what I nurst.

    Thus wept both these, and to his ruth proposde the utmost worst
Of what could chance them, yet he staid.[1] And now drew deadly
    neare
Mighty *Achilles*, yet he still kept deadly station there.
Looke how a Dragon when she sees a traveller bent upon
Her breeding den, her bosome fed with fell contagion,
Gathers her forces, sits him firme, and at his nearest pace
Wraps all her Caverne in her folds, and thrusts a horrid face
Out at his entry: *Hector* so with unextinguisht spirit
Stood great *Achilles*: stird no foot, but at the prominent turret
Bent to his bright shield, and resolv'd to beare falne heaven on it. . . .

[Hector wanted to retire but knew that he must either kill Achilles
or die 'for our citie with renowne, since all else fled but I.']

---

[1] Cf. V. 3. 50–93.

These thoughts employd his stay, and now *Achilles* comes, now
    neare
His *Mars*-like presence terribly came brandishing his speare.
His right arme shooke it, his bright armes like day came glittering on,
Like fire-light, or the light of heaven shot from the rising Sun.
This sight outwrought discourse, cold Feare shooke *Hector* from his
    stand.
No more stay now, all ports were left; he fled in feare the hand
Of that Feare-master, who hawk-like, ayres swiftest passenger,
That holds a timorous Dove in chace, and with command doth beare
His fierie onset: the Dove hasts, the Hawke comes whizzing on,
This way, and that, he turnes and windes, and cusses the Pigeon;
And till he trusse it, his great spirit layes hot charge on his wing:
So urg'd *Achilles Hectors* flight, so still Feares point did sting
His troubl'd spirit; his knees wrought hard; along the wall he flew
In that faire chariot way that runnes beneath the towre of view,
And *Troyes* wilde fig-tree, till they reacht, where those two mother
    springs,
Of deepe *Scamander*, pour'd abroad their silver murmurings. . . .
Both did their best, for neither now ranne for a sacrifice,
Or for the sacrificers hide (our runners usuall prise).
These ranne for tame-horse *Hectors* soule. And as two running Steeds,
Backt in some set race for a game that tries their swiftest speeds,
(A tripod, or a woman given for some mans funerals:)
Such speed made these men, and on foot, ranne thrice about the
    wals. . . .

[Jove would have liked to save Hector, but Pallas demanded his
death, and the god agreed. The pursuit continued.]

So, nor *Achilles* chace could reach the flight of *Hectors* pace,
Nor *Hectors* flight enlarge it selfe of swift *Achilles* chace.
   But how chanc't this? how all this time could *Hector* beare the knees
Of fierce *Achilles* with his owne, and keepe off Destinies,
If *Phœbus* (for his last and best) through all that course hath fail'd
To adde his succours to his nerves? and (as his foe assail'd)
Neare, and with him fed his scape. *Achilles* yet well knew
His knees would fetch him, and gave signes to some friends (making
    shew
Of shooting at him) to forbeare, lest they detracted so
From his full glory in first wounds, and in the overthrow
Make his hand last.[1] But when they reacht the fourth time the two
    founts,

---

[1] Contrast V. 7.

Then *Jove* his golden skales weigh'd up, and tooke the last accounts
Of Fate for *Hector*; putting in for him and *Peleus* sonne
Two fates of bitter death; of which high heaven receiv'd the one,
The other hell: so low declin'd the light of *Hectors* life.
Then *Phœbus* left him, when warres Queene came to resolve the strife,
In th'others knowledge: Now (said she) *Jove*-lov'd *Æacides*,
I hope at last to make renowne, performe a brave accesse
To all the Grecians; we shall now lay low this champions height,
Though never so insatiate was his great heart of fight.
Nor must he scape our pursuit still, though all the feet of *Jove*
Apollo bowes into a sphere, soliciting more love
To his most favour'd. Breathe thee then, stand firme, my selfe will
        hast,
And hearten *Hector* to change blowes. She went, and he stood fast,
Lean'd on his lance, and much was joy'd that single strokes should
        try
This fadging conflict. Then came close the changed deitie
To *Hector*, like Deiphobus in shape and voyce, and said:
   O brother, thou art too much urg'd, to be thus combatted
About our owne wals; let us stand, and force to a retreat
Th'insulting Chaser. *Hector* joy'd at this so kinde deceit,
And said: O good *Deiphobus*, thy love was most before
(Of all my brothers) deare to me, but now exceeding more.
It costs me honour that thus urg'd thou com'st to part the charge
Of my last fortunes; other friends keepe towne and leave at large
My rackt endevours. She replide: Good brother, tis most true
One after other King and Queene and all our friends did sue
(Even on their knees) to stay me there; such tremblings shake them
        all,
With this mans terror: but my minde so griev'd to see our wall
Girt with thy chases that to death I long'd to urge thy stay.
Come, fight we, thirsty of his bloud, no more let's feare to lay
Cost on our Lances, but approve, if bloudied with our spoyles
He can beare glory to their fleete, or shut up all their toyles
In his one sufferance on thy Lance. With this deceit she led,
And (both come neare) thus *Hector* spake: thrice I have compassed
This great towne (*Peleus* sonne) in flight, with aversation
That out of Fate put off my steps, but now all flight is flowne,
The short course set up, death or life. Our resolutions yet,
Must shun all rudenesse; and the gods before our valour set
For use of victorie, and they being worthiest witnesses
Of all vowes; since they keepe vowes best before their deities,
Let vowes of fit respect passe both, when Conquest hath bestow'd

Her wreath on either. Here I vow, no furie shall be show'd
That is not manly on thy corse; but, having spoil'd thy armes,
Resigne thy person, which sweare thou. These faire and temperate
termes
Farre fled *Achilles*, his browes bent, and out flew this reply:
　Hector, thou onely pestilence in all mortalitie
To my sere spirits; never set the point twixt thee and me
Any conditions, but as farre as men and Lyons flye
All termes of covenant, lambs and wolves: in so farre opposite state,
(Impossible for love t'attone) stand we, till our soules satiate
The god of souldiers; doe not dreame that our disjunction can
Endure condition. Therefore now all worth that fits a man
Call to thee, all particular parts that fit a souldier,
And they all this include (besides the skill and spirit of warre)
Hunger for slaughter, and a hate that eates thy heart, to eate
Thy foes heart. This stirs, this supplies in death the killing heate,
And all this needst thou. No more flight; *Pallas Athenia*
Will quickly cast thee to my lance; now, now together draw
All griefes for vengeance, both in me, and all my friends late dead
That bled thee, raging with thy Lance. This said, he brandished
His long Lance, and away it sung: which *Hector* giving view,
Stoupt low, stood firme, (foreseeing it best) and quite it overflew,
Fastening on earth. *Athenia* drew it, and gave her friend,
Unseene of *Hector*. *Hector* then thus spake: Thou want'st thy end
(God-like *Achilles*). Now I see thou hast not learn'd my fate,
Of *Jove* at all, as thy high words would bravely intimate;
Much tongue affects thee; cunning words well serve thee to prepare
Thy blowes with threats, that mine might faint with want of spirit
　to dare;
But my backe never turnes with breath; it was not borne to beare
Burthens of wounds; strike home before; drive at my breast thy
　speare,
As mine at thine shall; and try then, if heavens will favour thee
With scape of my Lance. O would *Jove* would take it after me,
And make thy bosome take it all; an easie end would crowne
Our difficult warres were thy soule fled, thou most bane of our towne.
　　Thus flew his dart, toucht at the midst of his vast shield, and flew
A huge way from it; but his heart wrath entred with the view
Of that hard scape, and heavy thoughts strooke through him, when
　he spide
His brother vanisht; and no lance beside left. Out he cride:
Deiphobus! another Lance! Lance nor *Deiphobus*
Stood neare his call. And then his minde saw all things ominous,

And thus suggested: Woe is me, the gods have cald, and I
Must meete Death here; *Deiphobus* I well hop't had beene by,
With his white shield; but our strong wals shield him, and this deceit
Flowes from *Minerva*; now, O now, ill death comes, no more flight,
No more recoverie: O *Jove*, this hath beene otherwise.
Thy bright sonne and thy selfe have set, the Greekes a greater prize
Of *Hectors* bloud then now, of which (even jealous) you had care;
But Fate now conquers; I am hers; and yet, not she shall share
In my renowne; that life is left to every noble spirit;
And that some great deed shall beget that all lives shall inherit.
  Thus forth his sword flew, sharpe and broad, and bore a deadly
    weight,
With which he rusht in: and looke how an Eagle from her height
Stoopes to the rapture of a Lambe, or cuffes a timorous Hare:
So fell in *Hector*, and at him *Achilles*; his mindes fare
Was fierce and mightie: his shield cast a Sun-like radiance;
Helme nodded; and his foure plumes shooke, and when he raisde his
    lance
Up *Hesperus* rose amongst th'evening starres. His bright and
    sparkling eyes
Lookt through the body of his foe, and sought through all that prise
The next way to his thirsted life. Of all wayes, onely one
Appear'd to him; and that was, where th'unequall winding bone
That joynes the shoulders and the necke, had place, and where there
    lay
The speeding way to death: and there his quicke eye could display
The place it sought; even through those armes, his friend *Patroclus*
    wore,
When *Hector* slue him. There he aim'd, and there his javelin tore
Sterne passage quite through *Hectors* necke; yet mist it so his throte,
It gave him powre to change some words; but downe to earth it got
His fainting body: then triumpht divine *Æacides*.
Hector, (said he) thy heart supposde that in my friends decease
Thy life was safe; my absent arme not car'd for: Foole! he left
One at the fleete that better'd him; and he it is that reft
Thy strong knees thus; and now the dogs and fowles, in foulest use
Shall teare thee up, thy corse exposde to all the Greekes abuse.
  He fainting said: Let me implore, even by thy knees and soule,
And thy great parents; doe not see a crueltie so foule
Inflicted on me; brasse and gold receive at any rate,
And quit my person; that the Peeres and Ladies of our state
May tombe it, and to sacred fire turne thy prophane decrees.
  Dog, (he replied) urge not my ruth by parents, soule, nor knees;

I would to God that any rage would let me eate thee raw,
Slic't into pieces; so beyond the right of any law
I tast thy merits; and beleeve, it flyes the force of man
To rescue thy head from the dogs. Give all the gold they can,
If tenne or twenty times so much, as friends would rate thy price,
Were tendred here, with vowes of more, to buy the cruelties
I here have vow'd, and after that thy father with his gold
Would free thy selfe; all that should faile, to let thy mother hold
Solemnities of death with thee and doe thee such a grace,
To mourne thy whole corse on a bed; which peecemeale Ile deface
With fowles and dogs. He (dying) said: I (knowing thee well)
    foresaw
Thy now tried tyrannie; nor hop't for any other law
Of nature, or of nations; and that feare, forc't much more
Then death my flight, which never toucht at *Hectors* foot before:
A soule of iron informes thee; marke, what vengeance th'equall fates
Will give me of thee, for this rage when in the Scæan gates
Phœbus and *Paris* meete with thee. Thus deaths hand closde his eyes,
His soule flying his faire lims to hell, mourning his destinies,
To part so with his youth and strength. Thus dead, thus *Thetis* sonne
His prophecie answer'd: Die thou now; when my short thred is
    spunne,
Ile beare it as the will of *Jove*. This said, his brazen speare
He drew and stucke by: then his armes (that all embrewed were)
He spoil'd his shoulders of. Then all the Greekes ran in to him
To see his person; and admir'd his terror-stirring lim:
Yet none stood by, that gave no wound to his so goodly forme;
When each to other said: O *Jove*, he is not in the storme
He came to fleete in with his fire, he handles now more soft.
    O friends, (said sterne *Æacides*) now that the gods have brought
This man thus downe, Ile freely say, he brought more bane to Greece
Then all his aiders. Try we then (thus arm'd at every peece,
And girding all Troy with our host) if now their hearts will leave
Their citie cleare; her cleare stay slaine and all their lives receive;
Or hold yet, *Hector* being no more. But why use I a word
Of any act, but what concernes my friend? dead, undeplor'd,
Unsepulcherd, he lies at fleete unthought on; never houre
Shall make his dead state while the quicke enjoyes me, and this
    powre
To move these movers. Though in hell men say, that such as dye,
Oblivion seiseth, yet in hell in me shall Memorie
Hold all her formes still of my friend. Now, (youths of Greece) to
    fleete

Beare we this body; *Pæans* sing, and all our navie greete
With endlesse honour; we have slaine *Hector*, the period
Of all Troyes glory; to whose worth all vow'd as to a god.
  This said, a worke not worthy him he set to: of both feete
He bor'd the nerves through from the heele to th'ankle; and then
    knit
Both to his chariot with a thong of whitleather; his head
Trailing the center. Up he got to chariot, where he laid
The armes repurchac't; and scourg'd on his horse, that freely flew.
A whirlewinde made of startl'd dust drave with them as they drew,
With which were all his black-browne curles knotted in heapes
    and fil'd.
And there lay Troyes late Gracious; by *Jupiter* exil'd
To all disgrace, in his owne land, and by his parents seene:
  When (like her sonnes head) all with dust Troyes miserable
    Queene
Distain'd her temples; plucking off her honor'd haire, and tore
Her royall garments, shrieking out. In like kinde *Priam* bore
His sacred person; like a wretch that never saw good day,
Broken with outcries. About both, the people prostrate lay;
Held downe with Clamor; all the towne vail'd with a cloud of teares.
Ilion, with all his tops on fire, and all the massacres
Left for the Greekes, could put on lookes of no more overthrow
Then now fraid life. And yet the king did all their lookes outshow.
The wretched people could not beare his soveraigne wretchednesse,
Plaguing himselfe so; thrusting out, and praying all the preasse
To open him the Dardan ports; that he alone might fetch
His dearest sonne in; and (all fil'd with tumbling) did beseech
Each man by name, thus: Loued friends, be you content; let me
(Though much ye grieve) be that poore meane to our sad remedie
Now in our wishes; I will goe, and pray this impious man,
(Author of horrors) making proofe, if ages reverence can
Excite his pittie. . . .

[In Book XXIII the Greeks performed the obsequies of Patroclus.
In Book XXIV Priam was granted the body of his son, which was
embalmed and then burned, as Troy mourned for him.]

II. Probable Source

From OVID'S METAMORPHOSES
translated by Arthur Golding (1567)

The. xv. Bookes of P. Ovidius Naso, entytuled Metamorphosis, translated oute of Latin into English meeter,
by Arthur Golding Gentleman, A worke very pleasaunt
and delectable.

With skill, heede, and judgement, this worke must be
read,

For else to the Reader it standes in small stead.
1567. Imprynted at London, by Willyam Seres.

[Paris slew Achilles and a dispute occurred about Achilles' armour]

[Bĸ. XII]

This was the onely thing wherof the old king *Priam* myght   670
Take comfort after *Hectors* death. That stout and valeant
   knyght
Achilles whoo had overthrowen so many men in fyght,
Was by that coward carpet knyght beereeved of his lyfe,
Whoo like a caytif stale away the *Spartane* princes wyfe.
But if of weapon womanish he had foreknowen it had
His destnye beene too lose his lyfe, he would have beene more
   glad
That Queene *Penthesileas* bill had slaine him out of hand.
Now was the feare of Phrygian folk, the onely glory, and
Defence of Greekes, that peerelesse prince in armes, *Achilles*
   turnd
Too asshes. That same God that had him armd, him also
   burnd.   680
Now is he dust: and of that great *Achilles* bydeth still
A thing of nought, that scarcely can a little coffin fill.
Howbeet his woorthy fame dooth lyve, and spreadeth over all
The world, a measure meete for such a persone too beefall.
This matcheth thee *Achilles* full. And this can never dye.
His target also (too thentent that men myght playnly spye
What wyghts it was) did move debate, and for his armour
   burst

Out deadly foode. Not *Diomed*, nor *Ajax Oylye* durst
Make clayme or chalendge too the same, nor *Atreus* yoonger
    sonne,
Nor yit his elder, though in armes much honour they had
    wonne.   690
Alone the sonnes of *Telamon* and *Laërt* did assay
Which of them twoo of that great pryse should beare the bell
    away.
But *Agamemnon* from himself the burthen putts, and cleeres
His handes of envye, causing all the Capteines and the Peeres
Of *Greece* too meete amid the camp toogither in a place,
Too whom he put the heering and the judgement of the cace.

[Bk. XIII]

The Lordes and Capteynes being set toogither with the King,   1
And all the souldiers standing round about them in a ring,
The owner of the sevenfold sheeld, too theis did *Ajax* ryse,⎫
And (as he could not brydle wrath) he cast his frowning eyes⎬
Uppon the shore, and on the fleete that there at Anchor lyes,⎭
And throwing up his handes, O God and must wee plead
    (quoth hee)
Our case before our shippes? and must *Ulysses* stand with mee?
But like a wretch he ran his way when *Hector* came with fyre,
Which I defending from theis shippes did force him too retyre.
It easyer is therefore with woordes in print too maynteine
    stryfe,   10
Than for too fyght it out with fists. But neyther I am ryfe
In woordes, nor hee in deedes. For looke how farre I him excell
In battell and in feates of armes: so farre beares hee the bell
From mee in talking. Neyther think I requisite too tell
My actes among you. You your selves have seene them verry
    well.
But let *Ulysses* tell you his doone all in hudther mudther,[1]
And wheruntoo the only nyght is privy and none other.
The pryse is great (I doo confesse) For which wee stryve.
    But yit
It is dishonour untoo mee, for that in clayming it
So bace a person standeth in contention for the same.   20
Too think it myne already ought too counted bee no shame
Nor pryde in mee: although the thing of ryght great valew bee
Of which *Ulysses* standes in hope. For now alreadye hee
Hath wonne the honour of this pryse, in that when he shall sit

---

[1] in hugger-mugger, secretly. Cf. *Ham.* IV.5.83.

Besydes the quisshon,[1] he may brag he strave with mee for it.
And though I wanted valiantnesse, yit should nobilitee
Make with mee. I of *Telamon* am knowne the sonne too bee
Who under valeant *Hercules* the walles of *Troy* did scale,
And in the shippe of *Pagasa* too *Colchos* land did sayle.
His father was that *Aeäcus* whoo executeth ryght   30
Among the ghostes where *Sisyphus* heaves up with all his myght
The massye stone ay tumbling downe. The hyghest *Jove* of all
Acknowledgeth this *Aeäcus*, and dooth his sonne him call.
Thus am I *Ajax* third from *Jove*. Yit let this Pedegree
O Achyves in this case of myne avaylable not bee,
Onlesse I proove it fully with *Achylles* too agree.
He was my brother, and I clayme that was my brothers. Why
Shouldst thou that art of *Sisyphs* blood, and for too filch and lye
Expressest him in every poynt, by foorged pedegree
Aly thee too the *Aeacyds*, as though we did not see   40
Thee too the house of *Aeäcus* a straunger for too bee?
And is it reason that you should this armour mee denye
Bycause I former was in armes, and needed not a spye
Too fetch mee foorth? Or think you him more woorthye it
    too have,
That came too warrefare hindermost, and feynd himself too
    rave,
Bycause he would have shund the warre? untill a suttler head
And more unprofitable for himself, sir *Palamed*
Escryde the crafty fetches of his fearefull hart, and drew
Him foorth a warfare which he sought so cowardly too eschew?
Must he now needes enjoy the best and richest armour? whoo   50
Would none at all have worne onlesse he forced were thertoo?
And I with shame bee put besyde my cousin germanes gifts,
Bycause too shun the formest brunts of warres I sought no
    shifts?
Would God this mischeef mayster had in verrye deede beene
    mad,
Or else beleeved so too bee: and that wee never had
Brought such a panion untoo *Troy*. . . .

[Ajax accuses Ulysses of treachery to Philoctetes and Palamedes]

Thus eyther by his murthring men or else by banishment
Abateth hee the Greekish strength. This is *Ulysses* fyght:
This is the feare he puttes men in. But though he had more
    might

---

[1] cuissue, O.F. cuisseau, thigh-armour.

Than *Nestor* hath in eloquence, he shalnot compasse mee   80
Too think his leawd abandoning of *Nestor* for too bee
No fault: who beeing cast behynd by wounding of his horse,
And slowe with age, with calling on *Ulysses* waxing hoarce,
Was nerethelesse betrayd by him.[1] Sir *Diomed* knowes this
    cryme
Is unsurmysde. For he himselfe did at that present tyme
Rebuke him oftentymes by name, and feercely him upbrayd
With flying from his fellowe so who stood in neede of ayd.
With ryghtfull eyes dooth God behold the deedes of mortall
    men.
Lo, he that helped not his freend wants help himself agen.
And as he did forsake his freend in tyme of neede: so hee   90
Did in the selfsame perrill fall forsaken for too bee.
He made a rod too beat himself. He calld and cryed out
Upon his fellowes.[2] Streight I came: and there I saw the lout
Bothe quake and shake for feare of death, and looke as pale
    as clout.
I set my sheeld betweene him and his foes, and him bestrid:
And savde the dastards lyfe: small prayse redoundes of that
    I did.
But if thou wilt contend with mee, lets to the selfe same place
Agein: bee wounded as thou wart: and in the foresayd case
Of feare, beset about with foes: cowch underneath my sheeld:
And then contend thou with mee there amid the open feeld.   100
Howbeet, I had no sooner rid this champion of his foes,
But where for woundes he scarce before could totter on his toes,
He ran away apace, as though he nought at all did ayle.
Anon commes *Hector* too the feeld and bringeth at his tayle
The Goddes. Not only thy hart there (*Ulysses*) did the fayle,
But even the stowtest courages and stomacks gan too quayle:
So great a terrour brought he in. Yit in the midds of all
His bloody ruffe, I coapt with him, and with a foyling fall
Did overthrowe him too the ground. Another tyme, when hee
Did make a chalendge, you my Lordes by lot did choose out
    mee,   110
And I did match him hand too hand.[3] Your wisshes were not
    vayne.
For if you aske mee what successe our combate did obteine,
I came away unvanquished. Behold, the men of *Troy*

---

[1] From *Iliad*, Bk. VIII.
[2] *Iliad*, Bk. XI.
[3] *Iliad*, Bk. VII.

Brought fyre and swoord, and all the feendes our navye too
    destroy.
And where was slye *Ulysses* then with all his talk so smooth?
This brest of myne was fayne too fence your thousand shippes
    forsooth,
The hope of your returning home. For saving that same day
So many shippes, this armour give. But (if that I shall say
The truth) the greater honour now this armour beares away,
And our renownes toogither link. For (as of reason ought)   120
An *Ajax* for this armour, not an armour now is sought
For *Ajax*. Let *Dulychius* match with theis, the horses whyght
Of *Rhesus*, dastard *Dolon*, and the coward carpetknyght
King *Priams Helen*, and the stelth of *Palladye* by nyght.
Of all theis things was nothing doone by day nor nothing
    wrought
Without the helpe of *Diomed*. And therefore if yee thought
Too give them too so small deserts, devyde the same, and let
Sir *Diomed* have the greater part. But what should *Ithacus* get
And if he had them? Who dooth all his matters in the dark,
Who never weareth armour, who shootes ay at his owne mark   130
Too trappe his fo by stelth unwares? The very headpeece may
With brightnesse of the glistring gold his privie feates bewray
And shew him lurking. Neyther well of force *Dulychius* were
The weyght of great *Achilles* helme uppon his pate too weare.
It cannot but a burthen bee (and that ryght great) too beare
(With those same shrimpish armes of his) *Achilles* myghty
    speare.
Agen his target graven with the whole howge world theron
Agrees not with a fearefull hand, and cheefly such a one
As taketh filching even by kynd. Thou Lozell thou doost seeke
A gift that will but weaken thee: which if the folk of Greeke   140
Shall give thee through theyr oversyght, it will bee untoo thee
Occasion, of thyne emnyes spoylde not feared for too bee.
And flyght (wherin thou coward, thou all others mayst out-
    brag)
Will hindred bee when after thee such masses thou shalt drag.
Moreover this thy sheeld that feeles so seeld the force of fyght
Is sound. But myne is gasht and hakt and stricken thurrough
    quyght
A thousand tymes, with bearing blowes. And therefore myne
    must walk
And put another in his stead. But what needes all this talk?
Lets now bee seene another whyle what eche of us can doo.

The thickest of our armed foes this armour throwe intoo,   150
And bid us fetch the same fro thence. And which of us dooth
    fetch
The same away, reward yee him therewith. Thus farre did
    stretch
The woordes of *Ajax*. At the ende whereof there did ensew
A muttring of the souldiers, till *Laertis* sonne the prew
Stood up, and raysed soberly his eyliddes from the ground
(On which he had a little whyle them pitched in a stound)
And looking on the noblemen who longd his woordes too heere,
He thus began with comly grace and sober pleasant cheere.
  My Lordes, if my desyre and yours myght erst have taken
    place,
  It should not at this present tyme have beene a dowtfull cace,   160
What person hath most ryght too this great pryse for which
    wee stryve.
Achilles should his armour have, and wee still him alyve.
Whom sith that cruell destinie too both of us denyes,
(With that same woord as though he wept, he wypte his
    watry eyes)
What wyght of reason rather ought too bee *Achilles* heyre
Than he through whom too this your camp *Achilles* did
    repayre?
Alonly let it not avayle sir *Ajax* heere, that hee
Is such a dolt and grossehead, as he shewes himself too bee:
Ne let my wit (which ay hath done you good O Greekes) hurt
    mee.
But suffer this mine eloquence (such as it is) which now   170
Dooth for his mayster speake, and oft ere this hath spoke for
    yow,
Bee undisdeynd. Let none refuse his owne good gifts he brings.
For as for stocke and auncetors, and other such like things
Wherof ourselves no fownders are, I scarcely dare them
    graunt
Too bee our owne. But forasmuch as *Ajax* makes his vaunt
Too bee the fowrth from *Jove*: even *Jove* the founder is also
Of my house: and than fowre descents I am from him no mo.
Laërtes is my father, and *Arcesius* his, and hee
Begotten was of *Jupiter*. And in this pedegree
Is neyther any damned soule, nor outlaw as yee see.   180
Moreover by my moothers syde I come of *Mercuree*,
Another honor too my house. Thus both by fathers syde
And moothers (as you may perceyve) I am too Goddes alyde.

But neyther for bycause I am a better gentleman
Than *Ajax* by the moothers syde, nor that my father can
Avouch himself ungiltye of his brothers blood, doo I
This armour clayme: wey you the case by merits uprightly.

[Ulysses describes his own part in the Trojan War, and speaks of
Ajax's 'blockish wit' and 'the rayling of this foolish dolt at mee.' He
tells Ajax:]

Thou hast a hand that serveth well in fyght,
Thou hast a wit that stands in neede of my direction ryght.
Thy force is witlesse: I have care of that that may ensew.
Thou well canst fyght: the king dooth choose the tymes for
    fyghting dew   440
By myne advyce. Thou only with thy body canst avayle,
But I with bodye and with mynd too profite doo not fayle...

[The armour is given to Ulysses, whereupon the enraged Ajax falls
on his sword and dies.]

III. Possible Source

From THE HYSTORYE SEGE AND DYSTRUCCYON OF TROYE

by John Lydgate (1513)

The hystorye Sege and dystruccyon of Troye [Colophon:]
Here endeth the Troye booke other wyse called the Sege
of Troye translated by John Lydgate monke of the
Monastery of Bery And Emprynted the yere of oure
Lorde a. M.CCCCC & XIII. by Richard Pynson
prynter unto the kynges noble grace.

BOOK II. CAP. xv[1]

[From Lydgate's description of some major characters.]

Oyleus Ayax was right corpulent,   4571
To be well cladde he sette all his entent.
In ryche araye he was full curyous.

---

[1] The punctuation is modern.

All though he were of body coursyous,
Of armes great with shulders square and brode,
It was of hym almoste an horse lode.
Hye of stature and boystous in a pres,
And of his speche rude and reckeles.
Ful many worde in ydell him asterte,
And but a cowarde was he of his herte.[1]   4580
   Another Ayax, Thelamonyous,
There was also, discrete and vertuous,
Wonder fayre and semely to beholde,
Whose heer was blacke and upward ay gan folde.
In compas wyde, rounde as any spere,
And of musyke was there none his pere,
Havynge a voyce full of melodye
Right well entuned as by armonye
And was inventyfe for to counterfete
Instrumentes bothe smale and grete   4590
In sturdy[2] wise longynge to musyke,
And for all this yet had he good practike
In armes eke and was a noble knyght.
No man more orped nor hardyer for to fyght.
Nor desyrous for to have vyctorye,
Devoyde of pompe hatynge all vaynglorye,
All ydle laude spent and blowe in vayne.
   Of Ulixes what shall I also sayne
That was so noble and worthy in his dayes,
Full of wyles and sleyghty at assayes.   4600
In menynge double and deceyvable
To forge a lesynge also wonder able.
With face playne he coude make it towghe,
Mery worded and but selde lowghe.
In counseylynge discrete and full prudent,
And in his tyme the moste eloquent,
And holpe to Grekes often in theyr nede.
   And for to speke of worthy Dyomede,
Full well compacte and growe well in lengthe,
Of sturdy porte, and famous eke of strengthe,   4610
Large brested and feers also of syghte,
And deceyvable of what ever he hyghte,[3]
Hasty, testyf, to smyte reckeles,

---

[1] Shakespeare's Ajax is a boaster, but no coward.
[2] sondry *MSS.*
[3] promised. Cf. Thersites on his deceit, V.1.92ff.

And medlynge aye, and but selde in pes;
To his servauntes full impacyent,
And baratous where that ever he went.
For lytell worthe of disposicyon,
And lecherous of complexyon,
And hadde in love ofte sythe his parte
Brennynge at herte of Cupids darte,   4620
And specheles full ofte felte sore. . . .
   And overmore to tell of Cryseyde
My penne stombleth, for longe or he deyde,
My mayster Chauncer dyde his dylygence
To discryve the greate excellence   4690
Of hir beaute and that so masterlye,
To take on me it were but hye folye
In any wyse to adde more thereto. . . .
Of hye nor lowe, but mene of stature,   4740
Hir sonnysshe heer lyke Phebus in his spere,
Bounde in a tresse bryghter than golde were
Downe at hir backe, lowe downe behynde,
Whiche with a threde of gold she wolde bynde
Fulle ofte sythe of a customaunce.
Therto she had so moche suffysaunce
Of kyndes werke without any mere,
And save hir browes joyned yfere,
No man coude in hir a lacke espyen.
And ferthermore to speke of hir eyen,   4750
They were so persynge hevenly and so clere
That an herte ne myghte hymselfe stere
Agayne hir shynynge that they ne wolde wounde
Thorugh out a breste (god wote) and beyounde . . .
Also she was, for all hir semelynesse,
Full symple and meke and full of sobernesse,
The beste nourysshed eke that myght be,
Goodly of speche, fulfylled of pyte,
Facundyous and therto ryght tretable,
And, as sayth Guydo, in love varyable;   4760
Of tendre herte and unstedfastnesse
He hir accuseth, and newfongylnesse . . .
   But Troylus sothly if I shall descryve,   4861
There was of herte no manlyer alyve,
Nor more lykly in armes to endure,
Well growen on hyghte and of good stature,
Yonge, fresshe and lusty, hardy as a lyowne,

Delyver and stronge as any champyowne,
And perygall of manhode and of dede,
He was to any that I can of rede.
In derrynge do this noble worthy wyght
For to fulfylle that longeth to a knyght, 4870
The seconde Ector for his worthynesse
He called was and for his hye prowesse.[1]
Durynge the werre he bare hym aye so wele,
Therto in love trewe as any stele,
Secre and wyse, stedfast of courage,
The most goodly also of vysage
That myght be, and most benygne of chere,
Without chaunge and of one herte entere.
He was alway faythfull, juste and stable,
Perseveraunt and of wyll immutable 4880
Upon what thynge he ones set his herte,
That doubylnesse myght him nat perverte
In his dedes, he was so hole and playne.
But of his foon the sothe for to sayne,
He was so ferse they myght hym nat withstande
Whan that he helde his blody swerde in hande:
Unto Grekes dethe and confusion,
To theim of Troye shelde and proteccion.
And his knyghthode shortly to accounte,
There myght in manhode no man hym surmounte 4890
Thorugh the worlde though men woulde seke
To reken all, Troyan nouther Greke;
None so named of famous hardynesse,
As bokes olde of hym bere wytnesse.
Except Ector there ne was such another.

Book III. Cap. xxii
[Hector's meeting with Ajax Telamon.]

For as he rode, this Ector cruellye 2036
Amonge Grekes slewe and bare all downe.
Casually he mette Thelamowne,
I mene Ayax, nye of his allye,
That of hate and cruell hote envye 2040
To Ector rode lyke as he were woode,
Albe to hym he was full nye of bloode.
Yet for all that this yonge lusty knyght

---

[1] Cf. IV.5.96–109.

Dyde his powre and his full myght
Without faynynge, to have borne hym downe,
Whose fader hyght also Thelamowne
That hym begat, the storye telleth thus,
Of Exyon suster to Pryamus.
And this Ayax flourynge in yonge age,
Fresshe and delyver and of grete courage,   2050
Sette on Ector of knyghtly hye prowesse,
And as they mette bothe in theyr woodnesse,
On theyr stedes these manly champyownes
Everyche on other lyke Tygres or lyownes
Began to falle and prowdely to assayle,
And furyously severe plate and mayle
Firste with speres longe, large and rounde,
And afterwarde with swerdes kene grounde.
And fyghtynge thus longe they contune,
Tyll it befylle of case or of Fortune,   2060
Token or sygne or some apparence
Or by naturis kyndely influence,
Whiche into hertes doth full depe myne,
Namely of theym that borne be of one lyne,
Whiche cause was peraunter of these twayne
Naturally theyr rancoure to restrayne,[1]
And theyr yre for to modefye,
Onely for they so nye were of allye,
Unwyst of outher and therof unsure
Tyll they were taught oonly of nature.   2070
For naturally blode wyll aye of kynde
Drawe unto blode where he may it fynde.
Whiche made Ector kyndely to adverte
To be mevyd and steryd in his herte,
Both of knyghthode and of gentyllesse
Whan he of Ayax sawe the worthynesse,
Spake unto him full benygnely
And sayd: Cosyn, I saye the trewely,
If thou lyste Grekes here forsake,
And come to Troye, I dare undertake,   2080
To thyne allyes and to thy kynrede,
Thou shalte be there without any drede
Full well receyved in partye and in all
Of them that be of the blode royall . . .

---

[1] Cf. IV.5.92–3.

And he answered agayne full humbly
That sythen he of berthe was a Greke,
And was of youthe amonge them forstryde eke
From the tyme of his natyvyte
And taken hadde the ordre and degre   2100
Of knyghthode eke amonges them aforne,
And over this bounde was and sworne
To be trewe to theyr nacyon,
Makynge of blode none excepcyon,
He swore he wolde conserve his beheste . . .

[At Ajax's request Hector forbore to pursue the flying Greeks and to burn their ships. This was a fatal mistake. In a later battle (cap. xxiiii)]

They ran togydre with a despytous chere   3586
Tyll shyvered was asondre many spere
On shyldes stronge them selfe for to were,
And ryven was on pecys many targe
And with herys rounde brode and large
On basenettes as they smyte and shrede
Full many knyght mortally gan blede.
In sothfastnesse and as I tell can,
The same day was slayne many a man
On outher parte, but most of Troye towne . . .   3595
For that day Fortune holpe them nought   3602
But tourned hole to theyr confusyowne;
And so they be repeyred to the towne,
And to theyr tentes Grekes faste them spede,
Tyll on the morowe they sent Dyomede
With Ulixes to Troye the cyte
For a trewes oonly for monthes thre
If kynge Pryam therto wolde assente . . .   3609
And the kynge benyngnely them herde,   3625
And by avyse prudently answerde
That therupon his honour for to save
At good leyser he wolde a counsayle have
With his lordes and fully hym governe
In this mater lyke as they discerne.   3630
      And to conclude shortly everychone
Assentyd be except Ector alone
Unto the trewes and ne wolde it nat denye;
But Ector sayde that of trecherye
Oonly, of slaughter and false Treson

Theyr axynge was, under occasion
Firste to berye Grekes that were dede
And under coloure therof out of drede
Afterwarde them selfe to vytayle;
For he wel knewe that theyr stuf gan fayle,   3640
And enfamyned leste they shulde dye,
They sought a space them selfe to purveye. . . .
Yet nevertheles how ever that it be   3653
Touchynge this trewes as for monthes thre
Sythen ye all assente and accorde,
Fro your sentence I wyll nat discorde
In no wyse to be varyaunt.
And thus the trewes confermyd was by graunt.
On outher syde them thought for the beste
Bycause they shulde in quyate and in reste   3660
The mene whyle ease them and releve
And they that felte theyr woundes sore greve
Myght have leyser them selfe to recure.
    And whyle the trewes dyde thus endure
They fylle in Tretee and in communynge
Of Athenor and Thoas the kynge,
That Athenor delyvered shulde be
For kynge Thoas to Troye the cyte,
And so Thoas shuld to Grekes home agayne
Oonly by eschaunge as ye have herde me sayne   3670
One for another as it accorded was.
    And in this whyle the bysshop hight Calchas
Remembred hym upon his doughter dere
Called Cryseyde with hir Eyen clere
Whom in Troye he had lefte behynde
Whan he wente, as the boke maketh mynde;
For whom he felte passyngly great smerte,
So tenderly she was set at his herte
And enprented both at eve and morowe;
And chefe cause and grounde of all his sorowe   3680
Was that she lefte behynde hym in the towne
Without comforte or consolacyowne . . .
Wherfore Calchas, the storye sayth certayne,
In his wyttes many wayes caste
How he myght whyle the trewes doth laste   3690
Recure his doughter by some maner way.
And as I fynde, upon a certayne day,
In his porte wonder humbly

With wepynge eye wente pyteously
In complaynynge of terys albe reyned,
Whose inwarde wo sothly was nat feyned,
And on his knees anone he falleth downe
Tofore the great kynge Agamenowne,
Beseechynge hym with all humylyte,
Of very mercy and of hye pyte,   3700
With other kynges syttynge in the place,
To have routhe and for to do hym grace,
And on his woo to have compassyon
That he may have restytucyon
Of his doughter whom he loved so,
Prayinge them all theyr dever for to do
That thorugh theyr prudent medyacyon
For Anthenor that was in theyr pryson
With kynge Thoas she myght eschaunged be,
If that them lyst of theyr benygnyte   3710
To hys requeste goodly to assente.[1]
And they hym graunt and forth anon they sente
To kynge Pryamus for to have Cryseyde
For Calchas sake, and therwithall they leyde
The charge for hir wonder specyally
On them that went for this Embassatry
To Troye towne and to kynge Pryamus;
To whome Calchas was so odyus
So hatefull eke thorugh out all the towne,
That this reporte was of hym up and downe,   3720
That he a Traytour was and also false,
Worthy to be enhonged by the halse
For his Treson and his doubylnesse . . .

[The Trojans were unwilling to release Cryseyde, but finally]

Who ever grutche, the kynge in Parlement
Hath therupon gyven Jugement
So utterly it may nat be repelyd,
For with his worde the sentence was asselyd   3750
That she must parte with hir eyen glade.
And of the sorowe playnely that she made
At hir partynge hereafter ye shal here
Whan it agayne cometh to my matere.

[1] III.3.

¶ *Howe durynge a Trewes of thre Monthes Ector walked*
into the Grekes hooste, And of the communycacyon of Achylles
and hym. Ca. xxv.[1]

... Lyke as I rede, on a certayne daye
Whan agreable was the morowe graye,   3760
Blandysshynge and pleasaunt of delyte,
Ector in herte caught an appetyte
(Lyke as Guydo lyketh for to wryte)
The same day Grekes to vysyte
Full well besene and wonder rychely,
With many worthy in his company
Of suche as he for the nones ches;
And to the tent firste of Achylles
I fynde in sothe this Troyan knyght
Upon his stede toke the waye ryght   3770
Full lyke a man as made is mencyon.
    Nowe hadde Achylles great affeccyon
In his herte bothe day and nyght
Of worthy Ector for to have a syght;
For never his lyfe by none occasyon
He myght of hym have none inspeccyon
Nor hym behold at good lyberte,
For unarmed he myght hym never se.
But wonder knyghtly as well in porte and chere
They had them both as they mette in fere,   3780
And right manly in theyr countenaunce;
And at the laste they felle in Dalyaunce.
    But Achylles firste began abreyde,
And unto hym even thus he seyde:
Ector (quod he) full pleasynge is to me
That I at leyser naked may the se,
Syth I of the never myght have syght
But whan thou were armed as a knyght;
And now to me it shall be full grevous
Whiche am to the so inly envyous,   3790
But thou of me, there is no more to sayne,
Be slayne anone with my handes twayne;
For this in sothe were hoolly my pleasaunce
By cruell deth to take on the vengeaunce.
For I full ofte in werre and eke in fyght
Have felte the vertue and the great myght
Of thy force thorugh many woundes kene
That upon me be full fresshe and grene.

[1] IV.5.226–69.

In many place by shedynge of my blode
Thou were on me so furyous and wode 3800
Aye compassynge to my destruccyowne. . . .
So am I fret of envyous rage
That it may never in my breste aswage 3820
Tyll the vengeaunce and the fatall sute
Of cruell deth be on the execute.
   And of one thynge moost is my grevaunce,
Whan I have fully remembraunce
And in my mynde consyderyd up and downe,
Howe thou madest a dyvysyowne
Of me alas and of Patroclus,
So yonge, so manly and so vertuous,
Whom I loved, as it was skylle and ryght,
Ryght as my selfe with all my full myght, 3830
With as hole herte and inly kyndenesse
As an[y] tunge may telle or expresse.
Now haste thou made a departysyon
Of us that were by hole affeccyon
Yknet in one of hertely allyaunce
Without partynge or disseveraunce,
So entyerly our faythfull hertes twayne
Ylaced were and locked in a chayne
Whiche myght nat for none adversyte
Of lyfe nor deth a sonder twynned be 3840
Tyll cruelly thou madest us departe;
Which thurgh my herte so inwardly doth darte
That it wyll never in soth out of my thoughte,
And, truste well, full dere shalbe boughte
The deth of hym, and be no thynge in were
Paraventure or endydbe this yere;
For upon the oonly for his sake
Of cruell deth vengeaunce shalbe take.
I the ensure, without other bonde,
If I may lyve, with myn owne honde 3850
I shall of deth do execucyon
Without abode or longe delacyon . . .
   To whom Ector nat to hastely 3870
Answerde agayne with sobre countenaunce,
Avysed well in all his dalyaunce
As he that was in no thynge rekles;
And even thus he spake to Achylles:
   Syr Achylles, without any fayle

Thou oughtest nat in herte to mervayle
Though with my power and my full myght
With herte and wyll or very dewe ryght
Day by day I thy deth conspyre . . .

[He described the evil wrought by the Greeks and challenged
Achilles to single combat.]

[And] if it happe thorugh thy hye renowne   3970
Me to venqusshe or put at outtraunce,
I wyll you make fully assuraunce
That firste my lorde Pryamus the kynge
Shall unto Grekes in all maner thynge
With sceptre and crowne hoolly hym submytte,
And in a poynt varye nouther flytte
Fully to yelde to your subjeccyowne
All his lordshyp within Troye towne;
And his lyges in captyvyte
Shall go theyr way out of this cyte,   3980
And leve it quyte in your governaunce
Without stryfe or any varyaunce. . . .

But let the day atwene us two be joyned,   4010
As I have sayde in condycyowne—
If in diffence oonly of this towne
I have victorye by fortune on the,
I axe nat but anone that ye
Breke up sege and the werre lete,
And suffer us to lyve in quyete,
Into Grece home whan ye are gone.
    To whiche thynge Achylles anone
Hote in his Ire and furyous also
Brennynge full hote for anger and for wo   4020
Assentyd is with a despytous chere . . .
And for his parte he caste a glove downe
In sygne and token of confirmacyowne   4030
For lyfe or deth that he wyll holde his day
Agayne Ector happe what happe may.
    Unto the whiche Ector lyfly sterte
And toke it up with as glad an herte
As ever yet dyde man or knyght
That quarell toke with his foo to fyght.

[But their allies would not agree to stake all on one fight.]

Alas Fortune, gery [1] and unstable
And redy aye for to be chaungeable!
What folk most trust in thy stormy face
Lyke theyr desyre the fully to embrace,   4080
Than is thy joye away to tourne and wrythe
Upon wretches thy power for to kythe.—
Recorde on Troylus that fro the whele, so lowe
By false envye thou hast overthrowe
Out of the joye whiche that he was inne,
From his lady to make him for to twynne
Whan he best wende for to have be suryd.
And of the woo that he hath enduryd
I must nowe helpe hym to complayne,
Whiche, as his herte felte so great payne,   4090
So inwarde wo and so great distresse,
More than I have cunnynge to expresse
Whan he knewe the partynge of Cryseyde,
Almost for woo and for payne he deyde;
And fully wyste she departe shall
By sentence and Jugement fynall
Of his fader gyven in Parlyament.
For whiche, with wo and tourment all to rent,
He was in poynt to have fallen in rage
That no man myght apease nor aswage   4100
The hyd paynes whiche in his breste gan dare.
For lyke a man in furye he gan fare,
And suche sorowe day and nyght to make
In complaynynge oonly for hir sake;
For whan he saw that she shulde aweye
He lever hadde playnely for to deye
Than to lyve behynde in hir absence;
For hym thought without hir presence
He was but dede, there is no more to sayne.
And into terys he began to rayne   4110
With whiche his eyen gan for to bolle.
And in his breste the syghes up to swolle
And the sobbynge of his sorowes depe,
That he ne can but rore and wepe:
So sore love his herte gan constrayne. [2]
    And she ne felte nat a lytell payne,
But wepte also and pyteously gan crye,

---

[1] changeable.
[2] Cf. his moderation in IV.2–4.

Desyrynge aye that she myght dye
Rather than parte fro hym out of Troye,
Hir owne knyght, hir lust, hir lyves joye,   4120
That by hir chekes the terys downe distylle,
And fro hir eyen the rounde droppes trylle,
And all fordewed have hir blacke wede,
And eke untrussed hir heer abrode gan sprede
Lyke to golde wyre, forrent and all to torne,
Yplucked of and nat with sherys shorne. . . .
And aye amonge hir lamentacyowne   4135
Ofte sythe she fyll in a swowne downe,
Dedely pale fordymmed in hir syght,
And ofte sayde: Alas, myn owne knyght,
Myn owne Troylous, alas, why shall we parte?
Rather let deth wyth his spere darte
Thorugh my herte and the veynes kerve,
And with his rage do me for to stryve
Rather, alas, than from my knyght to twynne.
And of this wo, O deth, that I am inne,
Why ne wylt thou come and helpe make an ende?
For how shulde I out of Troye wende,
He abyde, and I to Grekes goon,
There to dwelle amonge my cruell foon?
Alas, alas, I wofull creature,
How shulde I there in the werre endure,   4150
I wretched woman, but my selfe alone
Amonge the men of armes everychone?
    Thus gan she crye all the longe day.
This was hir complaynte with full great afray;
Hir pyteous noyse till it drewe to nyght
That unto hir hir owne trewe knyght
Full tryste and hevy came agaynes eve,
If he myght hir comforte or leve.
    But he in sothe hath Cryseyde founde
All in a swowne lyinge on the grounde;   4160
And pyteously unto hir he went
With wofull chere and hir in armes hent
And toke hir up, and than atwene them two
Began of newe such a dedely wo
That it was routhe and pyte for to sene.
For she of chere pale was and grene
And he of coloure pyke to asshes dede . . .
So wofully atwene them two it stode   4170

For she ne myght nat a worde yspeke,
And he was redy with deth to be wreke
Upon hym selfe his naked swerde besyde ...
She was as stylle and dumbe as any stone;
He had a mouthe but wordes had he none ...
[And] in good fayth if I shulde aryght
The processe hole of theyr both sorowe
That they made tyll the next morowe,   4190
Fro poynt to poynt it to specefye,
It wolde me full longe occupye
Of every thynge to make mencyon,
And tarye me in my translacyon
If I shulde in hir wo procede.
But me semeth that it is no nede,
Syth my mayster Chaucer here afore
In this mater hath so well hym bore
In his boke of Troylus and Cryseyde,
Whiche he made longe or that he deyde ...   4200

[Lydgate summarises the story, how Troilus]

With great laboure firste he came to grace
And so contynueth by certayne yeres space   4220
Tyll fortune gan upon hym frowne
That she fro hym must go out of towne
All sodaynely and never hym after se.
Lo here the ende of false felycyte!
Lo here the end of worldely brotylnesse!
Of flesshely luste to here the unstablenesse!
Lo here the double varyacyon
Of worldly blysse and transmutacyon—
This daye in myrthe, and in wo to morowe!
For aye the fyne alas of joye is sorowe ...   4230
The hole storye Chaucer can you telle,
If that ye lyste, no man better alyve,   4235
Nor the processe halfe so well descryve;
For he our Englysshe gylte with his sayes,
Rude and boystous firste by olde dayes,
That was full fer from all parfeccyon
And but of lytell reputacyon   4240
Tyll that he came and thorugh his poetrye
Gan our tunge firste to magnefye
And adourne it with his eloquence.
To whom honoure, laude and reverence
Thorugh out this lande gyven be and songe,

So that the laurer of our Englysshe tonge
Be to hym gyven for his excellence . . .
   And where I lefte I wyll agayne of Troye   4264
The storye telle, and firste how that Guydo
Within his boke speketh Troylus to,
Rebukynge hym full uncurteysly
That he so sette his herte folyly
Upon Cryseyde full of doubylnesse.
For in his boke as Guydo lyste expresse,   4270
That hir terys and hir complaynynge,
Hir wordes whyte, softe and blandysshynge,
Were meynt with faynynge and with flaterye,
And outwarde farsed with many a false lye.
For under hyd was all the varyaunce
Curyd above with fayned countenaunce,
As women can falsely terys borowe
In theyr herte, though there be no sorowe,
Lyke as they wolde of very trouthe deye.
They can thynke on and another seye. . . .   4280
And though so be that with a wofull eye   4290
They can outwarde wepe pyteously,
The tother eye can laffe covertly,
Whose sorowes all are tempryed with allyes,
And theyr coloure ever is meynt with rayes.
For upon chaunge and mutabylyte
Stande hole theyr truste and theyr suerte,
So that they be sure in doublynesse,
And alway double in theyr sykernesse . . .

[Lydgate disagrees with this and cites instances of female constancy.]

And though Guydo wryte they have of kynde
To be double, men shulde it goodly take,
And there agayne no maner grutchyng make.   4400
Nature in werkynge hath full great powere,
And it were harde for any that is here
The course of hir to holde or restreyne,
For she wyll nat be gyded by no reyne
To be coarted of hir dewe ryght.
Therfore eche man with all his full myght
Shulde thanke God and take pacyently.
For if women he double naturelly
Why shulde men ley on them the blame?
For though myn Auctor hyndre so their name   4410

In his wrytynge oonly of Cryseyde,
And upon hir suche a blame leyde,
My counsayle is lyghtly over passe
Where myssayth of hir in any place.
To hyndre women, outher eve or morowe,
Take no hede, but let them be with sorowe,
And skyppe over where ye lyste nat rede
Tyll ye come where that Dyomede
For hir was sent into Troye towne,
Where ceryously is made mencyowne   4420
Firste how that she to hym delyvered was
For Anthenor and for the kynge Thoas,
And how Troylus gan hir to conveye
With many other to brynge hir on the weye,
And after this how that Dyomede
By the waye gan hir brydell lede
Tyll he hir broughte to hir faders tent;
And how Calchas in full good entent
Receyved hir lodgyd there he lay,
And of hir speche durynge all that day,   4430
And all the maner hole and everydele,
All is rehersed ceryously and wele
In Troylus boke as ye have herde me sayne.
To wryte it ofte I holde it were but vayne.
But Guydo sayth, longe or it was nyght
How Cryseyde forsoke hir owne knyght
And gave hir herte unto Dyomede
Of tendernesse and of womanhede
That Troylus were in hir herte as colde
Without fyre as ben these asshys olde.   4440
I can none other excusacyon
But oonly kyndes transmutacyon
That is appropryd unto hir nature,
Selde or never stable to endure,
By experyence as men may ofte lere.—
But nowe agayne to my matere. . . .

[After the truce was over the Trojans suffered grievously.]

And whyle Troyans constrayned were so narowe,
Were it with spere, quarell or arowe,
Ector was wounded thorugh out the vyser   4525
Into the face, that lyke a ryver
The rede blode downe began to rayle

But his harneys thorugh his aventayle,
Wherof astoned whan they hadde a syght
Full many Troyan toke hym to the flyght   4530
And to the Cyte faste gan them drawe
And at the chase full many one was slawe
Or they myght out of the felde remewe,
And ever in one Grekes after sewe
Unto the walles almost of the towne,
Tyll that Ector the Troyan champyowne
Of his knyghthode gan to take hede.
Albe his wounde sore gan to blede,
Yet of manhode he gan them recomforte
And maugre them into the felde resorte,   4540
Namely whan he hadde inspeccyowne
On the walles and toures of the towne
How that Eleyne and Eccuba the quene
And his suster fayre Polycene
With many other lady gan beholde,
Hym thought anone his herte gan to colde
Of very shame his knyghtes shulde fle,
And lyke a Lyon in his cruelte
He made them tourne manly everychone . . .[1]   4549

[Hector killed Meryon and was himself attacked by Achilles, but retaliated.]

And on his creste that shone so bryght and clere
With suche a myght Ector hath hym smet
That he percyd thorughe his basenet
And racede eke from his aventayle
With that stroke many pece of mayle,   4570
That Achylles constrayned was of nede
Maugre his myght to stagre on his stede,
To enclyne and to bowe his backe.

[Hector warned Achilles that sooner or later he would kill him. Troylus slew six hundred men, but was attacked by Diomed.]

Whan Dyomede came with his meyne   4620
And many worthy rydynge hym aboute,
And Troylus mette amonges all the route
All sodaynely of hap or adventure
And hym unhorseth as it were his eure;
And after that anone he hent his stede

[1] Cf. I.2.1–36.

And bad a squyer that he shulde it lede
Unto Cryseyde oonly for his sake
Besechynge hir that she wolde it take
As for a gyfte of hir owne man,[1]
Syth he that day for hir love it wan   4630
Amyd the felde thorugh his great myght
Of hym that was whylom hir owne knyght;
And he in haste on his waye is went
And herof made unto hir present,
Prayinge hir in full humble wyse
This lytell gyfte that she nat despyse
But it receyve for a remembraunce
And with all this that it be pleasaunce
Or very pyte and of womanhede
On hir servaunt called Dyomede   4640
To remembre, that was become hir knyght.
And she anone with herte glad and lyght
Full womanly bad hym repayre agayne
Unto his lorde and playnely to hym sayne
That she ne myght of very kyndenesse
Of womanhede nor of gentyllesse,
Refuse hym platly from hir grace
That was to hir there in straunge place
So kynde founde and so counfortable
In every thynge, and so servycable.   4650

[Diomed grew sick with love and she kept him in doubt.]

But cunnyngly and in full sleyghty wyse
To kepe hym lowe under hir servyse,   4840
With delayes she helde hym forthe on honde,
And made hym in a weer to stonde
Full unsure betwene hope and dispayre.
And whan that grace shulde have had repayre
To put hym out of all hevynesse,
Daunger of newe brought hym in distresse,
And with a disdayne to encrease his payne,
Of double weer she brought hym in a trayne,
As women kan holde a man ful narowe
Whan he is hurte with cupydes arowe,   4850
To sette on hym many felle assayes,
Day by day to put hym in delayes
To stond unsure betwyxe hope and drede

[1] V.5.1–5.

Right as Cryseyde left Dyomede
Of entent to sette hym more a fyre . . .[1]
And in doute thus I lette hym dwelle,
And forth I wyll of the storye telle . . .   4868

¶ *Howe Andromecha Ectors wyfe hadde a vysyon in hir slepe that and hir*
housbonde fought on the morowe that he shuld be slayne. The whiche wold
not byleve hir, nouther fader nor moder. And how Achylles slewe hym.
Ca. xxvii.

[The Greeks, afflicted with a pestilence, obtained a truce for thirty
days.]

Whan the moreyne and the wofull rage
Of Pestylence began for to aswage
And the trewes were wered out and goon . . .   4890
Andronomccha thc faythfull trewe wyfe
Of worthy Ector hym lovynge as hir lyfe
By whom he hadde gete children two
Wonder semely and inly fayre also,   4900
And Lamedoute called was the tone,
So yonge the tother that it ne myght gone,
And Astronanta I rede that he hyghte,
Fetured well and passynge fayre of syghte,
And, as Guydo lysteth to endyte,
Of his moder at the pappes whyte
For very yonge that tyme was soukynge,
And with his arme hir brestys embrasynge,
And she that nyght, as made is mencyon,
Hadde in hir slepe a wonder vysyon . . .   4910
For in sothenesse slepynge as she lay,
Hir thoughte playnely if the next day
Ector went his fomen for to assayle
As he was wonte, armed in batayle,   4920
That he ne shulde escape utterly
In Fatys hondes to falle fynally . . .
Of whiche astonyd, streyght and short of breth
Where as she lay abrayde up on the deth,   4930
And with a syghe stynte for to slepe
And pytously braste out for to wepe
For the constraynte of hir hertely sorowe,
And specyally on the wofull morowe
Whan that she sawe this stocke of worthynesse
As he was wonte manfully hym dresse

[1] As in V.2.94–8.

To arme hym in stele borned bryght,
This Troyan wall, Ector, this worthy knyght,
She can no more, but at his fete felle downe
Lowly declarynge hir avysyowne   4940
With quakynge herte of very womanhede.[1]
Wherof god wote he toke lytell hede
But therof hadde indygnacyon
Platly affermynge that no discrecyon
Was to truste in suche fantasyes . . .
For drede of whiche the Lamentacyon   4956
Encrease gan of Andronomecha
And in hir swowne firste she cryed A[h]!
Sayeng, Alas, myn owne lorde so dere,
Your trewe wyfe, alas, why ne wyll ye here,   4960
Whiche of so faythfull hoole affeccyon
Desyreth aye your savacyon?
And up she rose, dedely of vysage,
And lyke a woman caught with sodayne rage
To kynge Pryam and Eccuba the quene
In haste she went hir selfe to bemene,
And of hir wyfely herte trewe as stele
Ceryously declared every dele
Hir pyteous dreme whiche thorugh myracle
To hir oonly by devyne oracle   4970
Ishewed was thorugh goddes purveaunce,
And tolde them eke the fynall ordynaunce
Of Fortunes false disposycyon
Fully purveyed to destruccyon
Of hir lorde without more delay,
Into the felde if he go that day. . . .

[Priam ordered Hector not to fight, but he persisted]

So hole in manhode was his herte sette   5045
Thate he anone without lenger lette
Agayne to arme hym was full dylygent,
Agayne the precept and commaundement
Of his Fader, and rode forth on his weye[2];
For fere of whiche, as she wolde deye,   5050
His wyfe of newe crye gan and shoute,
And with hir pappes also hangynge oute,
Hir lytell childe in hir armes twayne,

---

[1] V.3.1–12.
[2] V.3.62–70.

Afore hir lorde gan to wepe and playne,
Besechynge hym of routhe and pyte
If he wolde unto hir sorowe se,
At the leste for hir wyfely trouthe
That he of manhode have in herte routhe
Upon hir childe and on hir also
Whiche that she bare in hir armes two   5060
And nat myght hym from cryinge kepe
Whan he sawe his wofull moder wepe;
And knelynge downe unto him she sayde
In hir sobbynge as she myght abrayde:
Myne owne lorde, have mercy nowe on me
And on this lytell childe whiche that ye se
So pyteously afore you wepe and crye.
Have mercy, lorde, on us or we dye,
Have mercy eke upon this cyte,
Myn owne lorde, have mercy, or that we   5070
By cruell deth passe shall echone
For lacke of helpe, alas, whan ye are gone.
    This was the crye of Andromecha
With whom was eke hir suster Cassandra,[1]
Eccuba and fayre Polycene
And Eleyne the lusty fresshe quene,
Whiche all attones felle hym beforne
With heer untressyd and wepynge all to torne,
And loude gan to crye in the place,
Besechynge hym of mercy and of grace   5080
For thylke day to abyde in the towne . . .

[Andromache went again to Priam and he forced his son to stay
behind when Troilus and others went out to do great deeds. When
Margareton was slain however, Hector rushed out into the fight.]

But all this tyme Ector up and downe   5325
As he was wont playeth the lyowne
Amonge Grekes in many sondry place,
And with his swerde gan them so to enchace
That as the deth where they myght hym seen
They fledde afore hym lyke a swarme of been;
For none so hardy was hym to with sette.
And in this whyle a Grekysshe kynge he mette,
Were it of hap or of adventure,
The whiche in sothe on his Cote armure

---

[1] V.3.7-25.

Enbrouded hadde full many ryche stone
That gave a lyght whan the sonne shone
Full bryght and clere that joye was to sene,
For Perlys whyte and Emerawdys grene
Full many one were there in sette,
And on the cercle of his basenette, 5340
And rounde envyrowne of his aventayle,
In velvet fret all above the mayle,
Saffres ynde and other stones rede
Of arraye whan Ector taketh hede
Towardes hym faste gan hym drawe.
And firste I fynde howe he hath hym slawe,
And after that by force of his manhede
He hent hym up afore hym on his stede
And fast gan with hym for to ryde
From the wardes a lytell out asyde, 5350
At good leyser playnely if he may
To spoyle hym of his rych array,
Full glad and lyght of his newe Empryse.[1]
But out, alas, on false covetyse
Whose gredy fret the whiche is great pyte
In hertes may nat lyghtly staunched be!
The Etyk gnaweth by so great distresse
That it defaceth the hye worthynesse
Full ofte sythe of these conqueroures,
And of theyr fame rent away the floures . . . 5360
Lyke as ye may now of Ector rede 5370
That sodaynely was brought to his endynge
Oonly for spoylynge of this ryche kynge.
For of desyre to hym that he hadde
On hors backe out whan he hym ladde
Reklesly, the storye maketh mynde,
He caste his shelde at his backe behynde[2]
To welde hym selfe at more lyberte,
And for to have opportunyte
To spoyle hym and for no wyght spare;
So that his breste disarmed was and bare. 5380
Except his plates there was no diffence
Agayne the stroke to make resystence.
Alas, why was he tho so rekles,
This floure of knyghthode, of manhode pereles,

---

[1] V.6.27–31.
[2] Cf. V.8.1–4.

Whan that his foo all that ylke day
For hym alone in awayte so lay,
If in myschefe of hate and of envye
In the felde he myght hym ought espye.
  This Achylles, cruell and venymous,
Of hertely hate moste melancolyous,   5390
Whiche covertely hovynge hym besyde,
Whan that he sawe Ector disarmed ryde
He hente a spere sharpe grounde and kene,
And of Ire in his hatefull tene
All unwarely or Ector myght adverte,
Alas the whyle! he smote hym to the herte
Thorugh out the breste, that dede he fylle downe
Unto the erthe, this Troyan champyowne,
Thorugh neclygence oonly of his shelde.[1]
The deth of whom, whan Odemon behelde,   5400
The worthy kynge myght hym nat refrayne
But to Achylles rode with all his payne
And hyt hym so amyd of all the prees,
Maugre the myght of his Myrundones,
That for dede Guydo sayth certayne
Of that wounde he fyll grofelyng on the playne.[2]
But his knyghtes on a shelde alofte
They layde hym, and caryed hym full softe
Unto his tent in all the haste they can;
And there I leve this dedely wounded man   5410
Full sore syke tyll he may releve.
And after that, whan it drewe to eve,
They of Troye with great reverence
Dyde theyr laboure and theyr dylygence
The dede corps to carye into towne
Of worthy Ector, whan Tytan went downe;
And to the temple dolefully they wende,
And of that day this was the wofull ende.
I can no more, but thus the longe nyght
In hevynesse, as it is skylle and ryght,   5420
I wyll them leve and agayne retourne
To my mater, to helpe them for to mourne.

¶ *Of the complaynt that Lydgate maketh for the deth of the worthy Ector.*
Cap. xxviii.

---

[1] Cf. V.8.5–10, and the killing of Troilus below.
[2] Contrast V.8.21–22.

13—N.D.S.S.

[Lydgate says that he cannot call on the Muses to help him write this]

For no discorde is founde them amonge;   5436
In theyr musyke they be entunyd so
It fytte them noughte for to helpe in wo,
Nor with maters that be with mournyng shent,
As Tragedyes all to tore and rent   5440
In complaynynge pyteously in rage
In the Theatre with a dede vysage.[1]
To them, alas, I clepe dare nor crye
My troubled penne of grace for to guye,
Nouther to Clyo nor Callyope,
But to Allecto and Thesyphone,
And Megera that ever doth complayne
As they that lyve ever in wo and payne
Eternally and in tourment dwelle
With Cerberus depe downe in helle,   5450
Whom I must praye to be gracyous
To my mater whiche is so furyous.

[He describes the mourning for Hector, the embalming of his body,
and the tomb they made for him.]

Book IV

[Achilles, having fallen in love with Polyxena, refused to fight
against the Trojans, and rejected the arguments of Ulysses and
other nobles sent to ask for his aid.[2] Diomed did great deeds in battle
until he met Troilus.]

This Troylus rode and smote hym on the breste   2060
So myghtely that of very nede
Downe of his horse he smote Dyomede
Albe of wounde he hadde no damage,
And furyously Troylus in his rage
Of envye gan hym to abreyde
Whan he was downe, the love of Creseyde,
Of his deceyte and his Trecherye;
And Grekes than faste gan them hye
Amonge the hors in myschefe where he lay
To drawe hym out in all the haste they may,   2070
And on a shelde, brosyd and affrayde,
They bare hym home, so he was dismayde

---

[1] Lydgate knew Seneca's tragedies.
[2] Cf. III.3.191–216.

Of the stroke, home unto his Tent . . .

[Agamemnon obtained another truce.]

In whiche tyme of very womanhede   2132
Creseyde lyst no lenger for to tarye,
Though hir Fader were therto contrarye,
For to vysyte and to have a syght
Of Dyomede that was become hir knyght,
Which had of Troylus late caught a wounde,
And in his Tent whan she hath hym founde,
Benygnely upon his beddes syde
She set hir downe in the selfe tyde,   2140
And platly caste in hir owne thought
Touchynge Troylus that it was for nought
To lyve in hope of any more recure,
And thought she wold for no thynge be unsure
Of purveaunce nor without store;
She gave anone without any more
Hooly hir herte upon Dyomede.
Lo, what pyte is in womanhede,
What mercy eke and benygne routhe,
That newly can all hir olde trouthe   2150
Of nature lette slyppe asyde
Rather than they shulde se abyde
Any man in myschefe for theyr sake . . .

[Achilles lent his Myrmidons to Agamemnon, but Paris and Troilus
slew or wounded many of them]

And to Achilles lyenge in his tent,   2337
They repeyre forwounde and to rent,
Theyr herneys broke, bothe plate and mayle,
And of nombre I fynde that they fayle   2340
An hondred knyghtes slayne and deed, alas,
That after were founde in the Taas
Amyd the felde thorugh gyrt with many wounde
Of Troylus swerde, Ector the secounde.
Wherof Achilles whan he hadde a syght
So hevy was all the nexte nyght
In his bedde walowynge to and fro,
Devoyde of slepe for constreynt of his wo,
At his herte his wounde was so kene,
What for his men and fayre Polycene,   2350
Wyttynge well, if he dyde his payne

To be venged, he shulde nat attayne
In no wyse unto his desyre.
And thus he brent in a double fyre
Of love and Ire that made hym syghe sore.
But for the cause love was the more,
He was aferde agayne them of the towne
In his persone to do offencyowne,
Lyste Pryamus and Eccuba the quene
Offended were, and namely Polycene.   2360
And thus he stode in a double weer,
That at his herte satte hym wonder neer
With many wonder dyvers fantasye,
As have lovers that be in poynt to dye.[1]
Ryght even so fareth this wofull man
For very woo that no rede ne can . . .

¶ *How Achylles slewe the worthy Troylus Ectors brother unknyghtly, and
trayled hym aboute the felde at his hors tayle. Cap. xxxi.*

[When he saw the Greeks in danger of utter defeat, and was re-
proached for doing nothing, he forgot his love, rushed into the fight,
and was wounded by Troilus.]

For whan Achylles of his woundes grene   2622
Was fully curyd by a certayne day
He gan compasse in all that ever he may,
And ymagyne in his envyous herte
To be vengyed of his woundes smerte
Upon Troylus that stacke aye in his mynde,
At avauntage if he myght hym fynde.
To hym he bare so passyngly hatrede
In his herte brennynge as the glede   2630
Whiche day nor nyght may in no degre
Fully be queynt tyll he avengyd be.
The hoote rancour gan so on hym gnawe,
Avysed platly that he shalbe slawe
Of his hondes whan so that it falle.
And on a day to hym he gan calle
Myrundones his knyghtes everychone. . . .
Besechynge them for to do theyr payne   2650
Agayne this Troylus in the felde that day,
To catche hym at myschefe if they may,
And besely to do theyr dyllygence

---

[1] III.3.310–111.

On hym to have theyr full advertence
By one assent where so that he ryde;
All other thynge for to sette asyde,
And of nought ellys for to take hede
Saufe fynally agayne hym to procede;
If they myght catche hym in a trappe,
Within them selfe Troylous for to clappe,   2660
To enclose and sette hym rounde aboute
In all wyse that he go nat oute,[1]
And whan he were beset amonge them alle,
Nat to slee hym what so ever falle,
But thorugh theyr myght manly hym conserve
Tyll he hym selfe come and make hym sterve
With his swerde, he and none other wyght.
　　Loo here a manhode for to preyse aryght!
Vengeaunce of deth, of rancoure and of pryde,
Compassyd treason, knyghthode layde asyde,   2670
Worthynesse by envye slawe,
Falshede alofte, trauthe abacke ydrawe.
Alas, in armes that he shulde falle
Of Trecherye, there the bytter galle.
Shoulde in this worlde many knyght be founde
That be to trauthe of theyr ordre bounde.
Alas, alas, for now this Achylles
Conspyred hath with his Myrundones
The deth of one the worthyest wyght
That ever was, and the beste knyght.   2680
Alas for wo, my herte I fele dede
For his sake this story whan I rede . . .

[Troilus made havoc among the Greeks till noon.]

Whan Myrundones gadred all in one   2715
In compasse wyse rounde aboute hym gone
And furyously of one entencyowne
They made a cercle aboute hym envyrowne
Whan they sawe hym of helpe desolate;
But he of herte nat disconsolate   2720
Upon no syde, thorugh his manlyhede
Lyke a Lyon toke of them no hede,
But thorugh his famous knyghtly excellence
As a Tygre stondeth at diffence,
And manfully gan them to encoumbre,

[1] Used against Hector, V.7.1–8.

And gan to lesse and discrease theyr noumbre;
And some he maymeth and wounded to the dethe,
And some he made to yelde up the brethe,
And some he layde to the erth lowe,
And some he made for to overthrowe　　　　　2730
With his swerde of theyr blode all wete
At great myschefe under his hors fete
Upon his stede sturdy as a wall.
This worthy knyght, this man most marcyall
Playeth his pley amonge Myrundones,
Hym selfe, god wot, alone, all helpeles.
But tho, alas, what myght his force avayle
Whan thre thousand knyghtes hym assayle
On every parte bothe in lengthe and brede.
And cowardly firste they slewe his stede　　　　2740
With theyr sperys sharpe and quare grounde,
For whiche, alas, he stante now on the grounde
Without reskus, refute or socoure,
That was that day of Chyvalrye floure.
But welawaye, they have hym so beset
That from his hede they smote his basenet
And brake his harneys as they hym assayle,
And severe of stele the myghty stronge mayle.
He was disarmed both necke and hede,
Alas the whyle, and no wyght toke none hede　　2750
Of all his knyghtes longynge to the towne,
And yet alway this Troyan Champyowne
In knyghtly wyse, naked as he was,
Hym selfe diffendeth, tyll Achylles, alas,
Came rydynge in furyous and wode,
And whan he sawe how Troylus stode
Of longe fyghtynge awaped and amate,
And from his folke alone desolate,
Sole by hymselfe, at myschefe pyteously,
This Achylles wonder cruelly　　　　　　　2760
Behynde unwarely or that he toke hede,
With his swerde smyteth of his hede
And caste it forthe, of cruelly cursyd herte,
And thought platly it shulde hym nat asterte
To shewe his malys, this wolfe unmercyable,
Full unknyghtly to be more vengeable,
Upon the body that lay deed and colde.
Alas, that ever it shulde of knyght be tolde,

Wryte or rehersed to do so foule a dede,
Or in a boke, alas, that men shall rede   2770
Of any knyght a story so horryble,
Unto the erys passyngly odyble.
For this Achylles of cruelte, alas,
The deed corps toke out of the taas
And vengeably bonde it as I fynde
At the tayle of his hors behynde,
And hatefully that every wyght behelde,
Drewe it hym selfe endelonge the felde
Thorugh the renges and the wardes alle.[1]
     But O, alas, that ever it shulde falle   2780
A knyght to be in herte so cruell,
Or of hatrede so despytous fell,
To drawe a man after he were dede!
     O thou Omer, for shame be now rede
And be astoned, that holdest thy self so wyse,
On Achylles to sette such a pryse
In thy bokes, for his Chyvalrye.
Above echone doest hym magnefye
That was so sleyghty and so full of fraude.
Why gyvest thou hym so hye a pryse and laude?   2790
Certys Omer, for all thyne excellence
Of Rethoryke and of Eloquence,
Thy lusty songes and thy dytees smerte,
Thy hony mouthe that doth with sugre flete,
Yet in one thynge thou greatly arte to blame,
Causeles to gyve hym suche a name
With a tytle of Tryumphe and glorye;
So passyngly put hym in memorye
In thy bokes to saye and wryte so
Thurgh his knyghthod he slewe Ectorys two;   2800
Firste hym that was lyke unto none other,
And Troylus after that was his owne brother.
If thou arte meved of affeccyon
Whiche that thou haste to Grekes nacyon
To preyse hym so for thou canste endyte,
Thou shuldest aye for any favour wryte
The trouthe playnely, and be indifferent,
And saye the sothe clerely of entent.
For whan he slewe Ector in the felde
He was afore disarmed of his shelde,   2810

[1] Cf. Hector's body, V.10.4–5.

And besy eke in spoylynge of a kynge.
For if he hadde beware of his commynge
He hadde hym quyt, thorugh his Chyvalrye,
His false deseyt and his Trecherye,
That he ne hadde so lyghtly from hym gone.
Troylus also was naked and alone
Amyd thre thousande closyd and beshet
Whan Achylles hath his hede ofsmet
At his backe, of full cruell herte,
Whan he no thynge his treason dyde adverte.   2820
Was that a dede of a manly knyght,
To slee a man forweryed in fyght,
Faynt of travayle all the longe daye
Amonge so many stondynge at a bay,
A kynges sone and so hye borne,
Naked the hede, his armure all to torne,
Even at the deth on the selfe poynt
At disavauntage and playnely out of joynt
Of his lyfe standynge on the wrake? . . .
    Wherfore Omer preyse hym now no more;
Late nat his pryse thy ryall boke difface,   2835
But in all haste his renowne out arrace. . . .

[Achilles and his Myrmidons killed Menon in a similar way, but Achilles was killed by Paris and his body thrown to the dogs. Later Paris and Ajax Telamon killed each other.]

IV. Source

From THE RECUYELL OF THE HISTORYES OF TROYE

by Raoul Lefevre, translated by William Caxton (c. 1474).

Here begynneth the volume intituled and named the recuyell of the historyes of Troye composed and drawen out of dyverce bookes of latyn in to frensshe by the ryght venerable persone and worshipfull man. Raoul le ffevre . . . And translated and drawen out

of frensshe in to englysshe by Willyam Caxton mercer
of the cyte of London . . . Whiche sayd translacion and
werke was begonne in Brugis in the Countre of Flaundres
the fyrst day of marche the yere of the Incarnacion of
our said Lord god a thousand foure hundred sixty and
eyghte And ended and fynysshed in the holy cyte of
Colen the.xix. day of septembre the yere of our sayd
lord god a thousand foure honderd sixty and enleven.

BOOK III

¶ *How the kynge Priant reediffied the cyte of Troye more stronge than ever
hit was afore & of his sones and doughters. And how after many counceyllis
he sente Anthenor and Polydamas in to Grece for to remande his suster
Exione that Ayax mayntenyd.*

For to entre than in to the matere. Ye have herd here to fore at
the seconde destruccion of Troye how Hercules had taken prysonner
Priamus the sone of kynge Laomedon, and had put hym in prison.
How be hit Dares of Frigie sayth that his fader had sente hym to
meve warre in a strange contrey where he had ben right longe,
wherfore he was not at that disconfiture. This Pryamus had espowsid
and weddyd a moche noble lady doughter of Egypseus, kynge of
Trace, of whom he had fyve sones and thre doughters of grete beaulte.
The fyrste of the sones was named Hector, the most worthy & beste
knyght of the world. The second sone was named Parys and to
surname Alixandre, the whiche was the fayrest knyght of the world
and the beste shoter and drawer of a bowe. The thyrde was callyd
Deyphebus, ryght hardy and discrete. The fourthe was named
Helenus, a man of grete scyence and knewe all the artes lyberall.
The fifth & the laste was callid Troyllus that was one of the beste
knyghtes & aspre that was in his tyme.

Virgile recounteth that he had two other sonnes by hys wyf of
whom that one was named Polidorus. This Polidorus was sente by
kynge Pryamus with a grete foyson of gold unto a kynge his frende
for to have ayde ayenst the Grekes. But this kyng, seeyng that the
kynge Pryamus was at myschief ayenst the Grekes and also he beyng
mevyd with covetise, slew Polidorus and buryed hym in an ysle of
the see. That other sone was named Gaminedes, whom Jupiter
ravyshid and maad hym hys botyller in the stede of Hebe the
doughter of Juno whome he putte oute of that sayd office. The
eldest of the doughters of kynge Pryamus was named Cheusa,
whiche was wyf unto Eneas. And this Eneas was sone of Anchises

and of Venus of Munidie. The seconde doughter was named Cassandra and was a ryght noble vyrgyne, aourned [1] and lerned with scyences and knew thynges that were for to come. And the thirde was named Polixena that was the fayrest doughter and the beste fourmed that was knowen in alle the world. Yet above thise chyldren here to fore rehercid, Kyng Pryant had thretty bastard sones by dyverce women, that were valyant knyghtes, noble and hardy.

Whan than kyng Pryant was in a strange contrey occupied in the fete of warre (the quene and her children were with hym), the tidynges cam to hym that the kyng Laomeden his fader was slayn, his cyte destroyed, hys noble men put to deth, their doughters brought in servitude, and also his suster Exiona. Of thise tidynges he had grete sorowe, and wepte largely and made many lamentacions. . . .

[Priam's Troy]

In this cyte were sixe pryncipall gates, of whome that one was named Dardane, the seconde Tymbria, the thirde Helyas, the fourthe Chetas, the fifthe Troyenne and the sixthe Antenorides.[2] These gates were right grete and fayre and of stronge deffence. And ther were in the cyte ryche palayces with oute nombre the fayrest that ever were, and the fayrest houses ryche and well compassed. Also ther were in many parties of the cyte dyverse fayr places and playsaunt for the cytezeyns to esbatre[3] and playe. In this cyte were men of alle craftes and marchauntes that wente and cam fro alle the partyes of the world. In the myddell of the cyte ranne a grete ryver named Paucus whiche bare shyppis and dide grete prouffit and solace unto the habitaunts. Whan this cyte was thus made, the kyng Pryant dide do come alle the peple and habytaunts of the contre ther aboutes, and maad them dwelle in the cyte. And there come so many that ther was never cyte better aourned wyth peple and with noble men and cytezeyns than hit was. There were founden many games and playes as the chesse playe, the tables and the dyse and other dyverse games. In the moste apparaunt place of the cyte upon a roche the kynge Pryant dide do make hys ryche palays that was named Ylyon, that was one of the rycheste palays and stronge that ever was in the world. And hyt was of heyght fyve honderd paas wyth oute the heyghte of the towres, wherof was grete plente and so hyghe that hit semed to them that sawe hem fro ferre that they rought unto the hevene.[4]

[1] adorned.
[2] *TC*, Prol. 15-17.
[3] sport.
[4] Hence Marlowe's 'topless towers'.

¶ *How the kynge Pryant assemblid all his barons for to knowe whome he myght sende in to Grece for to gete agayn his suster Exione. And how Hector answerd and of his good counceyll. And how Parys exposed to hys fader the vysion and the promesse of the goddesse Venus &c.*

Whan the kynge Priaunt was thus adcertayned of the hate of the Grekes & by no fayr mene he coude recovere his suster, he was mevyd with grete yre and thoughte that he wold sende a grete navye in to Grece for to hurte and domage the Grekes . . .

[He addressed his sons in council.]

My sones ye have well in your memorye the deth of your grantfader, the servytude of your Aunte Exione, that men holdeth by your lyving in manere of a comyn woman. And ye be so puyssant me semeth that rayson shold enseygne yow for to employe yow to avenge this grete injurye and shame. And yf thys meve yow not therto, yet ye ought to do hyt to satysfye my wyll and pleasyr ffor I dye for sorowe and anguyssh to whiche ye ought and ben bounde for to remedye to your power, that have do yow so well be nourysshyd and brought furth. And thou, Hector, my ryght dere sone, that art the oldeste of thy bretherin, the moste wyse and the moste stronge: I praye the fyrst that thou empryse to putte in execucion thys my wyll, and that thou be duc and prynce of thy bretherin in thys werke, and alle the other shall obeye gladly unto the. And in lyke wyse shall doo alle they of this royame for the grete prowesse that they knowe in the. And knowe that from this day forth I dispoylle me of alle thys werke and putte hyt upon the that arte the moste stronge and aspre to mayntene the batayles. And I am auncyent and olde and may not forth on helpe my self so well as I was wonte to doo &c.

To these wordes answerd Hector right sobrely and swetely, saying, 'My fader and my ryght dere and soverayn lord, ther is none of alle your sones but that hit semeth to hym thyng humayne to desyre vengeance of thyse injuryes. And also to us that ben of hyghe noblesse a lytyll injurye ought to be grete. As hit is so that the qualyte of the persone groweth and mynnyssheth, so oughte the qualyte of the injurye.[1] And yf we desyre and have appetite to take vengeance of our injuryes, we forsake not ne leve the nature humayne, ffor in lyke wyse do and usen the dombe bestes in the same manyere, and nature enseigneth and gyveth hem therto. My ryght dere lord and fader, ther is none of alle your sones that oughte more to desyre the vengeance of the injurye & deth of our ayeul or granfader[2] than I,

---

[1] Cf. II.2.25–28.
[2] Laomedon, killed by Hercules.

that am the oldeste. But I will yf hit plese yow that ye considere in this empryse not onely the begynnyng but also the myddell and the ende to what thyng we may come here after, ffor otherwhyle lityll prouffyten some thynges well begonne that come unto an evyll ende. Than me thynketh that hit is moche more alowable to a man to absteine hym for to begynne thinges wherof the endes ben daungerous and wherof may come more evyll than good, ffor the thynge is not sayd ewrous or happy unto the tyme that hit come unto a good ende. I saye not thyse thynges for ony evyll or cowardyse, but onely to the ende that ye begynne not a thyng, and specyally that thynge that ye have on your herte to put hit lightly in ewre, but that ye fyrst be well counceyllyd . . . Exyone is not of so hyghe pryse that hit behoveth alle us to put us in peryll and doubte of deth for her. She hath ben now longe tyme there, where she is yet. Hit were better that she parforme forth her tyme, that I trowe hath but lityl tyme to lyve, than we sholde put us alle in suche peryllys. And mekely I beseche yow not to suppose in no maner that I saye these thynges for cowardyse, but I doubte the tournes of fortune and that under the shadowe of thys thynge she not bete ne destroye youre grete seignourye, and that we ne begynne thynge that we ought to leve for to eschewe more grete myschyef' &c:.

Whan Hector had maad an ende of hys answer, Parys was no thynge well contente therwyth. He stode up on hys feet and sayd in thys wyse: 'My ryght dere lord, I beseche yow to here me saye to what ende ye may come yf ye begynne the warre agaynst the Grekes. How be not we garnysshid of so many and noble chyvalrye as they ben? Certes that bee we, whyche in alle the world is none that may disconfyte. And therfore begynne ye hardely that empryse that ye have thoughte, and sende of your shyppis and of your peple to renne in Grece and to take the peple and domage the contre. And yf hyt please yow to sende me, I shall doo hit wyth a good wyll and herte, for I am certayne that yf ye sende me, that I shall doo grete domage unto the Grekes. And I shall take some noble lady of Grece and brynge her with me in to this royame. And by the comutacion of her ye may recovere your suster Exione. And yf ye wyll understand and knowe how I am certayn of this thynge, I shall saye hit to yow how the goddes have promysid hit to me . . .

[He told his vision of the goddesses.]

So than I saye yow this to the ende that ye sende me in to Grece, and that ye may have joye of that I shall doo there' &c.

After Parys spacke Deyphebus in thys manyere: 'My ryght dere lorde, yf in alle the werkys that men shold begynne, men shold avyse in all the particularytees and synguler thynges that myght happe or falle, ther shold never enterpryse ner no feet be doon ner maad by hardynes . . . Ye may not beleve better counceyll than that councel that Paris hath gyven to yow, ffor yf he brynge ony noble ladye, ye may lightly for to yelde her agayn have agayn your suster Exione, for whome we all suffre vilonye ynowhe.' After this spake Helenus, the fourthe sone of kyng Pryant, that said thus: 'Ha, ha, right puissant kynge and right soverayn domynatour upon us your humble subgettes & obeyssant sones, beware that coveytise of vengance put not yow in suche daunger as lyeth herein. Ye know well how I knowe and can the scyence to knowe the thynges future and to come, as ye have provyd many tymes with oute fyndyng fawte. The goddes forbede, that hit never come that Parys be sente in to Grece, ffor knowe ye for certayn that yf he goo to make ony assault ye shall see this noble and worshipfull cyte destroyed by the Grekes, the Troyans slayn and we alle that ben your chyldren.[1] . . .

Whan the kyng herde Helenus thus speke he was all abasshid and began to countrepeyse and thynke, and helde his peas and spake not of a grete whyle. And so dyde alle the other. Than arose upon his feet Troylus, the yongest sone of kynge Pryant, and began to speke in this manyere: 'O noble men and hardy, how be ye abasshid for the wordes of this coward preste here.[2] Is hit not the custome of prestes for to drede the batoylles by pusillanymyte and for to love the delyces and to fatte and encrasse hem & fylle their belyes with good wynes and wyth good metys? Who is he that belevyth that ony man may knowe the thynges to come but yf the goddes shewe hit hem by revelacion? Hyt is but folye for to tarye upon thys or to beleve suche thynges. Yf Helenus be a ferd, late hym goo in to the temple and synge the dyvyne servyce. And late the other take vengeance of their injuryes by force of armes. O ryght dere fader and lord, wherfore art thou so troublid for these wordes? Sende thy shippis in to Grece and thy knyghtes wyse and hardy, that may rendre to the Grekes theyr injuryes that they have doon to us.' All they that herde Troylus thus speke, they alowed hym sayng that he had well spoken. And thus they fynysshid their parlament and wente to dyner.

[Despite the prophecies of a knight named Pantheus it was resolved to send Paris against Greece.]

Whan this conclusion was comen to the knowleche of Cassandra, the doughter of kynge Pryant, she began to make so grete sorowe as

[1] Cf. Helenus's part in II.2.33–36.
[2] II.2.37 'brother priest'.

she had be folyssh or oute of her mynde, and began to crye an hyghe, sayng, 'Ha, ha, right noble cyte of Troye, what fayerye hath mevyd the to be brought to suche paryllis, for whiche thou shalt in shorte tyme be beten doun and thyne hyghe tourys ben demolisshid and destroyed unto the ground.[1] Ha, ha, quene Hecuba, for what synne hast thou deservyd the deth of thy children whiche shall be cruell and horrible. Wherfore detournest not thou Paris fro goyng in to Grece, whiche shall be cause of this evyll aventure?' And whan she had so cryed, she wente to her fader the kynge. And with wepyng, drowned in terys, prayd hym that he shold deporte hym and leve his empryse, and that she wiste by her scyence the grete evyllis and harmes that were comyng by this cause. But never for the dissuacions of Hector ne the monyssions ne warnynges of Cassandra, the kyng wold not change his purpoos, ne for Helenus his sone, ne for Pantheus &c.

¶ *How Parys and Deyphebus, Eneas, Anthenor and Polidamas were sente in to Grece, and how they ravysshyd Helayne oute of the temple of Venus with many prysonners and richesses and brought them to Troye where Parys espowsed the sayd Helayne.*[2]

. . . .

[The Greeks resolved to make war on Troy.]

In this place declareth Dares in his book the facions of the Grekes that were to fore Troye of the moste notable of them as he that sawe hem and behelde hem many tymes duryng the triews that was often tymes betwene bothe parties duryng the siege to fore the cyte; and he begynneth to speke of Helayne and sayth that she was so fayr that in the world no man coude fynde no fayrer woman ne better fourmed of alle membres. Agamenon was longe and whyte of body, strong of membres and well fourmed, lovyng labour, discrete, hardy and passing well bespoken. Menelaus was of mene stature, hardy in armes and corageous. Achilles was of right grete beaulte, blonke heeris & cryspe gray eyen, and grete, of amyable sighte, large brestes & brode sholdres, grete armes, his raynes hyghe ynowh, an hyghe man of grete stature and had no pareyll ne like to hym amonge alle the grekes, desiryng to fighte, large in yeftes, and outerageous in dispense. . . . Ayax of grete stature, grete and large in the sholdres, grete armes, and alleway was well clothyd and richely, and was of no grete empryse and spack lightly. Thelamon Ayax was a moche fayr knyght. He had black heeris, and herd gladly songe and he

---

[1] II.2.97–112.
[2] Referred to at II.2.72–79.

sange hym self gladly well. He was of grete prowesse, and a good man of warre, and with oute pompe. Ulixes was the moste fayr man among all the Grekes, but he was deceyvable and subtyll, and sayd his thynges joyously. He was a right grete lyar and was so well bespoken that he had none felawe ne like to hym. Dyomedes was grete and had a brode breste and mervayllous stronge, of a fiers regard and sight, false in his promesses, worthy in armes, desirous of victorye, dredde and redoubted. For he was gretly injuryous to his servantes, luxuryous, wherfore he suffryd many paynes. The duc Nestor was grete of membrys and longe and well bespoken, discrete and prouffitable, and gaf alleway good counceyll. Anone and sone he was strongly angry and anone peasid agayn. He was the moste trewe frend in the world. . . . Palamydes, sone of kynge Naulus, was of ryght fayre shapp and lene, hardy and amyable, a good man and large. Polydaryus was passing grete, fatte and swollen, hardy, orguyllous[1] and proude, withoute trouthe. . . . Brysayda, doughter of Calcas, was passing fayr, of mene stature, white and medlid with reed, and well made, swete & pytouse and whome many men lovyd for her beawte. For the love of her cam the kynge of Perse in to the ayde of the Grekis unto the siege tofore Troye.

Of them that were within Troye, the same Dares sayth fyrste of kynge Pryant that he was longe, gresle[2] and fayr, and had a lowe voys, ryght hardy, and that gladly eete erly in the morenyng, a man wythoute drede, and that hated flaterers. He was verytable and good justycyer, and gladly he herde synge & sownes of musycque, and strongly lovyd his knyghtes and enrichid them. Of alle his sones ther was none so hardy as was Hector, the oldest sone of kyng Pryant. This was he that passid in his tyme alle other knyghtes in puyssance and was a lityll besgue.[3] He was grete and had hard membres and myght souffre moche payne, and was moche heery and crispe and lisped. Ther yssued never oute of Troye so stronge a man ne so worthy. Ne ther yssued never oute of his mouthe a vyllaynous worde. He was never wery of fightyng in bataylle. Ther was never knyght better belovyd of his peple than he was. Parys was a passing fayr knyght and strong, soft heerid and trewe, swyft and swete of speche, tote mowthed, well drawyng a bowe, wyse and hardy in batayll and well assewryd and covetous of lordship. Deyphebus and Helenus were passing like of facion in suche wyse that a man myghte not well knowe that oon fro that other. And they

[1] arrogant. This word appears several times in Chaucer's first edition, the one probably used by Shakespeare. Cf. Prologue, 2.

[2] thin.

[3] stammering.

resamblid passing well the kynge Pryant, theyr fader. Deyphebus was wyse and hardy in armes, and Helenus was a moche wyse clerk.[1] Troylus was grete and of grete corage, well attempryd and sore belovyd of younge maydens. In force and gladnesse he resamblid moche to Hector, and was the seconde after hym of prowesse,[2] and ther was not in alle the royame a more strong ne more hardy yong man. Eneas had a grete body, discrete mervayllously in his werkis, well bespoken and attempryd in his wordes, full of good counceyll and of science connyng. He had his visage joyouse and the eyen clere and graye, and was the richest man of Troye after the kyng Pryant in townes and castellys. Anthenor was long and lene and spacke moche, but he was discrete and of grete industrye and whom the kynge Pryant lovyd gretely, and that gladly playd amonge his felawship, and was a ryght wyse man.[3] . . .

The quene Hecuba was a rude woman and semed better a man than a woman. She was a noble woman, passinge sage, debonayre and honeste and lovyng the werkes of charyte. Andrometha, the wyfe of Hector, was a passing fayr woman and whyte and that had fayr eyen and fayr heer. She was amonge alle other women ryght honeste and attempryd in her werkes. Cassandra was of fayr stature and clere, round mouthed, wyse, shynyng eyen. She lovyd virgynyte and knew moche of thynges to come by astronomye and other sciences. Polyxena was a moche fayr doughter and tendre, and was the verray raye of beawte, in whome nature fayllyd nothynge save only that she made her mortall. And she was the fayrest mayde that was in her tyme, and the beste fourmed.

[Wishing to prevent bloodshed Agamemnon asked the Greek leaders to send ambassadors to Priam.]

Ye may well knowe for trouthe that they have assemblid in the cyte of Troye grete power for to deffende them ayenst us, and also the cyte is passing grete and stronge. And ye knowe well that they ben upon theyr propre herytage, that is a thynge that dowblith theyr force and strength. For ye may take ensample of the crowe that otherwhyle deffendeth well her neste agayn the fawcion. I ne saye not these thynges for any doubte that I have but that we shall have victorye and that we ne shall destroye theyr cyte how well that hit is stronge, but onely for oure worshippe, to the ende that we be recomanded to have conduyted this werke by grete discrecion and with oute pryde. . . . Ye knowe well that it is not longe agoo that

[1] I.2.234 'a priest'.
[2] Cf. Ulysses, IV.5.109.
[3] I.2.197–200.

the kynge Pryant dide do requyre us by his specyall messangers that
we sholde rendre to hym his suster Exione, and that by our orguyell
and pryde we wolde not delyvere her agayn. And yf we had deliveryd
and sente her home agayn, these evyllys had never happend in the
yle of Cythare as they now been, and the quene Helayne, that is of
the moste noble of Grece, had never be ravysshyd ne ladde awaye.
And also we had not enterprysed the payne ne the laboure where we
now ben in. And ther is none of us that knoweth what shall happen
to hym good or evyll. And therfore yf ye seme good that we myghte
retorne in to our contrey with oute suffrynge of more payne with
oure honoure and worshippe, we shall sende unto the kynge Pryant
oure specyall messangers and bidde hym to sende and renvoye to us
Helayne freely and that he restore to us the domayges that Parys hath
doon in the yle of Cythare.[1] For yf he wyll so doo, oure retorne shall
be honourable and we may no more axe of hym by ryght. And yf he
reffuse thys we shall have two thynges that shall fyghte for us,
justyce and oure trewe quaryll, and oure puyssance excusid. And
whan men shall here of oure offres they shall gyve the wronge and
blame to the Trojans and to us the loose and preysyng. And we
shall ben excused of alle the domayges that we shall doon to them
after thyse offres. Therfore avyse yow amonge your self what thynge
ye wyll doo.

Than were there some felonnes that blamed this counceylle and
some alowed hit. And fynably they concluded to do soo as Agamenon
had sayd. Than they cheese for theyr messangers Dyomedes and
Ulixes for to goo to Troye and make theyr legacion,[2] whiche toke
theyr horses and went incontynent theder and cam to Troye aboute
mydday. And they wente strayt to the pallays of kynge Pryant and
toke theyr horses to kepe at the gate and after wente up in to the
halle. And in goyng up they mervayllyd hem gretly of the ryche
werke that they sawe in alle the pallays. . . .

[Ulysses delivered the Greek demands.]

Kinge Pryant, mervaylle the nothyng that we have no salewid the
for as moche as thou arte oure enemye mortell. The kynge
Agamenon, to whome we ben messangers, sendeth and comandeth
the by us that thou renvoye and sende to hym the quene Helayne
whome thou haste don to be ravysshid and betaken fro her husbonde, and that thou restore alle the domages that Parys thy sone
hath done in Grece. As yf thou so doo, I trowe thou shalt doo as a
wyse man. And yf thou doo not, beholde what evyllys may come to

---

[1] Cf. Nestor's message, II.2.1–7.
[2] This 'legation' may be the basis of the Admiral's Plot, Scene A.

the and to thyne, for thou shalt dye an evyll deth and alle thy men, and this noble cyte shall be destroyed.' Whan the kynge Pryant herde Ulixes thus speke, he answerd incontynent to Ulixes wyth oute demandyng counceylle, 'I mervaylle me gretly of thy wordes that requyrest of me that thynge that a man vaynquysshid and myght not deffende hym self no more wyth grete payne wolde accorde to the. . . . But had lever dye vylaynsly than to agree your requeste. And late Agamenon knowe that I desire never to have peas ne love wyth the Grekes that have doon to me so many dysplaysirs. And yf hit were not that ye ben messangers I shold make yow dye an evyll deth. Therfore go ye your way anone, for I may not see yow wyth oute displaysir in myn herte.' Than began Dyomedes to lawghe for despyte & sayd thus: 'Ha kynge, yf with oute displaysir mayste not see us that ben but tweyne, than thou shalt not be wythoute displaysir alle the dayes of thy lyfe. For thou shalt see fro hensforth to fore thyn eyen grete puissance of Grekes, the whiche shall come to fore thy cyte, and shall not cesse for tassaylle hit contynuelly, ayenst whome thou mayste not longe deffende the, but that thou and thyne finably shall receyve bytter deth. Therfore thou sholdest take counceyll in thy werkes yf thou were well avysed.

Than were there many Trojans that wolde have ronne upon the Grekes and drewe theyr swerdes for to have slayn them, but the kynge Pryant destourned hem, and sayd to hem that they sholde late two fooles saye theyr folye, and that hit was the nature of a fole to shewe folye and to a wyse man to suffre hit. 'Ha, a, syre,' sayd Eneas, 'what is that that ye saye, men shold shew to a foole his folye. And truly yf hit were not in your presence, this felawe that hath spoken so folyly to fore yow, shold receyve his deth by my hande. Hit apperteyneth not to hym to saye to yow suche venymous wordes ne menaces. And therfore I avyse hym that he go his way anone yf he cesse not to speke folyly.' Dyomedes that of no thyng was abasshyd answerd to Eneas and sayd, 'What some ever thou be, thou shewest well by thy wordes that thou arte right yll avysed and hoot in thy wordes. And I desire that I may ones fynde the in a place covenable that I may rewarde the for the wordes that thou hast sayd of me. I see well that the kynge is well ewrous [1] & happy to have suche a counceller as thou arte that counceyllest hym to do vylonnye.' Than Ulixes brack the wordes of Dyomedes ryght wysely and prayd hym to holde his peas, and after saide to kynge Pryant, 'We have understand alle that thou haste sayd and we shall goo and reporte hit unto our prynces.' And incontynent they wente and toke theyr horses and retorned unto theyr ooste. . . .

[1] Fr. heureux, happy.

[Before the second great battle Hector took over command from his father.]

This Hector was moche coragyous, stronge and victoryous in batayll, and a right wyse conduytour of men of armes. His shelde was alle of gold, and in the myddell a lyon of gowles. And how well that he was the laste that yssued out of his hous or of the cyte, yet passid he alleweye alle the bataylles and cam and putte hym self afore in the fyrst bataylle. The women that were in the cyte and alle the other wente upon the wallys for to beholde the batayles. There were the doughters of the kynge wyth the quene Helayne that had grete doubte and dyverce ymagynacyons in her self. . . .

[How Hector slew Patroclus.]

Whan alle the bataylles were ordeyned on that one side and on that other, and was no thyng to do but tassemble, than avauncyd hym Hector alle ther fyrst. And Patroclus cam ayenst hym as moche as his horse myghte renne, and smote hym so strongly wyth his spere in his shelde that he perchid hit thurghout, but more harme dyde he not. Than Hector assayllid Patroclus wyth his swerde and gaf hym so grete a strook upon his heed that he clefte hit in two peces and Patroclus fyll doun dede to the ground.[1] Whan Hector sawe hym ded he coveyted his armes, for they were ryght queynte and ryche, and a lightid doun of his horse for to take them. But the kynge Menon cam upon hym wyth thre thousand good knyghtes for to deffende the kynge Patroclus ayenst Hector, and sayd to hym thus: 'Ha, a, wolf ravysshyng and insacyable, certes the behoveth to seke thy praye in some other place, for here geteste thou none.' And than they assayllyd hym on alle sides and wolde have taken fro hym Galathee his hors[2] but Hector by his prowesse remounted, wolde they or not, and wende to have vengid hym on kynge Menon. But the kynge Glancion and the kynge Thesus and Archilogus his sone cam wyth thre thousand fightars, and than Hector leyd on and bete doun all afore hym. And the fyrst that he mette he gaf so grete a stroke that he slewe hym and after hym many mo he bete doun and slewe.

Thus began the bataylle on bothe sides and Hector cam agayn to the body of Patroclus for to have his armes. But the kyng Ydumeus of Crete cam ayenst hym with two thousand fyghtars, and the kynge Menon that had allway his eye to Hector letted hym and was so in the waye that Hector myght not have his armes that he sore desired and suffryd grete payne for as moche as he was on foote, but he

---

[1] Not shown in the play. V.5.13.
[2] V.5.20.

enforced hym wyth alle his corage and began to slee man and hors and to smyte of heedes, legges, feet and armes, and slewe fyften of the strengest that assayllyd hym.[1] In this mene while the kyng Menon toke the body of Patroclus to fore hym and bare hit unto his tente[2] as the Grekes contended to greve Hector and to take away his horse. . . .

In this day had the Trojans had vittorye of alle the Grekes yf fortune that is dyverse had wylle consentyd. For they myght have slayn hem alle and eschewyd the grete evyllys that after cam to them. Certes hit is not wysedom whan ony man fyndeth his enemye in grete perylle and fortune to offre his power to delivere hym therof, for hit happeth ofte tymes that he shall never recovere to have his enemye in the same caas but that fortune torne her backe. Thus hit happend this day to the unhappy Hector that was at the above of his enemyes and myght have slayn hem alle yf he had wolde, for they soughte no thynge but for to flee, whan by grete mysaventure cam afore hym in an encountre Thelamon Ayax that was sone of kynge Thelamon and Exione, and was cosyn germayn of Hector and of his brethern, whiche was wyse & vayllyant, whiche adressid hym ayenst Hector & deliveryd to hym a grete assault, and Hector to hym as they that were valyant bothe two.[3] And as they were fightyng they spak to geder and therby Hector knewe that he was his cosyn germaine, sone of his aunte.[4] And than Hector for curtoisye enbraced hym in his armes and made hym grete chiere and offryd to hym to do all his playsir yf he desired ony thynge of hym and prayed him that he wolde come to Troye with hym for to see his lignage of hys moder syde. But the sayd Thelamon, that entended no thynge but to his avauntage, sayde that he wolde not goo at thys tyme but prayd to Hector sayng that yf he lovyd hym so moche as he sayde that he wolde for his sake and at his instance do cesse the bataill for that day and that the Trojans shold leve the Grekes in pees. The unhappy Hector accorded to hym his requeste, and blewe an horn & made alle his peple to withdrawe in to the cyte. Than had the Trojans begonne to putte fyre in the shippes of the Grekes and had alle brente hem ne had Hector callyd them fro thens, wherof the Trojans were sory of the rapeell. This was the cause wherfore the Trojans lost to have the victorye, to the whiche they myght never after atteyne ne come, for fortune was to them contrarye. And therfore Virgile sayth, Non est misericordia in bello,

[1] Cf. V.5.19–35.
[2] V.5.17.
[3] No lottery here; cf. Homer and Shakespeare.
[4] IV.5.119–47.

that is to saye, There is no mercy in bataill. A man ought not to take misericorde but take the victorye who may gete hit.[1]

[In the fourth battle Hector fought Achilles and Troilus Diomed.]

There began mervayllously the bataylle . . . The kynge Menelaus recountrid Parys, and they knewe eche other well; and Menelaus smote hym so harde wyth his spere that he made hym a grete wounde and smote hym doun, wherof Parys was alle ashamed.[2] . . . Polidamas bete Palamydes and wounded hym sore,[3] and after mocqued hym by reproche. . . . The kynge Thoas and Achilles that were coyns assaylleden Hector and gaf hym many strokes, and drewe of his helme fro his hede & hurted hym in many places; and Hector gaf to hymso grete a stroke with his swerd that he cutte of half his nose.

To the rescows of Hector cam his bastard brethern that slewe many of the Grekes & toke the kynge Thoas & wounded & bete the kynge Agamenon in suche wise that he was born to his tentes as dede and the kyng Thoas was ladde prisonner to Troye. Menelaus contended to greve Parys, and Parys shotte to hym an arowe envenymed and wounded hym in suche wise that he was born in to his tente and as sone as Menelaus had bounden his wounde he cam agayn to the batayll for to greve Parys, yf he had founden hym. And he fonde hym & assayllid hym. But Eneas put hym self betwene hem bothe, for as moche as Parys was unarmed for to avente hym, and so Eneas lad hym in to the cyte to the ende that Menelaus shold not slee hym. Than Hector assayllyd Menelaus and wende to have taken hym, but ther cam to the rescows grete plente of chyvalrye of the Grekes wherfore Hector myght not come to his entente. And than he threstid in and smote amonge the other, and dide so moche with helpe of his folke that the Grekes fledde, and than the nyght cam on that made the batayll to cesse.

[In the fifth battle Hector slew three kings and Diomedes slew the Sagittary.]

Dyomedes slewe the kynge Antipus. Than the kynge Epistropus and the kynge Cedus assaylleden Hector, and Epistropus justed ayenst Hector and brak his spere upon hym and said to hym many vilayns wordes, wherof Hector was angry and in his grete yre gaf hym so grete a strook that he slewe hym, and after sayd to hym that he sholde goo & saye his vilaynous wordes to them that were dede suche as he

---

[1] Shakespeare does not make the fight so crucial.
[2] Cf. I.1.113–16.
[3] V.5.13–14, 'Palamedes sore hurt and bruis'd.'

was wonte to saye to lyvyng men . . . Than was Cedeus passyng sorrowfull of the deth of his broder, and amonestid a thousand knyghtis that he had to slee Hector. And they assaylled hym anone & bete hym of his hors. And than they cryed to kynge Cedeus for to sle Hector. And whan Hector apperceyvyd that, he gave hym so grete a strook that he cutte of his arme wherof he fyll for the angwyssh that he felte, and anone Hector slewe hym.[1] Aeneas slewe in his medlee the kynge Amphymacus. And ther wente togyder alle the most puyssant of Grekes and assaylled the Troians and slewe many of them. And they wente by so grete force that they put the Troians in a chaffe in the whiche Achilles slewe the kynge Philis. Wherof Hector had grete sorowe, and in his yre he slewe the kynge Dalpmee and the kynge Doreus. And thus by the puyssance of Hector the Troians recoverd the felde and slewe many Grekes.

Than yssued oute of Troye the kynge Epistropus with thre thousand knyghtes and they foureyed and threstyd amonge the Grekes, that reculed in theyr comyng, for as moche as he brought wyth hym a sagittarye, the same that afore is made mencion of.[2] This sagittarye was not armed but he bare a stronge bowe and a turquoys[3] that was full of arowes and shotte strongly. Whan the knyghtes of the Grekes sawe this mervayllous beste they had no wyll to goo forth, and they that were afore began to wythholde hem and wente aback. Amonge these thynges Hector slewe Polixenes the noble duc that fought sore ayenst hym. And by the strengthe of the Trojans and the horrour of the sagittarye the Grekes were reculyd unto theyr tentes. Hyt happend that Dyomedes to fore one of the tentes was assayllyd of the sagittarye and had this beste to fore hym and the Trojans on his back, and so behoved hym there to shewe his puyssance. The sagittarye had tho shotte an arowe to hym, and Dyomedes, that was not well assewryd, avaunsid hym nyghe unto hym and gaf hym so grete a stroke wyth his swerde, the whiche was not armed, that he slewe hym. And at that tyme hit was paste myddaye. And than the Grekes recoveryd the felde and made the Trojans to flee. And than entrecountryd Hector and Achylles and wyth force of theyr speres they faught bothe two and fylle bothe to the erthe. And as Achilles was fyrst remounted, he supposid to have ladde awaye Galathe the good horse of Hector, but Hector escryed to hys folke that they sholde not suffre hym to lede hym awaye. Than they ran upon Achilles and dyde so moche that they rescowed

---

[1] Most of the names in V.5.6–16 appear in this battle. Shakespeare probably glanced at Caxton fol. 299, and used them differently.

[2] 'A beste that behynde the myddes was an hors & tofore a man', i.e. a centaur. Cf. V.5. 14–15.

[3] quiver.

Galathe & rendryd hym to Hector that was right glad of hym. At this medle was Anthenor taken & sente to their tentes, notwithstandyng that Polidamas his sone dyde mervaylles of armes for to resscowe hym, but he myght not. And thus they faught to grete domage of that one partye and of that other unto that the nyght departed hem. . . .

[Diomedes and Ulysses were sent to ask for a truce.]

. . . the triews were accorded for thre monethes.[1] This triewes duryng, the kynge Thoas was deliveryd in the stede of Anthenor that they held prisoner, whom they sente to the Trojans. Calcas, that by the comandement of Appolyn had lefte the Trojans, had a passing fayr doughter and wyse named Breseyda. Chaucer in his booke that he made of Troylus named her Creseyda. For whiche doughter he prayd to kynge Agamenon and to the other prynces that they wolde requyre the kynge Pryant to sende Breseyda to hym. They prayde ynow to kynge Pryant at the instance of Calcas,[2] but the Trojans blamed sore Calcas and callid hym evyll and fals traytre and worthy to dye, that had lefte hys owne lande and his naturell lorde for to goo in to the companye of his mortall enemyes. Alleway at the petycion of the Grekes the kynge Pryant sente Breseyda to her fader.

The triews duryng, Hector wente hym on a day unto the tentes of the Grekes. And Achylles behelde hym gladly for as moche as he had never seen hym unarme.[3] And at the requeste of Achylles Hector wente in to hys tente. And as they spack to geder of many thynge, Achylles sayde to Hector, I have grete playsir to see the unarmed for as moche as I had never seen the to fore, but yet I shall have more playsir whan the day shall come that thou shalt dye of my hande, whyche thynge I moste desire. For I knowe the to be moche stronge and I have often tymes provyd hit unto the effusion of my blood, wherof I have grete anger. And yet have I more grete sorowe for as moche as thou slewest Patroclus, hym that I moste lovyd of the world. Than thou mayste beleve for certayn that be fore thys yere be past his deth shall be avengyd upon the by my hande. And also I wote well that thou desirest to slee me.[4] Hector answerd and sayde, Achilles yf I desire thy deth, mervaylle the nothynge therof, for as moche as thou deservest to be myn enemye mortall. Thou art come in to our lande for to destroye me and myne. I wyll well that thou

---

[1] This mission of Diomedes and Ulysses may have been shown in Scene F of the Admiral's Plot.

[2] Cf. Calchas in III.3.1–30.

[3] III.3.238–42; 276.

[4] Contrast Achilles' insolence in IV.5.229–50.

knowe that thy wordes fere me nothynge at all. But yet I have hope that wyth in two yere, yf I lyve and my swerde faylle me not, that thou shalt dye of myn handes. Not thou allonely but alle the moste grettest of the Grekes: for amonge yow ye have enterprysid a grete folye, and hit may none otherwyse come to yow therby but deth, and I am assewrid that thou shalt dye of my hande er I shall dye by thyne. And yf thou wene that thou be so stronge that thou maiste defende the ayenste me, make hit so that alle the barons of thyn ooste promyse and accorde that we fighte body ayenst body. And yf hit happen that thou vaynquysshe me, that my frendes and I shall be bannysshid oute of this royame and we shalle leve hit unto the Grekes. And therof I shall leve good plegge. And herein thou mayste prouffite to many other that may renne in grete danger yf they haunte the batayll. And yf hit happen that I vaynquysshe the, make that alle they of this ooste departe hens and suffre us to lyve in pees.[1] Achilles achauffid hym sore with these wordes and offryd hym to doo this batayll and gaf to Hector his gayge whiche Hector toke and resseyvyd gladly &c.

Whan Agamenon knewe of this haytye[2] and bargayn, he wente hym hastely unto the tente of Achylles with a grete companye of noble men whiche wolde in no wise accorde ne agree to this batayll, sayng that they wold not submytte hem so many noble men under the strengthe of one man. And the Trojans sayden in lyke wyse, save only the kynge Pryant that wolde gladly agreed for the grete strengthe that he felte in his sone Hector. Thus was the champe broken and Hector departed & wente agayn to Troye fro the Grekes.

Whan Troylus knewe certaynly that Breseyda shold be sente to her fader, he made grete sorowe, for she was his soverain lady of love, and in semblable wyse Breseyda lovyd strongly Troylus. And she made also the grettest sorowe of the world for to leve her soverayn lord in love. Ther was never seen so moche sorowe made betwene two lovers at their departyng. Who that lyste to here of alle theyr love, late hym rede the booke of Troyllus that Chawcer made wherin he shall fynde the storye hooll, whiche were to longe to wryte here. But fynably Breseyda was ledde unto the Grekes whome they receyved honourably. Amonge them was Diomedes that anone was enflamed with the love of Breseyda whan he sawe her so fayr, and in ridyng by her side he shewid her alle his corage and made to her many promesses and specially desired her love. And than when she knewe the corage of Diomedes she excused her, sayng that she wolde not agree to hym ne reffuse hym at that tyme, for her

---

[1] These conditions do not appear either in I.3.256–309, or in IV.5.65ff.
[2] bargain.

herte was not disposed at that tyme to answere otherwyse. Of this answere Dyomedes had grete joye, for as moche as he was not reffusid utterly. And he accompanyed her unto the tente of her fader, and halpe her doun of her hors and toke fro her one of her glovys that she helde in her handes, and she souffryd hym swetely. Calcas resceyvyd her wyth grete joye . . .

The comyng of Breseyda plesid moche to alle the Grekes. And they cam theder and fested her and demaunded of her tydynges of Troye and of the kynge Pryant and of them that were wyth inne. And she sayd unto hem as moche as she knewe curtoysly. Than alle the grettest that were there promysyd her to kepe her and holde her as dere as her doughter.[1] And than eche man wente in to hys owne tente and ther was none of hem but that gaf to her a jewell at the departyng. And than hit plesid her well to abide and dwelle wyth the Grekes and forgate anone the noble cyte of Troye and the love of the noble Troyllus. O how sone is the purpos of a woman chaungid and torned, certes more sonner than a man can saie or thinke. Now late had Breseyda blamed her fader of the vyce of trayson whiche she her self excersised in forgetyng her contre and her trewe frende Troyllus &c. . . .

[After three months the war began again.]

Achilles slewe many noble men, amonge the whyche he slewe the duc Biraon and Euforbe that was a moche noble man. Hector was this day sore hurte in the visage and bledde grete plente of blood and wyste not who had doon hyt, and therfore the Trojans reculed unto the walles. And whan Hector behelde and sawe upon the wallis the quene Hecuba, hys moder, and his susters, he had grete shame, and by grete yre assayllid the kynge Menon, cosyn of Achilles, and gaf hym so many strokes wyth his swerd upon hys helme that he slewe hym. Seeyng Achilles that, wende for to have enraged and toke a stronge spere and ranne aynest Hector and brake hys spere upon hym, but he coude not remeve hym. And Hector gaf hym wyth hys swerd so grete a strooke that he maad hym to tomble under hys horse, and sayd to hym, Achilles, Achilles, thou contendest to approche to me. Knowe that thou approchest thy deth. And as Achilles wold have answerd to Hector, Troyllus cam upon betwene them wyth a grete nombre of knyghtes and putte hym in the myddes of them. And there were slayn more than fyve honderd knyghtes of Grece and were put back by force. And Menelaus cam to the rescows wyth thre thousand fyghtyng men, and of the partye of the Trojans cam the kynge Ademon that justed

---

[1] Not in Chaucer. Shakespeare's Greeks are less respectful, IV.5.

ayenst Menelaus and smote hym and hurted hym in the vysage. And he and Troylus toke hym and had lad hym away yf Dyomedes had not come the sonner with a grete companye of knyghtes and fought with Troillous at his comyng and smote hym doun and toke hys horse and sente hit to Breseyda, and dyd do saye to her by his servant that hit was Troyllus horse, her love, that he had beten hym by his prowesse and prayd her fro than forth on that she wold holde hym for her love and frende &c.

Breseyda had grete joye of these tydynges, and sayd to the servaunt that he shold saye unto his lord that she myght not hate hym that wyth so good herte lovyd her. Whan Diomedes knewe the answer he was right joyous and threstid in amonge his enemyes. But the Trojans, that were stronger than they, maad the Grekes to goo a back and recule unto their tentes, and had slayn hem all yf the kynge Agamenon had not socowred hem with right grete strength. Than began the batayll horryble and mortall . . .

[After the sixth battle there was a truce of six months.]

Amonge all other thynges Diomedes suffred grete mysease for the love of Breseida and myght not ete ne reste for thynkyng on her, and requyred her many tymes of her love. And she answerd hym right wysely, gyvyng hym hope wyth oute certaynte of ony poynte, by the whyche Dyomedes was enflamed of alle poyntes in her love. Whan the sixe monthes were passid they began to fyghte by the space of twelve dayes contynuelly fro the mornyng unto the evenyng. And there were many slayn of that one syde and of that other. And than cam a grete mortalite amonge the Grekes in the oost of the grete hete that tho was, and therfore the kyng Agamenon requyred tryews whyche was agreed and accorded to hym &c.

Whan the triews was passid, the nyght to fore Andrometha the wyf of Hector, that hadde two fayr sones by hym, wherof that one had to name Laomedon and that other Astromatas, this Andrometha sawe that nyght a mervayllous vysion, and her semed yf Hector wente that day folowyng to the bataylle he shold be slayn. And she that had grete fere and drede of her husbond, wepyng sayd to hym, prayng hym that he wold not goo to the batayll that day. Wherof Hector blamed his wyf sayng that men shold not beleve ne gyve fayth to dremes, and wold not abyde ner tarye therfore.[1] Whan hyt was in the morenyng Andrometha wente unto the kynge Pryant and to the quene and tolde to them the veryte of her vysion, and prayd to them wyth alle her herte that they wold doo so moche to Hector that he shold not that day go to the bataylle &c.

[1] V.2.1-15.

Hit happend that day was fayre and cleer, and the Trojans armed them, and Troyllus yssued fyrste in to the batayll, after hym Eneas, after Parys, Deyphebus, Polidamas and the kynge Sarpedon, the kynge Epistropus, the kynge Croys and the kynge Philomenus, and after alle the prynces that were comen in the ayde of the Trojans, eche man in good ordenance. And the kyng Pryant sente to Hector that he shold kepe hym well that day fro goyng to batayll. Wherfore Hector was angry and sayd to his wyf many wordes reprochable, as he that knewe well that this defence cam by her requeste. How be hyt, notwithstandyng the deffence, he armed hym. And whan Andromeda sawe hym armed she toke her lytyll chyldren and fyll doun to the feet of her husbond and prayd hym humbly that he wold take of his armes, but he wold not doo hyt. And than she sayd to hym, At the leste yf ye wyll not have mercy on me, so have pytie of your lytyll children that I & they dye not a bitter deth or that we shall be ledde in servytude & bondage in to strange contreyes. With this poynte cam upon them the quene Hecuba & the quene Helayne and the susters of Hector and they knelid doun to fore his feet and prayd hym wyth wepyng teerys that he wold doo of his harnoys and unarme hym and come wyth them in to the halle. But never wold he doo hit for her prayers, but descended from the palays thus armed as he was and toke hys horse and wold have goon to bataylle. But at the requeste of Andromeda the kynge Pryant cam rennyng anone and toke hym by the brydell and sayd to hym so many thynges of one and other that he maad hym to retorne, but in no wyse he wold not unarme hym.[1]

Amonge all these thynges the batayll was mortall of the Grekes and of the Trojans. Diomedes and Troyllus justed to geder and at the assemble they grevyd eche other and wyth oute faylle eche of them had slayn other yf Menelaus had not come and departid them. Than the kynge Myseres of Frygye bete Menelaus and had taken hym whan Eneas cam and distrowblid them, and wold have slayn hym but the sayd Troyllus delyveryd hem and slewe many Grekes. Than cam the kynge Thelamon with thre thousand fyghtyng men and justid in hys comyng ayenst Polidamas and put hym to the worse and unhorsid hym. But Troyllus socourid hym and made hym to remounte on his hors. After cam Parys and Achilles on the other side that smote amonge the Trojans by so grete force wyth the helpe of hys peple that he putte hem to the flyght unto the cyte. And in this chasse Achilles slewe Margareton, one of the bastardes of kynge Pryant.[2]

---

[1] Shakespeare's Priam is not so successful. V.3.59–94.
[2] Called Margarelon in V.5.6 and V.6.13–23.

Whan Hector knewe that Achylles had slayn Margareton, he had grete sorowe and dyde anone do lase on hys helme and wente hym to the batayll that hys fader knewe not of. . . . And he threstid in to the grettest prees of the Grekes, and slewe as many as he coude areche. And the Grekes fledde afore hym, that ther was none so hardy that durst abide his strokes. And thus the Trojans retorned and slewe the Grekes on all sides . . .

Whan Achilles sawe that Hector slewe thus the nobles of Grece and so many other that it was mervayll to beholde, he thought that yf Hector were not slayn that the Grekes shold never have victorye, and also for as moche as he had slayn many kynges & prynces. He ranne upon hym mervayllously and a noble duc of Grece with hym named Polyceus and was come for the love of Achilles, the whyche had promysyd to gyve to hym hys suster in maryage. But Hector slewe the same duc anone seeyng Achilles. Than Achilles wenyng to avenge the deth of Policeus assayllyd Hector by grete yre. But Hector caste to hym a darte so fiersly and made hym a wounde in his thye, and than Achilles yssued out of the batayll and dide do bynde hys wounde and toke a grete spere in purpose to slee Hector yf he myght mete hym.[1] Amonge all these thynges Hector had taken a moche noble baron of Grece moche queyntly and rychely armed, and for to lede hym oute of the ooste at his ease had caste his shelde behynde hym at his backe and had lefte his breste discoverte.[2] And as he was in thys poynte and toke none hede of Achylles that cam pryvely unto hym and putte thys spere wyth in his body.[3] And Hector fyll doun dede to the ground. Whan the kynge Menon sawe Hector dede, he assayllyd Achylles by grete yre and bete hym doun to the ground and hurte hym strongly. And his men bare hym in to his tente upon hys shelde. Than for the deth of Hector were alle the Trojans disconfyte and reentryd in to theyr cyte beryng the body of Hector wyth grete sorowe and lamentacion.

¶ *Of the ryche sepulture of Hector and of the grete lamentacions and wepynges that the Trojans maad for his deth and how Palamydes was chosen duc and governour of the oost of the Grekes:*

Whan Hector was ded and his body born in to the cyte, ther is no tonge that coude expresse the sorowe that was maad in the cyte generally of men & women, and that ther was none but he had lever to have loste his owen sone than hym, and they sayd all that from thens forth they had loste alle her hope and truste of deffence. And

---

[1] Contrast V.6.13–21, where Hector apparently spares the exhausted Achilles.
[2] V.6.27–31; V.8.1–4.
[3] An unchivalrous act, but not so bad as in V.8.5–14, 21–22.

thus they demened ryght longe their sorowe. The noble kynges and prynces bare the body unto the palais of Ylyon. Than whan the kynge Pryant sawe hym, he fyll doun a swowne upon the body and was as ded for sorowe that unnethe they coude take hym awaye by force. There demened grete sorowe all his brethern. What myght men saye of the sorowe that his moder the quene made and after hys susters? O what sorowe maad hys wyf! Certes there can no man expresse alle the lamentacions that there were maad. . . .

[During a truce on the anniversary of Hector's death, Achilles visited Troy and saw Polixena in the temple.] . . . Than was Achilles shoten with the darte of love that stack hym to the herte so mervayllously that he coude not cesse to beholde her, and the more he behelde her the more he desired her. He was so asottyd on her that he thought on none other thynge, but abode in the temple unto the evenyng as longe as the quene was there. And whan she wente oute he conveyed his eye upon Polixena as ferre as he myght see her. And thys was the cause and the begynnyng of hys meschief. In thys sorowe Achilles retorned unto his tente, and whan he was leyde to slepe that nyght ther cam many thynges in his mynde and in his thoughte, and knewe than the daunger where Polixena had putte hym inne, and thought in hym self that the moste stronge men of the world coude not ner had not mowe vaynquysshe hym,[1] and the only regarde and syghte of a frayll mayde had vaynquisshid and overcome hym. And hym semed that ther is no medecyne of the world myght hele hym save she. . . . And than he torned hym to the walle and fyll in wepyng and drowned hym self in teres, and of necessite he muste thynke how he myght come to the love of Polixene, and so he coveryd and hydde his corage as well as he myghte.

¶ *How Achylles sente his secrete messanger unto Hecuba the quene of Troye for to requyre her doughter Polixena and of the answer, and how for the love of her the said Achilles assemblid the oost of the Grekes and counceyllid hem to departe and have pees with the Trojans.*

The nyght folowyng as Achilles was leyde on his bedde & myght not slepe, he thought that he wold sende be tymes hys messanger unto the quene Hecuba for to knowe yf he myght fyne wyth her that she wold gyve to hym her doughter Polixena to wyve, and he wold do so moche for her that he wold make the Grekes to reyse theyr syege and goo agayn in to theyr contrees hastely, and the pees shold be maad betwene them. Alle thus as he thought in the nyght

---

[1] ner . . . hym: nor had been able to vanquish him.

he put in execucion and sente his trewe messanger unto the quene for to requyre her doughter, and sayde to her the promyses that his lord had comanded hym. Whan the quene had understande the wordes of the messanger, she answerd hym discretly, how well that she hated Achilles more than ony man of the world, sayng, Frend, as moche as is in me, I am redy for to doo that thyng that thy mayster requyreth of me. So saye unto hym that I may not doo this thynge allone by my selfe, but I shall speke to my lorde and to Parys my sone. And thou shalt come the thirde day agayn and I shall saye to the thyn answere.

Whan the messanger herde the quene so speke, he retorned unto his lord and said to hym all that he had founde. And thus began Achylles to have hope to come to his entente. The quene Hecuba wente her anone unto the kynge Pryant her husbond, where as Paris was, and tolde to them all that Achilles had sente to her. And than the kynge henge doun his heed and was so a longe whyle wyth oute sayng of ony worde. And after said to his wyf, O how is hyt as me thynketh herde thynge to resceyve in to frendship and amytye hym that hath don to me so grete offence, that hath taken away the lyght of myn eyen in sleyng my dere sone Hector, and hath therin gyven hope to the Grekes to have the victorye. But alleway for to eschiewe the moste grete peryll to thende that myn other sones lose not theyr lyf, and that I may have reste in myn olde dayes, I me consente with yow that he have that he requyreth, alleway forseen that he doo fyrste that thynge that he hath promysid wyth oute ony decepcion. Parys agreed to this thynge lyghtly for as moche as in the promesses of Achilles was no thynge spoken of the quene Helayne &c.

At the thirde daye after, Achilles sente agayn hys messanger unto the quene, and as sone as he cam to fore her she sayd to hym, I have spoken to my husbonde and also to my sone Parys of the requeste and also of the promesse of thy lorde, and they be contente that hys requeste be agreed to hym, but that he doo fyrst that thynge that he hath promysed. And so thou mayst saye to hym that he may come to the chief & ende of his desire, and that he conduyte wysely and secretly thys thynge as moche as in hym is. The messanger toke leve of the quene and cam anone to hys mayster and counted to hym alle that the quene had sayd to hym.[1] Than began Achilles strongly to thynke how he myghte performe this that he had promysed to the kynge Pryant, and that hyt was a grevous thynge to doo and that hit was not alle in hys puyssance. But hit is a propre vyce unto the folissh lovers to promyse thynge that is hard to brynge aboute and dyfficyle for to come to the effecte of their loves. In lyke wyse

---

[1] These communications with Hecuba underlie V.1.39–46.

gloryfyed hym Achilles that for hys merytes or for gyvyng hys ayde to the Grekes he wold make them to leve theyr syege. And than Achilles by the counceyll of Palamydes assemblid all the kynges and noble men of the oost in parlament & sayd to them in this manere:

My frendes that be here assemblid for to brynge this warre to the ende, thenke ye not otherwhile on your self, how by grete legyerte, lightnes and folye and for to recovere the wif of Menelaus we have lefte oure contrees and landes, oure wyves and oure chyldren, and ben comen in to thys stronge lande where we have dyspendyd the owrys folyly and putte oure bodyes in daunger of deth and in grete infynyte laboure, and syn we have ben comen hether ther ben ryght many kynges and prynces ded, and I my self have shedde moche of my blood that never shold have happend yf we had not begonne this folye. Helayne is nothyng of so grete prys that ther behoveth to dye for her so many noble men. Ther ben ynowhe in the world of as noble and as fayr women as she is, of whome Menelaus myght have one or two yf he wolde.[1] And hit is not a light thynge to overcome the Trojans, as they that have a stronge cyte and well garnysshid of good fightars on horse backe and a foote, and hit ought to suffise to us that we have now slayn Hector and many other of theyr nobles by the whiche we myghte now retorne wyth oure honoure and worshippe. And yf we leve Helayne, have not we Exione, to whome Helayne may not compare in noblesse?

Than mevyd them the duc of Atthenes and the kynge Thoas and contraryed strongly to the wordes of Achilles and so dyde alle the other and sayd that he sayde neyther fayr ne well, wherof Achilles had grete sorowe, and comanded to his Myrondones that they shold not arme them no more ayenst the Trojans and that they shold not gyve no counceyll ne ayde unto the Grekes. Amonge these thynges vytaylles began to faylle amonge the Grekes and they had grete famyne. . . .

[Even when the Trojans defeated the Greeks and set fire to their ships Achilles would not fight.]

There was Ebes the sone of the kynge of Trace sore hurte wyth a spere and bare the tronchon in his body, and in that poynte he wente to the tente of Achylles where he restid hym that day and had reffused to goo to the bataylle for the love that he had to Polixene. Ebes reprochid strongly Achylles that he suffryd so destroye the peple of his contre and to dye vyllaynsly, and that he myght well helpe hem yf he wolde. And as sone as he had fynysshid his wordes one toke oute the tronchon of his body and anone he fyll doun dede in the presence of Achilles.

[1] Cf. Diomed's dispraise of Helen and the war in IV.1.54–74.

Anon after cam fro the batayll oon of the varlettis or servauntes of Achilles and Achilles demaunded hym tydynges of the ooste. 'Ha, a, syre,' sayd he, 'hit is this day myshappid to oure folk for the grete multitude of Trojans that ben comen upon them, and they have slayn alle that they cowde mete wyth. And I trowe ther is not lefte oon at home of the men of Troye but that every man is come to the bataylle. And therfore yf hit plese yow now, whilis that the Trojans ben wery, to come to the bataylle, ye shall gete to yow perpetuell memorye of worshyppe and of glorye, for by your prowesse ye shall in lytyll space have alle vaynquysshid hem, and they shall not dare deffende hem ayenst yow, they ben so wery.' Never wolde Achylles for the wordes of his varlet ne for the deth of Ebes chaunge his corage but dissimyled alle that he had seen and herde for the grete love that he had to Polixene. . . .

[The Greeks had to ask for a two months' truce to bury their dead.]

Duryng these triews the kynge Agamenon sente the duc Nestor, Ulixes & Dyomedes to speke to Achilles for to praye hym and amoneste hym to come to the ooste for to deffende hem ayenst the Trojans that slewe hem over mervayllously. Whan they were come unto hym he resseyvyd hem wyth grete joye. And than Ulixes sayd to hym, Syre Achilles, ne was hit not by your entencion and also owres alle of this ooste to leve oure contre and come renne upon kynge Pryant and destroye hym and his by force of armes and bete doun his cyte. For whens cometh this newe corage after so many hurtes and domages as we have resseyvyd in this lande by the Trojans, that have slayn so many kynges and prynces, pylled and robbed oure tentys and brente oure shippes? And we were now in hope to have vaynquysshid hem after that ye by your force and valeur have slayn Hector that was the verray tutor of the Trojans. And also now that Deyphebus is dede the Trojans ben therwyth put under foote. And than after this that ye have goten with so grete travayll, so grete worshippe and so good renome, wyll ye now lese alle attones and suffre your peple to be slayn cruelly that ye have so longe deffended with the effusion of your blood? Plese hit to yow fro hens forth to entretene & kepe your good renome[1] and defende your peple that wyth oute yow may not longe defende hem ayenst your enemyes, to the ende that we may come to the victorye by your prowesse, by the whiche we hope to attayne and come.[2]

Sire Ulixes, sayd than Achilles, yf we be come in to this lande for

---

[1] 'Good renown' is the theme of Achilles and Ulysses in III.3.74–190.

[2] Caxton's Ulysses, unlike Shakespeare's, knows nothing of Achilles' love for Polyxena; cf. III.3.193–214.

tho causes that ye have declared, we maye saye that grete folye was amonge us, that for the wyf of one of us, that is to wete of syre Menelaus, so many kynges and so hyghe princes be but in paryll of deth. Had hit not ben moche more wysdom for the noble Palamydes to have abyden in peas in his contree than for to be slayn here, and other kynges and prynces in lyke wyse? Certes, as the most grete partye of the worlde of noble men ben here now assemblid, yf they dye here, as many ben all redy dede, hit muste nedes folowe that the contrees shall be replenysshid and governed by villayns. Hector, that was so noble and so worthy, is he not dede? In lyke wyse I may dye lightly that am not so stronge as he was. And therfore how moche as ye requyre me to goo to bataylle, so moche payne and laboure lese ye. For I have no more entencion to putte me more in danger, and love better to lese my renomee than my lyf, for in the ende ther is no prowesse but hit be forgoten. Nestor and Dyomedes contendeden ynowh to drawe Achilles to their quarellis, but they myght never enduce hym to theyr porpose, ne the wordes of Agamenon neyther. And than he sayd to hem that they shold make pees with the Trojans to fore that they were alle slayn &c.

Than retorned these thre prynces unto Agamenon and sayde to hym alle that they had founde in Achilles. And Agamenon dyde hit to be knowen to the prynces of the ooste, whom he had assemblid for this cause, and demanded of them theyr avyse. Than stode up Menelaus sayng that hit shold be to us now grete vylonnye to seke pees wyth the Trojans syn that Hector and Deyphebus ben dede and slayn, and that for theyr deth the Trojans repute them as vaynquysshid and that wyth out Achilles they sholde well mayntene the warre agaynst the Trojans. To that answerd Ulixes & Nestor and sayde that hit was not mervayll though Menelaus desired the warre for affeccion to recovere his wyf and that Troye was not so disgarnysshid but that they had a newe Hector. That was Troyllus, that was a lityll lasse stronge and worthy than Hector. And ther was also another Deyphebus, and that was Parys whom we oughte to dowte as moche as the other. And therfore they counceyllid the pees and to retorne hom agayn to Grece. Than escryed the false traytour Calcas, whiche was traytour to the Trojans, and said, Ha, a, noble men, what thinke ye to doo ayenst the comandement of the goddes? Have not they promisid to yow the victorie, & will ye now leve hit? Certes that shold be grete folye. Take agayn corage to you & fighte ye agaynst the Trojans more stronglye than ye have doon to fore, and cesse not tyll ye have the victorie that the goddes have promisid to yow. And than with the wordes of the said Calcas the Grekes toke herte to hem, sayng veryly that they wold mayntene the warre ayenst the Trojans whether Achilles helpe hem or not, & that for him they wold not leve. . . .

¶ *Of many bataylles that were made on that one side & on that other to their bothe grete domage, & of certayn triews, and of the deth of the noble Troyllus that Achylles slewe ayenst his promys, and drewe hym at his horse tayll thurgh the oost . . .*

Whan the triews of two monethis were passid, they began to fyghte in bataylle right sharpely. There dyde Troyllus mervaylles of armes for to venge the deth of his broder. Dares saith in his book that he slewe that day a thousand knyghtes and the Grekes fledde to fore hym. And the bataylle endured to the nyght that departed hem. The day folowyng the fourtenth bataylle began harde and sharpe. There dide Dyomedes mervaylles of armes and slewe many Trojans and hurte hem, and addressid hym ayenst Troyllus one tyme that smote hym so harde that he smote hym doun to the erthe and was sore hurte, and reprochid hym of the love of Breseyda. Than the Grekes ran with grete strength and toke Dyomedes up & bare hym upon his shelde unto his tente. Menelaus that sawe Dyomedes so beten adressid hym ayenst Troyllus, but Troyllus, that had yet his spere hole, smote hym so harde that he bete hym doun to the erthe sore hurte and was born in to his tente by his men upon his shelde. Than Agamenon assemblid alle his strengthe and threstid in amonge the Trojans and slewe many. But Troyllus cam ayenst hym and smote hym doun of his hors, but he was anon remounted by the helpe of his folk.

Thus finysshid the bataylle that day. And Agamenon sente for to have triews for sixe monethis, which were agreed and accorded by kynge Pryant, how be hit that hit semed to some of his counceyll that he shold not accorded them so longe. Amonge these thinges Breseyda ayenst the will of her fader wente for to see Diomedes that laye sore hurte in his tente. And she knewe well that Troyllus that was her love had so hurte hym. Than retorned in her corage many purposes, and in the ende she sawe that she might never recovere Troyllus and therfore as sone as Diomedes were hole she wolde gyve to hym her love wyth oute lenger taryyng.[1]

Amonge these thinges the kynge Agamenon transported hym unto the tente of Achilles in the companye of duc Nestor and Achilles receyvyd hem wyth grete joye. And than Agamenon prayd hym that he wolde come forthon to the bataylle and suffre no more their peple thus to be slayn. But Achilles wold never molefye his corage for his wordes. How well for as moche as he lovyd Agamenon he

---

[1] This is the last mention of her in Caxton's translation.

agreed and consentid that his men shold go to batayll with oute hym. Wherof Agamenon and Nestor cowde hym grete thanke and thanked hym ynowhe, and after retorned in to theyr tentes. . . .

Whan the bataylle was fynyssid ayenst the even the Myrundones retorned unto the tente of Achilles, and ther was founden many of them hurte, and ther were an honderd of hem dede, wherof Achilles had moche sorowe. And hit was nyght he wente to bedde, and there he had many thoughtes, and purposid ones to go to the bataylle for to avenge the deth of his men; and another tyme he thoughte on the beawte of Polixene, and thoughte that yf he wente he shuld lese her love for alleway, and that the kynge Pryant and his wyf shold holde hym a deceyvour. For he had promysid them that he sholde helpe no more the Grekes. And how well he sayd in hym self that he had sente his men in to theyr ayde. And in this thought Achilles was many dayes . . . [His indecision lasted through the seventeenth battle and into the eighteenth, which was very fierce.] And above alle other Troyllus was angry, that smote in amonge the Grekes, that he had put hem to flight ne had the Mirondones have ben that resisted hym. And therfore Troyllus smote in amonge them and slewe so many and bete doun and dyde so moche that he made the Grekes to reboute hem in to theyr tentes, and descended a fote and entryd in to the tentes and slewe hem on alle sides. And there was so grete a crye that the sowne cam to Achilles that rested hym in his tente and demanded of one of his servantes that was ther what hit was. And he sayd to hym that the Trojans had vaynquys-shid the Grekes and slewe them with in theyr tentes whiche myghte no more deffende them. And wene ye to be sewre here? Nay, ye shall see anone more than fourty thousand Trojans that shall sle yow unarmed. And at this tyme they have slayn the most parte of your Myrundones, and they cesse not to slee them. And ther shall not abide one a lyve but yf they be socouryd.

At these wordes Achilles quoke for yre, and sette behynde hym the love of Polixene and dyde do arme hym hastely[1] and mounted on his hors and ran out all araged as a lyon and smote in amonge the Trojans and pershid hem, slewe and hurte them in suche wyse that anone his swerde was knowen and the blood ran in the felde alle aboute as he wente. Whan Troyllus knewe that Achilles faught with his swerde he adressid hym to hym and gaf hym so grete a strooke that he made hym a grete wounde and a depe, that he muste nedes cesse many dayes of comyng to bataylle. Troyllus was hurte also of the hand of Achilles but no thynge so sore. And bothe fyll doun to the ground. And the bataylle dured unto the nyght. And

[1] V.5.31–35.

on the morn they began agayn & endured unto the even and thus they faught sixe dayes contynuelly. Wherfore ther were many slayn on eyther partye. The kynge Pryant had grete sorowe of this that Achilles ayenst his promyse was come in to the batayll, and wende that he had made hym to understand thynge that was not, but rather for to deceyve hym than otherwyse, and reprochid his wyf to beleve so lightly hym. And Polixene sorowed than ynowhe, for she was plesid than to have had Achilles to her husbond.

Achilles amonge other thynges dyde do hele his woundes duryng sixe monethes of triews that they had goten, whiche woundes Troyllus had gyven hym. And he porposid to avenge hym and that Troyllus shold dye villaynsly by his hande. After these thynges the nynetenth batayll began wyth grete occision. And afore that Achilles entryd in to the bataylle he assemblid his Myrondones and prayd hem that they wolde entende to none other thynge but to enclose Troyllus and to holde hym wyth oute sleynge tyll he cam and that he wolde not be fer fro hem.[1] And they promysid hym that they so do wolde. And he smote in to the bataylle. And of that other syde cam Troyllus that began to slee and bete doun alle them that he raughte, and dyde so moche that aboute mydday he put the Grekes to flight. Than the Myrondones, that were well two thousand fyghtyng men and had not forgete the comandement of theyr lord, threstid in amonge the Trojans and recoverid the felde. And as they helde hem to geder & sought no man but Troyllus, they fonde hym that he foughte strongly & was enclosid on all parties but he slewe & wounded many. And as he was all allone amonge hem and had no man to socoure hym they slewe his horse and hurte hym in many places and araced of his heed his helme and his coyffe of yron. And he deffended hym the beste wyse he cowde. Than cam on Achilles whan he sawe Troyllus alle naked, and ran upon hym in a rage and smote of his heed and caste hit under the feet of the horse and toke the body and bonde hit to the taylle of his horse and so drewe hit after hym thurgh oute the ooste.[2] O what vylonnye was hit to drawe so the sone of so noble a kynge that was so worthy and so hardy! Certes yf ony noblesse had ben in Achilles he wold not have done this vylonye.[3]

Whan Parys knewe that Achilles had thus vylaynsly slayn Troyllus, he had grete sorowe, and so had Eneas and Polidamas, and dyde grete payne to recovere his body. But they myght not for the grete multytude of Grekis that resisted hem. On the other parte the kynge Menon deyde for sorowe for the deth of Troyllus and assayllyd Achylles and sayd to hym in reproche, 'Ha, a, evyll trayttre, what

---

[1] Cf. V.7.1–8.   [2] V.8.21–22.   [3] Cf. V.10.4–5.

cruelte hath mevyd the to bynde to the taylle of thy horse the sone
of so noble a prynce as the kynge Pryant is, and to drawe hym as he
were the moste vylayne of the worlde. Certes thou shalt abyd hit.'
And ran upon hym and smote hym so harde wyth his spere in his
breste that he made hym a grete wounde, and after gaf hym so many
strokes wyth his swerde that he bete hym doun to the ground. And
than was the body of Troyllus recoveryd wyth grete payne. . . .

[Shortly afterwards a truce was called for the burial of Troilus.
Queen Hecuba plotted with Paris to murder Achilles, whom she
invited to meet her in the Temple of Apollo to discuss his desire for
Polyxena. There Paris and his knights ran upon Achilles and slew
him. Paris ordered his body to be thrown 'to the hounds and to the
birds', but Priam let Agamemnon have the corpse. 'Tho arose a
grete sorowe amonge the Grekes, and sayd that they hadde alle
loste . . . And they made for Achilles a noble sepulture.' In the
next battle Ajax and Paris killed each other.]

V. Analogue

THE TESTAMENT OF CRESSEID
by Robert Henryson (1593 edition)

The Testament of Cresseid, Compylit be M. Robert
Henrysone, Sculmaister in Dunfermeling. Imprentit at
Edinburgh be Henrie Charteris. M.D.XCIII.

[The unfaithful Cresseid is warned of her punishment in a dream.]

> Than Cynthia, quhen Saturne past away,   330
> Out of hir sait discendit doun belyve,
> And red ane bill on Cresseid quhair scho lay,
> Contening this sentence diffinityve:
> 'Fra heit of bodie I the now depryve,
> And to thy seiknes sall be na recure,
> Bot in dolour thy dayis to Indure.
>
> 'Thy Cristall Ene minglit with blude I mak,
> Thy voice sa cleir unplesand hoir and hace,
> Thy lustie lyre ouirspred with spottis blak,
> And lumpis haw appeirand in thy face.   340

Quhair thou cummis, Ilk man sal fle the place.
This sall thow go begging fra hous to hous
With Cop and Clapper lyke ane Lazarous.'

This doolie dreame, this uglye visioun
Brocht to ane end Cresseid fra it awoik,
And all that Court and convocatioun
Vanischit away, than rais scho up and tuik
Ane poleist glas, and hir schaddow culd luik:
And quhen scho saw hir face sa deformait
Gif scho in hart was wa aneuch God wait.   350

Weiping full sair, 'Lo quhat it is' (quod sche)
'With fraward langage for to mufe and steir
Our craibit Goddis, and sa is sene on me?
My blaspheming now have I bocht full deir.
All eirdlie Joy and mirth I set areir.
Allace this day, allace this wofull tyde,
Quhen I began with my Goddis for to Chyde.'

Be this was said ane Chyld come fra the Hall
To warne Cresseid the Supper was reddy,
First knokkit at the dure, and syne culd call: 360
'Madame your Father biddis you cum in hy.
He hes merwell sa lang on grouf ye ly,
And sayis your prayers bene to lang sum deill.
The Goddis wait all your Intent full weill.'

Quod scho: 'Fair Chyld ga to my Father deir,
And pray him cum to speik with me anone.'
And sa he did, and said: 'Douchter quhat cheir?'
'Allace' (quod scho) 'Father my mirth is gone.'
'How sa?' (quod he), and scho can all expone
As I have tauld, the vengeance and the wraik   370
For hir trespas, Cupide on hir culd tak.

He luikit on hir uglye Lipper face,
The quhilk befor was quhyte as Lillie flour,
Wringand his handis oftymes he said allace
That he had levit to se that wofull hour,
For he knew weill that thair was na succour
To hir seiknes, and that dowblit his pane.
Thus was thair cair aneuch betuix thame twane.

Quhen they togidder murnit had full lang,
Quod Cresseid: 'Father, I wald not be kend,   380
Thairfoir in secreit wyse ye let me gang
Into yone Hospitall at the tounis end.
And thidder sum meit for Cheritie me send
To leif upon, for all mirth in this eird
Is weird.' fra me gane, sic is my wickit

Than in ane Mantill and ane bawer Hat,
With Cop and Clapper wonder prively,
He opnit ane secreit yet, and out thair at
Convoyit hir, that na man suld espy,
Unto ane Village half ane myle thairby,   390
Delyverit hir in at the Spittaill hous,
And daylie sent hir part of his Almous.

Sum knew her weill, & sum had na knawledge
Of hir becaus scho was sa deformait,
With bylis blak ouirspred in hir visage,
And hir fair colour faidit and alterait.
Yit thay presumit for hir hie regrait,
And still murning, scho was of Nobill kin:
With better will thairfoir they tuik hir in.

[After 'The Complaint of Cresseid' (nine stanzas), the story is
resumed.]

That samin tyme of Troy the Garnisoun,
Quhilk had to Chiftane worthie Troylus,
Throw Jeopardie of Weir had strikken doun
Knichtis of Grece in number mervellous,
With greit tryumphe and Laude victorious
Agane to Troy richt Royallie thay raid
The way quhair Cresseid with the Lipper baid.   490

Seing that companie thai come all with ane stevin
Thay gaif ane cry and schuik coppis gude speid,
Said 'Worthie Lordis for goddis lufe of Hevin,
To us Lipper part of your Almous deid.'
Than to thair cry Nobill Troylus tuik heid,
Having pietie, neir by the place can pas,
Quhair Cresseid sat, not witting quhat scho was.

Than upon him scho kest up baith hir Ene,
And with ane blenk it come into his thocht,

That he sumtime hir face befoir had sene. 500
Bot scho was in sic plye he knew hir nocht,
Yit than hir luik into his mynd it brocht
The sweit visage and amorous blenking
Of fair Cresseid sumtyme his awin darling.

Na wonder was, suppois in mynd that he
Tuik hir figure sa sone, and lo now quhy.
The Idole of ane thing, in cace may be
Sa deip Imprentit in the fantasy,
That it deludis the wittis outwardly,
And sa appeiris in forme and lyke estait, 510
Within the mynd as it was figurait.

Ane spark of lufe than till his hart culd spring
And kendlit all his bodie in ane fyre.
With hait Fewir ane sweit and trimbling
Him tuik, quhill he was reddie to expyre.
To beir his Scheild, his Breist began to tyre
Within ane quhyle he changit mony hew,
And nevertheless not ane ane uther knew.

For Knichtlie pietie and memoriall
Of fair Cresseid, ane Gyrdill can he tak, 520
Ane Purs of gold, and mony gay Jowall,
And in the Skirt of Cresseid doun can swak:
Than raid away, and not ane word spak,
Pensiwe in hart, quhill he come to the Toun,
And for greit care oft syis almaist fell doun.

The Lipper folk to Cresseid than can draw,
To se the equall distributioun
Of the Almous, bot quhen the gold thay saw,
Ilk ane to uther prewelie can roun,
And said: 'Yone Lord hes mair affectioun 530
How ever it be, unto yone Lazarous,
Than to us all, we knaw be his Almous.'

'Quhat Lord is yone' (quod scho) 'have ye na feill,
Hes done to us so greit humanitie?'
'Yes' (quod a Lipper man) 'I knaw him weill,
Schir Troylus it is, gentill and fre:'
Quhen Cresseid understude that it was he,
Stiffer than still, thair stert ane bitter stound
Throwout hir hart, and fell doun to the ground.

Quhen scho ouircome, with siching sair & sad,
With mony cairfull cry and cald ochane:
'Now is my breist with stormie stoundis stad,
Wrappit in wo, ane wretch full will of wane.'
Than swounit scho oft or scho culd refrane,
And ever in hir swouning cryit scho thus:
'O fals Cresseid and trew Knicht Troylus.

Thy lufe, thy lawtie, and thy gentilnes,
I countit small in my prosperitie.
Sa elevait I was in wantones,
And clam upon the sickill quheill sa hie,
All Faith and Lufe I promissit to the,
Was in the self fickill and frivolous:
O fals Cresseid, and trew Knicht Troilus.' . . .

VI. Possible Source

THE TROILUS AND CRESSIDA PLOT

(A)

     r 〉 $\overline{at}$ 〈..
     〉〈 〉reo〈 〉e,   〈
     〉 *Uliſſes*   *A*〈   x
     〉 *dore*   〈*He*〉*rrauld*〈

5   〈*Pr*〉*iam,*   *Hecto*〈   〉*eiph*〈
     〈*ex*〉*eunt*   [....] 〈   o〉*med,* 〈..
     & 〈*D*〉*eiphob*〈   〉 *the rest* &
     〈*He* 〉*aʰu*〉*lds, to* 〈   m〉 *Menalaus*

   3· *ſeuera*〈*ll*〉   〈...... ..〉*s* & *Diomede, to them Hect*

10   〈*T*〉*ucketts*   〈*D* 〉*hobus, to them Caſſandra ex*

(B)   *Alar*〈*ũ*〉   *Excurſions*

   excurſions   *Enter Hector* &   [*Antenor*] *exeu* (Priam: mr Jones)

(C)   *exc*〈.... 〉   *Enter A*〈   〉

(D)   *Alarũ*   〈 〉*ter Antenor purſue*〈*d* 〉*by Diome*

15   *to them Aiax, to the*〈*m*〉 *on the*
     walls Hector Paris 〈&〉 *D*〈*e*〉*iphob*
  〈......*etr..t*〉 & 〈*m*〉*ʳ H*〈*u*〉*nt*   *exeunt*

(E)   *E*〈*nte*〉*r Tro*〈*y*〉*l*〈 *s* &〉 *Pandarus*
     to t〈*h*〉*em Creſſida* & *a waight*〈

20.   *maid* wᵗʰ *a l*〈*ig*〉*ht, mʳ Jones his bo*
     exit〈 *w*〉*ai*〈*g*〉*htng maid, exeunt mar*
   〈   〉 *Pan*〈*da* 〉*to* 〈*h*〉*im Deiphobus, e*
     D〈*ei*〉*p*〈*h b* 〉*to him Helen* & *Pari*

24   *exit Panda*〈*r*〉*us, exeunt omne*

(F)   *E*〈*n*〉*ter Priam, Hect*〈*o*〉*r, Deiphobus, Pa*
     H〈*el* 〉 *Caſſandra ·* [*to them*] *exi*

27   *De*〈*i b*〉*us.* & *Enter* 〈 〉 *Uliſſes a*

(G)
28

)E⟨
) |D⟨e
.. ⟩ |
larŭ |Enter⟨   ....   (H) 30
Diomede, menalay⟨
& beat Hector in ·   *Antenor*

larŭ | Enter   Hector   and ⟨[Priam ᵐʳ J⟨o⟩nes]   (I)
                              ∧[*Antenor*] *exeun⟨t*

larŭ | Enter   Diomede   to   Achil⟨lis   Tent⟩   (J) 35
to   them   Menalay,   to   them   Uliſſes
to   them   Achillis   in   his. Tent   ·to
them · Aiax   wᵗʰ   patroclus   on   his
⟩ *back ·   exeunt*

Enter · Creſſida, wᵗʰ Beggars, pigg   (K) 40
Stephen, mʳ Jones his boy · &   mutes
to them Troylus, ⟨& Deipho⟩bus & proctor
exeunt

Ente⟨r ⟩Priam · Hector, Paris Hellena   (L)
Caſſan⟨d⟩ra Polixina to the⟨m⟩ Antenor   45

larŭ | Enter   D⟨ ⟩med · & Troylus · · to the⟨m⟩   (M)
Achillis · ⟨ ⟩o them Hector & Deipho⟨bus⟩
to them on · the walls Priam Paris
⟨*tr....t*⟩ *Hellen Polixina & Caſſan⟨dra⟩ to the⟨m⟩*
vliſſes Aiax Menalay &   H⟨e⟩a⟨r ⟩   50
Priam & they on . the wall desce⟨nd to th⟩em

[1] Printed by permission of the delegates of the Oxford University Press from W. W. Greg, *Dramatic Documents from the Elizabethan Playhouses*, Oxford. 1931. The line-numbers and lettering of scenes are Greg's.

TIMON OF ATHENS

INTRODUCTION

TIMON OF ATHENS was first printed in the First Folio of
1623 in the place between *Romeo and Juliet* and *Julius Caesar*
where *Troilus and Cressida* was originally intended to be[1] (v.
supra 83). Perhaps the play would have been printed later in
the volume but for the need to fill the gap left by the temporary
withdrawal of *Troilus*. Fill the gap it could not, for it is a much
shorter play. The condition of its text is such that it might not
have been printed but for the emergency in the printing house.

Doubts have been expressed about the extent of Shakespeare's
authorship of this incomplete tragedy,[2] but a common view
today is that the text represents Shakespeare's rough draft of a
play which he never finished, and that it was printed either
from his own 'foul papers' or from a scribe's copy made from
them.[3] If this be so then the play, however defective, may throw
light on Shakespeare's practice in composition. Some of the
many textual oddities may be due to the scribe or the compositors, but some may be accounted for by author's inconsistencies
not properly revised, e.g. the spellings Apemantus and Aper-
mantus, Ventidius, Ventidgius, Ventigius, etc. There are
wide discrepancies in the references to 'talents', which Professor
T. J. B. Spencer has accounted for by the theory that 'in the
course of writing the play Shakespeare (i) became aware that
he did not know the value of the talent, (ii) found out this
piece of information from some person or book, and (iii) then
in several places got his figures right.'[4] I incline to believe that
Shakespeare did not know the value of a talent, and (with
Mr Maxwell[5]) that he got into difficulties by conflating two

---

[1] For bibliographical discussions see W. W. Greg, *The Shakespeare First Folio.*
Oxford, 1955; J. W. Schroeder, *The Great Folio of 1623.* (1956); J. C. Maxwell,
ed. *Timon, Camb.* (1957), 87–97.

[2] Well summarized by J. C. Maxwell in *Camb.*

[3] Cf. E. K. Chambers, *WSh,* 1930, I, 482.

[4] 'Shakespeare Learns the Value of Money', *Sh Survey* VI, 1953.

[5] *Camb.* 95–7.

accounts, the one in Lucian's *Timon* whence he took Ventidius's debt and dowry, with small amounts [*inf.* 273], and that in Plutarch [*sup.* V. 255] where the amounts are larger.

In discussing the lineation of the Folio text Mr Maxwell suggests that 'in some of the rougher scenes, Shakespeare had probably not decided exactly what was to be verse and what prose.' This might well happen if the author were rapidly sketching out a scene to be elaborated later, and particularly, one might guess, where the material had to be invented rather than built up on an already existing prose version. Professor Ellis Fermor pointed out that some speeches have all the signs of notes for blank verse, e.g. Alcibiades' speech to the Senate (III.5).[1]

Both the texture and the structure of the play certainly leave much to be desired, yet the grandeur and intensity of certain speeches and the adroit handling of some situations suggest that parts had been carefully thought out and others left undecided. A study of the sources and analogues provided below will give the reader food for speculation about the nature of the piece and how Shakespeare might have developed it.

Timon, son of Echecratides, was born in the fifth century B.C. in Collytos, a district of Athens to the north-east of the Acropolis. He emerged into literature in the comedies of Aristophanes, who referred to him several times. Thus in *The Birds* Prometheus, accused of being the enemy of the gods, agrees: 'Yes, yes, like Timon. I'm a perfect Timon; just such another' (l. 1548). Another allusion occurs in the *Lysistrata*, where the women, in revolt against their menfolk, sing a song about Timon as a man who sensibly turned against his fellow men but was 'dear to all the womankind'.[2]

Plato is said by Plutarch to have referred to Timon. He was apparently a major character in two (lost) comedies, *Monotropos* (*The Solitary*) by Phrynichus (5th cent.) and another by Antiphanes (4th cent.).[3] A life of Timon was compiled by

---

[1] *Shakespeare the Dramatist*, 1961, pp. 163–6.

[2] 'Savage Timon, all forlorn, / Dwelt amongst the prickly thorn, / Visage-shrouded, Fury-born. / Dwelt alone, / Far away / Cursing men / Day by day; / Never saw his home again, / Kept aloof from haunts of men: / Hating men of evil mind, / Dear to all the womankind' (Loeb trans. by B. B. Rogers, III, 1946, p. 81, ll. 808–20).

[3] Cf. 'The Sources of *Timon of Athens*', by W. H. Clemons, *Princeton College Bulletin*, XV, 1904, 208–23.

Neanthes of Cyzicus (*c.* 200 B.C.) and he was the subject of many epigrams or epitaphs by other poets besides Callimachus.[1] Cicero in his fourth Tusculan oration declared that fear was the cause of much hatred, 'like the hatred of all mankind which is termed *misanthropos*, and like *inhospitality*' associated with Timon's name.[2] About the same date Strabo (64 B.C.–*c.* A.D. 21), writing about Alexandria in his *Geography*, declared that Antony in despair went to the extremity of the Mole, where he 'built a royal lodge which he called the Timonium. This was his last act, when, forsaken by his friends, he sailed away to Alexandria after his misfortune at Actium, having chosen to live the life of a Timon.'[3] Pausanias in his *Description of Attica*, after mentioning the monument of Plato, wrote, 'In this part of the country is seen the tower of Timon, the only man to see that there is no way to be happy except to shun other men.'[4]

In the first century A.D. Plutarch, probably remembering Strabo, introduced Timon into his *Life of Antony* [*supra* Vol. V. 304 and *inf.* Text I]. What he wrote there of Timon was brief, and though he declared, 'Many other things could we tell you of this Timon', he never did so. For him as for most other early writers Timon was the personification of surliness,[5] a hater of men and gods, the enemy of society and all that made for civilization. But the analogy with Antony shows that Plutarch regarded Timon as one who had been abandoned by his friends.

The development of the Timon legend into a tale of excessive liberality, base ingratitude, disillusionment, withdrawal and revenge was due to the dialogue *Timon, or the Misanthrope* by Lucian of Samosata (*c.* A.D. 125–180), a Syrian who settled in Athens and made the Greek satiric dialogue into an important literary form. It has been thought probable[6] that Lucian got the plan of his dialogue from the lost comedy by Antiphanes. This cannot be proved, but certain ingredients may well have originated in Aristophanes' comedy *Plutus* (388 B.C.): the blindness of Riches (caused by Zeus so that Riches would visit

---

[1] Clemons, *op. cit.*
[2] Trans. J. E. King, Loeb edn, 1945, IV, xi.
[3] Trans. H. L. Jones, Loeb edn, 1932, Vol. 8, Bk. xvii, 9.
[4] Trans. W. H. S. Jones, Loeb edn, 1918, Vol. 1, Bk. I, xxx, 4.
[5] But Theophrastus did not allude to Timon in his 'Character' of 'Surliness'.
[6] E.g. by A. M. Harman, the Loeb translator.

good and bad men alike); the description of the extreme types
(misers and prodigals) who abuse wealth; the discussion of the
virtues brought respectively by Riches and Poverty.[1]

Lucian begins with a long diatribe in which the poverty-
stricken Timon describes how he is ill-treated by his former
friends and demands that the Father of the Gods punish them.
At first Zeus does not recognize his former worshipper, but then
resolves to send Plutus (Riches) down to Timon with Hermes.
Riches is unwilling, since Timon got rid of his wealth so foolishly,
and there is some talk about the two extremes of prodigality
and miserliness. Riches however has to go with Hermes, and on
the way they discuss Riches' lameness and blindness, how he
hides his defects from men, and the evils that accompany him.
They find Timon digging, surrounded by Poverty and companion virtues. Riches wishes to withdraw, but Hermes
dismisses Poverty.

Timon no longer wants Riches, but he is forced to obey
Zeus, and when he digs up treasure he rejoices. The effect
however is to fortify him in his love of solitude and hatred of
mankind. Immediately he is beset by sycophants seeking his
gold, and the behaviour of four of them affords excellent satire
on toadies, hypocrites, liars, orators and philosophers. The
dialogue ends with Timon driving off all comers with showers
of stones.

Lucian's Timon is a study in disillusionment. The man who
has wasted his substance in misplaced generosity has rebelled
against mankind and the injustice of the gods. His life as a
farm-labourer is described as wretched, yet he claims that he
has learned virtue by poverty. What he *has* learned is self-
sufficiency, and when he finds the treasure he is not, as might
have been expected, reconciled to society or to divine justice.
He is strengthened by his visitors in his resolve to hoard his
gold, to shun his fellow men, and to live entirely for himself.
The genial prodigal becomes the churlish miser.

In early Christian days Lucian was admired for his style, his
wit, and his attacks on classical deities, sophistical orators and
philosophers. But in the Middle Ages he was little known
(because Greek was little understood) until Aurispa of Sicily
(who in 1423 brought over two hundred Greek MSS to Venice)

[1] Cf. Aristophanes trans. B. B. Rogers, Loeb. Vol. III, 1946.

reintroduced him into Italy, after which references to him began again. After the first printed edition of Lucian in Greek appeared in 1494–6, his work was rapidly translated and edited in Latin and Italian. Erasmus and his group loved Lucian. Erasmus not only translated into Latin many of the dialogues, including *Timon*, *The Cock*, the *Icaromenippus* and the *Banquet*, but imitated Lucian's manner in his dialogue *Ciceronianus*, in *The Praise of Folly*, and the *Colloquia*. Luther indeed called him disparagingly a 'second Lucian' (*Epistles*, ccclxiii). Sir Thomas More wrote Latin versions of the *Cynic*, the *Menippus* and the *Philopseudes* (published with Erasmus's), and on the continent Ulrich von Hutten, Melanchthon, Reuchlin, Budé and Rabelais translated or imitated Lucian. Many of the dialogues were translated into Italian by Lonigo (editions 1535, 1541) and into French ('purged of all offensive words') by Filbert Bretin (1581). There was no large English translation of the dialogues in the sixteenth century. The version of the *Timon* given below is based on the Italian of Lonigo [Text III]. In England in Shakespeare's time something of Lucian was known to Gabriel Harvey, Thomas Lodge, Marlowe, Nash, Dekker and Ben Jonson. Dekker indeed satirized Jonson as 'Lucian' in *Satiromastix*, IV, 2. Jonson drew on Lucian for his *Poetaster*, IV, 5, and for *Volpone*.

The Timon dialogue entered modern drama in the *Timone* of Matteo Maria Boiardo, author of the *Orlando Innamorato*. This verse-comedy, performed in about 1487 before Ercule, Duke of Este, at Ferrara, was mainly a translation and expansion of Lucian's text with new material ingeniously added. Passages from the play are translated in Text IV.

After introducing his play with a Prologue and an Argument spoken by Lucian himself, Boiardo divides it into five Acts supposed to take place on consecutive days. The fifth Act was original. *Timone* was one of those early Italian pieces, like Poliziano's *Orfeo* (1471), performed on two stage-levels, (one here representing Heaven, the other Earth (with a mountain— Hymettus—to link them)), and introducing Gods, men and allegorical personages. The acts are divided into scenes with simple stage directions. In the original text some of the costumes must have been described.

In the Prologue, spoken by Lucian, Boiardo gives Timon a

family background, describing how his father became wealthy by usury but lived meagrely, and died leaving his young son ignorant of the world. Hence the extravagance which has brought him to poverty and disillusion. The first three scenes follow Lucian's text closely, but Scene 4 shows Timon going to rest and hoping not to dream of men, who alone of beasts are hostile to their kind. This last is a commonplace going back to Pliny. Act II follows Lucian's discussions between Zeus and Plutus, and between Mercury and Plutus on their way to earth. At the beginning of Act III, Sc. 1, Boiardo inserts a passage in which Timon wishes that he could make the soil bring forth poisons and spread death, hunger and pestilence over the world, to slay all human beings. Poverty (protesting that she has taught Timon how he should live) is driven off by Mercury (III.2). Timon in III.3. declares that he has been better off with Poverty than formerly with Riches. When in III.4 he finds the Treasure he forgets all this in joy at the discovery and, gloating over the gold, resolves to hoard it and to keep himself solitary and selfish and to hate mankind, the most ungrateful of animals. His self-dedication to misanthropy follows Lucian. To cover a lapse of time passed over by Lucian, Boiardo starts IV.1 with a monologue in which Fame tells the audience that she has spread the news of Timon's new wealth. In IV.2 Timon still feels unhappy because wealth brings new anxieties, and decides to bury his treasure. Whereas Lucian gives him no time for this, Boiardo shows him searching around and finding the tomb of Timocrates. This introduces a new theme related to the main one, for Timocrates, like Timon's own father, was a miser, and his son Filocoro, after wasting his inheritance, is in prison for debt. Timon is amazed to find two urns of gold in the tomb and shows his inhumanity by determining to keep them for himself. IV.3–6 expose the visitors to Timon's wrath, after which he goes to rest.

　　Having exhausted Lucian's material, Boiardo in Act V develops the theme propounded in IV.2. In V.1 an allegorical character, Help (Ausilio), explains how Timocrates came to bury treasure in his grave. Meaning to help his extravagant son he gave Filocoro a sealed letter which after ten years he must bring to the tomb, and read there. In V.2 Timon's anxiety about his hoard is revealed in a dream about ants which he relates. In V.3 two new characters (Parmeno, Filocoro's freedman, and Siro a slave) enter with the letter, since the time is up and Filocoro cannot bring it to the tomb. Siro reads the letter and they realize that the tomb contains the wherewithal to free Filocoro. In V.4 Timon talks with the two servants and regrets his cupidity. He decides to return to his simple life of toil without Riches, but true to his misanthropic nature tries to drive Parmeno and Siro away. They however hide, intending to return to the tomb later. Timon curses the audience, offering them the rope round his waist to hang themselves (V.5). In V.6 Help ends the play somewhat lamely by saying that the treasure will be taken, Filocoro will get his father's gold and the two servants will share Timon's. All three will live happily, in moderation.

As R. Warwick Bond has pointed out,[1] Boiardo probably took hints from Plautus for his additions to Lucian. Ausilio (Help) who fills in gaps in the story for the audience's benefit may derive from the *Cistellaria* where in I.3 Auxilium enters quite unexpectedly and demands the audience's attention, 'so that I may give you a clear, trim outline of this play'. Maybe Timon's dream was suggested by a not dissimilar warning dream in *Mercator*, II.1. There are a buried crock of gold and a miser's anxiety about its safety in *Aulularia*, and a parallel to the letter-theme occurs in the *Trinummus* in which a father (not dead but gone abroad) has left much treasure concealed in his house to save it from his extravagant son.[2]

In Spain Pedro Mexía told the story of Timon in his *La Silva de varia lección* (1542). This was translated into French by Claude Gruget (1552), and from French into English by William Painter whose Novel 28 in his *Palace of Pleasure* told 'Of the straunge and beastlie nature of Timon of Athens, enemie to mankinde, with his death, buriall, and Epitaphe' [Text V]. Mexía stressed the sub-human, brutish quality of Timon, and made him live 'alone in a little cabane in the fieldes'. Timon chose his burial place so that the sea 'might beate upon and vexe his dead Carcas'. This account contained only one epitaph.

---

[1] 'Lucian and Boiardo in *Timon of Athens*', *MLR*, 26, 1931, 52–68.
[2] Cf. Loeb edition of Plautus, *Cistellaria*, Vol. II, *Mercator*, Vol. III, *Aulularia*, Vol. I, *Trinummus*, Vol. V.

There are many references to Timon in Elizabethan times. Noteworthy are the brief accounts in John Alday's *Theatrum Mundi* (1566) and Sir R. Barckley's *Discourse on the Felicitie of Man* (1598), both of whom substituted 'gibbets' for the fig-tree on which Timon offered to let the Athenians hang themselves. Alday's narrative, translated from the French of P. Boaistuau, is given below [Text VI].

The relationship between Shakespeare's play and the anonymous *Timon* preserved in Dyce MSS [1] has often been discussed. The latter is an academic play, probably written for school or college performance, and unlikely to have been played on a public stage. Parallels with the *Pedantius* of Anthony Wingfield, performed at Cambridge in 1580, made G. C. Moore Smith regard it as probably a Cambridge play. [2]

This *Timon* is a long clumsy pedantic piece in which a broadly comic sub-plot parallels the action and ideas of the main-plot. In the main-plot Timon, at the peak of his wealth and popularity, is warned by his servant Laches against prodigality, but glories in his generosity (I.1). When his friend Eutrapelus (I.2) is threatened by his usurer Abyssus, Timon gives him five talents. He feasts his parasites, and when Laches again warns him he turns the faithful man out-of-doors (I.5). Laches however returns disguised as a soldier (II.2) and takes service anew with his master (II.3). When Demeas the orator is arrested, Timon frees him with sixteen talents (II.4). Made 'lord' of a wedding-feast (II.5), he orders great conviviality and falls in love with the bride, who refuses the groom chosen by her father and gladly turns to Timon, not for love but for his wealth, saying, 'Who doth possesse most golde shall mee possesse' (III.2). They are about to be married when a shipwrecked sailor announces that all Timon's ships have been sunk, and he is ruined (III.5). At once his bride and all his friends forsake him, and Timon is distraught. In IV.1 Timon, now homeless, asks Demeas and Eutrapelus for 'houseroom'. They pretend not to know him, whereupon he utters a Senecan diatribe and falls to the ground. Lying there, he is mocked and wishes he could be some animal hostile to men (IV.2). When he

---

[1] First published by A. Dyce for the Shakespeare Society in 1842; and reprinted in Hazlitt, *Shakespeare's Library*, VI, 1875.

[2] *Pedantius*, ed. G. C. Moore Smith. Bang's *Materialien*, 1905; and *MLR*, iii, 143.

begs shelter of Hermogenes, the fiddler he has befriended, Hermogenes bids him go hang himself, and when two philosophers try to calm him with stoic commonplaces, he beats them and Hermogenes. He resolves to invite his false friends to a last banquet (IV.3).

At the feast the viands are all stones painted to resemble rich dishes. Timon drives out his betrayers. Only Laches is left (IV.5). In V.2 Timon tries to shake off his servant, and even when Laches reveals his identity to prove his fidelity, bids him keep his distance. They vie with each other in railing against human nature. When Timon finds gold (V.3) he wishes to throw it into the sea, but Laches prevails on him to use it to avenge himself. He decides to dwell alone, and 'Lett that day be unfortunate wherein I see a man', but he is soon besieged by many clients (V.4). In V.5 his mistress wants him back and the others cringe before him. Demeas brings the decree he has prepared for the Areopagus. Helped by Laches Timon drives them all away. Left alone on the stage he speaks the Epilogue in which he promises to change his nature if the audience will applaud.

Most of this material is obviously based on Lucian's *Timon*. The sub-plot also draws on the *Dialogues* and the *True History*. It concerns Gelasimus, a wealthy young fool, the prey of every shark, who under the influence of Pseudocheus, a lying Traveller who calls himself a 'Worldling', wishes to get into society, to marry Callimela the daughter of the miser Philargurus, and to voyage to the Antipodes. Promised the girl by her father, he disgusts her by his folly, and she rejects him for Timon. Gelasimus sells his property to the usurer Abyssus and gives the proceeds to Pseudocheus (IV.2) who offers to provide a flying horse (Pegasus) for the Antipodean journey but sails away with his booty leaving the penniless young gull a cap with ass's ears. Timon laughs at his grief, offers to help him find a cliff to jump over, and gives him a spade to dig with. After much ridicule Gelasimus woos Blattc, his former mistress' old nurse, but is driven away by Timon with the other fools and knaves. Other comic passages are provided by servants, the philosophers and the fiddler Hermogenes. Stilpo and Speusippus discourse scholastically about philosophy. There are good moments, but the sub-plot takes up too much of the play and the whole thing becomes wearisome. The influence of Plautus is obvious, and there are borrowings from Homer, Juvenal and Horace. The scenes concerning Timon are given below [Text VII].

Moore Smith dated the academic *Timon* 1581–1600, but Herford and Simpson find the influence of Jonson in several places.[1] The first meeting of Gelasimus and Pseudocheus (I.4) recalls that of Asotus with the traveller Amorphus in *Cynthia's Revels*, I.4.28ff. The surprised incomprehension of Gelasimus when Callimela rejects him (III.3), resembles that of Amorphus when Echo will not stay for him (*Cynthia's Revels*, I.3.24–45). Pseudocheus's absurd instructions to Gelasimus on wooing, I.4, recall Amorphus's instructions to Asotus. The name Philargyrus (the 'late-deceased' father of Asotus) is transferred to the father of Callimela.[2]

There are resemblances to *Every Man Out of His Humour*. Philargurus's servant Grunnio is called 'leane macilente Grunnio' (III.4). 'Gelasimus has a grotesque coat of arms (I.3) like Sogliardo's (*E.V.M.O.* III.1); . . . in IV.2 Timon lying on the ground comments on the dialogue, like Macilente (I.2).'

The cap with ass's ears sent by Pseudocheus to Gelasimus as a parting present (V.3) is reminiscent of the ass's ears placed on the tribune Asinius Lupus in *Poetaster* (V.3.130), which also contains a drinking song to Bacchus (III.1.8–12, cf. *Timon* I.2).

If the author of the academic *Timon* used Jonson's *Poetaster* (pubd. 1602), he must have written his play after 1601. G. A. Bonnard dates it later than this.[3] The faithful servant Laches (whose name was taken from that of one of the syco-phants in Lucian [*inf.* 277]) reminds one of Kent in *King Lear*, who is driven out for reproving his master, but returns in disguise and stays with Lear to the end. Shakespeare took this character from Perillus in the old play of *King Leir* (*c.* 1594?). But there is another resemblance to Shakespeare's play in the scene (V.3) where Timon invites the despairing Gelasimus to kill himself.

---

[1] G. C. Moore Smith, *op. cit.*; C. H. Herford and P. Simpson, ed. *Ben Jonson*, IX, Oxford, 1950, 482–5.

[2] Herford and Simpson err in supposing that he was the father of Gelasimus (*ibid.* 483). They also think that the cap with ass's ears was 'sent to Timon as a present'. It was sent to Gelasimus.

[3] 'Note sur les Sources de *Timon of Athens*', *Etudes Anglaises*, VII, 1, 1954, 59–69.

This passage with its likeness to *King Lear* IV.1.74ff. and IV.6 has no parallel in the old *Leir*. Shakespeare got it along with much else in the story of Gloucester and Edgar from the story of the blind King of Paphlagonia in Sidney's *Arcadia*. It is much more likely that the academic *Timon* drew on Shakespeare's *King Lear* than that it independently combined material from the old *Leir* play and Sidney's romance. It is unlikely that Shakespeare could ever have known the academic *Timon*, since there is no evidence that it was played publicly or at the Inns of Court. But there are other resemblances; the most remarkable being the banquet at which Timon insults his treacherous friends. In the academic *Timon* he offers them painted stones for food (*inf.* 328); in Shakespeare (III.6) 'covered dishes' which prove to contain hot water, but stones are implied in the line, 'One day he gives us diamonds, next day stones' (III.6.122). In both plays Timon throws the stones at his guests and drives them out. The painted stones come from late Roman history, for it was a prank of the youthful Emperor Heliogabalus so to trick his guests.[1] Bonnard suggests that the two plays made use of a common source.[2] This is possible, but I incline to date the academic *Timon* after Shakespeare's play, and after the publication of the first Quarto of *King Lear* (1608).

Shakespeare knew about Timon quite early in his career, for he mentioned him in *Love's Labours Lost*. During the satiric turn of the century many other writers referred to the savage critic of humanity. When Shakespeare began his play is quite uncertain. If the mood has something in common with those of *Troilus and Cressida, Hamlet, Lear* and *Coriolanus*, the style is nearer to the last two of these. Critics have dated it variously before and after *King Lear*. My own inclination is to place it after *Antony and Cleopatra* and before *Coriolanus*, in 1607–8.

Shakespeare's primary source was Plutarch's *Life of Antony* in which he found the general statement of Timon's misanthropy, a suggestion that (like Antony himself) he had been

---

[1] The incident was told by Aelius Lampridius in his *Historia Augusta* (Lyons, 1593, Vol. 2, 383). Camoens alluded to it in a redondilla: 'Se não quereis padecer'. I am indebted to Mr L. de Sousa Rebelo for assistance in tracing the story.

[2] The parallels between the academic play and Ben Jonson led Tucker Brooke (*Tudor Drama*, p. 411n.) to think that Jonson and the anonymous dramatist drew on a common source. More probably the latter echoed Jonson as he echoed Shakespeare.

abandoned by his friends, his relationships with Alcibiades and Apemantus, the anecdote of the fig-tree (V.1.206–13), and the tomb with its two epitaphs.

M. Bonnard[1] notes also that the penitent Senator's reference to 'decimation and a tithed death' (V.4.31) may come from Plutarch's account of how Antony punished the legions which fled from the Medes at the siege of Phraata:

> 'Antonius was so offended withall, that he executed the Decimation. For he divided his men by ten legions, and then of them he put the tenth legion to death on whom the lot fell.' (Wyndham, VI.41)

Other parts of the *Life of Antony* also influenced Shakespeare.[2] After another defeat his soldiers 'willingly offred to take the lotts of Decimation if he thought good' (VI.46). Six of the minor names in *Timon* come from the same *Life*: Lucius, Hortensius, Ventidius, Flavius, Lucilius and Philotus. Shakespeare seems to have taken hints from Antony's luxurious ways to eke out the thin account of Timon. Thus Antony 'ever simply trusted his men in all things ... For he was a plaine man, without suttletie' (VI.24). Trustfulness was one of Timon's early characteristics (II.2.142–5). Antony was surrounded by sycophants who 'gave themselves to riot and excesse, when they saw he delighted in it' (VI.23). His cofferer tried to warn him when Antony wished to give one of his friends twenty-five Myriads (a Decies). Antony called it 'but a trifle; and therefore he gave his friend as much more another tyme' (VI.5). This recalls the snubs received by Flavius the Steward for warning Timon of his empty coffer (II.2.143). Just as '*Antonie* did easely geve away great seignories, realmes, and mighty nations unto some private men' (*ante* V.283, and *A & C*, V.2.90–2), so Timon says

> Methinks I could deal kingdoms to my friends,
> And ne'er be weary. (I.2.223–4)

Shakespeare first read Plutarch years before he began to write his Roman plays, since Theseus in *A Midsummer Night's Dream* owes something to the 'Comparison of Theseus with

---

[1] *Etudes Anglaises*, vii, 1954, p. 62.
[2] E. A. J. Honigmann, '*Timon of Athens*', *ShQ*, xii, 1961, 1–20.

Romulus'. The *Life of Antony* was used for *Julius Caesar* and the latter portion of it—in which Timon appears—for *Antony and Cleopatra*. It may well be that *Timon* was written not long after this last play.

The introduction of Alcibiades was suggested by Plutarch's account of Timon. For more information about him Shakespeare turned to Plutarch's *Life*, which couples him with Coriolanus. There Alcibiades is presented as a man of infinite adaptability, naturally extravagant, luxurious and a seeker after popularity. In prosperity he was 'daintie in his fare, wantonly geven unto light women, riotous in bankets, vaine and womanishe in apparell' [Text II]; but although many feared his insolence and ambition, the Athenians bore with him for 'his courtesies, his liberallities, and noble expenses to shewe the people so great pleasure and pastime . . . and dyd cover his faultes with the best wordes and termes they could, calling them youthfull, and gentlemans sportes.' In his prodigality Alcibiades resembled somewhat Timon before his fall. The introduction of a servile Painter may have been suggested to Shakespeare by Plutarch's anecdote telling how Alcibiades 'kept Agatharchus the painter prisoner in his house by force, untill he had painted all his walles within, and when he had done, dyd let him goe and rewarded him very honestly for his paines.' In Plutarch Shakespeare found Timon's prophecy that Alcibiades was a danger to Athens. Shakespeare however sets the latter in a better light. He appears before the Senate to beg for the life of a friend condemned to death for committing manslaughter in a fit of passion. His appeal is refused and when he insists he is summarily banished.

This recalls the scene in *Richard III* (II.1.96–131) where Stanley begs of Edward IV 'a boon . . . for my service done:

> The forfeit sovereign of my servant's life;
> Who slew today a riotous gentleman
> Lately attendant on the Duke of Norfolk.'

The situation is different, but in each case mercy is refused. No doubt Shakespeare remembered Plutarch's statement that Alcibiades went into hiding because he would not trust the justice of his own country (*inf.* 256). But Alcibiades resembles Plutarch's Coriolanus in several respects. Coriolanus too was unjustly exiled. He led his army to the walls of Rome before withdrawing. Alcibiades in Shakespeare (but not in Plutarch) invests Athens and only then is admitted by the repentant Senators. As Mr Honigmann points out:

> 'While Shakespeare's Alcibiades . . . seems to be conceived as a professional soldier (cf. I.2.76ff., III.5.40ff.) whose sole interest is war, as with Coriolanus, Plutarch's Alcibiades figures in many other capacities'[1]

His anger against Athens resembles Coriolanus's, and he resolves at once to 'strike at Athens' (III.5.108–16) without any of the hesitation he shows in Plutarch's *Life*.

Plutarch makes much of Alcibiades' chameleon-like ability to colour his behaviour according to his environment. In this respect he is entirely unlike Timon who, as Apemantus says, knew only two extremes (IV.3.300). This contrast Shakespeare outlines, though it is not fully developed in the play as we have it. Both men are victims of ingratitude and injustice; both go into exile from the city; but their reactions differ. Whereas Timon sinks into misanthropy, spurning all society, and dies miserably alone. Alcibiades takes positive action, surrounded by an army and accompanied by his concubines. And whereas Timon is unforgiving to the last, Alcibiades shows moderation and mercy. Plutarch's *Life* contained much other evidence of the latter's restraint and patriotism. Although he helped Sparta, he refused to aid the foreigner Tisaphernes to destroy his country, and when recalled he waged successful wars on behalf of Athens. Maybe Shakespeare would have used some of this material had he finished his play. As it is, he includes only the decisive moments.

Plutarch gave him the concubine Timandra and her name; but no trace is kept of the affection for Alcibiades which she showed, according to Plutarch, after he had been murdered. There is nothing to counter Timon's vile abuse of her and Phrynia. She exists for Shakespeare merely so that Timon may revile sex as well as war—repeating the theme of *Troilus*.

The resemblances and common material in *Timon* and *Coriolanus* indicate that *Timon* was probably written first, since it is unlikely that after *Coriolanus* Shakespeare would want to draw

[1] *Ibid.* pp. 7–8.

on the same material or repeat himself so closely in mood and theme. More probably, while drafting *Timon* Shakespeare came to realize the thinness of his subject, and that Coriolanus would give a richer opportunity for a tragedy of wrath and ingratitude. I suspect that Shakespeare abandoned *Timon* to write *Coriolanus*.

Shakespeare certainly knew William Painter's *Palace of Pleasure* well, but Painter had nothing of importance to offer that was not in Plutarch, and omitted such features as the reason for Timon's misanthropy and one of the epitaphs. [Text V]. There is no sign that Shakespeare owed anything at all to John Alday or Sir R. Barckley.

Much of Shakespeare's material derives ultimately from Lucian's *Timon*. No English translation of this dialogue in Tudor times is known, but the dramatist may have read it in Erasmus' Latin version, in Italian, or in French. The reference to 'Plutus the god of gold' in connection with Timon's liberality ('He pours it out', I.1.284–5) recalls the complaints about him by Plutus in the Greek and Latin of Lucian. [Plutus became Richezza in Italian, and Richesse in French.][1]

Mercury's criticism of Timon provided the idea for Shakespeare's portrait of 'the great spendthrift, avoiding all that is unpleasant, allowing himself to expand in a foolish glow of lazy benevolence, and prompted as much by love of admiration and flattery as by a real charity' (R. W. Bond) Lucian is also the final source for the scenes in which Shakespeare's Timon shows his lavish generosity to friends in need, and for those in which they refuse to help him. Thus Shakespeare's Timon frees Ventidius from imprisonment for debt (I.1.95–110) as Lucian's Timon has helped Demeas. Similarly when Timon gives Lucilius money to marry the rich Old Athenian's daughter (I.1.110–52) this recalls Philiades in Lucian, who received 'a whole farm and two talents for his daughter as a reward for his praises'. The servile Poet in Acts I and V was probably suggested by Gnathonides who offered Timon a dithyrambic ode (*inf.* 273).

Timon's declaration that he deserves help from the Senators 'even to the state's best health' (II.2.198–200), which is supported by their later apologies and request that he lead the

[1] For the Greek version, and a translation, see the Loeb edition by A. M. Harmon, 1915, Vol. ii.

defence of Athens against Alcibiades (V.1.139–67) may have been suggested by Demeas's fictions about Timon's feats in war. In the play however the visitors after Timon has found gold do not include Ventidius or Lucilius, and the Senators who come to offer him power have less in common with Demeas than with the Romans who plead with Coriolanus. Apemantus here may be a substitute for Thrasycles; but Shakespeare leaves Lucian far behind in his handling of Timon's attitude.

Timon's apostrophe to gold (IV.3.378–89) differs greatly in tone from Lucian. The lines

> Whose blush doth thaw the consecrated snow
> That lies on Dian's lap,

have been thought to spring from Lucian's 'What maiden would not open her lap to receive so beautiful a lover . . .' (*inf.* 272).[1] But Lucian alludes to Danäe, not Diana. The claim[2] that Shakespeare echoed Lucian's phraseology is hardly substantiated, although there are suggestive parallels.

When Timon takes the name 'Misanthropos' (IV.3.54) this seems to derive from the same resolve in Lucian (*inf.* 272) rather than from Plutarch's marginal note 'Timon Misanthropos the Athenian'. This is inconclusive, but we can say that Shakespeare drew either directly from Lucian or from some work closely modelled on Lucian.

In Apemantus the influence of Plutarch and Lucian may be combined. He is mentioned by Plutarch as one whom Timon liked to have 'in his company, because he was much like of his nature and conditions, and also followed him in manner of life'. Plutarch also tells a surly anecdote which must have reminded Shakespeare of the legendary churlishness of the cynic philosopher Diogenes. At the beginning of the play when Timon is foolishly generous, Apemantus behaves like the cynics in Lucianic dialogues such as 'The Dream, or The Cock', 'Philosophies for Sale' and 'The Banquet'. In this last dialogue the cynic Alcidamas is the target of wit. When welcomed he replies rudely.[3] Shakespeare however may have developed the character and speech of Apemantus along the lines of Diogenes

---

[1] Cf. also IV.3.135–6: 'Hold up, you sluts, Your aprons mountant.'
[2] By K. Deighton, *Arden*, 1905.
[3] Cf. Bonnard, *op. cit.* pp. 61–2.

in John Lyly's play *Campaspe* (1584) [Text VII], where the cynic philosopher utters outrageous remarks and bandies words with Alexander the Great very much as he does with Timon.

In the first part of the play Apemantus acts as a cynical commentator on Timon's entourage and on Timon's folly in not seeing the 'small love among these sweet knaves'. 'Thou giv'st so long, Timon, I fear me thou wilt give away thyself in paper shortly. What needs these feasts, pomps, and vain-glories' (I.2.242-3).

Professor Farnham[1] suggests that Shakespeare took the contrast between Timon's later misanthropy and Apemantus's from Montaigne's essay 'Of Democritus and Heraclitus'. There Montaigne insists on the relativity of human opinions and the subjectivity which colours our attitudes. He likes Democritus's mockery of mankind more than Heraclitus's pity:

> 'methinkes we can never bee sufficiently despised, according to our merit . . . We are not so full of evill, as of voydnesse and inanitie. We are not so miserable, as base and abject. Even so *Diogenes*, who did nothing but trifle, toy, and dally with himselfe, in rumbling and rowling of his tub, and flurting at *Alexander*, accompting us but flies, and bladders puft with winde, was a more sharp, a more bitter, and a more stinging judge, and by consequence, more just and fitting my humour, than *Timon*, surnamed the hater of all mankinde. For looke what a man hateth, the same thing he takes to hart. *Timon* wisht all evill might light on us: He was passionate in desiring our ruine. He shunned and loathed our conversation, as dangerous and wicked, and of a depraved nature. Whereas the other so little regarded us, that wee could neither trouble nor alter him by our contagion; forsooke our company, not for feare, but for disdaine of our commerce: He never thought us capable or sufficient to doe either good or evill.'[2]

What Montaigne writes of Diogenes does not apply to Apemantus, who is no true lover of virtue indifferent to men's

---

[1] *Shakespeare's Tragic Frontier*, pp. 65-7.
[2] *The Essays of Michael Lord of Montaigne, done into English by John Florio*, ed. Thomas Seccombe, 1908, I, Ch. L, p. 418.

opinions, but a railer against society. Undoubtedly Apemantus represents the cynic philosophy, not as Montaigne saw it but as it was generally viewed (with disgust) in Elizabethan England. Hence the mocking allusions to dogs in connection with him. He is a Thersites, a railer on society, himself a dog who snarls at mankind (II.2). Some vestige of humane feeling he possesses, for he warns Timon, and in IV.3.283 offers him better food than roots. This scene in which the two pessimists revile each other's way of life shows the weakness of both their positions. Montaigne pointed out that men's opinions were often the result of their fortunes. Apemantus tells Timon (IV.3.203–19) that his nature has changed through

> A poor unmanly melancholy sprung
> From change of fortune.

He should turn flatterer to get back something of what he has lost. There is nothing philosophic in his 'sour cold habit' since he was forced into it, and cannot live contented in a voluntary wretchedness. Timon retorts that Apemantus is a railer because he has never known anything but poverty. His abstemiousness is enforced upon him, but he has no grounds for hating mankind since they have never flattered him or shown him ingratitude. The implication is that misanthropy is excusable only if the result of bitter experience. Otherwise it is unnatural and vicious. Apemantus's wish that the beasts should inherit the earth is fatuous, since the beasts prey on each other just as men do. Between them the two men reveal the inherent weakness in their hatred of their kind, and when they fall to 'flyting' and Timon drives Apemantus off with stones, it is a logical end for minds debased by peevish passion.

Structurally Shakespeare's play falls into three parts: Timon in prosperity (Act I); Timon ruined (Acts II–III); Timon self-banished (Acts IV–V).

The introductory conversation between the Poet and the Painter takes us at once into an atmosphere well known to Shakespeare in a period when great noblemen patronized the arts and welcomed the flattery of literary men in dedications, prefaces and panegyrics. One thinks of Shakespeare's regret in the Sonnets that he could not equal the style or flattery with which rival poets courted his friend. Doubtless Shakespeare recalled not only Lucian's Gnathonides but also the court of Alexander the Great in Lyly's *Campaspe*, with the great painter Apelles, no sycophant however, but a rival to Alexander himself. The smug pretentiousness of the Poet and the Painter with their artistic clichés is amusing, yet the Poet with his allegory of Fortune's hill issues a warning which the Painter recognizes and commends. Although "'Tis common', it is a major theme of the play, and the explicit enunciation suggests that this is to be a moral piece, simpler than usual in Shakespeare, not so much the subtle portrait of a complex character as an *exemplum* of ethical truths. When Timon enters he is in full spate of giving. He not only frees Ventidius from gaol, but offers 'to support him after' (I.1.96–110), and provides Lucilius with wealth enough to match the dowry of the Old Athenian's daughter (112–54). He accepts the offerings of the Poet and Painter and is gracious to the Jeweller and Merchant (or Mercer).

Apemantus on his first appearance shows himself a typical cynic of Diogenes' breed, denying the honesty of all Athenians, making 'lascivious apprehensions' and preferring plain-speech to any jewel (211–16). He is the enemy of lords and all feigning; he is 'opposite to humanity' (281) and hates the courtesy with which Timon greets Alcibiades.

Timon feasts Alcibiades and his other friends (I.2). He refuses to accept Ventidius's offer of repayment and chides Apemantus for his perpetually angry humour. Apemantus now criticises Timon's friends whom he regards as ravening traitors (I.2.23–53). He warns Timon against waste and says a selfish grace mistrustful of all mankind. The warlike temper of Alcibiades is shown very briefly (74–82), and he is addressed only once again. We see Timon's genial altruism and trust in mankind ('What need we have any friends, if we should ne'er have need of them . . . I have often wished myself poorer that I might come nearer to you. We are born to do benefits. . . ') He weeps with sensibility. There is a masque of Ladies dressed as Amazons, who oddly enough apparently represent the five senses, led by Cupid (a device invented by Timon (151)) on which Apemantus moralizes grimly, ending prophetically, 'Men shut their doors against a setting sun'. The Steward complains about his munificence in giving jewels, and when Timon accepts presents from Lucius and Lucullus, 'Not without fair reward', lets us

17

know that Timon's coffers are now empty, and 'what he speaks is all in debt: he owes For ev'ry word'. The reckless Timon reveals the extravagance of his bounty (208–20) and cares nothing for Apemantus's warnings, which are sound though they come from a tainted source.

At the beginning of Act II the first signs of Timon's approaching downfall appear when a Senator sends urgently for repayment of his loans (Sc. 1) and the servants of Isidore and Varro come on similar missions (II.2.1–13). Timon is incredulous. There is a dialogue apparently in the street (l. 73) between Apemantus and the Fool and Page of some woman who keeps a brothel. This leaves a loose end, for nothing comes of the letters which the Page is carrying to Timon and Alcibiades (II.2.79–85). Flavius explains his position to Timon, who defends his actions

> No villanous bounty yet hath pass'd my heart;
> Unwisely, not ignobly, have I given (176–7),

and, trusting his friends to help him, sends out his servants to ask for immediate aid. This is a short Act, in which Alcibiades appears only for a moment, and says nothing.

In Act III the shadows deepen. Timon's friends react variously but all unfavourably to his requests. Lucullus (Sc. 1) who expected a gift, refuses to lend money 'especially upon bare friendship, without security'. Lucius (Sc. 2), after declaring his gratitude, fails when the test comes, protesting that he is hard up. As in other Shakespearean plays we hear the comments of outsiders on the ethical situation. Sempronius (Sc. 3) pretends to be offended because Timon did not apply to him first, and refuses in a hypocritical huff. In the next scene Timon, forced to stay indoors, is besieged by creditors. His servants try to shield him, and he comes out raging and offering himself to them to be bled and cut to pieces (as theoretically a debtor could be punished in Rome). 'Creditors? Devils!' he cries and at once thinks of giving them a feast fit for devils, a barmecidal feast of illusions. After this the appearance (III.5) of Alcibiades before the Senate comes as a great surprise, and we never learn who the rash friend was who comitted violence, but the suggestion that he may be Timon himself[1] is incredible.

---

[1] Cf. U. Ellis-Fermor, *op. cit.*, pp. 169–70.

The scene however displays another kind of self-destructive generosity and another example of ingratitude. It also introduces a discussion on violence and the endurance of evil which is relevant to the entire play as well as to Alcibiades' own vengeful resolve at the close of the scene. Had Shakespeare developed his plot fully he would certainly have prepared for Alcibiades' appeal in some way. As it is, we have had no previous indication of his past relations with the Senate, nor indeed of his past life.

The condemned man was violent in defence of his honour; so will Alcibiades be, at the expense of his country. The feast in III.6 presents the bewilderment, hypocrisy and rising hopes of Timon's friends, his satiric grace (contrast Apemantus in I.2), and his maledictions, violence, and renunciation of mankind:

> Burn, house! sink, Athens! henceforth hated be
> Of Timon man and all humanity! (III.6.108–9)

In Act IV, Sc. 1, Timon has left Athens and curses the city, invoking confusion and disorder on all Athenians. That he is wrong in his sweeping condemnation is immediately proved when in IV.2 his servants mourn his downfall and Flavius resolves to follow him. The third scene carries on the mood of the first. Timon has not learned, like the Timon of Lucian and Boiardo, any of the compensations of poverty. There has been no time, and Shakespeare's hero knows no alleviation of his bitterness. He finds gold almost at once, and the first visitors arrive. Unlike previous Timons he is not tempted by riches, but prefers roots to 'yellow, glittering, precious gold', and expatiates on its power of corrupting men. He will use his treasure in accordance with its evil nature. This savage twist is peculiarly Shakespeare's.

The entry of Alcibiades and his concubines (two to suggest his licentious nature) enables Timon to begin his work of corrupting others. He gives Alcibiades gold in hope that he will plague Athens and the world with war, and gold to the two women (who gleefully humour his madness) on condition that they spread vice and venereal disease. He is unmoved when Alcibiades (himself in financial straits) offers him money and promises to come again. Left alone, he curses the earth, except for the root he craves and finds. A second visitor, Apemantus, arrives and in the wordy contest between them Timon spurns the philosophy nearest to his own misanthropy, and looks forward to death (IV.3.198–393). Next he is visited by two thieves, 'straggling soldiers' (IV.3.395–456), whom he encourages with gold to cut throats and break open shops, till they are greatly shocked. Fourth comes Flavius whose fidelity at last touches even Timon's bitter heart. He gives gold to this 'singly honest man' (IV.3.522) and, before sending him away, wishes him happiness, but that will be only if he lives for himself alone:

> thou shalt build from men;
> Hate all, curse all, show charity to none (IV.3.525–7)

If these visitations have shown the intensity of Timon's revulsion against humanity they have also shown the weakness of his moral generalisations, since Alcibiades and Flavius both wished to help him, and two of the thieves are converted ('I'll believe him as an enemy, and give over my trade.') Moreover the loyalty of Flavius makes Timon admit an exception to his condemnation: 'I do proclaim the honest man'; but this does not alleviate his insane wrath.

V.1. reintroduces the Poet and the Painter, eager to take advantage of Timon's new generosity ('Then this breaking of his has been but a try for his friends'). The Poet will offer to write a Satire moralizing on Timon's own experiences. But Timon speaks to them in Hamlet-like irony and drives them away. The Senators who come next (V.1.117ff.) beg Timon to take up 'absolute power' and drive back Alcibiades. Timon however (despite a faint relic of patriotism expressed at IV.3. 104–7) receives their appeal with revilings, and proves his love of his country by offering his fig-tree for Athenians to hang themselves. His final message suggests that he too will commit suicide:

> Say to Athens
> Timon hath made his everlasting mansion
> Upon the beached verge of the salt flood;
> Who once a day with his embossed froth
> The turbulent surge shall cover (V.1.215–19)

In a brief scene (V.2) in Athens two Senators anxiously await-

ing news of Timon's reaction to the invitation learn that
Alcibiades also has sent a messenger to ask

> His fellowship i' the cause against your city,
> In part for his sake mov'd.

We do not see Timon die. His seventh and last visitor, Alcibiades' messenger arrives (V.3) to find Timon dead in a rude
grave with an inscription. The last scene of the play (V.4)
shows Alcibiades before the walls of Athens receiving the
apologies of the Senators (who declare that they had previously
tried to recall both him and Timon). To their dignified
admission of guilt and their plea that the innocent should not
suffer with the guilty, Alcibiades replies with great magnanimity:

> Those enemies of Timon's and mine own
> Whom you yourselves shall sct out for reproof,
> Fall, and no more.

When the soldier brings news of Timon's death, Alcibiades
reads his epitaph (made from the two in Plutarch), and ends
the play with words of reconciliation; the sea which washes
over Timon is weeping 'on faults forgiven', and he himself
brings the olive with the sword and peace after war.

That *Timon* is an unsatisfactory play is obvious, but it is hard
to be sure whether its flaws are due to incompleteness or to
weaknesses inherent in the theme. As Miss Ellis-Fermor points
out, Timon is not given enough biographical background to
make him a whole man. The traits we are shown are so limited
that we scarcely know whether to like him or regard him as a
fool becoming a madman.

Is what we have the rough blocking in of a portrait which
could have been worked up into something more like Shakespeare's other tragic heroes? It seems much more likely that in
Timon Shakespeare was experimenting in a different, more
didactic, kind of play than usual. Like Boiardo he was drawn
by the Lucianic source in the direction of a moral *exemplum*.
Timon is conceived in terms of Apemantus's assertion: 'The
middle of humanity thou never knewest, but the extremity of
both ends' (IV.3.300–1). Plutarch presented one extremity;
Lucian indicated the previous existence of the other. Shakespeare developed them both but preserved the ethical antithesis.

So Timon does not develop; he merely swings from the extreme of benevolence to the extreme of misanthropy. In his first state he is, as the First Stranger declares, a man of 'right noble mind, illustrious virtue, / And honourable carriage'. He fulfils many of the requirements of true friendship as Cicero defined it. He is liberal 'not from the mean hope of a return, but solely from that satisfaction which nature has annexed to the exertion of benevolent actions'.[1] He regards friendship as 'a constant interchange and vicissitude of reciprocal good offices', (cf. I.2.90–107), and fulfils Cicero's requirement: 'A truly good man is upon many occasions extremely susceptible of tender sentiments, and his heart expands with joy or shrinks with sorrow as good or ill fortune accompanies his friend'. Such a man's benevolence is not 'confined to a single object; he extends it to every individual. For true virtue enlarges the soul with sentiments of universal philanthropy'. Timon personifies this Ciceronian view. He is not Aristotle's 'magnanimous' man, who 'is disposed to bestow, but ashamed to receive benefits', and who regards himself as superior to those who receive from him. He is one of Aristotle's 'liberal' men (*Ethics*, Bk. IV. Ch. i), but he lacks propriety and judgement. His gifts sometimes seem excessive, and he lacks the ability to discriminate the virtuous from the self-seekers in his choice of friends. When he says 'Unwisely, not ignobly, have I given', he speaks the truth, and illustrates Aristotle's saying that the prodigal 'does not seem to be bad in moral character, for it is not the mark of a wicked or an ungenerous man to be excessive in giving, and not receiving, but rather of a fool.'

So Timon is a noble fool who until his downfall retains our sympathy by reason of his idealism, sensitivity and trusting nature. So far in a sense his 'worst sin is, he does too much good' (IV.2.39). But from the moment when he curses Athens and mankind he becomes ignoble as well as foolish, and, as Cicero pointed out, he needs human company if only to rail against it.[2]

---

[1] Cicero, *Laelius, an Essay on Friendship*. Quotations are from the translation by W. Melmoth (1773).

[2] Cicero, *ibid.* 'Were there a man in the world of so morose and acrimonious a disposition as to shun (agreeably to what we are told of a certain Timon of Athens) all communication with his species, even such an odious misanthropist could not endure to be excluded from one associate, at least, before whom he might discharge the whole rancour and virulence of his heart.' Hence Apemantus.

The unnatural quality of Timon in the wilderness, the brutishness stressed by Painter, is suggested by the imagery of disorder and disease.

The play however is not only about Timon but also about Alcibiades, and if the uneven exposition of his part proves that the play is not, and probably never was, complete, his portrait and his importance especially towards the end of the tragedy are such as to indicate that the dramatist intended to draw a strong contrast between him and Timon. He used Plutarch's *Life of Alcibiades* but slightly, and deviated from what he found there.

Shakespeare seems to have drafted the Timon scenes fairly fully, leaving the Alcibiades theme in the first half of the play to be worked on later. Before his mysterious appeal to the Senate in III.5 he makes two brief appearances, not enough to establish his character or antecedents. Consequently neither the circumstances of his appeal for clemency nor his relationship to the state of Athens are made clear. Shakespeare must have intended to give more than this and maybe the letters carried by the Page in II.2 had something to do with these. Alcibiades does not appear in the brief Act II. Shakespeare's departure from Plutarch's explanation of Alcibiades' banishment is therefore important as indicating that hero's part in the texture of Timon's tragedy. Whereas in Plutarch he was exiled because in his absence enemies accused him of sacrilegious practices, here he suffers because he pleads for mercy for a good warrior who has slain a man to defend his honour and his life; that is, Alcibiades suffers because he is a true and generous friend.

It seems likely that the play was conceived as having two parallel actions, both concerned with the love of one's fellow-men, friendship and ingratitude, violence and the need for patience, moderation and forgiveness. Timon encounters ingratitude in private life, Alcibiades in public life; the rulers of Athens are as mean and merciless as the courtiers of Timon. Both men are generous to their friends, but whereas Timon is injudicious and extravagant, Alcibiades' generosity (though inadequately embodied in the action) was probably meant to be well balanced and just. Both men react violently in their disillusionment, but whereas Timon turns from idealistic love to relentless hatred of all men, Alcibiades is reconciled to Athens and will punish only those who have wronged him and Timon. While keeping Timon at the centre of his tragedy, Shakespeare could not possibly have portrayed Alcibiades as the subtle, adaptable and various man Plutarch made him, but he could well have developed him more than he apparently did.

So the play is not a tragedy like *Lear* or *Coriolanus*, but a Jacobean morality in which the characters are little more than embodiments of ethical attitudes. It is so unlike Shakespeare's other plays that one is tempted to assume that he drafted it for a special occasion, perhaps an academic one, and that he left it in fragmentary form because he realized that Timon was not a character worth further exploration since his extreme misanthropy and his self-severance from humanity made him suitable only for a didactic play, not for the kind of tragedy Shakespeare had written or was to write in *Lear*, *Antony and Cleopatra* or *Coriolanus*. Probably its survival and publication were an accident, but we can be glad of that since it may well provide our chief glimpse of Shakespeare in his dramatic workshop.

I. Source

PLUTARCH'S LIVES OF THE NOBLE GRECIANS AND ROMANES

translated by Sir Thomas North (1579)

From THE LIFE OF MARCUS ANTONIUS[1]

... This Timon was a citizen of Athens, that lived about the warre of Peloponnesus, as appeareth by Plato, and Aristophanes commedies[2]: in the which they mocked him, calling him a vyper, and malicious man unto mankind, to shunne all other mens companies, but the companie of young Alcibiades, a bolde and insolent youth, whom he woulde greatly feast, and make much of, and kissed him very gladly. Apemantus wondering at it, asked him the cause what he ment to make so muche of that young man alone, and to hate all others: Timon aunswered him, I do it sayd he, bicause I know that one day he shall do great mischiefe unto the Athenians. This Timon sometimes would have Apemantus in his companie, bicause he was much like to his nature and condicions, and also followed him in maner of life. On a time when they solemnly celebrated the feasts called Choæ at Athens, (to wit, the feasts of the dead, where they make sprincklings and sacrifices for the dead) and that they two then feasted together by them selves, Apemantus said unto the other: O, here is a trimme banket Timon. Timon aunswered againe, Yea, said he, so thou wert not here. It is reported of him also, that this Timon on a time (the people being assembled in the market place about dispatch of some affaires) got up into the pulpit for Orations, where the Orators commonly use to speake unto the people: and silence being made, everie man listning to heare what he would say, bicause it was a wonder to see him in that place: at length he began to speake in this maner: My Lordes of Athens, I have a litle yard in my house where there groweth a figge tree, on the which many

---

[1] See *supra*, Vol. V, p. 304 for the context.
[2] *In margin:* 'Plato, and Aristophanes testimony of Timon Misanthropus, what he was.'

citizens have hanged them selves: and bicause I meane to make some building upon the place, I thought good to let you all under-stand it, that before the figge tree be cut downe, if any of you be desperate, you may there in time goe hang your selves. He dyed in the citie of Hales, and was buried upon the sea side. Nowe it chaunced so, that the sea getting in, it compassed his tombe rounde about, that no man coulde come to it: and upon the same was wrytten this epitaph:

> Heere lyes a wretched corse, of wretched soule bereft,
> Seeke not my name: a plague consume you wicked wretches left.[1]

It is reported, that Timon him selfe when he lived made this epi-taphe: for that which is commonly rehearsed was not his, but made by the Poet Callimachus:

> Heere lye I Timon who alive all living men did hate,
> Passe by, and curse thy fill: but passe, and stay not here thy gate.

Many other things could we tell you of this Timon, but this litle shall suffice at this present.

II. Source

From

PLUTARCH'S LIFE OF ALCIBIADES
translated by Sir Thomas North (1579)

Alcibiades by his fathers side, was aunciently descended of Eurysaces, that was the sonne of Ajax, and by his mothers side, of Alcmæon: for his mother Dinomacha, was the daughter of Megacles.[2] ... Now for Alcibiades beawtie,[3] it made no matter if we speake not of it, yet I will a litle touche it by the waye: for he was wonderfull fayer, being a child, a boye, and a man, and that at all times, which made him marvelous amiable, and beloved of every man. For where Euripides sayeth, that of all the fayer times of the yere, the Autumne or latter season is the fayrest: that commonly falleth not out true. And yet it proved true in Alcibiades, though in

---

[1] *In margin:* The epitaphe of Timon Misanthropus.
[2] *In margin:* 'Alcibiades stocke.'
[3] *In margin:* 'Alcibiades beawtie.'

fewe other: for he was passing fayer even to his latter time, and of good temperature of bodie. They write of him also, that his tongue was somewhat fatte, and it dyd not become him ill, but gave him a certen naturall pleasaunt grace in his talke: which Aristophanes mentioneth, mocking one Theorus that dyd counterfeat a lisping grace with his tongue.[1] . . .

For his manners they altered and chaunged very oft with time, which is not to be wondred at, seing his marvelous great prosperitie, as also adversitie that followed him afterwards. But of all the great desiers he had, and that by nature he was most inclined to, was ambition,[2] seeking to have the upper hand in all things, and to be taken for the best persone: as appeareth by certaine of his dedes, and notable sayings in his youthe, extant in writing. One daye wrestling with a companion of his, that handled him hardly and thereby was likely to have geven him the fall: he got his fellowes arme in his mouth, and bit so harde, as he would have eaten it of. The other feeling him bite so harde, let goe his holde straight, and sayed unto him: What Alcibiades, bitest thou like a woman? No mary doe I not (quoth he) but like a lyon. Another time being but a litle boye, he played at skayles in the middest of the streete with other of his companions, and when his turne came about to throwe, there came a carte loden by chaunce that way: Alcibiades prayed the carter to staye a while, untill he had played out his game, bicause the skailes were set right in the high way where the carte should passe over. The carter was a stubborne knave, and would not staye for any request the boye could make, but drave his horse on still, in so much as other boyes gave backe to let him goe on: but Alcibiades fell flat to the grounde before the carte, and bad the carter drive over and he durste. The carter being afeard, plucked backe his horse to staye them: the neighbours flighted to see the daunger, ranne to the boye in all hast crying out. Afterwards when he was put to schoole to learne,[3] he was very obedient to all his masters that taught him any thing, saving that he disdained to learne to playe of the flute or recorder: saying, that it was no gentlemanly qualitie.[4] For, sayed he, to playe on the vyoll with a sticke, doth not alter mans favour, nor disgraceth any gentleman: but otherwise, to playe on the flute, his countenaunce altereth and chaungeth so ofte, that his familliar friends can scant knowe him. Moreover, the harpe or vyoll doth not let him that playeth on them, from speaking, or singing as he playeth:

---

[1] *In margin:* 'Alcibiades lisped by nature.'
[2] *In margin:* 'Alcibiades ambitious.'
[3] *In margin:* 'Alcibiades studies.'
[4] *In margin:* 'A vile thing to playe of a flute.'

where he that playeth on the flute, holdeth his mouth so harde to it, that it taketh not only his wordes from him, but his voyce. Therefore, sayed he, let the children of the Thebans playe on the flute, that cannot tell howe to speake: as for us Athenians, we have (as our forefathers tell us) for protectours and patrones of our countrie, the goddesse Pallas, and the god Apollo: of the which the one in olde time (as it is sayed) brake the flute, and the other pulled his skinne over his eares, that played upon the flute. Thus Alcibiades alledging these reasons, partely in sporte, and partely in good earnest: dyd not only him selfe leave to learne to playe on the flute, but he turned his companions mindes also quite from it. . . .

Now albeit the nobilitie of his house, his goodes, his worthines, and the great number of his kinsemen and friends made his waye open to take upon him government in the common weale. Yet the only waye he desired to winne the favour of the common people by, was the grace of his eloquence.[1] . . . His charge was great, and muche spoken of also, for keeping of ronning horses at games: not only bicause they were the best and swiftest, but for the number of coches he had besides. For never private persone, no nor any prince, that ever sent seven so well appointed coches, in all furniture, unto the games Olympicall, as he dyd[2]: nor that at one course hath borne awaye the first, the second, and the fourth prise, as Thucydides sayeth: or as Euripides reporteth, the third. For in that game, he excelled all men in honour and name that ever strived for victorie therein. . . . Howbeit the good affection divers citties did beare him, contending which should gratifie him best, dyd muche increase his fame and honour. . . .

Yet with all these goodly dedes and fayer wordes of Alcibiades, and with this great corage and quicknes of understanding, he had many great faultes and imperfections. For he was to[o] daintie in his fare, wantonly geven unto light women, riotous in bankets, vaine and womanishe in apparell: he[3] ware ever a long purple gowne that swept the market place as he walked up and downe, it had suche a traine, and was to riche and costely for him to weare. And following these vaine pleasures and delightes, when he was in his galley, he caused the planckes of the poope thereof to be cutte and broken up, that he might lye the softer: for his bed was not layed upon the overloppe, but laye upon girthes strained over the hole, cut out and fastened to the sides, and he caried to the warres with him a gilded scutchion, wherein he had no cognizaunce nor ordinary devise of

---

[1] *In margin:* 'Alcibiades marvelous eloquent.'
[2] *In margin:* 'Alcibiades victorie at the games Olympicall.'
[3] *In margin:* 'Alcibiades ryot.'

the Athenians, but only had the image of Cupide in it, holding lightning in his hande. The noble men, and best cittizens of Athens perceyving this, they hated his facions and conditions, and were muche offended at him, and were afeard withall of his rashnes and insolencie: he dyd so contemne the lawes and customes of their countrie, being manifest tokens of a man that aspired to be King, and would subvert and turne all over hand. And as for the good will of the common people towards him, the poet Aristophanes doth plainely expresse it in these wordes:

The people most desire, what most they hate to have:
and what their minde abhorres, even that they seeme to crave.

And in another place he sayed also, aggravating the suspition they had of him:

For state or common weale, muche better should it be,
to keepe within the countrie none suche lyons lookes as he.
But if they nedes will keepe, a lyon to their cost,
then must they nedes obey his will, for he will rule the roste.

For to saye truely: his curtesies, his liberallities, and noble expences to shewe the people so great pleasure and pastime as nothing could be more: the glorious memorie of his auncesters, the grace of his eloquence, the beawtie of his persone, the strength and valliantnes of his bodie, joyned together with his wisedome and experience in marshall affayers: were the very causes that made them to beare with him in all things, and that the Athenians dyd paciently endure all his light partes, and dyd cover his faultes, with the best wordes and termes they could, calling them youthfull, and gentlemens sportes. As when he kept Agartharchus the painter prisoner in his house by force, untill he had painted all his walles within: and when he had done, dyd let him goe, and rewarded him very honestly for his paines. . . .

[Alcibiades and Timon]

And on a daye as he came from the counsaill and assembly of the cittie, where he had made an excellent oration, to the great good liking and acceptation of all the hearers, and by meanes thereof had obteined the thing he desired, and was accompanied with a great traine that followed him to his honour: Timon, surnamed Misanthropus (as who would saye, Loup-garou, or the manhater) meeting Alcibiades thus accompanied, dyd not passe by him, nor gave him waye (as he was wont to doe to all other men) but went straight to him, and tooke him by the hande, and sayed: O, thou dost well my sonne, I can thee thancke, that thou goest on, and climest up still: for if ever thou be in authoritie, woe be unto those that followe thee, for they are utterly undone. When they had heard these wordes, those that stoode by fell a laughing: other reviled Timon, other againe marked well his wordes, and thought of them many a time after, suche sundry opinions they had of him for the unconstancie of his life, and waywardnes of his nature and conditions.

[During his absence at the wars Alcibiades was accused by his enemies of sacrilege.]

. . . they sent the galley called Salaminiana, commaunding those they sent by a speciall commission to seeke him out, in no case to attempt to take him by force, not to laye holde on him by violence: but to use him with all the good wordes and curteous manner that they possibly could, and to will him only to appeare in persone before the people, to aunswer to certaine accusations put up against him.[1] If otherwise they should have used force, they feared muche least the armie would have mutined on his behalfe within the countrie of their enemies, and that there would have growen some sedition amongest their souldiers. This might Alcibiades have easely done, if he had bene disposed. For the souldiers were very sorie to see him departe, perceyving that the warres should be drawen out now in length, and be much prolonged under Nicias, seeing Alcibiades was taken from them . . . Now Alcibiades for a farewell, disapointed the Athenians of winning the cittie of Messina: for they having intelligence by certaine private persones within the cittie, that it would yeld up into their handes, Alcibiades knowing them very well by their names, bewrayed them unto those that were the Syracusans friendes: whereupon all this practise was broken utterly. Afterwards when he came to the cittie of Thuries, so sone as he had landed, he went and hid him selfe incontinently in suche sorte, that such as sought for him, could not finde him. Yet there was one that knewe him where he was, and sayed: Why, how now Alcibiades, darest thou not trust the justice of thy countrie? Yes very well (quoth he) and it were in another matter: but my life standing upon it, I would not trust mine own mother, fearing least negligently she should put in the blacke beane, where she should cast in the white. For by the first, condemnation of death was signified: and by the other, pardone of life. But afterwards, hearing that the Athenians for malice had condemned him to death: Well, quoth he, they shall knowe I am yet alive. Now the manner of his accusation and indite-

---

[1] *In margin:* 'Alcibiades sent for to aunswer to his accusation.'

ment framed against him, was found written in this sorte[1]: Thessalus the sonne of Cimon, of the village of Laciades, hath accused, and doth accuse Alcibiades, the sonne of Clinias, of the village of Scambonides, to have offended against the goddesses, Ceres and Proserpina, counterfeating in mockery their holy mysteries, and shewing them to his familliar friends in his house, him selfe apparrelled and arrayed in a long vestement or cope, like unto the vestement the priest weareth when he sheweth these holy sacred mysteries: and naming him selfe the priest, Polytion the torche bearer, and Theodorus of the village of Phygea the verger, and the other lookers on, brethren, and fellowe scorners with them, and all done in manifest contempt and derision, of holy ceremonies and mysteries of the Eumolpides, the religious priests and ministers of the sacred temple of the cittie of Eleusin. So Alcibiades for his contempt and not appearing, was condemned,[2] and his goodes confiscate. Besides this condemnation, they decreed also, that all the religious priestes and women should banne and accurse him. But hereunto aunswered, one of the Nunnes called Theano, the daughter of Menon, of the village of Agraula, saying: that she was professed religious, to praye and to blesse, not to curse and banne. After this most grievous sentence and condemnation passed against him, Alcibiades departed out of the cittie of Thuries, and went into the countrie of Peloponnesus, where he continued a good season in the cittie of Argos. But in the ende fearing his enemies, and having no hope to returne againe to his owne countrie with any safety: he sent unto Sparta to have safe conduct and licence of the Lacedæmonians, that he might come and dwell in their countrie, promising them he would doe them more good being now their friend, then he ever dyd them hurte, while he was their enemie. The Lacedæmonians graunted his request, and receyved him very willingly into their cittie.[3]

[He helped them greatly against Athens.]

... And if he were welcome, and well esteemed in Sparta, for the service he dyd to the common wealth: muche more he wanne the love and good willes of private men, for that he lived after the Laconian manner. So as they that sawe his skinne scraped to the fleshe, and sawe him washe him selfe in cold water, and howe he dyd eate browne bread, and suppe of their blacke brothe: would have doubted (or to saye better, never have beleeved) that suche a man had ever kept cooke in his house, nor that he ever had seene so muche as a perfuming panne, or had touched clothe of tissue made

[1] *In margin:* 'Alcibiades accusation.'
[2] *In margin:* 'Alcibiades condemned being absent.'
[3] *In margin:* 'Alcibiades flyeth to Sparta.'

at Miletum. For among other qualities and properties he had (wherof he was full) this as they saye was one, whereby he most robbed mens hartes: that he could frame altogether with their manners and facions of life, transforming him selfe more easely to all manner of shapes, then the Camelion.[1] For it is reported, that the Camelion cannot take white culler: but Alcibiades could put apon him any manners, customes or facions, of what nation soever, and could followe, exercise, and counterfeate them when he would, aswell the good as the bad. For in Sparta, he was very paynefull, and in continuall exercise: he lived sparingly with litle, and led a straight life. In Ionia, to the contrary: there he lived daintely and superfluously, and gave him self to all mirthe and pleasure. In Thracia, he dranke ever, or was allwayes a horse backe. If he came to Tissaphernes, lieutenaunt of the mightie king of Persia: he farre exceeded the magnificence of Persia in pompe and sumptuousnes. And these things notwithstanding, never altered his naturall condition from one facion to another, neither dyd his manners (to saye truely) receyve all sortes of chaunges. But bicause peradventure, if he had shewed his naturall disposition, he might in divers places where he came, have offended those whose companie he kept, he dyd with such a viser and cloke disguise him selfe, to fit their manners, whom he companied with, by transforming him selfe into their naturall countenaunce.

Then were the Athenians sorie, and repented them when they had receyved so great losse and hurte, for that they had decreed so severely against Alcibiades,[2] who in like manner was very sorowfull, to see them brought to so harde termes, fearing, if the cittie of Athens came to destruction, that he him selfe should fall in the ende into the handes of the Lacedæmonians, who maliced him to the death. Now about that time, all the power of the Athenians were almost in the Ile of Samos, from whence with their armie by sea, they sought to suppresse the rebelles that were up against them, and to keepe all that which yet remained. For they were yet pretily strong to resist their enemies, at the least by sea: but they stoode in great feare of the power of Tisaphernes, and of the hundred and fiftie gallyes which were reported to be comming out of the countrie of Phenicia, to the ayde of their enemies, which if they had come, the cittie of Athens had bene utterly spoyled, and for ever without hope of recovery. . . .

[Alcibiades tried to help them but his overtures were rejected. Then an oligarchy of four hundred seized power in Athens.]

[1] *In margin:* 'Alcibiades more chaungeable then the camelion.'
[2] *In margin:* 'The inconstancie of the common people.'

Now the common people that remained still in the cittie, sturred not, but were quiet against their willes, for feare of daunger, bicause there were many of them slaine, that boldely tooke apon them in open presence to resist these foure hundred. But those that were in the campe, in the Ile of Samos, hearing these newes, were so grievously offended: that they resolved to returne incontinently againe, unto the haven of Piræa. First of all, they sent for Alcibiades, whom they chose their captaine [1]: then they commaunded him straightly to leade them against these tyrantes, who had usurped the libertie of the people of Athens. But nevertheles he dyd not therein, as another would have done in this case, seeing him selfe so sodainely crept againe in favour with the common people: for he dyd not thinke he should incontinently please and gratifie them in all things, though they had made him now their generall over all their shippes and so great an armie, being before but a banished man, a vacabond, and a fugitive. But to the contrarie, as it became a generall worthie of suche a charge, he considered with him selfe, that it was his parte wisely to staye those, who would in a rage and furie carelesly cast them selves awaye, and not suffer them to doe it. And truely Alcibiades was the cause of the preserving of the cittie of Athens at that time, from utter destruction. For if they had sodainly (according to their determination) departed from Samos to goe to Athens: the enemies finding no man to let them, might easely have wonne all the countrie of Ionia, of Hellespont, and of all the other Iles without stroke striking, whilest the Athenians were busie fighting one against another in civill warres, and within the compasse of their owne walles. This Alcibiades alone, and no other, dyd prevent, not only by persuading the whole armie, and declaring the inconvenience thereof, which would fall out apon their sodaine departure: but also by intreating some particularly aparte, and keeping a number backe by very force. . . .

[When the usurpers were driven out the Athenians invited Alcibiades to return home, but he would not do so until he had won great victories over the Spartans and the Persians.]

Now Alcibiades desirous in the ende to see his native countrie againe (or to speake more truely, that his contry men should see him) after he had so many times overthrowen their enemies in battell: he hoysed saile, and directed his course towardes Athens,[2] bringing with him all the gallyes of the Athenians richely furnished, and decked all about, with skutchines and targettes, and other armour

---

[1] *In margin:* 'Alcibiades called home from exile.'
[2] *In margin:* 'Alcibiades honourable return into his country.

and weapon gotten amongest the spoyles of his enemies. Moreover, he brought with him many other shippes, which he had wonne and broken in the warres, besides many ensignes and other ornaments: all which being compted together one with the other, made up the number of two hundred shippes. Furthermore, where Duris Samian writeth (who challengeth that he came of his house) that at his returne one Chrysogonus, an excellent player of the flute (that had wonne certaine of the Pythian games) dyd playe suche a note, that at the sounde thereof the galley slaves would keepe stroke with their owers, and that Callipides another excellent player of tragedies, playing the parte of a comedie, dyd sturre them to rowe, being in suche players garments as every master of suche science useth commonly to weare, presenting him selfe in Theater or stage before the people to shewe his arte: and that the admirall galley wherein him self was, entred the haven with a purple saile, as if some maske had come into a mans house after some great banket made: neither Ephorus, nor Theopompus, nor Xenophon, make any mention of this at all. Furthermore, me thinkes it should not be true, that he returning from exile after so long a banishment, and having passed over such sorowes and calamities as he had susteined, would so prowdly and presumptuously shewe him selfe unto the Athenians. But merely contrarie, it is most certain, that he returned in great feare and doubt. For when he was arrived in the haven of Piræa, he would not set foote a lande, before he first sawe his nephewe Euryptolemus, and divers other of his friendes from the batches of his shippe, standing apon the sandes in the haven mouthe. Who were come thither to receyve and welcome him, and tolde him that he might be bolde to lande, without feare of any thing. He was no soner landed, but all the people ranne out of every corner to see him, with so great love and affection, that they tooke no heede of the other captaines that came with him, but clustred all to him only, and cried out for joye to see him. Those that could come neere him, dyd welcome and imbrace him: but all the people wholy followed him. And some that came to him, put garlands of flowers upon his head: and those that could not come neere him, sawe him a farre of, and the olde folkes dyd pointe him out to the yonger sorte. But this common joye was mingled notwithstanding, with teares and sorowe, when they came to thinke upon their former misfortunes and calamities, and to compare them with their present prosperitie: waying with them selves also how they had not lost Sicilia, nor their hope in all things els had failed them, if they had delivered them selves and the charge of their armie into Alcibiades hands, when they sent for him to appeare in persone before them. Considering also how he found the cittie of Athens in manner put from their seigniorie and commandement on the sea, and on the other side how their force by lande was brought unto such extremitie, that Athens scantly could defend her suburbes, the cittie self being so devided and turmoiled with civill dissention: yet he gathered together those fewe, and small force that remained, and had now not only restored Athens to her former power and soveraintie on the sea, but had made her also a conquerer by lande. Now the decree for his repaire home againe, was past before by the people, at the instant request of Callias, the sonne of Callæschrus, who dyd preferre it: as he him selfe dyd testifie in his elegies, putting Alcibiades in remembraunce of the good turne he had done him, saying:

> I was the first that moved in open conference,
>   the peoples voyce to call thee home, when thou wert banisht
>   hence.
> So was I eke the first, which thereto gave consent,
>   and therefore maye I boldly saye, by truthe of suche intent:
> I was the only meane, to call thee home againe,
>   by suche request so rightly made, to move the peoples vayne.
> And this maye serve for pledge, what friendshippe I thee beare:
>   fast sealed with a faithfull tongue, as plainely shall appeare.

But notwithstanding, the people being assembled all in counsaill, Alcibiades came before them, and made an oration [1]: wherein he first lamented all his mishappes, and founde him selfe grieved a litle with the wronges they had offred him, yet he imputed all in the ende to his cursed fortune, and some spightfull god that envied his glorie and prosperitie. Then he dilated at large the great hope their enemies had to have advantage of them: and therewithall persuaded the people to be of good corage, and afeard of nothing that was to come. And to conclude, the people crowned him with crownes of golde, and chose him generall againe of Athens, with soveraine power and authoritie both by lande as by sea.[2] And at that very instant it was decreed by the people, that he should be restored againe to all his goodes, and that the priestes Eumolpides should absolve him of all their curses, and that the herauldes should with open proclamation revoke the execrations and cursinges they had thundered out against him before, by commaundement of the people. Whereto they all agreed, and were very willing, saving Theodorus the bishoppe, who sayed: I dyd neither excommunicate him, nor curse him, if he hath done no hurte to the common wealth. Now Alcibiades florished in his chiefest prosperitie, yet were there

---

[1] *In margin:* 'Alcibiades oration to the people.'
[2] *In margin:* 'Alcibiades chosen generall with soveraine authoritie.'

some notwithstanding that misliked very muche the time of his landing: saying it was very unluckie and unfortunate . . .

[Although Alcibiades alone stood between them and ruin, many leading Athenians still mistrusted him.]

For if ever man was overthrowen and envied, for the estimation they had of his vallure and sufficiency, truely Alcibiades was the man. For the notable and sundry services he had done, wanne him suche estimation of wisedome and valliantnes, that where he slacked in any service whatsoever, he was presently suspected, judging the ill successe not in that he could not, but for that he would not: and that where he undertooke any enterprise, nothing could withstand or lye in his waye. Hereupon the people persuading them selves, that immediatly after his departure, they should heare that the Ile of Chio was taken, with all the countrie of Ionia: they were angrie they could have no newes so sodainely from him as they looked for. Moreover, they dyd not consider the lacke of money he had, and specially making warre with suche enemies, as were ever relieved with the great king of Persiaes ayde, and that for necessities sake he was sundrie times driven to leave his campe, to seeke money where he could get it, to paye his souldiers, and to mainteine his armie.[1] . . .

[Accused of self-conceited neglect of his duties, Alcibiades was superseded. As a result, the Spartan Lysander captured Athens. Alcibiades took refuge with the Persian Pharnabazus, but Lysander asked the latter to get rid of the Athenian hero.]

Now was Alcibiades in a certen village of Phrygia, with a concubine of his called Timandra. So he thought he dreamed one night that he had put on his concubines apparell, and how she dandling him in her armes, had dressed his head, friseling his heare, and painted his face, as he had bene a woman.[2] Other saye, that he thought Magæus strake his head, and made his bodie to be burnt: and the voyce goeth, this vision was but a litle before his death. Those that were sent to kill him, durst not enter the house where he was, but set it a fire round about. Alcibiades spying the fire, got suche apparell and hanginges as he had, and threwe it on the fire, thinck-ing to have put it out: and so casting his cloke about his left arme, tooke his naked sworde in his other hande, and ranne out of the house, him selfe not once touched with fyer, saving his clothes were a litle singed. These murderers so sone as they spied him, drewe backe, and stoode a sonder, and durst not one of them come neere him, to

---

[1] Cf. IV.3.90–2.
[2] *In margin:* 'Alcibiades dreame in Phrygia before his death.'

stande and fight with him: but a farre of, they bestowed so many arrowes and dartes of him, that they killed him there.[1] Now when they had left him, Timandra went and tooke his bodie which she wrapped up in the best linnen she had, and buried him as honorably as she could possible, with suche things as she had, and could get together.[2]

III. Translation of Possible Source

THE DIALOGUE OF TIMON
by Lucian of Samosata[3]

translated by the editor from the Italian version of N. da Lonigo (1536)

I Dilettevoli Dialogi, le Vere narrationi, le facete epistole di Luciano Philosopho, di Greco in volgare tradotte per M. Nicolo da Lonigo, historiate, & di nuovo accuratamente reviste & emendate. MDXXXV. [Colophon] Stampati in Vinegia per Francesco Bindone, & Mapheo Pasini compagni . . . 1536.

DIALOGUE I

[In this Dialogue Lucian introduces Timon, who having become poor through his own prodigality, and then abandoned by his friends, complains about Jove for sleeping and not punishing the ungrateful.]

TIMON O genial, hospitable, sociable, domestic Jove, presider over oaths, cloud-masser, thunderer, lightning-sender, and by whatever other name you are given by lunatic poets, especially when they need help in their verses (because then with the multitude of your names you sustain the drooping verse and supply the lack of a rhyme), where now is your pealing thunder, your piercing lightning, and your terrible burning arrow? All these have already become fables, truly a poetic mist, where there is nothing but a parade of

---

[1] *In margin:* 'Alcibiades death.'
[2] *In margin:* 'Timandra the curtisan buried Alcibiades.'
[3] For a gay, colloquial version of Lucian see *The Works of Lucian of Samosata,* trans. H. W. Fowler and F. G. Fowler, Vol. I, Oxford, 1905.

words. Your weapons, which once were ever-ready and wounded at a great distance, are now, I don't know how, quite extinct, and so cold that there remains in you no spark of anger against evildoers. Wherefore anyone who wished to perjure himself would be more afraid of a stinking lantern-wick than of the flame of your thunderbolt, which once awed all the world; for it seems that you direct against them nothing more than an ember without smoke and flame, from which they fear no other wound than to be dirtied with soot.

[He goes on at some length, accusing Jove of idleness.]

And truly you are treated by men as your laziness deserves. No one makes sacrifices to you; no one gives you wreaths—except occasionally some victor in the Olympic Games, who does so, not because it seems necessary, but just to follow an antiquated custom; and so in a short time, O noble God, they have deprived you of your dignity. I do not say how many times they have robbed your Temple, and in the Olympic festivals they have dared to lay hands on you yourself, and you, styled High-Thunderer though you be, have not roused the dogs or called the neighbours to your help, so that by pursuing the thieves with shouts they might catch them while they were making ready to flee. You, the Slayer of the Giants and Conqueror of Titans, you remained seated, and, holding in your right hand the thunderbolt ten cubits long, you let yourself be fleeced.

O wondrous God, when will you stop taking so little notice of these things? When will you punish such injustice? How many Phætons, how many Deucalions, would be enough against the vast iniquities of human life? As to that let me leave others aside and mention myself alone. I who have raised high so many Athenians from poverty to wealth, succouring them in all their needs, and have scattered my riches abroad for my friends' benefit, now when I have become poor through my liberality, I am no longer recognized by them, nor do they now look at me, though they formerly loved me ardently, adored me, and stood hanging on my every nod. If walking along the road I meet any of them, they pass me by like the column of some ancient tomb thrown down on the ground by lapse of time, the letters on which no one cares to read. And some who see me a long way off turn away in another direction, fearing they might see a terrible spectacle to be shunned by everybody; notwithstanding that previously I was their salvation and their benefactor. So through my calamities I am reduced to this extremity, and having tied a sheepskin round me I till the soil, and have made myself a man's servant for four soldi a day, and philosophize in the wilderness with my mattock in my hand. The only thing I seem to gain by it is that I do not now see many men unworthily exalted, because this would be even more painful to me. Now, O son of Rhea and Saturn, shake off this long and profound slumber—for you have slept longer than ever Epimemides did. Pay a little attention to your thunderbolt, or freshen it up at Mount Aetna and, making a great blaze, show us something of the way of a virile, youthful Jove—unless the fable is true that they tell of you, and you lie buried in the island of Crete.

JOVE   Who is that, Mercury, shouting in such a loud voice from Athenian soil under the roots of Mount Hymettus, all dirty, unkempt and dreary? He seems to have his head bent low, digging the earth. A man of many words and audacious. Perhaps he's a philosopher? For otherwise he would not speak so bitterly against us.

MERCURY   What, father! Don't you recognize Timon, the son of Echecratides the Collytan? This is the man who used to invite us to complete and perfect sacrifices, and only a short time ago was rich and sacrificed hecatombs at your festival.

JOVE   Alas, what a change from that fine rich man surrounded by so many friends! What has happened to him that he has become so filthy, wretched, a digger of the earth, working for pay apparently, since he's carrying in his hand such a heavy mattock?

MERCURY   He was brought to this by his bounty, humanity and compassion towards all in want; or rather, to speak more correctly, by his ignorance, foolish habits, and small judgement of men, not realizing that he was giving his property to ravens and wolves. Even while the poor wretch was having his liver eaten by so many vultures, he thought they were his friends and well-wishers, who took pleasure in consuming it because of the love they bore him. When they had finally eaten him down to the bone, and sucked the marrow, they left him dry and stripped from top to toe, and now they no longer know him or condescend to look at him, or give him any help. That's why you see him in skins, with a hoe, having abandoned the city out of shame, tilling the soil in order to live, and afflicting himself when he thinks that those who have become rich through his kindnesses now despise him and do not even care to know if he is called Timon.

JOVE   Truly this man does not deserve to be despised and neglected, for the poor fellow complains with good cause. We should be like those scoundrelly flatterers if we forgot him who to honour us has burned on our altars so many legs of bulls and fine fat goats, so that I still have the scent of the flesh in my nostrils. But owing to my busyness and the loud tumult of perjurers and violent men and robbers, and also through fear of sacrilege—since these villains are numerous and difficult to keep under control, so that I hardly dare take my eyes off them—it is a long time since I even glanced at Attica, especially since philosophy and disputations began to occur among the Athenians, for with their fighting and shouting I have hardly been able to hear men's prayers, so that I must either sit with my ears closed, or be overwhelmed while they talk in loud voices of virtue, of incorporeal things, and other fictions. That is why I have not been able to attend to Timon, and although he is a good man I have neglected him.

Now, however, Mercury, take Riches with you and go immediately to him. Make Riches take Treasure along too and both stay with Timon, and tell them not to leave him as quickly as they did before, even though with his bounty he chases them out of his house. We shall consider later the ingratitude those flatterers have shown him, and we shall see that they suffer punishment when we have put our thunderbolt in order—for recently two of its rays got broken and blunted, when I fulminated with more force than usual against Anaxagoras the sophist, who was persuading his disciples that we Gods don't belong to the natural order—yet I missed him, for Pericles placed his hand before him, and the bolt, hitting the Temple of Castor and Pollux, set it on fire and itself narrowly missed being shattered on the stones. Nonetheless in the meantime it will be sufficient punishment for them to have their hearts tormented when they see that Timon has become rich.

MERCURY See how useful it is to shout loudly and to be troublesome and insolent, not only for those who plead their case [in court] but also for those who pray to the Gods! See Timon who from being a poor man will become immensely rich, because his shouting and free-speaking to Jove made God turn towards him. Whereas if he had stayed quiet and kept on digging with his head bent he would still be digging and nobody would take any notice of him.

RICHES I tell you, Jove, I don't want to go back to that man any more.

JOVE Why not, good Riches, when I have ordered it?

RICH. Because he has insulted me and chased me out and torn me to pieces and thrown me about as people do who toss out hot coals with their hands. Must I go back to be given over again into the hands of parasites and flatterers? Send me, Jove, to those who will feel gratitude for the gift, and esteem it, who care about me and desire me, and let those simpletons stay with Poverty who prefer her to me. Let the poor, who receive from her some skins and a pick, be contented when they earn fourpence and thoughtlessly throw away the gift of ten talents.

JOVE He will never treat you again like that, for (unless his body is incapable of feeling pain) he has been sufficiently punished by the mattock not to prefer Poverty to you another time. But you seem to me to have a very complaining nature, for now you blame Timon because he opened his doors for you and let you circulate freely, and did not keep you locked up and felt no jealousy about you. At other times you were discontented and angry with the rich, saying that you had been imprisoned by them, sealed up under lock and key, so that you could not put your head out into the daylight, and you used to complain of this to me, saying that you were suffocated in darkness, and because of it you looked quite pale and melancholy, having your fingers worn down with counting on them, and you threatened to flee if you found a suitable opportunity. You thought it a grievous state to have to remain a virgin like another Danäe in a chamber of bronze or iron, tended only by subtle and malicious teachers, namely Accounting and Usury. You would say that they acted irrationally because they loved you beyond measure. Although they could enjoy you, they had no mind to make use of you or express their love in action as they could safely have done, but they tended you watchfully, keeping their eyes always fixed on the seal and the key, thinking it sufficient enjoyment of you not to make you bear fruit but to keep others from making use of you, like the dog in the manger which doesn't himself eat the corn, but will not let the famished horse eat it. You mocked at them because they were parsimonious and miserly, and (strange thing!) jealous of themselves, and did not know that a cursed servant or steward was secretly robbing them and guzzling, leaving the unhappy master to watch all night, and count up his interest by the light of a narrow-necked lamp, with a thirsty wick. After complaining of such things, is it not unfair of you now to blame Timon, who has done just the opposite?

RICH. If you examine the facts you will find that I am justly annoyed by both, because the prodigality of Timon and his little care of me naturally displeased me; so too did those who on the contrary kept me shut up in darkness, so that I might become fatter and more corpulent through their care, neither wishing to touch me themselves nor to bring me into the light lest I be seen by somebody else. I used to regard them as mad and unjust men, because they held me—who had done them no wrong—fast in bonds that made me fester and go rotten, not realizing that after a little while they would depart and leave me to someone else, who would become supremely happy through me. I therefore praise neither these latter nor those others who are too free with me, but I duly commend those who know how to keep moderation in this matter and neither hold me too tightly nor throw me entirely away in their desire to do good. O Jove, if a man took for his lawful wife a beautiful young girl and then neither guarded her nor felt any jealousy of her, letting her go by day and by night wherever she wished, to converse with any men she liked, nay even himself leading her into temptation, opening the doors and being himself her pimp, inviting everyone in to her, would you believe that such a man loved her? I am sure, Jove, that you would say no, for you have been in love many times. On the other hand, if a man took to his house as his lawful wife a lady of gentle birth in order to procreate children, and then neither touched the virgin, however ripe in age and beauty she were, nor allowed other men to see her, but kept her sterile and bereft and imprisoned, all the time saying that he loved her, and demonstrating that it was so by the colour of his face, and the wasting of his flesh, and the hollowness of his eyes; who would not say that such a man was mad, since, when he ought to beget children and make his marriage fruitful, he let so lovely and lovable a girl fade away as if he tended all her life long a victim dedicated to Ceres. This I grieve for, seeing that by some I am kicked about, despoiled, torn up and kept all in a whirl, while by others I am kept tied up like a runaway slave.

JOVE   Why are you angry with them? For they are duly punished. These last stand with mouth dry and gaping, and like Tantalus they never eat or drink. The others have the food caught from their mouths by Harpies, as happened to Phineus. But go with a glad heart, for now you will find Timon more sensible and wise.

[As Riches and Mercury go they talk about the ways of men with wealth, and Riches tells how, though she is blind and often lame, she hoodwinks men with the help of Ignorance and Deceit and by wearing a lovely mask.]

RICHES   When a man opens his door to me just once, and receives me into his house, then secretly go in with me Pride, Ignorance, Arrogance, Sloth, Violence, Fraud, and a thousand other similar evils. The man, having his soul oppressed and busied by such qualities, admires things not in themselves admirable, and desires what he ought to flee, and above all is bewildered by me, who am the mother of all the evils which have entered as my henchmen into his house. But he could bear almost any thing else save let me go from him.

MERC.   O how smooth, elusive and difficult to hold you are, Riches! You offer nothing by which one can take firm hold of you, but you slip through one's fingers like an eel or a snake. Unlike you,

Poverty somehow or other attaches herself like birdlime, easily takes hold, having a thousand little claws with which she can grip, so that as soon as one approaches her one is caught and cannot easily disentangle oneself. But while we have been talking we have forgotten something very important.

RICH.   What is that?

MERC.   We have not brought Treasure with us, who is most necessary.

RICH.   Don't bother about that, for when I came to you I left him on earth. I counselled him to stay inside and keep the door bolted, and to open for nobody if he doesn't hear my voice.

MERC.   Let's go down into Attica; and hold fast to my cloak until we reach Timon's place.

RICH.   It is good of you to lead me by the hand, Mercury, for if you left me wandering by myself, I should run up against Hyperbolus or Cleon.[1] But what noise is that? It sounds like iron striking on stone.

MERC.   It is Timon who is digging near here on hilly and stony ground.

RICH.   What are you telling me?

MERC.   With him are Poverty, Toil, Endurance, Wisdom, Strength and many others serving under Hunger—much better companions than your henchmen.

RICH.   Then let us go away at once, since we shall never be able to do any good with a man besieged by such an army.

MERC.   Jove thinks otherwise, so we need not fear.

POVERTY   Where, Mercury, are you taking that woman whom you hold by the hand?

MERC.   We have been sent by Jove to this man Timon.

POV.   So now Riches comes to look up Timon again after I have taken charge of him, freed him from a sad and idle life, and made a noble man of him with Prudence and Toil! Do you think so little of me and do I seem so easy to injure that you wish to deprive me of the good I get by this man whom I have made virtuous? Do you wish to plunge him once more into riches, so that he'll become as he was before, or finally be returned to me like a tattered old gown?

MERC.   It is Jove's will, Poverty.

POV.   Then I'm going. Toil, Wisdom and all you other companions of mine, come with me! Perhaps this fellow will find out what a friend he had in me, who was a good helper, and teacher of virtue. While I've been with him he has always been healthy in

[1] Two base rulers of Athens satirized by Aristophanes in *The Knights* and *Peace*.

body and sound in mind, and has led a life fit for a good man, not depending on anyone but himself, and regarding other things as useless and superfluous.

MERC. They are going away; let us go to Timon.

TIMON Who are you, curse you? What have you come to do here, annoying a worker in the field, a hired man? Go away in good time, you rascals, or I'll lay you out with these clods and stones.

MERC. Don't do anything of the sort, Timon; don't throw, for you cannot strike these men (as you think them). I am Mercury and this is Riches. Hearing your cry, Jove has sent me to you, so that you may at once receive abundance and leave all toil behind.

TIM. Even if you are gods, you shall suffer. For I hate gods and men equally; and let this blind one be what she will, I am inclined to give her what for with my mattock.

RICH. Let's go, Mercury, for God's sake; don't you see that this fellow is melancholy-mad, and I fear he'll do me some injury.

MERC. Don't be so hostile, Timon. Leave this rudeness and asperity, stretch your hands out and take your chance of good fortune. Become a leading citizen in Athens, and pay no heed to ungrateful men, if only you may be happy.

TIM. I have no need of you; don't annoy me. All the riches I need is my mattock. For the rest I am happy enough if only nobody comes near me.

MERC. My good fellow, 'do you wish me to take back to Zeus words so inhuman, bitter and cruel'[1]? It is reasonable for you to hate men, from whom you have had so many wrongs, but not the Gods, who take such thought for you.

TIM. I thank you, Mercury, and Jove too, but I do not want this Riches.

MERC. Why not?

TIM. Because a long time ago she caused me many troubles, putting me in the hands of flatterers and traitors, rousing other men's hatred and envy against me, destroying me with pleasures and delights, and finally she abandoned me all of a sudden, perfidiously and treacherously. The good Poverty has kept me exercised in the manliest labour—has been most truthful and free with me in speech, and in return for my work has served me with necessaries, and has taught me to despise superfluities, to place my hope in myself alone, showing me what true riches are, not to be lost by the ways of flatterers, nor by false accusers, nor by the fury of the mob, the violence of a tyrant, nor Senators' decree. Fortified by toil, diligently

---

[1] From *Iliad*, XV, 202.

working this piece of ground, seeing none of the evil things done in the city, and having by the help of my mattock as much flour as will suffice me, I am contented. So go back, Mercury, and take Riches with you to Jove; it would be enough for me if he would make all men weep.

MER. Don't say that, good fellow, for they do not all deserve to weep, but leave your anger and such puerile feelings, and accept Riches. I warn you that the gifts of Jove are not to be despised.

RICH. Do you wish me to defend myself, Timon, or will you be furious if I speak?

TIM. Speak then, but not too long, nor with a preamble like some cursed orator. For Mercury's sake I'll put up with your words, provided that they're few.

RICH. It is really necessary to say quite a lot since your accusation was so long. But just consider whether I have injured you as you say. I was the cause of so many good things, honour, preferment, garlands and other delights, and you were admired and praised, esteemed by men, all because of me; and if you suffered wrongs through flatterers, I am not to blame. Rather in this respect I was harmed by you, since you drove me out so shamefully, and put me into the hands of scoundrels who, with toadying and feigned praise did you wrong. Finally you have said that I have betrayed and deceived you; but I could well accuse *you* of this, since I have been chased away by you in all sorts of ways, and tossed head first out of your windows. See how, instead of soft and delicate clothes, your revered Poverty has put a sheepskin about you. Mercury here is a witness that I begged Jove not to send me down to you, since you have been so unfriendly to me.

MERC. You see, Riches, how changed Timon is already; be a good friend and stay with him, and you, Timon, go on digging. Riches, make Treasure come below the place where he digs, for if you call he will obey you.

TIM. I must obey you, Mercury, and be rich once more, for who could do otherwise when the Gods wish it? But think how much trouble you are bringing back to me. Until now I was living in happiness and security, and now, although I have committed no offence, I shall take up a load of gold, and with it so many cares.

MERC. Be resolute, Timon, for love of me, and although it may seem unbearably hard to you, at least do what I say, so that your old flatterers may burst with envy. Now I must fly to heaven, beyond Mount Etna.

RICH. He seems to have gone off; I deduce it from the rustling of wings. You wait here and I'll send Treasure to you. Meanwhile go on digging. I order you, Treasure, to obey Timon, and let yourself be dug up. Dig, Timon, with your mattock as deeply as you can, for I'm going to help you.

TIM.   Now, mattock, be valiant for me, and do not tire of digging for the treasure underground. O admirable Jove, and friendly Coribanti, O Mercury, God of gain, whence comes so much gold? Could it be a dream? I fear that when I wake I shall find only burning coals. Yet here *is* gold, stamped, (*signato, rubicondo, ponderoso*) ruddy and weighty, and smooth in appearance. 'O gold, the best prosperity of men'[1] you shine like flaming fire by day as by night. Come my dearest friend and lover. Now I believe that Jove once turned himself into gold. What maiden would not open her lap (*non aprisse il grembo*) to receive so beautiful a lover if he came like rain through the roof of the house? O Midas, Crœsus, Offerings made in the isle of Delos, you are naught in comparison with Timon, and the King of Persia is not equal in his riches. My mattock and precious garb of skin, it were good to offer you here to the god Pan. I shall now buy all this land, and build a tower above the treasure, big enough for me alone, and I intend that, after my death, this tower shall also be my tomb.

Let this be my firm resolve for the rest of my life, not to entangle myself with anyone, not to know anyone, to despise all other men. Friends, strangers, companions, the altar of mercy, all these seem myths to me. To sympathize in suffering, to help with prayers, shall be to me a crime and a breach of good customs. My life shall be solitary, like that of wolves, and my only friend shall be Timon. All others I shall consider enemies and traitors, and I shall regard it as sacrilege to talk with any of them. If I happen only to see one of them, that day shall be accursed; and generally I shall make no distinction between men and statues of bronze or stone. I want no ambassadors to mediate any truce between me and them. I intend to have no league with them; solitude shall be the frontier between us. Tribes, citizenship, one's country itself, these names shall be of small account, and seem like the aspirations of mad men. Let Timon alone be rich, and consider nobody else. Let him give himself a good time, alone, without anyone's flattery and intolerable praise. Alone let him sacrifice to the gods, alone may he feast, and have no other neighbour than himself; and if it come to him to die, alone let him stretch forth his right hand, and set the garland on his head. The name most acceptable to him, let it be 'Misanthrope', which signifies 'hater of men'. May the qualities of his behaviour be these: harshness, asperity, hostility, wrath, inhumanity. If I see a man

---

[1] From Euripides' *Danäe*, according to Loeb editor.

burning in a fire, and you beg me to put it out, I shall scatter on him melted pitch and oil. If a man is drowning and stretches out his hands to me for aid, I shall submerge him again by the head so that he cannot get out of the water. Behaving thus I shall treat them as they deserve. This law is introduced by Timon, son of Echecratides, of Collytus, who also confirms it in his Senate. Now may all these resolutions be decreed; if he stays constant in this determination, life will be worth living. Let everyone realize that I have become rich, for this will be like a death-sentence to them.

But who is that? See what haste! They are all running, covered with dust, out of breath; I suppose because they have scented this gold. What must I do? Shall I climb on top of this little house and chase them off with stones thrown from high above, or just for this once shall we suspend our law, and speak only this time with them, so that they may have the greater hurt when they see themselves despised. This seems the better way; let us wait for them here. Let me see, who comes first? It's Gnathonides the flatterer, who when I asked him the other day for a little gift handed me a noose, although at my house he has often vomited entire vases of wine. He has done well to come, for he'll be the first of them all to suffer.

GNA. Didn't I say that the Gods would not forget Timon, the dear good fellow? God keep you, fairest Timon, the kindest man that ever toasted his friends.

TIM. The opposite to you, Gnathonides, more predatory than the vulture, and greatest scoundrel of all men!

GNA. You always like to jest, Timon; but where have you arranged the feast? I have brought you a fresh song from one of the new plays.

TIM. I'll make you sing elegies and dirges if I set upon you with this mattock.

GNA. Why do you beat me, Timon? I call you to witness, God Hercules! I'll haul you up before the Areopagus for this assault.

TIM. If you wait a while, perhaps I'll be charged with murdering you.

GNA. Don't do it. Instead heal this wound by scattering a little gold on it, for gold is a medicine that staunches blood very well.

TIM. You're still waiting?

GNA. I'm going; I'll leave you, since from being a good fellow you've become so unfriendly.

TIM. Who is this coming now? It's the bald Philiades, the most rascally flatterer that ever was. He had from me a whole farm and two talents for his daughter as a reward for his praises, when on hearing me sing he praised me above all others, swearing that my voice was sweeter than a swan's. A short time afterwards, when I was sick, I went to ask him for a little help, and the noble soul threatened to thrash me.

PHIL. You shameless fellows! Now you recognize Timon! Now Gnathonides has become his friend and drinking-mate! But he has been treated as he deserved, as an ungrateful person. We true old acquaintances and companions and helpers of Timon's, we are always diffident and anxious not to put a wrong foot forward. Good day, sir; take care not to trust those rascally toadies who care for nothing but your table: you need not believe any of them. They're all ungrateful and dreary people. I was bringing a talent for you to use in your need, but coming along I learned that you had found countless riches. I come therefore to advise you what to do, although you are too sagacious to need my counsel, for you could give advice to Nestor himself.

TIM. Indeed, Philiades. But come a little nearer so that I may caress you with my mattock.

PHIL. Brothers, he has broken my head with his hoe, the thankless wretch, because I advised him for the best.

TIM. See, another one, the orator Demea, comes, with a decree in his hand and claiming to be related to me. I paid the city treasury sixteen talents for this man because he had just been condemned and sent to gaol for not paying his fine. Moved with compassion I set him free. The other day—when the lot fell on him to distribute money to the Erechtheis tribe, I went for what should come to me by right, and he replied that he did not recognize me as a citizen of Athens.

DEMEA. Good day, Timon, Great Ornament of your parent stock, Pillar of Athens, Shield of Greece! Know now that the people are gathered together and both the councils await you, but first hear the decree which I have penned for you.

'Since Timon, son of Echecratides of Collytos, a man both good and wise, whose like is not to be found in Greece, has been at all times the benefactor of this city, and has been victor at the Olympic games in boxing and wrestling and in the foot-race, all in one day, also with the single and the four-horse chariot—'

TIM. But I have never seen the Olympic games!

DEM. You'll see them another time. It is best for all these things to be put in—

'and only recently he bore himself bravely for the defence of his country against the Acharnians, and cut to pieces two companies of Spartans'—

TIM.   Mind what you say! For I wasn't inscribed in the army along with the others because I had no weapons.

DEM.   You always speak so modestly; but we should be ungrateful if we did not record it—'moreover by making laws, giving counsel in the Senate, and being an army-leader, he has done valuable service to the republic. For all these reasons let the Senate resolve by decree, with the authority of the people, the Heleian magistrate, and the tribes, and with the consent of the citizens individually and as a whole, to erect a statue to Timon beside Athena's on the Acropolis, which shall hold a celestial thunderbolt in its hand, and have rays over the head, and be crowned with seven golden crowns; and let these crowns be granted today at the feast of Bacchus when new tragedies are performed; for today must be celebrated as the feast of Bacchus in Timon's honour. This resolution Demea the orator moved in the Senate, being a relative and disciple of Timon, because Timon is a splendid orator, and indeed can do anything else that he wishes.' This is the decree made in your name; I wanted also to bring my son to see you, whom I have called Timon after you.

TIM.   How is that possible Demea, since when I knew you you had never taken a wife?

DEM.   I shall take one now, if it please God, and beget children, and the first-born, which I'm sure will be a boy, I'll call Timon.

TIM.   I doubt whether you'll ever have anything more to do with women after getting a blow like this from me!

DEM.   Oh, what is this? You want to become tyrant? You begin beating free men when you yourself are not really a free man? You'll soon pay the penalty for this and for other crimes too, such as burning the Acropolis.

TIM.   No fire has burned the Acropolis as yet. See you rascal, how you make false accusations!

DEM.   You, aided by the Gods? You became rich because you broke into the treasury behind your house.

TIM.   It hasn't been broken into, so what you say is incredible.

DEM.   It *will* be broken into, but you have already got what was inside.

TIM.   Here's another blow for you!

DEM.   Oh, my shoulders!

TIM.   Don't cry so loud, or I'll give you a third blow. I should deserve ridicule if, having cut in pieces the two companies of Spartans, and without weapons too—I could not destroy a scoundrelly little dwarf like you. Also I should have been victor in boxing and wrestling all for nothing.

But who is this other man? It looks like Thrasicles the

philosopher: It *is* he, for he has a long beard, and his eyebrows are permanently uplifted. He looks angry with himself, making a Titan's face, and tossing his hair over his forehead; he looks like a Boreas or a Triton as Zeuxis used to paint them. He who in appearance is so correct, modest in his walk, and inconspicuous in dress, had disputed one morning about virtue, blamed those who followed their own lusts, and praised abstinence. When afterwards he got up and came to dine with me, and the slave handed him a large cup to drink, the stronger the wine the better he enjoyed it, and (like one who had drunk the water of Lethe) he showed effects quite contrary to his words of that morning. Snatching at the food with his hands like a voracious bird, shoving the other guests with his elbow, and always getting his beard full of gravy, he bends his body over like a dog, looking down with his head bent over into his bowl as if he expected to find virtue inside it, working away in the dishes with his finger, so as not to leave anything to wash up. And always he grumbles, even if he has a whole pig all to himself. These are the benefits of gluttons and insatiable eaters, getting drunk, and doing insane things in their cups, not only dancing and singing but falling into rages and insulting the others. Besides this, while he stays sitting over his wine, his mouth is full of words, and then especially he talks of modesty and temperance, and this when he is already almost drunk. He then begins to stammer and makes everybody laugh at him. After this he starts to vomit, and finally he needs must be carried bodily away, catching with both hands at the flute-girl as he goes. When he is sober he will yield to no man in lying or impudence, insolence or avarice, and he is the prince of flatterers, ever the readiest to swear what is untrue. Fraud goes before him and impudence follows him. Altogether he is a very astute, clever, and double-faced man, and he shall smart now because his kindness doesn't last very long. How strange that you have come so late, Thrasicles!

THRAS. I have not come for the same reasons as these others, Timon, who marvel at your riches, and have come running in the expectation of your money and sumptuous feasts, showing you great falsity and adulation, because you are a simple person who shares freely with others whatever you have. You know that a dry biscuit is enough for my dinner, and watercress and thyme the sweetest of foods, with a little of something else when I want to have a feast. My drink is water; this tattered gown pleases me more than any purple robe. Gold I prize no more than sea-sand. And because of you I have come so that you may not let yourself be corrupted by this deceitful, treacherous stuff, which has been the cause of unbearable ills to many a man. If you take my advice you will throw it all away into the sea as not necessary for a good man, one who can comprehend the riches of philosophy. Don't throw it into the deep sea, but wade in until the water is up to your armpits, then throw it a little way outside the rough water, and be careful that nobody sees you but myself. If you do not want to do this, take a better way. Thrust it out of your house and don't keep a farthing for yourself. Distribute it to those in need, five drachmas to this man, a mina to that, and half a talent to another, and if one of them's a philosopher it would be fair for him to receive two or three times as much. As for me, I do not ask for myself, but only to share it with my colleagues. It will be enough if you will fill me this bag, which hardly holds two Æginetan measures. A philosopher should be content with just a little, and not want more than one bagful.

TIM. What you say pleases me, Thrasicles, but before you fill your sack, bring your head forward a little, so that I may weigh it with my fist and measure it with my mattock.

THRAS. O Law and Liberty! I am being beaten by a scoundrel, and in a free city!

TIM. Why are you complaining, my good fellow? Perhaps I have made an error. I'll give you another four pecks[1] over the due measure.

Now what do I see? They are coming all together, Blepsias, Laches, Gniso and a whole host of people who want to suffer. Why stay here when I might climb this rock, and letting my mattock have a rest, for it must be tired, gather a lot of stones and throw them at them till it seems like a tempest.

BLEPSIAS. Don't throw, please Timon; we'll go away.

TIM. You won't get away without blood and wounds!

IV. Analogue

From TIMONE
by M. M. Boiardo (c. 1487)
translated by the editor

Timone Comedia del Magnifico Conte Matheo Maria Boiardo Conte de Scandiano, traducta da uno dialogo

---

[1] Loeb trans.

de Luciano a complacentia de lo illustrissimo Principe
Signore Hercule Estense Duca de Ferrara, etc.

PROLOGUE

*Enter Timon in the proscenium: Lucian turning towards the Spectators
speaks the following lines:*

Spectators all, I come to represent
Something triumphant Rome never beheld
In the ancient days of emperors, for ne'er
Throughout their realms or all their festivals
Could they make boast of this our Comedy . . .
Echecratides dwelt in Collytum,
Native of Athens and of gentle birth;
But gentleness he never understood.
Putting aside all manly works, he set
His heart alone on the pursuit of cash
With an unerring eye for the smallest gain.
By anxious care, deceit and usury
(And otherwise today you still can't get it)
He makes himself immeasurably rich,
But rich in secret; in his looks so poor
That by his neighbours he is pointed out
For grievous wretchedness and poverty:
Such use he made of the treasure he amassed.
But what's acquired cannot be aye retained
Even by a man of unchecked appetite;
So now, as always happens in such cases,
Echecratides died in sorry plight,
His spirit passing forth in grief and pain,
And joyously his heir took over all.
This heir was Timon, his legitimate son,
Who out of boyhood then was growing up.
He had not learned by sage experience
How pounds are made by adding ounce to ounce,
And how by pounds great weights are added up.
By his conspicuous and indecent waste
He managed his inheritance so ill,
He doomed himself without need of a judge.
Never foreseeing how things might befall,
From wealth's abundance he falls into need;
From need he tumbles into poverty,
And lastly come to shameful beggary,

He's jeered at, driven away by the very men
Who through his help live rich and fortunate.
All the vast treasure that his father left,
Palaces, villas, great possessions,
He has consumed through indiscriminate gifts,
And brought himself to such contemptible state
That he goes clad in sheepskins, with his head
And arms left bare. All this has turned his brain
From anger into madness; grim his life,
As wearily he digs the barren shore
To earn a bare subsistence with his hands.
His great resentment this exacerbates—
That once he was acceptable to all,
And now they both abuse and drive him off.
(This often happens to a luckless man
Who spends in vain and ne'er recoups his loss.
But as the Arabs in their proverb say:
　　'To water without salt the palm tree shoots,
　　　Makes branches green but withers dry the roots')
Now Timon, sunk in such an evil state,
Perceiving some men's base ingratitude,
Has formed a universal hate to all,
Regardless of the two or three who're good.
He also blames the Gods themselves because
They don't destroy the world in punishment.
But here he comes, and with his hoe equipped,
Walks grumbling to himself; from far I hear him.
I'd better go, for anyone he meets
Is set upon and hurt incredibly.

Act I

Scene 1

Enter Timon from the other side of the proscenium, and at first begins to hoe the ground; then, interrupting his work, he turns his face to the sky and speaks thus:

[He versifies the opening soliloquy in Lucian]

Scene 2

The curtains of the heavens open; Jove appears with Mercury in the costumes already described, and they speak to one another as appears below:

[The dialogue closely follows Lucian]

.　.　.　.　.　.　.　.　.

JOVE   How can it be that he's so thin and dark?
               Whatever's brought him to adversity,
               That now he's sad who formerly was so gay?

MERC.   His liberality has brought him low,
               His appetite for honour, faith in others,
               Or rather, his stupidity in truth,
               For having no experience at all
               Of the false world and its base flatterers,
               Imprudently distributing his wealth
               He made himself a prey to ravens and vultures.
               He did not know that every company
               Of suchlike folk is full of treacherous men,
               But the poor devil illustrates the fact,
               For having given this one and that so much,
               They shun him now and all abandon him;
               They do not even wish to hear him named;
               In Athens now they never mention him.

[Jove orders Mercury to take Riches down to Timon]

Scene 3

Mercury leaves Jove on his throne, and walking through the upper proscenium, says the following words, turning towards the spectators.

[Mercury wonders where he can find Riches, 'Who is blind and dwells most often with the wicked folk'.]

Scene 4

Timon passes beyond the mountain and before he arrives there says these words as he goes.

TIM.   This little at least of good has human life
               That sleep, which is so similar to death,
               Somewhat removes us from afflictions sad.
               Night to the sun already opes its doors,
               And I by sleeping shall forget my shames
               Since other means I lack to comfort me.
               Now I will pass beyond this mountain's base
               To lay me down within the little hut
               That I have built myself beside the spring.
               O may God Mercury vouchsafe me this,
               That I may have no dreams of human kind;
               For I could have no omen worse than that.
               What bear or tiger or wild beast more strange
               That has not with its kind some sympathy?

Only the asp rages against her children;
'Twixt her and men there's little difference.
He who plumbs nature to the depth will find,
Believe me, who have had experience,
The world holds no more evil beast than man.

*When Timon has passed the mountain the curtains close and, remaining so,
the scene is empty. The first Act is over.*

ACT II

Scene 1

*This second Act is all in the superior scene. Mercury brings Riches to
Jove, and they converse as below.*

[The dialogue, based on Lucian, shows Riches' fear of being
squandered again by Timon. Jove commands her to go down and
chase Poverty away from Timon.]

Scene 2

*Jove, rising from his seat, walks about and passes behind the curtains.
Mercury takes Riches by the hand and, walking through the proscenium and
often stopping, reasons with her as follows.*

[As in Lucian. At the end of the scene the curtains close and the
Act finishes.]

ACT III

Scene 1

*Enter Timon on the scene saying the first words which follow. With him
are Poverty and the other three companions.[1] Above them appear Mercury and
Riches, speaking together in the manner given below.*

TIM.　　For other's profit and my own great hurt,
　　　　From day to day, poor wretch, I till this ground,
　　　　Which even to look at all my pain renews.
　　　　Would I might sow it full of every herb
　　　　That unto man is most inimical,
　　　　Aconite, monkshood, poisonous weed,
　　　　Or make it bear, instead of ears of corn,
　　　　Fatality, hunger and pestilence.
　　　　For all my toil would never weigh on me
　　　　If only human progeny might perish
　　　　And I might see all human kind in pain.
　　　　O that the world were subject to my will!

[1] Toil, Prudence or Wisdom, and Endurance.

MER.   Follow me Riches, and attend thou well,
For we are now come down to the lower ground
Where Timon is, in Athens countryside.

[Riches wishes to retire.]

RICHES   But don't I seem to hear a sort of noise
Like iron clattering? ah, way of fear!
For he who's blind fears every little sound.

MER.   Timon it is, who in a stony soil
Digs just beyond. His hoe has struck a rock;
For truth to say his tillage goes but ill;
The ground is bare, barren of any plant,
No grass or vervain on it can be seen;
The soil is stony more than two feet deep.

RICH.   This is an evil place, not fit to live in;
You can be sure that I'm not blind to that.
Only this man who's mad could dwell therein.

MER.   Both Toil and Poverty are also with him,
And likewise Prudence and Endurance too,
Far better folk than her that comes with you.

RICH.   Then let us go, for I have not the power
To find a remedy for his condition;
He is beset and there's no hope for us.

MER.   We're here at Jove's behest. It pleases him.
They cannot set themselves against his will.
Since God is with us, who will be against us?
I in his name will give them their dismissal.

Scene 2

Poverty moves from her place and comes over to Mercury and they speak together thus.

[As in Lucian. Poverty agrees to go.]

POV.   Well then, I'll go since Jove has ordered it.
Come with me Toil, come Wisdom, all of you;
Maybe some day Timon to penitence
Will turn again, and see of what true friends
He has been deprived, who always have his mind
From every alien thought to goodness turned.
With little food I have preserved his health,
With constant labour I have made him sleep,
Teaching him to despise earth's vanities . . .

Scene 3

When Poverty and her companions have passed beyond the curtains, Timon raises his head, for he has been hoeing all the time that the above persons have been conversing. Now, turning to Mercury and Riches, in a harsh voice he says

Tell me who are you, lunatics or what?
That move around me making such a coil
Among these briars, where no man frequents?
Who has conducted you through these field-paths
Where an unfortunate has his shelter made
By pounding with his mattock sods and flints?
Why do you come a poor man to molest,
A hired labourer who works for pay?
May pustules numberless your bodies spot!
If you'll just wait, not Pluto nor his Minos
Can stop my twisting both your heads around.
What are you staying for? Why are you still waiting?
I'll gather a few stones and show my fury.
Just give me time to pick up this big rock!

[Mercury tells him his mission.]

TIM.   I have no need of you, and less of men,
Nor of my lot do I complain at all,
So long as no one looks at me, and names me.
With this my spade my living I can earn;
And when the sun shines or the rain comes down,
Despite mankind I warm myself or bathe.

[Mercury tells him not to blame the Gods for the faults of men.]

TIM.   Neither to you nor Jove I bear a grudge,
Rather I owe you every thanks I can;
But this blind cripple, I'll have none of her.
I am already sated, Mercury, with her,
And so much does her filthiness disgust me,
That lighter far all other burdens seem.
My life she filled one time with indolence,
And yet the more she showed me her affection,
Hate burned against me, envy was aroused.
With delicacies and abundance she
Destroyed my life and personality;
She made me timid, arrogant, unjust.
But that which most of all spurs me to anger,

Into the hands of false and rascally folk
She put me, then she fled, abandoning me.
No wonder I grow hot, for when I think
Of her false lightness I can hardly keep
Hold of my sanity. On the other hand
Poverty has tendered me compassion
And transformed hatred with her sympathy.
I found her always full of truthfulness,
And she has shown me how most easily
To withstand hardship. She alone has brought
True riches to me which shall ne'er be lost,
Neither by lying process, false accusers,
Nor tyrants' violence. She brought me out
From hands of flatterers; now my hope (self-centred)
Is to despise the errors of the world.
So now, O Mercury, lift yourself in flight;
Return to Jove and tell him my desire
Would be to see the entire world in pain,
Not to be named or to enrich myself,
Because I know too well this strumpet here,
Who flees one at the height and can't be held.

[Riches declares herself defeated by Poverty but Mercury forces
her to stay with Timon.]

Scene 4

*Riches stands uncertain, as if blind, and speaks as it seems [to Treasure]
underground, then flees quickly. Timon digs and finds the treasure and speaks
as will appear.*

. . . .

TIM.   My precious mattock, you must help me truly,
Take me for ever out of my great afflictions
So that I need have naught to do with others.
O Jove, good Mercury, wild nymphs of Bacchus!
Whence comes this gold so tawny and so bright?
Who carried it and placed it here before me?
What am I saying? Truly I am dreaming,
And when I wake I'll find but coals and fire.
This is indeed gold. No deceit; I touch it,
And it is stamped and ruddy, weighty. Gold!
Well may the pauper suffer the ills it brings!
O thou most fortunate and gracious gold,
Thou comforter of weary minds

Without whom no man either can be well, or rest,
I well believe that Jove once changed himself
Into your form, believe there's naught shut off
That your divine power cannot open or pass.
Where can there be a damsel so unwilling
As not to open her lap to such a lover,
And, if it please him, strip herself to the skin?
O Midas, Croesus, sparkling Offerings
Placed for Apollo in the isle of Delos,
What have you like to this? The King of Persia
Compared with me henceforth's not worth a straw.
By fortune now I am so lifted up
That wonder is I do not leap to the sky.
I'll build a tower in the middle of this field,
For I shall buy the whole of this terrain,
All, all, for I desire no neighbour near me.
Here, solitary, and crammed full of riches
I'll have my habitation while I live,
And here my sepulchre when I fall off.
No hindrance e'er shall change this firm resolve
By force of fortune or by miracle.
I do not wish to have to do with men;
Henceforth of all, acquaintances and strangers,
My only chosen friend shall Timon be.
He is a fool who stoops to do a service
Because his fellow weeps when he is sad,
And he who aids him has but little sense.
He that believes sweet pleadings and fair words
Will always in the end remain deceived,
For faith in man the sun no longer sees.
I do not want laws human or divine
Agreed among us, but let solitude
Be our sole end and limitation.
Would that I could exchange my likeness, for
This shape of man in every vice outdoes
The other beasts; most in ingratitude.
Tribes, suffrages, citizenship, and company,
Relations, friendship are to me empty names.
O may my nature be all rage and harshness,
Anger, perverseness and asperity!
Such qualities on all mankind I shall
Discharge abundantly, and if it happens
That anyone's on fire I'll pour upon him

Oil and flaming pitch in quantity;
And if't should be some man's in danger of drowning,
I'll lend a willing hand to suffocate him.
Hatred grows in me, and I do not wonder!
I ought to be more rude and difficult.
I am not Timon—I take another name—
I name myself the *Misanthrope* and say
That only such a name is fit for me,
Since it denotes 'the enemy of men'.
This is the true law and decree that should
Be passed by me alone in solitude,
And I shall keep it with a resolute mind.
O how I like to think this wealth was given
That all might burst with envy and vexation.
I see the sky's already turning grey
And birds begin to sing.
'Twere well I passed the mountain, and 'tis time
I sought a place to hide my newfound gold.

When Timon has gone the scene remains empty, and the third Act is ended.

Act IV

Scene 1

The fourth Act begins in which Fame in her proper costume enters on the scene and says the following words.

[Fame says that she has spread the news of Timon's discovery. He will soon be molested by people 'as greedy for gold as flies for hot milk'.]

Scene 2

As Timon appears Fame leaves. Timon speaks thus.

TIM.   Why can I not chase from my morbid soul
Anxiety and care as I have driven
All human consort? Trouble fast arrives,
Comes unexpected with a deer's swift flight,
But when it leaves 'tis with a tortoise pace.
This gold corrodes my every power and strength;
It also keeps me far from all repose;
Since I obtained it I am made its slave.
Leave it I cannot; and I dare not keep it.
Both true and wonderful is what I say:
By it I live happy and full of woe.
Easy it is to say and hard to do,

But I must needs put it away from me,
Yet cannot think where to conceal it best.
Such fear I have as I'm ashamed to tell.
Does not Timocrates lie buried here?
Beneath his bones my gold I'll safely hide.
O my misfortune and my happiness,
If there's security in any place
Surely I think that here you will be safe!
So simple is the mass of humankind
That fears the dead, and for religion's sake
Scruples will have to desecrate a grave.
With what fatigue and with what suffering
I dug this urn, and then with how much pain
And how much passion I've preserved it since.
And I must labour now with panting breath
To place it back in earth under this stone
Which is so heavy I can hardly lift it.
My darling gold, O if I leave you here,
Where must you rest that no one else may find you?
I'll place you well down in the lowest depth.
What do I see? O God, O Jove, O Jove,
O Mercury, Riches, lend your powers to help me.
Here lie two urns already, full of money!
So still the sea, the wind so favourable
That, without fishing, I have fish in the net.
Who placed this gold here in this great amount?
I think Timocrates despoils the dead
As he despoiled the living while on earth.
How comes it fortune and the heavens allow
That this man, being dead, has so much gold,
The while his living son is in such need?
Filocoro, his heir, in prison languishes;
And begs an obol from the passers-by.
But why should I relate another's woe?
What matters it to me his sorry state?
Thus let him be, or go from worse to worse.
I shall be sole heir to Timocrates;
Filocoro will stay in prison chains;
What should be his will nonetheless be mine.
But oh, what folk are these that come towards me?—
The life blood ebbs away from round my heart,
And hardly can my life sustain itself.—
These men are come seeking the vase of gold

That I have found with so much toil and pain.
I fear that they will follow in my tracks.
And I believe I recognize the first:
'Tis Gnathonides surely, that big swine
So full of nonsense and false flattery.
'Twas he who at a banquet in my house
Vomited a great puddle. In my need
Asking his help, he handed me a noose.
Well, let him come; he'll be no welcome guest,
Though as I gather by his visage he
Is jubilant and quite dissolved in laughter.
I'll see that he is weeping when he goes.

Scene 3

Gnathonides and others enter, but he alone presents himself to Timon and speaks thus.

[Gnathonides praises Timon's beauty (like the peacock's) and his nobility (like the ermine's). As in Lucian he offers Timon a song, and is beaten. Timon describes Filades, the bald man, the falsest under the sun.]

Scene 4

Gnathonides flees, and Filades comes from among the others and speaks to Timon.

[Filades says he was bringing a gift of money, but since Timon no longer needs it he will offer good counsel instead. He is beaten. Timon sees Demea approaching and describes how he got Demea out of gaol and was later refused a free ticket to the games.]

Scene 5

Filades leaving with a broken head, Demea comes forward with a decree or privilege in his hand, and as he gets near to Timon, bows to him and speaks thus.

[As in Lucian, Timon beats and abuses him. He goes on to describe his next visitor, Thrasicles, the hypocritical philosopher who preaches abstinence and practises sensuality.]

Scene 6

When Timon has spoken as above, he comes opposite Thrasicles, who is somewhat disconcerted and stands silent; but Timon speaks to him.

[Thrasicles praises his own abstinence 'My food is bread and herbs and roots'. He offers to distribute Timon's gold to the poor, and is soundly thrashed till he leaves.]

When Timon has gone out, the scene remains empty, and the fourth Act is finished.

ACT V

Scene 1

The fifth Act begins in which Help enters in his costume, and says the following words.

> [Help says how necessary he is for all men.]
> For so much need the strong man has of me,
> To be continued in his happiness
> As the poor man with naught needs help to raise him.
> This truth ne'er enters into Timon's mind,
> Who thinks the solitary man is blessed
> And gulls himself to have no need of others.
> But this belief is false; he is deluded.
> All men, however great, some time or other,
> Have need of help. But lest the crowd who listen
> Believe that I am come only to preach
> And make them a collection of proverbs,
> I have come here to give you help, spectators.

[He tells them that Timocrates had his treasure buried with him because he feared that his son was 'Wholly disposed to prodigal liberality', and he wished to save him. Before he died he made Filocoro promise to come to his grave after ten years, bringing a letter which he must read and then place by his father's head. Filocoro has run through the rest of his inheritance and is now in prison for debt. But the ten years being up he has sent his freedman Parmeno to the tomb with the letter.]

Scene 2

As Timon enters Help departs, and Timon comes forward saying the words written below.

TIM.   Pleasing above all other gods, fair Sleep
Bears hatred to both Poverty and Riches,
And to them both is strange, unsuitable.
Poverty cannot cease her waking habit
Because she cannot suffer further hardship,
So day and night busies herself with gain.
The other to preserve what she has gained

Is aye suspicious, dreads whate'er she hears,
In anguish lives and never can she sleep.
How comes it then that I, weary and sad
With thinking of those urns, cannot find rest?
Throughout the night I have not slept at all,
And when I closed my eyes in the hour of dawn,
Weighed down with labour and with misery,
In dream I seemed to see two tiny ants
Running around the gold, biting and predatory . . .
Whatever ants I find at work thereon
I'll kill them all as thievish enemies.
Woe's me, what folk are these who now approach?
Surely these are the ants I saw in dream.
Just see how small and brown they are; they move
Slowly and sly like wolves, and in their looks
They are like robbers.
Let them come near. Unless I change my mind,
With this my hoe I'll play them such a game
As neither of them will go away content.
They've stopped. Perhaps they're going another way.

Scene 3

Timon stays still. Parmeno and Siro converse as they slowly walk along.

[Siro, a slave, marvels that Parmeno still serves the master who freed him. Parmeno praises Filocoro who has fallen into need after lifting the burden of need from others. Parmeno is carrying Timocrates' letter to the tomb. Siro opens it and reads it aloud. It explains why the money was hidden.

'Take these urns which you find buried with me,
And learn to live more wisely and provide
So that you have no need to come again;
For you may here return just as you please,
But do not think to find another fortune.'

Scene 4

The two servants come towards the tomb. Timon accosts them with the following words, and they reply as will appear below.

TIM.   Where are you going, robbers of the tombs?
If you come here intending such a crime,
You have deserved all evils. Spoil a tomb?
You've come for that, you sacrilegious thieves!
But I shall punish you without a trial.

PAR. Good sir, don't do it. We are messengers
Who bear a letter to the god of the dead.
Justice requires that messengers be honoured.
'Tis common practice that the ambassador
May unmolested go from place to place.

[When they claim to be free citizens he denies it, and enters into a discussion with them about freedom. Siro says that although he served Chremes the latter was a slave to his business.]

TIM. Who then is free? Give me some proof I pray.
Your reasoning strikes so deep into my heart
That I myself can make no judgement on it.

SIRO A man is free who his own will obeys,
Who holds the rein firm on cupidity,
And is no prey to avarice, I say:
He does not fear descent to poverty
And worships not the pinnacle of wealth,
Nor changes quality with fortune's change.
Good and bad fame he holds in like contempt.
Find me a man sincere in such a way
And I'll afford you proof of liberty.

TIM. By the god Hercules, you speak the truth,
And in myself I witness it for you,
For I have lost the way of liberty.
By sheer bad luck I blundered into riches
And my small wisdom brought me little rest.
But truly with the griefs I now endure
I am worse off; but I must not complain,
Since if I suffer, I am wrong to grumble,
For well I know that harlot Riches keeps
Whoever has her mightily in doubt;
And he who lives in fear is never happy.
In a bad hour I wandered from the path,
And punishment comes quite inevitably.
Wherefore I shall take up my former life,
Uncouth and solitary till death ends it.
The other people, servile, mercenary,
Who dwell in the world, will certainly insult me
Because my nature's different and perverse.
Profane, accursèd be that hour in which
I see another human being unless
He's either dead or in the gravest plight.
On some far mountain or in some strange wood

I'll feed upon the fruits that there are born
And slake my thirst at a spring, and when the boughs
In winter are disrobed, in the hollow trunk
Of some great oak the leaves shall be my bed,
Or in some cavern I may shelter find.
But without help I cannot clothe myself:
For man is poorest of the animals,
Since every other's born already clad,
But man is naked, weak and beggarly,
Only possessed of falsity and guile.
But why not do at once as I have said?
Why do I not chase off these men before me,
Since I have taken every man for foe?
Be off with you! To the devil, both of you,
Go to the Dead Sea, for if you stay here,
I'll make you run away with pain and tears.
Have you not gone yet? Are you rooted there?
I'll give you a taste of how the peasant-boy
Drives off the donkey wandering in the fields.

SIRO   The man's not sane; his words and gestures show it.
It would be useless more to argue with him.

PAR.   It is his way to counter peace with strife.
But I regret that I have not obeyed
Filocoro's request about this letter.

SIRO   Casting around, I've thought about a plan,
That we should hide somewhere near here and wait
Until that fellow's gone. I can't believe
That he'll stay there all day. In peace and quiet
We can return to the tomb and do our task.

PAR.   Your counsel pleases me; let's go.

Scene 5

The two servants leave and a little afterwards Timon goes too, saying these words.

TIM.   Well: I have chased off those two ants who sniffed
The gold hid in my pit. And let them go, god curse them.
May such bad luck accompany them home
That one step breaks their legs, the next their necks.
You others who so gaily listen there,
Tell me if you want anything from me
Before I go, for I grow weary of you.
Although I have a wrathful, arrogant soul,

By unjust injuries struck down, destroyed,
To you I shall not show aversion,
For piety in me's not quite extinct.
And any one of you who likes may prove it:
I'll lend this cord with which I'm girded round
Most willingly for him to hang himself.

Scene 6

Timon having gone out, Help enters, and turning towards the Spectators peaks thus.

[Help says that the two servants are not returning to the stage but will find the treasure. They will share *Timon's* vase of gold and take Timocrates' two urns to Filocoro, who once out of prison will be, 'No longer prodigal but liberal, Keeping expenses and his gifts in reason'. Help finally tells the audience]

If by your efforts you don't earn my Help,
You must not hope for any aid from me.
To God I leave you; may He make you rich.

V. Analogue

From THE PALACE OF PLEASURE
by W. Painter (1566)

THE TWENTY-EIGHTH NOVELL

Of the straunge and beastlie nature of Timon of Athens, enemie to mankinde, with his death, buriall, and Epitaphe.

Al the beastes of the worlde do applye theimselves to other beastes of theyre kind, Timon of Athens onely excepted: of whose straunge nature Plutarche is astonied, in the life of Marcus Antonius. Plato and Aristophanes do report his marveylous nature, because hee was a man but by shape onely, in qualities hee was the capitall enemie of mankinde, which he confessed franckely utterly to abhorre and hate. He dwelt alone in a litle cabane in the fields not farre from Athenes, separated from all neighbours and company: he never wente to the citie, or to any other habitable place, except he were constrayned: he could not abide any mans company and conversation: he was never seen to goe to any mannes house, ne yet would suffer them to come to him. At the same time there was in Athenes another of like qualitie, called Apemantus, of the very same nature, differente from the naturall kinde of man, and lodged likewise in the middes of the fields. On a day they two being alone together at dinner, Apemantus said unto him: 'O Timon what a pleasant feast is this, and what a merie companie are wee, being no more but thou and I.' 'Naie (quoth Timon) it would be a merie banquet in deede, if there were none here but my selfe.'

Wherein he shewed how like a beast (in deede) he was: for he could not abide any other man, beinge not able to suffer the company of him, which was of like nature. And if by chaunce hee happened to goe to Athenes, it was onelye to speak with Alcibiades, who then was an excellente captaine there, wherat many did marveile: and therefore Apemantus demaunded of him, why he spake to no man, but to Alcibiades. 'I speake to him sometimes, said Timon, because I know that by his occasion, the Atheniens shall receive great hurt and trouble.' Which wordes many times he told to Alcibiades himselfe. He had a garden adjoyning to his house in the fields, wherin was a figge tree, whereuppon many desperate men ordinarily did hange themselves: in place whereof, he purposed to set up a house, and therefore was forced to cutte it downe, for which cause hee went to Athenes, and in the markette place, hee called the people about him, saying that hee had newes to telle them: when the people understoode that he was about to make a discourse unto them, which was wont to speake to no man, they marveiled, and the citizens on every parte of the citie, ranne to heare him: to whom he saide, that he purposed to cutte downe his figge tree, to builde a house upon the place where it stoode. 'Wherefore (quoth he) if there be any man amonges you all in this company, that is disposed to hang himselfe, let him come betimes, before it be cutte downe.' Having thus bestowed his charitie amonges the people, he retourned to his lodging, wher he lived a certaine time after, without alteration of nature; and because that nature chaunged not in his life time, he would not suffer that death should alter, or varie the same: for like as he lived a beastly and chorlish life, even so he required to have his funerall done after that maner. By his last will, he ordeined himselfe to be interred upon the sea shore, that the waves and surges might beate and vexe his dead carcas. Yea, and that if it were possible, his desire was to be buried in the depth of the sea: causing an epitaphe to be made, wherin was described the qualities of his brutishe life. Plutarche also reported an other to be made by Calimachus, much like to that which Timon made himselfe, whose owne soundeth to this effect in Englishe verse.

My wretched catife dayes,
  Expired now and past:
My carren corps interred here,
  Is faste in grounde:
In waltring waves of swel-
  ling sea, by surges cast,
My name if thou desire,
  The gods thee doe confounde.

VI. Analogue

From THEATRUM MUNDI
by P. Boaistuau
translated by John Alday [1566?] 1581 edition

Theatrum Mundi. The Theatre or rule of the world, wherin may be seene the running race and course of every mans life, as touching music and felicitie, wherein be contained wonderfull examples and learned devises, to the overthrow of vice and exalting of vertue. Where-unto is added a learned and pithie booke of the excellency of man written in the French and Latine tongues by Peter Boaistuau, Englished by John Alday, and by him perused, corrected and amended, the olde translation being corrupt. Imprinted at London by Thomas East, for John Wyght. 1581.

Timon

[The author points out how many ancient works, comparing men with the beasts] 'have written that among those that have breath, that goe and creepe upon the earth, there is none more miserable then man. Some more rigorous censors of the works of nature, have begun to blaspheme against hir, calling hir cruel stepmother, in the steed of gracious mother. Others have bewailed all the long daies of their life, the humane calamities, and have troden their steppes in teares, perswading themselves that all that maye be contemplated under the concavits of the Skies, is (as an Heraclite) no other thing then a very Theater of miserie, worthye of continuall plaints and perpetuall compassion. Other by an unmeasurable laughter (lyke a Democrite) have pursued the vices that raigne on the earth: who if hee wer revived at this present, and that he saw the disorder and confusion, that is in our Christian weale, should have just occasion, to redouble his laughter, and to mocke with open throte. There hath ben an other kinde, but naturallye more straunge: which not contenting them selves to murmure against nature, or to complaine of hir effects, but with a particular hatred have cleaved to man their like, thinking that nature had ordained him as a but, or white, against the which she would shoot and discharge all the arrowes of her wrath and malediction. Among the which, Timon a Philosopher of Athens, hath ben the moste affectioned Patriarke of his sect: the which declared himselfe open and chiefe enimie to men, and witnessed the same in the presence of all and also confirmed it by effect: for he would not be conversant or communicate with men, but remained all his life alone in a wildernes with the beasts, far from neighbors, for feare to be seene or visited of any, and being in this solicitude, would speake to no man, saving sometimes to a valiant Captaine of Athens named Alcybiades, and yet spake he not for any good will he did beare him, but for that hee did foresee that he shoulde be a scourge and tormenter of men: and specially because that his neighbors the Athenians had much harme to suffer by him. And not sufficed to have men only in horror and detestation, and to fly their company; as the company of a fierce and cruel beast, but in forsaking them, he sought their ruine, and invented all the meanes he could to extinguish humane kind. In consideration whereof he caused many Gibettes to be reared in his Garden, to the ende that the dispaired, and those that are wearie of their lyves, shoulde come thether to hang themselves: So that in certaine yeares after, having occasion to amplifie and to enlarge his solitarie place, he was constrained for to pull downe those Gibets, for the easier framing and furniture of his worke. And without greater deliberation hee went to Athens, whereas despitefully he did congregate the people like a Herauld that wold declare some new thing, and when they understood the barbarous and strainge voyce of this fearefull and ugly monster, and knowing of a long time his humour, they ranne sodainely for to heare him, as though it had bene some sodaine miracle . . . then he cried out saieng: Citizens of Athens, if any of you have any devotion to go hang himselfe, let him make hast to come quickly, for I wil cut downe my Gibets, for certein necessitie that I have: so that having used this charitie towardes them, he returned to his place, without speaking of any other thing, whereas he lyved many yeares without chaunging his opinion, and ceased not to philosophy the rest of his lyfe upon the miserie of man, untill such time as the panges of death began to oppresse him, then detesting our humanitie, even untill the last gaspe, ordeined expressively, that his body should not be buried in the earth, which is the common element and buriall for all, for feare that men should see his bones and ashes, but he straightly commaunded, that he might be buried upon the Sea side, to the ende that the rage of the waves might let the creatures to come neere: and then he willed that this Epitaph recited by Plutarch, should be graved on his Tombe.

> After my miserable life,
> I am buried under this wave:
> To know my name have no desire
> O Reader, whom God confound.

Behold how this poore Philosopher, after that he had long plunged himselfe in the contemplation of humaine miseries, had will never to have ben, or else to have bene transformed into the shape of some brute beast, for the great disdain he had in mens vices.

VII. Analogue

From TIMON
Anon. (after 1601)[1]

THE ACTORS NAMES

1	Timon
2	Laches his faythfull Servant
3	Eutrapelus a dissolute young man
4	Gelasimus a Cittie heyre
5	Pseudocheus A Lying Travailer
6	Demeas an Orator
7	Philargurus a Covetous churlish ould man
8	Hermogenes a fidler
9	Abyssus a Usurer
10	Lollio a Cuntrey Clowne Philargurus Sonne
11	Stilpo ⎫
12	Speusippus ⎭ Two lying Philosophers
13	Grunnio a leane Servant of Philargurus

---

[1] Text from Dyce MSS 52 (Victoria and Albert Museum, London), with punctuation modernized.

14   Abba   Tymons butler
15   Padio   Gelasimus Page
16–17   Two Serjeants
18   A Sailer
19   Callimela   Philargurus daughter
20   Blatte   her pratling Nurse

Scene

Athens

[I.1]

The first Act: Scen. 1ma

Enter Timon and Laches

TIM.   Laches hast thou receav'd my rents?
LACH.   Master I have,
And brought in sacks filled with goulden talents.
Is't your pleasure that I cast them into pryson?
TIM.   Into pryson, whye soe?
LACH.   Lett your chests be the pryson,
Your locks the keeper, and your keyes the porter,
Otherwise they'le fly away, swyfter then birds, or wyndes.
TIM.   I will noe miser bee.
Flye, gould, enjoye the sunn beames; 'tis not fitt
Bright gould should lye hidd in obscuritie;
I'le rather scatter it among the people.
Lett poore men somewhat take of my greate plenty;
I would not have them grieve that they went empty
From Timons threshould, and I will not see
My pensive freinds to pyne with penurie.
LACH.   Who beares a princelie mynd needes princelie wealth,
Or ells hee'le wither like a Rose in springe;
Nought wilbe left but thornes of povertie.
Master, thou art noe Kinge, noe Prince; doe well
Unto thie selfe, and all is well.
TIM.   Thou speakest like thie selfe, and in thy kinde:
Lett those that are borne slaves beare abject minds.
I Timon am, not Laches.
LACH.   I, poore Laches,
Not Timon; yf I were, I would not see
My goodes by crowes devoured as they bee.
TIM.   Is't even soe, my learned Counsaylor?
Rule thou this howse, be thou a Cittizen
Of Athens; I thy servant will attend;

Thou shalt correct me as thy bond slave, yes,
Thou shalt correct me, Laches; I will beare
As fitts a slave. By all the gods I sweare,
Bridle thy tounge, or I will cutt it out
And turne thee out of dores.

  LACH. Because I speake
The truth.

  TIM. But, peace once, once more, I saye.

  LACH. Yes, I'le not mutter; I'le as silent bee
As any Counsaylor without his Fee.

  TIM. Inglorious dayes leade they, whose inwarde parts
Apollo hath not made of better claye.
It is to me a Tryumph and a glorye,
That people fynger point at me, and saye,
This, this is he that his lardge wealth and store
Scatters among the Comons and the poore;
Hee doth not sitt at home and hugg himselfe,
Rubbing his greedy right hand with his gould,
Whilst poore men their misfortunes doe deplore
Under the open Ayre. Laches, bestrowe
The streetes with gould, and lett the people knowe
How bountifull the hands of Timon are.

  LACH. Soe Jove me love, I had rather rotten eggs
Or stincking pispotts cast upon theire heades.   [*Aside.*

  TIM. The noyse ascends to heav'n; Timons greate name
In the Gods eares resounds, to his greate fame.
This I heare willinglie, and 'tis farre sweeter
Then sound of harpe, or any pleasant meetre:
I, magnified by the peoples crye,
Shall mount in glorye to the heavens high.   [*Exeunt.*

[I.2]   Scen. 2da

 Enter Eutrapelus knocking at Timons dore [1] *and Abyssus the Usurer
following him, then Enter Timon and Laches.*

  EUT. Love, pleasure, joye, delight dwell in this howse.
How farest thou, my humane Jupiter?
What! art thou joviall?

  TIM. I envye not Jove himselfe.

  EUT. By Venus Lapp I sweare, thou seem'st to mee
To bee too sadd. Why walk'st thou not the streetes?
Thou scarce art knowne in tenn tavernes yett:

---

[1] These last four words inserted above in the MS.

Subdue the world with gould. See'st thou this Feind?

TIM.   What is hee?

EUT.   A gryping Usurer, Abyssus named.
That man that knowes him not will scarce believe
What a dam'd knave he is. I with my cloake
Muffled my face, myne hatt puld o're myne eyes,
I walked through the byewayes of the Towne,
The schooles, the Cinqueports, the markett places.
By nookes and crookes I went; yett this bloudhound
Sents, swyftlie followes, hath me at a Baye,
Nor hath departed from my side this daye.

TIM.   His love's officious.

[ABY.]   Eutrapelus, pay me my mony!

[EUT.]   Di'st ever heare a Cuckowe of a note
More inauspicious?

ABY.   Pay what thou ow'st Eutrapelus.
Thou from my Clamour never shalt goe free:
Where e're thou go'st I still will followe thee,
An Individuall mate; When thou shalt dyne,
I'le pull thye meate out of thie very mouth;
When thou wilt sleepe, I'le flye about thy bedd,
Like to a nyght mare; no, I will not lett
Thyne eyes to slumber or take any rest.

EUT.   Proceed'st thou still with thy ostreperous noyse?
Soe helpe me Bacchus, I had rather see
Medusas heade, the dreadfull Basiliske,
Hobgob[l]ins, yea, Infernall Cerberus.
Foh, turne him out of dores, least he infect
The whole howse with the odor of his breath.—
Out, out thou stinckard, mans grand enemye!

ABY.   Our Controversye law shall soone decide.
Thou shalt perceave what a fellowe I am:
I'le make the[e] looke wormes through the pryson grates,
Unlesse thou satisfie to me my debt
In good and lawfull mony.

EUT.   By greate Bellonas sheild, by th' thunderbolt
Of Panomphæan Jove, by Neptunes mace,
By the Acroceraunian mountaines,
And by the glistering Jemms of thye redd nose,
Goe hence, or els I'le crush thee like a crabb.
Looke to thy selfe, thou damned usurer!
Looke to thy selfe! I gyve thee fayre warning.

ABY.   Thou shalt not fright me with thye bugbeare wordes;

Thye mountaines of Acroceraunia,
Nor yett thy Panomphæan Jove I ffeare:
I aske what is my owne.

    EUT.   Thou logg, thou stock, thou Arcadian beast,
Know'st thou not what 'tis to be honored?
Is't not a Creditt and a grace to have
Me be thy debtour?

    LACH.   Leave him not, Abyssus.   *[Aside to Abyssus.*
Oh, how I long for the Confusion
Of this same rascall that confounds our howse!

    ABY.   Thou showld'st have paid the First of the Calends;
'Tis now the third day.

    LACH.   Send for the serjents.   *[Aside to Abyssus.*

    EUT.   Timon, lend me a litle goulden dust,
To free me from this Feind; some fower talents
Will doe it.

    TIM.   Yea, take fyve; while I have gould,
I will not see my Freinds to stand in neede.

    EUT.   Heroicke spiritt! I will thee adore,
And sacrifice to thee in Franckinsence.

    LACH.   I scarcelie am my selfe, I am starke madd:
The Gods and Goddesses confound this scabb!   *[Aside.*

    EUT.   Come hither: what's the totall somme?

    ABY.   This bill
Will certifie you, yf you read it.

    EUT.   Come not too neere;
I feare that shyning *Ignis Fatuus*
Which the lampe of thie nose doth beare aboute:
Approch thou not too nigh. Two hundred pownds:
Well, thou shall have it at the next exchainge;
Then there of me thy debt thou shalt receave.

    ABY.   If not, the[y] pryson thee.   *[Exit Abyssus.*

    EUT.   The apple of Tantalus now followe thee!—
O sweet'st of things, thou hast reedeem'd thy Freind!
In myrth and jollitie this daye I'le spend.   *[Hee sings.*

           Bringe me hither a Cupp
               Of wyne, filld to the bryms;
           Lett's always drinck all upp;
              I love a cupp that swyms.
                 God Bacchus, God Bacchus.
           Thee wee adore;
           Thee wee ymplore,
                Oh most sweete Iacchus!

TIM.   Eutrapelus, thou hold'st thyne owne; but why
Wearst thou a plume of Feathers in thy hatt?
Art thou a lover or a souldier?

EUT.   Bee souldiers they that list, rather I thinck
Its safer farr to quaffe, carouse, and drinck,
And to embrace a lasse within my bedd
At my owne home.

TIM.   True; where the pot's thy pyke,
Thy bedd thy horse, thy wenches merry make
A sheild and buckler to receave thy launce.

EUT.   Th'art in the right . . .
This plume of Feathers shee did gyve to me,
As a conspicuous symbole of her love.

TIM.   Truely, a worthy guift. But, surely, Venus
Was not a freind to my Nativitie:
I oft have watched at my sweete harts dore
And offer'd up whole Hecatombes of teares;
I putt on black apparell; at midnight
Plaid at her Window; on my sweete string'd lute
I sung her love songs. Nothing could her move;
But when shee sawe the shyning gould, 'My love,
Whye stand'st thou heere? what's my gate, a bandogg?
My hony, gyve me this; nay, yf thou lov'st me,
I prithee, gyve it me.' Her gowne is rent,
Or ells shee stands in neede of a gould ringe;
Somethinge shee wants, to crave shee wilbe bould:
The man shee loves not, but shee loves his gould.

EUT.   By Jove thou know'st theire cunning to a hayre.
But Timon shall I thirst within thie house?
I have not wett my lipps with wyne this daye.

TIM.   Come, lett us in; wee will not want for drincke.   [*Exeunt.*

[Scenes 3 and 4 introduce the sub-plot. The rich gull Gelasimus
shows his vanity (Sc. 3) and is fascinated by the tall stories of the
pretended traveller Pseudocheus (Sc. 4).]

[I.5]   Scen. 5ᵗʰ, Act. 1ᵐⁱ

Enter Tymon, Eutrapelus, Hermogenes, Laches.

EUT.   Heere doe wee live and have the world at will,
Fare dayntilie, drinck stiffly, lodge softlye:
If such delights be even among the Gods,
By Jupiter, I'le suffer both myne eares
To be bor'd thorough with a Coblers awle.

TIM.   My freinds shall drinck noe lees; with pleasant sack
My cupps shall flowe.

EUT.   That, that is ev'n sweeter
Than the Gods Nectar.

TIM.   I have noe leekes or garlike at my table.

EUT.   Wee feede on partridge, pheazant, plover, quaile,
Snipes, woodcocks, larks, Ambrosia it selfe.

TIM.   Is not he madd, that carefullie doth watch
A thowsand heapes of wheate, and dares not tast
One graine thereof? or he that drincketh lees,
Having his Cellours fraught with pleasing wynes?
I'le use my treasure, and possesse my wealth,
And spend my dayes in pleasure whilst I lyve.
Wee shall goe naked to our sepulchers,
And carry not one groate away with us.

EUT.   Thou speakst Sybilla's leafes; yf I one doit
Except one halfepeny beare to my grave,
Lett Charon thrust me as a greedy knave
Out of his boate forthwith into the lake!
Heare Tymon! Know'st thou what Hermogenes
Undyned would have? how well he sings and fidles?

Hermogenes sings.

Lovelie Venus sported,
And with Mars consorted,
While swarthy Vulcan in his shopp
At his forge did lympe and hopp.
The same the Sunne espied,
To Vulcan it descried:
Who, when that he reputed
Himselfe to be cornuted,
In a greate rage did stammer,
And swore by his greate hammer,
His bellowes, forge, and fire light,
That Injurie to requite.

He plac'd a nett of Wyre
Where Mars, to cool's desire,
Mett fayre Venus in the Woode,
There to doe what they thought good.
Mars being taken sweares;
Fayre Venus shedds forth teares:
The Gods spectators smyled

To see them thus beguiled.
Now, quoth Vulcan, I am glad;
My hornes ake not halfe soe bad.[1]

TIM.   Hermogenes thou hast deserv'd thye dynner.
HER.   Lett me have it then.
LACH.   Whye suffer you this fidler in your howse?
There's not a veryer knave in all the towne:
Yf he depart not, Master by your leave
I'le thrust him out of dores.
TIM.   Is't ev'n so?—Come hither Hermogenes:
Gyve him a Cuffe, a sound box on the eare;
Bee not afraid.
HER.   I am afraid of him,
Least he strike me againe.
TIM.   Why stand'st thou soe?
Strike him, I say.
LACH.   But yf thou touche me, I—
HER.   What then?
LACH.   I'le dash thy braynes out with thy Fiddle.
HER.   I will not touch him; Hercules himselfe
Would not abide his furious Countenance.
TIM.   Now strike, Hermogenes; his hands are bounde.
                                        [*Tymon houlds him.*
HER.   Lett mee see that; are they bound fast enough?
My hart is at the bottome of my hose.
TIM.   Why dost thou thus delaye?
HER.   Now, now I strike.   [*Hee strikes him.*
Have not I paid him soundlie?
LACH.   O yee gods!
What shall I saye? yf health it selfe desire
To save this familie, it cannot be.
HER.   By Jove, I made him bellow like a bull.
TIM.   Hermogenes, come hither; take this gould,
And buy the[e] brave apparrell; this same man
I'le gyve thee to attend thee.
HER.   O happie day!
EUT.   This Fidler I envye.
Would Laches had forbidden me the howse!—   [*Aside.*
Laches, dost see me Laches? I am a knave too, Laches.
LACH.   Spend and consume; gyve gould to this, to all;
Your riches are Immortall.

[1] The story appears in Lucian's *Dialogues of the Gods*, xvii.

TIM. I'le pull thye eyes out, yf thou add one word.

LACH. But I will speake; yf I were blynd, I'de speake.

TIM. What, art thou soe magnanimous? Be gone;
The dore is open. Freeze or sweate, thou knave;
Goe hang thie selfe!

LACH. Master, Farewell. Is this my loves reward?
Varletts, farewell, hatefull to gods and men:
You lusty fydler, yf I meete with thee,
I'le knock thye Braines out. *[Exit Laches.*

HER. Full glad am I hee's gon; I was afraid.

TIM. What dost thou with this totter'd habitt? I
Will have thee proudlie goe in rich apparell.
Hould up thye heade; I will maynteyne it.

EUT. This man this daye rose with his Arse upwards;
To daye a fidler and at night a Noble. *[Aside.*

HER. How I doe scorne theis raggs! I a fidler?
I goe a fidling? noe, not I, by Jove!
Sirra I must cast of thy company;
[He shewes his gould, given by Timon.
Thou art noe fitt companion for me;
Thy face I knowe not; thou three farthing Jack
Gett fellowes like thye selfe; this, this is it
[Shewes his gould againe.
Makes me a Noble man.—Dost heare me Tymon?
When shall wee goe to dynner? I suppose
I have a stomack like a dog.

TIM. Wee'le goe. *[Exeunt.*

[II.1]   Scen. 1ᵐᵃ, Act. 2ᵈⁱ

[Gelasimus, tutored by Pseudocheus, is betrothed to the reluctant Callimela, daughter of the miser Philargurus.]

PSEUD. What shall we doe, Gelasimus?

GEL. With all speede wee will goe to Timons howse,
Where feasts with myrth and laughter doe abound.
Come lett us goe; I cannot brooke delaye
Till I have tould them of my wedding daye.

[Exeunt.

[II.2]   Scen. 2ᵈᵃ, Act. 2ᵈⁱ

Enter Laches, and Hermogenes with a guilt Rapier.

LACH. My face I have disfigured, that unknowne
I may againe be plac'd in Timons howse.

Laches is turn'd to a souldier,
A resolute hackster with his scarrs and sword,
My wiskers hanging o're the overlipp.
All things agree.—Hoi! what a spunge comes here!
How spruse he is! whom see I? the Fidler
That gave me such a box; the very same.

HER.   What man would saye that I am a fidler?
I Hermogenes? where are my rent shoes?
Torne raggs? my Fidle? what this? my fiddle case?
                              [*He lookes on his Rapier.*
Good people, doe I wake, or doe I sleepe?
I cannot thinck my selfe Hermogenes.

LACH.   I'le make thee feele thy selfe Hermogenes.
                      [*He beats him, and hoodwincks him.*
HER.   Oh, oh, why do'st thou beate me soe? why, why
Do'st thou thus hoodwinck me? Lett me not lyve,
If that I am Hermogenes. The gods
I call to Wytnes, I ne're wrong'd any.
What do'st thou? I was borne this day, this day
I first saw light.

LACH.   My name is Nemesis.

HER.   O sweete, sweete Nemesis, what wouldst thou have?

LACH.   I am thy evill spyritt!

HER.   What, two of yee?
Oh, spare me, good evill spyritt!

LACH.   No, no;
Thou shalt be beate because thou art a knave.

HER.   Oh, oh, sweete Nemesis!

LACH.   I'le pluck thie eyes out.

HER.   O good ill spiritt, doe not soe torment mee!
Oh, oh!

LACH.   Farewell, fidler; farewell, Hermogenes.

HER.   What did he saye? Farewell? I know not well
Whether I lyve or noe: 'tis well, I breathe.
O Jove, O Sunne, suffer you this sinne?
Send Mercury from heaven to helpe me!
Blinde I am, altogeather Blynd, I see
Nothing but darke. O heavens, O earth, O seas!

LACH.   Good gods, from what a deadlie warr scapt I!
Holbeards were charg'd, and swords against me drawen:
I with my buckler did receave the blowes.

HER.   Good souldier, pyttie a poore blynd man.

LACH.   Who art?

HER.   Nemesis hath pluc't myne eyes out.

LACH.   What Nemesis?

HER.   My evill spiritt; I am
More blynde then any mole; prythee leade me
To Timons howse.

LACH.   Thou art not blynd; some man hath hoodwinckt thee.

HER.   Never perswade me; I am blynd I knowe;
My eyes are out.[1]

LACH.   I will restore thy sight;
Feare nothing. What, dost thou see as yet? yet?

HER.   O yee Immortall Gods! I see, I see!
Well done, O souldier! I gyve the[e] thancks.

LACH.   I am not fedd with thancks: what dost thou gyve?

HER.   Come, I will make thee one of Timons howse.

[II.3]   Scen. 3ª, Act. 2di

Enter to them Timon, Eutrapelus, Gelasimus, and Pseudocheus.

HER.   Tenn Furies puld my eyes out, tenn, by Jove.
This souldier restor'd my sight againe.
What, shalhe be thy servant?

TIM.   What's thy name?

LACH.   Machætes.

TIM.   Bee thou true; I receave thee.

GEL.   Save yee, nobles;—save you Timon, save you.
Eutrapelus, how fare you Joviall?

TIM.   Thou seem'st more neate, then thou wast wont to be.

GEL.   I am more merry. Knowe yee this same man?

TIM.   I ne'ere beheld his face before. What's he?

GEL.   This man is rare, and hath noe paralell:
Hath travaild Africa, Arabia,
And the remotest Iles; yea, there's noe nooke
Or crooke in land or sea, but he hath seene.

TIM.   What, in a Table Geographicall?

GEL.   I pray yee note the man.

EUT.   Hee doth so finger-beate his breast, I thinck
Hee is about to call his hart out.

TIM.   What doth he murmure thus? Frames he verses?
'Twere synn to interrupt him.

GEL.   No, not soe. Pseudocheus,
Theis noble sparkes desires your company.

---

[1] The incident reads like a parody of *Lear*, III.7.

21

PSEUD.   Save yee.
I was transported cleane beyond my selfe
With contemplacion of my Pegasus;
Wounders did obviate my memorye,
Which I saw in the Iland of the moone.
    TIM.   In what place of the earth may that Ile bee?
    PSEUD.   'Tis not in earth; 'tis pendant in the ayre;
Endymion there hath the dominion.
    GEL.   In the ayre!
    PSEUD.   Yes, pendant in the ayre.[1]
    HER.   O, strainge!
    PSEUD.   Pish, this is nothing: I cann tell
You of a many gallants, that did sell
Theire Mannours here, and built them castles there,
And now live like Cameleons by th'aire;
And strainger thinges then theis I oft have seene.
    TIM.   Come Pseudocheus, goe along and walke.
Your strainge discourse shalbe our table talke.

                                          [*Exeunt omnes.*

[II.4]   The second Acte: Scen. 4ª

Enter Demeas, two Sergeants, at one dore; Timon, Laches, Hermogenes,
Gelasimus, Pseudocheus, Eutrapelus, at another.

    DEM.   Where hale yee mee, yee knaves? where hale yee mee,
Getes, canniballs, yee cruell Scythians?
Looze mee yee varletts; I'me an orator;
Looze mee, I say.
    SERG. 1.   Good words I pray: wee doe but our office;
The Judges have committed thee to gaole.
    DEM.   Helpe mee yee Godds! What? shall an orator
Bee caste in prison? bound in iron chaines?
    SERG. 2.   Wert thou Demosthenes thou shouldst not scape.
    DEM.   O suffer mee to speake!
    EUT.   What is this tumult? is this Demeas
The orator?
    TIM.   H'st, peace, and let us patiently see
This Comedies Catastrophe.
    SERG. 1.   If all thy Rhetoricke can perswade us
Weele sette thee free at thine owne liberty.
    SERG. 2.   Goe to, bee not to tædious; beginne.

---

[1] From Lucian's *True History*, Bk. I.

DEM. By what faulte or fate of mine (luculent, not lutulent Sergeants) shall I say it is come to passe that I, an orator, not an arator, floridde, not horridde, should bee cast into prison by stolidde, not by solidde, persons? What have I done? what have I not done? Whom may I invocate? whom may I not invocate? . . .

[He goes on at great length.]

GEL. Hee hath composde a very dolefull speache.

SERG. 1. Art thou perswaded to dismisse him? speake.

SERG. 2. I feele some striving motion; but stay,
I knowe 'twill vanishe presently.

PSEUD. This orator hath stole all that he spoke:
I hearde olde Nestor speake this worde for worde
In the fortunate Ilands.

SERG. 1. I am perswaded, I will let him goe.

DEM. O eloquence, what canst not thou effecte?
Whom doe not sweeter wordes than hony move?
I thanke my Genius.

SERG. 2. Exult not soe:
I am perswaded Demeas, I am,
Thee to imprisonne. Come, my orator,
Not arator, my floridde, not horridde;
Bee sure of this, weele putte thee in sure ties,
Unles thou putte in sureties.

TIM. Dismisse him. I will sixteene talents pay
Unto the citizens.[1]

DEM. My Jupiter, my Jupiter!

TIM. Carry my name unto the Judges. I
Will satisfie this debte.

DEM. My Jupiter,
When I forgette thee, let mee as a prey
Bee cast alive to be devour'd of beasts!

TIM. Thy wishe is to to large. I doe desire
A gratefull minde, thats all that I require:
I putte my talents to strange usury,
To gaine mee friends, that they may followe mee . . .

DEM. If this, my Timon, I doe not performe,
Let Jove confounde mee with his thunderbolte!

LACH. This vowe, O Jove, remember! let him feele,
If hee be false, the strengthe of thy right hande!

GEL. Hast thou not a brother lives in Athenes,
That is a fidler?

[1] Cf. Lucian's *Timon*.

HER.   A fidler?

GEL.   Sweete sir,
Bee not soe angry, I did never see
One egge more like another. I will send
For him to morrow to my nuptialls,
Hee sings soe daintily.

EUT.   What, to thy wedding? wilt thou putte thy necke
Into a marr'age nooze?

GEL.   Why not? I her,
Shee mee doth love.

DEM.   A metaphore from the effecte.

GEL.   What more can I desire?

TIM.   A barraine foreheade, where hornes may not growe.
Oft other men beware by others hornes.
View Athenes, thou shalt Vulcanes ensignes see,
A common badge to men of eache degree;
How many hange their heades downe, leaste they splitte
The signe posts with their hornes; how many sitte
At home sicke of the headeache, and complaine
That they are like to the twi-horned moone.
This man lookes pale; another stands amazde:
In the meane while their wives are joviall;
They eate the tongues of nightingales, lambestones,
Potato pies, pick'ld oysters, marrowbones,
And drinke the purest wine that they can gette.
They have their garden houses; will bee sicke;
Then comes the Doctor with his clister pipe,
And makes them well: their husbands heades ake still.

DEM.   Sarcasmus, or a bitter jeste.

GEL.   Thinke you that I shall bee a horn'd Satyre? ha, ha, he!
As if I did not knowe what tricke men use! . . . [1]

EUT.   Hem, let us drinke, not idely spende the time.
Lets sacrifice to Bacchus boles of wine.   [*Exeunt.*

[II.5]   The fifth Scene

Enter Lollio at one dore; and Timon, Hermogenes, Gelasimus, Pseudo-cheus, Eutrapelus, at another, with feathers in their hatts; Demas, Laches, Obba.

LOL.   Call they this Athenes? Lord, what vaire buildings.

HER.   See yee that clowne? how hee admires all things?

───────────
[1] Thirty lines of comedy are omitted here.

EUT. I knowe him well. 'Tis Lollio, the sonne
Of covetous Philargurus, who ne're
Permits his sonne to frequent the cittie,
Least hee shoulde learne the Citties luxurie;
Hee lives at home, eates browne breade and butter,
Sometimes fat bacon.

LOL. Good godds, good gods, what preparation!
What a concourse of people! This zittie zunne
Seemes brighter than our country zunne. Lord, Lord,
How many starres see I! how nere they are!

[*The signe of the 7 stars.*

PSEUD. Thy hande may touche them with a ladders helpe. . . .

LOL. Jove blesse mee, how many divells are here!
Are they philosophers or brabbling lawiers?
They looke with such soure faces.

TIM. Eutrapelus, speake to him; say we are
The prime men of the cittie.

EUT. Save you, Lollio.

LOL. Save you, Eutrapelus:
Soe love mee Pan, I am gladde to see thee well.

EUT. What strange occasion brought you hither?

LOL. I am zente for to my zisters wedding.
Here are fine zights . . .

TIM. Most welcome unto Athenes!

LOL. Thanks, by Jove.

TIM. Wee longe have look'd for such a one, whom wee
Might substitute Prince ore the whole country.

GEL. Foh, how hee stinks of garlicke!

LACH. All are not muskified.

TIM. Putte on thy hatte; thou shalt bee our fellow.

LOL. Well bee it with thy oxen and thy ploughes,
Who gracest mee with such greate courtesy!
If once I see thee at my fathers house,
Ile give thee ale pragmaticall indeede,
Which if thou drinke, shall fuddle thee hande and foote.

PSEUD. Since I did taste the Nectar of the gods,
No wine or ale can please my pallat well.[1]

TIM. This day shall bee a day of sporte and mirthe:
Bring cuppes of wine; let's welcome our new Prince.

LOL. I am afraid least my behaviour
Bee to to rusticke.

---

[1] From Lucian's *Icaro-Menippus*, §27.

EUT.   Dost thou not know Philargurus his sonne?
Hee's Callimelas brother.
    GEL.   Is hee soe?—
Heare, youngest youth of youthes; I am betrothd
Unto thy sister, whom I meane to wedde.
    LOL.   Give mee thy hande.
How doth my fathers servant Grunnio?
    EUT.   Thee Timon wee electe as soveraigne,
Prince and commaunder of these Bacchanales.
What lawes dost thou ordaine?—Peace, ho, awhile!
    TIM.   That this our compotation may have
A prosp'rous evente, we will and commaunde
Whole hogsheades to bee empt'ed, platters fill'd,
None to depart, unles hee first obtayne
Leave of the prince: We also doe enacte
That all holde up their heades and laughe aloude,
Drinke much at one draughte, breathe not in their drinke;
That none goe out to pisse, that none doe spew
In any corner. He that shall offende
In one of these shall weare infixt
Uppon his hatte an asses eares, and drinke
Nothing but sour wine lees for three daies space.
    [ALL]   This acte wee ratifie, confirme, allow.
    LOL.   I thinke my father hath transgress'd these lawes.
He nothing drinkes but lees.
    TIM.   What, thy father?
Hee is not worthy to exchange olde shoes;
But thou art noble, and king of good fellowes.
    LOL.   Father! hee no more shall be my father.
I am a Prince; I scorne and renounce him.
    TIM.   Lollio, I drinke to thee this whole one.
    LOL.   Were it a whole hogsheade, I would pledge thee.
What if I drinke two? fill them to the brimme.
Wher's hee that shall marry with my sister?
I drinke this to thee super naculum.
    DEM.   This wee doe call at Athenes καθόλου
    TIM.   Sounde musicke! wee will daunce.   [*Sounde Musicke.*

    [They revel, and Timon joins in a bawdy song.]

[III.1]   The third Acte, the first Scene

[Lollio takes the revellers to his father's house. Callimela and her old nurse Blatte come out.]

        Enter Callimela and Blatte.

BLAT.   O mee, what tumulte is before my dores?

GEL.   My lady mistris, Calimele my queene,
Withdraw not backe your feete.

BLAT.   Save yee, young men. What is't that yee would have?

LOL.   Yee Myrmidons beholde olde Hecuba!
What? shall we stone her?

GEL.   My fellowe soulders, this shall bee my wife.
Is she not faire? how does my Calimele?

EUT.   Looke in her urinall, and thou shalt knowe.

CAL.   Let mee bee gone; I doe not love to bee
A laughing stocke.

GEL.   Sweete love bee not angry;
Uppon the mountain Paphlagonia
There is a stone—

CAL.   In Athenes Cittie is an arrant foole.

GEL.   Thats call'd—

CAL.   Gelasimus.

LOL.   Why binde yee not olde Hecuba, that bitche?

BLAT.   I olde Hecuba! I'me Blatte, the nurse!
What ayles the drunken foole?

EUT.   Timon, why are your eies fixt on the grounde?

TIM.   I feele a wounde.

EUT.   O Jupiter forbidde!

TIM.   Eutrapelus, this is not in Joves pow're.
I subjecte am to Venus tyranny!
These eies betraide my hearte, these were the gate
And onely way where love first entred in.
I saw and lov'd, and must my love enjoye.

EUT.   What sodaine metamorphosis is this?

TIM.   I love, extreamely love.

EUT.   What, Callimele?

TIM.   The very same.

LOL.   My sparrowe, my marrow, my sowe,
My hony, my cony, my cowe!—
Achilles is adry; a little more ale!
This house doth seeme to walke: what, have they
   feete?

Enter Philarg. at another dore [1]

Or doth it ride on horsebacke? Grunnio,
Am I not in the cloudes?

---

[1] This entry, several lines before he speaks, suggests that the play was prepared
for stage-presentation.

BLAT. Hence, Callimele.
Philargurus thy father is at hande.

[*Exeunt Callimela and Blatte.*

TIM.   I nothing see, my eies have loste their light.

PHIL.   What company is this before my dores?
O mee accurs'd! my hidden golde is founde.
What shall I doe? I am undone, undone!
Why hange I not myselfe? who and alas!
I to to longe have liv'd, who must bee forct
To ende my daies in povertie. Yee theeves,
Yee theeves, what seeke yee here?

EUT.   Lollio, thy father.

LOL.   My father hange himselfe! I'me Achilles;
I have this day three thousand Trojans slayne.

PHIL.   Yee theeves, restore what yee have tane away!

TIM.   Olde man, bee patient.

PHIL.   Ile binde yee hande and foote in iron chaines.
Runne Grunnio, call for the peoples helpe.

LOL.   Thou olde, outworne, worme eaten Animal,
What wouldst thou have? I am greate Achilles:
Unless thou kill mee i'th heele Achilles
Will nere bee slaine.

PHIL.   Lord, Lord, what a strange madnes may this bee!

GEL.   Feare not, Philargurus, thou hast noe cause.
I am thy sonne in lawe; all things are safe;
Noe man hath toucht the threshold of thy house.

PHIL.   O, but my sonne is madde!

LOL.   Hast not thou nappy ale? if thou deny,
My Myrmidons shall ruinate thy house.

PHIL.   To ploughe, thou slave! that I would have thee doe.
Gelasimus, withdraw these youngmen hence;
I am afraide and tremble every joynte
Leaste they finde out my golde. . . .

[After more fooling the drunken Lollio is carried indoors.]

[III.2]   The Seconde Scene

Philargurus, Callimela, Blatte, [*and Grunnio.*]

PHIL.   What, shall I suffer such corruption
Of manners in my sonne? s'deathe, hee shall feele
His fathers fury. What? doe I arise
Carefull before the crowing of the cocke,
And scorne noe gayne, no, not from the dunghill,

That, when I die, my sonne may bee left riche?
Ile rather hide my treasure in the earthe,
Where neither sunne or moone or humane eies
Hath ever peepte.

Enter Laches.

LACH. Save you, Philargurus.
PHIL. What wouldst thou have? bee briefe, or els bee gone.
LACH. My master wishes all the gods thy friendes.
PHIL. I all of them his foes, whoere hee bee.
Is this thy arrand?
LACH. Y'are too cholericke;
I come a joyfull messenger to thee.
Timon doth love thy daughter fervently,
Will take her without dowry if you please.
What say you? hee hath also sent these gemmes
To make accesse to Callimelas love.
PHIL. O happy mee! will Timon take, saist thou,
My daughter without dowry?
LACH. Soe it is.
PHIL. Callimela.
CAL. What's your pleasure, father?
PHIL. Venus doth favour thee above the rest;
A seconde person doth desire thy love,
A golden youthe: rejecte Gelasimus.
This is farre richer, and thee, Callimele,
Will take without a dowry.
CAL. Who doth possesse most golde shall mee possesse:
Let womans love bee never permanent.
LACH. Timon doth consecrate these costly gemmes
Unto the altars of thy beauty.
CAL. I take his gemmes, and send him backe my love;
Let that be like a gemme. . . .
. . . Tell Timon I am his.
LACH. Timon is blest:
How well doe beauty and milde love accorde!
PHIL. Without a dowry, that, remember that.
LACH. I speake the truthe.
PHIL. Grunnio, make broathe of these two fishes.
[*two spratts or the like.*
[*Exeunt Phil., Call., Blat., Grun.*
LACH. Soe are my masters goods consum'd: this way
Will bring him to the house of poverty.
O Jove, convert him, leaste hee feele to soone

To much the rodde of desp'rate misery,
Before his chests bee emptied, which hee
Had lefte by his forefathers fill'd with golde!
Well, howsoever fortune play her parte,
Laches from Timon never shall departe.   [*Exit Laches.*

[In III.3 Gelasimus grieves at losing Callimela. In III.4 'leane
macilente Grunnio', Philargurus's servant, describes his master's
meanness.]

[III.5]   Actus tertii, Scena quinta

   Enter Timon, Callimela, Philargurus, Gelasimus, Hermogenes, Pseudo-
cheus, Eutrapelus, Demeas, Laches, Blatte.

   TIM.   Soe I embrace thee in my armes, who art
My life and light.
   CAL.   O, how such sweete embraces I desire,
Who without thee am neither life nor light!
   GEL.   Shee sees not mee as yet; if once shee did
I know shee would put finger in the eye.
   CAL.   Thou art my Titan, I thy Cynthia;
From thy bright beames my beauty is deriv'd . . .
   GEL.   Can the kings daughter of th'Antipodes
Speake so compleately?
   PSEUD.   Shee hath a parrot
Can speake more elegantly.
   GEL.   That is well.
   TIM.   My life, why doe wee thus delay the time?
Ile plight to thee my trothe in Pallas temple.
Art thou well pleas'd with this, my hony?
   CAL.   What pleases Timon cannot mee displease.
   PHIL.   Timon, thou hast a wife morigerous;
Shee is the onely comfort of my age.
   LACH.   Thou li'st, thou thinkest thy gold a sweeter . . .
                                                      [*Aside.*

[Demeas begins a fatuous eulogy which Eutrapelus cuts short.]

   EUT.   —Let's hie to the temple.
Hermogenes, out of thy greasy throate
Sing us some sweete Epithalamion.
   LACH.   Heele croke it like a frogge, I knowe; I feare
Least this extravagant singing fidler
Hath quite forgotte his arte.   [*Aside.*
   HER.   I sing among the people! I! what, I!

Is not Hermogenes a noble? My page
Shall acte my parte: if hee sing not a song
Of sweeter harmony than Orpheus,
I never more will sattin breeches weare.

The Musicians playe, and Hermogenes page sings.

                A faire mayden creature,
                Than hony farre more sweete,
                Whom the godds for feature
                Might well desire to greete;
                Whose beauty Venus might
                Envy, as farre more bright,
                Hath felt God Cupids dart,
                That prick'd her at the hearte.
                Love's victor; hence the cries
                Of young men pierce the skies.
ALL.   Hymen, O Hymen Hymenæus, Hymen!
[PAGE.]   Let Hymens joyfull saffron weede
                Assiste them alwaies at their neede.
ALL.   Hymen, O Hymen Hymenæus, Hymen!
[PAGE.]   Let Phœbus hide his light,
                And day bee turn'd to night,
                That the new bride now may
                The bridegroomes flames allay;
                Let Cupid straw love flowres,
                Venus augment love houres.
ALL.   Hymen, O Hymen Hymenæus, Hymen!
[PAGE.]   Let Hymens joyfull saffron weede
                Assiste them alwaies at their neede.
ALL.   Hymen, O Hymen Hymenæus, Hymen!

Enter a shippwrackte Sayler.

SAY.   Immortall Gods, why mocke yee mortalls thus?—
Where shall I finde Timon, wretched Timon?
  TIM.   Who with such clamors interupts our joyes?
Speake what soe're it is.
  SAY.   I bring thee heavy newes; thy shippes are drown'd
In Neptunes waves, not one of them arriv'd.
  LACH.   The gods forbidde!
  SAY.   Neptune thy foe hath wrought thee this mishappe,
And swallow'd uppe thy gemmes in his vast wombe,
And never will restore them backe againe.   *[Exit Sayler.*
  TIM.   At lengthe I knowe what misery doth meane.
  PHIL.   Hence Callimele, hence from that beggers side.

GEL.   Thou would'st not have mee to thy sonne in law.
What, doth it yet repent thee?

PHIL.   Give mee my daughter, why dost thou claspe her?
Shees none of thine.

TIM.   Doth Callimele say soe?

CAL.   I loved Timon riche, not Timon poore;
Thou art not now the man thou wast before.

PHIL.   This is my wisedome, this shee learn'd of mee.

TIM.   Wealth being loste, the love which was remaines.
Why dost thou soe inconstantly revolte?
Beholde the light of Hymenæus lampes.
Why turnest thou thy face away from mee?
What, am I such an eiesore now to thee?

PHIL.   Away, away, thou poore three farthing Jacke!
Thou faggende of the people, get thee hence!
Touche not my daughter, thou.

TIM.   Callimela!

BLAT.   Thus goods and love are Shippewrackt both at once.
Come, I'le receave thee into favour, come.

PHIL.   Base povertie doth followe luxury:
Get home, and live by mending of olde shoes.
Spende not whole daies in drunken Bacchus cuppes;
Goe home thou slave, or here, with hunger pin'd,
Belche out thy soule: I hate a man thats poore;
Hees worse than any homicide.

TIM.   O thou whoe're thou art, that dost dispose
Of paines in hell, dismisse thou Tantalus!
This fellow is more worthy to endure
Dry schorching thirst, and yet to stande for aye
Up to the chinne in water.

HER.   Why dost thou not lament, Eutrapelus?

EUT.   My eies are of Pumice stone, I cannot.

GEL.   To morrow Callimela, I will sayle
To the Kings daughter of Antipodes.
Expect mee not thy sutor any more.

TIM.   Doth noe small sparcle of thy love remaine?

PHIL.   Hence, my sweete girle; vouchsafe him not one worde;
Hees worse than a crocodile or serpent,
Nay, worse than the divell himselfe.

GEL.   Why soe?

PHIL.   Because hees poore.

[Exeunt Phil., Call., and Blat.[1]

---

[1] This s.d. is not in the MS.

GEL. Ha, ha, he!
How melancholy walkes hee to and fro!—
Thou shalt, if that thou wilt, mende my olde shoes.

LACH. I will not see my master thus abus'd.
I'le rather die.—What dost? whom speakst thou to?
Hence, least thou feele my cholericke revenge;
And quickly to bee gone, I say; thou foole,
Dost thou deride my masters miseries?

GEL. Thou knowst not how I hate these souldiers
That looke soe furious. Come, let us goe;
I am even sicke to see his face; vah!

EUT. Weele goe along with thee.

[*Exeunt Gelasimus and Eutrapelus.*

HER. Thy masters harde misfortune I lamente.

[*Exit Hermog.*

DEM. Commend my love to bee at his commaunde.

[*Exit Demeas.*

LACH. The shadowes all are gone; noe sunne shines here.—
Master, why muse you thus? what thinke you on?
Why are your eyes soe fixed on the earth?
Pull up your spirits; all adversity
By patience is made more tolerable.

TIM. Great father of the Gods, what wickednes,
What impious sinne have I committed?
What, have I piss'd upon my fathers Urne?
Or have I poyson'd my forefathers? what,
What, what have I deserv'd, an innocent?

LACH. His countenance bewraies his vexed soule.   [*Aside.*

TIM. O Jove, O Jove,
Have I thy altar seldome visited?
Or have I beene to proud? or yet deny'd
To succour poore men in necessity?
Not this, nor that: Yee Gods have vow'd my fall.
Thou, thou hast vow'd it, Jove; against mee, then,
Discharge whole vollies of thy thunderclapps
And strike mee thorough with thy thunderbolte,
Or with a sodeine flashe of lighteninge
Destroy mee quicke from thy supernall throne.
I knowe not how to suffer povertie,
Who have soe oft reliev'd the poore with golde.

LACH. Leave of complaints; griefe augments misery.

TIM. I am besides myselfe, I knowe not how.
Hymen, why, Hymen, are thy lampes extincte?

Come light them once againe; my bride's at hande.
A fonde dreame Timon never shall dejecte.
My Callimele complaines, I stay to long;
I come, my light, in dreames Ile come to thee!

    LACH.   Where rushe you heade-long? master, Callimele
Hath lefte thee basely and ingratefully,
And hath despised thee, now thou art poore.

    TIM.   Thou speakst the truthe; shee's gone, shee's gone indeede.
O most inconstant sexe of womankinde,
Proude, cruell, stiffenecked, and more monstrous
Than any monster bredde in Africa!
Is this their faithfull love? the vowes they make?
Yee cursed Furies, thou, thou, Megæra,
Helpe to augmente my fury!

    LACH.   Comfort yourself, you have some friends yet lefte.

    TIM.   Is't possible a poore man should have friends?

    LACH.   Adversitie cannot parte faithefull friends.

    TIM.   Hee is deceav'd that lookes for faithe on earthe:
Faithe is in heaven, and scornes mortall men.
I am compelled by necessity
To prove my friends: thus poore and destitute,
I goe to seeke reliefe from other men.

                               [Exeunt Timon and Laches.

[IV.i.]   Actus quarti, Scena 1ma

    Enter Timon at one dore; Demeas and Eutrapelus at another.

    TIM.   Unhappy Timon doth salute his friends.

    DEM.   Whom speakes hee to? what, dost thou knowe this man?

    EUT.   I doe confesse that I have seene his face,
But where I cannot tell.

    TIM.   Afflicted and forsaken on each side,
And lefte to the wide worlde, I yee beseeche
To give mee house-roome; only this I aske,
A hole wherein to hide my misery.

    DEM.   Art thou a stranger? or Athenian?
What country? whats thy name?

    TIM.   Know'st thou not? ah, Demeas, know'st thou not?
This face, these hands thou heretofore didst knowe.
Am I soe soone forgotte and wholy chang'd?
And is there nothing now of Timon lefte?

    DEM.   Thou brazen face, I ne're sawe thee before.

    EUT.   This fellowe would insinuate, I thinke.

TIM.   Where hide yee your heads, yee heav'nly powers?
They doe despise their needy friend, yet live
And breathe a guilty soule. O supreme Jove,
Why doth thy right hande cease to punish sinne?
Strike one of these with thunder from above?
And with thy lightening revenge my cause!
Strike which thou wilt, thy hande it cannot erre.

DEM.   Ha, ha, he: how tragicall hee is:

TIM.   O yee ingratefull, have I freed yee
From bonds in prison to requite mee thus?
To trample o're mee in my misery?
True Scythians broode, cruell, ingratefull,
Yee make mee live in woe and heavines.
Tell mee, O tell mee, yee perfidious,
Where is your faith vow'd of your owne accorde?
Where are your vowes soe largely promised?
What? are they all gone with the winde?

DEM.   Come hither; I will give thee this one groate,
But thou must publish my munificence.

TIM.   Thus I returne it backe into thy face.
Ne're bende thy browes; proude threats I doe not feare.

EUT.   Come, let us hence; this man is lunaticke.

DEM.   Looke to thy braines, least in the plenilune
Thou waxe more madde. Farewell.

> [*Exeunt Demeas and Eutrapelus.*

Timon solus.

TIM.   Fire, water, sworde confounde yee! let the crowes
Feede on your peckt out entrailes, and your bones
Wante a sepulchre! worthy, O, worthy yee,
That thus have falsifi'd your faith to mee,
To dwell in Phlegeton: Rushe on me heav'n,
Soe that on them it rushe! Mount Caucasus
Fall on my shoulders, soe on them it fall!
Paine I respecte not. O holy Justice,
If thou inheritte heav'n, descende at once,
Ev'n all at once unto a wretches hands!
Make mee an Arbiter of Ghosts in hell,
That when they shall with an unhappy pace
Descende the silent house of Erebus,
They may feele paines that never tongue can tell!
But where am I? I doe lamente in vaine.
Noe earthe as yet reliev'd a wretches paine:

I am well pleas'd to goe unto the Ghosts.
Open thou earthe and swallowe mee alive!
Ile headelonge tumble into Styx his lake.
Wilt thou not open, earthe, at my requeste?
Must I survive against my will? then here
Shall bee my place: who on the earthe lies, hee
Can fall noe lower than the same, I see.   [*Timon lies downe.*

[IV.2]   Scena Secunda

[Gelasimus assigns his lands to the usurer Abyssus for gold in order
to journey to the Antipodes with the confidence trickster Pseudocheus. Blatte persuades him to renew his suit to Callimela. Timon,
lying on the ground, overhears the conversation.]

PSEUD.   What oxe is this that lieth on the ground?
TIM.   What's that to thee?
GEL.   Rise, arise.
TIM.   I will not.
GEL.   Art thou a foole?
TIM.   But art thou wise?
GEL.   Farewell.
TIM.   Bee hang'd!
GEL.   Ha, ha, he! how concisely the rogue speakes!
BLAT.   'Tis Timon; doe yee not knowe him?
GEL.   That were a thinge indeede ridiculous,
To knowe a man that's poore. Sirrah, take heede
Least that thou catche a coughe: heare you, Sirrah?
The ground's to colde a bed to lie uppon.
TIM.   Nothing.
GEL.   Thy hearing, therefore, is not good.
TIM.   And yet I am not deafe.
GEL.   What's this?
TIM.   Somethinge.
GEL.   What's this somethinge?
TIM.   Nothing, I say, nothing:
All things are made nothing.
PSEUD.   Thou bee a sonne in law unto a Kinge,
And yet vouchsafe to talke with such a one!
Hee hath not wherewith to buy a haltar.
TIM.   Soe, thou abhominable father of lies,
What mighty spoiles and triumphs thou hast gain'd,
Thus to despise a wretche in misery!
BLAT.   Why stay you thus, Gelasimus, to sende

By mee the kisse you promis'd Callimele?
Goe yee into the house.
   GEL.   Goe thou before;
Olde age is reverent; weele follow thee.
   BLAT.   That's kindely done to putte mee in before;
A kisse and that together will doe well.   [*Exeunt.*[1]
   TIM.   Greate Jove confounde yee!
   PSEUD.   Barke not so, thou dogge.
   TIM.   Thou, nature, take from mee this humane shape
And mee transforme into a dire serpent,
Or griesly Lyon, such a one as yet
Nere Lybia or Affrica hath seene,
Or els into a crocodile or bore;
What not? or with my Basiliscan eies
May I kill all I see, that at the length
These base ingratefull persons may descende
The pitte of hell thus would I bee reveng'd.

[IV.3]

[The philosophers Stilpo and Speusippus discuss the man in the moon with the fiddler Hermogenes. Timon appeals to Hermogenes.]

   TIM.   Hermogenes, remembrest thou thy vow?
Hermogenes!   [*Timon ariseth from the grounde.*
   HER.   What wouldst thou have?
   TIM.   Houseroome.
Suffer mee not perish with the colde,
Under the open ayre.
   HER.   Thou art troublesome.—
I hearde from Pseudocheus, a most skillfull Chronographer, that the moone was an Ilande pendante in the Ayre, and that there inhabite many Myriades of men.
   STIL.   Tis true, not circumscriptively as the last Spheare, nor repletively, but definitively as an angell; this hee spake tentatively not dogmatically.
   TIM.   What, wilt thou not vouchesafe to looke on mee?
   HER.   Bee gone, bee gone, thou art troublesome I say.
   TIM.   Thou thanklesse wretch, dost thou reject mee thus?
Thus proudly tramplest on my miseries?
   HER.   If thou are wretched, goe and hange thyselfe;
An haltar soone will mitigate thy griefe.
   STIL.   A man may hange himselfe 2 manner of waies; either

---

[1] They go out, but Pseudocheus, being last, hears Timon's curse.

22

aptitudinally and catachrestically, or perpendicularly and inhæsively:
choose which of these thou wilt.

TIM.   O Titan, seest thou this, and is it seene?
Eternall darknes ceaze uppon the day!
Yee Starres, goe backeward! and a fearefull fire
Burne up the Articke and Antarticke Pole!
Noe age, noe country yeelds a faithfull friende.
A cursed furie overflowes my breast.
I will consume this Cittie into dust
And ashes; where is fire? Tysiphone,
Bring here thy flames! I am to mischiefe bente:
These naked handes wante but some instrumente.

HER.   Stilpo, Speusippus, vent your Sentences.
Appease his fury; it doth rage to much.

SPEUS.   Man's like unto the Sea that ebbes and flowes,
And all things in this world unstable are.

STIL.   There's nothing on the earth that's permanent.
As cloudes disperse the force of Boreas,
Soe all things into nothing doe returne.

SPEUS.   Adversity cannot daunte a wise man.

STIL.   Art thou opprest with griefe? be patient.

SPEUS.   A heavy burthen patience makes light.

STIL.   Hath fortune left thee naked and forlorne?
Then clothe thyselfe with vertue.

SPEUS.   Vertue alone beatifies the minde.

STIL.   Shee is not blinde.

SPEUS.   She cannot be deceav'd.

STIL.   Shee doth despise no man.

SPEUS.   Shee none forsakes.

STIL.   Shee is not angry.

SPEUS.   Doth not change.

STIL.   Nor rage.

SPEUS.   With comfort shee relieves the grieved soule.

STIL.   Shees fairer every day than other.

SPEUS.   The nearer shee the fairer doth appeare.

TIM.   This grieves mee worse than all my poverty.
Hence, hence, yee varletts!

STIL.   The chiefest good in vertue doth consiste.

SPEUS. Whose rage is moderate, that man is wise.

STIL.   He that is wise is rich.

SPEUS.   Whome fortune quailes
Is poore and base.

TIM   Your counsaile hath deserv'd these thanks.

                                    [*Timon beates them.*

SPEUS. Oh, oh!
Oh! dost thou buffet a philosopher?
Will a free Cittie such a deede allowe?
  STIL. O, I am holy! oh, withdraw thy handes!
  HER. Ile runne away, and take mee to my heeles.
  TIM. Not soe, not soe; Ile recompence thy pride.
    [*Timon beates him, Herm. runnes away, Tim. followes him in at*
                              one dore, and enters at another.
  STIL. How doth thy heade, Speusippus?
  SPEUS. It doth ake,
As well posterioristically
As prioristically. Let us hence,
Least hee againe assault us with his fistes.
                          [*Exeunt Speus. and Stil.*
  TIM. What, hath hee thus escaped from my handes?
Thou Goddes[s] Nemesis, revenge my wrong!
Let him, O let him wander up and downe,
A wretche unknowne, through Cities and through townes!
Let him desire to die, and yet not die!
And when hees deade, rewarde him, Rhadamant,
According to his meritts: hee deserves
The paine of Sysiphus, thirste of Tantalus,
And in thy lake (Cocytus) to remaine.

Enter Laches.

  LACH. My masters voyce doth ecchoe in my eares.
How full of fury is his countenance!
His tongue doth threaten, and his hearte doth sighe;
The greatnes of his spirit will not downe.
  TIM. Thee, thee, O Sunne, I doe to witnesse call,
These harde misfortunes I have not deserv'd!
  LACH. But sitt uppon some other earthe and pray.
This place is barbarous: here their proude handes
Scorne to relieve a poore man in his neede.   [*Timon standes up.*
  TIM. O thou, revenge, come wholy to my hands!
I will revenge.
  LACH. That takes not griefe away.
  TIM. But it will lessen griefe; something Ile doe;
Ile not consume this day in idlenesse.
Invite these rascalls.
  LACH. What shall they doe here?
  TIM. I have prepared them a worthy feaste.

Goe call them therefore, tell them there remaines
Of soe much wealth as yet some overplus.

              [Exit Timon at one dore, Lach. at another.

[IV.4 Timon's servant Obba, setting the table, drives off the hungry Grunnio.]

[IV.5]

   Timon, Laches, Obba, Philargurus, Gelasimus, Pseudocheus, Demeas, Eutrapelus: Hermogenes, Stilpo, Speusippus come awhile after.

   TIM.   Furnish the table, sette on dainty cheare;
Timon doth bidde his friends their last farewell.

   PHIL.   Thou wisely dost; it is too late to spare
When all is spent; whom the Gods woulde have
To live but poorely, let him bee content.

   TIM.   What man is hee can wayle the losse of wealthe,
Guarded with such a friendly company?
Ill thrive my gold, it shall not wring one teare
From these mine eies, nor one sigh from my hearte.
My friends sticke close to mee, they will not starte.

   DEM.   Is hee madde? wee knew him not this morning.
Hath hee soe soone forgotte an injury?

              Now enter Herm., Stil., Speu., and drawe backe.

   LACHE.   Putte of fonde feare; why draw yee backe your feete?
   HER.   I feare my heade.
   TIM.   Much hayle Hermogenes,—
Save yee, philosophers.

   SPEUS.   Save yee, said hee?
Such words are better farre than stripes and blowes.

   TIM.   Y'are welcome all. Spende yee this day in mirthe,
Mixe laughter and conceits with this our feaste,
And lay aside all grave severitie.

   STIL.   There lie Philosopher. I put of all formalities, excentricall and concentricall universalities, before the thinge, in the thinge, and after the thinge, specifications categorematicall and syncategorematicall, hæcceities complete and ἁπλῶς, or incomplete and κατά τι.

   GEL.   Ha, ha, he! hee seemes like a dry heringe.

   TIM.   Expecte noe junketts, or yet dainty fare:
What cheare poore Timon hath, y'are welcome to.

   PHIL.   I love a piece of beefe.
   GEL.   I hony sopps.
   PSEUD.   Give mee a Phœnix stew'd in Ambergreece.
   DEM.   I love an Artichoke pie sok'd in marrow.

EUT. Fill platters with wine, weele eate it with spoones.

HER. I pray thee putte a pheasante on the table.

STIL. I pray thee let not mustard bee wanting.

SPEUS. Bee mindefull of fatte bacon, I doe love
To line my choppes well with the greeze thereof.

TIM. Weele wante for nothing; that shall bee my care.

[*Exit Timon.*

GEL. Philosophers say that mustarde is obnoxious to the memory.

STIL. Mustarde by itselfe is obnoxious to the memory by an accident.

HER. Heare yee my opinion, who am halfe a Philosopher.

EUT. Partly a fidler, partly a foole.

GEL. Thou art too bitter; peace.

HER. Mustarde originally and proximely is obnoxious to the memory instrumentally and remotely.

GEL. O ex'lent witty, and beyonde compare,
Thou shalt with mee to the Antipodes,
If that thou please: this ingenuity
I love in any man.

PHIL. Art thou resolved on thy journey?

GEL. Yes:
This morning I have play'd the Alchymist,
Converting all my lands to pure golde.

DEM. A Metalepsis or transumption from one thinge to another.

GEL. Pseudocheus,
How many miles thinke you that wee must goe?

PSEUD. Two thousande, 44.

STIL. What dost thou meane?
A number numbering? or numbered?

PSEUD. My eares attende not to these idle trifles.
Thou art a trifling Philosopher; peace.
Perseus, hee had a winged horse. . . .
Thou mounted uppon Pegasus shalt fly.
The shippe shall carry mee.

LACH. Let eache man take his place.

STIL. A place is a superficies concave.

SPEUS. Or convexe of a body ambient.

HER. True, if it bee considered entitatively not formally.
Before I leave Ile make these termes threedbare:
Now, as I live, they cost mee twenty pounds.   [*Aside.*

EUT. Some one bring water: these Philosophers
Washt not their uncleane hands this day.

STIL.   A litle inke adhæres in the superficies of my nayle.

SPEUS.   I writte the state of a quæstion this day,
'Whether the heavens bee made of stones?'

STIL.   It is made of stones stoned, not stoning.

DEM.   O Jupiter, hee speakes Solœcismes!

PHIL.   Where is thy master?

LACH.   Heele bee here anon;
In the meane time sitte downe.

GEL.   Philargurus,
Thy hoary haires deserve the highest place.

Enter Timon.

TIM.   O happy mee, equall to Jove himselfe!
I going touche the starres. Breake out O Joy,
And smother not thyselfe within my breast!
Soe many friends, soe many friends I see;
Not one hathe falsifi'de his faith to mee.
What, if I am opprest with povertie?
And griefe doth vexe mee? fortune left mee poore?
All this is nothing: they releeve my wants.
The one doth promise helpe, another golde,
A thirde a friendly welcome to his house
And entertainment; eache man actes his parte;
All promise counsaile and a faithfull hearte.

GEL.   Timon, thou art forgettefull of thy feast.

TIM.   Why doe yee not fall to? I am at home:
Ile standing suppe, or walking, if I please.—
Laches, bring here the Artichokes with speede.—
Eutrapelus, Demeas, Hermogenes,
I'le drinke this cuppe, a healthe to all your healths.

LACH.   Converte it into poison, O yee Gods!
Let it bee ratsbane to them!   [*Aside.*

GEL.   What, wilt thou have the legge or els the winge?

EUT.   Carve yee that capon.

DEM.   I will cutte him up,
And make a beaste of him.

PHIL.   Timon, this healthe to thee.

TIM.   Ile pledge you, sir.
These Artichokes do noe mans pallat please.

DEM.   I love them well, by Jove.

TIM.   Here, take them then!
                  [*Stones painted like to them; and throwes them at them.*
Nay, thou shalt have them, thou and all of yee.

Yee wicked, base, perfidious rascalls,
Thinke yee my hate's soe soone extinguished?

DEM.   O my heade!

HER.   O my cheekes!   [*Timon beates Herm. above all the reste.*

PHIL.   Is this a feaste?

GEL.   Truly a stony one.

STIL.   Stones sublunary have the same matter with the heavenly.

TIM.   If I Joves horridde thunderbolte did holde
Within my hande, thus, thus would I darte it!   [*Hee hitts Herm.*

HER.   Woe and alas, my braines are dashed out!

GEL.   Alas, alas, twill never bee my happe
To travaile now to the Antipodes!
Ah, that I had my Pegasus but here,
I'de fly away, by Jove!

                                                    [*Exeunt.*[1]

TIM.   Yee are a stony generation,
Or harder, if ought harder may bee founde;
Monsters of Scythia inhospitall,
Nay, very divells, hatefull to the Gods.

LACH.   Master they are gone.

TIM.   The pox goe with them;
And whatsoe're the horridde sounding sea
Or earthe produces, whatsoe're accursed
Lurks in the house of silent Erebus,
Let it, O, let it all sprawle forth, here, here,
Cocytus, flowe, and yee blacke foords of Styx!
Here barke thou Cerberus! and here, yee troopes
Of cursed furies, shake your fi'ry brands!
Earth's worse than hell: let hell chaunge place with earth
And Plutoes Regiment bee next the Sunne!

LACH.   Will this thy fury never be appeas'd?

TIM.   Never, never it; it will burne for ever;
It pleases mee to hate. Goe, Timon, goe,
Banishe thyselfe from mans society.
Farther than hell fly this inhumane City.
If there bee any exile to bee had,
There will I hide my heade.   [*Exit Timon.*

LACH.   Ile follow thee through sword, through fire and deathe;
If thou goe to the ghosts Ile bee thy page,
And lacky thee to the pale house of hell.
Thy misery shall make my faith excell.   [*Exit Laches.*

[In V.1 Gelasimus, off to the Antipodes, takes leave of his flatterers.]

---

[1] Leaving Timon alone with Laches.

[V.2]   Scen. 2da, Actus quinti

Enter Timon and Laches with 3 spades[1] *in their hands.*

TIM.   Begone, I saye, why dost thou follow me?
Why art thou yett soe instant?
   LACH.   Faith commaunds.
   TIM.   Faith; What is faith? where doth shee hide her head?
Under the rise or setting of the sunne?
Name thou the place.
   LACH.   Here in this brest.
   TIM.   Thou liest.
There is noe faith; tis but an idle name,
A shaddowe, or nearer unto nothing,
If any thinge.
   LACH.   Lett me but followe thee.
   TIM.   If thou wilt follow me, then chainge thy shape
Into a Hydra that's in Lerna bred,
Or some strainge Monster hatcht in Affrica.
Bee what thou art not, I will hugg thee then.
This former face I hate, detest, and flye.
   LACH.   What is the reason thou dost hate me thus?
Is this the recompence for all my paynes?

                              [*He discovers himselfe.*
Thou heretofore did'st turne me forth of dores,
When I did give thee true and good advice:
Doth the same fury now possesse thye mynd?
What wickednesse doth make me soe abhor'd?
   TIM.   Thou art a man, that's wickednesse enough.
I hate that fault, I hate all humane kinde,
I hate myselfe, and curse my parents ghosts.
   LACH.   Doth greife and rage thus overflowe theire bancks?
When will they Ebbe?
   TIM.   Thou sooner shalt unite
Water to Fyre, heav'n to hell, darke to light.
My mynd is constant with a burning hate,
And knowes [not][2] how to chainge. Forsake me then;
I thee desire my Foe and not my mate.
   LACH.   Thinck mee thy foe, soe that thou suffer me
To be thy mate; noe hardnes I'le refuse.
If thou commaund, my parents I'le despise,
Thou so commaunding, will them ever hate.

---

[1] Amended in MS. Originally *wth either a spade.*
[2] Missing from MS.

TIM.   Thou hast prevayled, be thou then my mate,
But thou must suffer me to hate thee still.
Touch not our hands, and exercise thie spade
In the remotest parte of all the ground.
O Jove that darts't thy peircing thunderboults,
Lett a dire Comett with his blazing streames
Threaten a deadly plauge from heav'n on earth!
   LACH.   Lett seas of bloudshedd overflow the Earth!
   TIM.   Men, woemen, children perish by the sword!
   LACH.   Lett funerall follow funerall, and noe parte
Of this world ruyne want!
   TIM.   Lett greife teeme greife,
And lett it be a punishment to lyve!
   LACH.   Lett harvest cease!
   TIM.   Lett rivers all wax drye,
The hunger pyned parent eate the sonne!
   LACH.   The sonne the parent!
   TIM.   All plagues fall on this generacion
And never cease! Heare me, O, heare me, Jove!
Ἐμειδ ζωντος γαῖα μιχθήτω πυρί,[1]
Lett Atlas burthen from his shoulders slide,
And the whole fabrick of the heavens fall downe!
While Timon lyves, yea, now while Timon prayes,
Returne Earth, into thy former Chaos!
Lett never sunn shyne to the world againe,
Or Luna with her brothers borrow'd light!
Lett Timon see all theis things come to passe!
Such a revenge best fitts such wickednesse.
        [*Timon diggs at one end of the stage, and Laches at the other.*

[V.3]   Scen. 3ª, Actus quinti
   *Enter Gelasimus booted and spurd, with a watch in one hand and a Riding
rodd in th'other.*

   GEL.   Hee bad me should expect my Pegasus
In theis same feilds; I wounder hee's not come.
Sirrah thou digger, did'st thou see this day
A wynged horse here?
   TIM.   Thee, Jove confound thee,
Who e're thou art! hell swallow thee alive,
And be tormented there among the spirites!
   GEL.   What ['s] this? Use rusticks thus to rage and curse?
I'le aske this other man. All hayle good man.

---

[1] From Suetonius 'Nero' *c.* 38 (Dyce).

LACH.　I will not; I had rather be sick than be the healthier for thy salutacion. I beseech Jove that some evill end may betyde!

GEL.　Now as I live, this thinge is very strainge.
Perchaunce theis men have stolne away my horse.
Ile aske one question more.
Leades this way to Pyræum, I pray you?

TIM.　This way leade thee to the gallowes!

[*He throwes dust on him.*

GEL.　O most base deede, to dusty my new cloathes!
By Jove, by Jove, I'de sue thee at the lawe
If I went not to the Antipodes.

Enter Pædio, with a Cappe made with Asses eares.

PÆD.　Where shall I fynd my master?

GEL.　What's the newes? speake; here I am.

PÆD.　Pseudocheus is shippt and gone to sea,
And sent to thee this guift.　　　　　　[*Delivers him the capp.*

GEL.　Oh, oh, my gould!
My Pegasus, my gould, my Pegasus!
What shall I doe? which shall I first lament?

[*He putts the capp* [*on*].

TIM.　What sweete content delighteth thus my eares?
Noe harmony's soe sweete as humane teares.
Water thye cheekes, and lett thyne eyes gush out
Whole seas of teares; weepe, sigh, mourne and complaine.

What, art thou wretched, and desir'st to dye?
Ile tell thee where are wild beasts, where's the sea,
Where's a steepe place upon a stony rock
That scytuated on a Mountaine high,
And underneath the roaring sea doth swell:
Wilt thou goe thither? drowne thyselfe from thence?
Ile be thy guide, and helpe thee at a push,
And when thou fall'st into the lowest hell,
I will rejoyce. What say'st thou, wilt thou dye?

GEL.　I am already dead.

TIM.　Thee therefore will I on theis shoulders beare;
Thy grave is made.

[*He offers to bury him in the earth he had digged.*

GEL.　O, suffer me a while
To walke like to a shaddowe on the earth!
Or, yf thou be soe pleased, Ile digg with thee.

TIM.　Put of theis asses eares.　　　　　[*He gives him a spade.*

GEL.   Theis were the true Armes of my graundfather.

[*He puts of his cap.*

TIM.   Soe maist thou wander as a laughing stock
Throughout the Cittie, and be made a scoffe,
A Noted fable to the laughing people,
A fit reward for this thy foolishnes. . . .

PÆD.   Master, I tooke you for an Athenian; I see now thou art
become an Arcadian. Other busynes calls me hence; I pray you,
gyve me leave to leave you.

GEL.   Yf my acquaintance meete thee by the waye,
Tell them that Pegasus gave me a fall.   [*Exit Pædio.*

TIM.   Againe with this my spade Ile wound the earth. [*He diggs.*
Why do'st not gape, and open thy wide Chincks?
Spew out thy Vapours, and a blustring noyse
Of winds breake forth thy adoperted denns?

[*He fynds gould.*

Whats this? I am amaz'd! what doe I see?
Sp[l]endour of gould reflects upon myne eyes:
Is Cynthia tralucent in the darke?
Where shall I turne myne eyes? What,[1] shall I hide
My new found treasure underneath[2] the earth,
Or shall I drowne it in the ocean?
Though all the world love thee, Timon hates thee.
Ile drowne thee in the seas profunditie.

[*He offers to goe drowne it.*

LACH.   Stay, master, stay; where runn you headlong thus?
TIM.   To drowne the ruyne of the world and me.
LACH.   The Gods would have thee to be fortunate.
TIM.   Figge for the gods! I wilbe miserable.
LACH.   Wilt thou be wretched of thy owne accord?
TIM.   Under bright gould lurks wretched miserie;
I speake it by experience.
LACH.   Under bright gould publique revenge doth lurke:
Keep it, yf you are wise, keepe it, I saye;
Thus maist thou be reveng'd of thy false friends,
Exterminating them owt of thie dores.
TIM.   Thou hast prevayled Laches.
Farr from the Cittie is a desart place,
Where the thick shaddowes of the Cypresse trees
Obscure the daye light, and Madge howlett whoopes:
That as a place Ile chuse for my repose.

---

[1] *Originally* Where.
[2] *Originally* Under.

Lett that day be unfortunate wherein
I see a man! thee alsoe will I flye,
As fearfull of thee.

    LACH.   I will followe thee.

    TIM.   Thy love doth vex me. Timon hates all men.
Yea I detest them with a deadlie hate;
Neither the gods themselves doe I affect.

[Exeunt Ti. and Lach.

    GEL.   O, yee good people, what will become of me?
My land is sould, and all my gould is fledd,
And nothing left me but this asses heade. . . .
Timon pul'd gould out from the earthes close Jawes:
What yf I alsoe digg? Come hither spade.
Digg out some gould, good spade.

[In V.4 Hermogenes and the philosophers find Gelasimus digging.
They all join the clients following Timon in his new prosperity.]

[V.5]   Scena Ult. Actus Ult.

    Enter Timon, Philargurus, Callimela, Blatte, Gelasimus, Hermogenes,
Eutrapelus, Laches, Stilpo, and Speusippus.

    TIM.   What Company is this that followes mee?
What would yee have?

    LACH.   They follow thee as crowes doe carrion.

    CALL.   My Timon, why turn'st thou away thye face?
I love thee better then myne eyes or soule:
Do'st thou dispise my love?

    TIM.   Thou can'st not wynn me with thy flattering tounge:
Peace, peace, thou queane, I sooner will receave
Megæra to my bedd, a hissing snake
Into my bosome.

    PHIL.   Timon, good Timon, be not soe perverse;
Drowne all things that are past in Lethes Floud.
I willinglie gyve thee my Calimele
To be thye wyfe.

    TIM.   Give her to Cerberus
Or to the Furies, to be tost in hell.

    BLAT.   Timon behould that face how fayre it is;
A dainty girle, neate and compleate throughout.
Now verylie thou hast a stony hart,
If that face move thee not; hould, embrace her,
Fasten sweete kisses on her Cherry lips.
What yf shee caste thee of? the falling out

Of lovers doth renewe and strengthen love:
Soe when I was a girle I did reject
Those woers whome I lov'd most heartely.

TIM.   Why urge yee me? my hart doth boyle with hate,
And will not stoope to any of your lures:
A burnt childe dreads the fyre.

CALL.   My honey, at the last be reconcild;
Bee not soe angry! sweete love, be merry!

BLAT.   Hee hath a face like one's that is at rack,
Hee lookes soe sowerlie.

TIM.   Is it this gould that doth allure your eyes?

PHIL.   Now as I live 'tis very glorious;
How like to fyre it shynes!

HER.   It b[l]yndes my eyes.

TIM.   Art thou in love with this gould, Callimele?
Thou then shalt marry it, kisse it sweetelie,
And it shall lye with thee in bedd.

CAL.   Ile not refuse what Timon doth commaund:
It shall lodge with me, yf you please.

LACH.   If gould
Gett children of thee, who shall father them?

PHIL.   Ile take a course for that; it shalbe gelt.

LACH.   Yes, geld it, yf thou doe fynd it in thy daughters bedd.
Master, good master, part not with that gould.

PHIL.   Timon, wilt thou dine at my house this day?

LACH.   Hee baites his hooke to gaine some of thy golde.
I know this fellowes crafty pollicy.

TIM.   Philargurus, doth this golde please your eies?

PHIL.   O my delight, my humor radicall,
My healthe, thou art farre brighter than the Sunne:
My youth returnes, my bearde doth budde afreshe,
When I beholde thee, my felicity.
Let mee embrace thee and kisse the[e] awhile.

LACH.   Tis vertue to abstaine from pleasing thinges.
Abstaine (good olde man); doe your fingers itche?

TIM.   Thou yesterday thy daughter didst commaunde
To parte from mee, and to forsake my side.
I was a begger worse than any dogge.

HER.   Worse than a snake, than the divell himselfe;
O base and most abhominable olde man,
Durst hee abuse brave generous Timon?

PHIL.   I was a dotarde, and a lier too,
When I soe saide; thou art another Jove.

EUT.   Away thou mony-monging Cormorant!
Thou art not worthy to see Timons face.

HER.   No nor to wipe his shoes; away Stinkarde!

BLAT.   Thou wicked knave, Ile scratche out both thine eies,
If thou provoke my master with such words.

TIM.   Yee crowes, ye vultures, yee doe gape in vaine.
I will make duckes and drakes with this my golde;
Ile scatter it and sowe it in the streetes,
Before your fingers touch a piece thereof.

HER.   O sweetest Timon, let mee kisse thy feete!
So love mee Jove, I'me gladde to see thee well.
I am your Servante, what is't you commaunde?
Impose that burthen that doth trouble thee
Uppon my shoulders.

LACH.   O most noble fidler,
A fidle is a fitter fardle for thy backe.

EUT.   Tavernes want takings, and vintners doe breake,
Now thou absentst thyselfe: forsake the woods,
Frequente the Citie; weele be Joviall,
Play the good fellowes.

TIM.   O faithfull friendes, in all my miseries
What whirlewinde tooke yee all away from mee?

HER.   Ile followe thee through fire to finde thee out,
To doe my Timon good.

TIM.   I know thy faith.
Thy hollow heart how full of holes it is.

EUT.   Thou alsoe well dost knowe my faithfullnesse:
I hate these double hollow hearted men
Whose tongues and heartes consent not both in one.

LACH.   Another Pylades!

GEL.   Timon, beholde mee alsoe; I am one
Of your retinue.

Enter Demeas.

DEM.   Give mee free passage; yee knowen and unknowen
persons, gette yee out of my way, least as I goe I offende any with
my heade, my elbow, or my breaste.

LACH.   Unlesse thy hornes offende I nothing feare.

DEM.   Wher's Athens piller? wher's my glory? Wher's Timon?
Thou hast blest myne eyes, now I see thee. Jove save thee, who art
the defence of Greece, and the whole worlds delight! the Court and
Countrey both salute thee.

LACH.   Thye eyes are purblynd; dost thou know this man?

DEM. Dost thinck me of soe weake a memory? Heare, my humane Jup[iter],[1] the decree that I have written concerning thee before the Areopig[ites].

[*He takes a pa[per] out of his [pocket].*]

Whereas Timon, the sonne of Echeratides the Collitensian, a Champion and a Wrestler, was in one day Victor of both in the Olympick games—

TIM. But I as yet neere saw th'Olympick games.

DEM. What of that? that makes noe matter; thou shalt see them hereafter.

TIM. I neere as yett bore armes out of Athens.

DEM. But thou shalt in the next warr,—*ffor theis Causes it seemes good to the Court and the Commonwealth, to the Magistrates severallie, to the Plebeians singulerlie, to all universallie, to place Timon in Pallas Temple, houlding a goulden thunderbolt in his hand.*

Demeas spake this suffragie, because he was Timons disciple, for Timon is alsoe easily the Prince of Rhetorick; in my orations I use to use his Metaphores.

HER. Peace, Oratour; wee alsoe ought to speake.

DEM. Would I had brought my litle sonne with me, whome I have called Timon after thy name.

TIM. How canst thou? for thy wyfe had never a child.

DEM. But shee shall have, and that shalbe borne shalbe a man child, and that man child shalbe named Timon.

TIM. Well hast thou said. Dissembling hypocrites, Thinke yee that I will be deceaved thus?

CALL. My Timon, my husband!

PHIL. My Sonne in lawe!

HER. My Mæcenas!

EUT. My protector!

DEM. My sublunary Jupiter!

LACH. Thou asse, why braist thou not among the reste?

GEL. Seest thou me not a woing of this maide Of 80 yeares? What say you, my Blatte? Art thou inflam'd with thy Gelasimus? If thou wilt have mee, Ile not seeke a wife Mong the Antipodes: what saies my chicke? My love? Sweete Timon, give thy asse some golde To buy some toy for this olde pretty maide.

STIL. Plato in his Acrostikes saith, it is better to give than receave.

SPE. Neither doth Aristotle dissent from Plato in his first of the Metaphysicks, the last text save one.

[1] The MS. is defective here.

STIL.   Every agent doth resuffer in his action. Wilt thou give? so thou shalt receave: wilt thou receave? then give. This therefore is the state of the quæstion: Timon is the terminus from whom; I the philosopher the terminus to whom; Timons hande is the medium, which mediating, first from himselfe generating, then by removing the impediment, gold is moved with a motion uniformally from Timon to mee in an instant.

TIM.   Why vexe yee mee, yee Furies? I protest,
And all the gods to witnesse invocate,
I doe abhorre the titles of a friende,
Of father, or companion. I curse
The Ayre yee breathe. I lothe to breathe that Aire.
I grieve that these mine eyes should see that Sunne,
My feete treade on that earthe yee treade upon.
I first will meete Jove thundring in the clouds,
Or in the wide devouring Scylla's gulfe
Or in Charybdis I will drowne myselfe,
Before Ile shew humanity to man.

[*He beates them with his spade.*

LACH.   Master, wilt thou that I drive them away?
See how well arm'd I am!

TIM.   Drive them to hell,
That Timons eies may never see them more.

PHIL.   O Timon [·   ·   ·   ·   ·]¹
To be thus handled?

HER.   Why dost thou [·   ·   ·   ·]

DEM.   Oh, wilt thou drive away thy Orator?
Have I not a decree concerning thee?

LACH.   I am your driver; hoi, gee, hence away!—
What, stand yee idle, my foolcosophers?—
Thou fidler, play the Hunts up on thy fidle.
Dost thou not see how they beginne to daunce?

GEL.   Sweete Timon,
Breake thou my heade with one small piece of gold.

[*Laches strikes him.*

Oh, oh.

LACH.   Get yee before mee then; bee gone, I say:
Thus I will follow Athenes²   [*Exeunt omnes.*

Timon Epilogue.

I now am left alone, this rascall route

---

¹ The MS. is defective.
² The copyist has omitted some words.

Hath left my side. What's this? I feele throughout
A sodeine change; my fury doth abate,
My hearte growes milde, and laies aside its hate.
Ile not affecte newe titles in my minde,
Or yet bee call'd the hater of Mankinde.
Timon doffs Timon, and with bended knee
Thus craves a favour, If our Comedie
And merry Scene deserve a Plaudite,
Let loving hands loude sounding in the Ayre,
Cause Timon to the Citty to repaire.[2]

VIII. Possible Source.

From CAMPASPE
by John Lyly (1584)

Campaspe, Played beefore the Queenes Majestie on newyeares day at night, by her Majesties Children, and the Children of Paules. Imprinted at London for Thomas Cadman, 1584.

Act I, Scene 3

Melipus, Plato, Aristotle, Crisippus, Crates, Cleanthes, Anaxarchus, Alexander, Hephestion, Parmenio, Clytus, Diogenes.

Enter Melippus

MELIP. I had never such a doe to warne schollers to come before a king. First, I cam to *Crisippus*, a tall leane old mad man, willing him presently to appeare before *Alexander*; he stoode staring on my face, neither moving his eies nor his body; I urging him to give some answer, hee tooke up a booke, sate downe, and saide nothing: *Melissa* his maid told me it was his manner, and that oftentimes she was fain to thrust meate into his mouth: for that he wold rather starve then ceasse studie. Well thoght I, seeing bookish men are so blockish, & so great clarkes such simple courtiers, I wil neither be partaker of their commons nor their commendations. From thence I came to *Plato* & to *Aristotle*, and to diverse other, none refusing to come, saving an olde obscure fellowe, who sitting in a tub turned

---

[2] If the private performance is successful the play may get a public showing?

23

towardes the sunne, reade Greeke to a yong boy; him when I willed to appeare before *Alexander*, he answeared, if *Alexander* wold faine see me, let him come to mee; if learne of me, lette him come to me; whatsoever it be, let him come to me: why, said I, he is a king; he answered, why, I am a Philosopher; why, but he is *Alexander*; I, but I am *Diogenes*. I was halfe angry to see one so crooked in his shape, to be so crabbed in his sayings. So going my way, I said, thou shalt repent it, if thou commest not to *Alexander*: nay, smiling answered he, *Alexander* may repent it, if he come not to *Diogenes*; vertue must be sought, not offered: and so turning himself to his cel, he grunted I know not what, like a pig under a tub. But I must be gone, the Philosophers are comming. [*Exit*.

Act II, Scene 1

Enter on one side Diogenes with a lantern; on the other Psyllus, Manes, Granichus.

PSYLLUS. Behold *Manes* where thy maister is, seeking either for bones for his dinner, or pinnes for his sleeves. I wil go salute him.

MANES. Doe so; but mum, not a woord you sawe *Manes*.

GRAN. Then stay thou behinde, and I will goe with *Psyllus*.

PSYLLUS. All haile *Diogenes* to your proper person.

DIOG. All hate to thy peevish conditions.

GRAN. O Dogge.

PSYLLUS. What dost thou seeke for here?

DIOG. For a man and a beast.

GRAN. That is easie without thy light to be found, bee not all these men?

DIOG. Called men.

GRAN. What beast is it thou lookest for?

DIOG. The beast my man, *Manes*.

PSYLLUS. He is a beast indeede that will serve thee.

DIOG. So is he that begat thee.

GRAN. What wouldest thou do, if thou shouldest find *Manes*?

DIOG. Give him leave to doo as hee hath done before.

GRAN. Whats that?

DIOG. To runne away.

PSYLLUS. Why, hast thou no neede of *Manes*?

DIOG. It were a shame for *Diogenes* to have neede of *Manes*, and for *Manes* to have no need of *Diogenes*.

GRAN. But put the case he were gone, wouldest thou entertaine any of us two?

DIOG. Upon condition.

PSYLLUS. What?

DIOG.   That you should tell me wherefore any of you both were good.

GRAN.   Why, I am a scholler, and well seene in Phylosophy.

PSYLLUS.   And I a prentice, and well seene in painting.

DIOG.   Well then *Granichus*, bee thou a painter to amend thine yll face, & thou *Psyllus* a Phylosopher, to correct thine evil manners. But who is that, *Manes*?

MANES.   I care not who I were, so I were not *Manes*.

GRAN.   You are taken tardie.

PSYLLUS.   Let us slip aside *Granichus*, to see the salutation betweene *Manes* and his maister.

DIOG.   *Manes*, thou knowest the last day I threw away my dish, to drink in my hand, because it was superfluous; now I am determined to put away my man, and serve my selfe: *Quia non egeo tui vel te.*

MANES.   Maister, you know a while a goe I ran awaye, so doe I meane to do againe, *quia scio tibi non esse argentum.*

DIOG.   I know I have no mony, neither will I have ever a man: for I was resolved longe sithence to put away both my slaves, money and *Manes*.

MANES.   So was I determined to shake of both my dogs, hunger and *Diogenes*.

PSYLLUS.   O sweete consent betweene a crowde[1] and a Jewes harp.

GRAN.   Come, let us reconcile them.

PSYLLUS.   It shall not neede: for this is their use, nowe do they dine one upon another.   [*Exit Diogenes.*

GRAN.   How now *Manes*, art thou gone from thy maister?

MANES.   Noe, I didde but nowe bynde my selfe to him.

PSYLLUS.   Why, you were at mortall jars.

MANES.   In faith no, we brake a bitter jest one uppon another.

GRAN.   Why, thou art as dogged as he.

PSYLLUS.   My father knew them both litle whelpes.

MANES.   Well, I will hie mee after my maister.

GRAN.   Why, is it supper time with *Diogenes*?

MANES.   I, with him at al times when he hath meate.

PSYLLUS.   Why then, every man to his home, and lette us steale out againe anone.

GRAN.   Where shall we meete?

PSYLLUS.   Why, at *Alæ vendibili suspensa hedera non est opus.*

MANES.   *O Psyllus, habeo te loco parentis*, thou blessest me.   [*Exeunt.*

---

[1] a fiddle.

Act IV, Scene 1

Solinus, Psyllus, Granichus, Manes, Diogenes, Populus.

Enter Solinus, Psyllus, Granichus

SOLI.   This is the place, the day, the time, that *Diogenes* hath appointed to flye.

PSYLLUS.   I will not loose the flight of so faire a fowle as *Diogenes* is, though my maister cogel my no bodie, as he threatned.

GRAN.   What *Psyllus*, will the beaste wag his winges to-day?

PSYLLUS.   We shall heare: for here commeth *Manes*: *Manes* will it be?

Enter Manes

MANES.   Be? he were best be as cunning as a Bee, or else shortly he will not be at all.

GRAN.   How is he furnished to fly? hath he feathers?

MANES.   Thou art an asse! Capons, Geese, & Owles have feathers. He hath found *Dedalus* old waxen wings, and hath beene peecing them this moneth, he is so broade in the shoulders. O you shall see him cut the ayre even like a Tortoys.

SOL.   Me thinkes so wise a man should not be so mad, his body must needes be to heavy.

MANES.   Why, hee hath eaten nothing this sevennight but corke and feathers.

PSYLLUS *(aside)*.   Tutch him *Manes*.

MANES.   He is so light, that he can scarse keepe him from flying at midnight.

Populus intrat.

MANES.   See they begin to flocke, and behold my mayster bustels himselfe to flye. (Diogenes *comes out of his tub.*)

DIOG.   Yee wicked and beewitched Atheneans, whose bodies make the earth to groane, and whose breathes infect the aire with stench. Come ye to see *Diogenes* fly? *Diogenes* commeth to see you sinke! yee call me dog: so I am, for I long to gnaw the boanes in your skins. Yee tearme me an hater of menne: no, I am a hater of your maners. Your lives dissolute, not fearing death, will prove your deaths desperate, not hoping for life: what do you els in Athens but sleepe in the day, and surfeite in the night: back Gods in the morning with pride, in the evening belly Gods with gluttonie! You flatter kings, & call them Gods: speake trueth of your selves, & confesse you are divels! From the Bee you have taken not the honney, but the wax to make your religion, framing it to the time, not to the trueth. Your filthy luste you colour under a courtly colour of love, injuries abroad under the title of policies at home, and secrete malice creepeth under the name of publick justice. You have caused *Alexander* to dry up springs & plant Vines, to sow roket and weede endiffe, to sheare sheepe, and shrine foxes. Al conscience is sealed at Athens. Swearing commeth of a hot mettal: lying of a quick wit: flattery of a flowing tongue: undecent talk of a mery disposition. Al things are lawfull at Athens. Either you thinke there are no Gods, or I must think ye are no men. You build as though you should live for ever, and surfet as though you should die to morow. None teacheth true Phylosophy but *Aristotle*, because he was the kings schoolemaister! O times! O menne! O coruption in manners! Remember that greene grasse must turne to dry hay. When you sleep, you are not sure to wake; and when you rise, not certeine to lye downe. Looke you never so hie, your heads must lye levell with your feete. Thus have I flowne over your disordered lives, and if you wil not amend your manners, I wil study to fly further from you, that I may be neerer to honesty.

SOL.   Thou ravest *Diogenes*, for thy life is different from thy words. Did not I see thee come out of a brothel house? was it not a shame?

DIOG.   It was no shame to go out, but a shame to goe in.

GRAN.   It were a good deede *Manes*, to beate thy maister.

MANES.   You were as good eate my maister.

ONE OF THE PEOPLE.   Hast thou made us all fooles, and wilt thou not flye?

DIOG.   I tell thee unlesse thou be honest, I will flye.

PEOPLE.   Dog! dog! take a boane!

DIOG.   Thy father neede feare no dogs, but dogs thy father.

PEOPLE.   We wil tel *Alexander*, that thou reprovest him behinde his back.

DIOG.   And I will tell him, that you flatter him before his face.

PEOPLE.   We wil cause al the boyes in the streete to hisse at thee.

DIOG.   Indeede I thinke the Athenians have their children ready for any vice, because they be Athenians.

MANES.   Why maister, meane you not to flye?

DIOG.   No *Manes*, not without wings.

MANES.   Every body will account you a lyar.

DIOG.   No, I warrant you: for I will alwaies say the Athenians are mischievous.

PSYLLUS.   I care not, it was sport ynogh for me to see these old huddles hit home.

GRAN.   Nor I.

PSYLLUS. Come, let us goe, and hereafter when I meane to raile upon any body openly, it shall be given out, I will flye.

[*Exeunt.*

.   .   .   .

Act V, Scene 1

(Enter, to) Diogenes, Sylvius, Perim, Milo, Trico, Manes.

SYL. I have brought my sons, *Diogenes*, to be taught of thee.

DIOG. What can thy sonnes doe?

SYL. You shall see their qualities: Daunce, sirha!

Then Perim daunceth

How like you this? doth he well?

DIOG. The better, the worser.

SYL. The Musicke very good.

DIOG. The Musitions very badde; who onelye study to have their stringes in tune, never framing their manners to order.

SYL. Now shall you see the other. Tumble, sirha!

Milo tumbleth

How like you this? why do you laugh?

DIOG. To see a wagge that was born to break his neck by distinie, to practise it by arte.

MILO. This dogge will bite me, I will not be with him.

DIOG. Feare not boy, dogges eate no thistles.

PERIM. I marvel what dog thou art, if thou be a dog.

DIOG. When I am hungry, a mastyve, and when my belly is full, a spaniell.

SYL. Doest thou beleeve that there are any gods, that thou art so dogged?

DIOG. I must needs beleeve there are gods: for I think thee an enimie to them.

SYL. Why so?

DIOG. Because thou hast taught one of thy sonnes to rule his legges, and not to follow learning; the other to bend his body every way, and his minde no way.

PERIM. Thou doest nothing but snarle, and barke like a dogge.

DIOG. It is the next way to drive away a theefe.

SYL. Now shall you heare the third, who singes like a Nightingall.

DIOG. I care not: for I have heard a Nightingall sing her selfe. . . .

SYL. Well *Diogenes*, I perceive my sonnes brooke not thy manners.

DIOG. I thought no lesse, when they knew my vertues.

SYL. Farewell *Diogenes*, thou needest not have scraped rootes, if thou would'st have followed *Alexander*.

DIOG. Nor thou have follow'd *Alexander*, if thou hadst scraped rootes. [*Exeunt.*

PERICLES
PRINCE OF TYRE

INTRODUCTION

OF ALL THE PLAYS discussed in these volumes *Pericles* was the only one not printed in the first Folio. It was entered in the Stationers' Register on 20 May 1608, for Edward Blount, but he did not publish it. The play appeared in 1609 as *The Late, And much admired Play, called Pericles, Prince of Tyre . . . As it hath been divers and sundry times acted by his Maiesties Servants, at the Globe on the Banck-side. By William Shakespeare. Imprinted at London for Henry Gosson . . .*

A second Quarto with some variant readings was published in the same year, another (Q3) in 1611, and in 1619 *Pericles* was one of several pieces which Jaggard and Pavier printed (Q4) for what was probably originally intended to be a large volume of works ascribed to Shakespeare, until protests by the King's Company thwarted the scheme. Other editions came out in 1630 (Q5) and 1635 (Q6). Obviously the piece remained very popular, but it was not incorporated into the Folio until 1664, with other doubtful plays.

There has always been discussion about the authenticity of *Pericles*. Dryden regarded it as an early work:

> Shakespeare's own Muse her Pericles first bore;
> The Prince of Tyre was elder than the Moor.

meaning, no doubt, that *Pericles* preceded *Titus Andronicus*. Rowe included it as Shakespeare's, and so did Malone and Steevens although Pope did not. Most critics held that the play was too disconnected and feebly written to be wholly Shakespeare's, but that 'he has certainly bestowed some decoration on its parts' (Malone).

The problems of the play's character and authorship are complicated by the unsatisfactory nature of Q1, which at times is almost unintelligible. There is much printing of verse as prose, especially in the second half; there is much irregular verse, or prose set out as verse, all to an extent unusual even in

349

Elizabethan dramatic printing. Moreover there are muddled scenes, confusions of speech and of action, repetitions of phrase and apparent omissions of necessary material. These features have suggested to many critics that Q1 was a reported text, made 'possibly with the aid of shorthand' (*WSh*.I.521) or by men whose memory failed them.

Recently Professor P. Edwards has argued most ingeniously from a detailed examination of the text that the play was put together by two reporters, one doing Acts I and II, the other Acts III–V; and that the printing was done by three compositors, each with his own idiosyncrasies.[1] The theory certainly explains much of the confusion in the play as it stands, but does not entirely solve the problems raised by the difference in tone and manner between the first and second halves. Professor Edwards inclines to believe that Shakespeare wrote the whole play, and that the differences in style are due to the reporters. It is remarkable however that so little of Shakespeare was retained by the first reporter.

The theory of reporting as the source of the text has been opposed by Hardin Craig[2] and C. J. Sisson[3] who have argued that Q1 was printed from a rough draft of the play which gave the compositors much trouble to decipher, and even to arrange correctly. If the 'foul papers' were in more than one handwriting, with revisions of the other author's text inserted by Shakespeare and (maybe) some new scenes added, this would explain many difficulties. But this would still leave unexplained some of Edwards's evidence in favour of a 'reported' text.

Acts I and II are indeed jejune, rigid, and apart from one or two passages, unlike anything in Shakespeare. Parts of the last three Acts resemble the later Shakespeare: thus the Brothel scenes (IV.2, 6) have something in common with *Measure for Measure*; Marina's short flower-speech (IV.1.13–17) anticipates Perdita's in *A Winter's Tale*; and frequently (e.g. in V.1–3) the mood and syntax and other stylistic features resemble those of the last plays.

Malone suggested that the piece was written by 'some friend whose interest the "gentle Shakespeare" was industrious to

[1] P. Edwards, 'An Approach to the Problem of *Pericles*', *Sh Survey*, 5, 1952, 25–49.
[2] H. Craig, '*Pericles* and *The Painefull Adventures*', *SPhil*, XLV, 1949, 100–5.
[3] C. J. Sisson, *New Readings in Shakespeare*, 1955, p. 296.

promote', so he improved the dialogue and strengthened the last Act. Without accepting the speculation about Shakespeare's friendship, I accept the conclusion (held by many other critics) [1] that he revised someone else's play.

As Professor J. C. Maxwell suggests, it is impossible to find in the Q1 text conclusive evidence as between collaboration and revision; but it is difficult to believe that, if Shakespeare had been collaborating fully with another dramatist, he would not have taken control and organized the whole play more dynamically. What scattered evidence there is of Shakespeare's manner in the first two acts, together with the greater amount in the last three, suggests that Shakespeare started with only a perfunctory interest in the play but became more involved after the shipwreck and especially as the story of Marina developed. Although internal evidence that Shakespeare revised an already existing play is indecisive, important external evidence can, I believe, be found. Consideration of this will be left until the nature of the basic source-material has been examined.

The story of *Pericles* is taken from that of Apollonius of Tyre, which probably sprang from a Greek romance similar in type to that of *Anthia and Habrokomes* written by Xenophon of Ephesus (which also has some elements in common with the Romeo and Juliet story).[2] The story survived in Greek manuscripts through the Middle Ages; one was printed in Venice in 1534; and the tale is still told orally by Greek shepherds.[3] A Christian Latin version had been made by the sixth century, including several riddles from Symposius which seem to date from the fifth century or earlier. The popularity of the story in the Middle Ages is proved by the survival of scores of MSS containing the Latin Historia. In the late twelfth century Godfrey of Viterbo included it as historical in his rhymed Latin *Pantheon, or Universal Chronicle* (first published in 1559 at Basle).

---

[1] E.g. Coleridge; cf. T. M. Raysor, *Coleridge's Shakespearian Criticism*, II, 209; K. Muir, *Shakespeare as Collaborator*, 1960, 56–76; J. C. Maxwell, *Camb.* 1956, xxii–xxv; F. D. Hoeniger, *New Arden*, 1963, lii–lxiii.

[2] See Vol. I, p. 269. For the full history of the saga see A. H. Smyth, *Shakespeare's Pericles and Apollonius of Tyre*, Philadelphia, 1898; S. Singer, *Apollonius von Tyrus*, Halle, 1895; E. Klebs, *Die Erzählung von Apollonius aus Tyrus*, Berlin, 1899.

[3] R. M. Dawkins, 'Modern Greek Oral Versions of Apollonios of Tyre', *MLR*, xxxvii, 1942, 169–84.

It was also taken into the *Gesta Romanorum* though perhaps not before the fourteenth century.

The story as it entered *Gesta Romanorum* was one of wanderings and search, but also of riddles to be solved, since not only Antiochus asked a riddle but the maiden tried to win the suffering Apollonius's interest by asking him several. In addition the story makes much of her terrible situation in the brothel. This feature of the romance was probably taken over from the legends of Christian saints, several of whom had been thus exposed, e.g. Theodora, Serapia and Denise.[1] The best known was the Roman St Agnes who probably suffered in about A.D. 304 at the age of thirteen, and whose holy day is January 21.

Soon after her death (*c.* 376) St Ambrose devoted to her some pages in his sermons *De Virginibus*.[2] Prudentius's hymn in her honour (No. XIV)[3] influenced many later writers, including the German nun Hroswitha. In England Agnes was praised in Latin by Abbot Aldhem (seventh century) and in Old English in Aelfric's *Passions* (tenth century). She was celebrated also by Adam of Saint Victor (twelfth century) and in the *Golden Legend* of Jacobus de Voragine.

The legend of St Agnes varies somewhat from writer to writer. According to Hroswitha and Saint Victor she was desired in marriage by the son of the Prefect of Rome. When she refused him he fell ill, and his father tried in vain to persuade her by gifts. Denounced as a Christian[4] she was ordered to worship idols. On refusing she was sent naked to the brothel, but her hair covered her like a cloak, hiding her from prurient eyes. An angel appeared beside her; the frequenters of the brothel were terrified,[5] and the Prefect's son fell dead when he seized the maiden. When his father mourned, Agnes revived the youth. A fire was prepared to burn her alive, but it burned the pagans, not the saint, so she was decapitated. Tharsia-Marina has obviously much in common with St Agnes.

---

[1] See *Acta Sanctorum*, April, III, 578; August, VI, 500; May, III, 451.
[2] Migne, *Patrologiae Latinae*, XVI, Col. 200–2.
[3] Cf. *Prudence*, ed. M. Lavarenne, t. IV, Paris, 1951, 190–200.
[4] See the early sermon by Bishop Maximus of Turin (Migne, LVII, col. 642–8).
[5] St Agnes probably appears in three stained-glass panels in the west window of North Tuddenham Church, Norfolk. One shows a man falling back from her in the brothel. (See M. R. James, *Suffolk and Norfolk*, 1930, p. 184.)

The saga of Apollonius passed all over Europe into the vernacular. Thus in Germany Heinrich von Neustadt wrote a poem in 20,893 lines in the fourteenth century; and a century later Heinrich Steinhöwel a prose history which was printed in 1471. In the Netherlands the story of Apollonius was printed in translations of *Gesta Romanorum* from 1481 onwards, and separately published in 1493. In Italy it appears in a fourteenth-century MS, and a version in *ottava rima* was frequently printed between 1486 and 1629. Spain has vernacular MSS, and Juan de Timoneda printed a version (from *Gesta Romanorum*) in 1576. The troubadours of Southern France knew the tale, which in the north was assimilated into the Carlovingian cycle. A prose version was printed *c*. 1480, and F. de Belleforest re-told it from *Gesta Romanorum* in his *Histoires Tragiques*, tom. 7, 1595.

England possesses the first of all known vernacular versions, an Anglo-Saxon prose-fragment now at Corpus Christi College, Cambridge, dating from the eleventh century. This contains the story as far as the betrothal of Apollonius to Aroestrates' daughter (unnamed); and the climax in the Temple of Diana with the marriage of Tharsia and Athenagoras.

The Bodleian Library, Oxford, has a fragment of a Middle English romance in rhymed verse dating from the early fifteenth century and containing about a tenth of the story (144 lines) from Apollonius's narrative in the Temple. The translator of this romance

> 'Was vicary, y understonde,
> At Wymborne mynstre in that stede'

(i.e. in Dorset).

Chaucer referred to the legend when he made his Man of Law praise him for not writing about rape and incest, in *The Legend of Good Women* and elsewhere, e.g. about Canace:

> (Of swiche cursed stories I sey fy).
> Or elles of Tyro Apollonious
> How that the cursed Kyng Antiochus
> Birafte his doghter of hir maydenhede,
> That is so horrible a tale for to rede,
> Whan he hir threw upon the pavement;

And therefore he, of ful avysement,
Nolde nevere write in none of his sermons
Of suche unkynde abhomynacions.

Chaucer's friend John Gower (*c.* 1327–1408) devoted Book VIII of his *Confessio Amantis* (1393) to 'Unlawful love', and most of that Book to the story of 'Apollinus', which he took from Godfrey of Viterbo's *Pantheon*.

Ostensibly warning the Lover against evil lust, the Priest obviously enjoys the later adventures of the hero, and, though his tale 'is a long process to here', he tells it fully. Apollinus is 'well grounded' and a good family man, and his story brings out the contrast between

What is to love in good manere,
And what to love in other wise.

Gower tells of the maiden's sufferings in the brothel less elaborately than *Gesta Romanorum*, and he omits altogether the visit and conversion of Athanagoras, who first appears when Apollinus reaches Mytelene.

Shakespeare knew Gower's work early in his career, and probably drew for the dénouement of *The Comedy of Errors*[1] on the reunion of Apollinus with his wife in the Temple of Diana at Ephesus. The *Confessio Amantis* is also a major source of *Pericles*. Some of the names come from Gower;[2] there are parallels in structure and idea; and the use of the poet Gower as the Chorus linking the episodes suggests a recent reading of, and admiration for, *Confessio Amantis*, which was printed first by Caxton (1483) and then by Berthelette (1533, 1554). The story is given below from Berthelette's 1554 edition with a few emendations in spelling, and useful variants supplied by G. C. Macaulay's edition (1901) [Text I].

In 1510 Wynkyn de Worde published a prose romance *Kynge Apollyn of Thyre*, translated by Robert Copland from a French romance which derived ultimately from the *Gesta Romanorum*. The first printed English version of the *Gesta*,

---

[1] Cf. Vol. I, 10–11.

[2] Some place-names, also Cerimon, Helicanus, Dionyza, Lichorida, Philoten and Thaisa (the wife in the play, the daughter in Gower). The chief resemblances will be discussed later. Twine calls the wife Lucina, the daughter Tharsia.

published by Richard Robinson (1577, 1610, 1620) did not include the story, perhaps because the translation was based on an MS which (like others in the Middle Ages) did not contain it.

The 153rd story of the Latin *Gesta*[1] was however the source of *The Patterne of Painefull Adventures*, by Laurence Twine, which, entered in S.R. in 1576, is extant now in two editions, one undated but possibly *c.* 1594, the other of 1607 (when it was attributed to Thomas Twine, Laurence's brother). Twine's romance is given below [Text II] from the earlier edition.

Confessio Amantis and *The Patterne of Painefull Adventures* were undoubtedly the main sources of the play, which interweaves material from them both in almost every scene, sometimes taking more from Gower, sometimes more from Twine (especially in the last two acts e.g. Lysimachus in the brothel). A few coincidences with other versions suggest that the dramatist 'knew some folklore version of the tale unknown to us' (*Camb.* xviii). 'Perillie' is a name assumed by Apollonius in a French MS in Vienna; Cerimon's helper Philemon (not in Gower, Machaon in Twine) is called Philominus in von Neustadt's poem; and in a Greek poem on the story printed in the sixteenth century there is a tournament at Pentapolis. Was there a ballad or lay in English (now lost), in which Apollonius became 'Perilles' or 'Pericles', perhaps because of the perils (*pericula*) he endured? Most editors have followed Steevens who suggested that it came from Pyrocles, a hero in Sidney's *Arcadia*.

The adventures of Pyrocles in *The Countess of Pembroke's Arcadia* (1590) certainly afford parallels to those of Apollonius. At the opening of Book I he is shipwrecked along with his friend Musidorus, who is saved, clinging to a chest, and provided with apparel by two shepherds. Pyrocles is rescued by pirates, and made their leader before being reunited to Musidorus. The latter soon finds a suit of armour belonging to his noble cousin Amphialus, dons it, and has exciting adventures. Pyrocles, for love of Philoclea, disguises himself as an Amazon.

In Book II, Ch. 7–10, we learn of a previous shipwreck

---

[1] Printed in an appendix by A. H. Smyth, *op. cit.* pp. 93–112.

24

suffered by the two friends, their wanderings and encounter with the blind king of Paphlagonia (a story used by Shakespeare in *King Lear*). Pyrocles' love for Philoclea comes to a climax in Book III when he believes her dead, and his grief is described at length (Ch. 22). At dawn he hears a woman in his chamber. She rebukes him for excessive grief and he goes to strike her but finds that she is Philoclea [Text III].

Incidents such as these suggest that the tale of Apollonius of Tyre was one of the stories Sidney had in mind when writing his *Arcadia*. They do not prove that the dramatist was thinking of Sidney's romance, but Sir Gerrard Herbert in a letter in 1619 wrote of seeing 'the play of Pirrocles, Prince of Tyre'.

Dr J. M. S. Tompkins has suggested that Shakespeare named him after Pericles in North's *Plutarch*,[1] for the Greek statesman was a pattern of endurance. Plutarch tells that when he lost his only legitimate son Pericles lay at home in misery and dejection for a time, till he was won back to public life by Alcibiades. His faithful companion Aspasia was not his wife, but his mistress. We do not know that it was Shakespeare who changed Apollonius into Pericles. Other names appear in Plutarch: Cleon was a rash fellow with a loud voice and brazen face ('Life of Nicias'); and Lysimachus was a general of Alexander's and king of Thrace, to whom the poet Philippides, being asked what he would like as a gift, answered, 'Anything but your secrets' ('Life of Demetrius'). A cruel man, he was unlike our Lysimachus, but note that the Philippides anecdote appears at 1.3.4–6.[2]

Almost as baffling, and more important, is the relationship of the play to the prose romance *The Painfull Adventures of Pericles, Prince of Tyre*, which George Wilkins published in 1608, a year before the play, but in the same year as Edward Blount's entry in S.R. The title-page relates the book to a recent Pericles play.[3] The nature of that play is among the many problems raised by the publication.

Wilkins was a minor dramatist whose tragedy *The Miseries*

---

[1] *RES*, n.s. iii, 1952, 322–4.

[2] *Camb.* pp. 101–2.

[3] *The Painfull Adventures of Pericles Prince of Tyre. Being The true History of the Play of Pericles, as it was lately presented by the worthy and ancient Poet John Gower.* At London. Printed by T.P. for Nat: Butter, 1608. Modern edn. by K. Muir, Liverpool, 1953.

of Enforced Mariage was written in 1606 and performed by the King's Men in 1607. He had previously written a moral pamphlet *Three Miseries of Barbary* (*c.* 1606); he also collaborated with T. Dekker in *Jests to Make you Merrie* (1607) and with J. Day and W. Rowley in *The Travels of Three English Brothers* (1607). Little more is known about him. It has been argued that he collaborated with Thomas Heywood,[1] but this remains unproven.[2]

Wilkins's novel is largely founded on Twine's recently republished *Patterne of Painefull Adventures* (1607) and on a *Pericles* performed by the King's Company, the success of which doubtless encouraged him to write a catchpenny work. His method was to interweave passages from Twine and from the play, and since he lifted many passages almost word for word from Twine, it may be assumed that he did the same with the play so far as he could, since it had not been published. From Twine he took incidents not in our play, and in others followed Twine rather than the play—e.g. his first chapter is Twine's with some sentimental expansion; in his Chapter 2 he plagiarized Twine's account of Apollonius's doings in Tharsus, especially the selling of the wheat, the charitable restoration of the price, and the description of the monument erected in the market-place; in Chapter 4 the storm is largely from Twine, and the charity of the fisherman (only one in the novels, three in the play). In Chapter 6 the harp-playing, the wooing of Pericles by Thaisa and also the wedding festivities are from Twine, Chapters 5–7 (the last somewhat lopped of the long descriptions of bride and bridegroom). The whole of Chapter 8 follows closely Twine's Chapter 10, including the nurse's disclosure to Tharsia (Marina) of her parentage, which is not in the play. In Chapter 11 Marina's Song is probably taken from Twine, although it may have been sung in the play (which omitted it when printed). In this chapter Wilkins omitted the riddles which came down to Twine (Chapter 17) from *Gesta Romanorum*, but included the striking of the girl by her father, which is only obscurely referred to in the play as we

---

[1] By H. D. Sykes; rebutted by A. M. Clark, *Thomas Heywood*, 1931, pp. 301–28.
[2] Cf. M. Grivelet, *Thomas Heywood et Le Drame Domestique Elizabéthain*, Paris, 1957, pp. 378–40; B. Maxwell, *Studies in the Shakespeare Apocrypha*, N.Y. 1956, Ch. 4.

have it. The winding up of the story after the play's ending is summarized from Twine.[1]

On the other hand Wilkins obviously followed a play with many likenesses to *Pericles* both for some incidents given in Twine and for others not in *The Patterne of Painefull Adventures*. At times he seems to be describing what he has seen or heard at a performance. The names of the characters are as in Shakespeare's play, except that Wilkins does not name Boult, the 'leno'. There are references to 'cues' and actors' 'parts' when characters enter or speak, and the narrative is often interrupted by dialogue. Sometimes this dialogue is unnecessary but like a dramatic exposition, as when in Chapter 3 Cleon describes the famine at Tarsus to his wife Dyonysa. The account in Chapter 4 (*inf.* 508) where the King and princess 'have placed themselves in a Gallery, to beholde the triumphes' of the Knights with their devices etc. is more clear and consistent than in the play's text (II.2). Similarly Helicanus' interview with Pericles is muddled in the play but clear and consecutive in Wilkins (Ch. 2).[2] How far he invented material it is impossible to be sure, but his borrowings from Twine and from the play are usually so close that we may well doubt whether he troubled to insert anything of his own except some stylistic flourishes and a little sentiment.

There are also many passages of blank verse or quasi-blank verse. Bearing in mind Wilkins's general slavishness, it seems more likely that he took these from a source-play than that he occasionally began to invent verse. And when we find that some of these passages are close to Q 1 we are driven to conclude that, having seen a Pericles play performed (perhaps more than once), Wilkins remembered what he could of it (maybe with the help of notes) and turned dramatic material into prose as he interwove it with matter from Twine.

The question at once arises, was the play the one with Shakespeare's hand in it, or an earlier version? Professor Edwards, believing that Shakespeare wrote the whole play, that there was no earlier version, and that the differences in style and content are due to the activities of two reporters and three compositors, argues that where Wilkins differs from the

[1] Cf. Wilkins, ed. K. Muir, pp. iv–vi.
[2] Cf. P. Edwards, *op. cit.* pp. 26–7, and *Camb.* pp. 111–13.

play it is because the text of the play is corrupt or incomplete or because he has misremembered or tampered with those parts of the play which he did not piece out from Twine.

Certainly there are many lines in Wilkins which resemble the play as we have it; but, as J. C. Maxwell notes, the like passages have few 'Shakespearian' qualities, although there are some, e.g. the 'Poore inche of Nature' speech (*inf.* 519 and III.1.27–37). On the whole Wilkins's quasi-verse passages are un-Shakespearean, but they often resemble in style Acts I and II in the play as reported, e.g. in the occasional use of an abstraction qualified by an epithet at the end of a sentence.

The verse passages from Wilkins sometimes supplement or correct the play's text; sometimes they seem to come from a version very different from that reported in Q1. This version may have contained several scenes not in Q1, including two which in the printed version are represented by Dumbshows. These, and the differences between the brothel-scenes, force me to the conclusion that Wilkins's novel was based on an earlier version of *Pericles* than that published in 1609. Wilkins's paraphrases may therefore help us to reconstruct something of the play as it was before Shakespeare revised it in 1608. I have re-created much of the latent verse,[1] and give it, with some commentary, in an Appendix.

Speculation has accumulated about the identity of the first author (or Shakespeare's collaborator), and the claims of Rowley, Heywood and others have been well discussed by Dr Hoeniger (*New Arden*, lvi–lxiii and App. B). Wilkins is most unlikely, for 'it would be odd if a habitual plagiarist were to follow his own composition so very much less than someone else's' (*ibid.*). The strongest case yet advanced is for John Day, author of *Law Tricks* (1604), *The Isle of Gulls* (1606), *Humour out of Breath* (1608) and *The Parliament of Bees* (1641), and collaborator in *The Travels of the Three English Brothers* (1607), but although Day may have influenced Shakespeare's romances by his tragi-comedies about parents and children separated and then reunited, the close parallels to *Pericles* are limited to II.1 and II.3.

I propose now to consider in some detail the use of the known

---

[1] K. Muir did so, more cautiously, in *Shakespeare as Collaborator*, pp. 56–70.

sources in the play. Gower as Prologue begins by announcing his return to tell the old profitable tale. The playwright seems to have had both *Confessio Amantis* and Twine's novel before him. Antiochus' 'chiefest seat' (18) comes from Twine. Unlike the two sources the play omits all details of the King's violation of his daughter and the reactions of her nurse, but gets from Gower the idea that habit made their incest seem 'no sin'. The play follows Gower in omitting Twine's assertion that Antiochus beheaded suitors who guessed his riddle as well as those who failed.

Act I, Scene 1 starts in mid-conversation and fittingly departs from the sources by having the daughter brought in to be admired by Pericles before he hears the riddle. The imagery of trees, fruits, Hesperides, dragon and chivalric heroes is peculiar to the play. Pericles conceives himself as a knightly champion in the lists.

The riddle itself follows Gower rather than Twine, but differs considerably from both, for the dramatist had difficulty in interpreting the Middle English version and so made the daughter instead of Antiochus the speaker, and reshaped the clues.[1] There seems to be a reference to the 'caskets' of *Gesta Romanorum* and *Merchant of Venice* in 76–7

> Fair glass of light, I lov'd you, and could still,
> Were not this glorious casket stor'd with ill.

(A 'glass of light' was probably a glass vessel with a candle in it.) The girl has indicated her liking for Pericles; he now repulses her, and her father's jealousy is aroused ('touch not, upon thy life').

The running images of 72–86 and the moral reflections in 96–102 may be Shakespearian. Pericles is more cautious than Apollonius. In Twine the King gives a respite of thirty days and tells Apollonius to return home; in the play, as in Gower, Pericles flees from Antioch, fearing for his life. In all versions he is followed by Antiochus' agent, but the latter's name, Thaliard, and the mention of poison and gold, are from Gower (511–19).

The dramatist in I.2 not only displays Pericles' disturbance of mind and fear for his people, but also shows Helicanus reproving his melancholy inactivity, extracting the reasons

---

[1] P. Goolden, 'Antiochus' Riddle in Gower and Shakespeare', *RES*, n.s. 6, 1955.

first and urging him to 'travel for a while'. The responsibility for the Prince's long absence from his city is thus not his alone, and proper arrangements are made for its government during his absence. Unlike Apollonius Pericles is not governed only by selfish fear, but is a 'true prince' with a sense of duty. Some attempt is thus made to transfer the fairy tale into terms of Renaissance political interests. Helicanus and his advice are developed from Gower 579–92 where a Tyrian citizen of that name warns Apollonius (in Tharsus) not to return to Tyre.

The essentially narrative basis of the story is preserved in I.3 where Thaliard, reaching Tyre, finds that Pericles has gone. The scene moves quickly to Tharsus, where the Governor, Cleon (not the citizen Stranguilio of Gower and Twine) describes to his wife Dionyza (as in Gower, Dionisiades in Twine) the famine in the city. Pericles comes bringing boundless supplies and seeking 'harbourage' ('herbergage', Gower).

The Prologue to Act II mentions the statue erected in Pericles' honour, gives a Dumbshow of Helicanus' messenger (Helicanus himself in Gower) bringing a warning to Pericles against returning home, and describes the tempest which shipwrecks him near Pentapolis. II.1 provides social comment and comic relief by introducing three fishermen instead of one, the other two being servants of the first (cf. 95–6). The play substitutes a jousting of knights in honour of the Princess's birthday for Gower's athletic games before the King (680–711) and Twine's game of tennis in which the King takes part (*inf.* 435). This sustains the chivalric tone, and introduces the discovery of Pericles' father's armour (II.1.120–43), and the parade of knights in II.2. The knights are suitors of the Princess, like those whom we hear described or see in *The Merchant of Venice*, I.2 and II.7, 9. No single origin of their emblems and mottoes has been discovered, but all except perhaps that of Pericles, 'the stranger knight' were well known from emblem-books at the time.[1]

The banquet scene, II.3, is elaborated from Gower and Twine, both of which seem to have been used. Twine, for instance, suggested that the Princess (Lucina) was already half in love with him, 'having already in hir heart professed to doe

---

[1] Cf. Henry Green, *Shakespeare and the Emblem Writers*, 1870, Chap. V.

him good' (cf. 72), and Gower (748–56) makes Apollonius very ready to reveal his name and birthplace though not his rank (cf. 81–5). In both sources the Princess plays the harp and the hero praises her but offers to show her another measure, his playing of which proves to her that he must be of gentle birth. In Twine his praise is qualified ('she is not yet come to perfection in musike'); the girl obtains for him a great reward and gets him invited to stay in the palace. The harping leads next day to Apollonius' being employed to teach Lucina music 'and other good qualities, wherein hee is skilfull' (Twine). The play substitutes a dance for the music. King Simonides encourages Pericles to dance with Thaisa, and then puts Pericles to sleep in the room next his own—a sign of high favour. In order to show Tyre's need of Pericles the play shifts the scene back to Tyre (II.4) where Helicanus has had news of the dire punishment of Antiochus and his daughter, which slightly resembles that of Antiochus Epiphanes in 2 *Maccabees*, IX, 7–10, who was afflicted with an incurable plague so that 'his flesh fell away, and the filthiness of his smell was noisome to all his army.' The nobles invite Helicanus to be their ruler. A loyal subject, he refuses to do this until another year has passed. Some noblemen leave to search for their lost prince.

In Pentapolis (II.5) on the morning after the banquet, the King tells the other suitors that Thaisa will not marry for another year, and persuades them to abandon their vain suit. Thaisa has written him a letter declaring her love for 'the strange knight'. This is related to Gower where the suitors are told to write letters to the Princess, each describing 'His name, his fader, and his good' (885), and she writes to her father that she will have none but Apollonius, whereupon the King dismisses the others, shows Apollonius the letter, and gets the Queen to agree to their marriage—albeit reluctantly, since nobody knows who Apollonius really is. Twine's heroine sickens for love (Ch. 6) and lies in bed until her father agrees to the marriage.

In the play Simonides agrees with her choice but, wishing to test Pericles, first commends the young prince for his 'sweet music this last night' (which we have not heard), and then, declaring that Thaisa wants him as her music master, shows him her letter and accuses him of bewitching his daughter. Pericles answers so manfully, and Thaisa supports him so well, that the King's assumed rage quickly turns to laughing approval. Defective though the text may be (Wilkins throws light upon it), this is an effective scene.

Passing over Twine's long account of the bridal festivities, the play follows Gower, whose Prologue to Act III, amusingly suggesting that 'every thynge was right honeste / Within hous, and eke withoute', lets us know that Pericles' wife conceives a child (cf. Gower, 962–82). A Dumbshow is used to show how Pericles came to depart hastily from Pentapolis. Gower explains that Antiochus and his daughter are dead (but not, as in Twine, that Pericles is heir to Antioch and should go there to claim it). Pericles must return at once to Tyre if he wishes to preserve his throne. Only now is his identity revealed to the Pentapolitans (cf. *Conf* 1019–27). With Thaisa and her nurse Lychorida he puts to sea, but halfway home a great storm breaks (described more fully in Gower than in Twine). At the beginning of III.1 Pericles calls on Neptune to still the tempest, and on Lucina, goddess of childbirth, to aid his wife. Lychorida however places a baby girl in his arms and tells him that Thaisa is dead. Pericles' grief is less lavishly portrayed than in the sources (in Gower he swoons twice). Maybe the text of the play omits something, but his address to the storm, his blessing of the child, and his farewell to Thaisa have much of Shakespeare in them. This, very probably, is where the dramatist became fully interested in the story and began to rewrite passages more frequently. As in Gower, Pericles does not protest against the casting of his wife's body overboard. After saying, 'That's your superstition', he accepts the sailors' custom, sees to the bestowal, and changes course for Tarsus.

III.2 takes place next morning at Ephesus, where the wise man Cerimon is tending in his home some shipwrecked people, and explains his kindly scientific philosophy before his servants bring in the chest salvaged from the sea. In Gower and Twine Cerimon finds it himself (*Conf* 1159–80); in Twine his scholar Machaon plays the major part in reviving Lucina and obtains as reward the money intended for her burial [*inf.* 449]. The writing in the chest follows Gower fairly closely.

The play now leaves Thaisa and shows the arrival of Pericles at Tarsus, where he names the baby Marina (III.3.12–13), and entrusts her to Cleon and Dionyza, who promise to cherish her (20–5). He swears not to trim his hair until she is married. This agrees with the sources—except that the child is called Thaise in *Confessio Amantis* and Tharsia in Twine.

We move back to Ephesus in III.4 where Thaisa, believing herself separated from Pericles for ever, goes to live in the Temple of Diana, accompanied by a niece of Cerimon (his daughter in Gower, 1256).

The Prologue to Act IV after telling us that Pericles got safely back to Tyre (Gower 1318–21), turns to Marina (now grown up to maidenhood) who by her superiority in beauty and talent over her companion, Cleon's daughter Philoten, has excited the envy and jealousy of Dionyza. After the death of the nurse Lychorida, Dionyza plots to have Marina murdered (Gower 1332–74). In Twine the dying nurse has told the girl Tharsia who her parents were (Ch. 10); Tharsia visits the nurse's tomb daily, and Dionisiades orders 'one of her countrey villaines called Theophilus' to slay the girl there and cast her body into the sea. In Gower the bondman Theophilus is ordered to take Thaise to the seashore and murder her there. In both sources he is unwilling, but will obey. The play combines motifs from both sources, for in IV.1 Marina has learned from the nurse of her parentage; the nurse's tomb is by the sea; Dionyza and her slave Leontine (whose name was suggested by that of the brothel-master Leonin in Gower 1418–9), wait there and interrupt the girl's mourning. Dionyza makes Marina go for a walk on the shore with the murderer, who reluctantly prepares to do his evil duty, interrupting her artless talk about her birth at sea in a storm and paying no heed to her appeal for life. Her prayers are heard by pirates who drive off the villain and take Marina on board their vessel. In Gower the would-be murderer runs away. The play, as in most of this scene, keeps nearer to Twine (Ch. 12) in making him lurk near by, and then go and tell Dionyza that the girl is dead.

IV.2 moves to the brothel in Mitylene where for the first time the play elaborates considerably on the story material as Pandar (the brothel-master), his man Boult, and the Bawd discuss the problems of their trade and particularly the difficulty of getting new wenches (1–40). Boult goes to search the market and returns with the Pirates and Marina. The contrast between her innocence and the crudity of her new surroundings is brought out (41–94). Boult is sent to advertise her attractions and offer her to the highest bidder. He returns; they gloat over her; the Bawd tries to instruct her in a whore's behaviour, and Boult is promised 'a morsel off the spit' (118–35). It is all very horrible but with much grotesque humour. Marina threatens suicide and calls on Diana to help her preserve her virginity. Little of this is in Gower except the 'crying' of her maidenhead (1424–28). In Twine Tharsia is sold in the market, and Athanagoras, the Prince of Mitylene, bids against a 'man-bawd' until, the price rising very high, he ceases to bid, intending to be the girl's first client and so have her virginity at less cost. Tharsia's innocence is shown when, being ordered to worship a priapic image, she assumes that the people must be 'Lapsatenians' (i.e. men of Lampsacus) who worship Priapus (mentioned in IV.6.4). Her tearful appeals for mercy are unheeded and she is paraded through the streets to attract custom. The play concentrates on incidents in the brothel itself.

The next two scenes are narrative-links, which make use of the suspense excited by the brothel-scene. In Tarsus (IV.3) Cleon, like Stranguilio in Twine, laments his wife's evil action. She has poisoned the murderer Leonine, so nobody but they knows of the crime. Cleon's weak character, his fear of Pericles' return, his wife's ruthlessness, are well revealed. This scene, with the erection of a statue of Marina near her father's, was suggested mainly by Twine (Ch. 12), but the order has been changed. In Gower it occurs after Thaisa has defeated all comers in the brothel (1506 foll.); in Twine it comes after the pirate-scene.

IV.4, a narration by Gower, tells how Pericles comes to Tarsus to see his daughter. A Dumbshow shows him with Cleon and Dionyza at Marina's 'tomb'. Gower tells us that he swears never to wash or to cut his hair. The scene stresses Pericles' 'mighty passion', the 'tempest which his mortal vessel bears'. In *Confessio Amantis* the incident follows that of IV.3 and tells how Apollonius got home after losing his wife, informed parliament of his adventures, held mourning for her and then (fourteen years later!) set off to fetch Thaise from Tarsus and found her 'dead' (1555–90).

Back in Mitylene (IV.5), we see (as in Gower 1431–9) the

influence of Marina's virtue on the gentlemen who have sought her favours. In Gower 'the sorowe whiche she made' robs them of all power to wrong her; in the play she preaches 'divinity' and cures their lust for ever; neither reflects the humour in Twine, who makes Athanagoras and another converted client enjoy watching many gentlemen who went in with their money 'and came foorth againe weeping'.

The result of this obstinacy (IV.6) is consternation in the brothel. Lord Lysimachus, the play's parallel to Twine's Athanagoras, comes in disguise to visit her. This is the first we have heard of him. Unlike Athanagoras he seems not to have previously known of the maiden's presence. Twine's Athanagoras, coming as her first customer (Ch. 13), in accordance with his previous intention, is moved with compassion when she tells her story and identity, and gives her money. A second young man Aportatus behaves in the same way; then he and Athanagoras watch the procession of clients. Gower's Athenagoras does not appear until he visits Apollinus' ship (1629ff.).

The behaviour of Lysimachus in IV.6 is highly ambiguous. He enters boisterously ('How now! How a dozen of virginities!' etc.), and is obviously well known to the Bawd and Boult. When Marina is brought to him he thinks her reluctance is just a lure, but he is very soon (99–113) convinced by her anguish. Hitherto there has been no suggestion that he was acting a part, but he now says, 'Had I brought hither a corrupted mind, / Thy speech had alter'd it', and having given her gold, protests,

> For me, be you thoughten
> That I came with no ill intent; for to me
> The very doors and windows savour vilely. (117–9)

One wonders whether originally the play followed Twine, or whether it included an earlier scene in which Lysimachus showed the audience that he meant the girl no ill or that he was there to investigate the brothel, and whether IV.6 (cf. Wilkins [534]) contained a much longer and more poignant interview between the Governor and Marina. As it is we are left wondering why Lysimachus had come, if not with 'ill intent'. Both Twine and Wilkins make it clear that the Governor wishes to enjoy her body, but (like her other visitors) is converted by her chastity. Before Lysimachus leaves he roundly condemns Boult and his trade. As in Gower (1440–84) and Twine (Ch. 14), the Bawd's man is now instructed to 'crack the glass of her virginity' (IV.6.130–63), but is persuaded by Marina's pleading to help her to get free and earn an honest living by teaching.

Gower's prologue to Act V describes Marina's success in her work and then how a storm drove Pericles to Mitylene after he had left Tarsus (*Conf.* 1485–1505, 1597–1619; Twine Ch. 15). Helicanus describes his grief for his wife and daughter when receiving Lysimachus on board (V.1.21ff.), but, unlike Twine (Ch. 16), the play does not make Lysimachus go below and have a conversation with Pericles. Instead Pericles is 'discovered' and will not speak. In Gower Athenagoras goes below but can get no reply (1651–6). Twine's Athanagoras has heard Tharsia's story in detail, so when he hears Apollonius's name he remembers 'that hee heard Tharsia call her father so'. He therefore has some inkling of what may happen, and it is he who thinks of sending for her to persuade Apollonius not to kill himself with grief. In the play Lysimachus does not know all Marina's story, and it is the First Lord who suggests that she might 'win some words' of the silent sufferer (V.1.43–4). A parallel with David's cure of King Saul by the power of music in 1 *Samuel*, xvi, 14–23 is perhaps implied but never made explicit; indeed in the play and Twine, where Marina sings, it is less obvious than in Gower, where Thaise both sings and plays the harp (1676–9). Apollonius in Twine speaks to her, gives her gold, and sends her away, whereupon Athanagoras gives her twice as much to go below deck again, return the gold and try again to charm him. She asks him three verse-riddles which come, not from Gower but from the *Gesta Romanorum* version—and Apollonius guesses them. Moved with sympathy, Tharsia then embraces Apollonius, urging him not to grieve so, and that his wife and daughter may possibly be alive. At this Apollonius is enraged and as she leans over him kicks her in the face so that she falls bleeding. This makes Tharsia lament and relate her sad history, so that Apollonius realizes who she is (Ch. 17).

The play is closer here to Gower. The *Confessio Amantis* mentions the 'demandes strange', the proverbs and problems with which she tried in vain to make him speak, but insists on

Apollonius' lack of response. When 'halfe in wrath he bad hir go' she came to him and touched him, whereat he struck her with his hand. Nothing is said of blood. At her mild protest he pulls himself together and asks her who she is. She tells her story and her father realizes her identity and takes her in his arms (*Conf.* 1682–1746).

The play may owe something to Twine also. Marina sings (and plays maybe) but Pericles will not even look at her and her maid (V.1.82). There is a curious hiatus before the next line (*Lys.* 'See, she will speak to him') which suggests that she may have been sent back to try again (as in Twine). Pericles now begins to take notice, and his ejaculations ('Hum! ha! (84)) suggest that at this point he pushes her away (as he later says he did 'when I perceiv'd thee' (128–9)). Undoubtedly Marina's dignified reference to her 'derivation from ... mighty kings' (91–2) comes from Thaise's pride in her 'lineage' (*Conf.* 1706) which leads naturally into her account of it. The play however handles the recognition more delicately and with more suspense, as Pericles perceives Marina's likeness to her mother and her charm; then the coincidences gradually grow and Pericles, scarcely able to believe his ears, calls on Helicanus and Lysimachus, until the mother's name completes the revelation. Pericles, overjoyed, calls for his robes, and is 'wild in my beholding' as he gazes on his daughter.

In Gower Athenagoras shows him the city and soon (being 'Wiveless ... unto that daie') asks for Thaise's hand and is married to her. In Twine he is a widower with a daughter and is married to Tharsia after the Bawd has been burned. The play postpones the union but reveals Lysimachus' hopes; and whereas both sources place Pericles' vision later, on shipboard on the way to Tyre *via* Tarsus, we see the Prince fall asleep under the influence of heavenly music immediately after his recognition of Marina. Told by Diana to go to Ephesus and relate his story publicly in the Temple of Diana, he does so (V.3) and is recognized by his long-lost wife. In the play Cerimon and Helicanus are present; the marriage of Lysimachus and Marina is to take place at Pentapolis, and the joy of the occasion is scarcely ruffled by news that Thaisa's father is dead. Pericles decides to spend the rest of his life in Pentapolis, letting Lysimachus and Marina reign in Tyre.

Thus the story is rounded off, and it is only left for Gower in his Epilogue to moralize on the characters and to tell how Cleon and his wife were punished by their own people.

Pericles belongs to a species of play which had long been known on the Elizabethan stage. Such pieces were mainly derived from medieval romances (many of which were still popular in sixteenth-century editions), but perhaps to some extent also from the biographical Morality plays which represented a series of adventures or phases in a life-history. Typical examples were *Sir Clyomon and Clamydes* (*c.* 1570), *Mucedorus* (pubd. 1598), *The Rare Triumphs of Love and Fortune* (pubd. 1589), T. Heywood's *Four Apprentices of London* (1594?), Peele's *Old Wives Tale* (1591–4) and Anthony Munday's Robin Hood plays (1598). They were numerous enough to elicit Jonson's mockery in the Prologue to the later version (1605–6?) of *Every Man in His Humour*, where he calls it an 'ill custom'

> To make a child now swaddled, to proceed
> Man, and then shoot up, in one beard and weed,
> Past three score years.

In the early Jacobean period when drama on the whole was becoming more concentrated in form, the rambling romantic play gained a new lease of life from the fashion for variety of mood, scene and situation (which affected the tragicomedies of Beaumont and Fletcher) and expressed a reaction against the comedy of Humours and the realism of Jonson and Middleton.

The presence of Gower in the play indicates that its author realized that his drama was deliberately archaic in form, making use of a 'Presenter' or Chorus to bridge gaps of time and place and to hold the ragged plot together. The device was well known, e.g. *The Spanish Tragedy* (with Revenge and the Ghost) *Henry V* (with Time as Chorus), and two plays of 1607, Barnabe Barnes's *The Divil's Charter* (with Guicciardine) and *The Travailes of the Three English Brothers*, by John Day, George Wilkins, and William Rowley (with Fame).[1] Shakespeare may well have rewritten some of Gower's speeches, which from Act III on are more Shakespearian in tone, and have some echoes

---

[1] See Hoeniger, *New Arden*, xix-xxiii.

of the Chorus in *Henry V*. On the other hand, the earlier Choruses are more studiously archaic, and imitate Gower's four-stress rhythm, whereas the later ones stray into five foot couplets and quatrains.

The Elizabethans on the whole agreed with Skelton that

> Gower's Englysh is old,
> And of no value is told.
> His mater is worth gold,
> And worthy to be enrol'd.
>
>   (*Philip Sparrow*)

Puttenham went further:

> 'Gower, saving for his good and grave moralities, had nothing in him highly to be commended, for his verse was homely and without measure, his wordes strained much deale out of the French writers, his ryme wrested, and in his inventions small subtillitie'
>
>   (*Arte of English Poesie*, 1589)

Yet Sidney honoured Gower with Chaucer as the two first important English poets, and Wilkins could try to attract readers by declaring that the play on which he based his novel was presented 'under the habit of ancient Gower, the famous English poet'.

In the play Gower is used not only to bind the piece together but to give it an 'atmosphere of the antique'.[1] In Acts I and II he uses obsolete words and forms (fere, been, perishen; Ne . . . escapen, yravished) and has a sententious prosiness not unlike his original. At the end he moralizes gently, not perhaps quite as the author of *Confessio Amantis* did, as one

> that wold ensamples telle
> By olde daies as they felle
>   (*Conf.* Bk. V),

but more in the manner of an Elizabethan preacher.

Though scornfully condemned by Ben Jonson as a 'mouldy tale'[2] *Pericles* remained popular until the closing of the theatres, largely no doubt owing to the variety of incidents and their

---

[1] R. M. Garrett, 'Gower in *Pericles*', *ShJb*, XLVIII, 1912, 13–20.
[2] 'Ode to Himselfe'.

romantic content, and in particular to the integrity of Pericles and the tender depiction of Marina which shine through the mutilated Quarto text.

As was noted above, Marina's ordeal in the brothel has something in common with that of early Christian saints, and especially Saint Agnes. There is no reason to suppose that Shakespeare thought so of it, but he was obviously eager to get as much pathos and moral beauty out of the situation as possible. His development of its 'social realism' is somewhat out of key with the rest of the play [1]; but he doubtless wished to introduce towards the end of the piece touches of humour balancing those of the fishermen in II.1, and to emphasize the contrast between Marina and her environment.

The situation had been used not long before in *The Oratour*, a translation by L. Piot from the French of A. Silvayn. [2] This book was a collection of a hundred rhetorical exercises or 'declamations', debating the ethical problems set by situations drawn from history and fiction. It included the Bond story used in *The Merchant of Venice* [3] and several debates on analogies to Isabella's situation in *Measure for Measure*. These last, like many others in the book, were translated from the *Controversia* of Seneca the Elder, which doubtless gave Silvayn the idea for his collection. [4] Declaration 53 (expanded from Seneca's Lib. 1, 2, 'Sacerdos Prostituta') has obvious affinities to Marina's plight, for it summarizes the adventures of a nun who, travelling to Sicily where she was to be an abbess, was captured by pirates and sold to a house of ill-fame, where she withstood temptation and killed a man who would have violated her. The problem debated was whether a woman who had gone through such experiences could fittingly be an abbess.

It is a striking coincidence, if nothing more, that Shakespeare used three stories closely analogous to those in Silvayn's book;

---

[1] Cf. J. Danby, *Poets on Fortune's Hill*, 1952, p. 101.

[2] Pseudonym of Alexandre van den Busche. *The Orator: Handling a hundred severall Discourses, in forme of Declamations . . . Written in French by Alexander Silvayn, and Englished by L.P. . . . 1596.* Cf. W. Elton, '*Pericles*: A new source or analogue', *JEGP*, xlviii, 1949, 138–9; and W. Nowottny, 'Shakespeare and *The Orator*', *Bull. de la Fac. des L. de Strasbourg*, 1965,

[3] Cf. Vol. I of this work, pp. 482–6.

[4] Cf. *Annaei Senecae Oratorum et Rhetorum Sententiae . . .* ed. A. Kiessling, Leipzig, 1872; E. M. Waith, '*Pericles* and Seneca the Elder', *JEGP*, L, 1951, 180–2.

so I give the 'Declamation' [Text V]. Even if Shakespeare knew Piot's translation, he was unaffected by doubts of Marina's worthiness. The ordeal is used to show innocence triumphant over the worst of people and circumstances, and to make the last scenes of the play a spectacle of virtue crowned with happiness.

The goddess Diana figures frequently in prayers and vows; Thaisa becomes her priestess, and Diana appears to Pericles in a vision. There is no reason to imagine that 'Shakespeare intended Thaisa's time in the temple to be a means of expiating the sin of taking the name of the goddess in vain'.[1] It is Simonides, not Thaisa, who says that Thaisa has sworn to Diana not to marry for a twelve month (II.4.2); but this is probably his own device to get rid of the suitors, since he already has her letter saying that she wants to marry Pericles.

As Professor Muir writes, there is no broken vow in the sources. And there is never a hint in *Pericles* that the goddess is angry. It is a Diana-play because it is a play set in pagan times and containing much about chastity. Pericles is chaste when faced with incest and in his relations with Thaisa. In her supposed bereavement she vows herself to the chaste goddess, and Marina is saint-like in her purity.

Nothing mars the simple antinomies of the play, where all is black or white, the bad very bad, the good very good. Pericles is buffeted by fortune but in the end the goddess rewards his endurance; and Professor Muir rightly terms it 'the converting of the wheel of fortune into the wheel of Providence'. The Christian promise of patient virtue ultimately blessed by God is set forth in terms of a medievalized pagan romance. As Professor Wilson Knight has shown,[2] the play is permeated with a sense of goodness, which operates in Pericles' honest revulsion against the evil in Antioch and his desire to spare his people, in the ceremonious benevolence displayed at the Court of Simonides, in Pericles' humility when he accepts his loss in the storm, in Marina's maidenly innocence made strong by adversity, and her gentle persistence in the healing mission which restores her father to himself, and to her.

---

[1] K. Muir, *Shakespeare as Collaborator*, 1960, pp. 80–1.
[2] G. Wilson Knight, *The Crown of Life*, 1948 edn. pp. 32–75.

Examples of moral contrast abound in the play. The incestuous depravity of Antiochus can be set over against the gracious paternal humour of Simonides ('a happy King, since he gains from his subjects the name of good by his government', II.1.108); the quiet grief of the widowed mother Thaisa contrasts with the murderous envy of Dionyza; and the rough Arcadian simplicities of the fishermen are opposed to the urban degeneracy of the brothel-keepers. Contrasts in theme and tone are worked out through imagery of riches and deprivation, storm and music, death and revival.

The resultant play, while still in the main a laborious attempt to follow faithfully the narrative in Gower and Twine, has numerous scenes which go well on the stage even in their present mutilated form: Pericles' encounter with the incestuous Antiochus and his daughter, all the scenes at Pentapolis, with their variety (Pericles and the fishermen, the parade of knights, Pericles and Simonides and Thaisa), the birth of Marina and loss of Thaisa, the latter's restoration to life, Marina in peril on the shore and in the brothel, and the two recognition scenes. The stiffness of movement in several of them may well be partly due to reporters' omissions and misplacements, but they probably also perpetuate the unsophisticated technique of a minor dramatist which Shakespeare did not trouble wholly to remedy.

If *Timon* is a play wholly conceived by Shakespeare but falteringly carried out and abandoned in mid-career, *Pericles* is probably a piece conceived, planned and perhaps written by someone else, which Shakespeare undertook to improve and did so perfunctorily (maybe in haste) except for the second half where the themes aroused his interest and so led him largely to rewrite and (in the brothel scenes) to replace the original material.

Looking forward to *Cymbeline* and *The Winter's Tale* we can see *Pericles* in perspective as a preliminary shot in a new romantic campaign directed towards popularizing and improving the episodic drama of parted families, wanderings and searches, suffering and happy reunions.

Pericles can never have been as good a play as these others, but working on it may well have turned Shakespeare's mind towards themes of a similar kind. After the series of great tragedies he probably had 'a firm sense of new plays to be written, but no clear knowledge of their nature' (Knight). At this critical moment the revision of *Pericles* brought back memories of situations and characters in his earlier romantic comedies, of Isabella the chaste and the healing Helena, of good brought out of evil by virtuous effort and the effects of time. It made him realize the value of the 'young daughter' theme for a new comedy of tenderness between parents and children, and the possibilities for tragicomedy of an opening fraught with tragic possibilities, leading after many meanderings to a happy dénouement. Above all the story of Apollonius with its oracular vision and temple scene helped to revive in Shakespeare the sense of an overriding benevolent Providence which he had rejected in *King Lear* and ignored in *Coriolanus*, and to evoke the note of healing and forgiveness (struck somewhat oddly at the end of *Timon*) which he was to seek in the last three romances. *Pericles* indeed stands in relation to these plays somewhat as *Two Gentlemen of Verona* stands with regard to the major comedies of the nineties, as a 'laboratory'[1] for experiments which he was to apply more fruitfully in the last years of his career.

[1] See *Sources*, I, 210.

I. Source

From CONFESSIO AMANTIS, Bk. VIII
by John Gower [1554 edn.]

Jo. Gower de confessione Amantis   Imprinted at London in Flete strete by Thomas Berthelette the .xii. daie of Marche. An. MDLIIII.

[The story of Apollonius of Tyre.]

Liber Octavus

CONFESSOR.   Lo thus, my sone, as I the saie,
   Thou might thy selfe be besaie
   Of that thou hast of other herde,
   For ever yet it hath so ferde,
   Of loves lust, if so befall,
   That it in other place falle,
   Than it is of the lawe sette.
   He which his love hathe so besette,
   Mote aferwarde repent hym sore.
   And every man is others lore.   260
   Of that befill in tyme er this,
   The present tyme whiche nowe is
   Maie ben enformed, how it stoode,
   And take that hym thynketh good,
   And leve that, whiche is nought so;
   But for to loke of tyme ago,
   Howe lust of love excedeth lawe,
   It ought for to be withdrawe.
   For every man it shulde drede,
   And nameliche in his sibrede,   270
   Which tourneth ofte to vengeance,
   Wherof a tale in remembrance,

Which is a long processe to here,
I thinke for to tellen here.

Omnibus est communis amor, sed et immoderatos
Quae facit excessus, non reputatur amans.
Sors tamen unde Venus attractat corda videre,
Quae rationis erunt, non ratione finit.

Hic loquitur adhuc contra incestuosos amantum coitus, Et narrat
mirabile exemplum de magno rege Antiocho, qui Uxore mortua
propriam filiam violavit, et quia filie matrimonium penes alios
impedire voluit, tale ab eo exiit edictum, quod si quis eam in
uxorem peteret, nisi quoddam problema questionis, quam ipse rex
proposuerat, veraciter solveret, capitali sentencia puniretur,
super quo veniens tandem discretus juvenis princeps Tyri
Appollinus questionem solvit. Nec tamen filiam habere potuit, sed
rex indignatus ipsum propter hoc in mortis odium recollegit, Unde
Appollinus a facie regis fugiens quam plura, prout inferius inti-
tulantur, propter amorem pericula passus est.

Of a cronike in daies gone,
The which is cleped Panteone,   280
In loves cause I rede thus,
Howe that the great Antiochus,
Of whom that Antioche toke
His firste name, as saith the boke,
Was coupled to a noble quene,
And had a doughter hem betwene.
But such fortune cam to honde,
That deth, which no kyng[1] may withstond,
But every life it mote obey,
This worthy quene toke awey.   290
   The kynge, which made mochel mone,
Tho stoode, as who saith, all hym one
Without wyfe: but netheles
His doughter, whiche was pereles
Of bewtee, dwelt about hym stille.
But whan a man hath welth at wille
The flesh is freel and falleth ofte,
And that this maide tendre and softe,
Whiche in hir fathers chambre dwelte,
Within a tyme wist and felte: 300
For likynge of concupiscence,
Without insight of conscience

[1] *suggests* kind.

The fader so with lustes blente,
That he cast all his hole entente
His owne doughter for to spille.
The kynge hath leiser at his wille,
With strengthe and whan he tyme seye
The yonge maiden he forleie.
And she was tender, and full of drede,
She couth nought hir maydenhede   310
Defende: and thus she hath forlore
The floure, whiche she hath longe bore.
It helpeth not all though she wepe,
For thei that shulde hir bodie kepe
Of women, were absent as than.
And thus this mayden goeth to man.
The wilde fader thus devoureth
His owne flesh, which none socoureth,
And that was cause of mochel care.
But after this unkinde fare   320
Out of the chambre goth the kinge.
And she laie still, and of this thinge
Within hir selfe suche sorowe made,
There was no wight, that might hir glade
For fere of thilke horrible vice.

With that came in the norice,
Whiche fro childhode hir had kepte,
And asketh, if she had slepte,
And why hir chere was unglad.
But she, whiche hath ben overlad,   330
Of that she might nought be wreke,
For shame couth unnethes speke.
And nethelesse mercy she praied
With wepynge eie, and thus she saied:

Alas, my suster, wele awaie
That ever I sigh this ilke daie.
Thinge which my bodie firste begate
In to this worlde, onelich that
My worldes worship hath berefte.
With that she swouneth nowe and efte,   340
And ever wisheth after deth,
So that welnie hir lacketh breth.

That other, which hir wordes herde,
In comfortynge of hir answerde,
To lete hir faders foule desyre

She wist no recoverire,
Whan thing is do, there is no bote,
So suffren they that suffren mote:
There was none other, whiche it wist.
Thus hath this kynge all that hym liste   350
Of his likinge and his plesance,
And last in suche a continuance,
And suche delite he toke therin,
Him thought that it was no sin.[1]
And she durst him no thinge withseye.
    But fame, which goeth every weye
To sondry reignes all aboute,
The greate beautee telleth oute
Of such a mayde of hie parage.
So that for love of mariage   360
The worthie princes come and sende,
As they, whiche all honour wende,
And knewe no thinge, howe that it stoode.
    The fader whan he understood
That thei his doughter thus besought,
With all his wit he cast and sought,
Howe that he mighte fynde a lette,
And suche a statute then he sette,
And in this wise his lawe taxeth,
That what man [that] his doughter axeth,   370
But if[2] he couth his question
Assoyle upon suggestion
Of certeyn thinges, that befell,
The which he wolde unto him tell,
He shulde in certeyn lese his hede.
    And thus there were many dede,
Her heades stonding on the gate,
Till at last longe and late,
For lacke of answere in this wise
The remenante, that weren wyse,   380
Eschewden to make assaie.

*De adventu Appolini in Antiochiam, ubi ipse filiam regis
Antiochi in uxorem postulavit.*

    Till it befil upon a daie
Appolinus the prince of Tyre,

---

[1] *Per.* Prologue I, 29–30.
[2] Unless.

Whiche hath to love a great desire,
As he whiche in his high moode,
   Was likinge of his hote blode,
A yonge, a freshe, a lustie knyght,
As he laie musynge on a nyght
Of the tidinges, whiche he herde,
He thought assaie howe that it ferde.   390
He was with worthie companie
Araied, and with good navie
To ship he goeth, the winde him driveth,
And saileth, till that he ariveth
Saufe in the porte of Antioche.
He londeth, and goeth to approche
The kynges courte, and his presence.
   Of every naturall science,
Whiche any clerke him couth teche,
Him couthe enough: and in his speche   400
Of wordes he was eloquente.
And whan he sigh the kynge present,
He praieth, he mote his doughter have.
   The kinge againe began to crave,
And tolde hym the condicion,
How fyrst unto his question
He mote answere, and faile nought,
Or with his heed it shall be bought.
And he him asketh, what it was.

Questio regis Antiochi : scelere vehor, materna carne vescor, quero
patrem meum, matris mee virum, uxoris mee filium.

   The king declareth him the caas   410
With sterne worde and stordie chere,
To him and saide in this manere:
   With felonie I am up bore,
I ete, and have it not forlore [1]
My moders flesshe, whose husbonde
My fader for to seche I fonde,
Which is the sonne eke of my wife
Herof I am inquisitife.
And who that can my tale save,
All quite he shall my doughter have.   420
Of his answere and if he faile,
He shall be dead withouten faile.

---

[1] forbore *1493* edn.

Forthy my sonne, quod the kinge,
Be wel advised of this thynge,
Whiche hath thy life in jeopardie.
   Appollinus for his partie,
Whan he that question had herde,
Unto the kinge he hath answerde,
And hath reherced one and one
The poyntes and saide therupon: 430
   The question, whiche thou hast spoke,
If thou wilt, that it be unloke,
It toucheth all the privitee
Betwene thyn owne childe and thee,
And stonte all holle upon you two.
   The kinge was wondre sorie tho,
And thought, if that he said it oute,
Then were he shamed all aboute.
With slie wordes and with felle
He sayth: My sonne, I shall the telle,   440
Though that thou be of litell witte,
It is no great mervaile as yit,
Thin age maie it not suffise.
But loke wel thou nought despise
Thyn owne life: for of my grace
Of thirtie daies [1] full a space
I graunte the to ben advised.
And thus with leve and tyme assised
This yonge prince forth he wente,
And understode wel what it mente.   450
Within his herte as he was lered,
That for to make hym afered,
The kinge his time hath so delaied.
Wherof he drad and was amaied
Of treson, that he deie shulde,
For he the kyng his southe tolde.
And sodeinly the nightes tide,
That more wolde he nought abide,
All prively his barge he hente,
And home ageine to Tyre he wente.   460
And in his owne witte he saied,
For drede if he the kynge bewrayed,
He knewe so well the kinges herte,
That deth ne shulde he nought asterte,

---

[1] I.1.116 'forty days longer'.

The kyng him wolde so pursewe.[1]
But he that wolde his deth eschewe,
And knewe all this tofore the honde,
Forsake he thought his owne londe,
That there wolde he not abide.
For well he knewe that on some side   470
This tyranne of his felonie,
By some manere of trecherie,
To greve his bodie will not leve.

De fuga Appollini per mare a regno suo.

Forthy withouten takinge leve
As priviliche as thei might,
He goeth him to the sea by night,
Her shippes that ben with whete laden,
Her takill redie tho thei maden,
And haleth sayle, and forth thei fare.
But for to tellen of the care,   480
That thei of Tyre began tho,
Whan that thei wist he was ago,
It is a pitee for to here.
They losten lust, they losten chere,
They toke upon hem suche penance,
There was no song, there was no daunce,
But every myrthe and melodie
To hem was then a maladie.
For unlust of that aventure
There was no man whiche toke tonsure.   490
In deadly clothes thei hem clothe,
The bathes and the stewes bothe
Thei shet in by every wey:
There was no life whiche lust [to] pley
Ne take of any joye kepe,
But for hir liege lorde to wepe,
And every wight saith as he couth:
Alas, the lustie floure of youth,
Our prince, our head, our governour,
Through whom we stonden in honour,   500
Without the comune assent,
That sodeinly is fro us went.
Such was the clamour of hem alle.

---

[1] Cf. Pericles' soliloquy I.2.1–33.

Qualiter Thaliartus miles, ut Appollinum veneno intoxicaret, ab Antiocho in Tyrum missus, ipso ibidem non invento Antiochiam rediit.

But see we nowe what is befalle
Upon the fyrst tale playne,
And tourne we thereto agayne.
  Antiochus the grete syre,
Whiche full of rancour and of yre
His herte bereth so as ye herde,
Of that this prynce of Tyre answerde.   510
  He had a felowe bacheler,
Which was his previe counceyler
And Taliart by name he hight.[1]
The kynge a stronge poyson hym dight
Within a boxe, and golde therto,[2]
In all haste and bad hym go
Streight unto Tyre, and for no coste
Ne spare, till he had lost
The prynce, whiche he wolde spille.
And whan the kynge hath said his will,   520
This Taliart in a galeye
With all the haste he toke his wey.
The wynde is good, they seilen blive,
Tyll he toke londe upon the rive
Of Tyre, and forth with all anone
Into the borough he gan to gone,
And toke his inne, and bode a throwe.
But for he wolde nought be knowe,
Disguised than he goth hym out.
He sigh the wepynge all about,   530
And axeth, what the cause was.
  And thei hym tolde all the cas,
Howe sodeynly the prynce is go.
And whan he sigh, that it was so,
And that his labour was in vayne,
Anone he tourneth home agayne.
And to the Kynge whan he cam nigh,
He tolde of that he herde and sigh,
How that the prynce of Tyre is fled.
So was he come ageyne unsped.   540
  The kynge was sorie for a while.

[1] Thaliard in Per. I.1.150–70.
[2] I.1.155.

But whan he sighe, that with no wile
He might acheve his crueltee,
He stynt his wrath, and let hym bee.[1]

Qualiter Appollinus in portu Tharsis applicuit, ubi in hospicio
cuiusdam magni viri nomine Strangulionis hospitatus est.

But over this now for to telle
Of adventures that befelle
Unto this prince, of which I tolde.
He hath his righte cours forth holde
By stone and nedell, till he cam
To Tharse, and ther his londe he nam.   550
A bourgeis riche of golde and fee
Was thilke time in that citee,
Which cleped was Stranguilio,
His wife was Dionyse also.
This yonge prince, as saith the boke,
With him his herbergage toke.
And it befill that citee so
Before tyme, and than also,
Through stronge famyn, which hem lad,
Was none, that any wheate had.[2]   560
Appolinus, whan that he herde
The mischefe howe the citee ferde,
All freliche of his owne gifte
His wheate amonge hem for to shifte,
The whiche by ship he had brought,
He yave and toke of hem right nought.
But sithen fyrst this worlde began,
Was never yet to suche a man
More joye made, than thei hym made.
For thei were all of hym so glade,   570
That thei for ever in remembrance
Made a figure in resemblance
Of hym and in a commen place
Thei set it up: so that his face
Might every maner man beholde,
So as the citee was beholde,
It was of laton[3] overgylte.
Thus hath he nought his yefte spilt.

---

[1] Contrast II *Chor.*, 23–6; and *inf.* 579–87.
[2] *Per.* expatiates on the famine, I.4.
[3] brass.

Qualiter Hellicanus civis Tyri Tharsim veniens Appolinum de insidiis Antiochi prenuntiavit.

Upon a tyme with a route,
This lord to pley goeth hym oute: 580
And in his waie of Tyre he mette
A man, which on his knees hym grette,
And Hellican by name he hight,[1]
Whiche praide his lorde to have insight
Upon hym selfe: and saide hym thus,
Howe that the great Antiochus
Awaiteth, if that he might hym spille.
That other thought, and helde hym stille,
And thanked hym of his warnynge,
And bad hym telle no tidynge, 590
Whan he to Tyre cam home ageyne,
That he in Tharse hym had seyne.

Qualiter Appolinus portum Tharsis relinquens, cum ipse per mare navigio securiorem quesivit, superveniente tempestate navis cum omnibus preter ipsum solum in eadem contentis juxta Pentapolim periclitabatur.

Fortune hath ever be muable
And maie no while stonde stable.
For nowe it hieth, nowe it loweth,
Nowe stant upright, nowe overthroweth,
Nowe full of blisse, and nowe of bale,
As in the tellynge of my tale
Here afterwarde a man maie lere,
Whiche is great routh for to here.[2] 600
This lord, which wolde done his best,
Within hym selfe hath litell rest,
And thought he wolde his place chaunge,
And seke a countrei more straunge.
Of Tharsiens his leve anone
He toke, and is to shippe ygone.
His cours he name with saile updrawe,
Where as fortune doth the lawe
And sheweth, as I shall reherse,
Howe she was to this lorde diverse, 610
The whiche upon the see she ferketh.

---

[1] Cf. II *Chor.* 17, 'Good Helicane hath stay'd at home'.
[2] This corresponds to II *Chor.*

The wynde arose, the wether derketh,
It blewe and made suche tempeste,
None anker maie the ship arest,
Which hath to broken all his gere.
The shipmen stoode in suche a fere,
Was none that might him selfe bestere,
But ever awaite upon the lere,
Whan that they shulden drenche at ones.
There was enough within the wones   620
Of wepynge and of sorowe tho.
The yonge kynge maketh mochel wo,
So for to se the ship travaile.
But all that might him nought availe.
The mast to brake, the sayle to roofe,
The ship upon the wawes droofe,
Till that thei see the londes coste.
Tho made a vowe the leste and moste,
Be so thei mighten come a londe.
But he which hath the se on honde,   630
Neptunus wolde nought accorde,
But all to brake cable and corde
Er thei to londe mighte approche.
The ship to clave upon a roche
And all goth downe into the depe.
But he, that all thinge maie kepe,
Unto this lorde was merciable
And brought him save upon a table,
Which to the londe him hath upbore,
The remenaunt was all forlore.   640
Therof he made mochel mone.[1]

Qualiter Appolinus nudus super litus jactabatur, ubi quidam piscator ipsum suo collobio vestiens, ad urbem Pentapolim direxit.

Thus was this yonge lorde alone
All naked in a poure plite.
His colour, which was whilom white,
Was than of water fade and pale,
And eke he was so sore a cale,
That he wist of him selfe no bote,
It helpe him no thynge for to mote,
To gete ageyn that he hath lore.

[1] II.1.1–12.

But she which hath his deth forbore,[1]   650
Fortune, though she will not yelpe,[2]
All sodeynly hath sente him helpe,
Whan him thought alle grace aweie.
There came a fisher[3] in the weye,
And sigh a man there naked stonde.
And whan that he hath understonde
The cause, he hath of hym great routh,
And onely of his poure trouth,
Of suche clothes as he hadde,[4]
With great pitee this lorde he cladde.   660
And he hym thonketh as he sholde,
And saith hym, that it shall be yolde,
If ever he gete his state ageyne,
And praith, that he wolde hym seyne,
If nigh were any towne for hym.
   He sayde: Ye, Pentapolim,
Where bothe kynge and quene dwellen.
Whan he this tale herde tellen,
He gladdeth hym and gan beseche,
That he the wey hym wolde teche.   670
And he hym taught: and forth he went,
And praid god with good entent,
To sende hym joye after his sorowe.
It was nought passed yet midmorowe.

Qualiter Appolino Pentapolim adveniente ludus gimnasii per urbem publice proclamatus est.

   Than thiderward[5] his wey he nam,
Where soone upon the noone he cam.
He ete suche as he might gete,
And forth anone whan he had ete,
He goth to se the towne aboute,
And cam there as he fonde a route   680
Of yonge lustie men withall.
And as it shulde tho befalle,
That daie was set of suche assise
That thei shulde in the londe gyse,
As he herde of[6] the people seie

---

[1] 1493. forlore 1554.   [2] 1493 though he wolde not yelpe.
[3] Three in II.1.   [4] Cf. II.1.81.
[5] 1493. afterwarde *1554*.   [6] 1493. was *1554*.

Her comune game than pleye.[1]
And cried was, that thei shulde come
Unto the game all and some
Of hem that ben deliver and wight,
To do such maistrie as they might.   690
Thei made hem naked as thei sholde,
For so that ilke game wolde,
And it was the custume, and use,
Amonge hem was no refuse.
The floure of all the towne was there,
And of the courte also there were,
And that was in a large place,
Right even before the kynges face,
Whiche Artestrates thanne hight.
The pley was pleyed right in his sight.   700
And who moste worthie was of dede,
Receive he shulde a certaine mede,
And in the citee bere a price.
  Appolinus, which ware and wise
Of every game couth an ende,
He thought assaie, howe so it wende.

Qualiter Appolinus ludum gimnasii vincens in aula regis ad cenam honorifice ceptus est.

  And fill among hem into game,
And there he wanne hym suche a name,
So as the kynge hym selfe accounteth,
That he all other men surmounteth,   710
And bare the price above hem alle.[2]
The kynge bad, that in to his halle
At souper tyme he shulde be brought.
And he cam than and lefte it nought,
Withoute companie alone.
Was none so semely of persone,
Of visage, and of limmes bothe,
If that he had what to clothe.
At souper tyme netheles
The kynge amiddes all the pres   720
Let clepe hym up amonge hem alle,
And bad his mareshall of his hall,
To setten hym in suche degree

---

[1] II.1.113, 'to joust and tourney'.
[2] Cf. II.2.

26

That he upon hym might see.
The kynge was soone sette and served,
And he whiche had his prise deserved
After the kynges owne worde,
Was made begyn a middel borde,
That bothe kynge and quene hym sie.
He sette and cast about his eie,   730
And sawe the lordes in estate,
And with hym selfe wexe in debate,
Thynkende what he had lore,
And such a sorowe he toke therfore,
That he sat ever stille, and thought,
As he whiche of no meate rought.[1]

Qualiter Appolinus in cena recumbens nihil comedit, sed doloroso
vultu, submisso capite, maxime ingemescebat, qui tandem a filia
regis confortatus Citharam plectens cunctis audientibus citharando
ultra modum complacuit.

The kynge behelde his hevinesse,
And of his grete gentilnesse
His doughter, which was fayre and good,
And at the borde before him stoode,   740
As it was thilke tyme usage,
He bad to go on his message
And fonde for to make him glade.[2]
And she did as hir fader bade.
And goth to him the softe paas,
And asketh whens, and what he was,
And praithe he shulde his thoughtes leve.
He saith: Madame by your leve,
My name is hote Appolinus,
And of my riches it is thus,   750
Upon the sea I have it lore.
The contrei, where as I was bore,
Where that my londe is, and my rente
I lefte at Tyre, whan that I wente,
The worship there, of which I ought,
Unto the god I there betought.[3]
And thus togider as thei two speke,
The tearis ranne downe by his cheke.
The king, whiche therof toke good kepe,
Had great pitee to see him wepe,   760

---

[1] Cf. II.3.1–56.   [2] II.3.58–74.   [3] *Ibid.* 75–89.

And for his doughter sende ageyn,
And praid hir fayre, and gan to sayn,
That she no lenger wolde dretche,
But that she wolde anone forth fetche
Hir harpe, and done all that she can
To glad with that sory man.
And she to doone hir faders hest,
Hir harpe fet, and in the feste
Upon a chaire, which thei fette,
Hir selfe next to this man she sette.[1]   770
With harpe both and eke with mouth
To him she did all that she couth,
To make him chere, and ever he sigheth,
And she him asketh, howe him liketh.

    Madame, certes wel, he saied,
But if ye the mesure plaied,
Whiche, if you list, I shall you lere,
It were a gladde thinge for to here.
A leve syr, tho quod she,
Nowe take the harpe, and lete me see,   780
Of what measure that ye mene.
Tho praith the kinge, tho praith the quene,
Forth with the lordes all arewe,
That he somme myrthe wolde shewe.

    He tak'th[2] the harpe, and in his wise
He tempreth, and of suche assise
Synginge he harpeth forth with all,
That as a voyce celestiall
Hem thought it sowned in her ere,
As though that it an angell were.   790
They gladen of his melodie,[3]
But moste of all the companie
The kynges doughter, whiche it herde,
And thought eke of that he answerde,
Whan that it was of her apposed,
Within hir herte hath well supposed,
That he is of great gentilnesse.
His dedes ben therof witnesse,
Forth with the wisdome of his lore,
It nedeth not to seche more.   800

[1] The play substitutes dancing, II.3.90–109.
[2] *1554* takth.
[3] Cf. the king, II.5.25–30.

He might not have suche manere,
Of gentill blood but if he were.
  Whan he hath harped all his fille,
The kinges hest to fulfille,
Aweie goth dishe, awaie goth cup,
Doun goth the borde, the cloth was up,
Thei risen, and gone oute of the halle.

Qualiter Appolinus cum rege pro filia sua erudienda retentus est.

  The kynge his chamberleyn let calle
And bad, that he by all weye
A chamber for this man purveie,   810
Whiche nighe his owne chambre bee.[1]
It shall be do me lorde, quod hee.
  Appolinus, of whom I mene,
Tho toke his leve of kynge and quene,
And of the worthie maide also,
Whiche praied unto hir fader tho,
That she might of the yonge man
Of tho sciences, whiche he can,
His lore have.[2] And in this wise
The kynge hir graunteth hir apprise   820
So that hym selfe therto assent.
Thus was accorded er thei wente,
That he with all that ever he maie
This yonge fayre freshe maie
Of that he couth shulde enforme.
And full assented in this forme,
Thei token leve as for that night.

*Qualiter filia regis Appolinum ornato apparatu vestiri fecit,
Et ipse ad puelle doctrinam, in quam pluribus familiariter
intendebat, unde placata puella in amorem Appollini exardescens
infirmabatur.*

  And whan it was on morowe right
Unto this yonge man of Tyre,
Of clothes, and of good attyre,   830
With golde and silver to dispende
This worthie yonge ladie sende.
And thus she made hym well at ease,
And he with all that he can please

---

[1] II.3.110–11.
[2] Cf. II.5.37–41.

Hir serveth well and faire ageine.
He taught hir, till she was certeyne
Of harpe, citole and of riote,
With many a tewne and many a note,
Upon musike, upon measure.
And of hir harpe the temprure   840
He taught hir eke, as he well couth.
    But as men seyne, that frele is youth,
With leiser and continuance
This mayde fill upon a chance,
That love hath made hym a quarele
Ageyne hir youth freshe and frele,
That maugre where she wolde or nought,
She mote with all hir hertes thought,
To love and to his lawe obey.
And that she shall full sore obeie.   850
For she wot never what it is,
But ever amonge she feleth this
Touchinge upon this man of Tyre,
Hir herte is hote as any fyre,
And otherwhile it is a cale.
Now is she redde, nowe is she pale,
Right after the condicion
Of hir imaginacion.
But ever amonge hir thoughtes all,
She thought, what[1] so may befalle,   860
Or that she laugh or that she wepe,
She wolde hir good name kepe
For fere of womannyshe shame.
    But what in ernest what in game,
She stant for love in such a plite,
That she hath lost all appetite
Of mete and drynke, of nightes rest,
As she that note what is the best.
But for to thynke all hir fille
She helde hir ofte tymes stille   870
Within hir chamber, and goth not out.
    The kinge was of hir lyfe in doute,
Whiche wist nothynge what it ment.

Qualiter tres filii principum filiam regis singillatim in uxorem
suis supplicationibus postularunt.

---

[1] whan *1554.* what *1493.*

But fill a tyme, as he out wente
To walke, of princes sonnes three
There came, and fill to his knee,
And eche of hem in sondrie wyse
Besought and profereth his service,
So that he might his doughter have.
The kynge, which wold her honour save,   880
Saieth, she is sicke, and of that speche
Tho was no time to beseche,[1]
But eche of hem to make a bille
He bad, and write his owne wille,
His name, his fader, and his good.
And whan she wist, howe that it stood,
And had her billes overseyne,
Thei shulden have answere ageyne.
Of this counseyle thei weren glad,
And written, as the kynge hem bad,   890
And every man his owne boke
Into the kynges honde betoke.
And he it to his doughter sende,
And praide hir for to make an ende
And write ageyne hir owne honde,
Right as she in her herte fonde.

Qualiter filia regis omnibus aliis relictis Appolinum in maritum
preelegit.

The billes weren well received,
But she hath all her loves weived:
And thought tho was tyme and space
To put hir in hir faders grace,   900
And wrote ageyne, and thus she sayde.
    The shame, which is in a mayde,
With speche dare nought be unloke,
But in writynge it maie be spoke.
So write I to you fader thus,
But if I have Appolinus,
Of all this worlde what so betide,
I will none other man abide.
And certes if I of him faile,
I wot right welle withoute faile,   910
Ye shall for me be doughterles.
This letter came, and there was prese

---

[1] Cf. II.5.1–13; their writing is omitted.

Tofore the kinge, there as he stode.
And whan that he it understode,
He yave hem answere by and by.
But that was doone so prively,
That none of others counseil wiste.
Thei toke her leve, and where hem list
Thei wente forth upon their wey.[1]

Qualiter rex et regina in maritagium filie sue cum Appollino
consencierunt.

The kynge ne wolde nought bewrey   920
The counseil for no maner hie,
But suffreth till he time sie,
    And whan that he to chambre is come,
He hath unto counseil nome
This man of Tyre, and lete hym see
The letter, and all the privitee,
The whiche his doughter to him sente.[2]
    And he his knee to grounde bente,
And thonketh him and hir also.[3]
And er thei wente then a two,   930
With good herte and with good corage,
Of full love and full mariage
The kinge and he be hole accorded.
And after, whan it was recorded
Unto the doughter, howe it stoode,
The yefte of all this worldes good
Ne shuld have made hir halfe so blithe,
And forth with all the kinge als swithe,[4]
For he woll have hir good assent,
Hath for the quene hir moder sente.   940
    The quene is come; and whan she herde
Of this mater, howe that it ferde,
She sigh debate, she sighe disease,
But if she wolde hir doughter please,
And is therto assented full,
Which is a dede wonderfull.
For no man knewe the soth cas,
But he hym selfe, what man he was,

---

[1] II.5.13–15.
[2] II.5.41–3.
[3] Contrast II.5.45–87.
[4] 1493 asswithe. II.5.88–93.

And nethelesse so as hem thought
His dedes to the soth wrought,   950
That he was come of gentill blood,
Him lacketh nought but worldes good.
And as therof is no dispeire,
For she shall be hir faders heyre,
And he was able to governe.
Thus wyll thei not the love werne
Of him and hir in no wise,
But all accorded thei devise
The daie and time of mariage.
Where love is lorde of the corage,   960
Him thenketh longe, er that he spede,
But at laste unto the dede.

Qualiter Appolinus filie regis nupsit, et prima nocte cum ea
concubiens ipsam impregnavit.

The time is come, and in her wise,
With great offrynge and sacrifice
Thei wedde, and make a great feste,
And every thynge was right honeste
Within hous, and eke withoute.
It was so doone, that all aboute,
Of great worship, and great noblesse,
There cried many a man largesse   970
Unto the lordes high and loude.
The knightes, that ben yonge and proude,
Thei juste firste, and after daunce.
The daie is go, the nightes chaunce
Hath derked all the bright sonne.
This lorde, which hath his love wonne,
Is go to bed with his wife,
Where as thei lede a lustie life,
And that was after somdele sene,
For as thei pleiden hem betwene,   980
Thei gete a childe betwene hem two,[1]
To whom fill after mochell wo.

Qualiter ambassiatores a Tyro in quadam navi Pentapolim
venientes, mortem regis Antiochi Appolino nunciaverunt.

Now have I tolde of the spousailes,
But for to speake of the mervailes

---

[1] III *Chor.*, 9–11.

Which afterwarde to hem befelle,
It is a wonder for to telle.
　　It fell a daie thei riden oute,
The kinge, and quene, and all the route,
To pleien hem upon the stronde,
Where as thei seen towarde the londe　　990
A ship sailyng of great arraie.
To knowe what it mene maie.
Till it be come thei abide,
Than see thei stonde on every side
Endlonge the shippes borde to shewe,
Of penounceals a ryche rewe.
　　They asken, whens the ship is come.
Fro Tyre, anone answerde some.
　　And over this thei saiden more
The cause why thei comen fore　　1000
Was for to seche, and for to fynde
Appollinus, which is of kynde
Her liege lorde: and he appereth,
And of the tale whiche he hereth
He was right glad; for they hym tolde,
That for vengeaunce, as god it wolde,
Antiochus as men maie witte,
With thonder and lightnyng is forsmitte.
His doughter hath the same chance[1]:
So ben thei both in o balance.　　1010
　　Forthy our liege lorde we seie,
In name of all the londe, and preie,
That lefte all other thynge to doone,
It like you to come soone,
And see your owne liege men,
With other that ben of your ken,
That live in longynge and desyre,
Till ye be come ageyne to Tyre.[2]
　　This tale after the kynge it had
Pentapolin all oversprad.　　1020
There was no joye for to seche,
For every man it had in speche,
And saiden all of one accorde:
A worthy kynge shall ben our lorde,
That thought us first an hevines,

---

[1] III *Chor.* Dumbshow, and 15–25.
[2] Cf. *Ibid.* 26–33.

Is shape us nowe to great gladnes.
Thus goth the tydynge over all.[1]

*Qualiter Appolino cum uxore sua impregnata a Pentapoli versus
Tyrum navigantibus contigit uxorem mortis articulo angustiatam,
in navi filiam, que postea Thaisis vocabatur, parere.*

But nede he mote, that nede shall.
Appolinus his leve toke,
To god and all the londe betoke,   1030
With all the people longe and brode,
That he no lenger there above.
 The kynge and quene sorowe made,
But yet somdele thei were glade
Of suche thynge, as thei herden tho.
And thus betwene the wele and wo
To ship he goth, his wife with childe,
The which was ever meke and milde,
And wolde not departe hym fro,
Suche love was betwene hem two.[2]   1040
 Lichorida for hir office
Was take, whiche was a norice,[3]
To wende with this yonge wife,
To whom was shape a wofull life.
 Within a time, as it betid,
Whan thei were in the sea amid,
Out of the north thei see a cloude,
The storme arose, the wynde loude
Thei blewen many a dredefull blaste,
The welken was all overcaste: 1050
The derke night the sonne hath under,
There was a great tempest of thunder.
The moone, and eke the sterres bothe
In blacke cloudes thei hem clothe,
Wherof their brighte loke thei hide.
 This yonge ladie wepte and cride,
To whom no comforte might availe,
Of childe she began travaile
Where she laie in a caban close.[4]
Her wofull lorde fro hir arose,   1060
And that was longe or any morowe,
So that in anguishe and in sorowe

---

[1] *Ibid.* 33–38.   [2] *Ibid.* 39–42.
[3] *Ibid.* 43–44.   [4] *Ibid.* 44–52.

She was delivered all by night
And deide in every mannes sight.
　But nethelesse for all this wo
A maide chylde was bore tho.

Qualiter Appolinus mortem uxoris sue planxit.

　Appolinus when he this knewe,
For sorowe a swoune he overthrewe,
That no man wist in hym no life.
And whan he woke, he said: Ah, wife,　　　1070
My joye, my lust, and my desyre,
My welth, and my recoverire,
Why shall I live, and thou shalt die?
Ha, thou fortune, I the defie,
Now hast thou do to me thy werst.
Ah herte, why ne wilt thou berst,
That forth with hir I mighte passe?
My peynes were well the lasse.
In such wepynge and suche crie
His dead wife, which laie hym bie,　　　1080
A thousande sithes he hir kiste.
Was never man that sawe ne wiste
A sorowe to his sorowe liche,
Was ever amonge upon the liche.
He fill swounynge, as he that thought
His owne deth, whiche he sought
Unto the goddes all above,
With many a pitous worde of love:
But suche wordes as tho were
Herde never no mannes eare　　　1090
But onely thilke, whiche he saide.[1]
The maister shipman came and praide
With other such, as ben therin,
And saine, that he maie nothinge winne
Ageyne the deth, but thei hym rede
He be well ware, and take hede:
The sea by weie of his nature
Receive maie no creature,
Within hym selfe as for to holde,
The whiche is dede. Forthy thei wolde,　　　1100
As thei counceilen all about
The dead bodie casten out.

[1] Not in the play, III.1.18-27.

For better it is, thei saiden all,
That it of hir so befalle,
Than if thei shulden all spille.[1]

*Qualiter suadentibus nautis corpus uxoris sue mortue in quadam
cista plumbo et ferro obtusa, que circumligata Appolinus cum
magno thesauro una cum quadam littera sub eius capite scripta
recludi, in mare proici fecit.*

The kynge, which understode her will,
And knew her counsaile that was trewe,
Began ageyn his sorowe newe,
With pitous herte, and thus to seie,
It is all reason that ye preye.   1110
I am (quod he) but one alone,
So wolde I not for my persone,
There fell suche adversitee,
But whan it maie no better bee,
Doth than thus upon my worde,
Let make a coffre stronge of borde,
That it be firme with lead and pitche.
Anone was made a coffer siche
All redie brought unto his honde.
And whan he sawe, and redie fonde   1120
This coffre made, and well englued,[2]
The dead bodie was besewed
In cloth of golde, and leide therin.
And for he wolde unto hir win
Upon some coste a sepulture,
Under hir head in adventure
Of gold he leyde sommes great,
And of jewels strong beyete
Forth with a letter,[3] and sayd thus:

Copia littere capiti uxoris sue supposite.

I, kynge of Tyre Appolinus   1130
Doth alle men for to witte,
That here and see this letter writte,
That helpeles without rede
Here lieth a kynges doughter dede,
And who that happeth hir to finde,

---

[1] III.1.38–55.
[2] III.1.71–73.
[3] III.1.66–68.

For charitee take in his mynde,
And do so, that she be begrave:
With this treasour, whiche he shall have.[1]
    Thus whan the letter was full spoke,
Thei have anone the coffre stoke   1140
And bounden it with yron faste,
That it maie with the wawes last,
And stoppen it by such a weie,
That it shall be within dreie,
So that no water might it greve.
And thus in hope, and good beleve,
Of that the corps shall well arive,
They cast it over borde as blive.

Qualiter Appollinus, uxoris sue corpore in mare projecto, Tyrum
relinquens, cursum suum versus Tharsim navigio dolens arripuit.

    The ship forthe on the wawes went.
The prince hath changed his entent,   1150
And saith, he will nought come at Tyre
As than, but all his desire
Is firste to sailen unto Tharse.[2]
The wyndie storme began to scarse,
The sonne arist, the weder clereth,
The shipman, which behinde stereth,
Whan that he sigh the wyndes saught,
Towards Tharse his cours he straught.

Qualiter corpus predicte defuncte super litus apud Ephesum
quidam medicus nomine Cerimon cum aliquibus suis discipulis
invenit, quod in hospicium portans, et extra cistam ponens
spiraculo vite in ea adhuc invento, ipsam plene sanitati restituit.

    But now to my matere ageyn,
To telle as olde bokes seyne,   1160
This dead corps, of whiche ye knowe,
With wynde and [water][3] was forth throwe,
Nowe here, now there, till at last
At Ephesus the sea upcast
The coffre, and all that was therin.
Of great mervaile now begyn
Maie here, who that sitteth still.
That god will save maie not spill.

---

[1] Cf. III.2.68–75.
[2] III.1.73–79.
[3] water *1483.*

Right as the corps was throwe a londe,
There cam walkynge upon the stronde,[1]　　　　1170
A worthie clerke and surgien,
And eke a great phisicien,
Of all the londe the wisest one,
Whiche hight maister Cerimone.
There were of his disciples some.
This maister is to the coffer come,
He peyseth there was somwhat in,
And bad hem beare it to his inne,
And goeth him selfe forthe with alle.
All that shall falle, falle shall.　　　　1180
　　Thei comen home, and tarie nought.
This coffer into his chamber is brought,
Whiche that thei finde faste stoke,
But thei with crafte it have unloke.
Thei loken in, where as thei founde,
A body deade, which was wounde
In cloth of golde, as I saide ere.
The tresour eke thei founden there,
Forthwith the letter, whiche thei rede,
And tho thei token better hede.　　　　1190
Unsowed was the body soone.
As he that knewe, what was to doone,
This noble clerk with alle haste
Began the veynes for to taste,
And sawe hir age was of youthe.
And with the craftes, whiche he couth,
He sought and found a signe of life.
With that this worthie kinges wife
Honestlie thei token oute,
And maden fyres all aboute.　　　　1200
Thei leied hir on a couche softe,
And with a shete warmed ofte
Hir colde breste began to heate,
Hir herte also to flacke and beate,
This maister hath hir every joynte
With certein oyle and balsam anoynte,
And put a licour in hir mouthe,
Whiche is to fewe clerkes couthe.
So that she covereth at laste.[2]

---

[1] III.2 is set in his house.
[2] III.2.59–98.

And first hir eien up she caste,　　　　　　1210
And whan she more of strength caught,
Hir armes both forth she straughte,
Helde up her honde, and pitouslie
She spake, and said: Where am I?
Where is my lorde, what worlde is this?
As she that wote not how it is.[1]

But Cerimone that worthie liche
Answerde anone upon hir[2] speche
And saide: Madame, ye ben here,
Where ye be save, as ye shall here　　　　1220
Hereafterwarde, forthy as nowe
My counceil is, comforteth you.[3]
For tristeth wel withoute faile,
There is no thinge, which shall you faile,
That ought of reason to be do.
Thus passen thei a daie or two.

Qualiter uxor Appollini sanata domum religionis petiit, ubi
sacro velamine munita, castam omni tempore vovit.

Thei speke of nought as for an ende,
Till she began somdele amende,
And wist hir selfe, what she mente.
Tho for to knowe her hole entente　　　　1230
This maister asketh all the caas,
Howe she cam there, and what she was.

Howe I came here, wote I nought,
Quod she, but well I am bethought
Of other thynges all about,
Fro poynte to poynte, and tolde him oute,
As ferforthly as she it wist.

And he hir tolde, howe in a chiste
The sea hir threwe upon the londe,
And what tresour with hir he fonde,　　　　1240
Whiche was all redy at hir wille,
As he that shope him to fulfille
With al his might, what thinge he sholde.

She thonketh him, that he so wolde,
And all hir herte she discloseth,
And saith him wel, that she supposeth,

---

[1] III.2.99–106.
[2] hir *1483*; his *1554*.
[3] Comfort yourself!

Hir lord be dreint, hir childe also.
So sawe she nought but all wo.
Wherof as to the worlde no more
Ne wil she torne, and praieth therfore,   1250
That in some temple of the citee,
To kepe and holde hir chastitee,
She might amonge the women dwell.[1]
Whan he this tale herde telle,
He was right glad and made hir knowen,
That he a doughter of his owen[2]
Hath, whiche he woll unto hir yeve
To serve, while thei both live,
In stede of that, whiche she hath loste.
Al onely at his owne coste   1260
She shall be rendred forth with hir.
    She saith, Graunte mercy leve sir,
God quite it you, there I ne maie.
And thus thei drive forth the daie
Till time cam, that she was hole.
And tho thei toke her counseyle hole
To shape upon good governance,
And made a worthie purveiance
Ageyne daie, whan thei be veiled.
And thus when that thei were counseiled,   1270
In blacke clothes thei hem cloth,
The doughter and the lady both,
And yolde hem to religion.
The feste, and the profession,
After the rule of that degree,
Was made with great solemnitee
Where as Diane is sanctified.
Thus stant this lady justified,
In ordre, where she thynketh to dwelle.[3]

*Qualiter Appolinus Tharsim navigans, filiam suam Thaisim
Strangulioni et Dionisie uxori sue educandum commendavit et
deinde Tyrum adiit, ubi cum inestimabili gaudio a suis receptus
est.*

    But now ageinwarde for to telle   1280
    In what plite that hir lord stode in.

[1] III.4.1–11.
[2] III.4.15, 'a niece of mine'.
[3] III.4.12ff.

He saileth, tyll that he maie wynne
The haven of Tharse, as I saide ere.
And whan he was arrived there,
Tho was it through the citee knowe,
Men mighte see within a throwe,
As who saith all the towne at ones
Thei come ageyne him for the nones
To yeven hym the reverence,
So glad thei were of his presence.   1290
   And though he were in his corage
Diseased, yet with glad visage
He made hem chere, and to his inne,
Where he whylom sojourned in,
He goth hym straught, and was received.
And whan the prees of people is weived,
He taketh his hoste unto hym tho
And saith: My frende Strangulio,
Lo thus, and thus it is befalle:
And thou thy selfe art one of all,   1300
Forthwith thy wife, whiche I most trist.
Forthy if it you both list,
My doughter Thaise¹ by your leve
I thynke shall with you bileve
As for a tyme: and thus I praie,
That she be kepte by all waie.²
And whan she hath of age more,
That she be set to bokes lore.
And this avowe to god I make,
That I shall never for hir sake   1310
My berde for no likynge shave,
Till it befalle, that I have
In covenable tyme of age
Besette hir unto mariage.³
   Thus thei accorde, and all is welle:
And for to resten hym somdele,
As for a while he ther sojourneth,
And than he taketh his leve, and tourneth
To ship, and goth hym home to Tyre,
Where every man with great desyre   1320
Awaiteth upon his comynge.

¹ Marina, III.3.12–13.
² III.3.
³ III.3.27–30.
27

But whan the ship cam in sailynge,
And they perceiven that it is he,
Was never yet in no citee
Such joye made, as thei tho made.
His herte also began to glade
Of that he seeth his people gladde.
    Lo thus fortune his happe hath ladde,[1]
In sondry wise he was travailed.
But how so ever he be assailed,   1330
His later ende shall be good.

*Qualiter Thaisis una cum Philotenna Strangulionis et Dionysie
filia, omnis sciencie et honestatis doctrina imbuta est, sed et
Thaisis Philotennam precellens in odium mortale per invidiam a
Dionysia recollecta est.*

    And for to speke how that it stoode
Of Thaise his doughter, where she dwelleth,
In Tharse as the cronike telleth
She was well kepte, she was well loked,
She was well taught, she was well boked:
So well she sped hir in hir youth,
That she of every wysedome couth,
That for to seche in every londe
So wise an other no man fonde,   1340
Ne so well taught at mannes eie.
But wo worth ever false envie.[2]
For it befill that tyme so,
A doughter hath Strangulio,
Whiche was cleped Philotenne.
But fame, whiche will ever renne,
Came all daie to her moders eare,
And saith, wher ever hir doughter were
With Thaise set in any place,
The common voyce, the common grace   1350
Was all upon that other mayde,
And of hir doughter no man sayde.
    Who was wroth but Dionyse than?
Hir thought a thousand yere till whan
She might be of Thaise wreke,
Of that she herde folke so speke.[3]

---

[1] IV *Chorus*, 1–2.
[2] IV *Chor.* 5–14.
[3] *Ibid.* 15–40.

And fill that ilke same tide,
That dead was trewe Lichoride,
Whiche had be servant to Thaise,
So that she was the wors at ease.[1]   1360
For she hath than no servise
But onely through this Dionyse,
Whiche was her deadly ennemie:
Through pure treson and envie,
She, that of all sorowe can,
Tho spake unto hir bondeman,
Whiche cleped was Theophilus,[2]
And made hym swere in counceill thus,
That he suche tyme as she hym set,
Shall come Thaise for to fette,   1370
And lede hir out of all sight,
Where that no man hir helpe might,
Upon the stronde nighe the sea,
And there he shall this maiden slea.
    This chorles herte is in a trance,
As he whiche drad hym of vengeance,
Whan tyme cometh an other daie:
But yet durst he not saie naie,
But swore, and said he shulde fulfill
Hir hestes at hir owne will.[3]   1380

Qualiter Dionysia Thaisim ut occideret Theophilo servo suo
tradidit, qui cum noctanter longius ab urbe ipsam prope litus
maris interficere proposuerat, pirate ibidem latitantes Thaisim
de manu carnificis eripuerunt, ipsamque usque civitatem Mitele-
nam ducentes, cuidem Leonino scortorum ibidem magistro
vendiderunt.

    The treason and eke time is shape,
So fell it that this churlishe knape
Hath lad this maiden where he wolde
Upon the stronde,[4] and what she sholde
She was adrad, and he out brayde
A rusty swerde, and to hir saide,
Thou shalt be dead. Alas, quod she,
Why shall I so? Lo thus, quod he,

---

[1] *Ibid.* 41–42.
[2] Leonine in IV.1; cf. *inf.* l. 1408.
[3] IV.1.1–12.
[4] Cf. IV.1.24–49.

My ladie Dionyse hath bede,
Thou shalt be murdred in this stede.   1390
   This maiden tho for feare shright,
And for the love of god allmight
She preith that for a litell stounde,
She mighte knele upon the grounde
Towarde the heven for to crave
Her wofull soule that she maie save.[1]
   And with this noyse, and with this crie,
Out of a barge faste by,
Which hid was there on scomer fare,[2]
Men sterten out and weren ware   1400
Of this felon, and he to go.
And she began to crie tho,
Ah, mercy, helpe for goddes sake.
Into the barge thei hir take,
As theves shulde, and forth thei wente.[3]
Upon the sea the wynde hem hent,
And maulgre where thei wolde or none,
Tofore the weder forth thei gone.
There helpe no saile, there helpe none ore,
Forstormed, and forblowen sore   1410
In great perill so forth thei drive,
Till at laste thei arrive
At Mitelene the citee.
In haven saufe and whan thei bee,
The maister shipman made him boune,
And goth him out into the towne,
And profereth Thaise for to selle.
   One Leonin it herde telle,
Which maister of the bordel was,
And bad hym gon a redie pas   1420
To fetchen her, and forth he went,
And Thaise out of his barge he hent,
And to the bordeler hir solde.[4]
And he that by hir body wolde
Take avantage, let do crie,
That what man wolde his lecherie
Attempte upon hir maidenhede,
Laie downe the golde, and he shulde spede.[5]

---

[1] Cf. IV.1.65–91.   [2] pirate-expedition.
[3] IV.1.91–95.   [4] Cf. IV.2.41–55.
[5] IV.2.58–63.

*Qualiter Leoninus Thaisim ad lupanar destinavit, Ubi dei
gracia preventa, ipsius virginitatem nullus violare potuit.*

And thus whan he hath cried it out,
In sight of all the people about,   1430
He ladde hir to the bordel tho,
No wonder though she were wo,
Close in a chambre by hir selfe,
Eche after other ten or twelfe
Of yonge men in to hir went.
But such a grace god hir sent,
That for the sorowe, whiche she made,
Was none of hem, which power hade
To done hir any vilanie.[1]

This Leonin let ever aspie,   1440
And wayteth after great beyete.[2]
But all for nought, she was forlete,
That no man wolde there come.
Whan he therof hath hede nome,[3]
And knewe, that she was yet a mayde,
Unto his owne man he sayde,
That he with strength ageyne hir leve,
Tho shulde hir maydenhode bereve.[4]
This man goth in, but so it ferde,
Whan he hir wofull pleintes herde,   1450
And he therof hath take kepe,
Hym list better for to wepe
Than do ought elles to the game.[5]
And thus she kepte hir self fro shame,
And kneled downe to therthe and prayde
Unto this man, and thus she sayde:
If so be, that thy maister wolde,
That I his good[6] encrees sholde,
It maie not falle by this weie,
But suffre me to go my weye   1460
Out of this hous, where I am in,
And I shall make hym for to wyn
In some place els of the towne,
Be so it be of religiowne,
Where that honeste women dwelle.[7]
And thus thou might thy maister telle,

---

[1] Hence IV.5.   [2] gain.   [3] taken heed.   [4] IV.6.130–54.
[5] Cf. *Ibid.* 161–81.   [6] *1554.* gold *1483.*   [7] IV.6.202.

That whan I have a chambre there,
Let hym do crie aie wide where,
What lorde, that hath his doughter dere,
And is in will that she shall lere   1470
Of suche a schole that is trewe,
I shall hir teche of thynges newe,
Whiche that none other woman can
In all this londe. [1] And tho this man
Hir tale hath herde, he goth ageyn
And tolde unto his maister pleyn
That she hath seyde: and therupon,
Whan that he sawe beyete none
At the bordell because of hir,
He bad his man to gon and spir   1480
A place, where she might abide,
That he maie wynne upon some side,
By that she can: [2] but at lest
Thus was she saufe of this tempest.

*Qualiter Thaisis a lupanari virgo liberata, inter sacras mulieres
hospicium habens, scientias, quibus edocta fuit, nobiles regni
puellas ibidem edocebat.*

He hath her fro the bordell take,
But that was not for goddes sake,
But for the lucre, as she hym tolde.
Nowe comen tho, that comen wolde
Of women in her lustie youth
To here and see, what thinge she couth.   1490
She can the wisedome of a clerke,
She can of any lustie werke,
Whiche to a gentill woman longeth,
And some of hem she underfongeth
To the citole, and to the harpe,
And whom it liketh for to carpe
Proverbes and demaundes slie,
An other suche thei never sie,
Whiche that science so well taught,
Wherof she great giftes caught,   1500
That she to Leonin hath wonne.
And thus hir name is so begonne
Of sondrie thynges that she techeth,

---

[1] IV.6.187–95.
[2] IV.6.196ff.

That all the londe to hir secheth
Of yonge women, for to lere.[1]

*Qualiter Theophilus ad Dionysiam mane rediens affirmavit se
Thaisim occidisse, super quo Dionysia una cum Strangulione
marito suo dolorem in publico confingentes, exequias et sepulturam
honorifice, quantum ad extra subdola conjectatione fieri
constituerunt.*

    Now lette we this maiden here
And speke of Dionyse agayne,
And of Theophile the vilayne,
Of whiche I spake of nowe tofore,
Whan thaise shulde have be forlore.   1510
This false chorle to his ladie
Whan he cam home all prively,
He saith: Madame, slayne I have
This mayde Thaise, and is begrave
In privy place, as ye me bede.
Forthy madame, taketh hede
And kepe counseyle, howe so it stonde.
This fende, whiche hath this understond,
Was glad and weneth it be sooth.
Now se hereafter how she dooth.[2]   1520
    She wepeth, she crieth, she compleyneth,
And of sickenes, which she feyneth
She saith, that Thaise sodeynly
By night is dead,[3] as she and I
Together lien nigh my lorde.
She was a woman of recorde,
And all is leved, that she seyth:
And for to yeve a more feith
Hir husbonde, and eke she both
In blacke clothes thei hem cloth,   1530
And make a great enterement.
And for the people shall be blent,
Of Thaise as for the remembrance,
After the riall olde usance,
A tombe of laton noble and riche,
With an ymage unto hir liche
Liggynge, above therupon,

[1] V *Chor.* 1–11; V.1.45–48.
[2] Compare IV.3.
[3] IV.3.15.

Thei made, and set it up anon.[1]
   Hir epitaphe of good assise
Was writte about: and in this wise   1540
It spake, O ye that this beholde,
Lo here lieth she, the whiche was holde
The fairest, and the floure of all,
Whose name Thaisis men call.
   The kynge of Tyre Appolinus
Hir father was, nowe lieth she thus.
Fourtene yere she was of age,
Whan deth hir toke to his viage.[2]

Qualiter Appolinus in regno suo apud Tyrum existens parlia-
mentum fieri constituit.

   Thus was this false treason hid,
Whiche afterward was wyde kid,   1550
As by the tale a man shall here.
But to declare my matere
To Tyre I thynke tourne ageyne,
And telle, as the cronikes seyne.
   Whan that the kynge was comen home,
And hath lefte in the salte fome
His wife, whiche he may not foryete,
For he some comforte wolde gete,
He lette sommone a parlement,
To whiche the lordes weren assent,   1560
And of the tyme he hath ben out,
He seeth the thynges all about,
And tolde hem eke howe he hath fare
While he was out of londe fare,
And praide hem alle to abide:
For he wolde at some[3] tide
Do shape for his wives mynde,
As he that wolde not be unkinde.
   Solempne was that ilke office,
And riche was the sacrifice,   1570
The feste rially was holde,
And therto was he well beholde.
For suche a wife as he had one,
In thilke daies was there none.

[1] IV.3.41–46.
[2] Cf. IV.4.32–43.
[3] atte same *1483*.

Qualiter Appolinus post parliamentum Tharsim pro Thaise filia sua querenda adiit, qua ibidem non inventa abinde navigio recessit.

Whan this was done, then he him thought
Upon his doughter, and besought
Suche of his lordes, as he wolde,[1]
That thei with him to Tharse sholde
To fette his doughter Thaise there,
And thei anone all redie were.   1580
To ship thei gone, and forth thei went,
Till thei the haven of Tharse hente.
Thei londe, and faile of that thei seche
By coverture and sleight of speche.
This false man Strangulio
And Dionyse his wife also,
That he the better trowe might,
Thei ladde him to have a sight,
Where that hir tombe was arraied,[2]
The lasse yet he was mispayde.   1590
   And netheles so as he durst,
He curseth, and saith all the wurst
Unto fortune, as to the blinde,
Which can no siker wey finde.
For hym she neweth ever amonge,
And medleth sorowe with his songe,
But sithe it maie no better be,
He thonketh god, and forth goth he
Sailynge towarde Tyre ageyne.
But sodeynly the wynde and reyne   1600
Began upon the sea debate,
So that he suffre mote algate.[3]

Qualiter navis Appolini ventis agitata portum urbis Mitelene in die quo festa Neptuni celebrari consueverunt, applicuit, sed ipse pre dolore Thaisis filie sue, quam mortuam reputabat, in fundo navis obscruo jacens lumen videre noluit.

The lawe, which Neptune ordeineth,
Wherof full ofte time he pleyneth
And held him wel the more esmaied

[1] IV.4.9–16.
[2] IV.4 Dumbshow.
[3] IV.4.23–31.

Of that he hath tofore assaied.
So that for pure sorowe and care,
Of that he seeth this world so fare,
The rest he leveth of his caban,
That for the counseil of no man, 1610
Ageyne therin he nolde come,
But hath beneth his place nome,
Where he wepynge alone laie,
There as he sawe no light of daie.
    And thus tofore the wynde thei drive,
Till longe and late thei arrive
With great distresse, as it was sene
Upon this towne of Mitelene,
Whiche was a noble citee tho.
And happeneth thilke tyme so, 1620
The lordes both, and the commune
The high festes of Neptune
Upon the stronde at rivage,
As it was custume and usage
Solempneliche thei be sigh.[1]
    Whan they this strange vessell sigh
Com in, and hath his saile avaled,
The towne therof hath spoke and taled.

Qualiter Atenagoras urbis Mitelene princeps navim Appolini investigans, ipsum sic contristatum nihilque respondentem consolari satagebat.

The lorde, which of that citee was,
Whose name is Atenagoras, 1630
Was there, and saide, he wolde see,
What ship it is, and who they bee,
That ben therin: and after soone,
Whan that he sigh it was to doone,
His barge was for him araied,
And he gotth foorth and hath assaied.[2]
He found the ship of great araie:
But what thynge it amounte maie,
He sigh thei maden hevy chere,
But well him thenketh by the manere, 1640
That thei ben worthie men of blood,
And asketh of hem howe it stood:

[1] V *Chor.* 16.
[2] V *Chor.* 17–20.

And thei him tellen all the caas,
Howe that her lorde fordrive was,
And whiche a sorowe that he made,
Of whiche there maie no man him glade.
He praieth that he her lorde maie see.
But thei him tolde it maie not bee.
For he lith in so derke a place,
That there maie no wight sen his face. 1650
    But for all that though hem be lothe,
He fonde the ladder, and downe he goeth,
And to him spake but none answere
Ageine of him ne might he here,[1]
For ought that he can do or seyne,
And thus he goeth him up ageyn.

Qualiter precepto principis, ut Appolinum consolaretur, Thaisis cum cithera sua ad ipsum in obscuro navis, ubi jacebat, producta est.

    Tho was there spoke in many wise
Amonges hem, that weren wise,
Nowe this, nowe that, but at last
The wisdome of the towne thus cast, 1660
That yonge Thaise was assent.
For if there be amendement
To glad with this wofull kynge,
She can so muche of every thynge,
That she shall glad him anon.[2]
    A messager for hir is gone,
And she came with hir harpe in honde,
And saide hem, that she wolde fonde
By all the weies, that she can,
To glad with this sory man. 1670
But what he was, she wist nought
But all the ship hir hath besought,
That she hir witte on him dispende,
In aunter if he might amende,
And sayn: it shall be well aquit.[3]
    Whan she hath understonden it,
She goeth hir doune, there as he laie,
Where that she harpeth many a laie,

[1] Cf. V.1.16–41.
[2] V.1.42–52.
[3] V.1.53–80.

And like an angell songe with alle.
But he no more than the walle 1680
Toke hede of any thynge he herde.[1]
  And whan she sawe that he so ferde,
She falleth with hym unto wordes,
And telleth him of sondrie bordes,
And asketh him demandes strange,
Whereof she made his herte change,
And to hir speche his eare he leyde
And hath mervaile, of that she sayde.
For in proverbe, and in probleme
She spake, and bad he shulde deme, 1690
In many a subtile question.
But he for no suggestion,
Whiche towarde hym she couthe stere,
He wolde not one worde answere.[2]
But as a mad man at laste,
His head wepynge awey he caste,
And halfe in wrath he bad hir go.
But yet she wolde not do so,
And in the derke forth she gothe,
Till she hym toucheth, and he wroth, 1700
And after hir with his honde
He smote[3]: and thus whan she him fonde
Diseased, courteisly she sayde,
Avoy my lorde, I am a mayde,
And if ye wyst, what I am,
And out of what linage I cam,
Ye wolde not be so salvage.[4]
With that he sobreth his corage
And put awey his hevie cher.

Qualiter, sicut deus destinavit patri, filiam inventam recognovit.

  But of hem two a man maie lere, 1710
What is to be so sibbe of bloode.
None wist of other howe it stoode,
And yet the father at laste
His herte upon this mayde caste,
That he hir loveth kyndely.

---

[1] *Ibid.* 80–81.
[2] Not in the play; compare Jurine.
[3] Cf. V.1.83–84; 95–101; 128–9.
[4] V.1.100–1.

And yet he wist never why,
But all was knowe er that thei went.
For god, [which]¹ wote her hole entent,
Her hertes both anone descloseth.
This kynge, unto this maide opposeth,   1720
And asketh first, what is hir name,
And where she lerned all this game,
And of what kyn she was come.
And she that hath his wordes nome,
Answereth, and saith: my name is Thaise,
That was sometyme well at aise.
In Tharse I was forthdrawe and fedde.
There I lerned, till I was spedde
Of that I can: my father eke
I not where that I shulde hym seke,   1730
He was a kynge men tolde me.
My moder dreint [was]² in the see.
Fro poynt to poynt all she hym tolde,
That she hath longe in herte holde,
And never durst make hir mone,
But onely to this lorde allone,
To whom hir herte can not hele,
Tourne it to wo, tourne it to wele,
Tourne it to good, tourne it to harme.³
     And he tho toke hir in his arme,   1740
But suche a joye as he tho made,
Was never sene, thus ben thei glade,
That sory hadden be toforne.⁴
Fro this daie forth fortune hath sworne
To set hym upwarde on the whele.
So goth the worlde, now wo, now wele.

Qualiter Athenagoras Appolinum de navi in hospicium
honorifice recollegit, et Thaisim, patre consenciente, in uxorem
duxit.

     This kynge hath founde newe grace,
So that out of his derke place,
He goth hym up in to the light,
And with hym cam that swete wight   1750
His doughter Thaise, and forth anone
They bothe into the caban gone,

---

¹ which *1483*: *not in 1554.*   ² was *1483*: *not in 1554.*
³ V.1.85–181.   ⁴ *Ibid.* V.1.192–225.

Whiche was ordeined for the kynge,
And there he did of all his thynge,
And was araied rially,[1]
And out he cam all openly,
Where Athenagoras he fonde,
Whiche was lorde of all the londe.
He praieth the kynge to come and see
His castell bothe, and his citee.   1760
And thus thei gone forth all in fere
This kyng, this lorde, this maiden dere.
This lorde tho made hem riche feste,
With every thynge, which was honeste
To plese with this worthy kinge:
Ther lacketh hem no maner thynge.
But yet for al his noble araie
Wiveles he was unto that daie,
As he that yet was of yonge age.
    So fill there into his corage   1770
The lustie wo, the glad payne
Of love, whiche no man restrayne
Yet never might as now tofore.
This lord thynketh all this world lore,
But if the kynge will doone hym grace.[2]
He waiteth tyme, he waiteth place,
Hym thought his herte wold tobreke,
Till he maie to this maide speke,
And to hir fader eke also
For mariage, and it fyll so,   1780
That all was doone, right as he thought,
His purpos to an ende he brought,
She wedded hym as for hir lorde,[3]
Thus ben thei all of one accorde.

Qualiter Appolinus una cum filia et eius marito navim in-
gredientes, a Mitilena usque Tharsim cursum proposuerunt, sed
Appolinus in somnis admonitus versus Ephesim, ut ibidem
templo Diane sacrificaret, vela per mare divertit.

Whan all was done right as thei wolde,
The kynge unto his sonne tolde
Of Tharse thilke traiterie,

---

[1] V.1.224, 'Give me my robes'.
[2] Cf. V.1.67–69; 261–3.
[3] Delayed in the play: V.2.9–13.

And said, how in his companie
His doughter and him selven eke,
Shall go vengeance for to seke.   1790
    The shippes were redy soone.
And whan thei sawe it was to doone,
Without let of any went,
With saile up drawe forth thei wente
Towarde Tharse upon the tide:
But he that wote what shall betide,
The hie god, which wolde hym kepe,
Whan that this kynge was fast a slepe
By nightes tyme he hath hym bede
To sayle unto another stede.   1800
To Ephesum he bad hym drawe,
And as it was that tyme lawe
He shall do there his sacrifice.
And eke he bad in all wise,
That in the temple amongest all
His fortune, as it is befalle,
Touchyng his doughter, and his wife,
He shall be knowe upon his life.[1]
    The king of this avision
Hath great imaginacion,   1810
What thinge it signifie maie.
And nethelesse whan it was daie,
He bad cast anker, and abode.
And while that he on anker rode,
The wynde, that was tofore strange,
Upon the poynte began to change,
And torneth thider, as it sholde.
Tho knew he well, that god it wolde,
And bad the maister make hym yare,
Tofore the wynde for he wolde fare   1820
To Ephesum, and so he dede.
And whan he came into the stede,
Where as he shulde londe, he londeth,
With all the haste he maie and fondeth
To shapen him in suche a wise,
That he maie by the morowe arise,
And doone after the mandement
Of hym, whiche hath hym thider sent.
And in the wise that he thought,

---

[1] V.1.235–52.

Upon the morowe so he wrought.   1830
His doughter and his sonne he nome,
And forth to the temple he come,
With a great route in companie,
His yeftes for to sacrifie.
  The citezens tho herden saie
Of suche a kynge that came to praie
Unto Diane the goddesse,
And lefte all other besinesse,
Thei comen thider for to see
The kinge and the solempnitee.   1840

*Qualiter Appolinus Ephesum in templo Diane sacrificans,
uxorem suam ibidem velatam invenit, qua secum assumpta in
navim versus Tyrum regressus est.*

  With worthie knightes environed
The kynge hym selfe hath abandoned
To the temple in good entente.
The dore is up, and in he wente,[1]
Where as with great devocion
Of holy contemplacion,
Within his herte he made his shrifte:
And after that a riche yifte
He offreth with great reverence,
And there in open audience,   1850
Of hem, that stoden all aboute,
He tolde hem, and declareth out
His happe, suche as him is befalle.
There was no thynge foryete of alle.
His wyfe, as it was goddes grace,
Whiche was professed in the place,
As she that was abbesse there,
Unto his tale hath leied hir ere.
She knewe the voyce, and the visage:
For pure joye as in a rage   1860
She straught to hym all at ones,
And fill a swoune upon the stones,[2]
Wherof the temple flore was paved.
She was anone with water laved
Till she came to hir selfe ageyne,
And than she began to seyne,
  Ah blessed be the high sonde

[1] As in V.3.   [2] V.3.1–15.

That I may se my husbonde,
Whiche whilom he and I were one.
 The kynge with that knew hir anone,   1870
And toke hir in his arme, and kist,[1]
And all the towne this soone it wist.
Tho was there joye many folde.
For every man this tale hath tolde,
As for miracle, and weren glade.
But never man such joye made,
As doth the kynge, which hath his wife.
And whan men herde, how that hir life
Was saved, and by whom it was,
Thei wondred all of suche a cas.   1880
Through all the londe arose the speche
Of maister Cerimon the leche,
And of the cure whiche he dede.[2]
The kynge hym selfe tho hath bede
And eke the quene forth with hym,
That he the towne of Ephesym
Woll leve, and go where as thei bee.[3]
For never man of his degree
Hath do to hem so mychell good.
And he his profite understoode,   1890
And graunteth with hem for to wende.
And thus thei maden there an ende,
And token leve, and gone to ship
With all the hole felauship.

Qualiter Appolinus una cum uxore et filia sua Tyrum applicuit.

 This kyng, whiche now hath his desire,
Saith, he woll holde his cours to Tyre.
They hadden wynde at will tho,
With topsayle coole, and forth thei go.
And stryken never till thei come
To Tyre, where as thei have nome,   1900
And londen hem with mochell blisse,
There was many a mouth to kisse,
Eche one welcometh other home.
But whan the quene to londe come
And Thaise hir doughter by hir side,

---

[1] V.3.15–45.
[2] *Ibid.* 59–63.
[3] He takes them to his house, V.3.64–68.

28

The whiche joie was thilke tide
There maie no mans tunge telle.
They sayden all, here cometh the welle
Of all womannishe grace.
The kynge hath take his roiall place,　　　　1910
The quene is into chambre go.
There was great feste araied tho.
Whan tyme was thei gone to mete,
All olde sorowes ben foryete,
And gladen hem with joyes newe.
The discoloured pale hewe
Is nowe become a ruddy cheke,
There was no mirth for to seke.

Qualiter Appolinus Athenagoram cum Thaise uxore super Tyrum coronari fecit.

But every man hath what he wolde,
The kynge as he well coude and sholde　　　1920
Makth to his people right good chere,
And after soone, as thou shalt here,
A parlement he hath sommoned,
Where he his doughter hath coroned,
Forthwith the lorde of Mitelene,
That on is kynge, that other quene.
And thus the fathers ordinance
This londe hath set in governance,
And sayde that he wolde wende
To Tharse, for to make an ende　　　　　1930
Of that his doughter was betraied,
Wherof were all men well paied.
And said, howe it was for to done.
The shippes weren redy sone.

Qualiter Appolinus a Tyro per mare versus Tharsim iter arripiens, vindictam contra Strangulionem et Dionysiam uxorem suam pro injuria, quam ipsi Thaisi filie sue intulerunt, judicialiter assecutus est.

A stronge power with him he toke,
Upon the skie he cast his loke,
And sigh the wynde was covenable,
Thei hale up ancre with the cable,
Thei saile on hie, the stere on honde,
Thei sailen, till thei come a londe　　　　1940

At Tharse nygh to the citee.
   And whan thei wisten it was hee,
The towne hath done hym reverence.
   He telleth hem the violence
Whiche the traitour Strangulio
And Dionyse hym had do
Touchynge his doughter, as ye herde.
And whan thei wiste, how it ferde,
As he whiche pees and love sought,
Unto the towne this he besought,   1950
To done him right in jugement.
   Anone thei weren both assente,
With strengthe of men, and comen soone,
And as hem thought it was to doone,
Atteynt thei weren by the lawe,
And demed to be honged and drawe,[1]
And brent, and with wynde to blowe,
That all the worlde it might knowe.
And upon this condicion
The dome in execucion   1960
Was put anone withoute faile.
And every man hath great mervaile,
Whiche herde tellen of this chance,
And thonketh goddes purveance,
Whiche doth mercy forth with justice.
Slain is the mordrer and the mordrice
Through very trouth of rightwisnesse,
And through mercy save is simplesse
Of hir, whom mercy preserveth.
Thus hath he wel, that wel deserveth.   1970

Qualiter Artestrate Pentapolim rege mortuo, ipsi de regno epistolas super hoc Appolino direxerunt, unde Appolinus una cum uxore sua ibidem advenientes, ad decus imperii cum magno gaudio coronati sunt.

   Whan all this thinge is doone and ended,
This kinge, which loved was and frended
A letter hath, which came to hym
By ship fro Pentapolim,
In whiche the londe hath to him writte,
That he wolde understonde and witte,
Howe in good mynde and in good pees

---

[1] 1483. *1554* And demed so honged and drawe,

Dead is the kinge Artestrates,
Wherof thei all of one accorde
Him praiden, as her liege lorde,   1980
That he the letter wol conceive,[1]
And come, his reigne to receive:
Whiche god hath yeve him, and fortune.
And thus besought the commune,
Forthwith the great lordes all.
   This kinge sighe howe it is befalle.
Fro Tharse and in prosperitee
He toke his leve of that citee,
And goeth him into ship ayene.
The wynde was good, the sea was pleyne,   1990
Hem nedeth not a riffe to slake,
Til thei Pentapolim have take.
The londe whiche herde of that tydinge
Was wonder glad of his cominge,
He resteth him a daie or two,
And toke his counceil to him tho,
And set a tyme of parlement,
Where al the londe of one assente,
Forthwith his wife have him croned,
Where all good him was forsoned.   2000
   Lo what it is to be well grounded.
For he hath first his love founded
Honestly as for to wedde,
Honestly his love he spedde,
And had chyldren with his wife,
And as him liste he led his life.
And in ensample his life was writte,
That all lovers mighten witte
Howe at laste it shal be sene
Of love what thei wolden mene.   2010
   For see nowe on that other side,
Antiochus with all his pride,
Whiche sette his love unkyndely,
His ende had sodeynly,
Set ageyn kynde upon vengeance,
And for his lust hath his penance.
   Lo thus my sonne, might thou lere,
What is to love in good manere,
And what to love in other wise.

[1]conceive *1483*; receyve *1558*.

The mede ariseth of the service, 2020
Fortune though she be not stable,
Yet at somtime is favourable
To hem, that ben of love trewe.
But certes it is for to rewe,
To see love agein kynde falle.
For that maketh sore a man to falle,
As thou might of tofore rede.
Forthy my sonne I wolde the rede
To let all other love aweie,
But if it be through suche a weie, 2030
As love and reason wold accorde.
For elles if that thou discorde,
And take luste as doeth a beste,
Thy love maie nought ben honeste.
For by no skille that I finde
Such luste is nought of loves kynde.

II. Source

THE PATTERNE OF
PAINEFULL ADVENTURES
by Laurence Twine

The Patterne of Painefull Adventures: Containing the most excellent, pleasant and variable Historie of the strange accidents that befell unto Prince Apollonius, the Lady Lucina his wife, and Tharsia his daughter. Wherein the uncertaintie of this world, and the fickle state of mans life are lively described, Gathered into English by Lawrence Twine Gentleman. Imprinted at London by Valentine Simmes for the Widow Newman. n.d. (1594?)

To the worshipfull

Master John Donning, Custo-
mer and Jurate of the towne
of Rie in Sussex

Being diversely mooved in mind, to signifie my good will and hartie love towardes you, gentle M. Donning, I could not devise any meanes more effectuall, then by presenting the same to you, which cost me some small labor and travel. Not seeming therby to acquite your manifold curtesies, towards me diversly extended, but rather to discharge me of the note of Ingratitude, which otherwise I might seeme to incurre. Wherefore in steede of a greater present to countervaile your friendlines, I am bold in the setting foorth of this simple Pamflet under your name, to make a proffer of my thankeful heart to you againe. Wherin though want of farther abilitie appeare, yet is there no let, but that a wel-willing heart may be exprest, yea in the smallest gift. Now if haply the argument hereof appeare unto you other than you could much wish, or I well afford, yet have I no feare of any great misliking, considering your natural disposition, which is to be delighted with honest pleasure, and commendable recreation, and not to lie evermore weltering, as it were, in dolefull dumpishnesse. Which thing did put me in the greater hope, that this worke would be the welcommer unto you, especially considering the delectable varietie, and the often changes and chances contained in this present historie, which cannot but much stirre up the mind and sences unto sundry affections. What ever it be take it I beseech you, in good part, in stead of some better thing which I might well affoord, promising the same when occasion shall serve, not being at this present so well furnished as I could wish of God: to whose good grace I recommend you and yours, both nowe and evermore.

Your worships to use,

LAURENCE TWINE.

THE TABLE

How *Antiochus* committed incest with his owne daughter, and beheaded such as sued unto her for marriage, if they coulde not resolve his questions. CHAP. 1.

How *Apollonius* arriving at Antiochia, resolved the King's question; and howe *Taliarchus* was sent to slay him. CHAP. 2.

How *Taliarchus*, not finding *Apollonius* at Tyrus, departeth joyfully; and *Apollonius* arriving at Tharsus, relieveth the citie with victuall. CHAP. 3.

How *Apollonius* departing from Tharsus by the perswasion of *Stranguilio* and *Dionisiades* his wife, committed shipwracke, and was relieved by *Altistrates* King of Pentapolis. CHAP. 4.

How *Lucina* king *Altistrates* daughter desirous to heare Apollonius adventures, fell in love with him. CHAP. 5.

How *Apollonius* is made Schoolemaster to *Lucina*; and how shee preferreth the love of him above all the Nobilitie of Pentapolis. CHAP 6.

How *Apollonius* was married to the Lady *Lucina*, and hearing of king *Antiochus* death, departeth with his wife towards his own country of Tyrus. CHAP. 7.

How faire *Lucina* died in travell of childe upon the sea, and being throwen into the water, was cast on land at Ephesus, and taken home by *Cerimon* a Physicion. CHAP. 8.

How *Lucina* was restored to life by one of *Cerimon* the Physicions schollers; and how *Cerimon* adopted hir to his daughter, and placed her in the Temple of *Diana*. CHAP. 9.

How *Apollonius* arriving at Tharsus, delivereth his yong daughter *Tharsia* unto *Stranguilio* and *Dionisiades* to be brought up, and how the Nurce, lying in her death bed declareth unto *Tharsia* who were hir parents. CHAP. 10.

How after the death of *Ligozides* the Nurce, *Dionisiades*, envying at the beautie of *Tharsia*, conspired her death, which should have been accomplished by a villaine of the countrey. CHAP. 11.

How certain Pirats rescued *Tharsia* when she shuld have been slaine, and carried hir unto the citie *Machilenta*, to be sold among other bondslaves. CHAP. 12.

How the Pirats which stole away *Tharsia*, brought her to the citie *Machilenta*, and sold her to a common bawd; and how she preserved her virginitie. CHAP. 13.

How *Tharsia* withstood a second assault of her virginitie, and by what meanes shee was preserved. CHAP. 14.

How *Apollonius* comming to Tharsus, and not finding his daughter, lamented her supposed death, and taking ship againe, was driven by a tempest to Machilenta where *Tharsia* was. CHAP. 15.

How *Athanagoras* prince of Machilenta seeing the beautie of *Apollonius* ship, went aboord of it, and did the best he could to comfort him. CHAP. 16.

How *Athanagoras* sent for *Tharsia*, to make her father *Apollonius* merrie, and how after long circumstance they came into knowledge one of another. CHAP. 17.

How *Apollonius* leaving off mourning, came into the citie Machilenta, where he commanded the bawd to be burned, and how *Tharsia* was married unto Prince *Athanagoras*. CHAP. 18.

How *Apollonius*, meaning to saile into his owne Countrey by Tharsus, was commanded by an Angell in the night to goe to Ephesus, and there to declare all his adventures in the Church, with a loud voice. CHAP. 19.

How *Apollonius* came to the knowledge of his wife the Ladie *Lucina*, and how they rejoyced at the meeting of ech other. CHAP. 20.

How *Apollonius* departed from Ephesus and sailed himselfe, his wife, his sonne and daughter unto Antiochia, and then to Tyrus, and from thence to Tharsus, where he revenged himselfe upon *Stranguilio* and *Dionisiades*. CHAP. 21.

How *Apollonius* sayled from Tharsus to visite his father in law *Altistrates*, king of Pentapolis, who died not long after *Apollonius* comming thither. CHAP. 22.

How *Apollonius* rewarded the fisherman that relieved him after he had suffered shipwracke: how he dealt also with old *Calamitus*, and likewise with the Pirates that stole away *Tharsia*. CHAP. 23.

How *Apollonius* had a yong sonne and heire by his wife *Lucina*, likewise of *Appolonus* age, and how hee died: with some other accidents thereunto incident. CHAP. 24.

CHAP. I

Howe Antiochus committed incest with his owne daughter, and beheaded such as sued unto her for marriage, if they coulde not resolve his questions.

The most famous and mightie king Antiochus, which builded the goodly citie of Antiochia in Syria,[1] and called it after his own name, as the chiefest seat of all his dominions, and most principal place of his abode, begat upon his wife one daughter, a most excellent and beautifull yoong Ladie. Who in processe of yeeres growing up as well in ripenesse of age, as perfection of beautie: many Princes and noble men resorted unto her for intreaty of marriage,[2] offering inestimable riches in jointure. Howbeit the king her father, evermore requiring deliberation, upon whom rather than other to bestow his daughter, perceived eftsoones an unlawfull concupiscence to boyle within his breast, which he augmented with an outragious flame of crueltie sparkling in his heart, so that he began to burne with the love of his owne childe, more than it was beseeming for a father. Thus being wrapped in the toyle of blind desire, hee sustained within himselfe a fierce conflict, wherein Madnesse put Modestie to flight, & he wholly yeelded himselfe unto love. Wherefore, not long after, on a certaine day hee came into his daughters chamber, and bidding all that were there for to depart, as though he had had some secret matter to conferre with her: the furious rage of lust pricking him forward thereunto, he violently forced her,[3] though seely maiden she withstood him long to her power, and threwe away all regard of his owne honestie, and unlosed the knot of her virginitie. Now when he was departed, and she, being alone, devised within her self

[1] Prologue I, 17–19.
[2] Prol. I, 31–34.
[3] Contrast Prol. I, 25–27.

what it were best for her to doe, sodainelie her nurse entred in, and perceiving her face al beblubbred with teares, What is the matter, deare childe and Madam (quoth she) that you sit thus sorrowfully? O, my beloved nurse, answered the Ladie, even nowe two noble names were lost within this chamber. Howe so, said the nurse? Because (quoth shee) before marriage, through wicked villanie I am most shamefully defiled. And when the nurse had heard these wordes, and looking about more diligently, perceived indeede what was done, being inraged with sorrowe and anger, and almost distract of her wittes. Alas, what wretch or rather infernal feend (quoth she) durst thus presumptuously defile the bed of a Princesse? Ungodlinesse hath done this deede (quoth the Ladie.) Why then doe you not tell it the King your father, saide the nurse? Ah nurse, answered the Ladie, Where is my father? For if you well understoode the matter, the name of Father is lost in me, so that I can have no remedie now but death onely. But the nurse nowe by a few wordes perceiving the whole tale, and weying that the yong Lady gave inkling of remedie by death, which she much feared, beganne to assuage her grief with comfortable wordes, and to withdrawe her minde from that mischievous purpose. Wherein she prevailed so effectually in short time, that she appeased the fresh bleeding of the greene wound, howbeit the scarre continued long time, as deeply stroken within her tender heart, before it could be throughlie cured.[1]

In the meane season, while this wicked father sheweth the countenance of a loving sire abroad in the eies of al his people, notwithstanding, within doores, and in his minde, he rejoyceth that he hath played the part of an husband with his daughter: which false resemblance of hateful marriage, to the intent he might alwaies enjoy, he invented a strange devise of wickednesse, to drive away all suters that should resort unto her, by propounding certaine questions, the effect and law whereof was thus published in writing: *Who so findeth out the solution of my question, shall have my daughter to wife, but who so faileth, shal lose his head.*[2]

Now, when Fame had blowen abroade the possibilitie to obtaine this Ladie, such was the singular report of her surpassing beautie, that many kings and men of great nobility repaired thither. And if haply any through skill or learning had found out the solution of the kings question, notwithstanding hee was beheaded as though hee had answered nothing to the purpose: and his head was set up at the gate to terrifie others that should come, who beholding there the present image of death, might advise them from assaying anie such

---

[1] Contrast Prol. I.29–30.
[2] Prol. I.35–38.

danger.[1] These outrages practised Antiochus, to the ende he might continue in filthie incest with his daughter.

CHAP. II

How Apollonius arriving at Antiochia resolved the kings question, and how Taliarchus was sent to slay him.

Whilest Antiochus thus continued in exercising tyrannie at Antiochia, a certaine yong Gentleman of Tyrus, Prince of the country, abounding in wealth, and very well learned, called Apollonius, arrived in the coast, and comming unto the citie of Antiochia, was brought into the kings presence. And when he had saluted him, the king demanded of him the cause of his comming thither.[2] Then saide the yoong prince, Sir, I require to have your daughter in marriage. The king hearing that which he was unwilling to heare, looking fiercely upon him, saide unto him: Doest thou know the conditions of the marriage. Yea sir king, said Apollonius, and I see it standing upon the gate. Then the king being sharply moved, and disdaining at him, said, Heare then the question which thou must resolve, or else die: *I am carried with mischiefe, I eate my mothers fleshe: I seeke my brother my mothers husband and I can not finde him.*[3] Apollonius having received the question, withdrew himselfe a while out of the kinges presence, and being desirous to understand what it meant, he found out the solution thereof in short space through the help of God, and returned againe to the king, saying; Your grace proposed a question unto me, I pray you heare the solution thereof. And whereas you said in your probleme, *I am carried with mischiefe*: you have not lied, for looke unto your owne selfe. But whereas you say further, *I eate my mothers flesh*, looke upon your daughter.[4]

Now the king, as soone as he perceived that Apollonius had resolved his probleme, fearing lest his wickednesse should be discovered, he looked upon him with a wrathful countenance, saying; Thou art farre wide from the solution of my demand, and hast hit no part of the meaning thereof: wherefore thou hast deserved to be beheaded. Howbeit, I will shew thee this courtesie, as to give thee thirtie daies[5] respite to bethinke thy selfe of this matter. Wherefore returne home into thine owne countrey,[6] and if thou canst find out the solution of my probleme, thou shalt have my daughter to wife:

---

[1] Prol. I.39–40.
[2] Shakespeare begins after this.
[3] Cf. I.1.64–71.
[4] Less directly hinted at I.1.93–108.
[5] I.1.118. 'Forty days'.
[6] Cf. I.1.119–20. He will keep him at Antioch.

If not thou shalt be beheaded. Then Apollonius being much troubled and molested in mind, accompanying himself with a sufficient train, tooke shipping, and returned into his owne countrey. But so soone as he was departed, Antiochus called unto him his steward, named Thaliarchus,[1] to whom he spake in maner following.

Thaliarchus, the only faithfull and trustie minister of my secrets: understand that Apollonius, prince of Tirus, hath found out the solution of my question. Wherefore, take shipping and followe him immediatly, and if thou canst not overtake him upon the sea, seeke him out when thou commest to Tirus, and slay him either with sword or poyson,[2] and when thou returnest I will bountifully reward thee. Taliarchus promised to accomplish his commandement with all diligence, and taking to him his shield, with monie sufficient for the journey, departed on his way, and shortly after arrived at the coast of Tirus. But Apollonius was come home unto his owne Pallace long time before, and withdrawing himselfe into his studie, perused all his bookes concerning the kings probleame, finding none other solution, than that which he had alreadie told the king.[3] And thus he said within himselfe: Surely, unlesse I be much deceived, Antiochus burneth with disordinate love of his daughter: and discoursing further with himselfe upon that point: What sayest thou now, or what intendest thou to doe, Apollonius, said he to himselfe? Thou hast resolved his probleme, and yet not received his daughter, and God hath therefore brought thee away that thou shouldest not die. Then brake hee off in the midst of these cogitations, and immediatly[4] commanded his ships to be prepared, and to be laden with an hundred thousand bushels of wheat,[5] and with great plenty of gold, silver and rich apparell: and taking unto him a few of his most trustiest servants, about midnight imbarked himself, and hoysing up his sails, committed himselfe to the wide sea. The day following, his subjects the citizens came unto the Pallace to have seene their Prince, but when they found him not there, the whole citie was forthwith surprised with wonderfull sorrowe, everie man lamenting that so worthy a Prince [was] so sodainly gone out of sight and knowledge, no man knew whether. Great was the grief, and wofull was the wayling which they made, every man lamenting his owne private estate and the commonwealths in generall, as it alwaies hapneth at the death or losse of a good Prince, which the inhabitants of Tirus tooke then so heavily, in respect of their great affection, that a long time after no barbers shops were opened, the common

---

[1] Thaliard in *Per.* [2] I.1.155.

[3] Not in *Per.* where he has no doubt.

[4] In *Per.* he is advised by Helicanus I.2.34ff. [5] I.4.95.

shews and plaies surceased, baines and hoat houses were shut up, taverns were not frequented, and no man repaired unto the Churches, al thing was full of sorrow and heavinesse, what shall I say? there was nothing but heavinesse.

CHAP. III

How Taliarchus not finding Apollonius at Tirus, departeth joyfully, and Apollonius arriving at Thasus, relieveth the citie with vittell.

In the middes of this sorrowful season, Taliarchus commeth to Tirus to execute the cruell commandement of Antiochus where, finding al-thing shut up, and a generall shew of mourning, meeting with a boy in the streete,[1] Tell me, said he, or I will slay thee, for what cause is al this citie thus drowned in heavines? To whom the child answered: My friend, doest thou not know the cause, that thou askest it of me? This citie mourneth because the Prince therof Apollonius, returning back from king Antiochus, can no where be found or heard of. Now, so soone as Taliarchus hearde these tidings, he returned joyfully unto his ships, and tooke his journey backe to Antiochia, and being landed, he hastened unto the king, and fell downe on his knees before him, saying: All haile most mightie Prince, rejoyce and be glad, for Apollonius being in feare of your grace is departeth no man knoweth whether. Then answered the king: He may well flie away from mee, but he shall never escape my handes. And immediatly he made proclamation, that whosoever could take that contemner of the king Apollonius prince of Tirus, and bring him alive into the kinges presence, should have an hundred talents of golde for his labour: and whosoever coulde bring his head, should have fiftie talentes. Which proclamation beeing published, not onely Apollonius enemies, but also his friendes, made all haste possible to seeke him out, allured thereto with covetousnesse of the money.[2] Thus was that poore Prince sought for about by sea and by land, through woodes and wilde deserts, but could not be found. Then the king commanded a great Navie of ships to be prepared to scoure the seas abroad, if haply they might meet with him, but for that every thing requireth a time ere it can be done, in the meane season Apollonius arriveth at Tharsus, where walking along by the sea side, he was espied by one of his owne servauntes, named Elinatus,[3] who landed there not long before, and overtooke him as he was going, and comming neere unto

---

[1] In I.3 he meets Helicanus.
[2] Contrast *Conf.* 544.
[3] In *Per.* Helicanus sends news. II *Chorus*, 17–26 and Dumbshow.

him with dutifull obeisance, said unto him: God save you prince
Apollonius. But he being saluted, did even so as noble men and
princes use to doe, set light by him. But Elinatus taking that
behaviour unkindly, saluted him againe saying: God save you
Prince Apollonius; salute me againe, and despise not povertie
beautified with honestie. And if you knewe that which I know, you
would take good heed to your self. Then answered Apollonius: If
you thinke good, I pray you tell me. Elinatus answered, you are by
proclamation commanded to be slaine. And who, said Apollonius,
dares commaund by proclamation, the prince of a countrey to be
slaine? Antiochus, said Elinatus. Antiochus! For what cause,
demanded Apollonius. For that, said Elinatus, thou wouldst be
unto his daughter which he himselfe is. Then demanded Apollonius,
For what summe of mony is my life sold by that proclamation?
Elinatus answered, whosoever can bring you alive unto the king
shall have an hundred talents of gold in recompence: but whoso
bringeth your head shall have fiftie talents of gold for his labour, and
therefore I advise you my lord, to flie unto some place for your
defence: and when he had so said he tooke his leave and departed.
But Apollonius called him againe, and said that hee would give him
an hundred talents of gold; for, said he, receive thus much now of
my povertie, where nothing is now left unto me but flight, and
pining misery. Thou hast deserved the reward, wherefore draw out
thy sword, and cut off my head, & present it to the king, as the most
joyfull sight in the world. Thus mayst thou win an hundred talents
of gold, and remaine without all blame or note of ingratitude, since
I my selfe have hyred thee in the kinges behalfe to gratefie him with
so acceptable a present. Then answered Elinatus: God forbid my
lord that by anie such sinister means I should deserve a reward.
In all my life I never consented to any such matter in my heart.
And, my lord, if the deed were good, the love of vertue were a sufficient force to allure any man thereunto. But since it respecteth your
life, to whome in consideration of the cause no man may doe
violence without villanie: I commit both you and your matter unto
God, who no doubt will be your defender: And when he had thus
said, he departed. But Apollonius walked forth along upon the
shoare, where he had gone not farre, but he descried a man afarre
off comming towardes him with heavie cheere and a sorrowfull
countenance, and his name was Stranguilio: a Tharsian borne, and
of good reputation in the citie.[1] To whom saide Apollonius, God
save you Stranguilio: and he likewise resaluted him saying, And you
likewise my good lord Apollonius: I pray you tel me, what is the

---

[1] Cf. I.4.21. Cleon is governor of Tarsus.

cause that you walk in this place thus troubled within your minde?
Apollonius answered: because, being promised to have king
Antiochus daughter to my wife, if I told him the true meaning of his
question, nowe that I have so done, I am notwithstanding restrained
from her. Wherefore I request you it may so be, that I may live
secretly in your citie; for why, I stand moreover in some doubt of
the kinges farther displeasure. Stranguilio answered: My lord
Apollonius, our citie at this present is verie poore, and not able to
sustaine the greatnesse of your dignitie: and even now we suffer
great penurie and want of vittell, insomuch that there remaineth
small hope of comfort unto our citizens, but that we shall all perish
by extreme famine: and now certes there resteth nothing but the
fearefull image of gastly death before our eies.[1] When Apollonius
heard these wordes, he said unto him: Then give thankes unto God,
who in my flight hath brought me a land into your costes. For I
have brought great store of provision with me, and will presently
give unto your citie an hundreth thousand bushels of wheate, if you
will onely conceale my comming hither. At these wordes Stranguilio
being strooken as it were into a sodaine amazednesse, as it happeneth
when a man is overjoyed with some glad tidinges, fell downe
prostrate before prince Apollonius feete, and saide: My lord
Apollonius, if you coulde, and also if it might please of your great
goodnesse, in such sort as you say, to succour this afflicted and
famished citie, we wil not onely receive you gladly, and conceale
your abode: but also if neede so require, willingly spend our lives
in your quarrell. Which promise of mine, to the intent you may
heare to be confirmed by the full consent of all the citizens, might it
please your Grace to enter into the citie, and I most willingly will
attend upon you. Apollonius agreed thereto, and when they came
into the citie, he mounted up into the place of judgment, to the
intent he might the better be heard, and gathering al the people
together: thus hee spake unto the whole multitude. Ye citizens of
Tharsus, whom penurie of vittell pincheth at this present: understand ye, that I Apollonius prince of Tirus, am determined presently
to relieve you: In respect of which benefite I trust ye will be so
thankfull as to conceale mine arriving hither. And know ye moreover, that not as being driven away through the malice of king
Antiochus, but sayling along by the Seas I am happily fallen into
your haven. Wherefore I meane to utter unto you an hundred
thousand bushels of wheate, paying no more than I bought it for
in mine own countrey, that is to say, eight peeces of brasse for everie
bushell.[2] When the citizens heard this, they gave a shout for joy

---

[1] I.4.7–55.   [2] Nothing in *Per.* I.4.88–96 about selling the corn.

crying, God save my Lord Apollonius, promising to live and die in
his quarrell, and they gave him wonderfull thankes, and the whole
citie was replenished with joy, and they went forthwith unto the
ships, and bought the corne. But Apollonius, doubting lest by this
deede, he should seeme to put off the dignitie of a prince, and put
on the countenance of a merchant rather than a giver, when he
had received the price of the wheate, he restored it backe againe to
the use and commoditie of the same citie. And when the citizens
perceived the great benefites which he had bestowed upon their
citie, they erected in the market place a monument in the memoriall
of him, his stature[1] made of brasse standing in a charret, holding
corne in his right hand, and spurning it with his left foot: and on
the baser foot of the pillar whereon it stoode, was ingraven in great
letters this superscription: Apollonius prince of Tirus gave a gift unto
the citie of Tharsus whereby hee delivered it from a cruel death.

CHAP. IV

How Apollonius departing from Tharsus by the perswasion of Stranguilio
and Dionisiades his wife, committed shipwracke, and was relieved by
Altistrates king of Pentapolis.

Thus had not Apollonius aboden many daies in the citie of Tharsus
but Stranguilio & Dionisiades[2] his wife, earnestly exhorted him, as
seeming very carefull and tender of his welfare, rather to addresse
himselfe unto Pentapolis or among the Tirenians, as a place most fit
for his securitie, where he might lie and hide himselfe in greatest
assurance & tranquilitie. Wherefore hereunto, he resolved himselfe,
and with convenient expedition prepared al things necessarie for
the journey. And when the day of his departure was come, he was
brought with great honour by the citizens unto his ships, where
with a courteous farewell on ech side given, the marriners weighed
anker, hoysed sailes, and away they goe, committing themselves to
the wind and water. Thus sailed they forth along in their course,
three days and three nights with prosperous winde and weather,
untill sodainly the whole face of heaven and sea began to change;
for the skie looked blacke and the Northerne wind arose, and the
tempest increased more and more, insomuch that prince Apollonius
and the Tyrians that were with him were much apalled, and began
to doubt of their lives. But, loe, immediatly, the wide blew fiercely
from the South-west, and the North came singing on the other side,
the rain powred down over their heads, and the sea yeelded forth

---

[1] statue. II *Chor.* 14.
[2] Dionyza in *Per.*

waves as it had beene mountanes of water, that the ships could no longer wrestle with the tempest, and especially the admirall, wherein the good prince himselfe fared, but needs must they yeeld unto the present calamitie. There might you have heard the winds whistling, the raine dashing, the sea roaring, the cables cracking, the tacklings breaking, the shippe tearing, the men miserable shouting out for their lives.[1] There might you have seene the sea searching the shippe, the bordes fleeting, the goods swimming, the treasure sincking, the men shifting to save themselves, where partly through violence of the tempest, and partly through darcknes of the night which then was come upon them, they were all drowned, onely Apollonius excepted,[2] who by the grace of God, and the helpe of a simple boord, was driven upon the shoare of the Pentapolitanes. And when he had recovered to land, wearie as he was, he stoode upon the shoare, and looked upon the calme sea, saying: O most false and untrustie sea! I will choose rather to fall into the handes of the most cruell king Antiochus, than venture to returne againe by thee into mine owne Countrey: thou hast shewed thy spite upon me, and devoured my trustie friendes and companions, by meanes whereof I am nowe left alone, and it is the providence of almightie God that I have escaped thy greedie jawes. Where shall I now finde comfort? or who will succour him in a strange place that is not knowen? And whilest he spake these wordes, hee sawe a man comming towardes him, and he was a rough fisherman,[3] with an hoode upon his head, and a filthie leatherne pelt upon his backe, unseemely clad, and homely to beholde. When hee drewe neare, Apollonius, the present necessitie constraining him thereto, fell down prostrate at his feet,[4] and powring forth a floud of teares he said unto him: whosoever thou art, take pitie upon a poore sea-wracked man, cast up nowe naked, and in simple state, yet borne of no base degree, but sprung foorth of nnoble paretage.[5] And that thou maiest in helping me knowe whome thou succourest: I am that Apollonius prince of Tyrus, whome most part of the worlde knoweth, and I beseech thee to preserve my life by shewing mee thy friendly reliefe. When the fisherman beheld the comlinesse and beautie of the yoong Gentleman, hee was moved with compassion towardes him, and lifted him up from the ground, and lead him into his house and feasted him with such fare as he presently had, and the more amplie to expresse his great affection towardes him, he

---

[1] Compare the storm in *Tempest*, I.i.

[2] II *Chor.* 36.

[3] Three fishermen in *Per.* II.i.

[4] In II.1.54ff. Pericles is more dignified and does not tell his name.

[5] II.1.64.

disrobed himselfe of his poore and simple cloke,[1] and dividing it into
two parts, gave the one halfe thereof unto Apollonius, saying: Take
here at my handes, such poore entertainment and furniture as I
have, and goe into the citie, where perhappes thou shalt finde some
of better abilitie, that will rue thine estate: and if thou doe not,
returne then againe hither unto mee, and thou shalt not want what
may be perfourmed by the povertie of a poore fisherman. And in the
meane time of this one thing onelie I put thee in mind, that when
thou shalt be restored to thy former dignitie, thou doe not despise to
thinke on the basenesse of the poor peece of garment. To which
Apollonius answered: If I remember not thee and it, I wish nothing
else but that I may sustaine the like shipwracke. And when hee had
saide so, he departed on the way which was taught him, and came
unto the citie gates, whereinto he entred. And while he was thinking
with himselfe which waie to seeke succor to sustaine his life, he saw
a boy running naked through the streete, girded only with a tuell
about his middle, and his head annointed with oyle, crying aloude,
and saying: Hearken all, as well citizens as strangers and servants,
hearken: Whosoever will be washed, let him come to the place of
exercise. When Apollonius heard this, he followed the boy, and
comming unto the place cast off his cloake, and stripped himselfe,
and entred into the Baine, and bathed himselfe with the liquour.
And looking about for some companion with whome he might
exercise himself according unto the manner of the place and
countrey, and finding none: sodainelie unlooked for entred in
Altistrates King of the whole land, accompanied with a great troupe
of servitours. Anone he beganne to exercise himselfe at tennis with
his men, which when Apollonius espied, he intruded himselfe
amongst them into the kings presence, and stroke back the ball to
the king, and served him in play with great swiftnes. But when the
king perceived the great nimblenesse and cunning which was in him,
surpassing the residue: stand aside (quoth he) unto his men, for me
thinkes this yong man is more cunning than I. When Apollonius
heard himselfe commended, hee stept foorth boldly into the middes
of the tennis court, and taking up a racket in his hand, he tossed the
ball skilfully, and with wonderful agilitie.[2] After play, he also washed
the king very reverently in the Baine: and when all was done, hee
tooke his leave duetifully, & so departed. When Apollonius was gone,
the king said unto them that were about him: I sweare unto you of
truth as I am a Prince, I was never exercised nor washed better then

---

[1] II.1.81.

[2] Cf. the tennis image in II.1.61–64, but the play substitutes for this incident
the tournament, II.2.

29

this day, and that by the diligence of a yong man I know not what
he is. And turning back, Go, said he unto one of his servants, and
know what that yong man is that hath with such duty & diligence
taken pains with me. The servant going after Apollonius, and seeing
him clad in a filthy fishers cloke, returned againe to the king, saying:
If it like your grace, the yong man is a sea-wracked man. How
knowest thou that? said the king. The servant answered: Though he
told me not so himselfe, yet his apparel bewraieth his state. Then
said the king to his servant: Go apace after him, & say unto him,
that the king desireth him to sup with him this night. Then the
servant made haste after Apollonius, & did the kings message to
him, which so soone as he heard, he granted thereto, much thanking
the kinges majestie, & came back with the servant. When they were
come to the gate, the servant went in first unto the king, saying:
The sea-wracked man, for whom your grace sent me, is come but is
ashamed to come into your presence, by reason of his base aray[1]:
whome the King commaunded immediatly to be clothed in seemely
apparell, and to be brought in to supper, and placed him at the
table with him, right overagainst himselfe. Immediately the boord
was furnished with all kinde of princelie fare, the guests fed apace,
every man on that which he liked, onelie Apollonius sate still and
eate nothing, but earnestlie beholding the golde, silver, and other
kingly furniture, whereof there was great plentie, hee could not
refraine from sheading teares.[2] Then saide one of the guests that
sate at the table, unto the king: This yoong man, I suppose, envieth
at your graces prosperitie. No, not so, answered the king, you suppose amisse; but he is sorie to remember that he hath lost more
wealth then this is:[3] and looking upon Apollonius with a smiling
countenance, Be mery yong man,[4] quoth he, and eate thy meate
with us, and trust in God, who doubtlesse will send thee better
fortune.

CHAP. V

*How Lucina King Altistrates daughter[5] desirous to heare Apollonius
adventures, fel in love with him.*

Now while they sate at meate, discoursing of this and such like
matters at the boord, suddenlie came in the kings daughter and
onlie child named Lucina, a singular beautifull ladie, and a maiden
now of ripe yeeres for marriage: and she approched nigh, and kissed
the king her father, and al the guests that sate with him at the table.

---

[1] Cf. II.3.23.   [2] Cf. II.3.29.   [3] Cf. II.3.37-47.
[4] Cf. II.3.48.   [5] Thaisa and Simonides in *Per*.

And when she had so done, she returned unto her father, and saide: Good father, I pray you, what yong man is this which sitteth in so honourable a place over against you, so sorrowfull and heavie?[1] O sweete daughter, answered the king, this yong man is a sea-wracked man, and hath done me great honour to day at the baines and place of exercise, for which cause I sent for him to sup with me; but I knowe not neither what, neither whence he is. If you be desirous to know these things, demaund of him, for you may understand all things; and peradventure when you shall knowe, you will be mooved with compassion towardes him. Nowe when the lady perceived hir fathers mind, she turned about unto Apollonius, and saide: Gentleman, whose grace and comlinesse sufficiently bewraieth the nobilitie of your birth, if it be not grievous unto you, shew me your name I beseech you, and your adventures.[2] Then answered Apollonius: Madam, if you aske my name, I have lost it in the sea: if you enquire of my nobilite, I have left that at Tyrus. Sir, I beseech you then said the Lady Lucina, tel me this more plainly, that I may understand. Then Apollonius, craving licence to speake, declared his name, his birth and nobilitie, and unripped the whole tragedie of his adventures in order as is before rehearsed, and when he had made an end of speaking, he burst foorth into most plentifull teares.[3] Which when the king beheld, he saide unto Lucina: deere daughter, you have done evill in requiring to know the yong mans name, and his adventures, wherein you have renued his forepassed griefes. But since nowe you have understoode all the trueth of him, it is meete, as it becommeth the daughter of a king, you likewise extend your liberalitie towards him, and whatsoever you give him I will see it be perfourmed. Then Lucina having already in hir heart professed to doe him good, and nowe perceiving very luckily her fathers mind to be inclined to the desired purpose, she cast a friendly looke upon him, saying: Apollonius, nowe lay sorrowe aside, for my father is determined to inrich you: and Apollonius, according to the curtesie that was in him, with sighes and sobbes at remembrance of that whereof he had so lately spoken, yeelded great thankes unto the faire ladie Lucina.

Then saide the king unto his daughter: Madame I pray you take your harpe into your handes, and play us some musike to refresh our guests withall, for we have all too long hearkened unto sorrowfull matters[4]: and when she had called for her harpe, she beganne to play so sweetely, that all that were in companie highly commended her, saying that in all their lives they never heard pleasanter

---

[1] Cf. II.3.53–65.
[2] II.3.73–4.
[3] II.3.81–85.
[4] *Per.* has dancing here.

harmonie. Thus whilest the guests, every man for his part much commended the ladies cunning, onely Apollonius spake nothing. Then saide the king unto him: You are too blame Apollonius, since all praise my daughter for her excellencie in musike, and you commend not her, or rather dispraise her by holding your peace. Apollonius answered: My soveraigne and good lord, might it please you to pardon me, & I will say what I think: The lady Lucina your daughter is pretily entred, but she is not yet come to perfection in musike. For proofe whereof, if it please your Grace to command the harp to be delivered unto me, she shal well perceive, that she shal heare that which she doth not yet know. The king answered: I see well Apollonius you have skill in all things, and is nothing to be wished in a gentleman, but you have perfectly learned it, wherfore, hold, I pray you take the harpe, and let us heare some part of your cunning. When Apollonius had received the harp, he went forth, and put a garland of flowers upon his head, and fastned his raiment in comly maner about him, and entred into the parlour againe, playing before the king, and the residue with such cunning and sweetnes, that he seemed rather to be Apollo then Apollonius, and the kings guests confessed that in al their lives they never heard the like before.[1] But when Lucina had heard and seene what was done, she felt hir selfe sodainely mooved within, and was sharpelie surprised with the love of Apollonius, and, turning to her father: Nowe suffer me good father, saide she, to give unto this yoong gentleman some reward, according as I shall think convenient. I give you leave to do so faire daughter, saide the king. Then she looking towards Apollonius, My lord Apollonius, said she, receive heere of my fathers liberalitie two hundred talents of gold, foure hundred poundes of silver, store of raiment, twentie men servants, and tenne handmaidens. Nowe therefore, said she unto the officers that stood by, bring hither all these things which I have here promised, and lay them downe in the parlour, in the presence of our friends. And immediatly they were all brought into their sight as she had commanded. When this was done, the guests arose from the table, and giving thankes unto the king and ladie Lucina, tooke their leave and departed. And Apollonius, thinking it likewise time for him to be gone: Most gratious king Altistrates (quoth he) thou which art a comforter of such as are in miserie; and thou also renowmed princesse, a favourer of philosophie, and lover of all good studies, I bid you now most heartily farewell: as for your great deserts toward me, I leave them to God to requite you with deserved recompence: and looking unto his servants which the ladie Lucina

---

[1] II.5.25–28 suggest that Pericles played. Compare Wilkins, Ch. vi.

had given him, Sirs, take up this geere, quoth hee, which is given me, and bring it away, and let us go seeke some lodgings.

When Lucina heard those words she was sodainlie stroken into a dump, fearing that she shoulde have lost her newe lover, before she had ever reaped anie fruit of his companie, and therefore turning to her father, said: I beseech you good father and gratious king, forasmuch as it has pleased you this day to inrich Apollonius with many great gifts, you would not suffer him now to depart so late, lest he be by some naughtie persons spoiled of the things which you have given him. The king willingly granted the ladies request, and commanded forthwith that there should be a faire lodging prepared for him and his, where he might lie honourably, and when he sawe convenient time he went to bed, and tooke his rest.

CHAP. VI

How Apollonius is made Schoolemaster to Lucina, and how she preferreth
the love of him, above all the nobilitie of Pentapolis.

When night was come, and every one was at rest, Lucina laie unquietly tumbling in her bed, alwaies thinking upon Apollonius, and could not sleep. Wherefore, in the morning she rose very early, & came in to the king her fathers chamber. Whom when her father saw, what is the matter, daughter Lucina, (quoth he) that contrary to custome you be stirring so earelie this morning? Deere father, quoth Lucina, I could take no rest al this night, for the desire I have to learn musicke of Apollonius; and therefore I pray you good father, to put me unto him to be instructed in the Art of Musicke, and other good qualities, wherein hee is skilfull.[1] When Altistrates hearde his daughters talke, he smiled within himselfe, when hee perceived the warmed affection kindled within her breast, which with so seemely a pretence she had covered, as the desire to learne, and determined in part presently to satisfie her request: and when time served, he sent a messenger for Apollonius. And when he was come, he said unto him: Apollonius my daughter much desireth to be your scholler, and therefore I pray you take her to your governement, and instruct her the best you can, and I will reward you to your contentation. Apollonius answered, gracious prince, I am moste willing to obey your commaundement. So hee tooke the ladie, and instructed her in the best maner he coulde, even as himselfe had learned: wherein she profited so well, that in short time she matched, or rather surpassed her maister. Thus increased shee not onely in learning, but grew also daily in more fervent love of

[1] Cf. II.5.30–40.

Apolonius, as, whether standing in doubt of her fathers resolute good wil if he were moved concerning marriage, or fearing the time woulde be deferred in respect whereof she was presently ready, in so much that she fell sicke and became weaker everie day than other.[1] When the king perceived his daughters infirmitie to increase, hee sent immediatlie throughout all the dominions for the learnedst phisitions to search out her griefe and to cure it, who examining her urine, and feeling her pulse, coulde finde out no manifest cause or substance of her disease. After a few dayes that this happened, three noble yong men of the same countrey, which had been suters a long time unto Lucina for marriage, came unto the Court, and being brought into the kinges presence, saluted him dutifully. To whom the king said, Gentlemen, what is the cause of your comming? They answered, your Grace hath oftentimes promised to bestow your daughter in marriage upon one of us, and this is the cause of our comming at this time. Wee are your subjectes, wealthie, and descended of noble families, might it therefore please your Grace to choose one among us three, to be your sonne in law. Then answered the king, you are come unto me at an unseasonable time, for my daughter now applieth her studie, and lieth sicke for the desire of learning, and the time is much unmeet for marriage.[2] But to the intent you shall not altogether loose your labour, nor that I will not seeme to deferre you too long, write your names every one severally in a peece of paper, and what joynter you will make, and I will send the writinges to my daughter, that she may choose him whom she best liketh of.[3] They did forthwith as the king had counselled them, and delivered the writings unto the king, which hee read, and signed them, and delivered them unto Apollonius, saying: Take here these billes, and deliver them to your scholler, which Apollonius received, and tooke them immediatly unto the ladie Lucina. Now when she sawe her schoolemaister whom she loved so entirely, she said unto him: Maister, what is the cause that you come alone into my chamber? Apollonius answered: Madame, I have brought writings from the king your father, which he willeth you to reade. Lucina then received the writinges, and brake them up, and when she had reade the names of the three noblemen her suters, shee threw away the billes, and looking upon Apollonius, said unto him: My welbeloved Schoolemaister Apollonius, doth it not greeve you that I shall be married unto another? Apollonius answered, No madame it greeveth not me, for whatsoever shall be for your

---

[1] Not in the play.
[2] Compare the reason in II.5.1–12.
[3] Not in *Per.*

honour, shall be unto me profitable. Then said Lucina, Maister, if
you loved me you woulde be sorie, and therewithall she called for
inke and paper, and wrote an answere unto her father in forme
following: Gracious king and deare father, forasmuch as of your
goodnesse you have given me free choice, and libertie to write my
minde: these are to let you understand, that I would marry with the
Sea-wrecked man, and with none other: your humble daughter,
Lucina.[1] And when she had sealed it, she delivered it unto Apollonius to be carried unto the king. When the king had received the
letters, he perused them, wherein he perceived his daughters minde,
not knowing whom she meant by the sea-wrecked man: and therefore turning himselfe towardes the three Noblemen, hee demaunded
of them which of them had suffered shipwracke? Then one of them
named Ardonius, answered, If it like your Grace, I have suffred
shipwrack. The other twaine named Munditius, and Carnillus,
when they hearde him say so, waxed wroth, and fel into termes of
outrage against him, saying: sicknesse, and the fiends of hell consume thee, for thy foule & impudent lie: doe not we, who are thy
equals both of birth and age, know right well that thou never wentest
almost out of this citie gates? And how couldest thou then suffer
shipwracke? Nowe when the king Altistrates could not finde out
which of them had suffered shipwrack, he looked towards Apollonius, saying: Take these letters and read them, for it may be that I
doe not knowe him whom thou knowest, who was present. Apollonius
receiving the letters, perused them quickly, and perceiving himselfe
to be loved, blushed wonderfully. Then said the king to Apollonius,
hast thou found the sea-wrecked man? But Apollonius answered
litle or nothing, wherein his wisedome the rather appeared according
to the saying of the wise man: *In many words there wanteth discretion*;
where as contrariwise, many an undiscreet person might be
accounted wise if hee had but this one point of wisdom, to hold his
tongue.[2] Wherin indeed consisteth the whole triall or rather insight
of a man, as signified the most wise Philosopher Socrates.

CHAP. VII

*How Apollonius was married to the ladie Lucina, and hearing of king
Antiochus death, departeth with his wife towards his owne country of Tyrus.*

But to returne againe to my storie from which I have digressed:
when king Altistrates perceived that Apollonius was the man whom
his daughter Lucina disposed in her heart to preferre in love before

[1] Cf. II.5.15–17.
[2] Cf. Pericles' doubts, II.5.42–48.

anie of the other three noble men, hee found meanes to put them off
for that present, saying that he would talke with them farther concerning that matter another time: who taking their leave, immediatly departed, but the king withdrew himself into the chamber
where his daughter lay sicke, and sayd unto her: whom have you
chosen to be your husband?[1] To whom Lucina humbling her selfe,
and with trickling teares, answered: Gratious Prince and deare
father, I have chosen in my heart the Sea-wrecked man, my schoolemaister Apollonius, for whom I most duetifully desire your fatherly
goodwil: when the king saw her teares, his heart bled inwardly with
compassion toward his childe whom hee loved tenderly, and he
kissed her, and saide unto her: My sweete Lucina be of good cheere,
and take not thought for anie thing, and assure thy selfe thou hast
chosen the man that I liked of assoone as I first sawe him: whom I
love no lesse than thee: that is to say, than if hee were my naturall
childe. And therefore since the matter is nowe thus fallen out, I
meane forthwith to appoint a day for your marriage, after that I
have broken the matter unto Apollonius. And when he had said that,
Lucina with blushing cheekes thanked her Father much, and he
departed. Nowe would I demand of lovers, whether Lucina rejoyced
or not? or whether there were anie better tidings in the worlde
coulde chance to a man or woman? I am sure they would answer no.
For such is the nature of this affection, that it preferreth the beloved
person above all earthly thinges, yea and heavenly too, unlesse
it be brideled with reason: as the same likewise though moderately,
and within the boundes of modest womanhoode, working the
woonted effect in the ladie Lucina, revived her so presently, that
shee forsooke her bed, and cast away her mourning apparrell, and
appeared as it had been a newe woman restored from death to life,
and that almost in a moment. The king being alone in the parlour
called for Apollonius, and when he was come, he said thus unto
him: Apollonius, the vertue which I have seene in thee, I have
testified by my liberalitie towards thee, and thy trustinesse is
prooved by committing mine onelie childe and daughter to thine
instruction. As these have caused mee to preferre thee, so have they
made my daughter to love thee, so that I am as well contented with
the one as I am well pleased with the other. And for thy part,
likewise I hope Apollonius, that as thou hast been glad to be my
client, thou wilt rejoyce as much to be my sonne in law. Tell me thy
minde out of hand, for I attend thine answere. Then Apollonius
much abashed at the kinges talke, falling downe upon his knees,
answered: Most gratious soveraigne, your wordes sound so strangely

---

[1] Cf. the King's pretended anger, II.5.49–83.

in mine eares, that I scarsly know how to give answer, & your
goodnesse hath been so great towardes me, that I can wish for no
more. But since it is your Graces pleasure that I should not be
indebted to many, but owe all thing unto you, as life, and wife,
honour, and goods, and all: you shall not find me unthankful,
howsoever God or fickle fortune deale with me, to remaine both
loyall and constant to you, and your daughter, whom above all
creatures, both for birth and beauty and good qualities, I love and
honour most intirely. Altistrates rejoiced much to heare so wise and
conformable an answere, and embracing Apollonius, called him
by the name of deare beloved sonne. The next day morning the
king addressed his messengers & purseuants, to assemble the
nobliest of his subjects and frends out of the confederat cities, and
countries, and to shew them that he had certaine affaires to com-
municat unto them: and when they were come altogither unto
Pentapolis, after due greeting, and accustomable intertainment
shewed as in the maner of great estates, he said thus unto them.
My loving friends, and faithfull subjects, my meaning was to let you
understand, that my daughter is desirous to marrie with her
schoolemaster Apollonius, and I am wel pleased therwith. Wherfore,
I beseech you all to rejoyce thereat, and be glad for my daughter
shalbe matched to a wise man. And know you moreover, that I
appoint this day six weekes for the solemnization day of the marriage,
at what time I desire you all to be here present, that like friends we
may rejoyce, and make merry togither: and when he had all said,
he dismissed the assembly. Now as the time wore away, so the
wedding day drue neere, and there was great preparation made
aswell for the feast, as for jewels, and rich clothes to furnish the
bridegroome, and bride withall, as althing els that appertaine to
the beautifying of so great a wedding. And when the day was come,
the king apparrelled in his princely robes with a diadem of great
price upon his head, accompanied his daughter Lucina and
Apollonius unto the Church, whom thousands of lordes and ladies
followed after, all cloathed in rich attire, and marshalled in comely
order. The bride woare on a gowne of cloth of gold cut, & drawen
out with cloth of silver, and a kirtle of crimsin velvet imbrodered
with pure golde, and thickly beset with oriental pearles. Her haire
hung downe in tresses fairely broided with a lace of gold, and a
Coronet upon her head set with pretious stones of inestimable value.
Her necke was bare, whereby her naked skinne appeared whiter
than the driven snowe, curiously bedecked with chaines of golde, and
every other lincke enameled with blacke amell. Great baudrickes
of perfect goldsmithes worke upon eche arme to fasten the sleeves

of her garment from sliding up at the wreast. Lastly, a massie collar of fine golde, made esse wise uppon her shoulders, hanging downe behinde and before, with a Diamond reaching downe unto her middle, esteemed in value at three-score thousand pound, which the king her father had sent unto her for a present, that morning while she was apparrelling. The bridegrome wore on a dublet and hosen of costly cloth of silver, garded with Goldsmithes worke of the same colour, and a gowne of purple Satten, embroidred with golde, and beset with rich stones. His cap was of fine blacke Velvet, all over bespangled with Rubies, set in gold and fastned on by loopes: the band of massie golde, beset with courses of stones in order, first a Rubie, then a Turkeis, then a Diamond, and so beginning againe with a Rubie. This was their raiment, and thus went they forth togither hand in hand, after whom, as is already declared, the lordes and ladies followed by three and three in a ranke. When the solemnities were done at the Church, and the wordes spoken, and the Princes joyned in marriage, they returned home and went to dinner. What shall I nowe speake of the noble cheare and Princely provision for this feast?[1] And after dinner of the exquisite Musicke, fine dauncing, heavenly singing, sweete devising, and pleasant communication among the estates? I may not discourse at large of the liberall challenges made and proclaimed at the tilt, barriers, running at the ring, *joco di can*,[2] managing fierce horses, running a foote and daunsing in armour: And at night of the gorgeous plaies, shewes, disguised speeches, masks and mummeries, with continuall harmony of all kindes of musicke, and banqueting in all delicacie: All these things I leave to the consideration of them which have seene the like in the Courts, and at the weddinges of Princes, where they have seene more than my simple pen is able to describe, or may be comprehended within the recital of so short an historie. When night was come, and revels were ended, the bride was brought to bed, and Apollonius tarried not long from her, where hee accomplished the duties of marriage, and faire Lucina conceived childe the same night.[3] The next daie, every man arose to feasting and jollitie, for the wedding triumphes continued an whole moneth. This while Lucinas bellie began to grow, and as it fortuned that the lord Apollonius and his ladie on a day walked along the sea side for their disporte, hee sawe a faire shippe fleeting under saile, which hee knew well to be of his countrey, and he hallowed unto the maister, whose name was Calamitus and asked of him of whence

[1] III *Chor.*, 4.
[2] jousting with canes.
[3] III *Chor.*, 11.

his ship was?[1] The maister answered, Of Tyrus. Thou hast named my country said Apollonius: Art thou then of Tyrus, said the maister? Yea, answered Apollonius. Then said the maister, knowest thou one Apollonius prince of that countrey? If thou doe, or shalt heare of him hereafter, bid him now be glad and rejoyce, for king Antiochus and his daughter are strooken dead with lightning from heaven. And the Citie of Antiochia with all the riches, and the whole kingdome are reserved for Apollonius.

With these words the ship being under saile, departed, & Apollonius being filled with gladnes, immediatly began to breake with his ladie to give him leave to go and receive his kingdom. But when faire Lucina heard him beginne to moove words of departing, she burst out into teares, saying: My Lorde, if you were nowe in some farre countrie, and heard say that I were neere my time to be delivered, you ought to make haste home unto me. But since you be nowe with me, and know in what case I am me thinks you should not now desire to depart from me. Howbeit, if your pleasure be so, and tarriance breede danger, and kingdomes want not heirs long, as I would not perswade you to tarry, so doe I request you to take me with you. This discreete answere pleased Apollonius well; wherefore he kissed his lady, and they agreed it should be so.[2] And when they were returned from walking, Lucina rejoycing, came unto the king her father, saying: Deare father, rejoice I beseech you, and be glad with my lord Apollonius and me, for the most cruell tyrant Antiochus and his daughter are by the just judgement of God destroied with lightning from heaven; and the kingdome and riches are reserved for us to inherite: Moreover, I pray you good father, let me have your goodwil to travel thither with my husband. The king rejoyced much at this tidings, and graunted her reasonable request, and also commaunded all things to be provided immediatly that were necessary for the journey. The shippes were strongly appointed and brought unto the shoare, and fraught with al things convenient, as golde, silver, apparell, bedding, vittels and armour. Moreover, whatsoever fortune might befal, the king prepared to sail with them Ligozides[3] the nurse, and a midwife, and all things meet for the childe whensoever Lucina shoulde neede them: and with great honour himselfe accompanieth them unto the sea side, when the time appointed for their departure was come; where with many teares, and great fatherly affection hee kissed his daughter, and embraced his sonne in law, and recommended them unto God, in

---

[1] Cf. the Messenger in III *Chor.*, Dumbshow and 21–32.

[2] III *Chor.*, 40–41.

[3] Lychorida in *Per.*

whom hee did wish unto them a most prosperous journey, and so returned unto his pallace.

CHAP. VIII

How faire Lucina died in travell of child upon the sea; and being throwen into the water, was cast on land at Ephesus, and taken home by Cerimon a Phisition.

The marriners immediatly merrily hoissed saile and departed; & when they had sailed two dayes, the master of the shippe warned Apollonius of a tempest approching, which nowe came on, and increased so fast, that all the companie was amazed, and Lucina, what with sea-sicknes & feare of danger, fel in labor of child, wherewith she was weakened, that there was no hope of recoverie, but she must now die: yet being first delivered of a faire daughter, insomuch that now all tokens of life were gone, and she appeared none other but to be dead. When Apollonius beheld this heavie spectacle, no heart was able to conceive his bitter grief, for like a mad man distracted he tore his cloths, and rent his haire, and laying himself upon the carkas, he uttered these wordes with great affection: O my deare lady and wife, the daughter of king Altistrates, what shall I now answer to thy father for thee? would God thou haddest remained with him at home, & if it had pleased God to have wrought this his pleasure in thee, it had rather chanced with thy loving father in his quiet land, than with me thy woful husband upon the wild seas. The whole company also made great lamentation for her, bewailing the death of so noble and beautifull a ladie, and so curteous a gentlewoman. Howbeit in the hotest of the sorrowe the governour of the ship came unto Apollonius, saying, My lord, plucke up your heart, and be of goode cheere, and consider I pray you that the ship may not abide to carie the dead carkas, and therefore command it to be cast into the sea, that we may the better escape.[1] Then answered Apollonius: What saiest thou varlet? wouldest thou have me cast this bodie into the sea, which received me into house and favour, when I was in miserie and drenched in the water, wherein I lost ship, goods & all? But taking further consultation, and advising himselfe what were best to do, he called certaine of his men unto him, & thus he devised with them. My trusty servants, whome this common mischance grieveth as wel as me, since sorowing wil not help that which is chanced, assist me, good sirs, to provide for the present necessity. Let us make forthwith a large chest, and bore the lid full of small holes, and we will seare

[1] III.1.38–55.

it all over within with pitch and rosen molten together, whereinto
we will put cunningly a sheete of lead, and in the same we will
inclose the tender corps of the wife of me, of all other a most unfortunate husband.[1] This was no sooner said, but it was almost
likewise done with sembable celer[i]tie. Then tooke they the body of
the faire lady Lucina, and arraied her in princely apparel, and layd
her into the chest, and Apollonius placed a great summe of golde at
her head, and a great treasure of silver at her feet, & he kissed her,
letting fall a flood of salt teares on hir face, and he wrote a bill, and
put in it also, the tenor whereof was in forme as foloweth: *Whosever
shal find this chest, I pray him to take ten pieces of gold for his paines, and to
bestowe tenne pieces more upon the buriall of the corpes; for it hath left
many teares to the parents and friends, with dolefull heaps of sorow and
heavines. But whosoever shall doe otherwise than the present griefe requireth,
let him die a shamefull death, and let there be none to bury his body.*[2] And
then closing all up verie safe, commaunded the chest to be lifted
overboorde into the sea: and willed the child to be nursed with all
diligence, that if ever fortune should so fall, he might present unto
good king Altistrates a neece[3] in steede of a daughter.

Now fleeted away the ship fast with the wind, and the coffin
tumbled backeward with the tide, and Apollonius could not keep
his eie from the bodie whereon his heart rested, until kenning failed,
and the sea rose up with a banke between. There were two days
passed, and the night was now at hand, when the next day morning
the waves rolled foorth this chest to the land, and cast it ashore on
the coast of Ephesus. Not farre from that place there dwelt a
physition[4] whose name was Cerimon, who by chaunce walking
abroad upon the shore that day with his schollers, found the chest
which the sea had cast up, & willed his servants to take it up, &
diligently to cary it to the next towne, where hee dwelt, and they
did so.[5] When Cerimon came home he opened the chest, marveling
what shuld be therein, and found a lady arrayed in princely apparell
and ornaments, very faire and beautifull to beholde.[6] Whose
excellencie in that respect as many as beheld, were strangely affectioned thereat, perceiving such an incomparable gleame of beautie
to be resident in her face, wherein nature had not committed the
least errour that might be devised, saving that shee made her not
immortall. The haire of her head was naturally as white as snowe,
under which appeared her goodly forehead, faire and large, wherein
was neither blemish nor wrinkle. Her eies were like two starres

---

[1] III.2.65–72.
[2] Cf. verse in III.2.65–75.
[3] grand-daughter.
[4] A 'lord' in *Per.* III.2 and Wilkins.
[5] Altered in *Per.* III.2.
[6] III.2.60–66.

turning about in their naturall course, not wantonly roving here and there, but modestly mooving as governed by reason, representing the stabilitie of a setled mind. Her eie brows decently commending the residue of her countenance. Her nose straight, as in were drawn with a line, comely dividing her cherry cheeks asunder, not reaching foorth too long, nor cut off too short, but of a commendable proportion. Hir necke was like the white alabaster shining like the bright sunne beames, woonderfully delighting the mindes of the beholders. Her bodie of comely stature, neither too high nor too lowe, not scregged with leanenesse, nor undecently corpulent, but in such equality consisting, that no man woulde wish it otherwise. From her shoulders sprang foorth her armes, representing two branches growing out of a tree, beautified with a white hand, and fingers long and slender, surpassing to behold. To be short, such was the excellencie of her beutie in each respect, that it could suffer no deformitie to accompany it, whereby also may be discerned a singular perfection of her minde, created by God and infused into her bodie, whereby it was mooved, and those good qualities of hers expressed in operation: so that all outward beautie of the bodie proceedeth from the inward beuty of the minde, from whence sprang up the olde and true saying of the wisest Philosophers, that the sundry nature of the forme or soule, diversely disposeth the matter according unto it owne qualitie: as it expresly appeared in the beutiful countenaunce and stature of this Ladies bodie, whereof Cerimon stoode amazedly taking the view.

CHAP. IX

How Lucina was restored to life by one of Cerimon the Phisitions schollers; and howe Cerimon adopted her to his daughter, and placed her in the temple of Diana.

The surpassing beauty of faire Lucina, being such as is before recited, no woonder it was though Cerimon were marvellously ravished at the sight, whereby his affection inforced him to breake out into these words: Alas good beautiful gentlewoman, what unhappy and cruell chance hath thus made thee away, and caused thee to be so wofully forsaken? And as he spake those wordes, hee perceived the golde that lay at her head, and the silver that lay at her feet, with a scroll of paper written, the which hee tooke up and read, the tenor whereof was this: *Whosoever shal finde this chest, I pray him for to take tenne pieces of golde for his paines, and to bestowe tenne peeces more on the buriall of the corps; for it hath left many teares to the parents and friends, with dolefull heapes of sorrowe and heavinesse. But whosoever shall doe otherwise than the present griefe requireth, let him die a shamefull death, and let there bee none to burie his bodie.* And as soone as he had read over the writing, he said unto his servants: now let us perfourme unto the bodie that which the sorrowe requireth; and I sweare to you, by the hope which I have to live, that I will bestow more money upon the accomplishing of the same, than the sorrowful scedul requireth. Wherfore, according to the maner of the buriall which was at that time to burn the bodies of the dead, and to burie the ashes, gathered up and put into pottes, he commaunded a pile of wood to be erected, and upon the top thereof he caused the body to be layed.[1]

Nowe Cerimon had a scholler in Physicke, whose name was Machaon, very towardly in his profession, of yeres but yong, but antient in wit and experience, who comming in while these things were doing, and beholding so beautifull a corps layd upon the pile, hee stoode still and wondered at it. Which thing Cerimon perceiving: Thou art come in good time saide hee to Machaon, and I looked for thee about this time. Take this flagon of precious ointment, and powre it uppon the corps, being the last ceremonie of the sepulture. Then came Machaon unto the corps, and pulled the clothes from the ladies bosome, and powred foorth the ointment, and bestowing it abroad with his hand, perceived some warmth in her breast, and that there was life in the body. Machaon stoode astonished, and hee felt her pulses, and layde his cheeke to her mouth, and examined all other tokens that he could devise, and he perceived how death strived with life within her, and that the conflict was daungerous and doubtfull, who should prevaile. Then saide he unto the servants: set fire unto the wood at the foure corners of the pile, and cause it to burne moderatly, and bring me hither a bed that I may take the body out of the chest, and lay it thereon.

This being done, he chafed the body against the fire, untill the blood which was congealed with colde, was wholly resolved. Then went Machaon unto his master Cerimon and saide: The woman whome thou thinkest to be dead, is alive, and that you may the better beleeve my saying, I will plainely proove it to be so. And when he had so saide, he tooke the body reverently in his armes, and bare it into his owne chamber, and layed it upon his bed groveling upon the breast. Then tooke he certaine hote and comfortable oyles, and warming them upon the coales, he dipped faire wooll therein,[2] and fomented all the bodie over therewith, until such time as the congealed blood and humours were throughly resolved, and the

---

[1] Cerimon in *Per.* thinks at once she may be alive (III.2.79–86) and does all the reviving.

[2] III.2.87 'the fire and cloths'.

spirits eftsoones recovered their wonted course, the veines waxed warme, the arteries beganne to beate, and the lungs drew in the fresh ayre againe, and she opened her eies and looked about, and being perfectly come to herselfe, What art thou, said shee unto Machaon? see thou touch me not otherwise than thou oughtest to do, for I am a Kings daughter, and the wife of a King. When Machaon heard her speak these words, he was exceeding glad, and he ran unto his master and saide: Sir, the woman liveth, and speaketh perfectly. Then answered Cerimon: My welbeloved schollar Machaon, I am glad of this fortunate chaunce, and I much commende thy wisedome, and praise thy learning, and cannot but extoll thy diligence. Wherefore be not unthankfull to thy knowledge, but receive here the reward which is due unto thee, namely, that which by the writing was appointed to be bestowed uppon her buriall: for thou hast restored her unto life, and shee hath brought with her great summes of mony. When he had so saide, they came unto her and saluted her, and caused her to be apparelled with wholsome and comfortable clothes, & to be refreshed with good meats. A few daies after, when she had fully recovered strength, and Cerimon by communication knew that she came of the stocke of a king, he sent for many of his friends to come unto him, and he adopted her for his owne daughter: and she with many tears requiring that she might not be touched by any man, for that intent her placed in the temple of Diana, which was there at Ephesus, to be preserved there inviolably among the religious women.[1]

CHAP. X

How Apollonius arriving at Tharsus, delivereth his yong daughter Tharsia unto Stranguilio and Dionisiades to be brought up; and how the nurce lying in her death-bed declareth unto Tharsia who were her parents.

Let us leave now a while the lady Lucina among the holy Nunnes in the temple of Diana at Ephesus, and let us looke backe unto sorrowful Apollonius, whose ship with fortunate winde, and the good providence of God directing the same, arrived at the shoare of Tharsus,[2] where hee immediatly came forth of the ship, and entred into the house of Stranguilio and Dionisiades, whom he saluted, and told them the heavy chances that had befallen him, both of the great stormes and tempests on the sea, which hee had indured, as also of the death of the good lady Lucina his wife: howbeit said he, God be thanked, my daughter remaineth alive, for the which I am very glad: wherfore, deare friends Stranguilio and Dionisiades,

[1] III.4.   [2] III.3

according to the trust which I have in you, I mean in some things to use your friendship, while I go about to recover the kingdome which is reserved for me. For I will not returne backe againe unto king Altistrates my father-in-law, whose daugher alas, I have lost in the sea, but meaning rather to exercise the trade of merchandize, I commit my daughter unto you, to bee nourished and brought up with your yoong daughter Philomacia, and I will that my daughter be called Tharsia.[1] Moreover I wil leave my deare wife Lucinas nurce here also, called Ligozides,[2] to tend the child, that she may be lesse troublesome unto you. And when hee had made an end of talking, he delivered the infant and the nurce unto Stranguilio, and therewithal great store of gold, silver, and raiment; and hee sware a solemne othe, that he would not poule his head, clip his beard, nor pare his nailes, untill hee had married his daughter at ripe yeares.[3] They wondred much at so strange an othe, promising faithfully to bring up his daugher with all diligence. When these things were ended according to his mind, Apollonius tooke his leave, departed unto his ship, and sailed into far countries, and unto the uppermost parts of Egypt. Therewhile the yoong maiden, Tharsia sprang up in yeeres, and when she was about five yeares olde, being free borne she was set to schoole with other free children, alwaies jointly accompanied with Philomacia,[4] being of the same age that she was of. The time passed forth a pace, & Tharsia grew up so wel in learning as in yeers until comming to the age of fourteene yeeres, one day when she returned from schoole, she found Ligozides her nurce sodainly falne sicke, and sitting beside her upon the bed, demanded of her the cause, and maner of her sickenesse. Then said the nurce unto her, hearken unto my wordes deare daughter Tharsia, and lay them up in thine heart. Whom thinkest thou to be thy father, and thy mother, and in what countrey supposest thou wast thou borne? Tharsia answered, why, nurce, why aske you me this question? Stranguilio is my father, Dionisiades my mother, and I was borne in Tharsus. Then sighed the nurce, and saide: No, sweete Tharsia, no, thou art deceived. But hearken unto me, and I will declare unto thee the beginning of thy birth, to the intent thou mayst know how to guide thy selfe after my death. Apollonius the prince of Tyrus is thy father, and Lucina king Altistrates daughter was thy mother, who being in travell with thee, died after thou wast borne, and thy father, Appollonius, inclosed her bodie in a chest with princely ornaments, laying twenty talents of gold at her head, and as much at her feete in silver, with a scedule written, and

---

[1] Marina in III.3.12–13.
[2] Lychorida in *Per.*
[3] III.3.27–30.
[4] Philoten in *Per.*

threw the chest overboord into the sea, that whether soever it were driven, it might suffice to burie her, according to her estate. Thus wast thou born upon the Sea; and thy fathers ship with much wrestling of contrarie windes, and with his unspeakeable griefe of minde arrived at this shoare, and brought thee in thy swading clothes unto this citie, where hee with great care delivered thee unto this thine hoste Stranguilio and Dionisiades his wife to be fostered up diligently, and left me heere also to attend upon thee. Moreover he sware an othe, that he would not poule his head, clip his beard, nor pare his nayles, untill he had married thee unto some man at ripe yeares. Wherefore now I admonishe thee, that if after my death thine hoste or thine hostesse, whom thou callest thy parents, shall haply offer thee any injurie, then runne thou into the market place, where thou shalt find the stature of thy father standing; and take hold of it, and cry aloud saying: O Citizens of Tharsus, I am his daughter, whose image this is: and the citizens being mindfull of thy fathers benefites, will doubtlesse revenge thine injurie. Then answered Tharsia: Deare nurce Ligozides, I take God to witnesse, if you had not told me thus much, I should utterly have been ignorant from whence I had come. And therefore now, good nurce, I thank thee with all my heart, and if ever need so require, thy counsel shal be followed: and while they were debating these matters betweene them, Ligozides being verie sicke and weake, gave up the ghost, and by the death of this present bodie, passed into the state of live everlasting.[1]

CHAP. XI

How after the death of Ligozides the nurce, Dionisiades envying at the beautie of Tharsia, conspired her death, which should have been accomplished by a villaine of the countrey.

Tharsia much lamented the death of Ligozides her nurce, and caused her bodie to be solemnly buried not farre of, in a field without the walles of the citie, and mourned for her an whole yeere following. But when the yeare was expired, she put off her mourning atire, and put on her other apparel, and frequented the schooles, and the studie of liberall Sciences as before. And whensoever she returned from schoole, she would receive no meate before she had visited her nurces sepulchre, which she did daily, entring thereinto, and carrying a flagon of wine with her, where she used to abide a space, and to call uppon her father and mother.[2] Now on a day it fortuned,

[1] IV *Chor.*, 41–42.
[2] IV.1.10–11.

that as she passed through the street with Dionisiades, and her companion Philomacia, the people beholding the beautie and comlinesse of Tharsia, said: Happy is that father that hath Tharsia to his daughter, but her companion that goeth with her, is foule and evill favoured.[1] When Dionisiades heard Tharsia commended, and her owne daughter Philomacia so dispraised, shee returned home wonderfull wroth, and withdrawing her self into a solitary place, began thus secretly to discourse of the matter. It is now fourteen years since Apollonius this foolish girles father departed from hence, and he never sendeth letters for her, nor any remembrance unto her, whereby I conjecture that he is dead. Ligozides her nurce is departed, and there is no bodie now of whom I should stande in feare, and therefore I will now slay her, and dresse up mine owne daughter in her apparell and jewels. When shee had thus resolved her selfe uppon this wicked purpose, in the meane while there came home one of their countrey villaines called Theophilus,[2] whom shee called, and said thus unto him: Theophilus, my trustie friend, if ever thou looke for libertie, or that I shoulde doe thee pleasure, doe so much for me as to slay Tharsia. Then said Theophilus: Alas mistresse, wherein hath that innocent maiden offended, that she should be slaine?[3] Dionisiades answered, Shee innocent! nay she is a wicked wretch, and therefore thou shalt not denie to fulfill my request, but doe as I commaund thee, or els I sweare by God thou shalt dearely repent it. But how shall I best doe it, Mistres, said the villaine? Shee aunswered: shee hath a custome, as soone as shee returneth home from Schoole, not to eate meat before that she have gone into her Nurces sepulchre, where I would have thee stand readie, with a dagger drawn in thine hand; and when she is come in, gripe her by the haire of the head, and so slay her: then take her bodie and cast it into the Sea, and when thou hast so done, I will make thee free, and besides reward thee liberally. Then tooke the villaine a dagger, and girded himselfe therewith, and with an heavy heart and weeping eies went forth towards the grave, saying within himselfe, Alas poore wretch that I am, alas poore Theophilus that canst not deserve thy libertie but by shedding of innocent bloud: and with that hee went into the grave and drue his dagger, and made him readie for the deede. Tharsia was now come from schoole, and made haste unto the grave with a flagon of wine as shee was wont to doe, and entred within the vau[l]t. Then the villaine rushed violently upon her, and caught her by the haire of the head, and threw her to the

---

[1] Cf. IV *Chor.*, 11–40.
[2] Leonine in *Per.*, which omits this scene of incitement.
[3] IV.1.9.

ground.[1] And while he was now readie to stab her with the dagger, poore silly Tharsia all amazed casting her eies upon him, knew the villain, and holding up her handes, said thus unto him: O, Theophilus against whom have I so greevously offended, that I must die therefore? The villaine answered, Thou hast not offended, but thy father hath, which left thee behind him in Stranguilios house with so great a treasure in mony, and princely ornaments. O, said the mayden, would to God he had not done so: but I pray thee Theophilus, since there is no hope for me to escape with life, give mee licence to say my praiers before I die. I give thee licence said the villaine, and I take God to record that I am constrained to murther thee against my will.

CHAP. XII

How certaine Pyrats rescued Tharsia when she should have been slaine, and carried her unto the citie Machilenta to be sold among other bondslaves.

As fortune, or rather the providence of God served, while Tharsia was devoutly making her praiers, certaine pyrats which were come aland, and stood under the side of an hill watching for some prey, beholding an armed man offering violence unto a mayden, cried unto him, and said: Thou cruel tyrant, that maiden is our prey and not thy victorie; and therfore hold thine hands from her, as thou lovest thy life.[2] When the villain heard that, he ran away as fast as he could, and hid himselfe behind the sepulchre. Then came the Pyrats and rescued Tharsia, and caried her away to their ships, and hoysed saile, and departed. And the villaine returned home to his mistres,[3] and saide unto her: that which you commaunded me to doe is dispatched, and therefore now I thinke it good that you put on a mourning garment, and I also, and let us counterfeit great sorrowe and heavinesse in the sight of all the people, and say that shee died of some greevous disease.[4] But Stranguilio himselfe consented not to this treason, but so soone as hee heard of the foule mischaunce, beeing as it were a mopte, and mated[5] with heavinesse and griefe, he clad himselfe in mourning aray, and lamented that wofull case, saying: Alas in what a mischiefe am I wrapped? what might I doe, or say herein? The father of this mayden delivered this citie from the peril of death; for this cities sake he suffered shipwracke, lost his goodes and endured penury, and now he is requited with evil for good. His daughter which he committed unto me to be

---

[1] Cf. IV.1.50ff. [2] IV.1.93–5. [3] Cf. IV.1.96–102.
[4] Cf. Dionyza, IV.3.14–18. [5] dejected, and overcome.

brought up, is now devoured by a most cruell Lionesse: thus I am deprived as it were of mine owne eies, & forced to bewaile the death of an innocent, and am utterly spoiled through the fierce biting of a moste venemous serpent. Then casting his eies up towards heaven, O God said hee, thou knowest that I am innocent from the bloud of silly Tharsia, which thou hast to require at Dionisiades handes, and therewithall he looked towards his wife, saying: Thou wicked woman, tell me, how hast thou made away prince Apollonius daughter? thou that livest both to the slaunder of God, and man?[1] Dionisiades answered in manie wordes evermore excusing herselfe, and, moderating the wrath of Stranguilio, shee counterfeited a fained sorrowe by attiring her selfe and her daughter in mourning apparell, and in disembling teares before the people of the citie, to whom shee saide: Dearly beloved friendes and Citizens of Tharsus, for this cause we doe weepe and mourne in your sight, because the joy of our eyes and staffe of our olde age, the Mayden Tharsia is dead, leaving unto us bitter teares, and sorrowfull heartes. Yet have we alreadie taken order for her funerals, and buried her according to her degree. These wordes were right greevous unto the people, and there was almost none that let not fall some teares for sorrowe. And they went with one accord unto the market place, whereas her fathers image stood, made of brasse, and erected also another unto her there with this inscription: *Unto the virgin Tharsia in liew of her fathers benefites, the Citizens of Tharsus have erected this monument.*[2]

CHAP. XIII

How the Pirats which stole away Tharsia brought her to the citie Machilenta, and sold her to a common bawd, and how she preserved her virginitie.

The meane time while these troubles were at Tharsus, the Pirats being in their course upon the Sea, by benefite of happie winde arrived at Machilenta,[3] and came into the citie. Nowe had they taken manie mo men and women besides Tharsia, whom all they brought a shoare, and set them to sell as slaves for money. Then came there sundrie to buy such as they lacked for their purposes, amongst whom a moste vile man-bawd,[4] beholding the beautie and tender yeeres of Tharsia, offered money largely for her. Howbeit Athanagoras, who was Prince of the same Citie,[5] beholding likewise the noble countenance, and regarding the great discretion of the mayden in communication, out-bid the bawd, and offered for her

---

[1] IV.3.2–39.   [2] Cf. IV.3.42–46.   [3] Mytilene in IV.2.
[4] A woman in *Per.* wife of the Pander.
[5] Lysimachus is 'governor of this country' IV.6.55.

ten sestercies of gold. But the bawd, being loth to loose so commodious a prey, offered twenty. And I wil give thirty said Athanagoras. Nay I wil give forty said the bawd: and I fiftie quoth Athanagoras, and so they continued in outbidding one an other untill the bawd offered an hundred sestercies of gold to be payed ready downe, and whosoever wil give more, saide he, I will yet give ten sestercies more than he. Then prince Athanagoras thus bethought him secretly in his minde: if I should contend with the bawd to buy her at so hie a price, I must needes sell other slaves to pay for her, which were both losse and shame unto me. Wherefore I will suffer him to buy her; and when he setteth her to hire, I will be the first man that shall come unto her, and I will gather the floure of her virginitie, which shall stand mee in as great steade as if I had bought her.[1] Then the bawd payed the money, and tooke the maiden and departed home,[2] and when he came into his house, hee brought her into a certaine chappel where stoode the idoll of Priapus made of gold, and garnished with pearls and pretious stones. This idoll was made after the shape of a man, with a mighty member unproportionable to the body, alwayes erected, whome bawds and leachers doe adore, making him their god, and worshipping him. Before this filthy idoll he commaunded Tharsia to fall downe.[3] But she answered, God forbid master, that I should worship such an idoll. But (sir) said she, are you a Lapsatenian? Why askest thou? said the bawd I aske, quoth she, because the Lapsatenians doe worship Priapus: this spake she of simplicitie, not knowing what he[4] was. Ah wretch, answered he, knowest thou not that thou arte come into the house of a covetous bawd? When Tharsia heard that, she fell downe at his feet and wept, saying: O master, take compassion upon my virginity, and do not hire out my body for so vile a gaine. The bawd answered, knowest thou not, that neither bawd nor hangman do regard teares or prayers? Then called he unto him a certaine villaine which was governour over his maids, and said unto him: Let this maiden be decked in virgins apparell, pretious and costly, and write upon her: whosoever defloureth Tharsia shal pay ten peeces of golde, and afterward she shall be common unto the people for one peece at a time.[5] The villaine fulfilled his masters commaundement, and the third day after that she was bought, shee was with great solemnitie conducted through the streete with musicke, the bawd himselfe

---

[1] Cf. IV.2.57–63.
[2] Lysimachus is not the first in IV.6 and is more ambiguous.
[3] Cf. IV.2.41–57.
[4] Hence perhaps IV.6.3–4.
[5] *orig.* she.

with a great multitude going before, and so conveyed unto the brothell house.[1] When shee was come thither, Athanagoras the Prince disguising his head and face because hee woulde not be knowen,[2] came first in unto her; whom when Tharsia sawe, she threw her selfe downe at his feete, and saide unto him: For the love of God, Gentleman, take pitty on me, and by the name of God I adjure and charge you, that you do no violence unto me, but bridle your lust, and hearken unto my unhappy estate, and consider diligently from whence I am sprung. My father was poore Apollonius prince of Tyrus, whome force constrained to forsake his owne countrey. My mother was daughter to Altistrates king of Pentapolis, who died in the birth of me, poore wretch, upon the sea. My father also is dead as was supposed, which caused Dionisiades wife of Stranguilio of Tharsus, to whom my father committed me of special trust to be brought up being but an infant, envying mine estate, and thirsting after my wealth, to seeke my death by the handes of a villaine; which had beene accomplished, and I would to God it had before I had seen this day, but that I was suddenly taken away by the pyrates which solde me unto this filthie bawd. With these or such like wordes declared shee her heavie fortune, eftsoones sobbing and bursting out into streames of tears, that for extreme griefe she could scarsly speake. When she had in this manner uttered her sorow, the good prince being astonied and mooved with compassion, said unto her: Be of good cheere Tharsia, for surely I rue thy case, and I my selfe have also a daughter at home,[3] to whome I doubt that the like chances may befall.

And when he had so said, he gave her twenty peeces of gold, saying: Holde heere a greater price or reward for thy virginitie, than thy master appointed: and say as much unto others that come unto thee as thou hast done to me, and thou shalt withstand them. Then Tharsia fell on her knees, and weeping saide unto him: Sir, I give you most hartie thankes for your great compassion and curtesie, and most hartily I beseech you upon my knees, not to descry unto any that which I have saide unto you. No surely, answered Athanagoras, unlesse I tell it unto my daughter, that she may take heede when she commeth unto the like yeares, that she fall not into the like mishappe: and when he had so saide, he let fall a fewe teares, and departed. Now as he was going he met with an other pilgrime that with like devotion came for to seeke the same saint, who demaunded of him how hee liked of the maidens company. Truly, answered

---

[1] Cf. IV.2.95.
[2] IV.6.16–17.
[3] Not in *Per.*

Athanagoras, never of any better. Then the yong man whose name was Aportatus entred into the chamber; and the maiden, after the manner, shut the doore to, and Athanagoras listned at the windowe. Then saide Aportatus unto Tharsia, How much did the prince give unto thee? She answered fortie peeces of golde. Then said he, receive here of me an whole pound weight of golde. The Prince which heard this talke thought then in his minde, the more that you do give her, the more she will weepe, as thinking that you would looke for recompence, the which shee meaneth not to perfourme.

The maiden received the money, and fell down on her knees at his feete, and declared unto him all her estate with teares, as is before shewed. When Aportatus heard that, he was mooved with compassion, and he tooke her up from the ground, saying: Arise Ladie Tharsia: we are al men, and subject to the like chances, & therewithall he departed. And when he came foorth he found prince Athanagoras before the doore laughing at him, to whom he said: Is it wel done, my liege, thus to delude a poore gentleman? was there none to whom you might beginne in teares but unto me only? Then communed they further of the matter, and sware an othe betweene themselves, that they would not bewray those words unto any, & they withdrew themselves aside into a secret place, to see the going in and comming foorth of other, and they sawe many which went in and gave their mony, and came foorth againe weeping.[1] Thus Tharsia through the grace of God, and faire perswasion, preserved her body undefiled.

CHAP. XIV

How Tharsia withstoode a second assault of her virginitie, and by what means she was preserved.

When night was come the master bawd used always to receive the money which his women had gotten by the use of their bodies the day before. And when it was demaunded of Tharsia, she brought him the mony, as the price and hire of her virginitie. Then said the bawd unto hir: It is wel doone Tharsia: use diligence hencefoorth, and see that you bring mee thus much mony every day. When the next day was past also, and the bawd understoode that she remained a virgin stil, he was offended, and called unto him the villaine that had charge over the maides, and said unto him: Sirra, how chanceth it that Tharsia remaineth a virgin still? take her unto thee, and spoile her of her maidenhead, or be sure thou shalt be whipped.[2]

[1] Contrast IV.5.
[2] IV.6.130–160.

Then said the villaine unto Tharsia, tel me, art thou yet a virgin? She answered, I am, and shalbe as long as God will suffer me. How then, saide he, hast thou gotten all this mony? She answered, with teares falling downe upon her knees, I have declared mine estate, humbly requesting all men to take compassion on my virginitie. And nowe likewise, falling then downe at his feete also, Take pitty on me, good friend, which am a poore captive, and the daughter of a king, and doe not defile me. The villaine answered: Our master the bawd is very covetous and greedie of money, and therefore I see no meanes for thee to continue a virgin. Whereunto Tharsia replied: I am skilful in the liberall sciences, and well exercised in all studies, and no man singeth or playeth on instruments better than I, wherefore bring mee into the market place of the citie that men may heare my cunning. Or let the people propound any maner of questions, and I will resolve them: and I doubt not but by this practise I shall get store of money daily. When the villaine heard this devise, and bewailed the maidens mishappe, he willingly gave consent thereto, and brake with the bawd his master touching that matter, who hearing of her skill, and hoping for the gaine, was easily perswaded.[1]

Now when she was brought into the market place, all the people came thronging to see and heare so learned a virgin, before whom shee uttered her cunning in musicke, and her eloquence in speaking, and answered manifestly unto all such questions as were propounded unto her with such perspicuitie, that all confessed themselves fully satisfied, and she wonne great fame thereby, and gained great summes of money.[2] But as for Prince Athanagoras, he had evermore a speciall regard in the preservation of her virginitie, none otherwise than if she had been his owne daughter, and rewarded the villaine very liberally for his diligent care over her.

CHAP. XV

How Apollonius comming to Tharsus, and not finding his daughter, lamented her supposed death; and taking shippe againe, was driven by a tempest to Machilenta where Tharsia was.

Returne we now againe unto Prince Apollonius, who whiles these things were doing at Machilenta when the fourteenth yeere was expired, arrived at Tharsus, and came into the citie unto the house of Stranguilio and Dionisiades, with whome he had left his yong daughter Tharsia.[3] Whome when Stranguilio beheld and knew, he

[1] Cf. IV.6.161ff.
[2] Cf. V *Chor.*, 1–11.
[3] Cf. IV.4, Dumbshow, etc.

ranne hastily unto his wife Dionisiades and saide: Thou reportedst
that Prince Apollonius was dead, and loe now where he is come to
require his daughter. What shall wee now doe, or say unto him?
Then cried she out, alas wretched husband and wife that we are,
let us quickely put on our mourning attire, and shead foorth teares,
and he wil beleeve us that his daughter died a naturall death. And
when they had apparelled themselves, they came foorth unto
Apollonius, who seeing them in mourning attire, said unto them:
My trusty friends, Stranguilio and Dionisiades, why weep ye thus at
my comming? & tell me, I pray you (which I rather beleeve)
whether these teares be not rather mine than yours. Not so (my
lord Apollonius) answered the wicked woman. And I woulde to God
some other body, and not mine husband or I, were inforced to tel
you these heavie tidings, that your deare daughter Tharsia is dead.
When Apollonius heard that word, hee was suddenly cut to the heart,
and his flesh trembled, and he coulde scarce stand on his legges, and
long time hee stoode amazed with his eies intentively fixed on the
ground, but at length recovering himselfe and taking fresh breath,
he cast up his eyes upon her, and saide: O woman, if my daughter
be dead, as thou sayest she is, is the money also and apparell perished
with her? She answered, some is, and some yet remaineth. And as
for your daughter, my Lorde, we were alwaies in good hope, that
when you came, you should have found her alive and merry. But to
the intent that you may the better beleeve us concerning her death,
we have a sufficient witnes. For our citizens being mindfull of your
benefites bestowed upon them, have erected unto her a monument
of brasse by yours, which you may go see if you please. And when she
had so saide, she brought foorth such money, jewels and apparell
which it pleased her to say were remaining of Tharsias store. And
Apollonius belieeving indeede that she was dead, saide unto his
servants: take up this stuffe and beare it away unto the ships, and I
will goe walke unto my daughters monument: and when he came
there, hee read the superscription in manner as is above written,[1]
and he fell suddenly, as it were into an outragious affection and
cursed his owne eies, saying: O most cruell eies, why can you not
yeelde foorth sufficient teares, and woorthily bewaile the death of
my deare daughter? and with that word, with griefe and extreme
sorrowe he fell into a sowne, from which so soone as ever he was
once revived, immediatelie hee went unto the shippes unto his
servauntes, unto whome hee saide, cast mee, I beseech you, unto the
very bottome of the sea, for I have no joy of my life, and my desire is
to yeelde up my Ghost in the water. But his servants used great

---

[1] Cf. IV.4.33–43.

perswasions with him to assuage his sorrowe, wherein presently they some deale preaviled, as they might in so wofull a case; and partly the time, which is a curer of all cares, continually mittigated some part of the griefe, and hee espying the winde to serve well for their departure, hoised up saile, and bid the land adue. They had not thus sailed long in their course, but the winde came about to a contrary quarter, and blew so stifly that it troubled both sea and shippes. The raine fell fiercely over head, the sea wrought wonderously under the ships, and to be short, the tempest was terrible for the time.[1] It was then thought best in that extremitie to strike saile, and let the helme go, and so suffer the shippe to drive with the tide, whither it shoulde please God to direct it.[2] But as joy evermore followeth heavinesse, so was this sharpe storme occasion of a sweet meeting of the father with the daughter, as in processe heereafter it shall appeare. For while Apollonius shippe runneth thus at random, it striketh upon the shoare of the Citie Machilenta, where at that present his daughter Tharsia remained.

Nowe it fortuned that this verie day of their arrivall was the birth day of Prince Apollonius,[3] and when as the Marriners sawe themselves so happily come to the land, both for the gladnesse of the one, and joy of the other, the master of the shippe, and all the whole company gave a great shout.

When Apollonius, who lay solitarily under the hatches, heard such a sodaine voice of mirth, hee called unto the master, and demaunded what it meant. The master aunswered, we rejoyce, and be you glad also with us my lorde, for this day we doe solemnize the feast of your birth. Then Apollonius sighed, and said himselfe: all keepe hollyday save I onely, and let it suffice unto my servants that I onely remaine in sorrowe and heavinesse: Howbeit, I give unto them ten peeces of goold, to buy what they will to keepe holyday withall. But whosoever shall call me unto the feast, or goe about to provoke me unto mirth, I commaund that his thighes shall be broken. So the cater tooke the money, and went aland, and provided necessaries, and returned againe unto the ship.

CHAP. XVI

How Athanagoras prince of Machilenta seeing the beautie of Apollonius ship, went aboord of it, and did the best he could to comfort him.

As fortune thereto served, and delight to take the fresh aire moved Athanagoras prince of the Citie, to walk toward the sea side,

[1] V *Chor.*, 13–14.
[2] IV.4.47–48.
[3] Cf. V *Chor.*, 16–17 'God Neptune's annual feast'.

he sawe Apollonius ships riding at anker: at the view wherof he tooke great pleasure, especially at the Admirall which was a great ship and a beautiful, wherin Apollonius himself was carried, the like wherof haply he had not seene often before. This was that Athanagoras that loved Tharsia so tenderly, and he haled unto the Marriners, and asked of whence that faire ship was? The Marriners answered, that she came now from Tharsus. Truly, said Athanagoras, it is a faire shippe, and well appointed, and of all that I have seene, I like best of her. Now when the Marriners heard their shippe so highly commended, they desired him to come aboord, whereunto he willingly graunted.[1] And when he was come abord, he sate downe with them at meat, and he drue his purse, and laid downe ten peeces of gold upon the table, saying, you shall not say that you have bidden an unthankfull person, take this small summe of money at my handes for a reward, and they thanked him. But when he was set downe, and beheld al that sate at the boord, he demaunded who was owner of the ship, and where he was? The maister[2] answered, our owner is sicke, and weake with sorrowe and taking thought, and needes will die. He lost his wife uppon the Sea, and his daughter in a strange land. Athanagoras said unto one of the servants called Ardalius: I will give thee two peeces of gold, to go down and tell thy master that the prince of this Citie desireth him to come up out of darknesse into light. The servaunt answered, I cannot buy new thighes for thy golde, and therefore get some man els to go on the errand, for he hath said that whosoever troubleth him, his thighes shall be broken. That law hath he made over you, said Athanagoras, and not over mee, and therefore I will go downe unto him: but first tell me, I pray you, what you call his name? They answered, Apollonius. And when he heard that name, hee remembred in his minde that hee heard Tharsia call her father so, and he went downe unto him where he lay,[3] whom when hee beheld, having a long beard, and rough fligged haire, and long nailes on his fingers, he was somewhat astonied, and called upon him with a soft voice, saying: Apollonius! When Apollonius heard himselfe named, thinking it had been some of his men that had called him, [he] arose up sodainly with a fierce countenance, and seeing a stranger looking verie comely and honourably attired, he held his peace. Then spake Athanagoras: Sir, I thinke you doe marvell, that I being a stranger, am so bold as to come to trouble you. You shall understand that I am prince of this citie, and my name is Athanagoras. I walked by

---

[1] Cf. V.1.3–10.
[2] Helicanus in *Per.* V.1.22–30.
[3] Cf. V.1.36 s.d. 'Pericles discovered'.

chance unto the Sea side, where beholding thy ships, especially commending this wherin thou art, for beautie and strength: I was by thy men desired to come aboord which I did, and have eaten with them. Then inquired I for the owner, and they told me thy name, and that thou remainest in great sorrow, and for that cause I am come downe unto thee to bring thee, if I may, out of darknesse into light, hoping that after this heavinesse God shal restore thee unto gladnesse. Apollonius lifted up his eies, saying: I thanke thee, my Lord, whosoever thou art, and I beseech thee not to trouble me longer, for I am not worthy to eate meat or make good cheare, & I will live no longer.[1] Athanagoras much mused at this answere, and wondred at the wilfulnesse of the man, and came up uppon the decke and saide unto the servauntes: I cannot perswade your lord to come up out of that darke place into the light: what way therefore, were I best to devise to bring him from his purpose, and to preserve him from an obstinate death? For it were great pitie that a notable gentleman should so consume away in hucker mucker, and die by a dishonourable death.

CHAP. XVII

How Athanagoras sent for Tharsia to make her father Apollonius merry; and how after long circumstance they came into knowledge one of another.

And as he was devising with himselfe, it came into his mind to send for the maiden Tharsia, for which purpose he called unto him one of his men, and saide unto him. Go unto the baud, desire him to send Tharsia hither unto me, for she hath wisdom, & can move pleasant talke, and perhaps she may perswade him not to die thus wilfully. The messenger went speedily, & returned immediatly, bringing the maiden Tharsia with him unto the ship.[2] Whom when Athanagoras beheld, come hither unto me Tharsia, quoth he, and shew now the uttermost of thy cunning and knowledge, in comforting the owner of the ship, which lieth in darknes and will receive no comfort, nor come abroad into the light, for the great sorrow that he taketh for his wife and his daughter. Goe unto him, good Tharsia, and prove if thou canst perswade him to come into the light: for it may be that God hath appointed by thy meanes, to bring him from sorrowe into gladnesse. Which thing if thou canst bring to passe, as I am a gentleman, I will give thee thirtie sestercies of gold, and as many of silver, and I will redeeme thee from the bawd for thirtie dayes.[3] When Tharsia heard this, she went boldly downe into the

[1] Cf. V.1.39–55.
[2] V.1.52, 64.
[3] V.1.70–80.

cabin unto him, and with a milde voice saluted him, saying: God save you sir whosoever you be, and be of good comfort, for an innocent virgin, whose life has been distressed by shipwracke, and her chastitie by dishonestie, and yet hath both preserved, saluteth thee. Then began she to record in verses, and therewithall to sing so sweetly, that Apollonius, notwithstanding his great sorrow, wondred at her. And these were the verses which she soong so pleasantly unto the instrument[1]:

> *Amongst the harlots foule I walke,*
>   *yet harlot none am I:*
> *The Rose amongst the Thorns grows,*
>   *and is not hurt thereby.*
> *The thiefe that stole me, sure I thinke,*
>   *is slaine before this time,*
> *A bawd me bought, yet am I not*
>   *defilde by fleshly crime.*
> *Were nothing pleasanter to me,*
>   *than parents mine to know:*
> *I am the issue of a king,*
>   *my bloud from kings doth flow.*[2]
> *I hope that God will mend my state,*
>   *and send a better day.*
> *Leave off your teares, plucke up your heart,*
>   *and banish care away.*
> *Shew gladnesse in your countenance,*
>   *cast up your cheerfull eyes:*
> *That God remaines that once of nought*
>   *created earth and skies.*
> *He will not let in care and thought*
>   *you still to live, and all for nought.*

When Apollonius heard her sing these verses, lifting up his eyes, and sighing he said: Alas poore wretch as I am, how long shall I strive with life, and abide this greevous conflict? Good maiden, I give hearty thanks both to your wisedome and nobilitie: requiting you with this one thing, that whensoever, if ever such occasion doe chance, I shall have desire to be merrie, I will then thinke on you, or if ever I be restored unto my kingdome. And perhaps, as you say, you are descended of the race of kings, and indeed you doe well represent the nobilitie of your parentage.[3] But nowe I pray you receive this reward at my handes, an hundred peeces of golde, and

---

[1] The words are not given in *Per.* V.1.81ff. Nor are there riddles.
[2] V.1.90–95.   [3] V.1.98–99.

depart from me and trouble me no longer, for my present griefe is
renued by your lamentable recitall, and I consume with continuall
sorrowe. When the maid had received the reward, shee was
about to depart. Then spake Athanagoras, wither goest thou
Tharsia,[1] quoth hee? hast thou taken paine without profite, and
canst thou not worke a deed of charitie, and relieve the man that wil
consume his life with mourning? Tharsia answered: I have done all
that I may, and he hath given me an hundred peeces of gold, and
desired me to depart. I wil give thee two hundred, said Athanagoras,
and goe downe unto him againe, and give him his money, and say
unto him, I seeke thy health and not thy money. Then went Tharsia
downe againe,[2] and set her selfe downe by him, and saide unto him:
Sir, if you bee determined to continue alwaies in this heavinesse,
give mee leave, I pray you, to reason a little with you. And I meane
to propose certaine parables unto you, which if you can resolve, I
will then depart, and restore your money. But Apollonius, not
willing to receive the money againe, but thankefully to accept
whatsoever shee should utter, without discouraging of her: albeit
in my troubles quoth he, I have none other felicitie but to weepe
and lament, yet because I will not want the ornamentes of your
wisedome, demaund of me whatsoever shall be your pleasure, and
while I am aunswering you, pardon me I pray you, if sometime I
give libertie unto my teares, and shall not be able to speak for
sobbing. Sir, I will beare with you somewhat in that respect said
Tharsia, and nowe if it please you I will begin:

> *A certaine house on earth there is,*
> *that rooms hath large and wide:*
> *The house makes noise, the guests make none,*
> *that therein doth abide;*
> *But house and guest continually,*
> *togither forth doe slide.*

Now if indeed you be a Prince, as your men say you are, it
behooveth you to be wiser than a simple maiden, and to resolve my
probleme. Apollonius answered: Maiden, to the intent you may not
thinke you were tolde a lie, hearken now to the resolution.

The house on the earth is the Sea or every great water, the fish is
the dumbe guest, which followeth the water whither soever it runne.
Sir, you have answered truely said Tharsia; and now I assaile you
the second time:

---

[1] V.1.95 'I will desist'.
[2] Cf. Marina, V.1.96–97.

In length forth long I runne,
faire daughter of the wood,
Accompanied with many a one,
of foote and force as good,
Through many waies I walke,
but steps appeare none where I stood.

Apollonius answered: If I might be so bold, and opportunitie
served thereto, I could declare unto you many things that you doe
not knowe, faire maiden, but not interrupting your questions whereunto I have to answere, wherein I much wonder at your yoong
yeares, so plentifully fraught with excellent knowledge. But to come
to the purpose: The daughter of the wood, is the tree whereof is
made the long ship, which is accompanied with many companions,
and walketh uppon the seas many wayes leaving no print, or foot-
steppes behinde. You have guessed right said Tharsia, and therefore
nowe I propose my third parable:

There is an house through which the fire
doth passe, and doth no harme:
Therein is heat, which none may moove
from thence, it is so warme.
A naked house, and in that house
guests naked doe desire
To dwell, from whence if boords you draw,
then fall you in the fire.

Apollonius answered: Maiden, this that you meane, were a meet
place for men that live in delight and pleasure. And the time hath
been, when I have also delighted in the bath and hoat-house, where
the heate entreth through the crevises of the boordes and chinkes of
the stones, and where by reason of sweating, it behooveth a man to
be naked. When he had done speaking, Tharsia wondering at his
wisedome, and the rather lamenting his discomfortablenesse, threw
her selfe uppon him, and with clasped armes embraced him, saying,
O good gentleman, hearken unto the voice of her that beseecheth
thee, and have respect to the suite of a virgin, that thinking it a far
unworthy thing that so wise a man should languish in griefe, and
die with sorrow. But if God of his goodness would restore unto thee
thy wife safe, whom thou so much lamentest: Or if thou shouldst find
thy daughter in good case, whom thou supposest to be dead, then
wouldest thou desire to live for joy. Then Apollonius fell in a rage,
and forgetting all courtesie, his unbridled affection stirring him thereunto, rose up sodainly, and stroke the maiden on the face with his
foote, so that shee fell to the ground, and the bloud gushed plentifully

out of her cheekes.[1] And like it is that shee was in a swoone, for so soone as shee came to her selfe, shee beganne to weepe, saying, O immortall God, which madest heaven and earth, looke uppon my afflictions, and take compassion uppon mee. I was borne among the waves and troublesome tempests of the sea.[2] My mother died in pangues and paines of childbed and buriall was denied her upon the earth, whom my father adorned with jewels, and laid twentie sestercies of gold at her head, and as much in silver at her feete, and inclosed her in a chest, and committed her to the Sea. As for mee unfortunate wretch, I was at Tharsus committed to Stranguilio and wicked Dionisiades his wife, whom my father put in trust with me, with mony & princely furniture, and their servants were commanded to slay me. And when I desired time to pray, which was granted me, there came pyrates in the meane while, and carried mee away, and brought me unto this wofull city, where I was solde to a most cruell bawd, and with much adoe have preserved my virginitie, and I see nothing ensuing but continuall sorrowe, whereof I feele both now and every day some part, and shall doe ever more and more, until it please God to restore me unto my father Apollonius.[3] Apollonius gave good eare unto her words, and was strangely moved within himselfe, knowing that all these signes and tokens were most certaine that she was his daughter, and hee cried out with a mighty voice and saide: O mercifull God, which beholdest heaven, earth and hell, and discoverest all the secretes therein, blessed bee thy most holy name for ever: and when he had said those words, he fell upon his daughter Tharsias necke, and kissed her, and for extreame joy wept bitterly, saying: O most sweete and onely daughter, the halfe part of my life, for the love of thee I lust not nowe to die, for I have found thee for whome I had desire to die onely. And therewithall he cryed out aloude, saying: Come hither my servants and frends, come ye al hither, and see now the end of all my sorrow, for I have found my deare daughter and onelie childe which I had lost. When the servants heard the noise, they came hastily togither, and with them prince Athanagoras; & when they came downe under the hatches, they found Apollonius weeping for joy, and leaning upon his daughters shoulders, and he said unto them: behold here my daughter, for whome I have mourned, beholde the one halfe of my life, and for whose sake I nowe desire to live.[4] And they all rejoyced and wept with him for company, and thanked God for that happy day.

---

[1] Pericles speaks roughly and pushes her away, V.i.98–101; 128.
[2] V.i.104–6.   [3] V.i.149–81.
[4] V.i.192–224.

31

CHAP. XVIII

Howe Apollonius leaving off mourning, came into the citie Machilenta, where he commaunded the bawd to be burned, and how Tharsia was married unto prince Athanagoras.

Tharsia hearing her fathers words, fell down at his feet and kissed him, saying: O father, blessed be God that hath given me the grace to see you, & that I may die with you. But Apollonius lifted up his heart, and cast away his mourning apparell, and put on other sweete and cleane raiment.[1] And when Athanagoras and the servants looked earnestly upon him, and upon his daughter, they wondred, saying, O my lord Apollonius, how like in countenance is your daughter Tharsia unto you? that if you had no other argument, this were sufficient proofe to shewe that she is your childe. Apollonius thanked them, saying, that now he stoode not in any doubt thereof. Then Tharsia beganne to discourse unto her father, howe she was sold unto the bawd, and howe hee thrust her into the common brothell, and by what meanes she alwayes preserved her chastitie, and howe much she was bounden unto good prince Athanagoras there present. Now Athanagoras was a widower, and a lusty yoong gentleman, and prince of the citie, as it is declared, who fearing lest Tharsia should be bestowed in marriage upon some other man, and using the benefite of the time, cast him selfe downe at Apollonius feete, and besought him for her, saying: Most noble Prince, I beseech you for the living Gods sake, which hath thus myraculously restored the father unto his daughter, bestowe not your daughter upon any other in marriage then me onely. I am prince of this citie, and through my meanes she hath continued a virgin, and by my procurement she is nowe come unto the knowledge of thee her father. Apollonius courteously embracing him answered: I thanke you most heartily, good Prince Athanagoras, for your friendly offer, which I may in no wise gainsay both in respect of your owne woorthinesse, and for the pleasure which you have shewed my daughter, and, therfore you have my goodwill to be her husband. Then, turning his face towards Tharsia, how say you my deare daughter, said he, are you contented to bee wife unto Athanagoras? Tharsia with blushing cheeks answered: Yea forsooth father, for since I came from Stranguilioes house, I never found rest nor pleasure saving through his alonely curtesie. Nowe whether Athanagoras rejoyced at this answere or not, I referre me to the judgement of those, who, being passionate with the same affection, would be well pleased with a joyntly grant of the like goodwil.[2]

---

[1] V.1.224. 'Give me my robes'.   [2] Cf. V.1.262-4; V.3.71-72.

When these matters were thus concluded, Apollonius mooved Athanagoras concerning revenge to be executed uppon the bawd. Then Athanagoras took his leave for a while of Apollonius and departeth unto the citie, and, calling al the citizens togither to the market place, he spake thus unto them: My friends and welbeloved citizens, understand ye that Apollonius, prince of Tyrus and father unto Tharsia, is arrived in our coast with a great fleete of ships, wherein hee hath brought a mighty army of men to destroy our city for the bawds sake, who placed his daughter in a common brothell, to hire out the use of her body for monie. Wherefore looke unto your selves, and advise your selves what you were best to doe, for it were pittie that the whole citie should perish for one wicked mans sake.

When as hee made an ende of this speech, the whole multitude trembled and was sore afraide, and foorthwith determined that they would all, as well men, women and children, goe foorth to see prince Apollonius, and to crave pardon of him. Not so, said Athanagoras, but we will desire him to come peaceablie into our citie, and what he list to commaund shall be fulfilled. The people liked well of that counsel, and committed the matter unto his discretion wholly to provide for their safetie. Then went he foorth unto Apollonius, and desired him in the peoples name to come into the citie, where he should be most heartily welcome. Apollonius refused not that friendly offer, but immediately prepared himselfe to goe with him, and caused his head to be polled, and his beard to be trimmed, and his nailes to be pared,[1] and put on a princely robe upon his backe, and a crowne of golde upon his head, and so passed foorth togither upon the way. And when they were come into the citie, the citizens saluted Apollonius, and hee was placed in the highest seate whence the prince was woont to give judgement, and his daughter Tharsia by his side, and he spake unto the people in this manner following: Good people of the city of Machilenta, you see the virgine Tharsia, whome I her father have found out this present day: hir hath the most filthie bawd, as much as in him lay, constrained to dishonest her body, to her utter destruction. From which his devillish purpose no intreatie could persuade him, no price could allure him. Wherfore my request unto you (good people) is, that I may have due revenge on him for the injury done unto my daughter. When the people heard his reasonable demaund, they cried out with one accord, saying: My lorde Apollonius, we judge that he be burned alive, and his goods be given unto the maiden Tharsia. The revenge pleased Apollonius well, and foorthwith they apprehended the

[1] Later in *Per.*, V.3.72–76.

bawd, and bound him hand and foot; and they made a great fire, and at Apollonius commaundement cast him alive into it, and burnt him to ashes. Then called Tharsia for the villaine, and saide unto him: Because by thy meanes, and all the citizens, I have hitherto remained a virgine even untill my fathers comming, my will is that thou be free; and moreover, I heere give unto thee two hundred peeces of gold for a reward. Secondly, she called for all the women that were in the bawdes brothell, and saide unto them: good women, whose chances, perhaps, hath beene as greevous unto you as mine was unto me, I set you al at liberty, and whereas heretofore you have gained money by hiring foorth the use of your bodies, receive of mee here this rewarde, that you may live hereafter more in the feare of God, and practise some more commendable way to sustaine necessitie; and therewithall she gave to everie one of them a rewarde, and so dismissed them. And when all these things were ended, Apollonius minding to depart, spake unto the people saying: Noble Prince Athanagoras, and beloved citizens of Machilenta, I acknow-ledge my selfe much bounden to you, and I yeeld you hearty thanks for all your benefites bestowed uppon me and my daughter. And now in recompence thereof I give unto you fifty poundes weight of golde to be divided amongst you, that when I am gone from you, you may be mindefull of me. The citizens thanked him, and bowed their heads in token of reverence; and they agreed together, and they erected two statues of brasse one unto him, another to his daughter in the market place of the citie, with these superscriptions written in their bases: *Unto Apollonius prince of Tyrus, the preserver of our houses; and unto his vertuous daughter Tharsia, a virgin, the mindefull citizens of Machilenta have erected those monuments.* But Apollonius remembring the great curtesie of Athanagoras, and his promise made unto him concerning Tharsia, appointed a short time for their mariage,[1] against which there was great provision as might be at so smal warning, the solemnities, riches, braverie, cost, feasts, revelles, intertainement, and all things else appertaining thereunto, and requisite for so great personages, I shall not here neede particularly to set downe, since every man may judge what belongeth to such a matter, and none can precisely describe this unlesse he had beene there present. Of this thing sure I am, that this mariage brought great pleasure to the father, contentment to the parties, and joy to all the people.

---

[1] Delayed until Pentapolis after the reunion with Thaisa, V.3.72–80.

CHAP. XIX

How Apollonius meaning to saile into his owne countrey by Tharsus, was commaunded by an Angel in the night to go to Ephesus, and there to declare all his adventures in the Church, with a loude voice.

The solemnities of the wedding being finished, Apollonius made haste to depart; and all things being in a readinesse, he tooke shipping with his sonne in lawe and his daughter, and weyghed anchor, and committed the sailes unto the winde, and went their way, directing their course evermore towarde Tharsus, by which Apollonius purposed to passe unto his owne countrie Tyrus. And when they had sailed one whole day, and night was come, that Apollonius laide him downe to rest, there appeared an Angell in his sleepe,[1] commaunding him to leave his course toward Tharsus, and to saile unto Ephesus, and to go into the Temple of Diana, accompanied with his sonne in lawe and his daughter, and there with a loude voyce to declare all his adventures, whatsocver had befallen him from his youth unto that present day.

When Apollonius awoke in the morning, he wondered at the vision, and called for Athanagoras his sonne in lawe and his daughter Tharsia, and declared it to them in order as is before recited. Thus saide he unto them, what counsell do you give me in this matter? They answered, whatsoever it pleaseth to you to doe that we shall like well of. Then Apollonius called unto him the Master of the shippe, and commaunded him to winde saile and coast towards Ephesus, which he did;[2] and immediately the winde served them so prosperously, that in fewe days they safely arrived there. Apollonius and his companie foorthwith forsooke their shippes, and came aland, and according to the commaundement of the Angell, tooke his journey to the Temple of Diana, whereas it is before mentioned, his long lamented wife lady Lucina, remained in vertuous life and holy contemplation among the religious Nunnes. And when he was come thither, he besought one of the Nunnes that had the keeping of the Temple that he might have licence to go in, and she willingly granted his request, and opened the doore unto him. By this time report was blowen abroad, that a certaine strange Prince was lately landed with his sonne in lawe and his daughter in very costly and rich ornaments, and gone into the Temple: and the ladie Lucina as desirous as the rest to see the strangers, decked her head with rich attire, and put on a purple robe, and, with convenient retinue attending upon her, came into the Temple.

Now Lucina was passing beautifull, and for the great love which

---

[1] Diana in V.1.240–51.   [2] V.1.252–6.

she bare unto chastitie all men reverenced her, and there was no virgin in al the number in like estimation unto her. Whom when Apollonius beheld, although he knew not what she was, yet such was the exceeding brightnes and majestie of her countenance, that he fel down at her feet, with his sonne in law likewise and his daughter, for hee thought shee glittered like a diademe, and exceeded the brightest starres in beautie. But Lucina curteously lifted them up from the ground, and bid them welcome, and afterward went to bestow the plate and ornaments of the temple in decent order, which thing was part of the Nunnes duety. Then Apollonius setled himselfe to doe as the Angell had commaunded him in the vision, and thus he beganne to say: I being borne Prince of Tyrus, was called Apollonius, and when in youth I had attained unto all kinde of knowledge, I resolved the cruel king Antiochus parable, to the intent to have married with his daughter, whome he most shamefully defiled, and kept her from all men to serve his owne filthie lust, and sought meanes to slay me. Then I fled away, and lost all my goodes in the sea, hardly escaping my selfe with life, and in my greatest extremitie I was courteously intertained by Altistrates king of Pentapolis, and so highly received into favor, that he left no kindes of favor on me untried, insomuch that hee bestowed upon mee his faire daughter and onelie childe Lucina to be my wife. But when Antiochus and his daughter by the just judgement of God, were stroken dead by lightning from heaven, I carried my wife with me to receive my kingdome, and she was delivered of this my daughter and hers upon the sea, and died in the travell, whome I enclosed in a chest, and threwe into the sea, laying twenty sestercies of golde at her head, and as much in silver at her feete, to the intent that they that should find her might have wherewithall to bury her honorably, leaving also a superscription that they might perceive with what griefe of her friends she died, and of what princelie parentage shee descended. Afterwardes I arrived at the citie of Tharsus, where I put in trust my yoong daughter to be brought up unto certain wicked persons, and from thence I departed unto the higher partes of Egypt. But when from that time fourteene yeeres were expired, and I returned thither to fetch my daughter, they told me that shee was dead, which I beleeving to be true, put on mourning attire, and desired nothing so much as to die, and while I was in that extremitie of sorrowe, and determined to have sayled unto Tyrus, while I was on my way upon the sea the winde turned, and there arose a tempest, and drave me unto the citie Machilenta, where my daughter was restored unto me.[1] Then went I with my sonne in law, and my

---

[1] Here Thaisa faints, V.3.1–14.

daughter once againe, to have sailed unto Tyrus by Tharsus; and as I was now in the journey, I was admonished in my sleepe by an Angell to turne my course unto Ephesus, and there in the temple to declare aloud al my adventures that had befallen me since my youth unto this present day, which hath hither to guided me in all my troubles, will nowe send an happy end unto all mine afflictions.

CHAP. XX

How Apollonius came to the knowledge of his wife the ladie Lucina, and how they rejoyced at the meeting of ech other.

The ladie Lucina was not so busie in executing her office in the Church, but that she gave also attentive eare unto her lord Apollonius talke, whom at first she knew not. But when shee heard the long discourse, whereby she knew by all signes that hee was her husband, and shee was his wife, her heart burned within her, and she could scarce temper her affections until hee had done talking. Yet measuring her love with modestie, as nowe of long time having learned the true trade of pacience, shee gave him libertie to make an end: which done, shee ran hastily unto him and embraced him hard in her armes, and woulde have kissed him. Which thing, when Apollonius sawe, hee was mooved with disdaine, and thrust her from him, as misliking such lightnesse in her whose modestie and good grace hee had so lately before commended in his heart, and nothing at all suspecting that she had been his wife. Then shee pouring foorth teares aboundantly, O my lord Apollonius, said she, the one halfe of my life, why deal you thus ungently with me? I am your wife, daughter unto Altistrates, king of Pentapolis, and my name is Lucina. And you are Apollonius, prince of Tyrus, my lord and deare husband, and you are my schoolemaister, which taught mee musicke: and moreover you are the Sea-wrecked man whom I especially loved above many, not for concupiscence sake, but for desire of wisedome. When Apollonius heard those words, he was sodainly astonied; and as the strangenes of the chance appalled him much: so the great joy revived his spirites againe, and he cast his eies earnestly uppon her, and immediatly called her to remembrance, and knew perfitly that it was shee indeede, and he went unto her, and fell uppon her necke, and for exceeding joy brast out into teares, and then lifting up his handes and eyes to heaven, hee saide: Blessed be the moste mightie God of heaven, which sitteth above and beholdeth the state of men on earth, and dealeth with them according to his great mercie: who nowe also of his unspeakeable goodnesse, hath restored unto mee my wife and my daughter. Then did hee most lovingly embrace and kisse his ladie, whom he supposed long before to be dead: and shee likewise requited him with the like fruites of good will and courtesie, whom she surely thought she should never have seene againe. And when they had continued a good space in intertaining the one another: O my most deare lord Apollonius, saide the lady Lucina, where is my childe, whereof I was delivered? Apollonius aunswered: my best beloved ladie, it was a daughter, and she was named Tharsia, and this is she, and there-withall he shewed her Tharsia. Then kissed and embraced she her daughter,[1] and likewise her sonne in law Athanagoras, and they greatly rejoyced one in another.

And when report heereof was spread abroad, there was great joy throughout all the Citie of Ephesus, and the report has blowen about in everie place how prince Apollonius had found out his ladie and wife among the Nunnes in the Temple. Then Lucina discoursed unto her lord and husband Apollonius, of all the strange accidents that happened unto her after his casting her forth into the Sea. Namely, howe her chest was cast on land at the coast of Ephesus, and taken up by a Phisition,[2] and how she was revived and by him adopted, and for preservation of her honestie, placed among the Nunnes in the Temple of Diana,[3] where hee there found her, accordingly as it appeareth before in the historie, wherefore they blessed the name of God, and yeelded most heartie thankes unto him, that hee had preserved them hitherto, and graunted them so joyfull a meeting.

CHAP. XXI

How Apollonius departed from Ephesus, and sailed himselfe, his wife, his sonne, and daughter unto Antiochia, and then to Tyrus, and from thence to Tharsus, where he revenged himselfe upon Stranguilio, and Dionisiades.

Apollonius and Lucina his wife, and the residue of their traine, having rested themselves and made merrie sufficient time at Ephesus, when the winde served, tooke leave of their friendes and went aboord of their ships, and lanched from the shore and departed unto Antiochia; where according as Calamitus the maister of the ship of Tyrus had tolde him before, the kingdome was reserved for him since the death of Antiochus. But when the citizens heard that he was arrived, they were all exceeding glad, and put on their bravest apparell, and garlandes of bayes upon their heads, and went forth

[1] V.3.44–48.
[2] Cf. Cerimon V.3.16–28; 56–68.
[3] V.3.24–25.

in procession to meet him, and brought him in triumph into the Citie, and crowned him king with all joy and gladnesse. And when all the solemnities of the coronation, the feastes, triumphes, largesses, and pardons were finished, hee abode with them certaine daies to dispose some matters in order that required redresse, and to establish certaine lawes for the due administration of justice. Which being all accomplished according to his desire, he tooke his leave of the Citizens, and with his wife, sonne, and daughter, departed to the sea, and sayled unto Tyrus his owne native country, where he was joyfully received of his subjects, and found his kingdome governed in good order. There placed he for his lieuetenant his sonne in lawe Athanagoras, which had married his daughter Tharsia, to rule the countrey in his absence,[1] and when he had aboden a convenient time amongst them to make merrie, and to provide necessaries for his farther affaires, he levied in shorter space a mightie armie of the best approoved souldiours, with sufficient store of money and munition, and taking with him moreover his lady, and his daughter Tharsia, tooke shipping in the haven, and had so prosperous winde, that in few dayes they landed in the coast of Tharsus. And when they were come all ashoare, they marched forward in battell aray, and came into the Citie to the great terrour of al the inhabitants. When he was come into the market place, he commaunded that Stranguilio and Dionisiades should be brought before him, which being done, he thus spake unto the people. Ye Citizens of Tharsus, I am come hither in armes as you see, not moved by my will, but constrained by injurie. Wherfore tell me, was I ever unthankfull unto your Citie in generall, or unto any of you al in particular? They all answered with one voice: no my lord, and therefore wee are ready all to spend our lives in thy quarrell: and as thou knowest well wee have erected heere, in perpetuall memorie of thee, a statue of brasse, because thou preservedst us from death, and our citie from utter destruction. Then said Apollonius, understand then this much my friends, that when I departed last from this citie, I committed my daughter in trust unto Stranguilio and his wife Dionisiades; and when I came to require her they would not deliver her unto me, nor tell me the trueth what is become of her. Immediatly they were both called forth to aunswere unto these matters before Apollonius, where falling downe on their knees before him, Dionisiades answered in this manner: My lord, I beseech you stand favourable unto my poore husband and mee, and not to beleeve any other thing concerning your daughter, then that shee is departed this life. And as for hir grave, you have seene it, and also the monument of brasse erected by the

---

[1] Cf. V.3.82.

whole citie in the memoriall of her, and moreover you have read the superscription. Then Apollonius commaunded his daughter to stand foorth in the presence of them all, and shee saide unto Dionisiades: beholde thou wicked woman, dead Tharsia is come to greete thee, who as thou diddest well hope, shoulde never have been forth comming to have bewrayed thy wickednesse. But when the miserable woman beheld Tharsia, her heart quaked for feare, and shee fell to the ground in a swoond: and when shee recovered againe, shee cried out upon the just judgment of God, and cursed the time that shee was borne. And all the people ranne thronging about Tharsia, and wondered at her, thinking howe greatly they had been of long time abused by Stranguilio, and Dionisiades; and they rejoyced much in her safetie, and all knew by her countenance that it was shee, and none other. O now, who were able to declare the bitter griefe and intolerable care which eftsoones assaied the wearisome consciences of these twaine, the husband and the wife when they sawe her living and in good liking before their faces, whose death they had so traiterously conspired. Even hell it selfe is not comparable unto so heavie a burden, the unspeakable weight whereof all men ought to feare, and none can sufficiently describe unlesse hee have been semblably plunged in the like gulfe of horrible desperation. Then Tharsia called for Theophilus Stranguilios villaine, and when he was come into her presence, shee saide unto him: Theophilus, aunswere mee aloud that all the people may heare, who sent thee forth to slay me? Hee aunswered, Dionisiades my Mistresse. What mooved her thereunto saide Tharsia? None other thing, I suppose, saide the villaine, but to enjoy the money and ornamentes, and also because thy beautie and comelinesse were commended above Philomacias her daughters. Nowe when the people heard this, they ranne uppon Stranguilio, and Dionisiades, and tooke them violently, and bound them, and drew them out of the citie, and stoned them to death,[1] and would likewise have slaine Theophilus the villaine, for that, that at his mistress commandement he would have murdered the innocent maiden. But Tharsia intreated for him, saying, Not so my deare friends. I pray you let me obtaine pardone for him at your handes; for unlesse he had given me respite to say my praiers, I had not been heere now to have spoken for him: and when she had said so, the furious multitude was appeased. And Apollonius gave many exceeding rich giftes unto the citie, and repared it strongly in many places where it was decaied, and abode there with them the space of three monthes in feasting and making merry before he departed.

---

[1] Burned in V.3.95–100.

CHAP. XXII

How Apollonius sailed from Tharsus to visite his father-in-law Altistrates king of Pentapolis, who died not long after Apollonius comming thither.

The terme of three monethes, that Apollonius purposed for his delight to remaine at Tharsus, was almost expired, and he commanded all things to be prepared for the journey; and when the day was come, hee made generall proclamation uppon paine of death every man to ship. And when the whole army was imbarked, he took ship himselfe with his wife and his daughter, being honourably accompanied by the citizens unto the water side; and after due courtesie on both sides done and received, he hoysed sayle and departed towardes Pentapolis king Altistrates Citie. And when they had sailed with prosperous winde ten dayes uppon the Sea, they discovered a farre off the Steeples and Towres of Pentapolis, and the Souldiers rejoyced and gave a shout for gladnesse that they were so neere to their wished land. Then they cast about and cut towards the haven, and cast anker, and landed all safe, and Apollonius with his wife and daughter after hee had taken order for the companie, rode unto the court unto king Altistrates, whom they found in good health, and merry.[1] And when Altistrates saw his sonne-in-lawe, his daughter and his neece Tharsia, hee bid them welcome, and rejoyced exceedingly, and sent for the Nobles of his land to keepe them companie, and gave them the best entertainment that hee could devise, and they sojourned with him an whole yeare in pleasure and pastime, whereof the king tooke as great comfort as was possible for a man to doe in any worldly felicitie. But as there was never yet any thing certaine or permanent in this mortall life, but alwaies we be requited with sowre sauce to our sweete meate, and when wee thinke ourselves surest in the top of joy, then tilt wee downe soonest into the bottome of sorrow, so fared it now unto those personages in the midst of their jollitie. For the good old king Altistrates fell sodainly sick which much appalled them all, and grew everie day weaker than other. Then were the Phisitions sent for in haste, who left nothing untried that appertained unto Art and experience to doe; and above all Apollonius and Lucina his wife plaied the parts of duetifull children, in tending their aged and weake father with all care and diligence possible. But alas olde age which of it selfe is an uncurable sickenesse, and had beene growing nowe well nigh an hundred yeares lacking seven upon him, accompanied with the intollerable paine of the gowt, and the stone of the bladder, had consumed naturall moisture, so that his force gave over

[1] Dead in V.3.78.

to the disease, and shortely after changed this transitorie life for a better. When report was spread abroad of the kings death, there was great sorrowe and lamentation made in all places, neither was there any that tooke not grievously the losse of so good a Prince. But to describe the inward affliction of Apollonius, and the teares of Lucina and Tharsia her daughter, woulde make any heart of flint to bleede, considering the tender affections of women above men, and howe prone they bee that way, yea, sometime (God knowes) in smaller cases than at the death of husband, father, or mother. But as al things have their time, so have sorrowe and teares also, which are best dried up with the towell of continuance; which gave nowe just occasion unto Apollonius to cast off drowsie sorrowe, and to provide for the funeralles of his father in lawe, which he accomplished with so seasonable expedition, and in so honourable a sort, as was seemely for so mighty a king, and so vertuous a prince, whome hee buried among the auntient race of kings his auncestours in the Temple within the citie of Pentapolis. Which beeing all finished, as it is also a worke of charitie to fulfill the will of the dead, he applied himselfe to execute his fathers testament, wherin he had given halfe his kingdome unto Apollonius, and the other halfe to Tharsia his neece, to have and to holde to them and to their heires for ever.

CHAP. XXIII

How Apollonius rewarded the fisherman that releeved him after he had suffered shipwracke: howe hee dealt also with olde Calamitus, and likewise with the Pyrates that stole away Tharsia.

By this time, when all cares were banished, and Apollonius injoyed his kingdome in quiet possession, he gave himselfe sometimes to delight as other Princes are wont to do. And it fortuned that on a day when he had dined, he walked foorth for recreation unto the sea side, with his wife and a fewe servants. And when hee came there, he sawe a small fisher boat fleeting under saile, which hee thought by all signes he should knowe well, for hee supposed it to be the fishermans boat which succoured him, when he had suffered shipwracke in sailing from Tharsus towardes Pentapolis. Wherefore hee commaunded some of his servantes, to take another shippe which rode at anchor there on the shore, to go after and take him, and to bring the fisherman unto him into the Coort. When the poore man saw himselfe boorded of so many and so gay a multitude, hee feared they had beene pyrates, and that they woulde have slaine him; and he fell downe on his knees, and besought them to have compassion upon him: he was but a poore fisherman, and had not that which they sought for: it were others that were more fit for their purpose to meete withall, such as ventured further in greater vesselles, carrying foorth great summes of money, and bringing home plenty of costly merchandize: As for him, they should not only find miserable povertie in ransacking his boat, but if they were also determined to take away his life from him, they should likewise with the same stroke bereave the lives of his poore wife, and many small Children, which were maintained by his hand onely. These or the like words uttered then the poore fisherman. But they smiling in their conceites, and mindefull of their Princes commaundement, bade him not feare that they would robbe him, but saide that he must goe with them, and brought him away unto the court. And when he was come into the kings presence, Apollonius knewe him well, and saide unto the Queene and the Nobles that were about him: Beholde, this is the man that received me into his house, and succoured mee when I suffered shipwracke, and shewed me the way into the Citie, by which meanes I came acquainted with good king Altistrates. And he rose out of his seate, and embraced him and said: I am Apollonius Prince of Tyrus whome thou diddest succour, and therefore bee of good cheere, for thou shalt be rewarded. And the poore fisherman wept exceedingly for joy. And Apollonius commaunded two hundred sestercies of gold to be given unto him, and thirty servants, and twenty handmaides, and fortie horses, and fiftie sutes of apparell, and a faire pallace to dwel in, and made him an earle, and used no man so familiarly as he did him all the dayes of his life. Nowe it was not long after that these things were done, but one called Calamitus the master of the ship of Tyrus, an olde man, who, as we have before declared, shewed unto Apollonius as hee was walking by the sea side with Lucina, that Antiochus and his daughter were dead, and the kingdome was reserved for him, came before Apollonius, and, falling downe on his knees: Remember me, my most gratious Lorde Apollonius saide hee, since the time I tolde your grace the good tidings of king Antiochus death.

Then king Apollonius tooke him up by the hand, and caused him to sit downe by him, and talked familiarly with him, and gave him great thankes, and made him a great lord in his countrey. Thus Apollonius busied himselfe, not onely in bestowing himselfe curteously at home, but he also provided as well for the quiet governement of the state abroad, as it appeared by the diligence of his officers, who having lately taken certaine pyrates upon the sea, brought them to Pentapolis, where Apollonius then remained, to have justice executed upon them. When they were arrived, they were found guilty of the facte of which they were accused, and the next day being appointed for them to suffer, when they came unto the gallowes, they confessed many robberies, and among store, how once at Tharsus they rescued a maide named Tharsia from a villaine that woulde have slaine her, and brought her to Machilenta, where they solde her to him that offered most money, and hee which bought her (as they thought) was a bawd. When the citizens, who were none of them ignorant of the Ladie Tharsias adventures, heard this, they stayed execution, and sent word unto king Apollonius, saying: May it please your grace to understand that we have certaine pyrates at the gallowes ready to be executed, and it appeareth that they be those that stole away the lady Tharsia your daughter from Tharsus, and sold her to the bawd at Machilenta. Which when we perceived, we thought it good to know your graces pleasure what shall be doone with them. Apollonius thanked them, and willed the pirats to be brought before him, & examined them diligently, and found that they were the same men indeede that had preserved Tharsias life. And he gave great thankes unto God and them, and imbraced them, & willingly pardoned them their lives.

And for that he knew that the sinister means which they hitherto had insued was caused most by constraint, for want of other trade or abilitie to live by, he therefore made them all knights, and gave them plenty of gold and silver, and indowed them also with great possessions.

CHAP. XXIV

How Apollonius had a yoong sonne and heire by his wife Lucina, likewise of Apollonius age, and how he died: with some other accidents thereunto incident.

While king Apollonius thus passed foorth his time in rewarding his friends which had doone him pleasure in his adversitie, the part of a thankeful and good natured man, and also unto his enemies in ministring justice with mercie, which is the duetie of a vertuous prince, the queene Lucina in the meane season conceived childe, and grewe every daie bigger bellied then other. And when the time came that she attended for a good houre, she was delivered of a faire sonne, whom some of the Ladies that were present saide hee was like Apollonius the father, other some, like king Altistrates the grandfather, and others judged otherwise, according as is the custome of women to doe, when as (God knoweth) there is no more likenesse betweene them saving that the childe hath the generall shape and proportion of a man, than is betweene Jacke fletcher and his bolt. Howbeit the boy was called Altistrates, after the grandfathers name, for whome there was much joy and triumphing, that it had pleased

God to send an heire male to governe the land, for whose life and preservation the people daily prayed, that as he was like to succeede his grandfather in place and name, so hee might also be successour to his father and grandfather in honour and vertue, which as they are the true goods, so are they the chiefest inheritance of a king, and to be preferred before the greedie seeking for large dominion and riches, which are the foolish scales whereby Fortune intrappeth us.

But to returne againe to our story, great was the care and provision for the diligent bringing up of this yoong gentleman: who as he grew up more and more every day to the strength of lusty youth, so his father Apollonius decayed continually through the infirmity of weake old age: Who having passed his life with one Ladie the faire Lucina, by whome hee had two beautifull children, the ladie Tharsia and yoong Altistrates, he lived to the age of fourescore and foure yeers, and obtained the empire of three kingdomes, to wit, Tyrus, Antiochia and Pentapolis, whome with the helpe of his sonne in lawe Athanagoras he governed peaceably and prosperously. Moreover, when hee had disposed the affaires of his realmes unto such of his nobilitie as were in credite about him, although at all times he had recourse unto his accustomed studies of humanitie, yet then especially he applied his vacant time to his booke, and hee wrote the whole storie and discourse of his owne life and adventures at large, the which he caused to be written foorth in two large volumes, whereof he sent one to the Temple of Diana at Ephesus, and placed the other in his owne library. Of which historie this is but a small abstract, promising if ever the whole chance to come into my hands, to set it forth with all fidelitie, diligence, and expedition. But when the fatall time was come that Apollonius olde age could no longer be sustained by the benefite of nature, he fell into certaine cold and drie diseases, in which case the knowledge of his physitions could stand him in little steed, either by their cunning or experience. For there is no remedie against olde age, which if the noble skill of phisicke could ever have found out, doubtlesse it would have obtained the means to have made the state of man immortall. Howbeit, God hath determined otherwise; and as he appointed all worldly things to have an end, so Apollonius had his dying day, wherein in perfect sense, and readie memorie, hee departed this transitorie life in the sweete armes of his loving ladie Lucina, and in the midst of his friendes, Nobles, Allies, kinsfolke, and children, in great honour, and love of all men. His kingdome of Tyrus he gave by will unto Athanagoras and his daughter Tharsia, and to their heires after them for ever[1]:

---

[1] V.3.82.

who lived long time togither, and had much issue, both boyes and girles. Unto the queene Ladie Lucina, he gave the two kingdomes of Antiochia and Pentapolis, for terme of her life, to deale or dispose at her pleasure; and after her decease unto his sonne lusty yoong Altistrates, and to his heires for ever: But Lucina, as she could not then be yoong, since Apollonius died so old, enjoyed not long her widows estate, but pining away with sorrow, and wearing with age, forsooke this present world also, and followed her deare lord into the everlasting kingdome that never shall have end, which so farre exceedeth the kingdome, which forthwith she left unto her yoong sonne Altistrates to inherite, as heavenly joyes surmount the earthly, and the bright sunne surpasseth the smallest starre.

III. Analogue

From

THE COUNTESS OF PEMBROKE'S ARCADIA

by Sir Philip Sidney (1590)[1]

(a) Book 1, Ch. 1.

[Two shepherds, Claius and Strephon, are praising their absent mistress Urania when they see a man in the sea.]

He was going on with his praises, but *Strephon* bad him stay, & looke: & so they both perceaved a thing which floted drawing nearer and nearer to the banke; but rather by the favourable working of the Sea, then by any selfe industrie. They doubted a while what it should be; till it was cast up even hard before then: at which time they fully saw that it was a man: Wherupon running for pitie sake unto him, they found his hands (as it should appeare, constanter frends to his life then his memorie) fast griping upon the edge of a square small coffer, which lay all under his breast: els in him selfe no shew of life, so as the boord seemed to bee but a beere to carry him a land to his Sepulchre. So drew they up a young man of so goodly shape, and well pleasing favour, that one would think death

---

[1] The Countesse of Pembrokes Aracadia, Written by Sir Philippe Sidnei. London. Printed for William Ponsonbie. *Anno Domini*, 1590.

had in him a lovely countenance; and, that though he were naked, nakednes was to him an apparrell. That sight increased their compassion, and their compassion called up their care; so that lifting his feete above his head, making a great deale of salt water to come out of his mouth, they layd him upon some of their garments, and fell to rub and chafe him, till they brought him to recover both breath the servant, & warmth the companion of living. At length, opening his eyes, he gave a great groane, (a dolefull note but a pleasaunt dittie) for by that, they found not onely life, but strength of life in him. They therefore continued on their charitable office, until (his spirits being well returned,) hee (without so much as thanking them for the paines) gate up, and looking round about to the uttermost lymittes of his sight, and crying upon the name of *Pyrocles*, nor seeing nor hearing cause of comfort: what (said he) and shall *Musidorus* live after *Pyrocles*? therewithall hee offered wilfully to cast destruction & himselfe againe into the sea: a strange sight to the shepheards, to whom it seemed, that before being in apparance dead had yet saved his life, and now comming to his life, shoulde be a cause to procure his death; but they ranne unto him, and pulling him backe, (then too feeble for them) by force stickled that unnatural fray. I pray you (said he) honest men, what such right have you in me, as not to suffer me to doe with my self what I list? and what pollicie have you to bestow a benefite where it is counted an injury? They hearing him speake in Greek (which was their naturall language) became the more tender hearted towards him; and considering by his calling and looking, that the losse of some deare friend was great cause of his sorow; told him they were poore men that were bound by course of humanitie to prevent so great a mischiefe; and that they wisht him, if opinion of some bodies perishing bred such desperate anguish in him, that he should be comforted by his owne proofe, who had lately escaped as apparant danger as any might be. No, no (said hee) it is not for me to attend so high a blissefulnesse: but since you take care of mee, I pray you finde meanes that some Barke may be provided, that will goe out of the haven, that if it be possible we may finde the body farre farre too precious a foode for fishes: and for the hire (said he) I have within this casket, of value sufficient to content them. *Claius* presently went to a Fisherman, & having agreed with him, and provided some apparrell for the naked stranger, he imbarked, and the Shepheards with him: and were no sooner gone beyond the mouth of the haven, but that some way into the sea they might discerne (as it were) a stayne of the waters colour, and by times some sparkes and smoke mounting thereout. But the young man no sooner saw it, but that beating his brest, he cried,

32

that there was the beginning of his ruine, intreating them to bend their course as neere unto it as they could: telling, how that smoake was but a small relique of a great fire, which had driven both him & his friend rather to committe themselves to the cold mercie of the sea, then to abide the hote crueltie of the fire: and that therefore, though they both had abandoned the ship, that he was (if any where) in that course to be met withall. They steared therefore as neere thetherward as they could: but when they came so neere as their eies were ful masters of the object, they saw a sight full of piteous strangenes: a ship, or rather the carkas of the shippe, or rather some few bones of the carkas, hulling there, part broken, part burned, part drowned: death having used more then one dart to that destruction. About it floted great store of very rich thinges, and many chestes which might promise no lesse. And amidst the precious things were a number of dead bodies, which likewise did not onely testifie both elements violence, but that the chiefe violence was growen of humane inhumanitie: for their bodies were ful of grisly wounds, & their bloud had (as it were) filled the wrinckles of the seas visage: which it seemed the sea woulde not wash away, that it might witnes it is not alwaies his fault, when we condemne his crueltie: in summe, a defeate, where the conquered kept both field and spoile: a shipwrack without storme or ill footing: and a wast of fire in the midst of water.

But a litle way off they saw the mast, whose proude height now lay along; like a widdow having lost her make of whom she held her honor: but upon the mast they saw a yong man (at least if he were a man) bearing shew of about 18 yeares of age, who sate (as on horsback) having nothing upon him but his shirt, which being wrought with blew silk & gold; had a kind of resemblance to the sea: on which the sun (then neare his Westerne home) did shoote some of his beames. His haire (which the young men of Greece used to weare very long) was stirred up & down with the wind, which seemed to have a sport to play with it, as the sea had to kisse his feet; himselfe full of admirable beautie, set foorth by the strangenes both of his seate & gesture: for, holding his head up full of unmoved majestie, he held a sworde aloft with his faire arme, which often he waved about his crowne as though he would threaten the world in that extremitie. But the fishermen, when they came so neere him, that it was time to throwe out a rope, by which hold they might draw him, their simplicity bred such amasement, & their amasement such a superstition, that (assuredly thinking it was some God begotten betweene *Neptune* and *Venus*, that had made all this terrible slaughter) as they went under sayle by him, held up their hands, and

made their prayers. Which when *Musidorus* sawe, though he were
almost as much ravished with joy, as they with astonishment, he
lept to the Mariner, and tooke the rope out of his hande and (saying,
doest thou live, and arte well? who answered, thou canst tell best,
since most of my well beyng standes in thee,) threwe it out, but
alreadie the shippe was past beyond *Pyrocles*: and therefore *Musidorus*
could doo no more but perswade the Mariners to cast about againe,
assuring them that hee was but a man, although of most divine
excellencies, and promising great rewardes for their paine.

And now they were alreadie come upon the staies; when one of
the saylers descried a Galley which came with sayles and oares
directlie in the chase of them; and streight perceaved it was a well
knowne Pirate, who hunted not onely for goodes but for bodies of
menne, which hee imployed eyther to bee his Galley slaves, or to
sell at the best market. Which when the Maister understood, he
commaunded forthwith to set on all the canvasse they could, and
flie homeward, leaving in that sort poore *Pyrocles* so neere to be
reskewed. But what did not *Musidorus* say? what did he not offer to
perswade them to venture the fight? But feare standing at the gates
of their eares, put back all perswasions: so that hee had nothing to
accompanie *Pyrocles*, but his eyes; nor to succour him, but his wishes.
Therefore praying for him, and casting a long look that way he saw
the Galley leave the pursuite of them, & turne to take up the spoiles
of the other wrack: and lastly he might well see them lift up the
yong man; and alas (said he to himselfe) deere *Pyrocles* shall that
bodie of thine be enchayned? shall those victorious handes of thine
be commaunded to base offices? shall vertue become a slave to those
that be slaves to viciousnes? Alas, better had it bene thou hadst
ended nobly thy noble daies: what death is so evill as unworthy
servitude? But that opinion soone ceased when he saw the gallie
setting upon an other ship, which held long and strong fight with
her: for then he began a fresh to feare the life of his friende, and to
wish well to the Pirates whome before he hated, least in their ruyne
hee might perish. But the fishermen made such speed into the haven,
that they absented his eyes from beholding the issue: where being
entred, he could procure neither them nor any other as then to put
themselves into the sea: so that beyng as full of sorrow for being
unable to doe any thing, as voide of counsell how to doe any thing,
besides, that sicknesse grew something upon him, the honest
shepheards *Strephon* and *Claius* (who being themselves true friends,
did the more perfectly judge the justnesse of his sorrowe) advise him,
that he should mitigate somwhat of his woe, since he had gotten
an amendment in fortune, being come from assured persuasion

of his death, to have no cause to dispaire of his life: as one that had lamented the death of his sheepe, should after know they were but strayed, would receive pleasure though readily hee knew not where to finde them.

(b) Book 1, Ch. 8.

[Pyrocles tells Musidorus of his adventures since the shipwreck.]

But first at *Musidorus* request, though in brief manner, his mind much running upon the strange storie of *Arcadia*, he did declare by what course of adventures he was come to make up their mutuall happinesse in meeting. When (cosin, said he) we had stript our selves, and were both leapt into the Sea, and swom a little toward the shoare, I found by reason of some wounds I had, that I should not be able to get the lande, and therefore turned backe againe to the mast of the shippe, where you found me, assuring my selfe, that if you came alive to the shore, you would seeke me; if you were lost, as I thought it as good to perishe as to live, so that place as good to perish in as an other. There I found my sworde among some of the shrowds, wishing (I must confesse) if I died, to be found with that in my hand, and withall waving it about my head, that saylers by it might have the better glimpse of me. There you missing me, I was taken up by Pyrates, who putting me under boorde prisoner, presentlie sett uppon another shippe, and mainteining a long fight, in the ende, put them all to the sworde. Amongst whom I might heare them greatlie prayse one younge man, who fought most valiantlie, whom (as love is carefull, and misfortune subject to doubtfulnes) I thought certainely to be you. And so holding you as dead, from that time till the time I sawe you, in trueth I sought nothing more then a noble ende, which perchance made me more hardie then otherwise I would have bene. Triall whereof came within two dayes after: for the Kinges of *Lacedæmon* having sett out some Galleys, under the charge of one of their Nephews to skowre the Sea of the Pyrates, they met with us, where our Captaine wanting men, was driven to arme some of his prisoners, with promise of libertie for well fighting: among whom I was one, and being boorded by the Admirall, it was my fortune to kil *Eurileon* the Kings nephew: but in the end they prevailed, & we were all taken prisoners: I not caring much what became of me (onely keeping the name of *Daiphantus*, according to the resolution you know is betweene us,) but beyng laid in the jayle of *Tenaria*, with speciall hate to me for the death of *Eurileon*, the popular sort of that towne conspired with the *Helots*, and so by night opened them the gates; where entring and

killing all of the gentle and riche faction, for honestie sake brake open
all prisons, and so delivered me; and I mooved with gratefulnesse,
and encouraged with carelesnesse of life, so behaved my selfe in
some conflictes they had in fewe dayes, that they barbarouslie thinking unsensible wonders of mee, and withall so much they better
trusting mee, as they heard I was hated of the Kinge of *Lacedæmon*,
(their chiefe Captayne beyng slaine as you knowe by the noble
Argalus, who helped thereunto by his perswasion) having borne a
great affection unto me, and to avoyde the daungerous emulation
whiche grewe among the chiefe, who should have the place, and all
so affected, as rather to have a straunger then a competitour, they
elected mee, (God wotte little prowde of that dignitie,) restoring
unto mee such thinges of mine as being taken first by the pyrates, and
then by the *Lacedæmonians*, they had gotten in the sacke of the towne.
Now being in it, so good was my successe with manie victories, that
I made a peace for them to their owne liking, . . .

(c) Book 1, Ch. 10.

[Calling himselfe Palladius, Musidorus is searching for Pyrocles
(Daiphantus) with Prince Clitophon.]

And so went they, making one place succeed to an other, in like
uncertaintie to their search, manie times encountring strange
adventures, worthy to be registred in the roulles of fame; but this
may not be omitted. As they past in a pleasant valley, (of either side
of which high hils lifted up their beetle-browes, as if they would
over looke the pleasantnes of their under-prospect) they were by the
daintines of the place, & the wearines of themselves, invited to light
from their horses; & pulling of their bits, that they might something refresh their mouths upon the grasse (which plentifully grewe,
brought up under the care of those wel shading trees,) they themselves laid them downe hard by the murmuring musicke of certain
waters, which spouted out of the side of the hils, and in the bottome
of the valley, made of many springs a pretie brooke, like a commonwealth of many families: but when they had a while harkened to the
persuasion of sleepe, they rose, and walkt onward in that shadie
place, till *Clitiphon* espied a peece of armour, & not far of an other
peece: and so the sight of one peece teaching him to looke for more,
he at length found all, with headpeece & shield, by the devise
whereof, . . . he streight knew it to be the armour of his cousin, the
noble *Amphialus*. Wherupon (fearing some inconvenience hapned
unto him) he told both his doubte, and his cause of doubte to
Palladius, who (considering therof) thought best to make no longer

stay, but to follow on: least perchance some violence were offered to so worthy a Knight, whom the fame of the world seemed to set in ballance with any Knight living. Yet with a sodaine conceipt, having long borne great honour to the name of *Amphialus, Palladius* thought best to take that armour, thinking thereby to learne by them that should know that armour, some newes of *Amphialus,* & yet not hinder him in the search of *Daiphantus* too. So he by the help of *Clitophon* quickly put on that armour, whereof there was no one piece wanting, though hacked in some places, bewraying some fight not long since passed. It was some-thing too great, but yet served well enough. [The armour belonged to Pyrocles.]

(d) Book 2, Ch. 7.

[The first shipwreck of Pyrocles and Musidorus on their way to the siege of Byzantium. Their first day on board was fine.]

And so the Princes delighting their conceats with confirming their knowledge, seing wherein the Sea-discipline differed from Land-service, they had for a day & almost a whole night, as pleasing entertainement, as the falsest hart could give to him he meanes worst to.

But by that the next morning began a little to make a guilden shewe of a good meaning, there arose even with the Sun, a vaile of darke cloudes before his face, which shortly (like inck powred into water) had blacked over all the face of heaven; preparing (as it were) a mournefull stage for a Tragedie to be plaied on. For forthwith the windes began to speake lowder, and as in a tumultuous kingdome, to thinke themselves fittest instruments of commaundement; and blowing whole stormes of hayle and raine upon them, they were sooner in daunger, then they coulde almost bethinke themselves of chaunge. For then the traiterous Sea began to swell in pride against the afflicted Navie, under which (while the heaven favoured them) it had layne so calmely, making mountaines of it selfe, over which the tossed and tottring ship shoulde clime, to be streight carried downe againe to a pit of hellish darkenesse; with such cruell blowes against the sides of the shippe (that which way soever it went, was still in his malice) that there was left neither power to stay, nor way to escape. And shortly had it so dissevered the loving companie, which the daie before had tarried together, that most of them never met againe, but were swallowed up in his never-satisfied mouth. Some indeed (as since was knowne) after long wandring returned into *Thessalia*; other recovered *Bizantium*, and served *Euarchus* in his warre. But in the ship wherein the Princes were (now left as much alone as proud Lords be when fortune fails them) though they employed all industrie to save themselves, yet what they did was rather for dutie to nature, then hope to escape. So ougly a darkenesse, as if it would prevent the nights comming, usurped the dayes right: which (accompanied sometimes with thunders, alwayes with horrible noyses of the chafing winds) made the masters and pilots so astonished, that they knew not how to direct, and if they knew they could scarcely (when they directed) heare their owne whistle. For the sea strave with the winds which should be lowder, & the shrouds of the ship with a ghastful noise to them that were in it, witnessed, that their ruine was the wager of the others contention, and the heaven roaring out thunders the more amazed them, as having those powers for enimies. Certainely there is no daunger carries with it more horror, then that which growes in those flowing kingdomes. For that dwelling place is unnaturall to mankind, and then the terriblenesse of the continuall motion, the dissolution of the fare being from comfort, the eye and the eare having ougly images ever before it, doth still vex the minde, even when it is best armed against it. But thus the day past (if that might be called a day) while the cunningest mariners were so conquered by the storme, as they thought it best with striking sailes to yeelde to be governed by it: the valiantest feeling inward dismayednesse, and yet the fearefullest ashamed fully to shew it, seeing that the Princes (who were to parte from the greatest fortunes) did in their counten-ances accuse no point of feare, but encouraging them to doo what might be done (putting their handes to everie most painefull office) taught them at one instant to promise themselves the best, and yet not to despise the worst. But so were they carryed by the tyrannie of the winde, and the treason of the sea, all that night, which the elder it was, the more wayward it shewed it selfe towards them: till the next morning (knowne to be a morning better by the houre-glasse, then by the day cleerenesse) having runne fortune as blindly, as it selfe ever was painted, lest the conclusion should not aunswere to the rest of the play, they were driven upon a rocke: which hidden with those outragious waves, did, as it were, closely dissemble his cruel mind, till with an unbeleeved violence (but to them that have tried it) the shippe ranne upon it; and seeming willinger to perish then to have her course stayed, redoubled her blowes, till she had broken her selfe in peeces; and as it were tearing out her owne bowels to feede the seas greedinesse, left nothing within it but des-paire of safetie, and expectation of a loathsome end. There was to be seene the diverse manner of minds in distresse: some sate upon the toppe of the poupe weeping and wailing, till the sea swallowed them; some one more able to abide death, then feare of death, cut his owne throate to prevent drowning; some prayed, and there wanted not of them which cursed, as if the heavens could not be more angrie then they were. But a monstrous crie begotten of manie roaring vowes, was able to infect with feare a minde that had not prevented it with the power of reason.

But the Princes using the passions of fearing evill, and desiring to escape, onely to serve the rule of vertue, not to abandon ones selfe, lept to a ribbe of the shippe, which broken from his fellowes, floted with more likelyhood to doo service, then any other limme of that ruinous bodie; upon which there had gotten alreadie two brethren, well knowne servants of theirs; and streight they foure were carried out of sight, in that huge rising of the sea, from the rest of the shippe.

(e) Book 3, Ch. 23.

[Pyrocles (Zelmane) is mourning the supposed death of Philoclea.]

Then stopping his woordes with sighes, drowning his sighes in teares, & drying againe his teares in rage, he would sitte a while in a wandring muse, which represented nothing but vexations unto him: then throwing himselfe somtimes upon the floore, and sometimes upon the bedde: then up againe, till walking was wearisome, and rest loathsome: and so neither suffering foode, nor sleepe to helpe his afflicted nature, all that day and night he did nothing, but weepe *Philoclea*, sigh *Philoclea*, and crie out *Philoclea*: till as it happened (at that time upon his bed) towarde the dawning of the day, he heard one stirre in his chamber, by the motion of garments; and he with an angry voice asked, Who was there? A poore Gentlewoman (answered the partie) that wish long life unto you. And I soone death to you (said he) for the horrible curse you have given me. Certainely (said she) an unkinde answere, and far unworthy the excellencie of your mind; but not unsutable to the rest of your behaviour. For most parte of this night I have hearde you (being let into your chamber, you never perceiving it, so was your minde estraunged from your senses) and have hearde nothing of *Zelmane*, in *Zelmane*, nothing but weake waylings, fitter for some nurse of a village, then so famous a creature as you are. O God (cried out *Pyrocles*) that thou wert a man that usest these wordes unto me. I tell thee I am sory: I tell thee I will be sory in despite of thee, and all them that would have me joyfull. And yet (replied she) perchaunce *Philoclea* is not dead, whom you so much bemone. I would we were both dead of that condition, said *Pyrocles*. See the folly of your passion (said she) as though you should be neerer to her, you being dead, and she alive; then she being dead, & you alive: & if she be dead, was she not borne to die? what then do you crie out for? not for her, who must have died one time or other; but for some fewe yeares: so as it is time, & this world that seeme so lovely things, and not *Philoclea* unto you. O noble Sisters (cried *Pyrocles*) now you be gone (who were the onely exalters of all womankind) what is left in that sex, but babling, and businesse? And truly (said she) I will yet a little longer trouble you. Nay, I pray you doo (said *Pyrocles*) for I wishe for nothing in my shorte life, but mischiefes, and combers: and I am content you shall be one of them. In truth (said she) you would thinke your selfe a greatly priviledged person, if since the strongest buildings, and lastingest monarchies are subject to end, onely your *Philoclea* (because she is yours) should be exempted. But indeede you bemone your selfe, who have lost a friende: you cannot her, who hath in one act both preserved her honour, and lefte the miseries of this worlde. O womans philosophie, childish follie (said *Pyrocles*) as though if I do bemone my selfe, I have not reason to doo so, having lost more then any Monarchie, nay then my life can be woorth unto me. Alas (said she) comforte your selfe, Nature did not forget her skill, when she had made them: you shall find many their superiours, and perchaunce such, as (when your eyes shall looke abroad) your selfe will like better.

But that speech put all good manners out of the conceit of *Pyrocles*; in so much, that leaping out of his bed, he ran to have striken her: but comming neere her (the morning then winning the field of darknesse) he saw, or he thought he sawe, indeede, the very face of *Philoclea*; the same sweetenesse, the same grace, the same beautie: with which carried into a divine astonishment, he fell downe at her feete. Most blessed Angell (said he) well haste thou done to take that shape, since thou wouldest submit thy selfe to mortall sense; for a more Angelicall forme could not have bene created for thee. Alas, even by that excellent beautie, so beloved of me, let it be lawfull for me to aske of thee, what is the cause, that she, that heavenly creature, whose forme you have taken, should by the heavens be destined to so unripe an ende? Why should unjustice so prevaile? Why was she seene to the world, so soone to be ravished from us? Why was she not suffered to live, to teach the world perfection? Doo not deceive thy selfe (answered she) I am no Angell; I am *Philoclea*, the same *Philoclea*, so truely loving you, so truly beloved of you. If it be so (said he) that you are indeede the soule of *Philoclea*, you have done well to keepe your owne figure: for no heaven could have given you a better. Then alas, why have you taken the paines to leave your blisfull seat to come to this place most wretched, to me, who am wretchednes it selfe, & not rather obtain for me, that I might come where you are, there eternally to behold, & eternally to love your beauties? you know (I know) that I desire nothing but death, which I only stay, to be justly revenged of your unjust murtherers. Deare *Pyrocles* (said she) I am thy *Philoclea*, and as yet living: not murdred, as you supposed, and therefore to be comforted. And with that gave him her hand. But the sweet touch of that hande, seemed to his astraied powers so heavenly a thing, that it rather for a while confirmed him in his former beliefe: till she, with vehement protestations (and desire that it might be so, helping to perswade that it was so) brought him to yeeld; yet doubtfully to yeelde to this height of al comfort, that *Philoclea lived*.

IV. Analogue

THE PAINFULL ADVENTURES OF PERICLES PRINCE OF TYRE

by George Wilkins (1608)[1]

The Painfull Adventures of Pericles Prince of Tyre. Being the true History of the Play of *Pericles*, as it was lately presented by the worthy and ancient Poet John Gower. At London Printed by T.P. for Nat: Butter, 1608.

The Argument of the whole Historie

Antiochus the Great, who was the first founder of *Antioch*, the most famous Citty in all *Syria*, having one onelie daughter, in the prime and glory of her youth, fell in most unnaturall love with her; and what by the power of his perswasions, and feare of his tyranny, he so prevailed with her yeelding heart, that he became maister of his desires; which to continue to himself, his daughter being for her beauty desired in marriage of many great princes, he made this law, That whoso presumed to desire her in marriage, and could not unfold the meaning of his questions, for that attempt should loose his life. Fearelesse of this Lawe, many Princes adventured, and in their rashnesse perished: amongst the number PERICLES the Prince of

---

[1] Text based on the B.M. copy (C 34.1.8) with punctuation occasionally modified. For the Dedication by George Wilkins to 'Maister Henry Fermor', a Middlesex J.P., see K. Muir's valuable edition (Liverpool, 1953).

Tyre, and neighbour to this tyrant King *Antiochus*, was the last who undertooke to resolve this Riddle, which he accordingly, through his great wisedome, performed: and finding both the subtiltie and sinne of the Tyrant, for his owne safetie fled secretly from *Antioch* backe to *Tyre*, and there acquainted *Helycanus* a grave Counsellour of his with the proceedings, as also with his present feare what might succeed, from whose counsell he tooke advise, for a space to leave his kingdome, and betake himselfe to travell; to which yeelding, *Pericles* puts to sea, arives at *Tharsus*, which he finds (thorow the dearth of corne) in much distresse: he there relieves *Cleon* and *Dyonysa* with their distressed City, with the provision which he brought of purpose; but by his good Counsellour *Helycanus* hearing newes of *Antiochus* death, he intends for *Tyre*, puts againe to Sea, suffers shipwracke, his shippes and men all lost, till (as it were) Fortune tyred with his mis-happes, he is throwne upon the shoare, releeved by certaine poore Fishermen, and by an Armour of his which they by chaunce dragged up in their nettes, his misfortunes being a little repaired, *Pericles* arrives at the Court of good *Symonides* King of *Pentapolis*, where through his noblenesse both in Armes and Arts, he winnes the love of faire *Thaysa* the kings daughter, and by her fathers consent marries her.

In this absence of his, and, for which absence the *Tyrians* his subjects muteny, would elect *Helycanus* (whome *Pericles* ordained his substitute in his absence) their King, which passion of theirs *Helycanus* by his grave perswasions subdewed, and wonne them to goe in quest of their lost Prince *Pericles*: In this search he is found, and with his wife *Thaysa*, who is now with childe, and *Lycorida* her Nurse; having taken leave of his kingly Father, puts againe for *Tyre*, but with the terrour of a tempest at Sea, his Queene falles in travell, is delivered of a daughter, whome hee names *Marina*, in which childe-birth his Queene dies, she is throwne overboorde, at departure of whome *Pericles* altereth his course from Tyre, being a shorter cut, to his hoste *Cleon* in *Tharsus*; hee there leaves his yoong daughter to be fostered up, vowing to himselfe a solitary and pensive life for the losse of his Queene.

Thaysa thus supposed dead, and in the seas buried, is the next morning on the shore taken up at *Ephesus* by *Cerimon* a most skilfull Physition, who by his Arte practised upon this Queene, so prevailed, that after five houres intraunced, she is by his skill brought to able health againe, and by her owne request, by him placed to live a Votary in *Dianaes* Temple at *Ephesus*. *Marina Pericles* sea-borne daughter, is by this growen to discreete yeares, she is envied of *Dyonysa Cleons* wife, her foster mother, for that *Marinaes* perfection exceedeth a daughter of hers, *Marina* by this envy of hers should have beene murthered, but being rescued by certaine Pyrates, is as it were reserved to a greater mishap, for by them she is carried to *Metelyne*, sold to the devils broker a bawd, to have bin trained up in that infection, shee is courted of many, and how wonderfully she preserves her chastitie.

Pericles returnes from Tyre toward *Tharsus*, to visite the hospitable *Cleon*, *Dyonysa*, and his yoong daughter *Marina*, where by *Dyonysaes* dissembling teares, and a Toombe that was erected for her, *Pericles* is brought to beleeve, that his *Marina* lies there buryed, and that shee died of her naturall death, for whose losse hee teares his haire, throwes off his garments, forsweares the societie of men, or any other comfort. In which passion for many moneths continuing, hee at last arrives at *Metelyne*, when being seene and pittied by *Lysimachus* the Governour, his daughter (though of him unknowen so) is by the Governour sent for, who by her excellent skill in Song, and pleasant-nesse in discourse, with relating the story of her owne mishap, shee so winnes againe her fathers lost sences, that hee knowes her for his childe, shee him for her father; in which over-joy, as if his sences were nowe all confounded, *Pericles* falles asleepe, where in a dreame he is by *Diana* warned to goe to *Ephesus*, and there to make his sacrifice. *Pericles* obayes, and there comes to the knowledge of *Thaysa* his wife, with their severall Joyes that they three so strangely divided, are as strangely mette. *Lysimachus* the Governour marrieth *Marina*, and *Pericles* leaving his mourning, causeth the bawde to be burned. Of his revenge to *Cleon* and *Dyonysa*, his rewarding of the Fishermen that releeved him, his justice toward the Pyrats that made sale of his daughter, his returne backe to his kingdome, and of him and his wifes deaths. Onely intreating the Reader to receive this Historie in the same maner as it was under the habite of ancient *Gower* the famous English Poet, by the Kings Majesties Players excellently presented.

The names of the Personages mentioned in this Historie.

John Gower the Presenter.
Antiochus that built Antioch
His daughter.
Pericles Prince of *Tyre*.
Thalyart a villaine.
Helycamus ⎫ Twoo grave
Eschines ⎭ Counsellors.
Cleon Governor of *Tharsus*.
Dyonysa his wife.

Five Princes.
Lycorida a Nurse.
Cerimon a Phisition.
Marina Pericles daughter.
A Murtherer.
Pirates.
A Bawde.
A *Leno*.
A Pander.

Two or three Fishermen.   *Lysimachus* Governour of *Meteline*.
Symonides king of *Pentapolis*
Thaysa his daughter.   *Diana* Goddesse of chastitie.

The
Painfull Adventures of Pericles
Prince of Tyre.

The first Chapter

Wherein *Gower* describes[1] how *Antiochus* surnamed the
Great committed incest with his daughter, and beheaded
such as sued to her for marriage, if they could not resolve
his question, placing their heades upon the top of his
Castle gate, whereby to astonish all others that came to
attempt the like.

The great and mighty King *Antiochus*, who was as cruell in tyranny,
as hee was powerfull in possessions, seeking more to enrich himselfe
by shewes, than to renown his name by vertue, caused to be built the
goodly Cittie of *Antioch* in *Syria*, and called it after his owne name,
as the chiefest seate of all his Dominions, and principall place of his
abode. This *Antiochus* had increase by his Queene one onely daughter,
so excellent in beauty, as if Nature and all Perfection had long
studied to seeme onely absolute at her birth. This Ladie growing to
like ripenesse of age, as shee had full endowment of outward ornaments, was resorted unto by many youthfull Princes, who desired her
in marriage, offering to make her Joynture as noble in possessions,
as shee by beauty was royall in her selfe. While the King her father
evermore requiring deliberation upon whome rather than other to
bestow this his so inestimable a Jewell, he beganne sodainely to have
an unlawfull concupiscence to growe in himselfe, which hee augmented with an outragious flame of cruelty sparkling in his hart,
and accompted her so worthy in the world, that shee was too worthy
for any, but himselfe. Thus being wrapped with this unnaturall love,
he sustained such a conflict in his thoughts, wherein Madnesse puts
Modesty to flight, giving over his affections to the unlawfulnesse of
his will, rather then subdued them with the remembraunce of the
evill hee had then in practise, so that not long after comming into
his daughters Chamber, and commaunding all that were neere at
her attendance to depart, as if he had had some carefull and fatherly
busines, the necessitie of whose import desired some private

[1] As in *Per.* I *Chor.*, 17ff. This chapter expands Twine's Ch. 1 with occasional
phrases from the dramatic source.

conference with her, he beganne to make motion of that unjust love to her, which even Lust it selfe, had it not in a father beene so brased with impudencie, would have blusht but even to have thought upon. Much perswasion, though to little reason, he used, as, that he was her father, whome shee was bound to obey, he was a King that had power to commaund, he was in love, and his love was resistlesse, and if resistlesse, therefore pittilesse, either to youth, blood, or beauty: In briefe, he was a tyrant and would execute his will. These wordes thus uttered with that vehement passion which such sinnefull Lovers fitte themselves unto in such desires, and such immodest sillables were by him contracted together, that my penne grubbes to recite them, and made the schoole of his daughters thoughts, (wherein were never taught such evills) to wonder at the strange-nesse, as understanding them not, and at last, to demaund of her unkingly father, what hee meant by this, when he forgetting the feare of heaven, love to his childe, or reputation amongst men; though by her withstoode with prayers and teares, (while the power of weaknesse could withstand)[1] throwing away all regard of his owne honesty, hee unloosed the knotte of her virginitie, and so left this weeping braunch to wyther by the stocke that brought her foorth; so fast came the wet from the sentinells of her ransackt cittie, that it is improper to say they dropped and rayned downe teares, but rather, that with great flouds they powred out water. It is beyond imagination to thinke whether her eyes had power to receive her sorrowes brine so fast as her heart did send it to them. In briefe, they were nowe no more to be called eyes, for griefes water had blinded them: and for wordes, she had not one to utter, for betwixt her hearts intent, and tongues utterance, there lay such a pile of lamentable cogitations, that she had no leisure to make up any of them into wordes, till at the last, a Nurse that attended her com-ming in, and finding her face blubbered with teares, which shee knew were strange guests to the table of her beauty, first standing in amaze thereat, at last, by the care shee had in charge of her, being more inheartned; Deare childe and Madam (quoth shee) why sit you so sorrowfully? which question, getting way betwixt griefe and her utteraunce, Oh my beloved Nurse, answered the Lady, even now two noble names were lost within this Chamber, the name of both a Father, and a Child. The meaning of which secret the Nurse understanding not, shee intreated her to be more plaine, that by knowing the cause of her griefe, shee might use meanes to redresse it, or else, that her selfe in her owne wisdome would alay the violence of that tempest which did wrong to so goodly a building. But shee

---

[1] Contrast I *Chor.*, 26, 'did provoke'.

loath to be the bellowes of her owne shame, and blushing more to rehearse than her Father was to commit, sate sighing, and continued silent, untill *Antiochus*, not satisfied with the fruite obtained by his former desire, returned, and like him that by stealth hath filched a taste from foorth a goodly Orchard, is not therewith contented, but eyther waiteth his opportunity to steale, till hee be glutted with his stealth, or so adventurous, that hee is taken, to his everlasting shame; so this *Antiochus* comming backe into the Chamber, and finding his daughter as full of wette, as winter is, commaunded the absence of the Nurse (which shee accordingly obeying) he beganne to perswade her, that actions past are not to be redeemed, that whats in secret done, is no sinne, since the concealement excuses it, that evills are no evills, if not thought upon, and that himselfe her Father had that power to gag all mouthes from speaking, if it were knowen. Besides her state, his greatnes, his kingdome, her beauty, were ornaments enow to draw the greatest Princes to joyne with her in marriage, and hee would further it. So with these and such like perswasions prevayling with his daughter, they long continued in these foule and unjust imbracements, till at last, the custome of sinne made it accompted no sinne.[1] And while this wicked Father shewed the countenaunce of a loving sire abroad in the eyes of his subjects, notwithstanding at home he rejoyceth to have played the parte of a husband with his owne childe, with false resemblaunce of marriage: and to the intent he might alwayes enjoy her, he invented a strange pollicie, to compell away all suters from desiring her in marriage, by propounding strange questions, the effect and true meaning whereof was thus published in writing, *Whoso attempteth and resolveth me of my Question, shall have my Daughter to wife: But whoso attempteth and faileth, shall loose his head.*

Which will of his, when Fame had blowne abroad, and that by this his Lawe there was found a possibilitie for the obtayning of this Lady, such was the singular report of her surpassing beautie, that many Princes, and men of great Nobilitie, to that purpose repaired thither, who not beeing able to explane his Riddle propounded, lost their heades, which to the terrifying of others that should attempt the like, were placed for open view on the toppe of his Castle gate.

The second Chapter

How *Pericles* arriving at *Antioch*, resolved the Kings Question: And how *Thalyart Antiochus* Steward was sent to murther him.

Whilest *Antiochus* continued thus exercising his tyranies on the

---

[1] I *Chor.* 30, 'account no sin'.

lives of severall princes, *Pericles* the Prince of *Tyre*, wonne with the wonderfull report of this Ladies beauty, was (as other Princes before) drawne to the undertaking of this desparate adventure; and approching neere *Antioch*, where there were no sooner newes that he was comming, but there was as great a preparation for the receiving of him, the Lords and Peeres in their richest ornaments to intertaine him; the people with their greedy and unsatisfied eyes to gaze upon him; for in that part of the world there was in those dayes no Prince so noble in Armes, or excellent in Artes, and had so generall and deserved a report by fame as *Pericles* Prince of *Tyre*. Which drew both Peere and People, with a joyfull and free desire to allow him their imbracements, and to wish him happy successe, requiring no other but such a happy Soveraigne to hope in: for so cunningly had *Antiochus* dealt in this incest with his daughter, that it was yet unsuspected of the neerest that attended him. With which solemnity and suffrages, being brought into the presence of the tyrant, and by him demaunded the cause of his arrivall at *Antioch*: and being by the Prince answered, that it was in love to his daughter, and in hope to enjoy her by resolving of his question, *Antiochus* then first beganne to perswade him from the enterprise, and to discourage him from his proceedings, by shewing him the frightfull heads of the former Princes, placed upon his Castle wall, and like to whome he must expect himselfe to be, if like them (as it was most like) hee failed in his attempt. But *Pericles* armed with these noble armours, Faithfulnesse and Courage, and making himselfe fitte for Death, if Death prooved fitte for him, replyed, That he was come now to meete Death willingly, if so were his misfortune, or to be made ever fortunate, by enjoying so glorious a beauty as was inthrond in his princely daughter, and was there now placed before him: which the tyrant receiving with an angry brow, threw downe the Riddle, bidding him, since perswasions could not alter him, to reade and die, being in himselfe confident the mysterie thereof was not to be unfolded: which the Prince taking up, read aloude, the purpose of which was in these wordes:

> *I am no viper, yet I feede*
> *On mothers flesh, that did me breede;*
> *I sought a husband, in which labour*
> *I found that kindnesse from a father:*
> *Hee's Father, Sonne, and Husband milde,*
> *I Mother, Wife, and yet his Childe:*
> *How this may be, and yet in two,*
> *As you will live, resolve it you.*[1]

[1] Almost verbatim as in play, I.i.64. Contrast Twine's version.

Which secret, whilest Prince *Pericles* was reading, *Antiochus* daughter, whether it were, that shee now lothed that unnecessary custome in which shee had so long continued, or that her owne affection taught her to be in love with his perfections, our storie leaves unmentioned: but this for certaine, all the time that the Prince was studying with what trueth to unfolde this darke *Enigma*, Desire flew in a robe of glowing blushes into her cheekes, and love inforced her to deliver thus much from hir owne tongue,[1] that he was sole soveraigne of all her wishes, and he the gentleman (of all her eies had ever yet behelde) to whome shee wished a thriving happinesse.[2] By which time the Prince having fully considered upon what he had read, and found the meaning, both of the secret, and their abhominable sinnes, *Antiochus* rising up, demanded the solution of his Question, or to attend the sentence of his death. But the gentle Prince wisely foreknowing, that it is as dangerous to play with tyrants evills, as the Flie to sport with the Candles flame, rather seemed to dissemble what he knew, than to discover his insight to *Antiochus* knowledge, yet so circumspectly,[3] that *Antiochus* suspected, or at least, his owne knowen guilt made him so suspect, that hee had found the meaning of his foule desire, and their more foule actions; and seeming (as it were) then to pitty him whom now in soule he hated, and that he rather required his future happinesse, than any blemish to his present fortunes, he tolde him, that for the honour of his name, the noblenesse of his woorth, nay his owne deere and present love to him (were it not against the dignity and state of his owne love) in his tender and princely disposition, he could from the whole world select him as a choice husband for his daughter, since hee found him so farre wide from revealing of the secret; yet thus farre hee should perceive his love should extend towardes him, which before time had not beene seene to stretch it selfe to any of those decaied princes, of whose falls, his eies were carefull witnesses, that for forty dayes he gave him onely longer respite, if by which time (and with all the indevours, counsell and advise hee could use) he can finde out what was yet concealed from him, it should be evident how gladly he would rejoyce to joy in such a sonne,[4] rather than have cause of sorrow by his untimely ruine: And in the meane time, in his owne Court, by the royaltie of his entertainment hee should perceive his welcom. With which, and other such like gratulations their presences being divided, *Antiochus* betooke himselfe to his Chamber, and princely *Pericles* to diligent consultations of his present estate, where when hee had a while considered with him-

---

[1] Note the blank verse lines here.
[2] I.1.59–60.
[3] Cf. *Per.* I.1.91–108.
[4] Paraphrases I.1.116–120.

selfe, that what he had found, was true, and this substantially was
the true meaning of his Riddle, hee was become both father, sonne,
and husband by his uncomely and abhorred actions with his owne
child, and shee a devourer of her mothers flesh, by the unlawfull
couplings with her owne father, and the defiling of her mothers bed,
and that this curtesie of *Antiochus* toward him, was but his hypocrisie,
to have his sinne concealed,[1] till he found fit occasion to take fit
revenge (by the instruments of tyrants,) poyson, treason, or by any
meanes, he resolved himselfe with all expedition, (the next darknesse being his best conductor,) to flie backe to *Tyre*,[2] which he
effecting, and *Antiochus* being now private in his lodging, and
ruminating with himselfe, that *Pericles* had found out the secret of
his evill, which hee in more secret had committed; and knowing,
that he had now[3] power to rip him open to the world, and make his
name so odious, that as now heaven did, so at the knowledge
thereof all good men would contemne him. And in this study, not
knowing how otherwise to helpe himselfe from this reproofe, he
hastily calleth for one *Thalyart*, who was Steward of his housholde,[4]
and in many things before had received the imbracement of his
minde; this *Thalyart*, (as *Pericles* fore-thought,) hee presently bribde
with gold, and furthered with poyson, to be this harmles gentlemans
executioner.[5] To which purpose, as hee was about to receive his
othe, there came hastily a Messenger that brought him newes, the
Tyrian shippes were that night departed his harbor, and that by
intelligence hee had learned the Prince also was fled for *Tyre*: at
whose escape *Antiochus* storming, but not desisting from his former
practise, hee commaunded his murthering minister[6] *Thalyart*, to
dispatch his best performance after him, sometime perswading him,
at others threatning him, in *Tyre* to see him, in *Tyre* to kil him, or
back to *Antioch* never to returne. Which villainous mind of his as
ready to yeeld, as the tyrant was to commaund,[7] *Thaliart* in all
secresie is shipt from *Antioch*, while *Pericles* in this interim is arrived at
Tyre, where, knowing what was past, and fearing what might succeed,
not to himself, but for the care he had of his subjects, remembring
his power, too weake if occasion were offred, to contend with the
greatnes of *Antiochus*: he was so troubled in mind,[8] that no advise of
counsell could perswade him, no delights of the eye content him,
neither any pleasure whatsoever comfort him, but still taking to
heart, that should *Antiochus* make warre upon him, as fearing lest he
should speake his shame which he intended not to reveale, his
misfortune should be the ruine of his harmlesse people.

---

[1] Paraphrase of I.1.121–31.   [2] I.1.134–42.   [3] no *1608*; now *Muir*.
[4] The incident follows I.1.14.   [5] I.1.155–6.
[6] Cf. Lady Macbeth I.5.48.   [7] I.1.161–71.   [8] Cf. I.2.1–33.

In this sorrowe consisting, one *Helycanus* a grave and wise Counsellor of his (as a good Prince is ever knowne by his prudent Counsell)
as much greeved in mind for his Princes distemperature, as his
Prince was troubled with the feare of his subjects mishap, came
hastily into the chamber to him, and finding him so distasting mirth,
that he abandoned all familiar society, he boldely beganne to
reproove him,[1] and not sparingly tolde him, he did not wel so to
abuse himselfe, to waste his body there with pyning sorrow, upon
whose safety depended the lives and prosperity of a whole kingdome,
that it was ill in him to doe it, and no lesse in his counsell to suffer
him, without contradicting it. At which, although the Prince bent
his brow stearnely against him, he left not to go forward, but plainly
tolde him, it was as fit for him being a Prince to heare of his owne
errour, as it was lawfull for his authority to commaund, that while he
lived so shut up, so unseene, so carelesse of his government, order
might be disorder for all him, and what detriment soever his subjects
should receive by this his neglect, it were injustice to be required at
his hands, which chiding of this good olde Lord, the gentle Prince
curteously receiving, tooke him into his armes, thankt him that he
was no flatterer, and commaunding him to seat himselfe by him,
he from poynt to poynt related to him all the occurrents past,[2] and
that his present sorrow was for the feare he had of *Antiochus* tyranny,
his present studies were for the good of his subjects, his present care
was for the continuing safety of his kingdome, of which himselfe was
a member, which for slacknesse chide him[3]: which uprightnes of
this Prince calling teares into the olde mans eies, and compelling his
knees to the earth, he humbly asked his pardon, confirming that
what he had spoke, sprung from the power of his dutie, and grew
not from the nature of disobedience. When *Pericles* no longer
suffring such honored aged knees to stoope to his youth, lifting him
up,[4] desired of him that his counsell now would teach him how to
avoide that danger, which his feare gave him cause to mistrust:
which in this manner was by the good *Helicanus* advised, and by
princely *Pericles* yeelded unto, that he should forthwith betake
himselfe to travel,[5] keeping his intent whither, as private from his
subjects, as his journey was suddaine, that upon his trust he should
leave the government, grounding which counsel upon this principle,
Absence abates that edge that Presence whets. In breefe, *Pericles*
knew *Helicanus* trusty, and consented: so with store of corne and all
necessaries fit for a kingly voyage, he in secret hath shipt himselfe

---

[1] Not in Twine. The whole scene is clearer here than in *Per.* I.2.
[2] Cf. I.2.70–83.   [3] I.2.84–95.
[4] I.2.59.   [5] I.2.106, 'go travel for a while'.

from *Tyre*. *Helycanus* is protector of the kingdome in his absence[1]: and our Story now hath brought us to the landing of *Thaliart*,[2] with a body fraught as full of treason against Pericles, as his maister *Antiochus* was of tyranny, who no sooner a shore, but he had his eares fild with the generall lamentation of the *Tyrian* people, the aged sighed, the youth wept, all mourned, helping one another how to make up sorrow to the highest heape, as if with the absence of their Prince they had lost their Prince,[3] and with his losse they had present feeling of a succeeding overthrow, which the vilaine understanding, and finding himselfe, both bereft of his purpose, and his maister of his intent, he, as traitors do, stole backe to *Antioch* resolving *Antiochus* of what he knew[4]: by which time, the clamors of the multitude being for a time pacified by the wisedome of *Helicanus*, and the peace of the common wealth by his prudence defended, our princely *Pericles* with spread sailes, faire winds, and full successe, is now arrived at *Tharsus*.

The third Chapter

How *Pericles* arriving at *Tharsus* releeved the Cittie, almost famished for want of foode, and how *Helycanus* sent him word of what had happened at *Tyre*, with his departure from *Tharsus*.

Prince *Pericles* by the advise of his good Counsellor *Helicanus*, having left *Tyre*, and intended his whole course for *Tharsus*, of which City lord *Cleon* was governor, who at this instance with *Dyonysa* his wife, were relating the present miseries wherein themselves and their Citty *Tharsus* consisted[5]: the ground of which forced lamentation was, to see the power of change, that this their City, who not two summers younger, did so excell in pompe, and bore a state, whom all hir neighbors envied for her greatnes, to whom strangers resorted, as to the schoole of variety, where they might best enrich their understandings with experience, whose houses were like so many Courts for Kings, rather than sleeping places for subjects, whose people were curious in their diet, rich in attire, envious in lookes, where was plenty in aboundance, pride in fulnesse, nothing in scarcenesse, but Charitie and Love, the dignitie of whose pallats the whole riches of Nature could hardly satisfie, the ornaments of whose attire Art it selfe with all invention could not content,[6] are

---

[1] I.2.115ff.   [2] As in I.3.
[3] Omits the meeting with Helicanus in I.3.
[4] Omits Antiochus's sending out a fleet to catch Apollonius.
[5] Based on I.4.1–55.   [6] Cf. I.4.21–31.

now so altered, that in steade of downy beds, they make their pillowes on boords, in stead of full furnished tables, hunger calles now out for so much bread, as may but satisfie life: sacke-cloth is now their wearing instead of silke, teares instead of inticing glaunces, are now the acquaintance of their eyes, in briefe, riot hath heere lost all her dominion, and now is no excesse, but whats in sorrow, heere standes one weeping,[1] and there lies another dying, so sharpe are hungers teeth, and so ravenous the devouring mouth of famine, that all pittie is exiled betweene the husband and the wife, nay all tendernesse betweene the mother and the children,[2] faintnesse hath now got that emperie over strength, there is none so whole to releeve the sicke, neither have the living sufficiencie to give buriall to the dead.[3] Thus while this *Cleon* Lord Governour of *Tharsus*, and *Dyonysa* his Lady, with interchanging wordes were describing the sorrows which their almost unpeopled Citty felt, who from the height of multiplication were substracted, almost to nothing: (for, what is life, if it want sustenaunce?) a fainting messenger came slowely into them,[4] his fearefull lookes described that he brought sorrowe, and in slowe wordes hee delivered this, that upon their coastes there was discovered a fleete of shippes making thitherward, which *Cleon* supposing to be an army, which some neighbour nation (taking advantage of their present mishap) had sent for their utter overthrowe, hee commaunded the bringer, upon their landing, to this purpose to salute their Generall, That *Tharsus* was subdewed before their comming, and that it was small conquest to subdew where there was no abilitie to resist,[5] that they desired but this, that their citty might still stand, and that for the riches which their prosperitie had purchased, they freely resigned to them, they though their enemies, (for humanities sake) in the place of breeding, would affoord them buriall. *Pericles* by this is landed, and no sooner entred into their unshut gates, but his princely eies were partaking witnesses of their widowed desolation. The messenger by this also hath delivered the pleasure of the Governour, which the Prince weeping to attend, who rather came to releeve than to ransacke, he demaunded of the fellow, where the Governour was, and foorthwith to be conducted to him, which being effected, in the market place they mette, where *Pericles* without further hinderance delivered to him, that his thoughts were deceved, to suppose them for enimies, who were now come to them for comfortable friends, and those his shippes which their feares might cause them to think were fraughted with their destruction, were intreasured with corne for their reliefe: at which

---

[1] I.2.47.   [2] *Ibid.* 42–46.   [3] *Ibid.* 48–49.
[4] *Ibid.* 58 'in haste'.   [5] Close to I.4.65–68; 84.

the feeble soules not having strength enough to give a showte for joy, gazing on him, and heaven, fell on their knees, and wept.[1] But *Pericles* going to the place of Judgement, causing all the living to be assembled thither, thus freely delivered to them: You Cittizens of *Tharsus*, whom penury of victuall pincheth at this present, Know you, that I *Pericles* Prince of *Tyre* am come purposely to releeve you, in respect of which benefit I doubt not but you will be thus thanke-full as to conceale my arriving heere, and for a while to give me safe harborage, and hospitalitie for my shippes and men,[2] since by the tyranny of *Antiochus*, though not driven, yet for a while I am desirous to leave mine owne Countrey, and continue my residence heere with you, in recompence of which love, I have brought with me a hundred thousand bushells of wheate, which equally for your releefe shall be distributed amongst you, each man paying for every bushell eight peeces of brasse, the price bestowed thereon in my owne Country.[3] At which, as if the verie name of bread only had power to renew strength in them, they gave a great showt, offering their Citty to him as his owne, and their repaired strength in his defence: with which corne their necessities being supplied, and every man willingly paying his eight peeces of brasse, as hee had appoynted, *Pericles* demaunded for the Governour and the chiefe men of the governement, disdaining to bee a Merchant to sell corne, but out of his princely magnificence, bestowed the whole revenew thereof to the beautifying of their Citty. Which when the Cittizens under-stoode, to gratifie these large benefites, and to acknowledge him their patron and releever sent them by the gods, they erected in the Market place a monument in the memoriall of him, and made his statue of brasse, standing in a Charriot, holding corne in his right hand, and spurning it with his left foote, and on the bases of the pillar whereon it stoode, was ingraven in great Letters this in-scription: *Pericles Prince of Tyre gave a gift unto the City of Tharsus, whereby he delivered it from cruell death.*[4] So a while we desire the Reader to leave *Pericles* heartning up the decayed Cittizens of *Tharsus*, and turne their eyes to good *Helycanus* at *Tyre*.

Good *Helycanus* as provident at home, as his Prince was prosperous abroad, let no occasion slip wherein hee might send word to *Tharsus* of what occurrents soever had happened in his absence,[5] the chiefe of which was, that *Thalyart* by *Antiochus* was sent, with purpose to murther him, and that *Antiochus*, though fayling in his practise by

---

[1] *Ibid.* 85–98.   [2] *Ibid.* 99–100.
[3] Not in *Per.* but in Twine.
[4] From Twine. Cf. II *Chor.*, 13–14.
[5] II *Chor.*, Dumbshow and 17–26. Cf. *Elinatus* in Twine, Ch. iii.

his absence, seemed not yet to desist from like intents, but that he againe, suborned such like Instruments to the like treason, advising him withall for his more certaine safetie, for a while to leave *Tharsus*, as a refuge too neere the reach of the tyrant. To which *Pericles* consenting, hee takes his leave of his hoste *Cleon* and *Dyonysa*,[1] and the Cittizens as sory to leave him, as sorrow can bee for the lacke of comfort.

The fourth Chapter

How *Pericles* puts foorth to Sea, suffers shipwrecke, is relieved by certaine poore Fishermen, at last arrives at *Simonides* Court, king of *Pentapolis*, where in feates of Armes hee exceedeth all the Princes that came to honor the birth day of his faire daughter *Thaysa*, and with purpose also to sue to hir for marriage.

Prince *Pericles* having thus releeved *Tharsus*, and bin warnd (for the avoydance of a greater danger) by his good Counsellour *Hely-canus* to forsake the Citie, though not without much sorrow of the Citizens for his departure, he is once againe at sea, seeking a new refuge, and accounting any countrey his best Inne, where he found the best safety. No sooner were his woodden castles floating on the unconstant deepes: but as if *Neptune* himselfe, chiefe soveraigne of that watery empire, would have come in person to have given calme gratulations, and friendly welcomes to this curteous prince, the whole nation of the flouds were at quiet, there were no windes blustering, no surges rising, no raines showring, no tempest storming, but all calmenesse was upon the face of this kingdome, only a troupe of cheerfull Dolphins,[2] as Ambassadours, sent from their kingly Maister, came dauncing on the waters, for the entertaining of him. At which, his joyfull Marriners being scarce from sight of land, with pleasant notes spread forth their comely sailes, and with their brasen keeles, cut an easie passage on the greene medowes of the flouds. At last, Fortune having brought him heere, where she might make him the fittest Tennis-ball for her sport: even as sodainely as thought, this was the alteration: the Heavens beganne to thunder, and the skies shone with flashes of fire: day now had no other shew but only name, for darkenes was on the whole face of the waters, hills of seas were about him, one sometimes tossing him even to the face of heaven, while another sought to sincke him to the roofe of hell, some cryed, others laboured, hee onely prayed: at last, two

---

[1] In Twine his hosts advise him to go.

[2] Contrast II.1.25.

ravenous billowes meeting, the one, with intent to stoppe up all clamour, and the other, to wash away all labour, his vessels no longer able to wrestle with the tempest, were all split. In briefe, he was shipwrackt, his good friends and subjectes all were lost, nothing left to helpe him but distresse, and nothing to complaine unto but his misery. O calamity! there might you have heard the windes whistling, the raine dashing, the sea roaring, the cables cracking, the tacklings breaking, the ship tearing, the men miserably crying out to save their lives: there might you have seene the sea searching the ship, the boordes fleeting, the goodes swimming, the treasure sincking, and the poore soules shifting to save themselves, but all in vaine, for partly by the violence of the tempest, and partly thorow that dismall darkenesse, which unfortunately was come upon them, they were all drowned, gentle *Pericles* only excepted, till (as it were Fortune being tyred with this mishap) by the helpe of a plancke, which in this distresse hee got holde on, hee was, with much labour, and more feare, driven on the shore of *Pentapolis*,[1] where a while complaining him of his mishaps,[2] and accusing the Gods of this injury doone to his innocencie, not knowing on what shoare, whether friend or foe he had, being certayne *Fishermen*,[3] who had also suffered in the former tempest, and had beene witnesses of his untimely shipwracke: (the day being cleered againe) were come out from their homely cottages to dry and repaire their nettes, who being busied about their work, and no whit regarding his lamentation, passed away their labour with discourse to this purpose, in comparing the Sea to Brokers and Usurers, who seeme faire, and looke lovely till they have got men into their clutches, when one tumbles them, and an other tosses them, but seldome leaving untill they have suncke them. Againe comparing our rich men to Whales, that make a great shew in the worlde, rowling and tumbling up and downe, but are good for little, but to sincke others: that the fishes live in the sea, as the powerfull on shoare, the great ones eate up the little ones [4]: with which morall observations[5] driving out their labor, and prince *Pericles*, wondring that from the finny subjects of the sea these poore countrey people learned the infirmities of men, more than mans obduracy and dulnes could learne one of another: at length over-charged with cold which the extreamity of water had pressed him with, and no longer being able to endure, he was compelled to de-maund their simple helpe,[6] offering to their eares the mishap of his

---

[1] Much of this storm is verbatim from Twine, Ch. iv.

[2] II.1.1–11. [3] One in Twine, three in II.1.

[4] II.1.27–36. [5] *Ibid.* 37 'A pretty moral'.

[6] *Ibid.* 58–79.

shipwracke, which hee was no sooner about to relate, but they remembred their eies, not without much sorrow, to have bin the witnesses thereof: and beholding the comely feature of this Gentleman, the chiefe of these Fishermen was mooved with compassion toward him, and lifting him up from the ground, himselfe with the helpe of his men, led him to his house, where with such fare as they presently had, or they could readily provide,[1] they with a hearty welcome feasted him, and the more to expresse their tendernesse to his misfortune, the master dishabited himselfe of his outward apparell to warme and cherish him,[2] which curtesy[3] *Pericles* as curteously receiving, vowing, if ever his fortunes came to their ancient height, their curtesies should not die unrecompensed, and being somewhat repayred in heart by their releefe, he demaunded of the country on the which he was driven, of the name of the King, and of the manner of the governement. When the maister Fisherman commaunding his servants to goe dragge up some other nettes, which yet were abroade, he seated himselfe by him, and of the question he demaunded to this purpose, resolved him: Our countrey heere on the which you are driven sir, is called *Pentapolis*, and our good king thereof is called *Symonides*: the Good King call you him? quoth *Pericles*. Yea, and rightly so called sir, quoth the poore Fisherman, who so governes his kingdome with justice and uprightnesse, that he is no readier to commaund, than we his subjects are willing to obey.[4] He is a happy King, quoth *Pericles*, since he gaines the name of Good by his governement, and then demaunded how farre his Court was distant from that place: wherein he was resolved, some halfe a dayes journey, and from point to point also informed, that the King had a princely daughter named *Thaysa*, in whome was Beauty so joyned with Vertue, that it was as yet unresolved which of them deserved the greater comparison: and in memory of whose birth day, her father yeerely celebrated feasts and triumphes, in the honour of which, many Princes and Knights from farre and remote Countries came, partly to approove their chivalry, but especially (being her fathers only child,) in hope to gaine her love[5]: which name of Chivalry to approove, that all the violence of the water had not power to quench the noblenesse of his minde. *Pericles* sighing to himselfe he broke out thus: Were but my fortunes aunswerable to my desires some should feele that I would be one there.[6] When as if all the gods had given a plaudite to his wordes, the Fishermen, who before were sent out by their Maister to dragge out the other nettes, having found somwhat in the botome

---

[1] *Ibid.* 82–85.
[2] *Ibid.* 81.
[3] curteous *1608* curtesy *Muir.*
[4] II.1.101–9.
[5] II.1.110–14. Not in Twine.
[6] II.1.115–16.

too ponderous for their strength to pull up, they beganne to lewre[1]
and hallow to their Maister for more helpe, crying that there was a
fish hung in their net, like a poore mans case in the Lawe, it would
hardly come out; but Industry being a prevayling workeman,
before helpe came, up came the Fish expected, but prooved indeede
to be a rusty armour.[2] At the name of which word Armour, *Pericles*
being rowzed, he desired of the poore Fishermen, that he who better
than they, was acquainted with such furniture, might have the view
of it. In briefe, what hee could aske of them, was granted: the
Armour is by *Pericles* viewed, and knowne to be a defence which his
father at his last will gave him in charge to keepe, that it might
proove to be a defender of the sonne, which he had knowne to be a
preserver of the father: so accompting all his other losses nothing,
since he had that agayne, whereby his father could not challenge
him of disobedience: and thanking Fortune, that after all her crosses,
shee had yet given him somewhat to repayre his fortunes, begging
this Armour of the Fishermen, and telling them, that with it hee
would shew the vertue hee had learned in Armes, and trie his
chivalry for their Princesse *Thaysa*, which they applauding, and one
furnishing him with an old gowne to make Caparisons for his horse,
which horse hee provided with a Jewel, whom all the raptures of the
sea could not bereave from his arme, and other furnishing him with
the long sideskirtes of their cassockes, to make him bases, his Armour
rusted: and thus disgracefully habilited, Prince *Pericles* with their
conduct is gone to the court of *Symonides*,[3] where the Fishermen had
foretolde him was all the preparation, that eyther Art or Industrie
might attaine unto, to solemnize the birth day of faire *Thaysa* the
good King *Symonides* daughter. This is the day, this *Symonides* Court,
where the King himselfe, with the Princesse his daughter, have
placed themselves in a Gallery,[4] to beholde the triumphes of severall
Princes, who in honour of the Princes birth day, but more in hope
to have her love, came purposely thither, to approove their chivalrie.
They thus seated, and Prince *Pericles*, as well as his owne providing,
and the Fishermens care could furnish him, likewise came to the
court. In this maner also 5 severall princes (their horses richly
caparasoned, but themselves more richly armed, their Pages before
them bearing their Devices on their shields) entred then the Tilting
place. The first a prince of *Macedon*,[5] and the Device hee bore upon
his shield, was a blacke Ethiope reaching at the Sunne, the word,

---

[1] call. [2] II.1.120–23.
[3] The whole incident is close to II.1.124ff.
[4] Maybe a memory of the stage-setting for II.2.
[5] Cf. II.2.17–22 'of Sparta'.

Lux tua vita mihi: which being by the knights Page delivered to the Lady, and from her presented to the King her father, hee made playne to her the meaning of each imprese: and for this first, it was, that the Macedonian Prince loved her so well hee helde his life of her. The second, a Prince of *Corinth*,[1] and the Device hee bare upon his shield was a wreathe of Chivalry, the word, *Me pompæ provexet apex*, the desire of renowne drew him to this enterprise. The third of *Antioch*,[2] and his Device was an armed Knight, being conquered by a Lady, the word, *Pue per dolcera qui per sforsa*: more by lenitie than by force. The fourth of *Sparta*,[3] and the Device he bare was a mans arme environed with a cloude, holding out golde thats by the touch-stone tride, the word, *Sic spectanda fides*, so faith is to be looked into. The fift of *Athens*,[4] and his Device was a flaming Torch turned downeward, the word, *Qui me alit me extinguit*, that which gives me life gives me death. The sixt and last was *Pericles* Prince of *Tyre*, who having neither Page to deliver his shield, nor shield to deliver, mak-ing his Device according to his fortunes, which was a withered Braunch being onely greene at the top, which prooved the abating of his body, decayed not the noblenesse of his minde, his word, *In hac spe vivo*, In that hope I live.[5] Himselfe with a most gracefull curtesie presented it unto her, which shee as curteously received, whilest the Peeres attending on the King forbare not to scoffe, both at his presence, and the present hee brought, being himselfe in a rusty Armour, the Caparison of his horse of plaine country russet, and his owne Bases but the skirtes of a poore Fishermans coate, which the King mildely reprooving them for, hee tolde them, that as Vertue was not to be approoved by wordes, but by actions, so the outward habite was the least table of the inward minde, and counselling them not to condemne ere they had cause to accuse.[6] They went forward to the triumph, in which noble exercise they came almost all as short of *Pericles* perfections, as a body dying, of a life flourishing. To be short, both of Court and Commons, the praises of none were spoken of, but of the meane Knights[7] (for by any other name he was yet unknowne to any.) But the Triumphes being ended, *Pericles* as chiefe, (for in this dayes honour hee was Champion) with all the other Princes, were by the Kings Marshall conducted into the Presence, where *Symonides* and his daughter *Thaysa*, with a most stately banquet stayed to give them a thankefull intertainment. At

---

[1] Cf. II.2.28–30 'The third of Antioch'.
[2] Cf. II.2.23–7 'the second . . . A prince of Macedon'.
[3] The fifth, not named, in II.2.36–8.
[4] The fourth, not named, in II.2.32–3.
[5] II.2.39–47.   [6] II.2.48–57.   [7] II.2.58ff.

whose entraunce, the Lady first saluting *Pericles*, gave him a wreathe
of Chivalry, welcommed him as her knight and guest, and crowned
him King of that dayes noble enterprise.[1] In the end, all being seated
by the Marshall at a table, placed directly over-against where the
king and his daughter sate,[2] as it were by some divine operation,
both King and daughter at one instant were so strucke in love with
the noblenesse of his woorth, that they could not spare so much time
to satisfie themselves with the delicacie of their viands, for talking of
his prayses[3]: while *Pericles* on the other side observing the dignity
wherein the King sate, that so many Princes came to honour him,
so many Peeres stoode ready to attend him, hee was strucke with
present sorrow, by remembring the losse of his owne.[4] Which the
good *Symonides* taking note of, and accusing himselfe before there
was cause, that *Pericles* spirites were dumpt into their melancholy,
through some dislike of the slackenesse hee found in his entertainement, or neglect of his woorth, calling for a boule of wine, hee dranke
to him, and so much further honoured him, that he made his
daughter rise from her seate to beare it to him, and withall, willing
her to demaund of him his name, Countrey, and fortunes, a message
(gentle Lady) shee was as ready to obey unto, as her Father was to
commaund, rejoycing that shee had any occasion offered her
whereby shee might speake unto him.[5] *Pericles* by this time hath
pledged the King, and by his daughter (according to his request)
thus returneth what hee is, that hee was a Gentleman of *Tyre*, his
name *Pericles*, his education beene in Artes and Armes, who looking
for adventures in the world, was by the rough and unconstant Seas,
most unfortunately bereft both of shippes and men, and after shipwrecke, throwen upon that shoare.[6] Which mis-haps of his the king
understanding of, hee was strucke with present pitty to him, and
rising from his state, he came foorthwith and imbraced him, bade
him be cheered, and tolde him, that whatsoever misfortune had
impayred him of, Fortune, by his helpe, could repayre to him, for
both himselfe and Countrey should be his friendes, and presently
calling for a goodly milke white Steede, and a payre of golden
spurres, them first hee bestowed uppon him, telling him, they were
the prises due to his merite, and ordained for that dayes enterprise:
which kingly curtesie *Pericles* as thankefully accepted.[7] Much time
beeing spent in dauncing and other revells, the night beeing
growne olde, the King commaunded the Knights shoulde be conducted to their lodgings, giving order, that *Pericles* Chamber should

---

[1] II.3.1–11.   [2] II.3.17–27.   [3] Cf. II.3.28–36.
[4] II.3.37–56.   [5] II.3.56–80.   [6] As in II.3.81–5.
[7] accepting. *1608*.

be next his owne, where wee will leave them to take quiet rest,[1] and returne backe to *Tyre*.

The fift Chapter

How *Helicanus* heard newes of *Antiochus* and his daughters deaths, and of his sending of other Lords in search of their Prince *Pericles*.

Antiochus, who as before is discoursed, having committed with his owne daughter so foule a sinne, shamed not in the same foulenesse to remaine in it with her, neither had shee that touch of grace, by repentaunce to constraine him to abstinence, or by perswasion to deny his continuance: long, like those miserable serpents did their greatnesse flourish, who use fairest shewes for fowlest evills, till one day himselfe seated with her in a Charriot, made of the purest golde, attended by his peeres, and gased on by his people, both apparrelled all in Jewells, to out face suspition, and beget wonder (as if that glorious outsides were a wall could keepe heavens eye from knowing our intents) in great magnificence rode they through *Antioch*: But see the Justice of the Highest, though sinne flatter, and man persevere, yet surely Heaven at length dooth punish. For as thus they rode, gazing to be gazed upon, and prowd to be accompted so, Vengeance with a deadly arrow drawne from foorth the quiver of his wrath, prepared by lightning, and shot on by thunder, hitte, and strucke dead these prowd incestuous creatures where they sate, leaving their faces blasted, and their bodies such a contemptfull object on the earth, that all those eyes, but now with reverence looked upon them, all hands that served them, and all knees adored them, scorned now to touch them, loathd now to looke upon them, and disdained now to give them buriall.[2] Nay, such is heavens hate to these and such like sinnes, and such his indignation to his present evill, that twixt his stroke and death, hee lent not so much mercy to their lives, wherein they had time to crie out; Justice, be mercifull, for we repent us. They thus dead, thus contemned, and insteede of kingly monument for their bodies left, to be intoombed in the bowelles of ravenous fowles, if fowles would eate on them. The strangenesse[3] of their deaths were soone rumored over that part of the world, and as soone brought to the eares of *Helycanus*, who was a carefull watchman to have knowledge of whatsoever hapned in *Antioch*, and by his knowledge to prevent what daunger might succeede, eyther to his Prince, or to his subjectes in his absence, of

---

[1] II.3.109ff. No dancing in Twine.
[2] II.4.1–12.   [3] II.4.13 'very strange'.

which tragedy he having notice, presently he imparted the news thereof to his grave and familiar friend Lord *Eschines*,[1] and now told him what till now hee had concealed, namely of their incest together, and that onely for the displeasure which princely *Pericles* feared *Antiochus* bore towardes him, and might extend to his people, by his knowledge thereof, hee thus long by his counsell had discontinued from his kingdome.

Now it hapned that these tydings arrived to his eares, just at the instant, when his grave counsell could no longer alay the head-strong multitude from their uncivil and giddy muteny: and the reason of them (who most commonly are unreasonable in their actions) to drawe themselves to this faction, was, that they supposed their prince was dead, and that being dead, the kingdome was left without a successefull inheritor, that they had bin onelie by *Helicanus* with vaine hope of *Pericles* returne, deluded, and that even now the power being, by his death, in their hands, they would create to themselves a new soveraigne, and Helycanus should be the man.[2] Many reasons hee used to perswade them, many Arguments to withstand them: nothing but this onely prevailed with them, that since he only knew their Prince was gone to travell, and that, that travell was undertaken for their good, they would abstaine but for three months longer from bestowing that dignity which they calld their love, though it was his dislike upon him, and if by that time (which they with him should still hope for) the gods were not pleased for their perpetuall good to restore unto them their absent Prince, hee then with all willingnesse would accept of their suffrages. This then (though with much trouble) was at last by the whole multitude accepted, and for that time they were all pacified, when *Helicanus* assembling all the peeres unto him, by the advise of all, chose some from the rest, and after his best instructions, or rather by perswasions and grave counsell given, hee sent them to inquire of their Prince,[3] who lately left at *Pentapolis* was highly honoured by good *Symonides*.

The sixt Chapter

How Prince *Pericles* is married to *Thaysa* king *Symonides* daughter, and how after he hath heard newes of *Antiochus* death, hee with his wife departeth toward his owne Country of *Tyre*.

Prince *Pericles* having had (as before is mentioned) his lodging directed next adjoyning to the kings bed-chamber, whereas all the

---

[1] Escanes in II.4.1–16. [2] II.4.17ff. [3] II.4.49–56.

other Princes uppon their comming to their lodgings betooke themselves to their pillowes, and to the nourishment of a quiet sleepe, he of the Gentlemen that attended him, (for it is to be noted, that upon the grace that the king had bestowed on him, there was of his Officers toward him no attendance wanting) hee desired that hee might be left private, onely that for his instant solace they would pleasure him with some delightfull Instrument, with which, and his former practise hee intended to passe away the tediousnesse of the night insteade of more fitting slumbers.[1]

His wil was presently obeyed in all things since their master had commaunded he should be disobeyed in nothing: the Instrument is brought him, and as hee had formerly wished, the Chamber is disfurnished of any other company but himselfe, where presently hee beganne to compell such heavenly voyces from the sencelesse workemanship, as if *Apollo* himselfe had now beene fingering on it, and as if the whole Sinode of the gods, had placed their deities round about him of purpose, to have beene delighted with his skill, and to have given prayses to the excellencie of his art, nor was this sound only the ravisher of al hearers, but from his owne cleere breast hee sent much cheerefull notes, which by him were made up so answerable to the others sound, that they seemed one onely consort of musike, and had so much delicacie, and out of discordes making up so excellent a conjunction, that they had had power to have drawne backe an eare, halfe way within the grave, to have listned unto it, for thus much by our story we are certaine of, that the good *Symonides* (being by the height of night, and the former dayes exercise, in the ripenesse of his contentfull sleepe) hee rejoyced to be awakend by it, and not accompting it a disease that troubled him in the hearing, but a pleasure wherewith hee still wished to be delighted. In briefe, hee was so satisfied to heare him thus expresse his excellence, that hee accompted his Court happy to entertaine so worthy a guest, and himselfe more happy in his acquaintance. But day that hath still that soveraigntie to drawe backe the empire of the night, though a while shee in darkenesse usurpe, brought the morning on, and while the king was studying with what aunswerable present, wherewith to gratifie this noble Prince for his last nights musicke, a Gentlewoman (whose service was thither commaunded by his Daughter) brought him a Letter, whose in-side had a sute to him to this purpose.

The Lady Thaysaes Letter to the King her Father

My most noble Father, what my blushing modesty forbids me to speake, let your fatherly love excuse that I write. I am subdude by love, yet not inthralld

---

[1] *Per.* omits this scene, but cf. II.5.25–28.

through the licentiousnes of a loose desire, but made prisoner in that noble battell twixt Affection and Zeale: I have no life but in this liberty, neither any liberty but in this thraldome, nor shall your tender selfe, weighing my affections truely in the Scale of your Judgement, have cause to contradict me, since him I love hath as much merite in him, to challenge the title of a Sonne, as I blood of yours to inherite the name of daughter: then if you shall refuse to give him me in marriage, deny not I pray you to to make ready for my funerall.

Tis the stranger Pericles.[1]

Which request of hers, when the king her father had thus understood of, hee beganne first to examine with him selfe, what vertue was in this choice, that should bind her thoughts to this liking, and what succeeding comfort hee might expect, the expectation of which, might invite him to his consent. First hee beganne to remember himselfe, that he came unto his Court but poore, and for poverty, quoth the good king, tis a woorkemanship, that Nature makes uppe even for others to contemne, and, which in these times, is growne odious to keepe companie withall, that to marrie her which was his onely childe, and the expectation of his subjectes, with one of so lowe blood and meane discent, would returne rather a dishonour than a dignitie to his name, since Parents rather expect the advauncement of Titles, and the raising of their houses, in the uniting of their issue, than the declining: but in the end, when hee had put all the Interjections he could between her love and his liking, his uprightnesse made him see, that in vertue consisted mans onely perfection, and in him, as her befitting Court, she thought it fittest to keepe her royall residence, and in that opinion allowing of his daughters choice, hee thought himselfe happy to live Father to such a vertuous sonne, and his daughter more happy to be coupled to so noble a husband.[2] And as hee was now thus contracting them together in his rejoycing thoughts, even in the instant came in *Pericles*, to give his Grace that salutation which the morning required of him, when the king intending to dissemble that in shew, which hee had determined on in heart,[3] hee first tolde him, that his daughter had that morning sent unto him that Letter, wherein shee intreated of him, that his Grace would be pleased, that himselfe (whom shee knew to call by no other name but the Stranger *Pericles*) might become her Schoolemaister, of whose rarity in musicke, excellencie in song, with comelinesse in dauncing, not onely shee had heard, but himselfe had borne testimonie to be the best, that ever their judgements had

[1] The letter is not cited in *Per.*
[2] II.5.15–22.
[3] II.5.23.

had cause to judge of. When *Pericles*, though willing to yeelde any courtesies to so gratious a Lady, and not disdaining to be commaunded any services by so good a Lord, yet replyed, Though all his abilities were at his Graces pleasure, yet he thought himselfe unwoorthy to be his daughters schoolemaister[1]: I but quoth *Symonides*, shee will not be denied to be your Scholler, and for manifest proofe thereof heere is her owne Character, which to that purpose shee hath sent unto us, and we to that purpose give you leave to reade: which *Pericles* overlooking, and finding the whole tenour thereof to be, that his daughter from all the other Princes, nay from the whole worlde, sollicited him for her husband, he straitway rather conjectured it to be some subtiltie of the father to betray his life,[2] than any constancy of the princesse to love him: and foorthwith prostrating himselfe at the kings feete, hee desired that his Grace would no way seeke to staine the noblenesse of his minde, by any way seeking to intrappe the life of so harmelesse a Gentleman,[3] or that with evill he would conclude so much good which he already had begunne toward him, protesting, that for his part, his thoughts had never that ambition, so much as to ayme at the love of his daughter, nor any action of his, gave cause of his princely displesure[4]: but the king faining still an angry brow, turned toward him, and tolde him, that like a traitour, hee lyed.[5] Traytour, quoth *Pericles*? I, traytour, quoth the king, that thus disguised, art stolne into my Court, with the witchcraft[6] of thy actions to bewitch the yeelding spirit of my tender Childe. Which name of Traytor being againe redoubled, *Pericles* then, insteade of humblenesse seemed not to forget his auntient courage, but boldely replyed, That were it any in his Court, except himselfe, durst call him traytor, even in his bosome he would write the lie: affirming, that he came into his Court in search of honour, and not to be a rebell to his State, his bloud was yet untainted, but with the heate, got by the wrong the king had offered him, and that he boldly durst, and did defie, himselfe, his subjectes, and the prowdest danger, that eyther tyranny or treason could inflict upon him.[7] Which noblenesse of his, the king inwardly commending, though otherwise dissembling, he answered, he should proove it otherwise, since by his daughters hand, it there was evident, both his practise and her consent therein. Which wordes were no sooner uttered, but *Thaysa* (who ever since she sent her Father her Letter, could not containe her selfe in any quiet, till she heard of his answer) came now in, as it had beene her parte, to make aunswere to her Fathers last sillable, when prince

---

[1] II.5.39–40. [2] II.5.44. [3] II.5.46.
[4] II.5.46–54. [5] *Ibid.* 55. [6] *Ibid.* 49–50. [7] *Ibid.* 56–64.

34

Pericles yeelding his body toward her, in most curteous manner demaunded of her by the hope she had of heaven, or the desire she had to have her best wishes fulfilled heere in the worlde, that shee would now satisfie, her now displeased Father, if ever he, by motion, or by letters, by amorous glaunces, or by any meanes that Lovers use to compasse their disseignes, had sought to be a friend in the noblenesse of her thoughts, or a copartner in the worthinesse of her love, when she as constant to finish, as she was forward to attempt, againe required of him, that suppose he had, who durst take offence thereat, since that it was her pleasure to give him to knowe that he had power to desire no more than she had willingnesse to performe?[1] How minion, quoth her Father (taking her off at the very word, who dare be displeased withall?) Is this a fit match for you? a stragling *Theseus* borne we knowe not where, one that hath neither bloud nor merite for thee to hope for, or himselfe to challenge even the least allowaunce of thy perfections, when she humbling her princely knees before her Father, besought him to consider, that suppose his birth were base (when his life shewed him not to be so) yet hee had vertue, which is the very ground of all nobilitie, enough to make him noble: she intreated him to remember that she was in love, the power of which love was not to be confined by the power of his will. And my most royall Father, quoth shee, what with my penne I have in secret written unto you, with my tongue now I openly confirme, which is, that I have no life but in his love, neither any being but in the enjoying of his worth. But daughter (quoth *Symonides*) equalles to equalls, good to good is joyned, this not being so, the bavine of your minde in rashnesse kindled, must againe be quenched, or purchase our displeasure. And for you sir (speaking to prince *Pericles*) first learne to know, I banish you my Court, and yet scorning that our kingly inragement should stoope so lowe, for that your ambition sir, Ile have your life. Be constant, quoth *Thaysa*, for everie droppe of blood hee sheades of yours, he shall draw an other from his onely childe. In briefe, the king continued still his rage, the Lady her constancie, while *Pericles* stoode amazed at both, till at last the Father being no longer able to subdue that which he desired as much as shee, catching them both rashly by the handes, as if hee meant strait to have inforced them to imprisonment, he clapt them hand in hand, while they as lovingly joyned lip to lip, and with tears trickling from his aged eyes, adopted him his happy sonne, and bade them live together as man and wife.[2] What joy there was at this coupling, those that are Lovers and enjoy their wishes, can better

---

[1] II.5.66–72.
[2] Cf. II.5.73–88.

conceive, than my pen can set downe; the one rejoycing to be made happy by so good and gentle a Lord, the other as happy to be inriched by so vertuous a Lady. What preparation there was for their marriage, is sufficiently expressed in this, that she was the onely daughter to a king, and had her fathers liking in her love: what speede there was to that marriage, let those judge who have the thoughtes of *Thaysa* at this instant, only conceive the solempnities at the Temple are doone, the feast in most solempne order finished, the day spent in musicke, dauncing, singing, and all Courtly communication, halfe of the night in maskes and other courtly shewes, and the other halfe in the happy and lawfull imbracements of these most happy Lovers. The discourse at large of the liberall Chalenges made and proclaimed, at Tilt, Barriers, running at the Ring, *ioco di can*, mannaging fierce horses, running on foote, and dauncing in armours, of the stately presented Playes, Shewes disguised, Speeches, Maskes and Mummeries, with continuall harmony of all kindes of Musicke, with banquetting in all delicacie, I leave to the consideration of them who have behelde the like in Courtes, and at the wedding of princes,[1] rather than afford them to the description of my penne, only let such conceive, all things in due order were accomplished, the dueties of marriage performed: and faire *Thaysa* this night is conceived with child.[2]

The next day Joy dwelling thorow the whole kingdom for this conjunction, every man arose to feasting and jollity, for the wedding triumphs continued a whole moneth, while Time with his feathered wings, so fanned away the houres, and with his slippery feete, so glided over the dayes, that nine Moones had almost chaunged their light, ere halfe the time was thought to be expired,[3] when it happened, that as the good *Symonides* and princely *Pericles* with his faire *Thaysa* were walking in the garden adjoyning to their pallace, one of the Lords, who (as before) were sent by grave and carefull *Helycanus*, in search of their absent Prince, came hastily in to them, who uppon his knee delivered unto the yoong Prince a Letter, which being opened the contents therein spake thus unto him: That *Antiochus* and his daughter (as is before described) were with the violence of lightning (shot from heaven,) strucke sodainely dead. And moreover, that by the consent of the generall voyces the Cittie of *Antioch*, with all the riches therein, and the whole kingdome were reserved for his possession and princely government.[4] Which Letter when he had read, he presently imparted the news thereof to his kingly Father, who uppon view received, hee strait knew (what

---

[1] Verbatim from Twine.
[2] III *Chor.*, 9–11.
[3] Note the verse here.
[4] III *Chor.*, 21–39.

untill then the modesty of *Pericles* had concealed) that his sonne whome from poverty hee advanced to be the bedfellow of his daughter, was Prince of *Tyre*, who for the feare he had of *Antiochus*, had forsooke his kingdome, and now had given unto him the kingdome of *Antiochus* for recompence, that grave *Helycanus* had not without much labour, appeased the stubborne mutiny of the *Tyrians*, who in his absence would have elected him their king, and that to avoyde a future insurrection, [and keep] [1] (his whole state) in safety, how necessary it was for him to make a speedy returne, which gladnesse *Symonides* imparted to his Daughter, who as gladly received them. While *Pericles* intending a while to leave his deerest deere behinde him, considering how dangerous it was for her to travell by sea, being with childe, and so neere her time, he beganne to intreate of his kingly father of all necessarie provision for his departure, since the safety of twoo kingdomes did importune so much: when on the other side *Thaysa* falling at her fathers feete, her teares speaking in her sute faster than her wordes, shee humbly requested, that as his reverend age tendered her, or the prosperitie of the Infant wherewith shee thought her selfe happy to be imburthened, hee would not permitte her to remaine behinde him. Which teares of hers prevayled [2] with the aged King, though compelling his teares to take a loth and sorrowfull departure of her. Their Shippes being strongly appoynted, and fraught with all things convenient as golde, silver, apparrell, bedding, victualls, and armour, and fearing what too unfortunately hapned, causing an aged Nurse called *Lycorida* a Midwife, with other handmaides to attend her, they [3] are shipt, and on shoare, the one gasing after the other with a greedy desire, untill the high usurping waters tooke away the sight from them both. [4]

The seaventh Chapter

How faire *Thaysa* died in travell of childe-birth uppon the Sea, and being throwen for buriall in the waters, was cast ashoare at *Ephesus*, and how by the excellent labour of Lord *Cerimon* a skilfull Physition, she was restored to her life againe, and by her owne request placed to live a Votary in the Temple of *Diana*.

Prince *Pericles*, with his Queene *Thaysa*, being thus on shippe-boorde, and their marriners merrily having hoysed uppe their sayles, their vessels, as prowde of such a fraught wherewith they were enriched, galloped cheerefully on the Ocean. Fortune did now

---

[1] *1608* omits some words.   [2] prevayling *1608*.
[3] her. They *1608*.   [4] III *Chor.*, 40–44.

seeme to looke fairely, neyther was there promise of any other alteration, the day looked lovely, and the sea smiled for joy, to have her
bosome pressed with these burthens: But nothing in this world that
is permanent, Time is the father of Fortune, hee is slippery, and then
of necessitie must his childe be fickle: and this was his alteration, a
cloude seemed to arise from forth the south, which being by the
Maister and Marriners beheld, they tolde Prince *Pericles*, that it was
messenger of a storme, which was no sooner spoken, but as if the
heavens had conspired with the waters, and the windes bin assistant
to both, they kept such a blustering, and such an unruely stirre, that
none could be heard to speake but themselves, seas of waters were
received into their ships while others fought against them to expell
them out. Stop[1] the lecage there, cries out one, hale uppe the maine
bowlings there calles out another,[2] and with their confusion (neither
understanding other, since the storme had gotte the maistery) they
made such a hideous noyse, that it had had power to have awakened
Death, and to have affrighted Patience: nor could it choose then but
bring much terror to our sea-sicke Queene, who had beene used to
better attendance, than was now offered her by these ill tutored
servantes Winde and Water: but they who neither respect birth nor
blood, prayers nor threats, time nor occasion, continued still their
boysterous havocke. With which stirre (good Lady) her eies and
eares, having not till then bin acquainted, she is strucke into such a
hasty fright, that welladay she falles in travell, is delivered of a
daughter, and in this childe-birth dies, while her princely husband
being above the hatches, is one while praying to heaven for her safe
deliverance, an other while suffering for the sorow wherwith he knew
his Queene was imburthened, he chid the contrary storme (as if it
had been sensible of hearing) to be so unmanerly, in this unfitting
season, and when so good a Queene was in labor, to keep such a
blustering[3]: thus while the good Prince remayned reprooving the
one, and pittying the other, up comes *Lycorida* the Nurse, sent along
by good *Symonides* with his daughter, and into his armes delivers his
Sea-borne Babe,[4] which he taking to kisse, and pittying it with these
words: Poore inch of Nature (quoth he) thou arte as rudely welcome
to the worlde, as ever Princesse Babe was, and hast as chiding a
nativitie, as fire, ayre, earth, and water can affoord thee,[5] when,
as if he had forgot himselfe, he abruptly breaks out: but say *Licorida*;
how doth my Queene? O sir (quoth she) she hath now passed all
daungers, and hath given uppe her griefes by ending her life. At
which wordes, no tongue is able to expresse the tide of sorrowe that

[1] out, stop *1608*. [2] Cf. III.1.43–4. [3] III.1.1–14.
[4] III.1.14–18. [5] III.1.27–37.

over-bounded *Pericles*, first looking on his Babe, and then crying out for the mother, pittying the one that had lost her bringer ere shee had scarce saluted the worlde, lamenting for himselfe that had beene bereft of so inestimable a Jewell by the losse of his wife, in which sorrowe as he would have proceeded, uppe came the Maister to him, who for that the storme continued still in his tempestuous height, brake off his sorrowe with these sillables. Sir, the necessitie of the time affoordes no delay, and we must intreate you to be contented, to have the dead body of your Queene throwne over-boorde.[1] How varlet! quoth *Pericles*, interrupting him, wouldest thou have me cast that body into the sea for buriall, who being in misery received me into favour? We must intreate you to temperance sir (quoth the Maister) as you respect your owne safety, or the prosperitie of that prety Babe in your armes. At the naming of which word Babe, *Pericles* looking mournfully upon it, shooke his head, and wept. But the Maister going on, tolde him, that by long experience they had tried, that a shippe may not abide to carry a dead carcasse, nor would the lingering tempest cease while the dead body remayned with them. But the Prince seeking againe to perswade them, tolde them, that it was but the fondnes of their superstition to thinke so. Call it by what you shal please sir (quoth the Maister) but we that by long practise have tried the proofe of it, if not with your graunt, then without your consent (for your owne safety, which wee with all duety tender) must so dispose of it.[2] So calling for his servants about him, he willed one of them, to bring him a chest, which he foorthwith caused to be well bitumed[3] and well leaded for her coffin, then taking up the body of his (even in death) faire *Thaysa*, he arrayed her in princely apparrell, placing a Crowne of golde uppon her head, with his owne hands, (not without store of funerall teares) he layed her in that Toombe, then placed hee also store of golde at her head, and great treasure of silver at her feete, and having written this Letter which he layd upon her breast, with fresh water flowing in his eyes, as loath to leave her sight, he nayled up the Chest, the Tenor of which writing was in forme as followeth;

> *If ere it hap this Chest be driven*
> *On any shoare, on coast or haven,*
> *I Pericles the Prince of Tyre,*
> *(That loosing her, lost all desire,)*
> *Intreate you give her burying,*
> *Since she was daughter to a King:*

[1] III.1.47-49.
[2] III.1.48-55.
[3] III.1.72 'Caulk'd and bitum'd ready'.

This golde I give you as a fee,
The Gods requite your charitie.[1]

The Chest then being nayled up close, he commaunded it to be
lifted over-boorde, and then naming his Childe *Marina*, for that she
was borne uppon the Sea, he directed his Maister to alter the
course from Tyre, (being a shorter cutte to *Tharsus*) and for whose
safety he thither intended, where with his hoste *Cleon* and *Dionysa*
his wife, he intended to leave his little infant, to be fostered and
brought up.[2] The dead body being thus throwne over-boorde, when
as if Fortune had bethought her, that shee had wrought her utmost
spight to him, by bereaving him of so great a comfort, even in the
instant the tempest ceaseth, where we will leave Prince *Pericles*
uppon calme waters, though not with a calme minde,[3] sayling to
Tharsus: and beholde, the next morning, by which time, the waves
had rouled, from wave to wave this Chest to land, and cast it ashoare
on the coast of *Ephesus*, in which Citty lived a Lord[4] called *Cerimon*,
who, though of noble bloud, and great possessions, yet was he so
addicted to studie, and in searching out the excellencie of Arts, that
his felicitie consisted in contemplation,[5] wisely fore-knowing, so icie
is the state of riches, that it is thawed to nothing, by the least adversitie, that carelesse heires may dispend, and riot consume them,
when one vertue, and our deserved fame attendeth immortality,
this consideration made him so to apply his time in Letters, and in
searching out the nature of Simples, that he grew so excellent in the
secret of Physicke, as if *Apollo* himselfe, or another *Aesculapius* had
beene his Schoolemaister: nor was he of this plentie a niggard to
the needie, but so bountifull to the distressed, that his house and
hand were accompted the hospitalls for the diseased. This Lord
Cerimon had his residence built so neare the shoare, that in his
windowes he over-looked the Sea.[6] and being this morning in
conference with some that came to him both for helpe for themselves,
and reliefe for others[7]; and some that were relating the crueltie of
the last nights tempest, on a sodayne casting his eye from foorth his
casement towards the maine, he might espie the waters, as it were,
playing with the Chest wherein the dead Queene was incoffind, and
which was upon the sodayne, by a more eager billow, cast on his
bankes, when presently thinking it to be the remnant of some
shippewracke, caused in the last nights storme, calling for his
servants, hee foorthwith commaunded them to have it brought
uppe to him as forfeited unto him, being cast on his ground, which

---

[1] Cf. III.2.68–75. [2] III.1.73ff. [3] winde, *1608*; minde, *Muir*.
[4] III.2.2 'my lord'. [5] III.2.21–48. [6] III.2.14.
[7] III.2.1–6; 12–20.

accordingly performed, hee as presently gave charge it should be opened, when not without much wonder he straitway viewed the dead body of the Queene, so crowned, so royally apparelled, so intreasured as before,[1] and taking up the writing which he likewise found placed upon her breast, hee read it to the Gentlemen, who at that time accompanied him, and knowing it thereby to be the dead Queene to Prince *Pericles*. Now surely, quoth *Cerimon*,[2] thou hast a bodie even drowned with woe for the losse of so goodly a creature[3]: for Gentlemen, sayde he, as you may perceive, such was the excellencie of her beauty, that grimme Death himselfe hath not power to suffer any deformitie to accompany it. Then laying his hand gently upon her cheeke, he bethought him that life had not lost all the workemanshippe that Nature had bestowed uppon her, for even at the opening of the Chest, and as it were she then receiving fresh aire, he might perceve, a new but calm glowing to reespire in her cheeks.[4] With which being somewhat amazed, Now surely Gentlemen, quoth hee turning to them, who were greedily set round about him, this Queene hath not long beene intraunced, and I have read of some Egyptians, who after foure houres death, (if man may call it so) have raised impoverished bodies, like to this, unto their former health,[5] nor can it be disparagement to me to use my best practise on this Queene: to which by the Gentlemen that accompanyed him hee was incouraged to attempt, since that the recovery of her could not but appeare to be a worke of wonder, and since that his fortune was so successefull in his ministring, that all *Ephesus* was repleate with his helpe. So calling for a servant of his to attend him with certayne boxes which he named were in his studie, as also with fire and necessary linnen,[6] invoking *Apollo* to be gratious to his empericke, and the worke in hand, he began to apply to her, First pulling downe the clothes from off the Ladies bosome, he powred uppon her a most precious oyntment, and bestowing it abroad with his hand, perceived some warmth in her breast, and that there was life in the body, whereat somewhat astonished, he felt her pulses, layde his cheeke to her mouth, and examining all other tokens that he could devise, he perceived how death strove with life within her, and that the conflict was dangerous, and doubtfull who should prevaile. Which beeing done, he chafed the body against the fire, untill the bloud which was congealed with colde was wholly dissolved, when powring a precious liquor into her mouth, hee perceived warmth more and more to encrease in her, and the golden

---

[1] III.2.65 'balm'd and entreasur'd'.
[2] *Pericles, 1608*.
[3] III.2.68–77.
[4] cheeks, with *1608*.
[5] Better than III.2.84–6.
[6] III.2.80–1, 87.

fringes of her eyes a litle to part: then calling softly to the Gentlemen who were witnesses about him, he bade them that they should commaund some still musicke to sound.[1] For certainely quoth he, I thinke this Queene will live, and suppose that she hath bin much abused, for she hath not beene long intraunced,[2] condemning them for rashnesse so hastily to throwe her over-boorde. And when he had so said, he tooke the body reverently into his armes, and bare it into his owne Chamber, and layed it upon his bed groveling upon the breast, then tooke hee certaine hote and comfortable oiles, and warming them upon the coles, he dipped faire wooll therein, and fomented all the bodie over therewith, untill such time as the congealed bloud and humours were thorowly resolved, and the spirites in due forme recovered their woonted course, the veines waxed warme, the arteries beganne to beate, and the lungs drew in the fresh ayre againe, and being perfectly come to her selfe,[3] lifting up those now againe pricelesse diamonds of her eyes,[4] O Lord (quoth shee) where am I? for it seemeth to me that I have beene in a strange Countrey. And wheres my Lord I pray you? I long to speake with him.[5] But *Cerimon*, who best knew, that now with any thing to dis-comfort her, might breede a relapse, which would be unrecoverable,[6] intreated her to be cheered, for her Lord was well, and that anone, when the time was more fitting, and that her decayed spirites were repayred, hee would gladly speake with her: So, as it were, being but newly awaked from death, to the great amasement of the beholders, she presently fell into a most comfortable slumber, which Lord *Cerimon* giving charge none should disturbe her of, he in the meane time, and against she should awake, provided cherishing meates, and as her strength grew, gave wholesome clothes to refresh her with. But not long after, weakenesse being banished from her, and *Cerimon*, by communication knew, that shee came of the stocke of a King, he sent for many of his friendes to come unto him, and adopted her for his owne daughter, and related unto her, howe after so greevous a tempest, in what manner shee was found. In which tempest she supposing her kingly husband to be shipwrecked, shee with many teares intreated, that since he had given her life, he would be pleased to give her leave to live unknowne to any man. To which *Cerimon* accorded: and for that intent placed her in the Temple of *Diana*, which was there consecrated at *Ephesus*.[7]

---

[1] III.2.88–91.
[2] *Ibid.* 93–5.
[3] Close to Twine.
[4] III.2.99–102.
[5] *Ibid.* 105–6.
[6] III.2.109–10.
[7] III.4.

The eight Chapter

How *Pericles* arriving at *Tharsus,* delivereth his yoong daughter *Marina* unto *Cleon* and *Dyonysa* to be fostered up: and how *Lycorida* the Nurse lying uppon her death-bed, declareth unto *Marina* who were her parents.

Having thus left the recovered *Thaysa* amongst the holy Nunnes in the Temple of Diana at *Ephesus,* our Storie biddeth us looke backe unto sorrowfull *Pericles,* whose shippe with fortunate winde, favour of the heavens, and providence of his pylate, arrived at the shoare of *Tharsus,* where upon his landing hee was curteously received by *Cleon* and *Dyonysa,*[1] whome he as curteously saluted, telling them the heavie chaunces which had befallen him, both of the great stormes and tempests on the Sea, which he with patience had indured, as also of the death of the good Lady *Thaysa,* which he not without much sorrow suffered, onely quoth he, I have heere left a little picture of her, who for it was given unto me at Sea, I have named *Marina,*[2] and I thanke the heavens, is so like unto her, that I never doe looke uppon it, but with much comfort, in whose protection and education I meane to use your friendship, while I goe on in travell to receive the kingdome of *Antiochus,*[3] which is reserved for mee. And if you will ever shew your gratitude, for my former charitie extended towardes you, and all this Citty in a former distresse, the gods have given this cause, to proove your thankefulnesse. When both vowing by solemne oath, their care should be on her, as reason unto themselves, who is the guider of mans life: he satisfied with that their promise, thanked them, telling them moreover, that with them also he woulde leave *Lycorida* her mothers nurse, (and given unto him by her good father *Symonides*) that shee might be a nurse unto her child, only further requesting them, and so charging *Lycorida,* that if it pleased the gods to lend her life to the yeeres of understanding, they should not till his returne, make knowne unto her, that she was a braunch sproong from him, but onely be brought uppe as the daughter of *Cleon* and *Dyonysa,* lest that the knowledge of her high birth, should make her growe prowd to their instructions. Of which having likewise promise, he delivered the infant and the nurse to *Cleon,* and therewithall, great sums of golde, silver, and apparrell, and vowing solemnely by othe to himselfe, his head should grow uncisserd, his beard untrimmed, himselfe in all uncomely, since he had lost his Queene, and till he had married his daughter at ripe years.[4] When they much wondring at so strange a resolve, and promising to be most faithfull with all diligence according to his

[1] III.3.
[2] III.3.12–13.
[3] Back to Tyre in *Per.* IV *Chor.*
[4] III.3.25–32.

directions, *Pericles* tooke his leave, departed with his Ship, sayling
even to the uttermost parts of all *Egypt*, while his yoong daughter
Marina grew up to more able discretion, and when she was fully
attaind to 5 yeers of age, being to her selfe knowne no other but to
be free borne, she was set to Schoole with other free children,
alwayes joyntly accompanied with one onely daughter that *Dionysa*
had, being of the same time that she was of, where growing up,
aswel in learning, as in number of yeeres, untill she came to the
reckoning of foureteene, one day when she returned from Schoole,
she found *Lycorida* her Nurse sodainely fallen sicke,[1] and sitting beside
her upon the bed, she as in care of her, demaunded the cause and
manner of her sickenesse: when the Nurse finding her disease to
have no hope of recovery, but a harbinger that came before to
prepare a lodging for death, answered her to this purpose; For my
sickenesse, quoth she, it matters not (deare childe) since it is as
necessary to be sicke, as it is needefull to die, onely I intreate of you
to hearken unto a dying womans wordes that loveth you, and laying
them uppe in your heart, perswade your selfe, that in these houres no
sinner should, or can be so wretched, to spare a minute to finde time
to lie. Knowe then, that you are not the daughter of *Cleon* and
Dyonysa, as you till this have supposed: but hearken unto me, and I
will declare unto thee the beginning of thy birth, that thou mayest
knowe how to guide thy selfe after my death: *Pericles* the Prince of
Tyre is thy father, and *Thaysa* king *Symonides* daughter was thy
mother: which father and mother departed from thy grandsir[e] at
Pentapolis toward their kingdom of *Tyre*, thy mother being at Sea,
fell in travell with thee, and died after thou wert borne: when thy
Father *Pericles* inclosed her body in a Chest with princely ornaments,
laying twenty talents of golde at her head, and as much at her feete
in silver; with a Scedule written, containing the dignitie of her
birth, and maner of her death, then caused he the Chest to be
thrown over-boorde into the Sea, thorow a superstitious opinion
which the mariners beleeved, leaving her body so inriched, to the
intent, that whither soever it were driven, they that found it, in
regarde of the riches, would bury her according to her estate. Thus
Lady were you borne uppon the waters, and your fathers Ship
with much wrestling of contrary windes, and with his unspeakeable
griefe of minde, arrived at this shoare, and brought thee in thy
swadling clowtes unto this Citty, where he with great care delivered
thee unto this thine hoste *Cleon* and *Dyonysa* his wife, diligently to
be fostered up, and left me heere also to attend uppon thee, swearing
this oath to keepe inviolate, his haire should be uncisserd, his face

[1] Not in *Per.*

untrimmed, himselfe in all things uncomely continually to mourne for your dead mother, untill your ripe yeares gave him occasion to marry you to some prince worthy your birth and beauty; wherefore I now admonish you, that if after my death, thine hoste or hostesse, whom thou calst thy parents, shall happly offer thee any injury, or discurteously taking advantage of thy absent father as unbefitting thine estate intertain thee, haste thee into the market place, where thou shalt finde a Statue erected to thy father standing, take hold of it, and crie aloude; You cittizens of *Tharsus*, I am his daughter whose Image this is, who being mindefull of thy fathers benefits will doubtlesse revenge thy injurie. When *Marina* thanking *Lycorida* for making that known to her, which till then was unknowne, and happly either thorow Time or Death might have beene buried in her ignorance: and vowing, if ever neede should so require (of which as yet she had no cause to doubt) her counsell should be followed. And so *Lycorida* through sickenesse growing more weake, and *Marina* for this knowledge and advise still tending on her, in her armes at last shee gave up the Ghost.[1]

The ninth Chapter

How after the death of *Lycorida* the Nurse *Dyonysa* envying at the beauty of *Marina*, hired a servant of hers to have murderd her, and how she was rescued by certaine Pyrates, and by them carried to the Cittie of *Meteline*, where among other bondslaves, shee was solde to a common Bawde.

Marina having thus by *Lycoridaes* meanes had knowledge of her parentes, and *Lycorida* having beene in her life, her most carefull Nurse, shee (not without just cause) lamented her death, and caused her body to be solempnely interred, in a field without the walles of the Cittie, raising a monument in remembrance of her, vowing to her selfe a yeares solemne sadnesse, and that her eies also for so long a time should daily pay their dewy offerings, as lamenting the losse of so good a friend.

But this decree of hers being accomplished, and all the rites thereof faithfully fulfilled, she dismissed her bodie of her mourning attire, and againe apparrelled her selfe as before, in her most costly habilliments, frequenting the Schooles, and diligently endevouring the studies of the Liberall Sciences, wherein she so out-went in perfection, the labours of all that were studious with her, that shee was rather used amongst them as their Schoolemistris to instruct, than

[1] Close to Twine. IV *Chor.* 42.

their fellow Scholler to learne, onely for her recreation betwixt the
houres of study, dauncing, singing, sowing, or what experience
soever (for in no action was she unexpert)[1] as also every morning,
and at noone, before she made her meale she forgotte not to revisite
her Nurses sepulchre: and entring into the monument, upon her
knees she there offered her funerall teares for the losse of her mother,
and desiring the gods in their holy Synode to protect the safety of her
father, accusing her selfe as an unfortunate childe, whose beeing,
caused the death of her mother, so good a Queene, and the sorrow
of her father, so curteous a Prince: and in very deede, the whole
course of her life was so affable and curteous, that she wonne
the love of all and every man, accompting his tongue (the father of
speech) a trewant, which was not liberall in her prayses: so that it
fortuned as she passed along the streete, with *Dyonysa* her daughter,
who was her companion and Schoolefellow, and who till then she
supposed had beene her sister. The people, as at other times, came
running out of their doores with greedy desire to looke upon her;
and beholding the beauty and comelinesse of *Marina* so farre to out-
shine *Dyonysaes* daughter,[2] who went side by side with her, could
not containe themselves from crying out, Happy is that father who
hath *Marina* to his daughter, but her Companion that goeth with
her is fowle and ill-favoured. Which when *Dyonysa* heard, her envy
of those prayses bred in her a contempt, and that contempt soone
transformed it selfe into wrath, all which shee for the instant dissembling, yet at her comming home withdrawing her selfe into a
private walke, she in this maner with her selfe beganne to discourse;
It is now quoth she, foureteene yeers since *Pericles* this out-shining
gerles father departed this our Citty, in all which time we have not
received so much as a Letter, to signifie that he remembers her, or
any other token, to manifest he hath a desire to acknowledge her,
whereby I have reason to conjecture, that he is either surely dead,
or not regardes her, though I must confesse, at his departure from
hence, and his committing her to our protection, he left her not
unfurnished of all things fitting the education of his childe, and a
princesse of her birth, both of golde, plate, and apparrell, even
competent enough to foster her according to her degree, nay (if
neede were) to marry her according to her blood. But what of all
this? he is absent, and *Lycorida* her Nurse is dead: Shee in beauty
out-shines my childe, and I have her fathers treasure in possession,
(though given for her use) shall make my daughter out-shine her.
What though I knowe her father did releeve our Citty? I agayne

[1] IV *Chor.*, 5-11; 21-29.
[2] *Ibid.* 11-35.

doe knowe, that but few in these dayes requite benefites with thankes, longer than while they are in receiving. In briefe, I envy her, and she shall perish for it. With the which wordes she had no sooner concluded, but in comes a servant of hers, and she now intended to make him the divells. With this *Leonine* she thus began to interprete her will: *Leonine* quoth she, thou knowst *Marina*. And madame, quoth he, for a most vertuous Gentlewoman. Talke not of vertue, quoth *Dyonysa*, for thats not the businesse which we have in hand; but I must have thee learne to know her now, that thou mayest never know her afterward, I understand you not quoth *Leonine*. When she replied, Take this at large then, Thou art my bond-slave, whom I have power to enfranchise or captive, if thou wilt obey me, first then receive this golde as the earnest which promiseth unto thee a greater reward: but if thou deny to accomplish my desire, in bondage and imprisonment, I will fetter thee, and by no other meanes conclude my revenge, but by thy death. Speake on my taske then good Madam, quoth *Leonine*, For what is it that a bondman will not attempt for liberty, which is deerer to man then life, and what not I then? Thou knowest, quoth *Dyonysa* then, that *Marina* hath a custome, as soone as shee returneth home from schoole, not to eate meate before she have gone to visite the sepulchre of her nurse.[1] There at her next devotion, doe thou meete her, stand ready, and with thy weapon drawne, sodainely kill her. How kill her quoth *Leonine*, why tis an acte unconscionable, and deserves damnation but to conspire in thought, since she is a creature so harmlesse, that even Innocencie it selfe cannot be more pure, nor inwardly be more decently arrayed than is her minde: yet to fulfill your pleasure, for the hope of golde, and the releasement of my bondage, were she as spotlesse as Trueth, heere are two monsters (drawing his sworde into his hand) shall effect it for you,[2] when she rewarding him with more golde, and commending his resolution, he goes forward to attend for her at *Lycoridaes* Toombe, and *Marina* being returned from Schoole, is also come thither to offer on the monument her diurnall devotion, when on the sodaine, while her knees kissed the earth, and her eyes saluted heaven, while prayers were in her mouth, and teares in her eyes, all tributary offerings, given unto the gods for the prosperitie of her father, on the sodaine toward her, out rushed this *Leonine*,[3] and with a looke as cruell as his heart, and speech as harsh as his intent, he resolved her in blunt wordes, that he was come to kill her, that hee was hired unto it by *Dyonysa* her

[1] IV.i.10–12.
[2] IV.i.9.
[3] In IV.i. Dionyza is present.

foster mother, that she was too good for men, and therefore he would send her to the gods, that if she would pray, pray, for hee had sworne to kill her, and he would kill her, and a thousand more, ere he would be damned for perjury. When she that was on her knees before making her orisons to heaven, was now compelled to turne her intreaties to him: and first demaunded of him what offence her ignoraunce had done (for wittingly shee knew shee coulde doe none) eyther to him, that (as himselfe said) came to murther her, or to her that hired him.[1] But the villaine neyther regarding her innocencie or teares, though showred in aboundaunce, but drawing out his sword wherewith to have shed her blood, and have damned his own soule, there were certaine pyrates that were newly put to water, in at a Creeke neare adjoyning, where the villaine intended this most inhumane murther, and being come up ashoare to forrage, for what pillage soever they could happen upon, even as he was about to have given the fatall blow, whom all her intreaties could not perswade him from, beholding so bloudy a villaine, offering violence to so goodly a beauty, they running all at once toward him cried out aloude; Holde monstrous wretch, as thou lovest thy life, hold, for that Mayden is our prey, and not thy victory.[2] Which when the villaine heard, and perceiving his intent to be intercepted, making his heeles his best defence, till having fledde some distance from them, and observing them not to pursue, he secretly stole backe, to note what the event would be, which was, that the pyrates who had thus rescued *Marina*, carried her to their shippes, hoysed sayles, and departed. At which the vilaine returned home to his Mistris, declaring to her that he had doone what she commaunded him to doe, namely murthered *Marina*, and from the toppe of a high cliffe, throwne her body downe for buriall into the Sea,[3] advising her withall, that since it was done, the chiefest meanes to avoyde suspition, was, to put on mourning garments,[4] and by counterfeiting a great sorrow, in the sight of the people report, that she was dead of some daungerous disease: and withall, to bleare the eies of the multitude (who with faire shewes are soone flattered) neere to her fathers Statue to erect a monument for her. According whereunto, she attyred her selfe and her daughter in solempne attire, and counterfeiting a fained sorrow, and dissembling teares. And going now to erect her monument (to the view of which, all the Citizens flocked) Shee in publike assembly thus spake unto them. Deere

[1] IV.1.65–81.
[2] IV.1.92–5.
[3] IV.1.96–9.
[4] The next passage comes from Twine (Ch. xii), except the *Epitaph*.

Friends and Cittizens of *Tharsus*, If you shall happly wonder, why we thus unwoontedly weep and mourne in your sight, it is because the joy of our eyes and staffe of our olde age *Marina* is dead, whose absence hath left unto us nothing but salt teares, and sorrowfull harts, as if by her death we were divided from all comfort, yet have we here taken order for her funeralls, and buried her (as heere you see) according to her degree, which losse of hers was right grievous to all the people, nor was there any that was capable of sorrowe, but spent it for her, so that with one voyce and willing handes, they attended *Dyonysa* to the Market place whereas her fathers Image stoode, made of brasse, and erected also another to her with this Inscription:

> *Marinaes Epitaph.*
> *The fairest, chastest, and most best lies heere,*
> *Who wythred in her spring of yeere:*
> *In Natures garden, though by growth a Bud,*
> *Shee was the chiefest flower, she was good.*[1]

So with this flattery, (which is like a Skreene before the gravest Judgements) deceiving the Cittizens, and all doone, unsuspected she returned home, when *Cleon*, who not at all consented to this treason, but so soone as he heard therof, being strucke into amazement, he apparelled himselfe in mourning garments, lamenting the untimely ruine of so goodly a Lady, saying to himselfe, Alas now, what mischiefe am I wrapped in, what might I do or say heerein? The Father of that Virgine delivered this Citty from the perill of death, for this Citties sake hee suffered shipwracke, lost his goodes, and endured penury, and now he is requited with evill for good, his daughter which hee committed by my care to be brought up, is now devoured by the cruelty of my wife, so that I am deprived, as it were, of mine owne eyes, and forced to bewaile the death of that Innocent, she in whose presence, as in the fortune of mine own posterity I shoulde have had delight. And then demaunding of Dyonysa how she could give prince *Pericles* accompt of his childe, having robbed him of his childe, how shc could appease the fury of his wrath, if her acte were knowne to him? or how alay the displeasure of the gods, from whome nothing can be hid. For *Pericles* quoth she, if such a pious innocent as your selfe do not reveale it unto him,[2] how should he come to the knowledge thereof, since that the whole Citty is satisfied by the monument I caused to be erected, and by our dissembling outside, that she died naturally, and for the gods, let

---

[1] Cf. IV.4.33–43.
[2] IV.3.12–19.

them that list be of the minde to thinke they can make stones speake, and raise them up in evidence, for my parte I have my wish, I have my safety, and feare no daunger till it fall upon me. But *Cleon* rather cursing then commending this obduracy in her, he continued mourning unfainedly, but she according to her sinful condition.[1] By this time the pirats (who before rescued *Marina*, when she should have beene slaine by trecherous *Leonine*) are now arived at *Meteline*, and in the Market place of the Cittie, according to the custome, amongst other bondslaves, offered her to be solde, whither all sorts of people, comming to supply their purposes, *Marina* was not without much commendations gazed upon of the buyers, come commending her beauty, others her sober countenaunce, all pittying her mishap, and praysing her perfections, which prayses of her, were so spread through the Citty, that from all parts they came crowding to see her, amongst the number of which, was a *Leno* or bawde, yet one who had not set up shop, and kept trade for himselfe, but was yet but journey-man to the devill. This *Leno* amongst others, staring upon her, and knowing her face to be a fit faire signe for his maisters house, and with which signe he made no doubt, but to lodge under their roofe, all th'intemperate (even from youth to age) thorow the whole Citty, hee foorthwith demaunded the price, intending to buy her, at what rate soever, and in the end, went thorow, and bargained to have her, paying a hundred Sestercies of golde, and so presently having given earnest, he takes *Marina*, and the rest of the Pirates home with him to his Maisters house, *Marina* was there to be taught how to give her body uppe a prostitute to sinne, and the Pirates for their new stuffe to receive their money.[2]

The tenth Chapter

How *Marina* being thus solde to a Bawde, preserved her virginitie, and how shee converted all that ever came to make hire of her beauty from the loosenesse of their desires.

Marina was no sooner thus concluded for, by the hee Bawde, but the Pyrates were as soone brought home to his masters house, and received their payment, when after their departure, she giving commaund to the Pander her man, that he should goe backe into the Market place, and there with open crie proclaime, what a picture of Nature they had at home, for every lascivious eie to gaze upon.[3] The she Bawd beganne to instruct her, with what complement

[1] IV.3.25ff.
[2] IV.2.41–57.
[3] IV.2.58–64

35

she should entertaine her customers: she first asked her, if she were a virgine. When *Marina* replyed, she thanked the Gods, shee never knew what it was to be otherwise. In so being quoth the she bawde, you have beene well: but now in plaine tearmes I must teach you how to be worse. It is not goodnesse in you (quoth *Marina*) to teach me to be so. For[1] goodnes answerd the bawd, it is a Lecture, such as we use seldome, and our consciences never reade one to another, and therefore attend unto me: you must now be like a stake for every man to shoote at, you must be like a foord that must receive all waters, you must have the benefite of all nations, and seeme to take delight in all men.[2] I thanke my starres, answered *Marina*, I am displeased with none: for by this answere it appeared such was the puritie of her minde, that she understoode not what this devills sollicitor pleaded unto her: but she quickely taking her off, told in more immodest phrase, that shee had payde for her, and that she and all her body was hers, that will ye nill ye she must now be what she her selfe had beene (and there is seldome any bawde, but before time, hath beene a whoore) that to conclude, shee had bought her like a beast, and shee meant to hire her out.

When she understanding unwillingly what all these wordes tended unto, she fell prostrate at her feete, and with teares showred downe in aboundaunce, she intreated her, not to make hire of her bodie to so diseasefull a use, which shee hoped the gods had ordained to a more happy purpose. When the bawde answered her, Come, come, these droppes availe thee not, thou arte now mine, and I will make my best of thee: and I must now learne you to know, we whom the worlde calles Bawdes, but more properly are to be stiled Factors for men, are in this like the hangman, neither to regard prayers, nor teares, but our owne profite. So calling for her slave, which was governour over her she-houshold,[3] this was her appoyntment unto him, Goe quoth shee and take this Mayden, as shee is thus decked in costly apparrell (for it is to be remembred, that the former Pirates had no way dispoyled her of her ornaments, with purpose to prise her at the higher rate) and leading her along, this be the crie thorow the whole Citty, That whosoever desireth the purchase of so wondrous a beauty, shall for his first enjoying her, pay tenne peeces of golde, and that afterward shee shall be common unto the people for one peece at a time. Which will of hers, *Marina* being no way able to resist, but with her sorrowe, onely desiring of the good gods, to be protectors of her chastitie: She with this her slave was hurried

---

[1] So, for *1608*.
[2] Cf. IV.2.69–82; 92–4.
[3] Boult in *Per.*

along, and who with the tenour of his priapine proclamation, had
so awaked the intemperaunce of the whole Cittie, that against her
returne, of high and low there was a full crowding at the doore,
every man carrying his money in his hand, and thinking him the
happiest man that might first have accesse.[1] But heaven who is still
a protector of Vertue against Vice, ordayned this for *Marina*, that
the sending her abroad, with purpose, first to shew her, and after,
to make sale of her to the worlde, was the onely meanes to defend
her in the state of her virginitie. For as she was (as before is saide)
led along, and thousands of people wondring about her, and
flocking as it had beene so many flies, to infect so delicate a pre-
servative, it happened that *Lysimachus* the cheefe governour of
Meteline, looking out at his windowe, to observe what strange
occasion drew the giddy havocke of people, to muster themselves
into such throngs: he, not without great admiration observed, that
it was to make boote of so pretious a beauty, whose inflaming
colours which Nature had with her best Arte placed uppon her face,
compelled him to censure, that she was rather a deserving bedfellow for a Prince, than a play-fellow for so rascally an assembly:
so pittying awhile her misfortune, that it was so hard to be throwne
into the jaws of two such poisonous and devouring serpents, a Pandar,
and a Bawde, yet at last, being inflamed with a little sinnefull
concupiscence, by the power of her face, he resolved himselfe that
since shee must fall, it were farre more fitter, into his owne armes,
whose authoritie could stretch to doe her good, than into the hote
imbracements of many, to her utter ruine[2]; so presently dismissing
away a servant of his, he gave him charge, to give in charge to the
Bawd, that at the returne home, of this new peece of merchandise of
hers, as shee respected, or in time of neede would be beholding to
his favour, (and Heavens forfend but Bawdes nowe and then should
stand in neede of authoritie) she should keepe her private from the
conference of any, for hee himselfe that night late in the evening, in
secret, and in some disguise, would (for her guests sake) visite her
house. There needed no further incouragement to bid the Bawde
stirre up her damnable limbes to make all fit. It was enough in this,
that the Governour had sent worde, it was he that was to come.
But having given the best garnish she could to her sinnefull habitation: and *Marina* being returned home againe by the Pandar, who
had ledde her up and downe as Beare-heards leade beares, for shew
first, and to be baited after: Shee tooke her up with her into a private
Chamber, when the fruite of her instructions were, how she should

[1] IV.2.95–117.
[2] Athanagoras is cruder in Twine Ch. 13.

now learne to behave her selfe, for she had fortunes comming uppon her, she was nowe to be received, respected, and regarded of a man that was honourable. Heaven graunt that I may finde him so, quoth *Marina.* Thou needest not doubt it sweete heart, quoth the Bawde, for though I tell it thee in private, which for a million he would not have to be knowne publikely: Hee is no woorse a man thou arte shortly to deale withall, than the Governour of this whole Citty, a Gentleman that is curteous, a favourer of our calling, one that will as soone have his hand in his pocket, as such a pretty dilling as thou shalt come in his eye, and not as most of our Gentlemen doe, drawe it out empty, but filling it full of golde, will most *Jove*-like rayne it downe in to his *Danaes* lap. In briefe, he is a Nobleman, and, which is a thing which we respect more than his nobilitie, he is liberall: he is curteous, and thou mayest commaund him, he is vertuous and thou mayest learne of him. All these indeede, answered *Marina,* are properties due unto so worthy a Gentleman, whom you picture him to be: and if he be liberall in good, I shall be glad to taste of his bountie: if curteous, I shall as willingly become his servant: and if vertuous, it shal be in me no way to make him vicious. Well, well, well, sayes the Bawde, we must have no more of this puling, and I must have you learne to know, that vice is as hereditary to our house, as the olde barne to your countrey beggar.[1] But as shee would have proceeded with more of these her divelish counsells, hastily into the Chamber came the Pandar unto them, who as hote as a toste, with his haste to bring the newes, he told them, that the Lorde *Lysimachus* was come,[2] and as if the word Come had beene his kew, he entred the Chamber with the master bawde, when the whole frie of sinners cursying about him, he very largely, as the Prologue to his entertainment, distributed golde among them, and then as roundly demaunded, for that same fresh peece of stuffe, which by their proclamation they tolde, they had now to make sale of, and he of set purpose was come to have a sight of.[3]

When they all poynting toward *Marina,* told him there shee was, and for our selves, quoth they, we having done the office of right Chamberlaines, brought you together, we will shut the doore after us, and so leave you.[4] Who no sooner departed, but *Lysimachus* the Governour began to demaund of her the performaunce of that for which he came. When shee prostrating her selfe at his feete, intreated him to take pitty of her, and from poynt to poynt (excepting her birth, and death of her parents) discoursed unto him the whole story

[1] IV.6.51–64.   [2] IV.6.16.
[3] IV.6.21.   [4] IV.6.67–8.

of her misfortunes: as that by the practise of *Dyonysa,* and cruelty of *Leonine,* she should have beene murthered. And how it pleased the Gods to rescue her from that ruine by certaine Pyrates, who after solde her to this brothell, where, most unhappy, he was witnesse she remayned. Then gentle Sir, quoth shee, since heaven hath been so gratious, to restore me from death, let not their good to me, be a meanes for you, to be author of my more misfortune. But the Governour suspecting these teares, but to be some new cunning, which her matron the Bawde had instructed her in, to drawe him to a more large expence[1]: He as freely tolde her so, and now beganne to be more rough with her, urging her, that he was the Governour, whose authoritie coulde wincke at those blemishes, her selfe, and that sinnefull house could cast uppon her, or his displeasure punish at his owne pleasure, which displeasure of mine, thy beauty shall not priviledge thee from, nor my affection, which hath drawen me unto this place abate, if thou with further lingering withstand me. By which wordes, she understanding him to be as confident in evill, as she was constant in good, she intreated him but to be heard, and thus she beganne.

If as you say (my Lorde) you are the Governour, let not your authoritie, which should teach you to rule others, be the meanes to make you mis-governe your selfe: If the eminence of your place came unto you by discent, and the royalty of your blood, let not your life proove your birth a bastard: If it were throwne upon you by opinion, make good, that opinion was the cause to make you great.[2] What reason is there in your Justice,who hath power over all, to undoe any? If you take from mee mine honour, you are like him, that makes a gappe into forbidden ground, after whome too many enter, and you are guiltie of all their evilles: my life is yet unspotted, my chastitie unstained in thought. Then if your violence deface this building, the workemanship of heaven, made up for good, and not to be the exercise of sinnes intemperaunce, you do kill your owne honour, abuse your owne justice, and impoverish me. Why, quoth *Lysimachus,* this house wherein thou livest, is even the receptacle of all mens sinnes, and nurse of wickednesse, and how canst thou then be otherwise then naught, that livest in it?[3] It is not good, answered *Marina,* when you that are the Governour, who should live well, the better to be bolde to punish evill, doe knowe that there is such a roofe, and yet come under it. Is there a necessitie (my yet good Lord) if there be fire before me, that I must strait then thither flie

[1] Cf. IV.2.119–24.
[2] IV.6.99–101.
[3] IV.6.83–4.

and burne my selfe? Or if suppose this house (which too too many feele such houses are) should be the Doctors patrimony, and Surgeons feeding; folowes it therefore, that I must needs infect my self to give them maintenance? O my good Lord, kill me, but not deflower me, punish me how you please, so you spare my chastitie, and since it is all the dowry that both the Gods have given, and men have left to me, do not you take it from me; make me your servant, I will willingly obey you; make mee your bond-woman, I will accompt it freedome; let me be the worst that is called vile, so I may still live honest, I am content: or if you thinke it is too blessed a happinesse to have me so, let me even now, now in this minute die, and Ile accompt my death more happy than my birth.[1] With which wordes (being spoken upon her knees) while her eyes were the glasses that carried the water of her mis-hap, the good Gentlewoman being mooved, hee lift her up with his hands, and even then imbraced her in his hart, saying aside: Now surely this is Virtues image, or rather, Vertues selfe, sent downe from heaven, a while to raigne on earth, to teach us what we should be. So in steede of willing her to drie her eyes, he wiped the wet himselfe off, and could have found in his heart, with modest thoughts to have kissed her, but that hee feared the offer would offend her. This onely hee sayde, Lady, for such your vertues are, a farre more worthy stile your beuty challenges, and no way lesse your beauty can promise me that you are, I hither came with thoughtes intemperate, foule and deformed, the which your paines so well have laved, that they are now white, continue still to all so, and for my parte, who hither came but to have payd the price, a peece of golde for your virginitie, now give you twenty to releeve your honesty.[2] It shall become you still to be even as you are, a peece of goodnesse,[3] the best wrought uppe, that ever Nature made, and if that any shall inforce you ill, if you but send to me, I am your friend. With which promise, leaving her presence, she most humbly thanked the Gods for the preservation of her chastitie, and the reformation of his mind.

Lysimachus though departed thus, intended not to leave her so, but with diligent eyes to attend, how shee behaved her selfe to all other, who should have admittance to her, and for that purpose, having power to commaund the Bawde, hee placed himselfe in the next Chamber where he might heare, even to a sillable, whatsoere passed, where he was no sooner setled with a former charge given to the bawd, that any man should have accesse to her, but by turnes,

---

[1] For possible verse here see Appendix.
[2] Contrast IV.6.110–16.
[3] IV.6.120–1.

he heard she had also won others, and preserved herselfe from them, as she had formerly done against him, gaining tenne times as much of profite by her prayers and teares, as she should have doone by prostituting her beauty to their willes[1]: at last, all of them being departed, and the house unfrequented, onely of their owne housholde, and of the Governour, the bawde standing ready at the doore, as hee should goe out, making his obeysaunce unto him as hee should returne, in hope of his fee or rewarde, hee with an angry brow turned towards him, saying, Villaine, thou hast a house heere, the weight of whose sinne would sincke the foundation, even unto hell, did not the vertue of one that is lodged therein, keepe it standing[2]; and so, as it were inraged, giving them nothing, he departed. By which displeasure of his, the whole swarme of bawdes (as truely it was) ghessed, that their new tenaunt, had not beene pliant to his will: and all rushing in hastily uppon her, first taking away the golde which the charitie (and not injury of all who had beene there) had given her to releeve her with, they cried against her, they should be all undoone by her, their house would grow uncustomed, and their trading would fall to decay, by her squeamishnesse, and want of familiaritie to their Clients, resolving now, that there was no way to bring her unto their bowe, but by having her ravished.[3] For it is to be noted, not any that parted the house besides *Lysimachus*, but even as he did, so they in like manner rayled against them, so forcibly had hir perswasions prevailed with them: whereupon, for that purpose they gave her up to the Pandar, who first agreed for her, saying; That he that had bargained for the whole joynt, it was fittest for him to cut a morsell from off the spit.[4] So leaving them together, and telling him, they gave her up to his power, to doe even what he would with her: the man and wife (though both bawdes) departed, when the pandar going to her, tolde her, that he, his master, nor their antient family would as thus long they had beene, he undoone by ere a Puritane peece[5] of them all. And therefore quoth he; Come on and resolve your selfe without more whining, for I am but the bawdes servant.[6] The bawde hath commaunded me, and every servant by the Indenture of his duety, is bound to obey his master: So catching her rashly by the hand, as he would have inforced her to his will; she first calling on *Diana* patronesse of Chastitie to defend her, fell likewise downe at his feete, and besought him but to heare her: which being graunted, she demaunded of him

[1] Cf. IV.5.   [2] IV.6.127–9.
[3] IV.6.4–5; 136–7.   [4] IV.2.132–6.
[5] Cf. IV.6.9 'make a puritan of the devil'.
[6] IV.6.150–63.

what thing he could wish himselfe[1] to be, which was more vile than he was, or more hatefull than he would make himselfe to be? Why my master or my mistris (quoth the villaine) I thinke, who have all the sinnes subject to mankind raigning in them, and are (indeede) as bad as the Divell himselfe: yet (quoth *Marina*) thou goest about to be worse then they, and to doe an office at their setting on, which thy master himselfe hath more pitty then to attempt,[2] to robbe me of mine honour, which in spite of them and thee, the Gods (who I hope will protect it still) have till this breathing protected, to leprous my chast thoghts, with remembrance of so foule a deede, which thou then shalt have doone, to damne thine owne soule, by undooing of mine.[3] At which word, the Villaine being strucke into some remorce, and standing in a pawse, *Marina* went forward, and tolde him; If thou wantest golde, there is some for thee[4] (part of that she had reserved which before was given hir, from the bawdes knowledge:) or if thou wantest maintenaunce, provide mee but some residence in an honest house, and I have experience in many things which shall labour for thee, as namely, I am skilfull in the seaven Liberall Sciences, well exercised in all studies, and dare approove this, that my skill in singing and playing on Instruments exceeds any in the citty: therefore (quoth she) as thou before didst proclame my beuty in the market to the open world, whereby to have made me a common prostitute, so now agayne proclame my vertues unto them, and I doubt not but this honorable citty will affoord schollers sufficient, the instructing of whome will returne profite enough,[5] both to repay the Maister what hee payed out for me, provide an honester course for thee then this thou livest in, and give a quiet content unto my selfe. Sooth (quoth the Villaine) being now mooved unto much more compassion of her; If you have (as you say) these qualities, I will labour with my Master, and doe my best for your release. If not (answered *Marina*) I give thee free leave to bring me backe againe, and prostitute me to that course which was first pretended for me. In[6] briefe, the Villaine so laboured with the bawde his maister, that though hee woulde not give her leave to depart his house,[7] yet in hope of the profit, which would come in by her other qualities, she should stay in his house, and none, with her former greevances disturbe her, and withall, charged the Pander to set up a Bill in the Market place, of her excellencie in speaking, and singing. At the report of which there crowded as many to the bawdes

---

[1] IV.6.164–8 clarify this.
[3] More latent verse here.
[5] IV.6.191–95.
[7] Cf. IV.6.200–7.

[2] IV.6.169–70.
[4] IV.6.189.
[6] IV.6.196–9.

great profite to be delighted with her woorth, as there came before to have made spoyle of her vertue, and not any man but gave her money largely, and departed contented,[1] onely above the rest the Lorde *Lysimachus* had evermore an especiall regarde in the preservation of her safety no otherwise than if she had beene descended from himselfe, and rewarded the villaine very liberally for the diligent care hee had over her.[2]

The eleventh Chapter

How *Pericles* after foureteene yeeres absence, arrived at *Tharsus*, and not finding his daughter, lamented her supposed death: and how taking ship againe, he was by crosse windes driven to *Meteline*, where his daughter *Marina* was: and how by the meanes of Prince *Lysimachus* comming aboorde his shippe to comforte him, he came to the knowledge of his lost daughter, and also of his wife *Thaysa*.

Having thus preserved *Marina*, our Story gives us now leave to returne againe to Prince *Pericles*, who after foureteene yeares absence arrived at *Tharsus*,[3] and was received into the house of *Cleon* and *Dyonysa*, with whome hee had left his yoong daughter *Marina* to be fostered up. At the newes of whose comming, *Cleon* and *Dyonysa* againe apparrelled themselves in mournfull habites, went out to meete him: who when *Pericles* beheld in so sad an out-side; My trusty friends, what cause inforceth you to give so sad a welcome to my entertainement? O my good Lord, answered *Dyonysa*, would any tongue but ours might be the herald of your mis-hap: but sorrowes pipes will burst, have they not vent, and you of force must knowe *Marina* is dead. Which when *Pericles* heard, the very word Death seemed like an edge that cut his heart, his flesh trembled, and his strength failed: yet in that agony a long time standing amased, with his eyes intentively fixed on the ground, and at length recovering himselfe, and taking breath, hee first cast his eyes uppe to heaven, saying; O you Gods! extreamity of passion dooth make mee almost ready to accuse you of injustice. And then throwing his eyes greedily upon her. But woman, quoth hee, If (as thou sayest) my most deere *Marina* be dead, is the money and the treasure which I also left with you for her, perished with her? When she aunswered; Some is, and some yet remaineth. And as for your daughter (my Lord)

[1] Cf. V *Chor.*, 1–11.
[2] Close to Twine.
[3] Cf. IV.4. Wilkins follows Twine.

lest you shoulde anie way suspect us, we have sufficient witnesse: for
our Citizens being mindefull of your benefites bestowed uppon
them, have erected unto her a monument of brasse fast by yours.
And when she had so said, she brought foorth such money, jewells,
and apparrell as it pleased her to say were remayning of *Marinaes*
store. Whereuppon *Pericles* giving credite to this report of her death,
he commaunded his servants to take up what she had brought, and
beare them to his shippes, while he himselfe would goe visite his
daughters monument. Which when he beheld, and had read the
Epitaph, as before written, his affection brake out into his eies, and
he expressed more actuall sorrow for the losse of her then Inditement
can expresse: first, tumbling himselfe uppon her monument, he then
fell into a swownd, as if, since he might not leave all his life with her,
yet he would leave halfe at least, from which trance being at the
length recovered, hee apparrelles himselfe in sacke-cloth,[1] running
hastily unto his shippes, desireth the Sea to take him into their
wombe, since neither land nor water was fortunate unto him; for
the one had bereft him of a daughter, the other of a wife. But as
befitted them, being most careful of his safety, they used their best
perswasions, to asswage this tempest of his sorrow; presently, as
much as might be in such a case, they prevayled, and partly by
time, which is a curer of all cares, continually mittigated some part
of the griefe. When hee perceiving the winde to stand fitte for their
departure, hee hoysed uppe sailes, and gave farewell to the shoare,
nor had they long sailed in their course, but the winde came about
into a contrary quarter, and blew so fiercely that it troubled both
sea and shippes, the raine fell fiercely from above, and the sea
wrought woonderously underneath, so that the tempest being
terrible for the time, it was in that extreamitie thought fittest to
strike sayle, to let the Helme goe, and to suffer the shippe to drive
with the tide, whither it would please the gods to direct it[2]: But
as Joy evermore succeedeth Heavinesse, so was this sharpe storme
occasion of a joyfull meeting, betwixt this sorrowful father, and his
lost daughter; for while Prince *Pericles* shippe is thus governed at
randon, by fortune it striketh uppon the shoare of the Cittie *Meteline*,
where now *Marina* remained, of whose death he (as before) being
fully perswaded, in whose life he had hope his decayed comfortes
should againe have had new growth. And being now agayne at sea,
he vowed to himselfe never more to have fellowshippe or conference
with any man, charging all his folowers, of whome *Helycanus* was one,
that none of them upon the paine of his displeasure (and who is

[1] IV.4.29.
[2] IV.4.46–8.

ignorant that the displeasure of kings is as daungerous as death) should dare to speake unto him: no not so much as they who attended him with meate, and withall commaunded them, that they should not ordayne for him any more but so small a competence, as might even scarcely maintaine nature, accompting now that life which he possessed, tedious to him, and wishing death in the most unfriendly languishment. In which state while he consisted, pining of his body, and perplexed in minde, it happened, that at one selfe same time Lord *Helycanus* going from the Princes shippe, and landing on the shoare,[1] the Governour *Lysimachus*, who (as before is mentioned) tenderd *Marina*, was standing at the haven, and noting *Pericles* ships riding there at anker, he beganne with himselfe to commend the comelinesse of the vessells, and applaude the state they uphelde in their burthens, and in especially, that of the Admirall wherein the Prince himselfe was, who seeing *Helycanus* come on shoare, and his grave and reverent[2] countenaunce promising him, to be a father of experience, and worthy of his conference, hee in curteous manner saluted him, and demaunded of him, of whence those shippes were, for sir quoth he, by their armes and ensignes I perceive they are strangers to our harbours, as also that it would please him to deliver to him who was the owner of them, when *Helycanus*, as in the whole Storie, discoursed unto him his misfortunes, as also of his former woorth, and his present languishment, from which he could not be remooved, neither by his owne wisedome, nor by the counsell of his friends. When *Lysimachus* pittying his ruine, intreated *Helycanus* that he might speake with him, whereby to try if his perswasions had power to prevayle with him more then the will of himselfe, or power of his subjects. Which being by *Helycanus* graunted, he foorthwith conducted him downe where his Maister lay[3]: whom when *Lysimachus* beheld, so attired from the ordinary habite of other men, as with a long over-growne beard, diffused hayre, undecent nayles on his fingers, and himselfe lying uppon his cowch groveling on his face. He somewhat astonished at the strangenes thereof, called unto him with a soft voice, Prince *Pericles*, who hearing himselfe named, and thinking it to be some of his men, that called upon him contrary to his commaundement, hee arose up sodainely with a fierce counten-aunce: but seeing him to be a stranger, verie comely and honourably attyred, hee shruncke himselfe downe uppon his pillow, and held his peace. When *Lysimachus* demaunded of *Helycanus* if it were his custome to be so silent to all men. Sir, it is quoth he, and hath continued so

---

[1] In *Per.* V.1. Lysimachus comes out to the ship.
[2] V.1.14.
[3] As in Twine. Cf. V.1.35.

for the space of this moneth, neither dare any of us his subjects, though we suffer much sorrow for him, by our perswasions seeke to alter him. Now surely quoth *Lysimachus*, though his misfortunes have beene great, and by which he hath great cause for this sorrow, it is great pitty he should continue thus perverse and obstinate, or so noble a gentleman come to so dishonorable a death: and thereuppon bethinking with himselfe what honourable meanes he might use to recover him. He sodainely remembring the wisedom that he had known *Marina* had in perswasion: and having heard since of her excellent skill in musicke, singing and dauncing: he by the consent of *Helycanus* caused her to be sent for, resolving with himselfe, that if the excellencie of her ministry had no power to worke on him, all phisicke was in vaine, and he from thence would resigne him over to his grave. The messenger speedily is returned, bringing *Marina* along with him: whome when *Lysimachus* beheld, *Marina* quoth he, let me request of thee, thy help and uttermost knowledge in comforting the owner of this shippe which lieth in darkenesse, and will receive no comfort, nor come abroade into the light, for the sorrow that he conceiveth through the losse of a wife and a daughter. From which if thou recover him, and to his former health restore him, I will, as I am a Gentleman, give thee in recompence thirtie sistercies of golde, and as many of silver, and though the bawd hath bought thee, according to the laws of our citty, from whom no authoritie can compell thee, yet for thirtie dayes will I redeeme thee.[1] Which when *Marina* heard, shee went boldely downe into the cabine to him, and with a milde voyce saluted him, saying; God save you sir, and be of good comfort, for an innocent Virgin, whose life hath bin distressed by shipwrack, and her chastity by dishonesty, and hath yet bin preserved from both, thus curteously saluteth thee: but perceiving him to yeeld her no answer, she began to record in verses, and therewithall to sing so sweetely, that *Pericles*, notwithstanding his great sorrow, woondered at her, at last, taking up another instrument unto his eares she preferred this[2]:

> *Amongst the harlots foule I walke,*
> *Yet harlot none am I;*
> *The Rose amongst the Thornes doth grow,*
> *And is not hurt thereby.*
> *The Thiefe that stole me sure I thinke,*
> *Is slaine before this time.*
> *A Bawde me bought, yet am I not*
> *Defilde by fleshly crime:*

[1] Cf. V.i.70–5.
[2] The song (not given in the play) is largely from Twine.

Nothing were pleasanter to me,
Then parents mine to know.
I am the issue of a King,
My blood from Kings dooth flowe:
In time the heavens may mend my state,
And send a better day,
For sorrow addes unto our griefes,
But helps not any way:
Shew gladnesse in your countenaunce,
Cast up your cheerefull eies,
That God remaines, that once of nought
Created Earth and Skies.

With this Musicke of *Marinaes*, as with no delight else was he a whit altered, but lay groveling on his face, onely casting an eye uppon her, as hee waere rather discontented than delighted with her indevour. Whereupon she beganne with morall precepts to reproove him, and tolde him, that hee was borne a Prince, whose dignity being to governe others, it was most foule in him to misgoverne himselfe. Which while he continued in that sullen estate, he did no lesse, thus to mourne for the losse of a wife and childe, or at any of his owne misfortunes, approved that he was an enemy to the authoritie of the heavens, whose power was to dispose of him and his, at their pleasure: and that it was as unfitte for him to repine (for his continuing sorrow shewed he did no lesse) against their determinations and their unaltered willes, as it was for the Giants to make warre against the Gods, who were confounded in their enterprise. Not fitte to sorrow, quoth he, rising up like a Cloude, that bespeakes thunder; presumptuous bewty in a childe, how darest thou urge so much? and therewithall, in this rash distemperature, strucke her on the face.[1] When she, who never untill that time knew what blowes were, fell sodainely in a swowne: but beeing againe recovered, shee cryed out; O humilitie! ordained especially for Princes, who having power over all, should contemne none, whither art thou fled? then weeping a while; And O you Gods! creators both of heaven and earth, looke uppon my afflictions, and take compassion uppon me, that am unfortunate in all things. I have bin tossed from wrong to injurie,[2] I was borne amongest the waves and troublesome tempests of the Sea, my mother died in paines and pangs of child-birth, and buriall was denyed her on the earth, whome my father adorned with Jewelles layd golde at her head, and silver at her feete, and inclosing

[1] As in Twine; cf. V.1.98–101; 128.
[2] V.1.132.

her in a Chest, committed her to the Sea: As for me unfortunate wretch, my father, who with princely furniture, put me (in trust) to *Cleon* and *Dyonysa*, who commanded a servant of theirs to murder me, from whose cruelty by Pirates I was rescewed, brought by them to this Citty, and sold to have beene hackneyd by a common Bawde, though (I thanke the heavens) I have preserved my chastity; and now after al these crosses, for my curtesies to be strucke thus to bleeding! O cruell fate! By which tale of hers, *Pericles* being mooved, since by all the circumstances he ghessed she was his childe, and yet not knowing whether he might beleeve himselfe to be awake, or in a dreame, he beganne agayne to capitulate with her, of her former relation, as namely, where she was borne, who were her parents, and what her name was. To the which she answered, My name is *Marina*, and so called because I was borne upon the sea.[1] O my *Marina* cryed out *Pericles*, being strucke into such an extasie of joy that hee was not able to containe himselfe! willing her agayne to discourse unto him the storie of her misfortunes, for hee could not heare too much.[2] Which she obeying him in, and he knowing her to be his childe, seeing that the supposed dead was risen again, he falls on hir necke, and kisses her, calles upon *Helycanus* to come unto him, shewes him his daughter, biddes him to kneele to her,[3] thanketh *Lysimachus* that so fortunately had brought her to begette life in the father who begot her; so one while weeping at others joying, and his senses being masterd by a gentle conquerour, in that extreamitie of passion he fell into a slumber: in which sweet sleepe of his, hee was by *Diana* warned to hie to *Ephesus*: and there upon the Altare of that Goddesse to offer uppe his sacrifice before the Priests, and there to discourse the whole progresse of his life[4]: which he remembring, being awake, he accordingly shipped himselfe with *Lysimachus*, *Marina*, and his owne subjects to perfourme. Who landing at *Ephesus*, and giving notice of the purpose, for which he was come, he was by all the Priests and Votaries attended to the Temple[5]; and being brought to the Altare, this was the substance of his sacrifice, I *Pericles* borne Prince of *Tyre*, who having in youth attained to all kinde of knowledge, resolved the Riddle of *Antiochus*, to the intent to have married his daughter, whome he most shamefully defiled. To preserve my selfe from whose anger, I fled to sea, suffered shipwracke, was curteously entertained by good *Symonides* king of *Pentapolis*, and after espoused his faire daughter *Thaysa*. At the naming of whome, she her selfe being by, could not choose but

---

[1] V.1.156–8.   [2] V.1.192–203.   [3] V.1.219.
[4] Wilkins and the play agree (against Twine) in this order of events.
[5] V.3.

starte: for in this Temple was she placed to be a Nunne, by Lord *Cerimon*, who preserved her life. But *Pericles* going on, when *Antiochus* and his daughter, quoth he, were by lightning strucke dead from heaven, I conducted my Queene with me from her fathers Court, with purpose to receive againe my kingdome: where upon the sea shee was delivered of this my daughter, in that travell she died, whom I inclosed in a Chest, and threw it into the Sea. When *Thaysa* standing by, and no longer being able to temper her affections, being assured he was her Lord, shee ranne hastily unto him, imbraced him in her armes, and would have kissed him.[1] Which when *Pericles* sawe, hee was mooved with disdaine, and thrust her from him, accusing her for lightnes, whose modesty and good grace hee at his first entrance did commend, when she falling at his feete, and powring foorth her teares aboundantly, gladnesse compelled her to crie out, O my Lord *Pericles*, deale not ungently with me, I am your wife, daughter unto *Symonides*, my name is *Thaysa*, you were my Schoolemaister, and instructed me in musicke, you are that Prince whome I loved, not for concupiscence, but desire of wisedome, I am she which was delivered and died at the sea, and by your owne hands was buryed in the deepes; which wordes of hers, Lord *Cerimon* standing by, he was ready to averre, but it needed not[2]: for *Pericles*, though at the first astonished, joy had now so revived his spirites, that hee knew her to be herselfe: but throwing his head into her bosome, having nothing but this to utter, he cried aloude, O you heavens! my misfortunes were now againe blessings, since wee are agayne contracted; so giving his daughter to her armes to embrace her as a child and *Lysimachus* to enfolde her as a wife, and giving order the solemnity of marriage should strait be provided for[3]: he then caused the bawd to be burnt, who with so much labor had sought to violate her princely chastitie, whilest *Marina* rewarded the pandar, who had beene so faithfull to hir: and then after he had seene hir mariage with *Lisimachus*, he leaveth *Ephesus*, and intendes for *Tyre*, taking *Pentapolis* in his way, where by the death of good *Symonides*, as lawful heire, he was made soveraigne. He also highly rewarded the poore Fisher-men, who had relieved him. From thence he arrived at *Tharsus*, where hee revenged himselfe of *Cleon* and *Dyonysa*, by stoning them to death. From thence to *Tyre*, where peaceably he was received into his kingdome, and given also possession of all the territories of *Antiochus*, where by his wife, though in the declining of both their yeeres, it pleased the Gods to blesse him with a sonne, who

---

[1] She faints at V.3.15.
[2] He does so at V.3.21–5.
[3] V.3.70–2.

growing to the lusty strength of youth, and the father declining to his grave, age being no longer able to be sustained by the benefite of nature, fell into certayne colde and dry diseases: in which case, the knowledge of his Physitions, could stand him in little steade, eyther by their cunning or experience, (so as no remedie being to be found against death) being in perfect memorie, he departed this life in the armes of his beloved *Thaysa,* and in the middest of his friendes, nobles, alies and children in great honour, his kingdome of *Tyrus* he gave by will to *Lysimachus* and his daughter *Marina,* and to their heires after them for ever, who lived long together, and had much comfort by their issue.[1] Unto his Queene *Thaysa* he gave the two kingdomes of *Antioch* and *Pentapolis* for tearme of her life, and at her death to descend to her yong sonne *Symonides.* But *Thaysa* who could not then be yong since *Pericles* died olde, continued not long in her widows estate, but pining much with sorrow, and wearing with age forsooke the present worlde, leaving her two kingdomes (according to his fathers will) to her yoong sonne *Symonides.*

V. Analogue

From THE ORATOR
by Alexander Silvayn (A. Van den Busche)
translated by Lazarus Piot (1596)

The Oratour: Handling a hundred severall Discourses, in forme of Declamations: Some of the Arguments being drawne from Titus Livius and other ancient Writers; the rest of the Authors owne invention: Part of which are of matters happened in our Age. Written in French by Alexander Silvayn, and Englished by L.P. London. Printed by Adam Islip. 1596.

DECLAMATION, 53

Of her who having killed a man being in the stewes, claimed for her chastity and innocencie to be an Abbesse.

   The order of the religious women is such, as they must be pure, chast, and free from all crime, but the Abbesse must be the chastest of all the rest.

[1] V.3.82.

Whereupon it chanced that a certaine yoong Nunne of Naples was to saile into Sicilie to be an Abbesse there, but her misfortune was such, that she was taken upon the sea by Pyrats, they sould her unto a bawd in Barbarie, who put the said Nunne into a Brothelhouse to get monie by her, but she declaring her misfortune unto such men as came to take their pleasure of her, did so win them by her persuasions, that they giving her the accustomed reward, left her a virgin: untill that on a time there came unto her an insolent souldior, who would in no sort regard her speech but having paied his monie, would by force have had his will of her, and as he was striving with her, she drew his dagger forth of his sheath, and slue him, for the which she was put in prison but being before the Judges, shee was not onely acquited of the murther, but also they sent her back unto Sicilie unto the place whether shee was determined to goe. She being there arrived, they would not receive her for Abbesse, but said:

This woman here which would be an Abbesse, should yet have ben in the Brothelhouse, if she had not murthered a man; but can she be chast, comming from such a place? Nay let us see whether it be lawfull to receive such into monasteries, whom the stewes and the prison forsaketh, Seeing the order of religion may very lawfully be denied, even unto those as doe but onely passe by such places? She saith fortune constrained mee unto these inconveniences, therefore ought every one to have compassion upon me: but wee say that those which are worthie of pittie, are unworthie of a prelateship, neither is it a custome amongst us, that such places as are of greatest honours should be bestowed in recompence of sustained harms, seeing that the only freeing them from their said harms may serve for a sufficient recompence of their passed miseries. Likewise, we may consider how smally she deserved by the little care her parents took of her distresse, not onely in suffering her to be lost or taken away, but being taken never sought either to recover her, or once to seeke her out: and what did the Pyrats see in her that they rather sold her unto a pandor, then to a Princesse, or to some other honourable ladie? If she knew how to persuade so manie men to leave her a Virgine, (as she saith) wherefore could she not persuade her mistresse to suffer her to gaine her living by some other means, rather then to put her forth to so vild a use; or els why did she not as *Hippo* the faire Grecian did, who leaped into the sea so soone as she perceived that she was taken by Pyrats.[1] Alasse if this woman obtaine the Abbesseship, greatlie are the Nunnes of this order to be pittied, if amongst them there cannot bee found one more chast then an harlot, or more innocent then a murtherer. She cannot be chast

---

[1] Not accurate. Hippo, daughter of Scedasus, killed herself after being ravished by the ambassadors of Sparta (*Pausanias*, 9.*c*.13).

36

inough to rule over us, especiallie seeing she saith; I knew how to persuade all those that came unto me: the which sheweth a certain token of her immodestie, for otherwise how could she have pratled so well in that place where such as were modest would have burst into teares, and without being able to speake one onlie word, would have died for shame. Let us then take the case thus: that in her there are three do claime to be Abbesse, the first, is one taken by Pyrats, the second such a one as hath lived in the stewes, & the third she that murthered a man, of whom the best is farre unworthie of anie honour.

The Answere

God herein was minded to shew his power, by making this woman free in bondage, chast in a dishonest place, and most innocent in committing murther to defend her chastitie. I know not whether anie did ever deserve the place of Abbesse so well as she: but I am sure there would bee somewhat to doe to depose all the Abbesses that are lesse worthie then shee. How chast she is, the blood of the slaine souldior doth testifie; how innocent she is, the Judges doe declare; how happie she is, her returne doth shew. Wherefore it is verie manifest that God would never have preserved her from so manie perrils, if it had not ben to serve him in some worthie place. Therefore the same God which hath protected her, is himselfe alone a further testimonie of her chastitie, and he onely is able to comprehend her admirable valor.

APPENDIX

Pericles and the Verse in Wilkins's *Painfull Adventures*[1]

What light do Wilkins's verse-paraphrases throw on the history of *Pericles*? It is no longer believed by many that Wilkins himself wrote the earlier play and used it for his novel. *Pericles* has little in common with his acknowledged plays, and Miss Spiker has shown that he did not know the play which he paraphrased very thoroughly[2]; hence he found Twine's *Patterne of Painefull Adventures* useful to fill in gaps. But he was a verse-dramatist, and it may be suggested that he might easily have dropped into verse when writing prose—though I do not know that this is commonly found in the prose of other verse-dramatists. There are however only a few metrical lines in Twine's story, and Wilkins rarely broke into verse in transcribing him. The frequency and length of his metrical passages elsewhere, and only there, suggest, not that Wilkins was spontaneously bursting with poetic feeling whenever he ceased stealing from Twine, but that he was at times paraphrasing or quoting a play. This play had numerous resemblances (the names of characters, the organization of many scenes, many lines and expressions) to *Pericles* as we have it. But the 'verse-fossils' also indicate that the source-play contained matter not in the 1609 Q. In what follows I have tried to reconstruct the main verse-passages in the novel, keeping as close to Wilkins's words as possible.

(a) When the hero is pondering Antiochus's riddle Twine does not mention the incestuous daughter's presence. In the play she is there, and Pericles praises her beauty. She wishes him success in two extraordinarily bad lines of verse (I.1.59-60)

> 'Of all 'say'd yet, mayst thou prove prosperous!
> Of all 'say'd yet, I wish thee happiness.'

In Wilkins we find:

> 'all the time that the Prince was studying with what trueth to
> unfolde this darke *Enigma*, Desire flew in a robe of glowing blushes

[1] A shortened version of an essay contributed to the *Bulletin de la Faculté des Lettres de Strasbourg*, 1965.

[2] 'George Wilkins and the Authorship of *Pericles*', SPhil, xxx, 1933, 551-70.

into her cheekes, and love inforced her to deliver thus much from hir owne tongue, that he was sole soveraigne of all her wishes, and he the gentleman (of all her eies had ever yet behelde) to whome shee wished a thriving happinesse.'

[*supra* 499]

Is it not likely that this embodies a soliloquy or 'aside'?

> Desire flows in a robe of glowing blushes
> Into my cheeks; and love enforces me
> Declare that he is the sole sovereign
> Of all my wishes, he the gentleman
> (Of all my eyes have ever yet beheld)
> To whom I wish a prosperous happiness.

It is, of course, often impossible to be sure how nearly Wilkins's paraphrases kept to the text since he frequently marred the metre and flattened the style, as memory failed or his prosaic purpose suggested. The above passage however may well be one of the many in which his version supplements or corrects the Q text.

(b) When Antiochus demands the solution of his riddle Twine makes the hero tell him to look into himself and upon his daughter. In the play he declines to tell ('' 'Twould braid yourself too near for me to tell it') but hints his knowledge. Wilkins gives no speech in *oratio recta* but has a rhetorical flourish (*ibid.*) which may come from a brief 'aside' by the Prince:

> ''Tis dangerous to play with tyrants vice
> As for the Fly to sport with Candle's flame.
> I'll rather then dissemble what I know,
> Than my insight discover to the King.'

(c) Pericles' scene with Helicanus in II.i has troubled many editors, for it is obviously corrupt and out of order. This led P. Edwards[1] to suggest a reconstruction which Hoeniger (*Arden*, Appendix C) carried out, pointing out that Wilkins's version of the scene (*supra* 501) may provide 'a clue for the missing piece of dialogue' where Helicanus chides Pericles for his retiredness.

Working on the assumption (justified by other passages) that Wilkins tended to paraphrase speeches into *oratio obliqua*, I suggest that the missing lines went something like this:

> HEL. (kneeling) You do not well, so to abuse yourself
>   To waste your body here in pining sorrow,
>   Upon whose safety all our lives depend

[1] *Sh. Survey*, 5, 1952, pp. 26–7.

And all your kingdom's (great) prosperity.
If ill in you to do't, 'twere ill in me
To suffer you without reproving it.

[Pericles answers angrily.]

HEL. As fitting 'tis for you, although a Prince,
To hear of your own error, as 'tis right
For your authority to order us.
But while you live so shut up, so unseen,
So careless of your government, our order
May turn disorder (?); and what detriment
Your subjects may receive by your neglect,
It were injustice to require of me.

[Pericles bids him rise, then tells his story (I.2.59–100).]

If Wilkins is to be trusted, Helicanus kneels again and begs his master's pardon. Pericles lifts him up and asks his advice. This advice, now given in lines 101–14, may have included lines such as the following:

Therefore my lord, go travel for a while (I.2.106)
Your purpose private as your journey's sudden,
Leaving the government into my trust . . .
Upon this principle my counsel's set,
'Absence abates the edge that Presence whets'.

(*supra* 501)

(d) After the banquet, in which Wilkins and the play agree pretty closely (e.g. in Pericles' formal declaration of his identity: 'A gentleman of Tyre, my name, Pericles . . .' (II.3.81ff.)). Simonides gives the stranger Knight a lodging next his own. In the play as we have it our next sight of Pericles is in the morning after the King has dismissed the rival suitors (II.5). Wilkins however begins his Sixth Chapter with a scene in which Pericles, in his bedchamber, plays the harp and sings so beautifully that Simonides 'rejoyced to be awakened by it' and congratulates himself on entertaining so worthy a guest. This scene probably came from the play and was substituted for Twine's elaborate account of the princess playing at the feast and the hero's (somewhat boastful) demonstration of his superior skill with the harp. It seems possible to rescue something of this lost or deleted scene:

PER. (to the Gentlemen)   Pray leave me private, but for present
solace,
Provide me some delightful instrument

With which and with my former practice on't
I'll pass away the tediousness of night
Instead of proper sleep.

1ST GENT.   Your will's obeyed
In all things.
2ND GENT.   Here's the instrument.
PER.   Now leave me . . .

[Pericles plays for a while, then sings. In the next room the King
awakes and listens.]

KING   He compels
Such heavenly voices from the senseless work
As if Apollo's self were fingering it,
And all the Synod of the Gods had plac'd
Themselves, to be delighted with his skill,
And praises give to his arts excellence.
Nor this alone his hearers ravishes;
From his clear breast he sends such cheerful notes,
Made up so answerable to the other's sound,
That voice and harp seem one consort of music
With so much delicacy, and out of discord
Making so excellent a conjunction,
That they'd have power to draw back an ear
From halfway in the grave to hearken to't . . .

        .   .   .   .

'Tis no disease that troubles me to hear,
But pleasure which will ever give delight . . .
                        I'm so satisfied
To hear him thus express his excellence,
I count my Court happy to entertain
A guest so worthy, and more happy I
To be acquainted with him . . .
Now day that ever hath the sovereignty
Back to withdraw his empire from the night,
Though for a while in dark she may usurp,
Brings morning on . . .
And I must find some answerable gift
Wherewith to gratify this noble prince
For last night's music . . .

(e) In *Pericles* II.5 the King, on the morning after the feast, reads
Thaysa's letter, dismisses the Knights whom Pericles has defeated
and tests Pericles by accusing him of presumption.

Wilkins here ignores the suitors (*supra* 513) and prefaces the test on Pericles by telling how the King received his daughter's letter (which is given in full), and deliberated whether to accept her choice. This reads like the description of a dramatic scene, and although Wilkins's prose here does not fall so easily into metre as sometimes elsewhere, probably the King's soliloquy went something like this:

SIMONIDES   What virtue's in this choice that binds her thoughts
        To this (particular) liking? And what comfort
        May follow after, whose expectancy
        Might my consent invite? And first, he comes
        But poor into my court, and poverty
        Is Nature's work for others to contemn,
        And in these days is grown so odious
        That should I marry her, my only child,
        The only expectation of my realm,
        With one of such low blood and mean descent,
        'Twould bring dishonour more than dignity,
        Since Parents rather will expect t'advance
        Their titles and the raising of their house
        In joining of their issue, than decline . . .
                . . . But, having put
        These interjections 'twixt her love and his,
        The man's uprightness makes me recognise
        Our sole perfection doth in virtue lie;
        And therefore she thinks best, as in her Court,
        In him to place her royal residence . . .
        In that opinion I allow her choice,
        And happy think myself to live as sire
        To such a virtuous son; more happy she
        If she be coupled to so noble a husband . . .
        Soft, here he comes: I must dissemble it. (II.5.23)

(f) Pericles now enters, and Wilkins (*supra* 514) gives the gist of the rest of the scene (II.5.37ff.), often coming close to the Q text but often supplementing it with additional lines. Some of these Professor Edwards thinks worthy of incorporation in the text. I would go further and regard the whole of what follows as probably representing passages in the play as Wilkins knew it:

SIMONIDES.   Traitor, thou liest!
PER.   Traitor?
SIM.   Aye, traitor! (II.5.54)
        That thus disguised art stolne into my Court,

With witchcraft of thy actions to bewitch[1]
The yielding spirit of my tender child.
Thou art a traitor!

PER.   Were't any in thy Court
Except thyself dared call me traitor,
Even in his bosom I would write the lie . . .
I came into your Court in search of honour,
And not to be a rebel to your State.
My blood's as yet untaint, save with the heat
Got by the wrong that you have offer'd me,
And now I boldly dare and do defy
Yourself, your subjects, and the proudest danger
That Tyranny or treason can inflict . . .

SIM. (aside)   I do commend his courage.
                              (*to Pericles*) No? I'll prove it,
Since by my daughter's hand 'tis evident—
Your practice (base) and her consent therein.
                                        (*Enter Thaysa*)[2]

PER. (to Thaysa)   . . . I beg you
By th'hope you have of Heav'n, by your desire
To have your dearest wish fulfill'd on earth,
To satisfy your now displeased father,
If ever I, by motion or by letters,
By amorous glances or by any means
That lovers use to compass their designs,
Have sought to be a friend in your (high) thoughts
Or a co-partner in your worthy love.

THAYSA   [Why sir, say if you had,   (II.5.71–2)
Who takes offence at that would make me glad?]

SIM.   How minion! Is this a fit match for you?
A straggling Theseus born we know not where,
One that hath neither (noble) blood nor merit
For thee to hope for, or himself to challenge
Even the least allowance of thy worth?

THAYSA (kneeling)   My noble Father I beseech you think:
Suppose his birth were base (although his life
Shows that he is not so) yet he hath virtue
(Which is the ground of all nobility)
Enough to make him noble. Royal father,
What with my pen I have in secret writ,

---

[1] Cf. II.5.49: 'Thou hast bewitch'd my daughter.'
[2] 'Which wordes were no sooner uttered, but *Thaysa* . . . came now in, as it had
beene her parte . . .' (*supra* 515).

Now with my tongue I openly confirm,
That I no life possess save in his love,
Nor can exist but to enjoy his worth.

SIM.   ... But, my daughter,
Equals to equals, good to good is joined.
This not being so, the bavin of your mind,
In rashness kindled, must again be quench'd,
Or purchase our displeasure.
                              (*to Pericles*) As for you, sir,
First you must know, I banish you my Court
And though I scorn my rage should stoop so low,
For your ambition, sir, I'll have your life.

THAYSA   Be constant, Pericles.
For every drop of blood he sheds of yours,
He'll draw another from his only child ...

        .   .   .   .

SIM.   I here adopt you as my happy son,
        And bid you live together, man and wife.

(g) A Dumbshow at the beginning of Act III, with forty-six lines by the presenter Gower, covers the period between Pericles' wedding and his departure for Tyre with his pregnant wife and the nurse Lychorida.

Wilkins's account is based on Twine, but also shows signs of dramatic origin, and contains a few lines of quasi-verse which might have been spoken after Gower's prologue (not in *W.*) when 'the good *Symonides* and princely *Pericles* with his faire *Thaysa* were walking in the garden adjoyning to their pallace':

Times feathered wings so fanned away the hours,
His slippery feet so glided o'er the days,
That nine (pale) Moons had almost changed their light,
Ere half the time was thought to be expired.

A lord from Tyre 'came hastily in to them, who uppon his knee delivered unto the yoong Prince a Letter, which being opened the contents therein spake thus unto him':

That (King) Antiochus and his daughter are
With violence of lightning shot from heav'n,
Struck suddenly dead.
Moreover by consent of the general voice
The city of Antioch with the wealth therein
And that whole kingdom are reserved for thee
Now to possess and govern as their prince.

The letter further informed Pericles that Helicanus had 'not without much labour'

> Appeased the stubborn mutiny of the *Tyrians*,
> Who in your absence would elect (have made) him King.
> So to avoid a future insurrection,
> And to preserve your state's security,
> 'Tis needful that you make a swift return . . .

Pericles means to leave Thaysa behind, but she falls at her father's feet and begs to be allowed to go. He tearfully gives permission, and they sail away.

(h) In *The Painfull Adventures* (Ch. 7) Pericles is on deck reviling the storm and praying for his wife's safe deliverance when the nurse comes and puts his 'Sea-borne Babe' into his arms before telling him that his wife is dead (contrast III.1.1–37). He addresses the child:

> Poor inch of Nature,
> Thou art as rudely welcome to the world,
> As ever Prince's babe was.
> Thou hast as chiding a nativity
> As fire, air, earth and water can afford thee—

(when, as if he had forgot himselfe, he abruptly breaks out:)

> But say Lycorida, how doth my Queen?
> LYC. O Sir, she now hath passed all danger, and
> Hath given up her griefs by ending life.

As a reporter Wilkins was untrustworthy, since his aim was to tell the story, but here he departed from Twine (who made Pericles present at his wife's 'death' and ignored the child) and followed what he had seen and heard. The phrase 'Poor inch of Nature' must have been in the play. But what about Wilkins's different order of events which omits the moving speeches of Lychorida, III.1.14–22?

(i) Wilkins begins his eighth Chapter by telling how Pericles left his daughter Marina in the care of Cleon and Dyonysa at Tarsus, the city which he had relieved of famine. His narrative agrees with that of *Pericles*, III.3, but contains some near-verse which I venture to reconstruct thus:

> PER. (after describing the death of Thaysa) . . . Only
> I here have left a little picture of her
> Which for that it was given me at sea,
> I've named Marina. And, I thank the heav'ns,

Is so like her that I ne'er look on it
But with much comfort. For this child's protection
And education I would use your friendship,
While I go on in travel to receive
Antiochus' kingdom, which is kept for me.
And if you'd ever show your gratitude
For the charity extended towards you
And all your City in a past distress,
The gods have giv'n this cause to prove your thanks.

CLE. & DYON. We swear in solemn oath our care shall be
Of her, as Reason to ourselves, which is
The guider of man's life . . .

PER. I thank you for your promise. Let me add,
I leave Lycorida, her mother's nurse
That she may be a nurse unto her babe;
And this I do request and charge you with,
That if it please the gods to lend her life
To years of understanding, you shall not
Till my return make known unto the child
That she's a branch sprung up from Pericles,
But only bring her up as your own daughter,
Lest that the knowledge of her lofty birth
Make her grow proud to your instructions . . .

(j) In the play (IV.1) we see Dyonyza reminding Leonine of his
oath and sending Marina with him to be murdered. We do not see
her broaching the crime to her slave; only the Prologue has

And cursed Dionyza hath
The pregnant instrument of wrath
Prest for this blow. (43-45)

Wilkins however (*supra* 528) gives a scene with dialogue (differing
considerably from that in Twine), and this scene again contains
enough quasi-metrical writing to make it seem likely to have come
in part from a play:

[Dyonysa out of envy and greed decides to remove Marina.]

DYON. What though I know her father did relieve
Our (starving) city, I do also know
That few these days give thanks for benefits
Longer than while they are receiving. Brief,
I envy her, and she shall die for it . . .

['With the which wordes she had no sooner concluded, but in comes
a servant of hers . . .']

DYON. Say Leonine, thou know'st Marina?

LEON. Aye, madam, for a virtuous Gentlewoman.

DYON.   Talk not of virtue,
That's not the business which we have in hand;
But I must have thee learn to know her now,
That thou maist never know her afterward.

LEON. I understand you not.

DYON.   Take this at large, then;
Thou art my bond-slave, whom I have in power
T'enfranchise or captive; if thou'lt obey,
Receive this gold as earnest promising
Greater reward. If thou deny my will,
In prison and in bonds I'll fetter thee,
And by no other means conclude my vengeance
But by thy death.

LEON.   Speak on; my task, good Madam!
What will a bondman not attempt for freedom
(Dearer to man than life), and what not I?

DYON. Thou knowest that Marina hath a custom,
As soon as she returneth home from school,
Not to eat meat before she's gone to visit
The sepulchre of her (beloved) nurse.
There at her next devotions do thou meet her;
Stand ready, and with dagger drawn in hand
Suddenly kill her.

LEON.   How! Kill her!
Why, 'twere an act unconscionable and deserves
Complete damnation but to conspire in thought;
Since she's a creature (made) so harmless, that
Ev'n Innocence itself is not more pure,
Nor inwardly's more decently arrayed
Than is her mind. Yet, to fulfil your wish,
For hope of gold and my release from bonds,
Were she unstained as Truth, here are two monsters
                    (*'drawing his sworde into his hand'*)
Shall it perform for you . . .

(k) The differences between the brothel scenes in the three versions, and particularly between Wilkins and the present play have caused much debate.

Wilkins probably makes use of Twine, but differs considerably in detail. He introduces a 'She-Bawd' who tries to instruct Marina 'with what compliment she should entertaine her customers'. The Governor of Mitylene, seeing her led through the street, is struck by

her beauty and determines 'that since shee must fall, it were farre
more fitter, into his owne armes, whose authoritie could stretch to
doe her good, than into the hote imbracements of many, to her utter
ruine.' He sends word of his coming to the Bawd, who prepares
Marina to receive Lysimachus (*supra.* 534).

Some of the Bawd's speeches seem to be based on verse, though
here the metre is difficult to construct satisfactorily, and I may be
wrong.

The Bawd calls the Governor 'honourable'.

MARINA   Heav'n grant I find him so.

BAWD   Thou need'st not doubt,
Sweetheart, for though I tell thee it in private,
Which for a million he would not have known
In public, he's no less a man, with whom
Thou shortly art to deal, than the Governor
Of this whole City, and a Gentleman
That's courteous, and a favourer of our calling;
One that will quickly have his hand in's pocket
When such a pretty dilling meets his eye,
Nor draw't out empty as most Gentlemen do,
But, fillèd full of gold like Jove himself,
Will rain it down into his Danäe's lap.
In brief he is a Nobleman, and, that
Which we respect more than nobility,
He's liberal, courteous, and thou may'st command him;
He's virtuous, and thou may'st learn from him.

MARINA   All these indeed are properties enough,
Apt to so good a man as you depict.
If he be liberal, I shall be glad
To taste his bounty, and shall willingly
Become his servant; if he's virtuous
It shall not be for me to make him vicious.

BAWD   Well, Well, Well.
An end to puling. I must have you know
Vice is hereditary to our house
As is the old barn to your country beggar.

PANDAR   The Lord Lysimachus is come.

Lysimachus enters, distributing gold and demanding their 'fresh
piece of stuff'. When Marina is left alone with him she throws
herself at his feet and pours out much of her story. Here verse
appears more plainly, and the ensuing dialogue may be sketched
thus:

MARINA   Then gentle Sir,
Since heav'n hath been so gracious to restore me,
Let not its good to me be means for you
To be the author of my more misfortune . . .

LYSIM.   I am the Governor, whose authority
Can wink at all those blemishes which you
And this (most) sinful house may cast upon you;
Or my displeasure punish them at will;
From which thy beauty shall not privilege thee,
Nor my desire abate, which drew me here,
If thou with further lingering withstand me.

MARINA   If, as you say, you are the Governor,
Let not authority, which teaches rule,
Be means to make you rule yourself amiss.
If eminence came to you by descent,
Let not your life prove you in birth a bastard.
If it were thrust upon you by opinion,
Make good the opinion that did make you great.
              . . . What reason's in
Your justice, which has power over all,
To undo any? If you take from me
Mine honour, you are like to him that makes
A gap into forbidden ground, whom after
Too many enter, and yourself are guilty
Of all their evils. Yet my life is pure,
My chastity unstainèd even in thought;
Then if your violence deface this building,
(The workmanship of heav'n, made up for good,
And not to be the exercise of lust),
You kill your honour, and abuse your justice,
And me impoverish also.

LYS.   Why, this house
Wherein thou liv'st is a receptacle
Of all men's sins, a nurse of wickedness.
How canst thou then be otherwise than naught
That liv'st in it?

MAR.   It is not good when you
That are the Governor, and should live well,
The better to be bold to punish evil,
Do know there's such a roof, yet come beneath it.
Is there a need (my yet good Lord) if I
See fire before me that I straight must fly
And burn myself? Or else, suppose this house

(As too too many feel such houses are)
Should be the doctor's patrimony and
The surgeon's feeding, follows it that I
Must needs infect myself to give them maint'nance?
O my good Lord, kill me but not deflow'r me,
Punish me how you please but spare my chastity,
And since 'tis all the dowry gods have giv'n
And men have left me, do not take it from me.
Make me your servant, I will joy t'obey you;
Make me your bondmaid, I'll account it freedom;
If I may be the worst that's callèd vile,
So I may still live honest, I'm content;
Or if you think it too much happiness
To have me stay so, prithee, let me now,
Now in this minute die, and I'll account
My death more happy than my birth . . .
LYSIM.　Now surely this is Virtue's image, nay,
Virtue herself sent down from heav'n, a while
To reign on earth and teach what we should be!
                              (*He wipes away her tears*)
Lady, though such your virtues are, a far
More worthy style your beauty challenges,
And nothing less your beauty promises
Than what you are. Alas, I hither came
With thoughts intemperate, deform'd and foul;
The which your tears have laved till they are white.
Continue still to all so; for my part,
Who hither came but to have paid the price,
A piece of gold for your virginity,
Here's twenty to relieve your honesty.
It shall become you ever to remain
Even as you are now, a piece of goodness,
The best wrought up that ever Nature made.
If any man shall threaten you with ill,
Do you but send to me, I am your friend.
                              (*Exit.*)

(1) When she is handed over to the Pandar to be ravished,
Marina pleads with him (*supra* 538).

MARINA　What couldst thou wish thine enemy to be,
          Viler than thou art now, more hateful yet
          Than thou wouldst make thyself to be?
PANDAR   Indeed
          My master or my mistress, who, I think,

Have all the sins to which mankind's subject
Reigning in them as bad as Satan's self.
MARINA   Thou goest about to be yet worse than they,
And do an office at their setting on
Which e'en thy master pitied to attempt—
To rob me of mine honour (which the Gods
In spite of all have till this breath protected),
And leper my chaste thoughts with memory of
So foul a deed, which thou shalt then have done
To damn thine own soul by undoing mine.
If thou desirest gold, there's some for thee,
Or if thou wantest maintenance, provide
Some residence within an honest house.
I have experience in many things
To labour for thee . . .
I'm skilful in the seven liberal arts,
Well exercised in studies, and can prove
My skill in song and playing instruments
Surpasses any in the city; hence
As thou before my beauty did proclaim
In open market to the world, whereby
To make of me a common prostitute,
So now again proclaim my virtues to them.
I doubt not but this honourable city
Will yield sufficient scholars . . .
And give to me content and quiet.
PANDAR   Sooth,
If you have, as you say, these qualities,
I'll labour with my Master for your freedom.
MARINA   If not, I give thee leave to bring me back
And prostitute me to that course which was
Pretended for me . . .

                                        (Cf. IV.6.156–201)

(m) One last short transcript should be given. When Pericles
(after fourteen years absence) returns to Tarsus to take home his
daughter, the play summarises what happens in a Dumbshow.
Wilkins (*supra* 539) draws mainly on Twine, and writes almost
entirely in prose, but the first exchanges between Pericles and
Dyonysa suggest metre:

PER.   My trusty friends, what cause inforceth you
        To give so sad a welcome to my coming (entertainment).
DYON.   O my good Lord, would any tongue but ours
        Might be the heralds of your (sad) mishap.

But sorrow's pipes will burst, have they not vent,
And you perforce must know, Marina's dead.

Are we to conclude that Wilkins started to praphrase Twine in verse of his own and then stopped, or rather that these four lines were all that he had remembered (or noted) of the dialogue in a scene acted out on the stage?

Looking back over the passages here reconstructed, and others not included, one realizes that they can at best outline the text they represent. Sometimes the text is obviously close to the 1609 Q, and may be used to support Professor Edwards's contention that Wilkins worked throughout from the play which was later mis-reported and badly printed in that volume. In some passages, where Wilkins differs from the play, he seems to supply lines omitted from the printed text or helps us to reorganise the latter (e.g. (a), (c), (f), (h), (l)). Professor Edwards argues persuasively that the play was written once and for all by Shakespeare but sadly spoiled in trans-mission. There are however in Wilkins several considerable passages (not in Twine or Q) in which the arrangement and the 'verse-fossils' suggest that the play which he reported was not the Q ver-sion. Some of these are passages which are not entirely necessary in a dramatic presentation of the romance, and which make an extremely episodic piece unbearably long. Passage (d), for example, with its pleasant display of Pericles' powers with harp song and of Simonides' good musical taste, is not essential. But in *Pericles*, II.5.25–8, the King says:

I am beholding to you
For your sweet music this last night. I do
Protest my ears were never better fed
With such delightful pleasing harmony.

As the play stands, *we* have not heard this music. It seems highly probable that there had been such a scene as Wilkins provides. Did Shakespeare write it? It seems more likely that the music scene was in an earlier version, and that Shakespeare, in revising and tighten-ing the action, cut it out.

Likewise Shakespeare may have cut Simonides' receipt of his daughter's letter and the soliloquy (e) in which he deliberates whether to let her marry the stranger-Knight; also the scene (j) where Dyonysa first orders her slave to kill Marina. About the Dumbshows I am more doubtful, but it is possible that Shakespeare substituted for scenes with dialogue in the original play (cf. (g), (m)), the Dumbshow in the Prologue to Act III and that at the tomb of Marina in IV.4.

37

The greatest crux concerns the brothel scenes and Lysimachus' part. The prose brothel-talk in IV.2 and IV.6, with its reminiscences of *Measure for Measure*, is Shakespearean. On the whole it is well reported in Q; but it is not represented in Wilkins. Was it in the play when he saw it, or was it added afterwards?

If my guess is correct, the Bawd originally spoke to Marina in verse at times; Lysimachus' intention in coming to the brothel was frankly just to enjoy the girl; Marina's appeal to him was lengthy and rhetorical (Passage k). In Q, however, the Bawd speaks prose; Lysimachus' motives are not properly explained—with the brothel-keepers he is coarsely jocular, with Marina curious but urgent, then turning to pity with surprising speed. His assertions,

> Had I brought hither a corrupted mind,
> Thy speech had altered it (IV.6.112–13)

and

> I came with no ill intent (*ibid.* 118)

are difficult to reconcile with his previous attitude. As Edwards suggests (*op. cit.* p. 45), he may possibly mean that 'he is not to be thought of as a hardened villain, but only as a pleasure-seeker now seeing for the first time that thoughtlessness may be a crime.' But this is hardly adequate. Maybe the Q reporters omitted some speeches between lines 94 and 102. Even so the scene reads more like an improved but somewhat hastily composed rewriting of the scene represented in Wilkins than vice-versa.

Consideration of the verse-relics in *The Painfull Adventures* and of the differences between Q and Wilkins not found in Twine leads me to conclude that Q represents a revision of an earlier play which was even more sprawling than now, that the piece when Wilkins saw it already contained the character-names used by Shakespeare, and that it was mainly written in a style like that which still pre-dominates in Acts I and II, though with occasional flashes of poetic feeling. Some difficulties are lessened if we imagine that the play had already been touched up a little by Shakespeare, but that he had not yet shortened it, or rewritten the brothel-scenes, or inserted some of the speeches not found in Wilkins which strengthen it here and there.

BIBLIOGRAPHY

I. For relevant general studies relating to Sources and Analogues, see Bibliographies in Vol. I, pp. 515–8, Vol. V, pp. 564–5.
II. Editions and Criticism of Individual Plays

Titus Andronicus
1. Editions of (*a*) the Play, (*b*) Sources and Analogues
(*a*) Fl 1623. Q1 1594. *The Most Lamentable Romaine Tragedie of Titus Andronicus: As it was Plaide by the Right Honourable the Earle of Darbie, Earle of Pembrooke, and Earle of Sussex their Servants. Printed by John Danter . . . sold by Edward White and Thomas Millington,* 1594.
Q2 1600. Q3 1611.
Modern edns.: Facsimile of Q1, J. Q. Adams, N.Y. 1937; Facsimile of Q2, J. O. Halliwell, 1867; A. Symons, 1885; A. Morgan, *Bankside* (parallel text), 1890; H. B. Baildon, *Arden*, 1904; A. M. Witherspoon, *Yale*, 1926; J. Dover Wilson, *Camb.* 1948; J. C. Maxwell, *New Arden*, 1953; S. Barnet, *Signet*, 1964.
(*b*) [Anon.] *The History of Titus Andronicus, The Renowned Roman General. Newly Translated from the Italian Copy printed at Rome* . . . C. Dicey. (n.d.) [Unique copy in Folger Library.] (Contains also the Ballad 'You Noble Minds, and famous martial Wights'.)
[Anon.] A Lamentable Ballad of the Tragical end of a Gallant Lord and a Vertuous Lady. . . . Printed by and for A. Milbourn (n.d.). Reprinted in *The Roxburghe Ballads*, ed. C. Hindley, 2 vols. 1873/4, Vol. 2.
[Anon.] *Tragaedia von Tito Andronico*, 1620. Modern trans.: A. Cohn, in *Shakespeare in Germany*, 1865.
BANDELLO, M. M. *Novelle.* La Prima, Seconda, Terza Parte de le Novelle del Bandello. In Lucca per il Busdrago. 3 Vols. 1554 (Vol. 3, Nov. 21 (Moor)). Modern edn.: G. Brognologio, 5 Vols. Bari, 1910–12.
BELLEFOREST, F. DE. *Des Histoires Tragiques: Tome Second. Extraicts de l'Italien de Bandel . . . enrichies outre l'invention de l'Autheur,* Paris, I. Bruneau, 1565 (Hist. 31 (Moor)).
GIBBON, E. *Decline and Fall of the Roman Empire,* ed. J. B. Bury, 7 Vols. 1909–14 (Ch. xxvi, xxxi).

565

GOULART, S. *Thresor d'Histoires Admirables et Memorables de nostre temps* . . . P. Marceau, 1610.

JOHNSON, R. ed. *The Golden Garland of Princely pleasures and delicate Delights* . . . A.M. for Thomas Longley, 1620.

MASUCCIO OF SALERNO. *Il Novellino*. Milan 1483; Venice 1484, 1492, etc. Modern trans.: W. G. Waters, 2 vols. 1895 (Vol. 2. Nov. 22. (Moor)).

OVID. *The XV Bookes of P. Ovidius Naso, entytuled Metamorphosis translated oute of Latin into English meeter, by Arthur Golding* . . . 1567. Willyam Seres (Bk. VI). Modern edn.: W. H. D. Rouse, *Shakespeare's Ovid*, 1904; 1961.

PERCY, BP. T. *Reliques of Ancient English Poetry*, 3 vols. 1715, 1717, 1775. Ed. H. B. Wheatley, 1876–7, 1891.

PLUTARCH. *Lives of the Noble Grecians and Romanes*, trans. Sir T. North, 1579 (Scipio and Publicola). Modern edn.: G. Wyndham, 2 vols. 1895.

SENECA, LUCIUS ANNAEUS. *The Seconde Tragedie of Seneca entituled Thyestes faithfully Englished by Jasper Heywood*. Imprinted in the hous late Thomas Berthelettes, 1560. Modern edns.: H. de Vocht, *Materialien*, Bd. 41, 1913; in A. K. McIlwraith, *Five Elizabethan Tragedies*, 1950.

VOS, JAN. *Aran en Titus*, Amsterdam, 1641. See A. Cohn, *ShJb*, xxiii, 1888.

2. Critical Studies of Sources, etc.

BOLTON, J. S. G. '*Titus Andronicus*: Shakespeare at Thirty', *SPhil*, xxx, 1933.

BROOKE, C. F. T. '*Titus Andronicus* and Shakespeare', *MLN*, xxxiv, 1919.

CLARK, E. G. 'Titus and Vespasian', *MLN*, xli, 1926.

CRAWFORD, CHARLES. 'The Date and Authenticity of *T.A.*', *ShJb*, xxxvi, 1900.

FULLER, H. DE W. 'The Sources of *T.A.*', *PMLA*, xvi, 1901.

GRAY, H. D. 'The Authorship of *T.A.*', Flügel Memorial Volume, Palo Alto, 1916.

GRAY, H. D. 'Shakespeare's Share in *T.A.*', *PhilQ*, v, 1926.

GREG, W. W. 'Titus Andronicus', *MLR*, xiv, 1919.

GROSART, A. B. 'Was R. Greene substantially the Author of *T.A.*?' *EngStud*, xxii, 1896.

HILL, R. F. 'The composition of *T.A.*', *Sh Survey*, 10, 1957.

KELLER, W. 'Titus Andronicus: ein Vortrag.' *ShJb*, lxxix, 1938, 137–62.

KOEPPEL, E. 'Beiträge zur Geschichte des Elisabethanischen Dramas', *EngStud*, xvi, 1892, 365–71.

LAW, R. A. 'The Roman Background of *T.A.*', *SPhil*, xl, 1943.

PARROTT, T. M. 'Shakespeare's Revision of *T.A.*', *MLR*, xiv, 1919.

PRICE, H. T. 'The Authorship of *T.A.*', *JEGP*, xlii, 1943.

SAMPLEY, A. M. 'Plot Structure in Peele's Plays as a Test of Authorship', *PMLA*, li, 1936, 689–701.
SARGENT, R. M. 'The Source of *T.A.*', *SPhil*, xlvi, 1949.
THOMSON, J. A. K. *Shakespeare and the Classics*, 1952.
WAITH, E. M. 'The Metamorphosis of Violence in *T.A.*', *Sh Survey*, 10, 1957, pp. 39–49.

Troilus and Cressida

1. Editions of (*a*) the Play, (*b*) Sources and Analogues
(*a*) Q 1609. Two issues: (i) *The Historie of Troylus and Cresseida. As it was acted by the Kings Majesties servants at the Globe.* Written by William Shakespeare. London. Imprinted by G. Eld for R. Bonian and H. Walley . . . 1609; (ii) *The Famous Historie of Troylus and Cresseid. Excellently expressing the beginning of their loves, with the conceited wooing of Pandarus Prince of Licia.* Written by William Shakespeare . . . (new title and epistle).
   Modern edns.: Facsimiles Q(i) J. O. Halliwell, 1871; Q(ii) J. O. Halliwell, 1863; H. P. Stokes, 1886; W. W. Greg, 1952.
   Fl 1623. Modern edns.: A. Morgan, *Bankside* (parallel text), 1889; K. Deighton, *Arden*, 1906; J. S. P. Tatlock, *Tudor*, 1912; N. B. Paradise, *Yale*, 1927; H. N. Hillebrand & T. W. Baldwin, *Var*, 1953; A. Walker, *Camb.* 1957.
(*b*) [Anon.] *The Rare Triumphs of Love and Fortune.* 1589. Modern edns.: J. P. Collier, 1851; Dodsley, vi, 1874.
   [Anon.] *Gest Hystoriale*, ed. G. A. Panton and D. Donaldson, *EETS.* O.S. Nos. 39, 56, 1869, 1874.
   [Anon.] *Siege of Troy*, ed, C. H. A. Wager, N.Y. 1899; L. Hibler-Lebmannsport, Graz, 1928.
   BENOIT DE SAINTE-MAURE. *Le Roman de Troie*, ed. A. Joly, 2 vols. Paris, 1870–1; Leopold Costans, 6 vols. Paris, 1904–12. Modern trans.: R. K. Gordon (extracts), 1934.
   BOCCACCIO, G. *Phylostrato che tracta de lo inamoramento de Troylo e Gryseida. Et de molte altre infinite battaglie*, 1498, 1501, 1528. Modern trans.: W. M. Rossetti, 1873; N. E. Griffin and A. B. Myrick, Philadelphia, 1929; R. K. Gordon, 1934.
   CHAPMAN, GEORGE. *Seaven Bookes of the Iliades* . . . J. Windet, 1598; *Homer Prince of Poets. Translated according to the Greek, in twelve Bookes of his Iliads* [1610?]; *The Iliads of Homer* . . . R. Field for N. Butter [1611]. Modern edns.: R. Hooper, 1858; H. Morley, 1883; Oxford, 1931.
   CHAUCER, G. *Works*, 3 pts. Pynson, 1526; ed. W. Thynne, 1532, 1542. 1590?. Facsimile: ed. W. W. Skeat, 1905. *The Workes of G. C.* ed. John Stow, 1561. *The Workes of our Antient and Lerned English Poet, G. C.*, ed. Thomas Speght, 1598, 1602, 1687. Modern edn.: *The Works*, ed. A. W.

Pollard, etc. 1898. *The Complete Works*, ed. F. N. Robinson, Boston, 1933. *Troilus and Criseyde*, ed. R. K. Root, Princeton, 1926.

COLLIER, J. P. *Old Ballads*, Percy Society, Vol. I, 1840.

COLONNE, GUIDO DELLE. (*Historia Troiana*) *Incipit prologus supra hystoria destructionis troie compositâ per judicem guidonem de columpna messanen.* 1475, 1477, 1480, etc. Modern edn.: N. E. Griffin, Camb. Mass., 1936.

COOPER, T. *Thesaurus Linguae Romanae et Britannicae . . .* Berthelet for H. Wykes, 1565, 1573, 1578, 1584, 1587.

DARES PHRYGIUS. (*De Excidio Troiae Historia*). *Incipit hystoria troiana daretis frigii.* Cologne 1472?; Venice 1472? Lyons, 1480? etc. In Henisch, G., *Belli Troiani Scriptores praecipui, Dictys Cretensis, Dares Phrygius et Homerus . . .* 1573. Ital. trans.: P. Lauro, 1543; T. Porcacchi, 1570.

DICTYS CRETENSIS. [*Ephemeris Belli Troiani*] *Incipit prologus in troianam hystoriam dyctys cretensis.* Cologne, *c.* 1470, 1477, 1498, etc. Modern edns.: Valpy, 1825; F. Meister, Leipzig, 1872.

HOMER. *Works*, ed. D. Chalcondylas and G. Accaiuoli, 1488; ed. A. P. Manutius, Venice, 1504, 1517; ed. A. Francinus, Florence, 1519; Louvain, 1523, 1535; Venice, 1524, 1537; Basle, 1535, etc. Latin trans.: Lorenzo Valla, 1474, 1502, 1522; Spondanus, 1583. French: Jehan Samxon, 1530; Hugues Salel, 1545–70, 1580, 1584, 1599. English: Arthur Hall, *Ten Books of Homers Iliades, Translated out of French . . .* R. Newberie, 1581 (Bks. I–X). G. Chapman (*supra*).

LE FEVRE, RAOUL. *Cy commence le volume Initule le receuil des histoires de troyes . . . Bruges*, 1476? [ed. W. Caxton?] Lyons, 1494; Paris, 1498, etc. *The Recuyell of the Historyes of Troye*, trans. W. Caxton Bruges (*c.* 1474). Modern edn.: H. O. Sommer, 2 vols. 1894.

LYDGATE, JOHN. [Troy-Book] *The hystorye Sege and dystruccyon of Troye.* R. Pynson, 1513; revised R. Braham, 1555. Modern edn.: H. Bergen, *EETS*, Ex-ser. Nos. 97, 103, 106, 126, 1906–35.

TURBERVILE, GEORGE. *Epitaphes, Epigrams, Songs and Sonets . . .* H. Denham, 1567, 1570. Modern edns.: A. Chalmers, *Eng. Poets*, Vol. 2, 1810; J. P. Collier, 1870?

2. Critical Studies of Sources, etc.

ACHESON, A. *Shakespeare and the Rival Poet*, 1903.

ALEXANDER, P. 'Troilus and Cressida, 1609', *4 Library*, IX, 1928, 267–86.

[Anon.] *The Return from Parnassus*, in *Three Parnassus Plays*, ed. J. B. Leishman, 1949.

BOYLE, R. '*Troilus and Cressida*'. *Eng Stud*, xxx, 1902, 21–59.

BULLOUGH, G. 'The Lost *Troilus and Cressida*', in *Essays and Studies*, n.s. 17, 1964, ed. W. A. Armstrong, pp. 24–40.

CAMPBELL, O. J. *Comicall Satyre and Shakespeare's Troilus and Cressida*, San Marino, 1938.

COLLINS, J. CHURTON. 'Had Shakespeare read the Greek Tragedies?' in *Studies in Shakespeare*, N.Y. 1904.

DAWSON, GILES E. 'A Bibliographical Problem in the First Folio', *4 Library*, xxii, 1941, 26–33.

ELTON, W. 'Shakespeare's Portrait of Ajax in *T.C*', *PMLA*, lxiii, 1948, 744–8.

EVANS, G. B. 'Pandarus' House?' *MLN*, lxii, 1947, 33–5.

GRIFFIN, N. E. 'UnHomeric Elements in the Story of Troy', *JEGP*, vii, 1908, 32–52.

HENDERSON, W. B. D. *Shakespeare's T.C. Yet Deeper in Its Tradition*. Parrott Presentation Volume, Princeton, 1935, pp. 127–56.

HENSLOWE'S DIARY, ed. W. W. Greg, 2 vols. 1904–8; ed. R. A. Foakes and R. T. Rickert, 1961.

HERTZBERG, W. 'Die Quellen der Troilus-Sage in ihrem Verhältniss zu Shakespeares *T.C.*', *ShJb*, vi, 1871, 169–225.

KELLER, WOLFGANG. 'Shakespeares *Troilus und Cressida*', *ShJb*, lxvi, 1930, 182–207.

KER, W. P. *Essays on Medieval Literature*, 1905.

KNIGHT, G. W. *The Wheel of Fire*, Oxford, 1930.

LAWRENCE, W. W. 'The Love-Story in *T.C.*' in *Shakespeare Studies by Members of . . . Columbia University*, ed. J. B. Matthews and A. H. Thorndike, N.Y. 1916.

LAWRENCE, W. W. *Shakespeare's Problem Comedies*, N.Y. 1931.

LAWRENCE, W. W. 'Troilus, Cressida and Thersites', *MLR*, xxxvii, 1942, 422–37.

MCMANAWAY, J. G. Review in *Sh Survey*, 5, 1952, 144–52.

MURRY, J. M. *Countries of the Mind*, 1922.

PALMER, J. F. '*Troilus and Cressida*', in *Roy. Soc. of Lit. Trans.*, 1893.

PALMER, JOHN. *Comedy*, 1914.

PARROTT, T. M. *Shakespearean Comedy*, N.Y. 1949.

PARSONS, A. E. 'The Trojan Legend in England', *MLR*, xxiv, 1929.

PARTRIDGE, ERIC. *Shakespeare's Bawdy*, 1947.

PRESSON, R. K. *Shakespeare's Troilus and Cressida and the Legends of Troy*, Madison, 1953.

REYNOLDS, G. F. '*T.C.* on the Elizabethan Stage', *J. Q. Adams Memorial Studies*, Washington, 1948.

ROLLINS, H. E. 'The Troilus-Cressida Story from Chaucer to Shakespeare', *PMLA*, xxxii, 1917, 383–429.

SAINTSBURY, G. 'Shakespeare and the Grand Style', *Essays and Studies of the English Association*, i, 1910, 113–35.

SCHIRMER, W. F. *John Lydgate*, 1961.

SEWELL, A. 'Notes on the Integrity of *T.C.*', *RES*, xix, 1943, 120–7.

SMALL, R. A. *The Stage Quarrel between Ben Jonson and the So-Called Poetasters*, Breslau, 1899.

SPENCER, THEODORE. *Shakespeare and the Nature of Man*. N.Y. 1942.

STAMM, R. 'The Glass of Pandar's Praise', *Essays and Studies of the Eng.Assn.* n.s. 17, 1964.

STEIN, ELIZABETH. 'Caxton's *Recuyell* and Shakespeare's *Troilus*', *MLN*, xlv, 1930, 114–16.

TATLOCK, J. S. P. 'The Siege of Troy in Elizabethan Literature, especially in Shakespeare and Heywood', *PMLA*, xxx, 1915, 673–770.

TAYLOR, G. C. 'Shakespeare's Attitude towards Love and Honour in *T.C.*', *PMLA*, xlv, 1930, 781–6.

ULRICI, H. 'Ist *T.C.* Comedy oder Tragedy oder History?' *ShJb*, ix, 1874, 26–40.

WALKER, ALICE. 'The Textual Problem of *T.C.*', *MLR*, xlv, 1950, 459–64.

WELLS, J. E. *Manual of the Writings in Middle English*, New Haven. 1918–35.

YOUNG, KARL. *The Origin and Development of the Story of Troilus and Criseyde*, Chaucer Soc. 2nd Ser. 41, 1908.

Timon of Athens

1. Editions of (a) the Play, (b) Sources and Analogues.

(a) Fl 1623. Modern edns.: K. Deighton, *Arden*, 1905, 1929. J. C. Maxwell, *Camb.* 1957.

(b) [Anon.] *Timon*. ed. A. Dyce, *Sh.Soc.* 1842; Collier–Hazlitt, *ShLib*, vi, 1875.

ARISTOPHANES. *The Birds*; in *Works*, trans. B. B. Rogers. (Loeb edn.) iii. 1946.

ARISTOTLE. *Ethics*, trans. R. W. Browne. 1853. (Bk. IV, Ch. 1).

BARCKLEY, SIR R. *Discourse of the Felicitie of Man*, 1598. Reprinted in Collier–Hazlitt, *ShLib*, IV, 1875.

BOAISTUAU, P. *Theatrum Mundi. The Theatre or rule of the world . . . written in the French and Latine tongues by Peter Boaistuau, Englished by John Alday . . .* Thomas East for John Wyght, 1581. Earlier edns. 1566? 1574.

BOIARDO, M. M. *Timone. Comedia del Magnifico Conte Matheo Maria Boiardo . . .* Scandiano, 1500; Bologna, 1503.

BRETIN, FILBERT. *Les Œuvres de Lucian, traduites du Grec, par F. Bretin.* 1583.

CALLIMACHUS AND LUCOPHRON, trans. A. W. Mair (Loeb edn.), 1921.

CICERO, M. T. *Tusculan Disputations*, trans. J. E. King (Loeb edn.), 1945.

CICERO, M. T. *Laelius, an Essay on Friendship*, trans. W. Melmoth, 1773.

ERASMUS, DESIDERIO. *Luciani viri q̄ divertissimi complura opuscula longe festivissima ab Erasmo Roterdamo et Thoma Moro interpretibus optimis in latinorum linguam traducta.* 1506 [Paris]; 1516, 1528, etc.

LONIGO, NICOLO DA. *I Dilettevoli Dialogi, le Vere narrationi, le facete epistole di Luciano Philosopho . . . tradotte per M. Nicolò da Lonigo,* Venice, 1536.

LUCIAN. *Works:* Gk. 1496; Venice, 1503, 1522; Hague, 1526, 1535; Basle, 1545. Latin trans. J. Micyllum, etc. Frankfurt, 1543, 1549. French trans.: Filbert Bretin Aussonois . . . Repurges de parolles impudiques et profanes, Paris, 1583. (See Lonigo). English trans.: *Works,* trans. H. W. & F. G. Fowler, 4 vols. 1905; A. M. Harman. (Loeb edn.), ii, 1961.

LYLY, JOHN. *Campaspe* . . . Thomas Cadman. 1584. Modern edn.: in *Dramatic Works,* ed. F. W. Fairholt, 2 vols. 1892. *Complete Works,* ed. R. W. Bond, 3 vols. 1902.

MEXIA, PEDRO. *La Silva de varia leccion.* Antwerp, 1544. French trans.: C. Gruget, Paris, 1552. English trans.: T. Fortescue, 1571.

MONTAIGNE. *The Essays of Michael, Lord of Montaigne, done into English by John Florio,* ed. Thomas Seccombe, Vol. 1, 1908.

PAINTER, WILLIAM. *Palace of Pleasure* 1566, (Vol. 1, Novel 28), Reprinted in Collier–Hazlitt, *ShLib,* IV, 1875. Modern edn.: J. Jacobs, 1890.

PAUSANIAS. *Description of Attica,* trans. W. H. S. Jones (Loeb edn.), Vol. I, 1918.

PLAUTUS. *Comedies,* trans. P. Nixon, 5 vols. 1917–38. Vol. II, *Casina, Cistellaria;* III, *Mercator, Mostellaria;* IV, *Pseudolus;* V, *Trinummus.*

PLUTARCH. *Lives of the Noble Grecians and Romanes,* trans. Sir T. North, 1579. (Antony and Alcibiades). Modern edn.: G. Wyndham, Vol. 2, 1895.

STRABO. *Geography,* trans. H. L. Jones. (Loeb edn.), viii, 1932.

2. Critical Studies of Sources, etc.

ADAMS, J. Q. '*Timon of Athens* and the Irregularities of Fl', *JEGP,* vii, 1908, 53–63.

ADAMS, J. Q. 'The Timon Plays', *JEGP,* ix, 1910, 506ff.

ANDERSON, R. L. 'Excessive Goodness as a Tragic Flaw', *Sh. Assoc. Bull,* xix, 1944, 85–96.

BOND, R. W. 'Lucian and Boiardo in *Timon of Athens*', *MLR,* xxv, 1930; xxvi, 1931.

BONNARD, G. A. 'Note sur les Sources de *Timon of Athens*', *Etudes Anglaises,* vii, 1954, 59–69.

BROOKE, C. F. T. *Tudor Drama,* 1912.

BROWN, HUNTINGTON. 'Enter the Shakespearean Tragic Hero', *Essays in Criticism,* III, 1953, 285–302.

CLEMONS, W. H. 'The Sources of Timon'. *Princeton Coll. Bull.* xv, 1904, 208–23.

COLLINS, A. S. '*Timon of Athens*: a Reconsideration', *RES*, xxii, 1946.

DRAPER, J. W. 'The Theme of *Timon of Athens*', *MLR*, xxix, 1934.

DRAPER, J. W. 'The Psychology of Shakespeare's Timon', *MLR*, xxxv, 1940.

ELLIS-FERMOR, U. '*Timon of Athens*, an unfinished play', *RES*, xviii, 1942, 270–83. Also in *Shakespeare the Dramatist*, 1961.

FARNHAM, W. *Shakespeare's Tragic Frontier.* Berkeley, 1950.

GREG, W. W. *The Shakespeare First Folio*, Oxford, 1955.

HAUG, R. A. 'The Authorship of *Timon of Athens*.' *Sh. Assoc. Bull.* xv, 1940.

HERFORD, C. H. and SIMPSON, P. & E., edd. *Works of Ben Jonson*, IX, Oxford, 1950.

HONIGMANN, E. A. J. 'Timon of Athens', *ShQ*, xii, 1961, 1–20.

KNIGHT, G. W. *The Wheel of Fire*, 1930.

MOORE SMITH, G. C. ed. *Pedantius* (1581). *Materialien*, viii, 1905, and *MLR*, iii, 1908, 143.

MUIR, K. '*Timon of Athens* and the Cash-Nexus', *Mod. Quart. Miscellany*, 1, 1946.

MÜLLER, A. *Über die Quellen aus denen Shakespeare den Timon entnommen hat.* Jena, 1873.

PARROTT, T. M. *The Problem of Timon*, Sh. Assoc. Pamphlet. 1923.

PETTET, E. C. '*Timon of Athens*: the Disruption of Feudal Morality', *RES*, xxiii, 1947.

ROBERTSON, J. M. *Shakespeare and Chapman*, 1917.

SCHROEDER, J. W. *The Great Folio of 1623*, 1956.

SPENCER, T. J. B. 'Shakespeare Learns the Value of Money', *Sh Survey*, 6, 1953.

WECTER, D. 'Shakespeare's Purpose in *Timon*', *PMLA*, xliii, 1928, 701–21.

WRIGHT, E. H. *The Authorship of Timon*, N.Y., 1910.

Pericles, Prince of Tyre

1. Editions of (*a*) the Play, (*b*) Sources and Analogues

(*a*) Q1 1609. *The Late, And much admired Play, Called Pericles, Prince of Tyre . . . As it hath been divers and sundry times acted by his Majesties Servants, at the Globe on the Banck-side.* By William Shakespeare . . . Imprinted (by William White) for Henry Gosson . . . 1609. Modern edns.: Facsimile, C. Praetorius, 1886 (*Sh.Qq.* xxi, ed. P. Z. Round); S. Lee, 1905; *Sh.Qq.* 5. 1940.

Q2 1609. Modern edn.: Facsimile, C. Praetorius, 1886 (*Sh.Qq.* xxii, ed. P. Z. Round). Q3 1611; Q4 1619; Q5 1630; Q6 1635.

(Not in F1, F2). F3, 2nd issue, 1664. *And unto this Impression is added seven Playes, never before Printed in Folio. viz. Pericles Prince of Tyre* . . .
Modern edns.: A. Morgan, *Bankside* (parallel text), 1891. E. Malone, 1790; C. H. Herford, *Eversley*, 1899; K. Deighton, *Arden*, 1907, 1925; A. R. Bellinger, *Yale*, 1925; P. Alexander, *Tudor Sh.*, 1951; J. C. Maxwell, *Camb.*, 1956; F. D. Hoeniger, *New Arden*, 1963.

(b) [Anon.] *Gesta Romanorum*, ed. G. Oesterley, Berlin, 1872. [153rd Tale.] Latin Tale reprinted in A. H. Smyth, *Shakespeare's Pericles and Apollonius of Tyre*, 1898.

BARNES, BARNABE. *The Divil's Charter*, 1607.
BELLEFOREST, F. DE. *Le Septiesme Tome des Histoires Tragiques.* Lyon, 1595 (Hist. 3me).
COPLAND, ROBERT. *King Appolyn of Tyre*, 1510–15.
GODFREY DE VITERBO. *Pantheon, Sive Universitatis Libri*, Basle, 1559. Modern edn.: Migne, *Patrologiae* Vol. 198, 1844.
GOWER, JOHN. *This book is intituled Confessio Amantis* . . . W. Caxton. 1493; *Jo. Gower de Confessione Amantis* . . . T. Berthelette, 1554. Modern edns.: Collier–Hazlitt, *ShLib*, vi, 1875; *Works*, ed. G. C. Macaulay, iii, 1901.
LYLY, JOHN. *Campaspe*, 1594. Modern edn.: *Works*, ed. R. W. Bond, 1902.
SIDNEY, SIR P. *The Countesse of Pembrokes Arcadia*, 1590. Modern edn.: A. Feuillerat, 1912.
TWINE, LAURENCE. *The Patterne of Painefull Adventures*, 1576?, 1594?, 1607. Modern edns.: Collier–Hazlitt, *ShLib*, vi, 1875.
WEISER, M. (Velserus). *Narratio Eorum Quae Contigerunt Apollonio Tyrio.* 1595.
WILKINS, GEORGE. *The Miseries of Inforst Marriage. As it is now playd by his Majesties Servants. By George Wilkins. For George Vincent. 1607.* Modern edns.: Dodsley, iv, 1874; J. S. Farmer, *S.F.T.* 1913; *MalSoc.* 1964.
WILKINS, GEORGE. *The Painfull Adventures of Pericles, Prince of Tyre. T.P. for N. Butter. 1608.* Modern edn.: K. Muir, Liverpool, 1953.

2. Critical Studies of Sources, etc.
ARTHOS, J. 'Pericles, Prince of Tyre', *ShQ*, iv, 1953.
BAKER, H. T. 'The Relation of Shakespeare's *Pericles* to G. Wilkins's novel', in *PMLA*, 23, n.s. 16, 1908, 100–18.
BOYLE, R. '*Pericles*' *EngStud*, 5, 1882, 363–9.
BOYLE, R. 'On Wilkins's share in the play called Shakespeare's *Pericles*'. *Trans. New Sh. Soc.* 1882, 321ff.
CLARK, A. M. *Thomas Heywood, Playwright and Miscellanist*, 1931.
COWL, R. P. *The Authorship of Pericles* n.d, [1927]

CRAIG, H. '*Pericles* and *The Painfull Adventures*', *SPhil*, XLV, 1949, 100–5.

CRAIG, H. 'Review of Shakespearean Scholarship in 1952' *ShQ*, iv, No. 2, 1953.

DAWKINS, R. M. 'Modern Greek Oral Versions of Apollonius of Tyre', *MLR*, 1942, xxxvii, 172ff.

DELIUS, N. 'Über Shakespeares Pericles, Prince of Tyre', *ShJb*, 3, 1868, 175–204.

EDWARDS, P. 'An Approach to the Problem of *Pericles*', *Sh Survey*, 5, 1952.

ELTON, W. '*Pericles*: A new Source or Analogue'. *JEGP*, xlviii, 1949, 138–9.

FLEAY, F. G. 'On the Play of *Pericles*', *Trans. New Sh. Soc.* 1874, 195ff.

GARRETT, R. M. 'Gower in *Pericles*', *ShJb*, 48, 1912, 13–20.

GRAVES, T. S. 'On the date and significance of *Pericles*', *MPhil*, 13, 1915–16, 545–56.

GRAY, H. D. 'Heywood's *Pericles* revised by Shakespeare', *PMLA*, 40, 1925, 507–29.

GREEN, H. *Shakespeare and the Emblem Writers*, 1870.

GREG, W. W. *The Editorial Problem in Shakespeare*, 1942.

HASTINGS, W. 'Shakespeare's part in *Pericles*', *Sh. Assoc. Bull.* XIV, No. 2, 1939, 67–85.

HERFORD, C. H. and SIMPSON, P. & E. edd. *Works of Ben Jonson*, II vols., 1925–52.

KLEBS, E. *Die Erzählung von Apollonius aus Tyrus*, Berlin, 1899.

MAXWELL, BALDWIN. *Studies in the Shakespeare Apocrypha*, 1956.

MUIR, K. 'The Problem of *Pericles*', in *English Studies*, xxv, 1949, 65–83.

MUIR, K. *Shakespeare as Collaborator*, 1960.

PARROTT, T. M. '*Pericles*: the Play and the Novel', *Sh.Assoc. Bull.* xxiii. 1948.

POLLARD, A. W. *Shakespeare's Folios and Quartos*, 1909.

RAITH, J. *Die alt und mittelenglischen Apollonius–Bruchstücke*, Munich 1956.

SINGER, S. *Apollonius von Tyrus*, Halle, 1895.

SINGER, S. 'Apollonius von Tyrus', in *Aufsätze und Vorträge*, 1912, pp. 79–103.

SISSON, C. J. *New Readings in Shakespeare*, 1955.

SMYTH, A. H. *Shakespeare's Pericles and Apollonius of Tyre*, Philadelphia, 1898.

SPIKER, SINA. 'George Wilkins and the authorship of *Pericles*', *SPhil*, 30, 1933, 551–70.

SYKES, H. DUGDALE. 'Wilkins and Shakespeare's *Pericles*', in *Sidelights on Shakespeare*, Stratford, 1919, pp. 143–203.

THOMAS, DANIEL L. 'On the Play *Pericles*', *EngStud*, 39, 1908, 210–39.

TOMPKINS, J. M. S. 'Why Pericles?' *RES* n.s. iii, 1952, 322–4.

WAITH, E. M. '*Pericles* and Seneca the Elder', *MLN*, L, 1951, 180–2.

INDEX TO THE INTRODUCTIONS

Acta Sanctorum, 352n
Adams, J. Q., 3n, 83n
Admiral's Company, 98, 99
Agamemnon, 26
Agnes, St, 352
A Knack to Know a Knave, 5
Alday, J., 232, 239
Alexander, P., 83, 86
Ammianus Marcellinus, 10
Ancient Songs and Ballads, 15
Antiphanes, 226
Antonio, 30
Antony and Cleopatra, 235, 237, 250
Apollonius of Tyre story, 351–6
Aran und Titus, 6
Aristotle, 248
Aristophanes, 226, 227
Arte of English Poesie, 370

Barbour, J., 92
Barckley, Sir R., 232, 239
Barnet, Sylvan, 7
Bandello, M., 14, 20
Bartholomew Fair, 4
Beaumont and Fletcher, 369
Belleforest, F. de, 14, 353
Benoit de Sainte-Maure, 90, 91
Berthelette, T., 354
Boaistuau, P., 232
Boccaccio, G., 13, 90, 91
Boiardo, M. M., 229–31, 245, 247
Bond, R. W., 231, 239
Bonnard, G. A., 234–6, 240n
Bradbrook, M. C., 31
Brooke, C. F. T., 85, 235n

Callimachus, 227
Camoens, L. V. de, 235n

Campaspe, 242–3
Campbell, O. J., 86, 109n, 110n
Caxton, W., 89, 92, 93–5, 98, 101,
    103–8, 354
Chambers, E. K., 83, 225n
Chapman, G., 84, 86–101
Chaucer, G., vii, 90–100, 104–7,
    109, 353, 370
Chettle, H., 98, 100
Cicero, M. T., 28, 227, 248
Claris and Laris, 91
Clark, A. M., 357n
Clemons, W. H., 226n, 227n
Cohn, A., 6n
Collier, J. P., 96n, 97n
Comedy of Errors, 354
Cooper, T., 94
Copland, R., 354
Coriolanus, 83, 235, 237–9, 250, 374
Craig, H., 350
Cymbeline, 13, 373
Cynthia's Revels, 234

Danby, J., 371n
Dares Phrygius, 90–3
Dawkins, R. M., 351n
Day, J., 359, 369
De Bello Troiano, 92
De Excidio Troiae Historiae, 90
Deighton, K., 240n
Dekker, T., 85, 98–100, 229
Dictys the Cretan, 90–1
Dido Queen of Carthage, 17
Dolce, L., 26
Donne, J., 86
Dowden, E., 85
Dryden, J., 349
Dyce, A., 232

Edwards, P., 350, 358n
Ellis-Fermor, U., 226, 244n, 247
Elton, W., 85n, 371n
Ephemeris Belli Troiani, 90
Erasmus, D., 229, 239
Essex, E. of, 102, 104
Euripides, 26
Every Man out of his Humour, 234

Farnham, W., 241
Folger Shakespeare Library, vii, 3, 7
Foole upon Foole, 84
Fuller, H. de W., 6

Garnier, R., 30
Gascoigne, G., 26, 97
Geoffrey of Monmouth, 91
Gesta Romanorum, 352–4, 357, 360, 367
Gest Hystoriale, 92
Gibbon, E., 9, 10
Godfrey of Viterbo, 351, 354
Golden Garland, 11
Goolden, P., 360n
Gorboduc, 26
Goulart, S., 14, 20
Gower, J., 29, 354–5, 360–70, 373
Green, H., 361n
Greg, W. W., vii, 6n, 83, 84n, 97, 98, 225n
Grimald, N., 96
Grivelet, M., 357n
Guido delle Colonne, 90–3

Hall, A., 87
Hamlet, 22, 85, 235
Harrison, G. B., 85, 86
Henry IV, 3, 108
Henry V, 86, 369, 370
Henry VI, 32
Henry VIII, 83
Henryson, R., 96–100
Henslowe, E., 5, 6, 84
Herford, C. H. and Simpson, P., 234
Heywood, T., 98, 357, 369
Historia Troiana, 90, 92
Hoeniger, F. D., 351n, 359, 369n

Homer, 86–91, 94, 95, 98, 102, 103, 107, 108, 110, 111, 234
Honigmann, E. A., 236, 238
Horace, 234
Hotson, L., 84

Il Filostrato, 90–1
Iliad (trans.), 87n

Johnson, R., 11
Jonson, B., 4, 84, 86, 110, 229, 234, 369, 370
Joseph of Exeter, 90, 92
Julius Caesar, 83, 225, 237
Juvenal, 234

Keller, W., 20n
Ker, W. P., 91–2
King John, 25
King Lear, 111, 234–5, 250, 356, 374
King Leir, 234–5
Kinwelmersh, F., 26
Knight, G. W., 108, 372, 374
Koeppel, E., 15
Kyd, T., 4, 22–3, 30, 32, 369

Lampridius, Aelius, 235n
Law, R. A., 24n, 25, 26n
Lefevre, R., 93, 101
Locrine, 29
Lonigo, N. da, 229
Love Labours Wonne, 84
Lucian, 225, 229–33, 239–40, 243–7
Lydgate, J., 89, 92–111
Lyly, J., 241, 243
Lysistrata, 226

Malone, E., 349, 350
Marlowe, C., 17n, 18n, 20, 32, 229
Marston, J., 86
Masuccio, 13, 14n
Maxwell, B., 357n
Maxwell, J. C., 3n, 5, 17, 27n, 29, 32n, 225, 226, 351, 359
Measure for Measure, 85, 371
Merchant of Venice, 360, 361, 371
Meres, F., 4, 84

Mexía, P., 231
Middleton, T., 369
Midsummer Night's Dream, 236
Mirror for Magistrates, 12
Montaigne, M., 241–2
Moore Smith, G. C., 232, 234
More, Sir T., 229
Mucedorus, 369
Muir, K., viii, 351n, 358n, 359n, 372
Murry, J. M., 85

North, Sir T., 25, 356
Nowottny, W., 371n

Ovid, 12–13, 18, 23, 26, 28–32, 88–9, 93, 102, 108

Painter, W., 231, 239
Palmer, J. F., 88, 110
Patrologiae Latinae, 352n
Pausanias, 227
Peele, G., 32, 369
Pembroke, Countess of, 30, 355
Pericles, vii, 349–74
Percy's *Reliques*, 11
Phaedra, 27, 30
Piot, L., 371–2
Plautus, 231, 234
Plutarch, vii, 22–6, 32, 226, 227, 235–9, 240, 247–50, 356
Plutus, 227
Presson, R. K., 88n
Pope, A., 349
Price, H. T., 29n, 32n
Prudentius, 352

Ramsay, W., 22
Rape of Lucrece, The, 32, 88
Rare Triumphs, 96
Ravenscroft, E., 4–5
Rebelo, L. de Sousa, 235n
Recuyell of the Historyes of Troye, 92, 93–5, 101–7
Return from Parnassus, The, 85
Richard II, 33
Richard III, 20, 24n, 32, 237
Robertson, J. M., 84

Rollins, H. E., 96, 100n
Romeo and Juliet, 83, 225, 351
Rowe, N., 349
Rowley, W., 369
Roxburghe Ballads, 11, 15

Saint Marie Magdalen's Conversion, 85
Salel, H., 87
Sargent, R. M., 11–12
Scipio, 243–4
Seneca, 12–13, 21, 23, 26–7, 32
Seege of Troye, 92
Shirburn Ballads, 11
Sidney, Sir P., 235, 356, 370
Silvayn, A., 371–2
Sir Clyomon and Clamydes, 369
Sisson, C. J., 350
Skelton, J., 96, 97, 370
Small, R. A., 94–5
Smyth, A. H., 351n, 355n
Spencer, T. J. B., 225
Spencer, Th., 111
Strabo, 227
Sykes, H. D., 357n

Taming of the Shrew, The, 32
Tatlock, J. S. P., 84n, 87n, 98–9
Testament of Cresseid, 96, 99
Theodosius, 8
Thomson, J. A. K., 27n
Thyestes, 13, 26–27
Tillyard, E. M. W., 25
Timon of Athens, vii, 83, 225–50, 373
Timon (Dyce MSS), 232–5
Tittus and Vespacia, 3, 6
Titus Andronicus (play, 3–33; 349; (ballad), 3, 11–12; (prose), 3, 7–10, 12–14, 16–20
Tompkins, J. M. S., 356
Tragaedia von Tito Andronico, 6
Troilus and Cressida, 83–111, 225, 235
Troublesome Raigne of King John, 5, 25
Twine, L., vii, 355, 357–68, 373
Two Gentlemen of Verona, 33, 374

Venus and Adonis, 32
Virgil, 86, 93

Waith, E. M., 31, 371
Walker, A., 83n
Whetstone, G., 97
Whitaker, V., 32n
Wilkins, G., vii, 356–9, 363, 366, 369, 370
Wilson, J. D., 32n, 86

Wingfield, A., 232
Winter's Tale, The, 373
Wynkyn de Worde, 94, 354

Xenophon, 351

Young, K., 91n